THE ART OF
GOOD
HOUSEKEEPING

THE ART OF GOOD HOUSEKEEPING

Edited by Helen Harrison

Consultant Editor, Trisha Schofield
Head of Testing, Good Housekeeping Institute

COLLINS & BROWN

First published in the United Kingdom in 2010 by
Collins & Brown
10 Southcombe Street
London
W14 0RA

An imprint of Anova Books Company Ltd

The Good Housekeeping website is
www.allboutyou.com/goodhousekeeping

10 9 8 7 6 5 4 3 2 1

ISBN 978-1-84340-568-9

A catalogue record for this book is available from the British Library.

All illustrations by Beci Orpin, www.beciorpin.com
Reproduction by Rival Colour UK Ltd
Printed and bound by 1010 Printing International Ltd, China

This book can be ordered direct from the publisher at
www.anovabooks.com

Acknowledgements

With special thanks to Katie Hewett, Caroline Bloor, Tony Cable,
Brian Clegg, Victoria Fterig and Judith Moore.

Contents

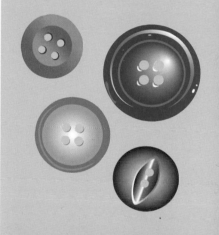

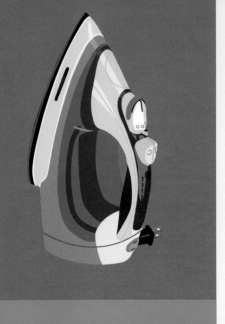

3 Cleaning the Home

4 Creative DIY in the Home

5 Safety and Security

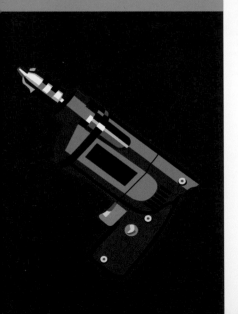

6 Household Emergencies

7 Moving House

8 Useful Information

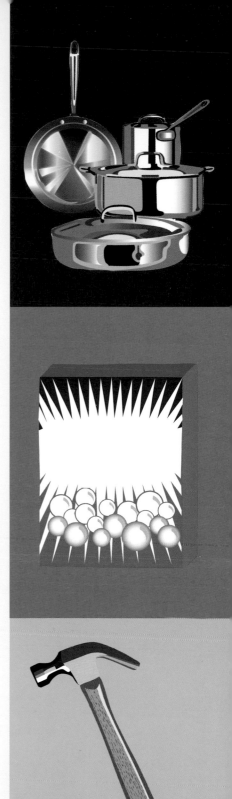

Introduction

Within two years of its successful launch in 1922, *Good Housekeeping* Magazine set up the Good Housekeeping Institute to test products and recipes, provide household information and champion the rights of consumers. In an era when housewives were finding the transition to a servantless society quite a struggle, the pressure to keep up standards without outside help was enormous. In addition, the 1920s were proving to be an exhilarating time for women, full of opportunities in the form of careers, cinema, cars and clothes, quite apart from finally being granted the right to vote! For women to take full advantage of all these new changes, ideas and innovations, it was vital they had access to independent advice they could trust. This was exactly what the Good Housekeeping Institute set out to achieve and, more than 80 years later, it is still helping women (and men too!) make informed choices about the mind-boggling variety of products and services available on today's market. Our lifestyles may have changed beyond all imagination – we now have access to a variety of labour-saving devices and technology that our predecessors would have given their eye-teeth for, and these help make running a smooth home no longer quite the chore it once was. If anything though, the access to such variety can make making the right choices even more difficult and overwhelming. Our experience is that today's modern working women need and appreciate our services just as much as ever. As well as producing tried-and-tested reports and many other practical features for the magazine, our team of professional researchers continue to respond to many thousands of your consumer enquiries for assistance and advice each year.

Our latest book, *The Art of Good Housekeeping*, aims to give the solutions to hundreds of these queries in one easy-to-use guide, and help make managing your life easier and more straightforward. With most households these days having both partners working outside the home, time truly is of the essence – the less hours you have to spend running your home, the more time you will have for the activities you really enjoy. This is exactly what this book will help you to do. Within it, you will find a condensed version of all the Good Housekeeping Institute's practical expertise, built up over many years.

We have distilled this experience into reliable advice that you can use when you buy and equip a new home – most of us are more discerning than ever about spending money and want to make sure we're getting good value, whether it's buying furnishings, a whole new bathroom or even just a replacement small appliance, such as a kettle or toaster. Our buying guides will help you ensure you get the best deal, whether you shop online or in-store. Hiring reliable tradespeople and service providers is important too, so there's information on how to go about finding them and making sure they do a good job. Protecting, maintaining and cleaning your home and its contents is also covered – for example, dealing with inevitable problems such as unblocking a sink or removing stains from clothing. You'll find out how to keep your taps gleaming, look after appliances, get answers to common laundry problems and which cleaning materials are best for the job at hand – in fact, everything you need to know to keep your home gleaming and fresh at all times. There's also step-by-step instructions for a variety of DIY projects, decorating techniques for special paint effects, such as stippling and marbling, how to fix things and creative ideas for making curtains and other soft furnishings. When emergencies like fires, burglaries or accidental injuries occur, our sensible advice will help you be able to deal with them quickly, safely and effectively. And as it's also vital to understand your rights in relation to your home and the law, we've even provided answers to some of the more frequently asked legal questions, such as what to do about noisy neighbours or whether you need planning permission for building projects.

Every chapter is packed with tried and tested advice you can trust, and a wealth of facts, tips and cross references to lead you to all the information you need as quickly as possible. We've even provided a section giving details of the Good Housekeeping Institute's own invaluable contacts book, listing all the products, suppliers and useful organisations mentioned in the book. We hope that you'll be able to dip in and out of this book whenever you're faced with a new household challenge and be able to find the correct answers to all your domestic dilemmas – just think of it like having the GHI's team of professional consumer experts right there alongside you in your home at all times!

We've made every effort to ensure that all the information in this book is as comprehensive, accurate and up-to-date as possible, but if you have any comments, queries or tips for the the next edition, please e-mail them to us at: **artofgoodhousekeeping@anovabooks.com**

Equipping Your Home

Many of the enquiries received by GHI each year concern products – which ones to buy and where to find them. In this section, you will find a wealth of practical information on how to equip your home with the best – what to buy, features worth paying extra for, how to choose a tradesperson, shopping strategies to get the best price and advice on consumer rights.

Your New Home

Setting up a new home is an exciting time: it represents a fresh start, it gives you the opportunity to create your own individual space and it gives you the chance to think about how you can add value. Equipping your home is the first step, and before you start it is useful to think about your needs, room by room.

PLANNING YOUR SPACE

Whether moving into a new home or even refurbishing an existing one, good planning will make the most of your space.

Indoors
STORAGE

Think carefully about your storage needs and incorporate them in your plan from the start. Make a list of everything you own and decide where in your home you want to store it. Although this is a good time to clear clutter, you should make allowances for a few new possessions too.

KITCHENS

Traditional free-standing kitchens furnished with individual pieces of furniture, such as dressers and tables, can be very attractive, but they require a large room to work effectively. The average kitchen is around $8m^2/86ft^2$, which doesn't give you much space for storing food, pots and pans, tools, china and appliances. A fitted kitchen is often the best option; careful planning will make the most of restricted space. Many stores offer free advice and planning tools to help with the first stages.

DINING ROOM

Do you need a separate room or would you benefit from combining it with the kitchen? A light, spacious kitchen-diner with patio doors onto a terrace is likely to add value to your home and provide an ideal everyday family space.

LIVING AREAS

Consider the activities you will use the space for. Do you want an informal family room, or an adult haven where you can close the door? Plan your space and storage accordingly, including space for children's toys if there is no play space in their bedrooms.

BEDROOMS

If you don't have enough bedrooms consider a loft conversion, which is usually less expensive than moving house. Depending on the available space, you could either add two children's bedrooms or a master bedroom suite. If similar houses in your street already have conversions, ask your neighbours if you can view them. If you like the

Traffic flow through rooms

Public spaces in your home – living areas, family rooms, kitchens and dining rooms – should flow into other rooms to encourage all the space to be used. Open-plan living optimises this, but if you prefer separate living rooms you still need to make them easy to move around.

- Make sure that furniture doesn't block a route through your home. As an example, if you have to navigate around the kitchen table to the back door, the garden will be used less.

- In a small room, place furniture against walls, with the largest piece on the longest wall, so that there is circulation space in the middle.

- In larger rooms group furniture away from walls to create distinct areas and aid traffic flow.

- Too many doors in a small room can turn it into a corridor, so look at ways to reconfigure the space to avoid this.

- Bedrooms should be separate from the public spaces and are best sited near bathrooms.

results and they are happy, then ask them for their contractor's details.

To make the most of existing space look at solutions such as bunk beds for shared children's rooms, mezzanine beds in high-ceilinged rooms and storage that makes use of spaces over doors or windows. If clothes storage is a problem in a master bedroom but you have a large bathroom, consider converting part of the bathroom space into a dressing area.

BATHROOMS

If you have a family, you may want to consider whether there is space to add an en-suite to the master bedroom. Or can you make adjustments to an existing bathroom by adding a separate shower, for example.

UTILITY

A space for laundry appliances and cleaning materials frees up space in a small kitchen and can be used as a feeding and sleeping area for pets.

HOME OFFICE

If you have a rarely used guest bedroom you could install a wallbed or sofabed and free up space to use as a home office. If you don't want to use an existing bedroom there are several options: under the stairs or in a hallway, or as part of an attic or basement conversion.

FLOORING

For kitchens and bathrooms, install any new flooring after old fittings have been taken out, and the plumbing and electrical work done, but before units and fittings are installed. Tiling a complete area may cost a little more in tiles but more than makes up for this in the labour time saved cutting around units. It also means that when you change an appliance and your new one is slightly smaller you won't have to renew your flooring.

Outdoors
TERRACE OR PATIO

An area of paving or decking next to the house is practical and easy to maintain. If you have a very small town garden you might want to pave or deck the whole area; your garden will look larger and you won't need to find somewhere to store the mower. In a medium or large garden you will probably have space for a lawn.

BOUNDARIES

Upgrading a tired fence will transform the look of your garden, and if you choose a closely boarded style you can increase your privacy. Fences are available in a range of styles, from period rustic to sleek contemporary.

FRONT OF HOUSE

Make sure that your property looks inviting from the street – it will be more pleasant to return home to, and will help attract buyers when you come to sell your house. If you don't have a garage but you do have a reasonably sized front garden, you may want to consider setting aside some of the area to create a paved parking space. Bear in mind, however, that these are usually subject to local authority permission.

TIP

To get the most out of your conversion it is usually better to consult an architect or specialist attic conversion company, rather than a general builder.

Decorative features

Finishing touches like pictures and candles add atmosphere and personality to your home. You don't have to start from scratch to improve a room. Carefully chosen details can refresh a tired scheme.

- **MIRRORS** Can be used to brighten every room in the house.

- **PICTURES** Whether you choose a painting, print or photograph, pictures will inject personality and colour into your home. Choose a mixture of wall-hung, shelf displayed and tabletop pictures to add interest. Consider your choice of frame as well as image to reflect the style of your home.

- **HOUSEPLANTS** From a kitchen herb trough to a steam-loving fern in the bathroom, a careful plant choice can enhance your home. Most plants will thrive in moderate light, but not in direct sunlight or too far from a natural light source.

- **FLOWERS** You don't have to take flower-arranging classes to decorate your home with flowers – a simple bunch of roses or tulips in a vibrant colour will lift any room on a dull day. Use a proprietary flower food and change the water regularly to prolong the life of your flowers.

Shopping for the Home

Whether you are buying goods, paying for a service or shopping on the Internet, these guidelines will help you shop safely and well.

SHOPPING FROM HOME

If you shop from home – whether by phone, mail order or the Internet – there are regulations that give you extra rights on top of those set out above. You are entitled to:

- ⊙ Clear information before placing an order (such as the trader's contact details and policy on returning/exchanging goods).
- ⊙ Written confirmation (by letter, fax or e-mail) of purchases.
- ⊙ A 'cooling-off' period during which you can cancel the order and get a refund.
- ⊙ A full refund if the goods do not arrive on time (within 30 days or on an agreed date).
- ⊙ Protection if anyone uses your credit or debit card fraudulently.

Internet shopping

Before buying goods via the Internet, make sure you are dealing with a reputable company. The following details should be included on the seller's website:

- ⊙ The full name and postal address of the company – not just the e-mail address – and the phone number, so you know who you are dealing with and how to get in touch if things go wrong.
- ⊙ How long it will take for the items to be delivered.
- ⊙ The company's refund policy.
- ⊙ A reminder of your cancellation rights. You can change your mind and send items back within seven days of receiving them, although some goods such as food may not be covered.
- ⊙ What data the company is collecting, how it will be used and for how long it will be stored.

Internet security

Make sure your credit card details do not fall into the wrong hands when you shop online. In a credit charge transaction, you are sharing valuable information. Only do it if you trust the company you are buying from. Never type in your details on a site that does not promise security or encryption services. Look for the closed padlock or unbroken key symbol in the corner of the web page. The beginning of the online retailer's Internet address will change from 'http' to 'https' when a connection is secure. In some new browsers, the address bar may also turn green to indicate that a site has an additional level of security. For more information on Internet security, go to www.cardwatch.org.uk, the UK banking industry initiative that aims to raise awareness of card fraud prevention.

Purchasing tips

- ⊙ **WHEN YOU BUY GOODS** Goods must be of satisfactory quality (durable, safe and free from minor defects), fit for their purpose and exactly as described.

- ⊙ **WHEN YOU PAY FOR A SERVICE** Any service, for example, from a builder or tradesman, should be carried out with reasonable skill and care, within a reasonable time and at a reasonable charge, if no price has been fixed in advance.

- ⊙ **WHEN YOU BUY BY CREDIT CARD** Using your credit card gives you extra protection for items over £100 in value. If you have a problem and complaining to the retailer has got you nowhere (or if the retailer goes out of business), you should be able to claim against the card issuer.

TIP

For free advice and information on shopping from home, visit the Office of Fair Trading website at www.oft.gov.uk.

IF YOU ARE UNHAPPY WITH GOODS OR SERVICES: YOUR RIGHTS

- You are within your rights to cancel goods and services if they have not been delivered, or work has not been completed by an agreed date.
- The responsibility for faulty goods lies with the retailer, not the manufacturer.
- You have the same rights when you buy in a sale as at any other time – goods should be free from defects, apart from those specifically pointed out to you when you buy.
- There is no set time limit on returning faulty goods – you do not automatically lose your rights after a certain period, but it is wise to return them or inform the retailer as soon as you notice the problem.

- Firms cannot disclaim responsibility for loss or damage to your property just by putting up a sign saying that they do.
- If you are unable to come to a satisfactory solution with the retailer or manufacturer, contact the Government's Consumer Direct service (see Useful Organisations) for advice. Here, you can speak to regionally-based consumer advisors who are specially trained to give assistance and advice on all kinds of consumer issues.

TEN ESSENTIAL SHOPPING TIPS

1 Start with the name and full model number of the item you want, so you can easily check the price in your favourite shop over the phone or on its website.

2 To save money, be ready to switch to an all-but-identical model, or one lacking a feature you don't really need.

3 Look for special offers on discontinued or superseded models that retailers want to clear.

4 Shop around at a few outlets, including at least one with a price-matching promise.

5 If you are happy to buy online, start by trawling for the best bargains using a price comparison website such as www.pricerunner.co.uk, which checks the prices of both high street and Internet retailers.

6 Don't assume nationwide chains will always offer better prices than a local independent outlet. With a local independent retailer, it may also be easier to negotiate a discount.

7 Check whether delivery and fitting are included in the price. If not, don't forget to ask how much they will cost and take this into consideration when comparing prices.

8 Ask if any add-ons are included for free, such as an extra year's warranty or service agreement.

9 Try haggling – you may be able to negotiate a discount for buying two or more items, or have delivery or fitting thrown in for no charge.

10 If you're not bothered about buying a slightly used item, look on auction sites such as www.ebay.co.uk or search for companies that specialise in offering ex-display models – you can often buy goods at huge discounts through these sources, but bear in mind they will usually come without the guarantees or warranties offered with brand new products.

Finding the best deal

When it comes to shopping for the home, the best savings are usually to be found on the Internet, and it can pay to shop around. Remember though that delivery costs could wipe out part or all of the apparent saving, and that prices do not remain static – Internet retailers in particular may alter prices on a daily basis, so grab good deals when you can. Look out for price-matching pledges – under these types of schemes, if you find the identical product in a competitor's outlet for a lower price after you have bought it, the store will refund the difference or even beat the lower price.

USING TRADESMEN

If you need someone reliable and trustworthy to provide services in your home, here are some helpful guidelines.

Obtaining recommendations

If no one you know can recommend someone, there are several ways to arrive at a shortlist of firms to ask for a quote:

- ⊙ Through one of the find-a-tradesmen schemes or trade associations (see the box opposite).
- ⊙ Via a local consumer group's list – your local council should be able to tell you how to contact these organisations; some councils even run their own 'reputable trader' lists.
- ⊙ From your household insurer.
- ⊙ By asking neighbours and looking in local newspapers.

Don't even consider having a job done by someone 'doing work in your area' unless you can talk to at least one householder prepared to recommend their workmanship, reliability and punctuality. Be wary of tradesmen you can only contact by phone, especially a mobile – if things go wrong, they can be hard to find.

Signing the contract

Once you have decided upon the right person for the job, it's important to insist upon a written contract. Think carefully about what you want done before you sign it because changing your mind halfway through, or asking for extras gives the firm a golden opportunity to inflate the bill – of course sometimes, unexpected extra work will be required, but make sure you agree any additional costs in writing before it starts.

Make sure the work specifies a start date, completion date, costs and cancellation rights. Check if subcontractors will be used and who is responsible for the quality and timing of their work. If the job is large, it is reasonable to agree to stage payments, but be suspicious of any company that asks for a sizeable deposit or money for materials. Always obtain a written receipt whenever money changes hands – if possible, pay by credit card if the bill is for £100 or more as this will give you extra protection if things go wrong. Check the company has public liability insurance, and that it covers any damage to your house, and make sure you receive a written guarantee for parts and a properly backed guarantee for the work done. Finally, do not pay the bill in full until after the work is completed to your satisfaction.

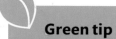

Green tip

Try looking for the items you require on Freecycle (www.uk.freecycle.org), a grass roots organisation that matches people who have things to get rid of with people who can use them. Freecycle aims to reduce unnecessary waste by keeping unwanted, but perfectly usable items, out of landfill sites – a highly commendable goal and better still, it's all completely free!

Shop for quality

- ● Ask at least three firms for a quote and make it clear that you want to inspect at least one similar job before you give the go-ahead. Write down exactly what you want done before the tradesmen visit, so you can be sure you are comparing like for like. When the quotes arrive, here are some things to look out for:

- ● Is it written on company letterhead? Tatty bits of paper are not a good sign.

- ● Does it include a detailed breakdown of costs and VAT?

- ● Does it indicate how long the job will take?

- ● Do quantities of raw materials vary between quotes? (Skimping on coats of paint may indicate that standards are not high enough, for example.)

- ● Is it clear which, if any, materials are included in the price?

- ● Is it clear when deposits and stage payments are expected?

- ● Is the tradesman easy to get hold of, and happy to answer any questions in detail?

TRADE ASSOCIATIONS AND 'REPUTABLE TRADER' SCHEMES

TRADE ASSOCIATIONS

ELECTRICAL CONTRACTORS' ASSOCIATION This association has a register of members who must follow a code of fair trading. All electrical work is covered by an insurance-backed warranty and bond scheme.

💻 www.eca.co.uk
☎ 020 7313 4800

FEDERATION OF MASTER BUILDERS The federation has a code of practice, an arbitration scheme and an optional insurance-backed warranty scheme.

💻 www.fmb.org.uk
☎ 020 7242 7583

HEATING AND VENTILATING CONTRACTORS' ASSOCIATION This association has a consumer Code of Fair Trading that provides a complaints procedure including a conciliation service and referral to binding arbitration. It also has a Guaranteed Installer scheme.

💻 www.hvca.org.uk
☎ 020 7313 4900

CHARTERED INSTITUTE OF PLUMBING AND HEATING ENGINEERING Will help you find qualified plumbers in your area.

💻 www.ciphe.org.uk
☎ 01708 472791

NATIONAL FEDERATION OF ROOFING CONTRACTORS Has a code of practice and optional one-year guarantee scheme.

💻 www.nfrc.co.uk
☎ 020 7638 7663

GAS SAFE REGISTER™ By law, anyone working on gas installations and appliances in your home must be on the Gas Safe Register™. Every engineer carries a Gas Safe Register ID card with their own unique licence number, showing the type of gas work they are qualified to do. Before any gas work is carried out, always make sure you ask to see their Gas Safe Register ID card.

💻 www.gassaferegister.co.uk
☎ 0800 408 5500

NEED TO KNOW

As of 1 April 2009, Gas Safe Register™ replaced the longstanding CORGI gas registration scheme as Great Britain's gas safety authority. CORGI registration is no longer valid, so don't accept CORGI membership as proof of competency when choosing a gas installer.

REPUTABLE TRADER SCHEMES

LOCAL AUTHORITY ASSURED TRADER SCHEME NETWORK

All the Local Authority Assured Trader Scheme Network (LAATSN) member schemes have to meet minimum standards and aim to give consumers a reliable way of finding businesses they can trust. Your local council can tell you if they are a member of this scheme or visit the Office of Fair Trading's website (www.oft.gov.uk) for a list of members.

TRUSTMARK Trustmark is a scheme endorsed by the Department of Business, Innovation, and Skill, supported by trade bodies and consumer groups, to help people find reliable and reputable tradesmen. Firms can be awarded the logo by a Trustmark approved scheme operator, but must comply with Government-endorsed standards covering technical competence and good customer service.

💻 www.trustmark.org.uk
☎ 01344 630 804

PROBLEM SOLVED Respected consumer journalist Alison Cork established Problem Solved to help people find the best (and worst!) tradesmen in their area. It now has a database of over 60,000 local traders recommended and vetted by their own customers.

💻 www.problemsolved.co.uk
☎ 020 7290 6060

Equipping a Kitchen

The kitchen is one of the most hardworking areas in the house, and therefore its planning needs careful attention.

KITCHEN PLANNING

When planning a new kitchen, even if you are using a professional, it is wise to do a plan yourself. Although a professional kitchen planner is very experienced, only you know how you will use your kitchen. If you are not involved, minor details may be overlooked which will be irritating and make your kitchen less easy to work in.

However, if you decide not to do your own plan you will still need to spend time thinking about your new kitchen because a professional plan will only be as good as your briefing.

Areas to consider

- How much can you afford?
- What activities do you use your kitchen for? For example, cooking only, eating in, socialising, laundry, or supervising children while cooking?
- Will the kitchen be used for any specialised cooking such as stir-frying in a wok, or large-scale preserving?
- How many people will use the kitchen? One person, two adults, or a large family with young children?
- Do you want to eat in the kitchen? Will you include a breakfast bar or table (fold-away if space is tight) and do you want to obscure the food preparation area from the dining area?
- What is the maximum number of seats required, and what is the minimum (in a small area) that will be satisfactory?
- Which appliances do you want to include and will you be keeping any existing appliances?
- How much storage space do you need? For example: food that is chilled, frozen, dry, bought in bulk; cleaning products in lockable cupboards away from children; china and glass; rubbish disposal.

Drawing a scale plan

The first step is to draw an accurate scale plan of your existing kitchen. Use graph paper and a scale of 1:20, so that 30mm/1.2in represents 600mm/2ft, which is the depth of many kitchen units.

Include all permanent features such as windows and sills, doors (mark the swing areas), chimney breast (external and recess dimensions), mains water supplies and stopcocks, waste outlets and soil pipes, boiler and controls, pipework, radiators and valves, and power points. Note which walls are internal and which are external. Include the ceiling height.

Starting points

- Be prepared to take some time to get the kitchen right.
- Think about how you use your current kitchen.
- Make a list of its good and bad features.
- Ask friends for their experiences and any grievances.

MAKING STRUCTURAL CHANGES

- If you are short of space you may decide to change the shape of the kitchen. You will need to weigh up the inconvenience of leaving the kitchen as it is with the cost of carrying out the alterations. Relatively easy jobs include raising a window sill or knocking out a larder.
- Moving walls is more costly, but could make all the difference. You may have to apply for approval for alterations under the Building Regulations, depending on the type of alteration (minor or major). Contact your local authority for advice. If a professional is carrying out structural work for you, ask if they have obtained the correct permission, because ultimately you will be responsible.
- Plumbing, wiring and drainage should conform to regulations. If worried about these, contact The Royal Institute of Chartered Surveyors (see Useful Organisations), who will put you in touch with a building surveyor in your area. They will survey the kitchen and highlight any problems. Surveyors usually charge an hourly fee and a kitchen survey usually takes about two hours.

Measuring tips

- Use a metal tape measure.
- Measure walls at floor and ceiling level, and at worktop height.
- Watch out for uneven flooring and corners.
- Double check all measurements.
- Take overall wall dimensions, then step dimensions, then compare to plus or minus 10mm/.

MEASURING THE KITCHEN

It is important to measure your kitchen accurately, as even the smallest inaccuracies at this stage will be vital when it comes to installation. You will need two people to do a proper job and it may take a few hours, depending on the size of the room. It is very important to measure everything in metric, as kitchen units and components are always sold in metric sizes. Do not try to convert inches into metric later.

DESIGNING THE LAYOUT

Once you have the basic shape of your kitchen on paper you can work on the layout. Templates of the standard kitchen units and components on a scale of 1:20 are printed on page 21. Photocopy, and use them to help plan the layout. Alternatively, use card shapes (drawn to scale) of the appliances and furniture you want to include. By moving the shapes around the plan it is possible to assess the pros and cons of different layouts. Aim to create maximum storage space and to position the largest area of worksurface between the cooker and sink. Allow for swing areas of doors and windows and the door openings of storage units.

The virtual kitchen

You can find excellent, computerised virtual kitchen planning tools on the Internet these days that will help you mark out your space, try out ideas and see how your kitchen might look. To find one, try looking on the websites of kitchen suppliers such as Ikea (www.ikea.com) and Magnet (www.magnet.co.uk).

WORK TRIANGLE

The three main activity areas in a kitchen are food storage (fridge and food cupboards), preparation (sink and worktops) and cooking (oven or hob, depending on what you use most frequently).

Start your plan by positioning the fridge, sink and oven and draw a line in the shape of a triangle between them. The total sum of the three sides of the triangle should be between 3.6m/12ft and 6.6m/22ft. If too long you will find yourself doing tiresome legwork, but if too short it will be cramped. The cooking and sink points should be connected by an unbroken worktop, even if this turns a corner.

In a modern kitchen there is often more than one triangle in operation: for example, if you use a microwave as well as your cooker, or two people use the kitchen at the same time.

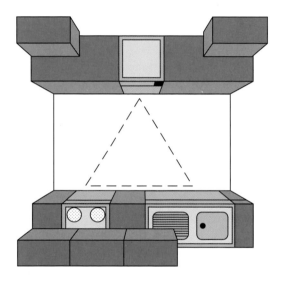

LEFT Basic work triangle

Basic kitchen shapes

Kitchens are available in many shapes and sizes but there are only five practical layouts that will provide maximum working efficiency. You should be able to match one of these layouts to your own kitchen.

SINGLE GALLEY LAYOUT

In a single galley kitchen, the units and appliances are lined up against one wall. Most suitable for one or two people, it can be fitted into a very narrow space, but it will need a 3m/10ft run of interrupted wall space. The room should be at least 1.8m/6ft wide to allow space for two people to pass each other.

The sink should be placed in the middle with the fridge and cooker at either end with, ideally, the doors of each opening away from the sink for easy access. Allocate as much worktop space as possible. Choose built-under appliances so you do not lose any of the limited worktop space.

Eating usually has to take place elsewhere, unless a pull-out or flap-down dining table can be included on the wall facing the main run of kitchen units.

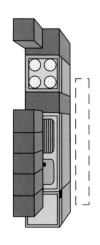

ABOVE Single galley layout

TEMPLATES FOR KITCHEN UNITS

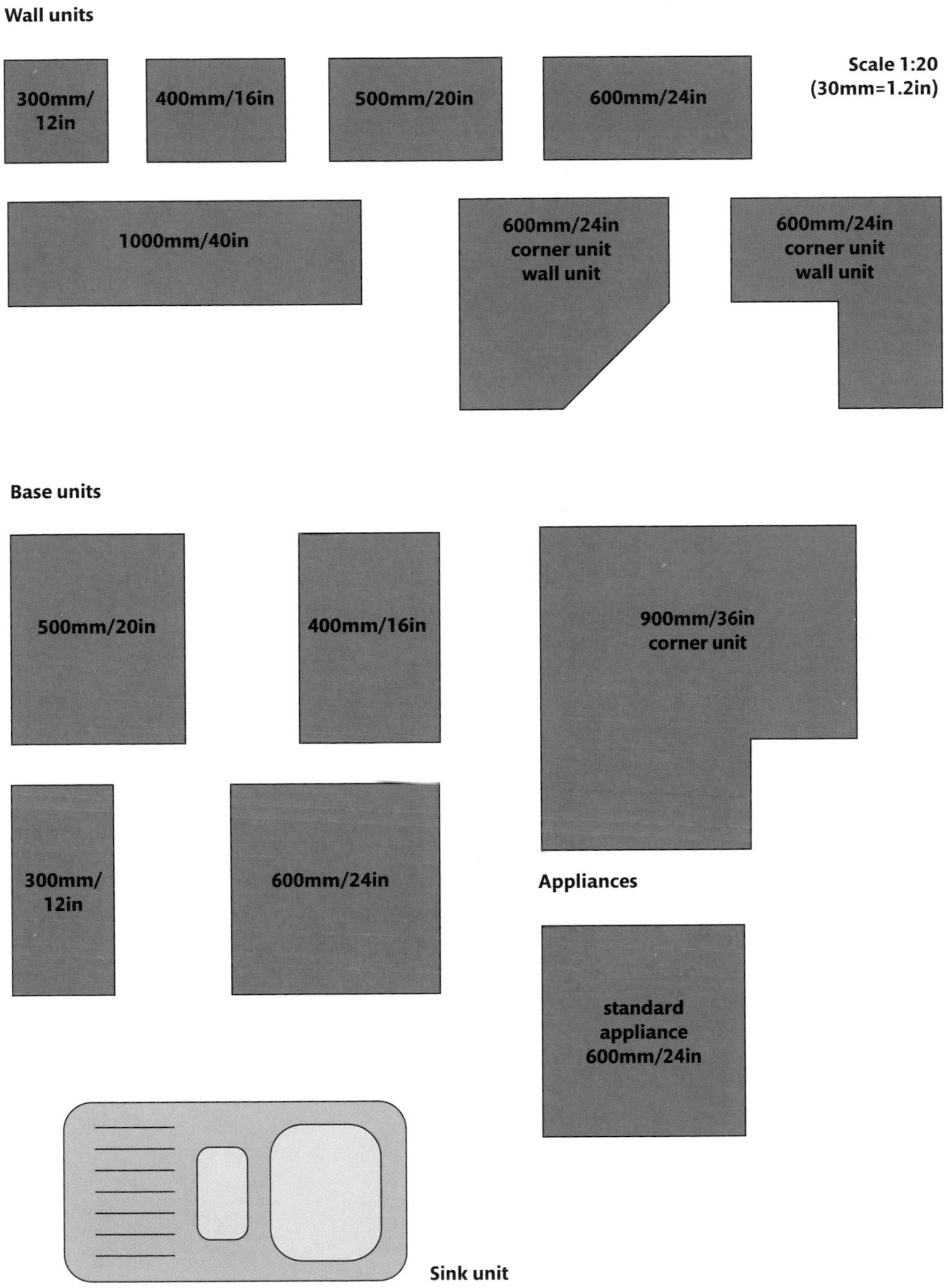

Wall units

Scale 1:20
(30mm=1.2in)

300mm/
12in

400mm/16in

500mm/20in

600mm/24in

1000mm/40in

600mm/24in
corner unit
wall unit

600mm/24in
corner unit
wall unit

Base units

500mm/20in

400mm/16in

900mm/36in
corner unit

300mm/
12in

600mm/24in

Appliances

standard
appliance
600mm/24in

Sink unit

DOUBLE GALLEY LAYOUT

In a double galley kitchen the units and appliances are lined along facing walls. Most layouts will be dictated by the position of existing doors and windows but, ideally, the sink and cooker/hob should be on one side with the fridge and the main storage area opposite. This is an easy layout for one or two people to work in, although traffic through the kitchen can be a problem if there are doors at both ends.

There needs to be at least 1.2m/4ft between facing units, otherwise it will be difficult to bend down to get something from a low-level cupboard. Use 500mm/20in-deep units instead of the standard 600mm/24in.

It's possible to create a feeling of more space by using glass-fronted cabinets instead of those with solid doors.

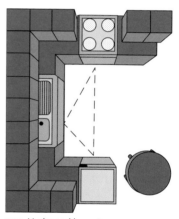

LEFT Double galley layout

U-SHAPED LAYOUT

In a U-shaped kitchen, units and appliances are positioned along three walls. It is the most flexible layout and works well in both a small and a large kitchen. There needs to be at least 1.2m/4ft of space between the legs of the U-shape, but in a larger kitchen make sure you keep to the dimensions of the work triangle to prevent unnecessary walking.

This layout can often incorporate a dining area or breakfast bar. This is probably the best layout for both working and safety.

L-SHAPED LAYOUT

In an L-shaped kitchen the units and appliances are arranged on two adjacent walls. It is suitable for most rooms, except very narrow rooms or rooms with lots of doors. It is a good choice for an awkwardly shaped room because the sides of the L can be adapted to suit most shapes. The work triangle will not be interrupted by through traffic.

It is important to make sure the corner is used effectively, so use a carousel unit or consider a corner sink. Separate the sink, cooker/hob and fridge with stretches of worktop to avoid the three areas of activity becoming congested.

This layout is ideal for incorporating an eating area. It should be able to accommodate two cooks without them constantly getting in each other's way.

LEFT U-shaped layout

FILLING IN THE GAPS

- When designing a kitchen there are often gaps that are the wrong length to accommodate a unit, which is an irritating waste of space. Use the gap to house trays, store wine or buy a custom-made fitting to fill the space, such as a telescopic towel rail. If the gap is large, fit some shelves or consider whether you can use it as an area in which to place your rubbish bin.
- Gaps around a free-standing cooker collect crumbs and food spills so it is a good idea to fill them with a worksurface. If you have a large gap, and cannot afford to fit more units, consider fitting a breakfast bar.

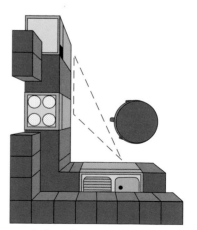

LEFT L-shaped layout

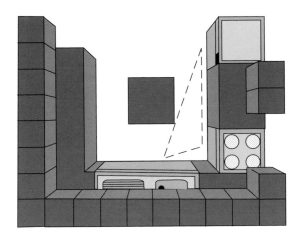

LEFT Island layout

ISLAND LAYOUT

An island layout is usually a U-shaped or L-shaped kitchen with an island of units in the centre. This layout is only suitable for large kitchens. The island can be used for a hob or sink, but the necessary services (gas or electricity, or water) and cooker-hood ducting will have to be brought to the centre of the room and this is costly. The space between the hob and sink must be a working area only and not a general thoroughfare. It is usually used as an additional worksurface, which can be positioned at a different working height.

To add definition to the island think about what will be placed above it. If the island houses a hob, a cooker hood is ideal, or place a light source or decorative rack for cooking pans or dried flowers above it. Careful planning is needed to avoid wasteful journeys around the island.

Plug points

⊙ For each large, fixed appliance, have a fused switch control fitted above worktop level with a cable outlet box behind the appliance to suit.

⊙ Fit at least four double plugs at around 200mm/8in above the worktop height.

Safety

See Home Safety, Kitchen, pages 350–1.

SAFETY PLANNING CONSIDERATIONS

⊙ Avoid people using the kitchen work triangle as a passageway through to the cloakroom or garden.

⊙ Avoid changes in floor level between kitchen and dining areas, to avoid tripping when carrying hot food.

⊙ Avoid fixing units directly above a table.

The human factor

If you have children you may want to situate the hob so you can watch what is cooking and still keep an eye on the children in an adjoining room. This arrangement may mean you have to walk further to the fridge, but it is the most practical solution for you.

POSITIONING COMPONENTS AND APPLIANCES

STORAGE UNITS

DO

✔ Keep food storage near the preparation area.

✔ Provide accessible storage for commonly used items.

✔ Use the ends of base and wall units to store jars and cookery books.

DON'T

✘ Position storage cupboards too high.

✘ Interrupt the work triangle with tall units. Tall storage for brooms and cleaning materials should not interrupt worksurface runs. Keep tall units together.

SINK

DO

✔ Position with worksurface either side for stacking dishes.

✔ Allow room for a second person to stand on the drainer side.

✔ Position within a feasible reach of a waste outlet or internal soil pipe.

DON'T

✘ Think you have to position it under the window if you want to use the view for another purpose.

✘ Position opposite a hob.

The average worktop height is up to 910mm/36in, but if you are tall or short you may find this height uncomfortable. To change the working height, the base plinth can be adjusted at the fitting stage, or place timber on top of the base units before fitting the worktop. Choose the timber to match the units.

Lighting

See Lighting, Kitchen, page 122.

Ventilation

See Cooker Hoods, pages 39–40.

BUYING KITCHEN COMPONENTS

Which kitchen?

Where you buy your kitchen from depends on how much you have to spend and how much work you are prepared to do yourself. The more you do, the cheaper it will be, although savings on installation may not be as significant as they first appear.

INSTALLING IT YOURSELF

Only consider installing a kitchen if you are a competent DIYer. This is the cheapest option but takes the most effort on your part. It will take longer than an experienced fitter and cause greater inconvenience, and you may need to take time off work.

Consider the cost of hiring tools, such as a jigsaw, if you don't have them already. It may be a more cost effective option to reduce your budget on the units so that you can hire a professional fitter.

TIP
When you have decided on your plan, use masking tape on the floor and walls to check that the layout works.

TIP
It is worth investing in a rechargeable screwdriver if assembling the units yourself.

POSITIONING APPLIANCES

OVEN/FREE-STANDING COOKER

DO

✔ Position with worksurface on one side for putting down pans.

DON'T

✖ Position in a corner.

✖ Position near or adjacent to a door.

✖ Position under a window.

✖ Position next to the fridge or freezer

HOB

DO

✔ Position with worksurface either side for putting down pans.

✔ Position near deep cupboards or drawers for pan storage.

DON'T

✖ Position in a corner, unless at an angle across it.

✖ Position near a window.

✖ Position under wall units without a cooker hood or extractor fan.

✖ Position near the eating area because children can reach across and touch the rings.

✖ Position too close to tall units or walls or at the end of a run of units.

✖ Position opposite the sink in an access way.

WASHING MACHINE OR WASHER-DRIER

DO

✔ Position near sink for plumbing.

DON'T

✖ Position in the work triangle.

TUMBLE-DRIER

DO

✔ Position near the washing machine. Consider stacking it on top if there is space.

✔ Ensure there is access to the outside for a vented drier.

✔ Ensure it is positioned in a well-ventilated area.

DISHWASHER

DO

✔ Position near the sink for plumbing.

✔ Position near the crockery cupboard, for easy unloading.

DON'T

✖ Position in a corner.

FRIDGES AND FREEZERS

DO

✔ Allow room for the door to open fully, in order to remove shelves for cleaning/adjustment.

✔ Position large fridge-freezers with worksurface on one side to put down food.

✔ Some fridge-freezers require ventilation around the back and sides – check manufacturer's instructions.

DON'T

✖ Position next to the cooker unless suitably insulated.

EMPLOYING YOUR OWN FITTERS

The responsibility for installing the kitchen is handed over to one or more fitters, whom you can supervise. This option usually works out cheaper than employing the supplier's installation service.

It is better to employ one fitter for the entire job, but check he is qualified to install both gas and electricity. If you employ more than one fitter, have an initial meeting with all the parties involved to sort out any problems before they occur.

You can buy kitchens for installation from builders' merchants, DIY stores, furniture stores and some kitchen specialists. These retailers will still offer a planning service but the complexity of the layout drawn up varies. Kitchen specialists and retailers offfer computer-aided design with perspective 3D drawings. Remember the plan can only be as good as the measurements you have taken.

INSTALLATION USING THE SUPPLIER'S FITTERS

This is the easiest but most expensive option.

Once a basic plan has been agreed using your measurements, the responsibility for checking the measurements and installation is taken on by the supplier. This option is available from DIY and furniture stores and kitchen specialists.

Using a fitting service from the supplier allows greater tailoring of the kitchen to suit your needs. Cupboards can be specifically made or tailored to exact measurements. Contact the Kitchen Bathroom Bedroom Specialists Association (see Useful Organisations) for independent kitchen specialists in your area.

Direct sales companies do not have high-street showrooms. Their costs should be less because they do not have high overheads. However, you do not have the same opportunity to see a fitted example unless they can provide a previous customer for you to visit. It is very unwise to buy a kitchen without visiting a fitted example first. You may feel pressurised having had the firm round for planning in your home.

If you do not choose the supplier's fitters, always check the guarantee. Some are invalidated if you arrange installation yourself.

Choosing a kitchen supplier

- Ask contacts for recommendations.
- Visit a showroom or ask for recent customers who you can visit, to judge the quality of the materials and fitting.
- Take your measurements and scale drawing with you.
- Get more than one quote.

Uneven floors and walls

When installing a kitchen, one of the biggest problems is uneven floors and walls, so adjustable fittings on units are useful. Look for adjustable hinges, to make alignment easier. Wall units should have adjustable brackets that will allow you to alter the wall unit height slightly. Adjustable legs compensate for changes in floor level.

BUY EX-DISPLAY?

Consider buying an ex-display kitchen. You can find top-of-the-range brands and make great savings on the cost, and the kitchen will typically be virtually unused. However, you will usually have to buy 'as seen' so if guarantees are important, this may not be the right option for you. Alno Kitchens (see Manufacturers, Retailers and Service Providers) have a list of ex-display kitchens for sale on their website. Another company to try is The Used Kitchen Company (see Manufacturers, Retailers and Service Providers).

CHOOSING THE UNITS

You may have firm ideas on the final look of your kitchen, but do not overlook the quality of the units you are choosing.

Flat pack or rigid?
The first choice to make is between self-assembly, flat-pack units or factory-assembled, rigid units. Flat-pack units tend to be cheaper than rigid because of mass production. Over the past five years the quality of flat pack has greatly improved, making it sturdier than some rigid furniture.

Flat pack units are joined together either with screw and dowel, or a cam and dowel fitting. A cam and dowel fitting is the easiest to assemble: you just fit the two parts together and only have to turn with a screwdriver once. With a screw and dowel you have to do all the work with a screwdriver. All units should be attached to the walls. The screw should penetrate at least 25mm/1in into the brickwork of the wall.

Sizes
Wall and floor units start at 200mm/8in wide (although 300mm/12in is more common) and usually increase in 100mm/4in steps to 600mm/24in wide for single cupboards and 1,200mm/47in wide for double units. With some of the most basic flat-pack units there is less flexibility in size; with expensive units there is more.

Wall units are usually 300mm/12in deep, but the Continental depth is 350mm/14in. Wall units can go up to the ceiling, but these taller units are generally more expensive than standard units.

The standard depth for most base units is 550–560mm/21½–22in; with the door thickness and worktop overhang, brings the base run depth to 600mm/24in. A few manufacturers have a 500mm/20in depth option; many will offer wall units (300–350mm/12–14in deep) as base units. You can space base units out from the wall to achieve any intermediate depth.

SELF CHECKS

It is important to judge the quality of the kitchen in the showroom, and there are a number of checks you can do.

- The carcass of units is often made from melamine-faced chipboard that is available in two thicknesses. Quality depends on density as well as thickness. Look inside the units and check that all exposed edges are sealed. If not the chipboard can be weakened by moisture.
- Door hinges should be metal, as plastic is not strong enough.
- Doors should open fully.
- For maximum versatility, the shelves in units should be adjustable.
- Drawer units should have full-height back panels to stop things falling down the back.
- Drawers should be fitted with stops so they will not fall out of the unit when opened fully.
- Drawers should run smoothly with a weight inside. Try placing something inside.
- Runners with ball bearings will run more smoothly than basic runners. Runners need to be metal and not plastic.
- Glass fronts of units should be safety (laminated) glass.
- Check that unit doors and drawers are soft closing.

Doors

When buying a kitchen, many people spend the most time choosing the doors. Although they give the kitchen its overall look, they do not have to withstand as much wear and tear as the other components.

The main choices are between coloured and wood effect, wood veneer, solid wood and metals such as stainless steel. If you have children, you may want to consider having child-resistant locks fitted on your doors.

Green tip

If you choose solid wood doors, try to make sure the wood comes from a sustainable farming source.

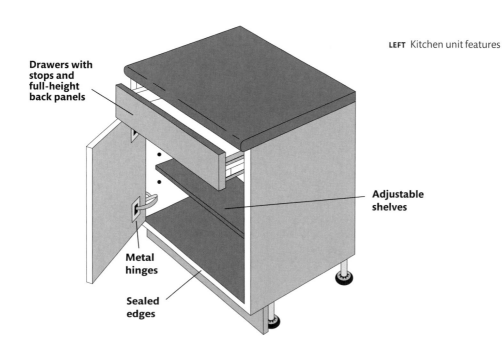

LEFT Kitchen unit features

Drawers with stops and full-height back panels

Adjustable shelves

Metal hinges

Sealed edges

CHOOSING CUPBOARD DOORS

- ⊙ **STAINLESS STEEL AND ALUMINIUM** Stainless steel and metals, such as aluminium and zinc, are also popular choices for kitchen doors. Metals are durable and look professional, but can be costly and difficult to keep clean.
- ⊙ **COLOURED/WOOD EFFECT** Medium-density fibreboard (MDF) or chipboard is covered with laminate, Polyvinyl Chloride (PVC) or melamine. MDF is a smoother base than chipboard. A wide range of colours and patterns are available in both matt and high gloss. More and more manufacturers are introducing bright colours into their ranges. These doors are available in a wide price range.
- ⊙ **WOOD VENEER** MDF or chipboard is covered with a thin layer of wood. This sort of door gives the look of solid wood and is generally less expensive and more environmentally friendly (if from sustainably farmed sources). There is often less variation than with solid wood, so they give a more standard look.
- ⊙ **SOLID WOOD** Popular solid wood doors are oak and limed woods, while others are hand painted. They are the most expensive option, but cheaper ones can change colour, swell or shrink with increasing age. Before buying, discuss the different qualities of different types of wood and how they have been treated.
- ⊙ **INTEGRATED APPLIANCE DOORS** Some manufacturers make integrated appliances, which have special fixings so they can be fitted with a door to give a uniform finish. The doors are available as a full door or an appliance door, which leaves the control panel exposed. Integrated appliances usually cost more and are not as widely available as standard appliances.

Worksurfaces

The worksurface gets the most wear and tear in a kitchen, so buy the best quality you can afford. Worksurfaces are usually 600mm/24in deep, but most manufacturers make deeper ones for eating areas or peninsula units. If you have the room and want extra worksurface area, set floor units away from the wall and use a deeper worktop.

The average height of a worktop is up to 910mm/36in, but if you do not find this comfortable it can sometimes be raised or lowered accordingly.

TIP
It is usually worth having worktops fitted professionally even if you are fitting everything else yourself.

CERAMIC TILES

Available either glazed or unglazed. Check the tiles you choose are suitable for worktops. Tiles should be vitrified and fixed using epoxy resin. Any spills should be cleaned up immediately. Tiles can be prone to scratching. Another problem is that the grouting between the tiles can become dirty. The worksurface will be uneven so is not suitable for rolling dough.

LAMINATES

These are the most popular option and are available in a wide range of colours, finishes and textures. Laminate worktops consist of a thin sheet of laminate on a chipboard base. There is a great difference between the top and bottom ranges in price and quality and, basically, you get what you pay for.

Most laminates will withstand temperatures of up to 180°C/356°F. High-pressure laminates are heat resistant to 230°C/446°F. Some cheaper ranges will not withstand high temperatures and may become quickly damaged.

The chipboard used varies in quality depending on the thickness and density. The thickness of laminate worktops varies from 25mm/1in to 40mm/1½in. Always choose the thickest you can afford. The weight of a good-quality worktop is an indication of the chipboard density.

The underside of a worktop can be water damaged if appliances, such as a dishwasher, are placed underneath. To prevent this the underside of most worksurfaces is protected by the manufacturers with a resin coating or a foil lining. If the worktop is not sealed, you can seal it yourself at the time of installation, with wax or oil-based paint.

The supplier will usually cut the worktop to the size you require. If cutting the worktop yourself, use a circular saw and cut from the underside. Have a practice on an offcut first to check the effect on the laminate, because some blades are unsuitable. The front of the worktop can be square edged or rounded (post-formed). A rounded edge is less likely to chip but is more difficult to join at the internal corners.

TIP

If having a worktop delivered, check the condition before signing for it because due to their large size they are often dropped or knocked in transit.

MAN-MADE SOLID SURFACES

Consist of a composite material that is the same colour and texture throughout (e.g. Corian). A variety of colours are available and the worktop can be shaped, carved or inlaid. Joints are virtually invisible, so it gives a smooth and seamless finish. However, this sort of worksurface is expensive, and should only be fitted by experts. White Corian needs vigilance to avoid staining and scratching.

NATURAL SOLID SURFACES

A natural, solid surface (e.g. granite) looks good, but is not as practical as man-made solid surfaces because you cannot have as many inlays or carved features, and joints will show. Natural surfaces are also prone to scratches and chips. However, they are cool to the touch and so excellent for making pastry. It is possible to fit natural solid worksurfaces yourself, but as they are very expensive, it's perhaps more advisable to use a professional installer.

STAINLESS STEEL

Surface marks easily but the scratches blend together over time to give a uniform patina. Stainless steel is hygienic and requires hardly any maintenance to keep it looking good. It is resistant to heat and cold and very durable, and sinks can be pressed out of worktops to give a completely seamless finish. Upfront costs are quite high, but considering the lifespan of the product, very economical over time.

WOOD

A hardwood worktop looks extremely attractive, but is also expensive and high maintenance. Susceptible to damp, avoid using wood next to a butler-type sink where it is difficult to form a watertight seal. To protect wood above a washing machine or dishwasher from condensation, you will need to use a special moisture-resistant paper on the underside of the worksurface. Wood needs oiling regularly and can usually be sanded if scratches become too noticeable.

CARE AND CLEANING
See A–Z of Cleaning and Caring for Surfaces, Worktops, page 237.

Sinks

Although the popularity of dishwashers means sinks are used less, most households still need one that is a good size. Sink units are usually about 1m/3ft wide, but a variety of sizes are available. For an easy-to-wipe-down flush finish, choose between an integrated or undermounted design that sits level with the worksurface or a top-mounted sink that is raised above the worktop. If space is very tight, consider opting for a circular sink with no drainer, or a corner sink. When buying, check the position of the tap-hole – reversible sinks have a hole at the front and the back, and the hole that is not used can be used for pop-up waste control, which allows you to operate the plug by turning a knob rather than pulling the plug out by hand – useful when the water in the sink is very hot or dirty. Think about which side you would like your draining board to be and whether accessories such as strainer baskets or a waste disposal unit would be a useful addition.

SINK MATERIALS

- ⦿ **ACRYLIC** A good budget choice, acrylic sinks come in many colours, and are lightweight and easy to install. They are stain resistant and can be purchased with antibacterial coatings, but tend to be less heat resistant than some other kitchen sink materials.
- ⦿ **CERAMIC** Available in traditional designs such as the butler or Belfast – ideal if you need a deep, spacious sink. For a less rustic look, consider more contemporary designs that are set into the worktop. Ceramic is hardwearing and durable, stain, scratch and heat resistant, but can chip.
- ⦿ **COMPOSITES** A combination of an acrylic substance with added mineral particles such as silica, quartz or granite (e.g. Corian), which give added strength and depth of colour and are resistant to high temperatures. Sinks are fully integrated into the worksurface for a streamlined look, with no seams or joins to trap dirt. With light colours you will need to mop up spills immediately to avoid staining.

- ⦿ **COPPER** Copper sinks are becoming an increasingly popular choice and make a stunning addition to any kitchen. Although expensive, they are extremely resistant to scratching and staining, and their appearance actually improves with time. An additional benefit is that copper is naturally antibacterial and studies have shown that germs survive for far shorter periods on its surface than compared with stainless steel, so it's also a good sanitary choice.
- ⦿ **ENAMEL** Usually enamelled cast-iron or mild steel, with a glass-like finish. Available in matt or gloss, and in a range of colours. Can be vulnerable to chips and scratches.
- ⦿ **STAINLESS STEEL** The most popular choice for sinks – it is resistant to high temperatures, durable and easy to clean. However, it can dull and scratches quite easily, although scratches become less obvious with time. Available in different grades: 18/10 is good quality and will not distort. Stainless steel is noisy, but a vibration damper (usually a self-adhesive fibre pad) will help to keep the noise levels down.

Taps

Taps do not automatically fit all sinks so check that they are the correct size and reach for the sink bowl. If you choose a shallow sink, buy tall taps to give clearance for filling buckets. It is often possible to buy the taps as part of a complete pack with the sink. All water fittings and their installation must satisfy your local water supplier's by-laws, so check before installing them.

Check that the taps and the sink are a good match before you buy. Coloured taps may not be exactly the same colour as a coloured sink, so compare carefully. Chrome taps are the most popular type of metal tap in the kitchen. Gold and brass finishes are available but they are not very practical for a sink that is frequently used because they can discolour.

For more than one bowl choose swivelling mixer taps that can reach all the bowls.

Some taps are available with a pull-out spray. These are ideal for filling large containers with water, for cleaning large items and cleaning the sink itself.

HOT-WATER TAPS

A new addition to the market are taps, such as those available from Quooker (see Manufacturers, Retailers and Service Providers), which dispense boiling water. You simply turn the tap and boiling water for your tea or coffee comes out instantly. The water is stored in a tank (usually of around 3 litre/⅓ gallon capacity) and is very well-insulated, so requires little energy to keep it hot – running costs are estimated at around 3p per day. For safety, handles are childproof and the water comes out in a fine spray, rather than a solid jet. Hot-water taps are a stylish and practical addition to any kitchen, but do come at a price. Expect to pay upwards of £600 for a basic model!

Floors

See Flooring, page 143.

Appliances

See Large Electrical Appliances, pages 34–52.

PURCHASING THE KITCHEN

Check that the contract includes:

- Total price.
- Dates that payments are to be made. (A deposit of up to 25 per cent is reasonable, with the final payment when work is completed.)
- Exactly what is included in the price.
- Dates that work will start and finish. (Stipulate that 'time is of the essence' to help prevent major delays.)

Guarantees

Expect a guarantee of five years to cover cabinets and worktops against problems arising from faulty materials and manufacture. Members of the Kitchen Bathroom Bedroom Specialists Association (see Useful

Organisations) operate an insurance-backed deposit protection scheme called Consumer Care or a more comprehensive Consumer Care Plus Scheme, which covers the deposit, advanced payments, work-in-progress and gives a six-year warranty.

APPLIANCES

See Large Electrical Appliances, pages 34–52.

INSTALLATION

Bad installation is the cause of most problems in a kitchen. Ask for a written quotation of how long it will take: usually a working week. Sometimes new jobs will come to light during the installation, such as moving a pipe, so be prepared to pay extra.

Before installation, make sure you are definitely happy with your plan, as changing your mind any later will be expensive.

If the units are flat pack you can either collect them yourself from the store (many rent out roof racks) or have the units delivered.

If you are required to sign an acceptance form after installation make sure you thoroughly check the work first, and that the acceptance is subject to a reassessment after an appropriate period of normal use.

DIY

Only consider installing a kitchen yourself if you are competent at DIY. To give an idea on equipment, you will need an electric jigsaw, a spirit level, a power drill, plane, work bench, screwdrivers, electric glue gun, plumber's wrench, hacksaw, plumber's tape, wire strippers, electric cable and cable clips.

Installation tips

- Allocate space for short-term storage of kitchen items.
- Empty cupboards, remove curtains and unscrew kitchen accessories.
- Keep doors shut to reduce dust spreading.
- Allocate parking space for the fitter's van.

IMPORTANT
All gas appliances must be fitted by a member of the Gas Safe Register™ (see Useful Organisations).

Large Electrical Appliances

Appliances such as cookers, dishwashers and fridges are some of the most expensive items bought for the home. They are used with such frequency that an informed choice can make all the difference to the enjoyment of using the kitchen. When it comes to these items, the best savings are usually to be found on the Internet, but it always pays to shop around. Bear in mind that delivery costs could wipe out any savings on price, and that prices can change daily, so grab bargains while you can.

COOKING APPLIANCES

Hobs

Hob cooking has become increasingly popular. We are steaming and stir-frying more, reflecting healthy eating trends. The most popular hob configuration is one large burner, two medium and a simmerer, but you can also buy domino hobs that allow you to mix and match your burners according to your requirements. When buying a new hob, check heat output specifications – some do not get hot enough for searing meat or stir-frying. Built-in hobs are usually 60cm/23½in wide, but 70cm/27½in widths are becoming more popular with extra burners that can still fit into a 60cm/23½in cut-out on the worksurface.

Green tip

Induction hobs use a third less power than traditional ceramic hobs, and 50 per cent less power than gas, so are a good environmentally friendly choice.

ELECTRIC SEALED PLATE HOBS

Sealed plate hobs have declined in popularity. They are normally the cheapest to buy, but are quite expensive to run. The heating element is covered by a solid metal plate. Compared with other electric hobs, these are slow to heat up and cool down, and it can be difficult to maintain a low temperature for simmering. They are also quite fiddly to clean.

ABOVE Electric sealed plate hob

ELECTRIC GLASS-TOPPED HOBS

The heating systems are hidden beneath the tough ceramic glass surface. Patterned zones on the glass surface indicate the size and position of the heat source. All have a safety device that prevents the ceramic glass from overheating. Glass-topped hobs fit flush to the surface of the kitchen worktop, so are practical and easy to clean. There are three main types of ceramic glass hob to choose from:

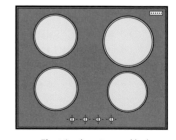

ABOVE Electric glass-topped hob

HALOGEN Work by from infrared lamps under the glass and heat up extremely quickly. They are faster, but usually more expensive than traditional radiant heat ceramic glass hobs.

INDUCTION Induction hobs heat the pan directly via a spiral copper coil beneath the glass surface, which transfers energy directly to the pan. The coil is not activated until an iron-based magnetic pan is placed on to it, so the glass itself does not need to heat up for cooking. When the pan is removed from the heat, the hob goes cold, thus reducing the risk of burns. Induction hobs were initially very costly to buy but are becoming increasingly affordable.

They are economical to run, easy to use and highly responsive. Not suitable for anyone fitted with a pacemaker.

RADIANT less costly than halogen ceramic glass hobs, but also slower to heat.

GAS HOBS

Gas is still one of the most popular choices for a hob. It is fast, responsive and can be used with all types of pan. Most gas hobs can be dismantled for easier cleaning, but it can still be fiddly to keep them looking their best. Go for a hob with a variety of burner ratings that will suit different types of cooking. If you use a wok frequently, a gas hob is probably the best choice.

ABOVE Gas hob with barbecue grill

FEATURES TO LOOK FOR ON ALL HOBS

Expect to find the following on all built-in hobs; some of these may be less common on free-standing cookers:

- **AUTOMATIC IGNITION** Will spark gas alight when controls are turned and pushed in.
- **AUTOMATIC SWITCHOUT/TIMEOUT** Heat switches off if left unattended for a long period.
- **CHILD-SAFETY CONTROLS** Touch controls that can be locked to prevent children altering settings or switching on the hob.
- **COATED PAN SUPPORTS** Much easier to clean than bare stainless steel.
- **DUAL ELEMENT** Saves energy by matching the size of the element to the size of the pan – select only the inner ring for smaller pans, or the outer and inner ring for larger pans.
- **ELECTRONIC BOIL START/AUTOMATIC HEAT REDUCE** Zone heats up to the highest setting then reduces after a set time to simmer.
- **FISH KETTLE/CASSEROLE ZONE** Elongated cooking zone that can accommodate a fish kettle or long casserole dish.
- **FLAME FAILURE PROTECTION** If the burner goes out accidentally, flame will re-light automatically or gas stops running.
- **HOT HOB LIGHT** Comes on when hob rings are still hot.
- **OVERSPILL PROTECTION** Detects when liquid has boiled over and turns the power off.

- **POWER BOOST** Increases the wattage on one or two rings by up to 800W for quick boiling, but reduces the wattage of zones operating on the same side by around 700W.
- **RANGE OF HEAT OUTPUTS** Low to maintain a good simmer and high for quick heating/stir-frying etc.
- **REMOVABLE PAN SUPPORTS** Can be taken apart and washed. Consider weight and robustness.
- **REMOVABLE CONTROLS** For easy cleaning.
- **TIMER** Can be set so hob will switch off automatically after a prescribed period of time.
- **ULTRA RAPID BURNERS** For bringing water to the boil or frying food in a wok.

IMPORTANT

Any gas hob must be fitted by a member of the Gas Safe Register™ (see Useful Organisations)

SPECIAL HOB TYPES

- ⊙ **BARBECUE GRILL** Built-in hob that simulates barbecue cooking. Look for one with a removable lava-stone tray for easy cleaning. Most must be used in conjunction with an extractor fan.
- ⊙ **DOMINO** Normally two-ring hobs that can be combined with other hobs to provide a range of cooking techniques, such as a two-ring gas burner with a barbecue grill, or a gas wok burner with an electric griddle. You can mix and match according to your needs. Joining strips are usually required for a neat finish.

- ⊙ **DUAL FUEL** These allow you to combine two different fuel types, such as gas and electric, electric and induction, or even gas and induction.
- ⊙ **GRIDDLE HOB** These have a flat cooking surface that fits flush with the worktop. Food items, such as steaks, eggs can be placed directly on to the hob without the need for a pan.
- ⊙ **TEPPANYAKI** The ultimate griddle hob, these are designed to emulate Japanese fat-free 'hot-plate' cooking. Very sleek and attractive, but extremely expensive.

Ovens and grills (including microwave ovens)

Consider whether you need a double rather than a single oven – a second oven is ideal for warming food and plates – and whether to choose a built-in model or one that fits underneath the worksurface. Single ovens have a grill that cannot be used at the same time as the oven, so they are not as versatile as a double oven. Built-under ovens slot under the worksurface but you will have to bend in order to reach the oven and grill.

ELECTRIC OVENS

Electric is the most popular fuel type. Choose from:

CONVENTIONAL (STATIC) These are less widely available now and generally found in basic models. Electric elements are in the sides or top and bottom of the oven. These have zoned heating: the top of the oven is usually hotter than the bottom. Some top and bottom elements work independently, which is ideal for base crisping, or browning the surface of some foods.

FAN-OPERATED Most electric cookers now have a fan to circulate heat more evenly, so the temperature is the same throughout the oven.

In 'fan-assisted' types, the air is heated by electric elements in the oven sides, while in convection ovens the element is wrapped around the fan. The advantages are:

- ⊙ Cooking is quicker.
- ⊙ Colour is even, but usually paler and less glossy than on food cooked in a conventional oven.
- ⊙ Pre-heating is usually unnecessary.
- ⊙ Repositioning shelves is unnecessary, as is swapping trays halfway through cooking.
- ⊙ Good for batch baking (cooking on more than one shelf) because of the even heat distribution.
- ⊙ Cooking times and temperatures are always less than traditional ovens but by variable amounts depending on the make of cooker. So follow the manufacturer's instructions carefully.
- ⊙ The food surface may be drier and less crisp.

Changing oven types

Changing from a static to a fan oven takes some adjustment. Always follow manufacturers' instructions for cooking times and temperatures, or if you are trying an old favourite recipe reduce the heat by about 10°C/50°F and the time by 10–15 minutes. You can always return the dish for further cooking. Leave space around dishes and at the sides to allow the air currents to circulate. Check whether the manufacturer recommends grilling with the oven door open or closed.

Green tip

Since 2003, electric ovens have had to be graded from A–G for energy efficiency. Look for an A-rated oven for the best energy efficiency.

MULTI-FUNCTION This type of oven is a combination of a fan and a conventional oven. It therefore provides the user with the maximum versatility. Each option can be used separately or together depending on the type of food you are cooking and the grill can be used with the fan, giving a similar effect to a rotisserie. A multi-function oven is ideal for batch baking and traditional cooking.

GAS OVENS

CONVENTIONAL (BRITISH) GAS OVENS The temperature in the middle of the oven relates to the selected gas mark. The top shelf is slightly hotter, lower shelf slightly cooler and the base cooler still. 'Zoned heat' is ideal for cooking complete meals, where dishes require different temperatures. Gas is a much moister form of heat than electric, particularly noticeable in baking. It results in food with a glossy appearance on the outside and a moist texture inside.

IMPORTED GAS OVENS Many built-in gas cookers sold in the UK are of European origin. The burners are concealed under the base of the oven, so food is crisped from underneath. They are ideal for pizzas and pastries, but you must avoid using the base plate of the oven as a shelf. Heat distribution differs from that in a conventional gas oven, so always follow the manufacturer's instructions carefully. Cooking techniques are similar to fan cooking, and heat is more evenly distributed throughout the oven, so you will have to reduce cooking times and temperatures. The amount of reduction does vary depending on the make of cooker, so again, always follow the manufacturer's instructions carefully.

RANGE OVENS

These have either two side-by-side ovens or one extra-wide oven with an internal grill, plus a storage or warming compartment and a substantial hob. You will not, however, get more cooking space than with a conventional oven – external dimensions are larger but the oven may be of normal size or even smaller. Check the number of shelves supplied and usable space. In most cases, the hobs put range cookers in a class of their own because they are quick, powerful and versatile, and most have the advantage of including useful extras such as a wok burner, an extra burner for fish kettles, a griddle or barbecue plates and warming zones.

HEAT STORAGE OVENS

Heat storage or Aga-type cookers use stored heat. They take approximately six hours to heat up, so are kept on at all times. Heat inside the oven stays relatively constant, but there is a large variation in temperature between gradients, so the user must move items up and down to control cooking rates. They look beautiful and help to warm the home, but can be expensive to run and require practice to use effectively. Aga-type cookers can use various types of fuel, including electricity, gas, oil, wood and solid fuel. Most, except all electric, require a flue and are very heavy to install.

ABOVE Slot-in oven

ABOVE Built-in oven

ABOVE Range oven

ABOVE Heat storage oven

GRILLS

Grilling is done by intense radiant heat at close range. It is quick, and provides even browning over the whole heated area. Depending on the type of cooker, there is a grill either at the top of the main oven cavity, in the small oven, in both ovens, or in a separate grill cavity.

ELECTRIC GRILLS Most cookers and microwaves with grills use radiant elements that require about five minutes of pre-heating. On the more expensive cookers, grills are faster and more efficient and require little or no pre-heating.

GAS GRILLS Sometimes separate or in the main oven cavity. There are three types to choose from:

FRET BURNERS Are situated either at the back or in the middle of the grill cavity. They require no pre-heating, but browning can be uneven, especially when the grill pan is at full capacity.

SURFACE COMBUSTION BURNERS Are concealed behind mesh. This provides a more even heat distribution, resulting in even browning.

POINTS TO LOOK FOR ON ALL OVENS AND GRILLS

- ⊙ If you batch bake and cook traditional foods, opt for a multi-function oven. If you only cook traditional foods choose a static type; otherwise a fan oven is better for batch baking, quick cooking (reheating ready meals) and defrosting.
- ⊙ Double ovens offer more versatility and are good for families. Electric cookers, where the main oven is fan or multi-function, have a smaller, traditional second oven. Make sure you can fit some of your popular weekday cookware in it; some second ovens tend to be very shallow.
- ⊙ Alternatively, look for a separate grill and main oven for versatility and convenience.
- ⊙ Check for cool-touch oven doors, especially useful if you have young children. Even on a high temperature the oven door will remain warm only.
- ⊙ Eye-level grills are the most convenient to use. Otherwise, check that a grill below the hob is comfortable for you to use.
- ⊙ To save money and energy choose a half-grill facility for small batches of grilling.
- ⊙ Check the oven is at a comfortable height for loading.
- ⊙ Choose side-opening or drop-down doors to suit your needs.

- ⊙ Clearly marked and easy-to-use controls. Some are illuminated for easier use.
- ⊙ On gas appliances look for safety and flame-failure devices.
- ⊙ BSI approval or equivalent Continental standards.
- ⊙ Storage drawer and plate-warming racks. Grill can double for plate warming.
- ⊙ Reversible door hanging to fit in with your kitchen layout.
- ⊙ Stay-clean liners make cleaning easier. They may need replacing during the lifetime of the cooker. Normal linings are less expensive and may be cleaned with an oven cleaner. Top-range ovens use a high temperature pyrolitic cleaning system that cleans every part of the oven's interior. During the cleaning cycle the internal temperature rises to around 260°C/500°F and soiling is converted into ash, which collects on the floor of the oven, and can then easily be swept out.
- ⊙ Minute minders may be useful.
- ⊙ An oven light and clear door viewing panel.
- ⊙ Automatic timers that will switch the oven on when you are out.
- ⊙ Child-proof controls.

INSTALLING OVENS AND GRILLS

⊙ **BUILT-IN/UNDER** These have become increasingly popular as more people opt for fitted kitchens. Compared with free-standing or slot-in models they can be installed at the most convenient height and position. Fuels can be combined offering maximum versatility. Before choosing, decide whether you want built-in or built-under. With a built-in, the oven is set into a column-style housing unit, so a cupboard and worktop space is lost. If space is limited choose a built-under unit which slots under the worktop. Remember you will have to bend to use the oven and grill. Built-in ovens come in standard sizes. A single model will fit into a space 600mm/24in wide, deep and high, and a double oven will fit into a space 600mm/24in wide and deep, and 900mm/35in high. Electric double ovens require a special cooker socket, but single ovens use an ordinary 13-amp socket.

⊙ **FREE-STANDING** More traditional in design because they can have an eye-level grill. This is normally available on gas cookers only. Most electric models have fan or fan-assisted ovens, while only the more expensive models have multi-function ovens. Check the oven is a comfortable height. Some models have a storage drawer, which raises the oven above ground level. The hob is usually the less expensive radiant, sealed plate or gas.

⊙ **SLOT-IN** Gives a built-in look. It is streamlined because the cooker is the same height as the adjoining worksurface. Unlike a built-in cooker, you can take it with you when you move. Grills are low level, situated in the main oven cavity or in the second smaller oven. Some manufacturers recommend grilling with the door open, others with the door closed. Consider this if you have children around. The type of hob depends on the price. Top of the range have either ceramic, halogen or a combination. Some cookers have a gas hob and an electric oven, i.e. dual fuel.

CERAMIC GRILLS Situated behind a heat-resistant glass panel giving a very even heat distribution. Easy to clean, but takes longer than a normal gas grill to heat up. Once pre-heated, grilling is very fast.

HALOGEN GRILLS Only found in microwave ovens. (See Microwave Ovens, pages 40–42.)

Cooker hoods

These can be installed above built-under or free-standing slot-in cookers to draw grease, odours and steam from the air. There are two types available: recirculating and ducted, and both require some sort of grease filter. Cooker hoods come in two widths, 600mm/24in or 900mm/35in. Because hoods rely on moving air in order to operate, they can be noisy when used.

If you are fitting a hood above a gas hob there should be a minimum space of 750mm/30in between the two appliances. For electric hoods, the minimum height clearance is 450mm/18in – measurements can vary though, so always follow the manufacturer's instructions.

TIP
To work out the extraction rate you need, calculate the volume of the room in cubic metres/feet, and then multiply by ten to allow for ten changes of air per hour.

RECIRCULATING

These are the most popular type and the cheapest. They require no external ducting so can be sited on an internal wall, but are less efficient as filtered air is returned to the kitchen. Consider only if you live in a flat or if your cooker is situated too far from an external wall. Two filters are required for this type of extractor – a charcoal filter to absorb smells and a grease filter.

DUCTED

If your hob is on an outside wall, choose a ducted hood. They are more expensive than recirculating but performance is superior. Stale air is ducted through pipes to the outside, so no charcoal filter is necessary. For the most efficient air flow make sure the pipework to the outside wall is as short as possible. A grease filter is necessary.

Microwave ovens

Microwave ovens work by generating electromagnetic waves. These are produced by a device inside the oven called a magnetron. Microwave energy travels through the air but no heat is generated until it is absorbed by the food. That is why it works so fast – because no energy is wasted. Microwaves can pass through certain substances without harming them, such as plastic, china, paper and glass, but will not pass through metal (metal reflects the waves, which is why it cannot be used in most microwave ovens).

A microwave oven will cook, heat, reheat and defrost, but will not crisp or brown food. Combination microwave ovens are more flexible and allow you to cook by microwave only, grill only or convection heat only; you can also use the microwave and grill together. Microwave power is measured in watts from 600–1100W – the higher the wattage, the quicker food will cook. Not all microwaves and combination ovens defrost well – some start to cook food even when on the lowest setting.

TIP
The cooker hood is only as effective as the filters are clean, so make sure to clean or change these in accordance with the manufacturer's instructions.

When comparing models, the turntable size and interior height are more important than volume. For family use, the turntable diameter should ideally be at least 30cm/12in and interior height more than 20cm/8in to accommodate larger portions of food. If thinking of buying a simple model with dial controls, check the calibrations for the first five minutes clearly show the all-important seconds. If, like most households, you use your microwave oven mainly to defrost and reheat food, it's probably not worth buying a model with an enormous variety of weird and wonderful programmes.

POWER LEVELS

- When cooking by microwave the most frequently used power settings are high, medium and low, and it is unnecessary to have nine or ten power levels.
- Whatever the wattage of your microwave, the High/Full setting will always be 100 per cent of the power output.
- Some combination ovens only have pre-set programmes for combination cooking. This means the microwave power level and convection temperature is pre-set, e.g. medium microwave and 180°C/350°F. These can limit your choice if you want to use recipes other than just those in the instruction manual. A model that allows you to select your own settings is the most versatile.
- Make sure the oven has a full range of temperatures available for convection cooking.

MICROWAVE OVEN FEATURES TO LOOK FOR

- **AUTO COOK/REHEAT/DEFROST** Automatically calculates power and length of cooking time.
- **AUTO PRE-HEAT** Maintains the requested oven temperature for a set period, then automatically switches off.
- **AUTO WEIGHT COOK** Automatically calculates the cooking time according to the weight of the food.
- **CHAOS DEFROST** Uses random pulses of microwave energy to reduce defrosting times even further.
- **DELAY START** Programmes the oven to come on automatically at a set time of day.
- **ONE-TOUCH CONTROLS** For reheating specific foods, such as fish or milk, at the press of a button.

- **QUARTZ GRILL (BULBS SET BEHIND METAL MESH)** Quick to heat and easy to clean. Less powerful than a conventional oven grill, but suitable for surface browning of food.
- **RADIANT GRILL (AS IN A CONVENTIONAL OVEN)** Better for cooking thicker foods, such as pork chops, but does require pre-heating and is not as powerful as a conventional oven grill.
- **SENSOR COOKING** Detects the level of moisture in food and the oven's humidity and adjusts power levels and cooking time accordingly, for the best results.
- **STAND TIMER** Can be set for a rest period during multi-stage cooking programmes or at the end of cooking, during which food continues to cook due to residual heat.

WHERE TO SITE A MICROWAVE OVEN

Microwaves are usually sited on a worksurface. They need to be placed with a gap of about 15cm/6in above and behind for ventilation. This is particularly important for a combination oven, because a lot of air is dispelled when using the dual function. Microwave ovens can be hung on the wall using special brackets to save space. If a microwave is built into a kitchen you will need a ventilation kit, available from the manufacturer.

MICROWAVE COOKWARE

See Microwave Cookware, pages 75–6.

ACCESSORIES

BASIC

TURNTABLE To ensure even cooking, food must be turned. If your microwave has a turntable (as do most models) this will be done automatically. With a turntable, reheating is more even, and there is no need to keep interrupting the programme and turning the dish during cooking.

DEFROSTING RACK A defrosting rack is useful because it raises the food off the oven floor or turntable allowing the food to be defrosted from below as well as from above.

MICROWAVE AND GRILL/COMBINATION OVEN

COOKING RACK Cooking racks are useful to raise the food nearer to the grill element to speed up the browning process. You will need a high rack for grilling small items such as sausages and a low rack so you can fit in larger cooking dishes such as a dish of cauliflower cheese.

DRIP PAN A drip pan is useful to catch fat and make cleaning easier. Some ovens have splash guards that are placed over the drip tray to prevent the fat splashing up into the oven.

BUILT-IN SHELVES It can be difficult to remove a high rack with food balanced on it from a hot oven. To get around this some ovens have built-in shelves that make removing the food easier. Turn the food to ensure even reheating.

MICROWAVE SAFETY

Microwave ovens are safe appliances. They will only work if the door is firmly shut. A microwave door has at least two switches, which will cut off the power if the door is not shut properly. Keep the oven door and hinges clean and inspect regularly for corrosion.

If you are worried about microwave leakage, contact the manufacturer, who will send a service engineer to check the oven with accurate equipment.

Microwave leakage detectors are available from electrical stores, but they are not always completely accurate.

Green tip

Some microwave ovens use a lot of energy when in standby mode – if you're concerned about energy use and the environment, buy a model with an energy-safe mode. This reduces the amount of power used, with power only being drawn for the clock.

Microwave cooking tips

- After heating, always check food is piping hot throughout. If you have a food thermometer check it reaches 70°C/158°F in the centre. Feel the middle underside of the container: it should be hot.

- The outer edges of food will cook first in a microwave oven. Place thicker parts of food at the outside of the cooking container and thinner parts at the centre.

- Stir food or rotate dishes during cooking to ensure even heating.

- Where a recipe specifies standing time it is important to follow it exactly. The heat within the food continues to cook it even when it has been removed from the oven and the standing time is calculated to take account of this.

- Leave any covered food vented, so that steam can escape while it cooks.

- Don't operate your microwave oven while it is empty – the microwaves will bounce off the interior and could damage the oven.

COOLING APPLIANCES

Freezers

There are two main types available, upright and chest freezers (more suitable for larger or awkward-shaped items). However, you can also now buy free-standing or built-in drawer freezers, where each drawer can be opened individually and is its own freezer compartment. Choosing the type depends upon where the freezer is to be situated and the space available. Both usually have an area for fast freezing of food.

CLIMATE CLASS

When choosing a freezer, it is important to look for the 'climate class' rating, which tells you the range of temperatures with which it can cope. N (normal) is for a room with a temperature range of 16–32°C/61–90°F. If your room drops below 16°C/61°F at night – or you keep your freezer in a garage, where temperatures can fall as low as 10°C/50°F – an SN (sub-normal) model might be more suitable. An ST (sub tropical) model is for places with temperatures between 18–38°C/64–100°F.

INSTALLATION

Always allow a 2.5cm/1in space around the back, sides and top of the freezer for ventilation, otherwise the condenser will have to work harder and the freezer will not run so efficiently. After your new freezer is delivered you need to leave it sitting for around six hours before plugging it in. This

---

FREEZER FEATURES TO LOOK FOR

- ⊙ **AUDIBLE SIGNAL** To warn if the door has been left open, or internal temperature is too high to store food safely.
- ⊙ **CHILDPROOF FEATURES** To stop temperature of freezer being altered accidentally. Look for a temperature dial that can only be turned with a coin, or buttons that have to be unlocked before settings can be changed.
- ⊙ **CLEAR INDICATOR LIGHTS AND DIGITAL TEMPERATURE DISPLAYS** Help you make sure the freezer is at the correct temperature.
- ⊙ **COLD ACCUMULATION BLOCK** A block that is frozen and stored in the freezer to increase the length of time the freezer stays cold in the event of a power failure.
- ⊙ **ENCLOSED CONDENSER PLATE** Makes cleaning easier as dust will not collect on it.
- ⊙ **FAST-FREEZE** Helps keep temperature low when you add large quantities of fresh food. Some models automatically revert to the normal setting once food is frozen; others have to be switched back manually.

- ⊙ **FREEZER TRAY** Small tray at the top or bottom of the freezer that is useful for freezing small items such as berries and herbs, and for ice-cube trays.
- ⊙ **FROST-FREE** No need to defrost – it incorporates a heater that comes on periodically to eliminate ice, and a fan that circulates cold air around the cavity. Frost-free models tend to be slightly more expensive and may be noisier to run than standard models.
- ⊙ **PULL-OUT DRAINAGE SPOUT** Allows water to be drained away more easily when you defrost the freezer.
- ⊙ **STURDY DRAWERS** Easier to pack and clean than shelves as they can be removed, and keep the cold better than mesh drawers. Before you buy, check that drawers glide easily and that there are stops at the back.

allows the gases inside to settle. Once you have switched it on, try to leave it overnight to get to the correct temperature before packing with food.

Fridges and fridge-freezers

The fridge is one of the most important appliances in your home, so it's worth spending a bit of time to make sure you choose the right model. There are two main types of fridge – larder fridges (where all the space can be used for storing fresh food) and those with an ice box compartment for storing commercially frozen food and making ice cubes. The ice box will have a star rating to indicate how long food can safely be stored. With a combined fridge-freezer, you will need to decide which compartment you want to be bigger, and whether you want the fridge or the freezer to be on top.

AMERICAN-STYLE FRIDGE-FREEZERS

Becoming more and more popular, these are usually wider than standard fridge-freezers, with the typical configuration being side-by-side doors that open in opposite directions from the centre. They offer larger than average capacities and can look very attractive. Most models are frost-free and have several cooling zones in different areas. Water filters and ice-cube makers are also often standard (but bear in mind, you may need to get these plumbed in (some have built-in water tanks so you don't need to plumb them in)). However, fitting an American-style fridge-freezer one into a typical British kitchen can be a tight squeeze as they can be up to three times wider than a standard fridge-freezer. The large size of the evaporating unit means they can also be quite noisy to run.

INSTALLATION

FREE-STANDING For efficient and safe operation, fridges and freezers should have a gap of at least 3cm/1⅛in around the sides and top of the unit. (Check with manufacturer for exact details.) When installing

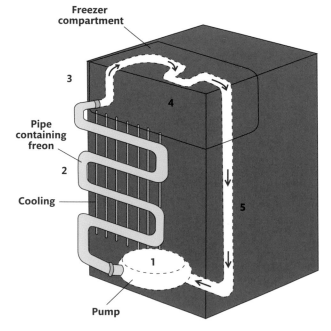

Freezer compartment

3

4

Pipe containing freon

2

Cooling

5

1

Pump

LEFT Fridge features

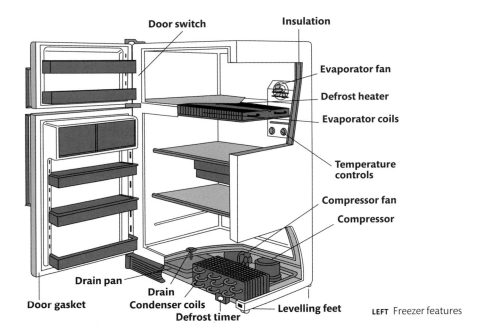

Door switch · Insulation · Evaporator fan · Defrost heater · Evaporator coils · Temperature controls · Compressor fan · Compressor · Drain pan · Drain · Condenser coils · Defrost timer · Door gasket · Levelling feet

LEFT Freezer features

your new fridge/fridge-freezer, always keep it upright and leave to
stand for least six hours before switching on to allow the gases inside
to settle.

BUILT-IN Built-in fridges and freezers are fitted into the kitchen units,
often with a matching door. The fitting is usually secure at the top
with height adjustments made at the base.

FRIDGE/FRIDGE-FREEZER FEATURES TO LOOK FOR

- **AUTO-DEFROST** Defrost water in the fridge
  drains into a trough at the back of the appliance
  and evaporates.

- **DIGITAL DISPLAYS, INDICATOR LIGHTS AND
  AUDIBLE SIGNALS** Allow you to monitor
  temperature easily, and will also let you know if
  the door has been left open or if there is a fault
  with the appliance.

- **EXTRA STORAGE COMPARTMENTS IN THE
  DOOR** Handy for items you need to keep upright
  or for storing smaller items.

- **FRIDGE SHELVES THAT SPLIT IN TWO (OR ARE
  HINGED)** Help with storing bottles and bulky
  items.

- **HUMIDITY CONTROLS ON SALAD, MEAT AND
  CHEESE DRAWERS** These allow you to alter the
  air flow and temperature to help keep food
  fresher for longer and in peak condition.

- **REVERSIBLE DOORS** This allows you to change
  the door to either left or right-sided opening
  according to what is best suited to your kitchen.

- **SEPARATE CONTROLS (FOR FRIDGE-
  FREEZERS)** Allow you to set the fridge and
  freezer controls independently of each other.

- **SOLID DRAWERS IN FREEZER/GLASS SHELVES
  IN FRIDGE** Retain cold more effectively than
  mesh drawers and are easier to pack and clean.
  Check that the drawers and shelves glide easily
  and that there are stops on the back.

- **VACATION/HOLIDAY MODE** Useful feature that
  allows you to switch off the fridge compartment,
  but leave the freezer running while you are away.

- **WATER FILTERS AND ICE-CUBE MAKERS**
  Great for providing a constant supply of cooled,
  filtered water and ice, but may need plumbing
  into the main water supply.

Green tips

✳ All fridges/fridge-freezers are awarded an energy efficiency rating between A++–G. After central heating, fridges and fridge-freezers are the biggest users of energy because they stay switched on throughout the year, so it's worth buying one with a good rating. Choose a model with an A++ rating for the best energy efficiency.

✳ Don't open the fridge/fridge-freezer more often than is necessary or leave the door open for long periods. Check door seals regularly to ensure a tight fit – the seal should be able to hold a sheet of paper firmly in place.

✳ Don't overfill your fridge – this restricts air circulation, making it harder to maintain the correct temperature and thus using more energy. For best results, leave it around 20 per cent empty.

✳ Fridges and fridge-freezers use less energy when placed in a cool environment, so don't site your fridge next to a cooker, radiator or boiler.

✳ Under the Waste Electrical and Electronic Equipment Directive, retailers are obliged to help customers recycle their old appliances. When you are buying a new one, ask in the shop whether they will take away your old fridge/fridge-freezer. Most will charge a small fee for this service – if you prefer to deal things yourself, then contact your council to find the nearest recycling site. Alternatively, if the item is still in working order, you may be able to find it a new home by using Freecycle (www.uk.freecycle.org, see Useful Organisations).

STAR RATINGS AND STORAGE TIMES

Commercially frozen foods can be stored in an ice box or freezer compartment depending upon its rating, as follows:

✱ 1 week Compartment at –6°C/21°F

✱✱ 1 month Compartment at –12°C/10°F

✱✱✱ 3 months Compartment at –18°C/0°F

NB Compartments with 1–3 stars cannot be used for freezing down fresh food; this can only be done in a four-star freezer compartment.

✱✱✱✱ 6 months (depending upon food type; refer to manufacturer's instruction book) Compartment at –18°C/0°F

RECOMMENDED OPERATION TEMPERATURES

Fridge: 0°C–5°C/32–41°F

Zero/Chiller Compartment: 0°C–3°C/32–37°F

Freezer: –18°C/0°F

WASHING APPLIANCES

Dishwashers

Dishwashers are one of those appliances we wonder how we ever managed without. They save time and make washing-up an easy task. Dishwashers are more hygienic than washing-up by hand. The dishwasher's high wash temperatures – hotter than your hands can bear – and efficiency of the dishwasher detergents play an important role in this result. Dishwashers use less power and water than traditional washing-up, so are also more environmentally friendly.

Look for features that make using the machine easier, and bear in mind that special programmes like 'delicates' are only worth paying extra for if you will use them regularly. It makes sense to go for the biggest machine (i.e. largest number of place settings) you can accommodate in your kitchen, but if space is limited, compact and slimline models are available. Most dishwashers take in cold water only (cold fill) and offer a range of programmes for optimum cleaning efficiency. There will usually be at least three programmes, with the main one being at 65°C/149°F. Features to look for include:

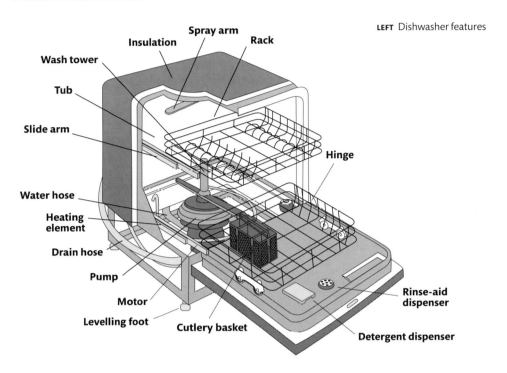

LEFT Dishwasher features

Spray arm
Insulation
Rack
Wash tower
Tub
Slide arm
Hinge
Water hose
Heating element
Drain hose
Pump
Motor
Levelling foot
Cutlery basket
Rinse-aid dispenser
Detergent dispenser

DISHWASHER FEATURES TO LOOK FOR

- ⊙ **ANTI-FLOODING DEVICE** Offers peace of mind. For extra protection, check when you buy a machine that its inlet pipe has a leak sensor that turns off water if it floods.
- ⊙ **BASKETS** Should be height adjustable to accommodate glasses and larger plates, sturdy, smooth-running and stay on, even when pulled right out. There should be enough room in the top basket for large plates and pans without obstructing the spray arm.
- ⊙ **CHILD-SAFETY LOCK** Prevents door from being opened during the wash cycle.
- ⊙ **DELAY START** Allows you to set the machine to start washing automatically after a time delay.

- ⊙ **FOLDABLE PLATE RACKS** These help you to make the most of mixed loads.
- ⊙ **HYDROSENSOR** Alters the amount of water used by monitoring how dirty it is as it is pumped from the machine. Sensors identify when dishes are clean and can then automatically end the programme, saving water.
- ⊙ **PRE-RINSE** Useful for rinsing plates before washing a full load.
- ⊙ **SALT AND RINSE-AID INDICATORS** Let you know when to refill.

Green tip

* Dishwashers are rated according to energy use and drying. Choose a model rated as A for both to get the best environmental performance.
* Choose a model with an 'eco' programme that uses less energy and water.
* Use the coolest setting possible to achieve acceptable results.
* Ensure the machine is full whenever you use it.
* Look for dishwashing detergents that are biodegradable and free of phosphates.

Items unsuitable for dishwashers

* **ALUMINIUM PANS** (Including hard-anodised, non-stick coated and cast aluminium). React with detergent and discolour.
* **ANTIQUE OR HAND-PAINTED CHINA** Colours will fade.
* **CAST-IRON PANS** Rust if uncoated.
* **CUTLERY WITH BONE, WOOD, PEARL OR PLASTIC HANDLES** Handles can crack, swell and distort; check with the manufacturer.
* **LEAD CRYSTAL** May crack or dull or become etched with limescale.
* **UNGLAZED POTTERY** May crack.
* **WOODEN ITEMS** Will swell and eventually crack unless specially treated.

DRYING CYCLE

Full-sized dishwashers usually have a drying cycle. There are two different methods used:

HOT AIR DRYING (ELEMENT) Most effective drying method but uses slightly more electricity. An element heats the air to dry items in the dishwasher.

RESIDUAL HEAT (HOT RINSE) Uses the residual heat from the final rinse to dry the load.

Tumble-driers

There are two types, vented or condenser. Vented driers are more common. Whether you choose a vented or a condenser drier will depend on where you need to put it. A condenser can go anywhere as it does not have a hose – instead, the hot air produced is turned back into water and collected in a built-in container, which must be emptied regularly. Vented driers use a hose to pass steam through a window, wall or door to the outside, so you need access to one of these within reach of the hose. If you don't have much space, then consider choosing a compact model, which can sit on a worktop or even be wall-mounted – or choose a model that can be stacked on top of your washing machine.

Most tumble-driers are quite simple to operate and will have a timer to select the period for drying, and a high or low heat selector button. Other machines are most sophisticated and have a range of programmes to choose from. Here are some features to look out for:

ANTI-CREASE Tumbles clothes without hot air after drying time has ended to help prevent creases forming.

COOL-DOWN PHASE Allows clothes to cool slowly, reducing shrinkage, as the heater switches off for the last few minutes.

RESERVOIR FULL ALERT Lights or alarm that lets you know when it's time to empty the water collecting container on a condenser drier.

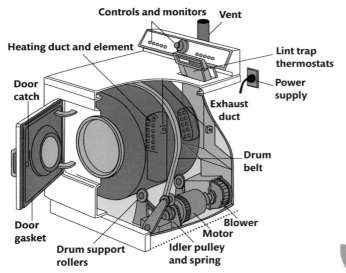

Controls and monitors Vent

Heating duct and element

Door catch

Lint trap
thermostats

Power supply

Exhaust duct

Drum belt

Door gasket

Blower
Motor

Drum support rollers

Idler pulley and spring

STEAM OPTION Some models have a steam progamme which reduces creasing so there is minimal ironing required.

SENSOR DRYING Will dry to a set moisture level – they are useful for eliminating guesswork in setting drying time and help to reduce unnecessary energy use.

Washing machines

Buying washing machine these days can be daunting. There is such a bewildering array of features to choose from, designed to improve cleaning power and increase efficiency. The best thing to do is think about how often you use your machine and what sort of loads you wash most often. This will help you narrow down which features will be of most use, and which machine will be the most efficient and economical for your particular household.

The most common type of washing machine has a porthole door at the front. Manufacturers are continually bringing out higher capacity models, with some claiming to wash up to 9kg/20lb of cottons and 4kg/9lb of synthetics (one set of double bed linen), however this can be a very tight squeeze! Standard dimensions to fit under a kitchen worktop measure 850mm/33½in high, 600mm/24in wide and 600mm/24in deep. Slimline models are the same height but not as deep: 450mm/18in or 320mm/13in.

INSTALLATION

Before installation, transit straps must be removed – these are usually located at the back of the machine. Machines preferably should be sited on a solid floor, but if you must put them on a suspended floor, then it is a good idea to screw a 2.5cm/1in thick suitably sized piece of MDF or solid plywood to the floor on which the machine will sit – this helps to reduce vibration and will prolong the life of the machine. Ensure the machine is level and plumbing hoses are not kinked or twisted before pushing it into place.

Green tip

✱ Tumble-driers are one of the more expensive appliances to run in your home, so choose a model with a good energy efficiency rating. Ratings go from A–G, with A being the best choice. You could also consider buying a gas-powered tumble-drier – typically, these cost far less to run and have a much smaller carbon footprint than standard driers.

✱ To avoid energy wastage, always try to dry similar fabrics together and don't overload your machine – most driers will take around 6kg/13lb dry weight of clothing.

✱ Reuse the water from the condenser reservoir to water plants or put in your iron.

✱ Clean the 'fluff filter' after each use to maintain tiptop energy performance.

✱ The most environmentally friendly option is not to use your drier at all! So, if you have a garden or outside drying area, always hang your washing on a line to dry whenever weather permits!

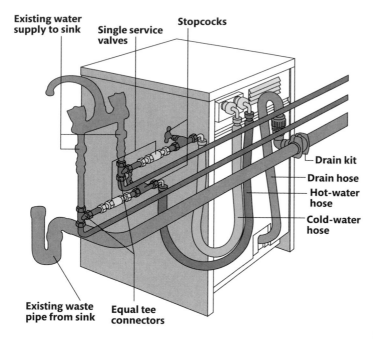

Existing water
supply to sink

Single service
valves

Stopcocks

Drain kit

Drain hose

Hot-water
hose

Cold-water
hose

Existing waste
pipe from sink

Equal tee
connectors

LEFT Washing machine features

WASH PROGRAMMES

The main programme dial selects the wash cycle, which is set to correspond to wash care labels on clothes (see Understanding Laundry Symbols, page 240). Some machines automatically set the temperature while others have a separate temperature control. This gives greater flexibility to use lower temperatures with different wash cycles.

Spin speeds are usually automatically set, depending upon the programme selected. Full agitation cotton washes have a maximum spin, while the easy-care and wool programmes with less agitation use a lower spin. Spin speeds can often be lowered using an option button.

LESS COMMON MACHINE TYPES

◉ **AUTOMATIC TOP LOADERS** These are designed to sit level with an adjacent worktop. The controls may protrude higher, and space is needed to open the lid. (Height from 850mm/33 ½in plus lid; width from about 400mm/16in to 600mm/24in; depth 600mm/24in.) The plumbing needed is the same as for an automatic washing machine (cold and hot water supply and a drain hose). The wash programmes are the same as for front-loading machines, corresponding to clothes care labels, but extra features and options will be less sophisticated.

◉ **TWIN TUB** These are not automatic and are filled from the kitchen taps, so need to be pulled out for use. They will slot under a worktop for storage when not in use. There are two compartments, one for washing and rinsing and one for spinning. Clothes are agitated in the water either by a central spindle-mounted paddle or an agitator on the back of the compartment. The clothes are moved manually over to the second drum for spinning. Twin tubs are good for households with small washes that can be finished quickly. Height 750mm/30in; width 760mm/30in; depth 460mm/18in. Twin tubs will wash a maximum load of about 3kg/6lb of cottons, and 2kg/4lb of synthetics.

WASHING MACHINE FEATURES AND PROGRAMMES

- ⊙ **ANTI-CREASE CYCLE** Periodically tumbles clothes for up to 30 minutes after washing.
- ⊙ **BRACKET HINGES** Allow the door to open 180° for easy loading and unloading.
- ⊙ **COUNTERBALANCES** Usually a concrete slab in the top or base of the machine designed to reduce vibration during spinning. On expensive models, these cradle the drum, reducing noise and wear.
- ⊙ **DELAY START** Allows you to programme the machine to come on at a predetermined later time. Useful if you want your laundry ready to hang up when you come home from work.
- ⊙ **DRIP-DRY/NO SPIN** Useful for delicate items as it completes a wash programme without a final spin.
- ⊙ **EXTRA RINSE** Good for people with sensitive skin or allergic conditions as it removes even more detergent from laundry.
- ⊙ **DUVET** Special programme for pillows and duvets.
- ⊙ **FRESHEN UP FUNCTION** A quick wash (usually of around 15–30 minutes) to freshen up very lightly soiled clothing.
- ⊙ **FUZZY LOGIC** Sensors that monitor the wash cycle to ensure you get optimum wash performance. Systems detect level of soiling, size of wash load etc. and can then determine the length of wash time and amount of water required, improving cleaning performance and energy efficiency.
- ⊙ **GENTLE/DELICATES PROGRAMMES** Reduce the amount of agitation in the wash to suit delicate items.
- ⊙ **MEMORY FUNCTION** Recalls additional options selected the last time a programme was run.
- ⊙ **SOAK** Useful for pre-soaking heavily soiled and stained items.
- ⊙ **STEAM PROGRAMME** Some machines include a steam programme to improve stain removal, sterile wash loads and reduce creasing.
- ⊙ **SUPER/STAIN/INTENSIVE WASH** Heavy-duty programmes suitable for heavily soiled loads.
- ⊙ **THICK INNER DRUM** Drums, springs and heavy-duty bearings need to be robust enough to withstand high spin speeds. Rap it sharply with your knuckles – the deeper the sound, the thicker the drum.
- ⊙ **VARIABLE SPIN SPEED** Allows you to reduce the spin speed to protect woollens, silks and other delicates.
- ⊙ **WASH INDICATORS** Digital displays that allow you to see how far the wash has progressed, and how much time is remaining until the end of the cycle.

Green tips

* Try reducing your normal wash temperature to 30°C instead of 40°C. You may need to use a special low temperature detergent, but don't expect it to remove heavy soiling. Using the lower temperature will save you money, is kinder to the environment and helps reduce carbon emissions. For bedding and towels stick to a higher temperature and a powder detergent that contains bleach to kill any lurking bacteria.

* Buy a triple A-rated machine for maximum energy efficiency and don't just dump your old model. Most retailers will take the old one away when they deliver the new model, or you can find your nearest recycling site by contacting your local council.

A lower spin speed (e.g. 900 rpm) does not necessarily mean that the spin is not as thorough as a high speed spin; the machine may spin for longer to compensate.

A rinse-and-hold option (also called delay spin or Creaseguard) stops the machine during the final rinse when the easy-care programmes are used. This holds the clothes in the water and the machine will not spin until it is reset. This reduces creasing, as clothes can be removed from the drum immediately after spinning rather than left sitting wet in the drum at the end of a wash.

Washer-driers

These look just like automatic washing machines but are also able to tumble-dry in the same drum. They are convenient, carrying out both operations where space is limited. The machine has to be plumbed in where a washing machine would normally fit. The washing capacities are similar to full-sized washing machines but you can only dry half the maximum load, 2.5kg/5½ lb cotton, so you must remove half the load after washing. For drying, the water is condensed using cold water and is pumped away down the washing-machine piping. As the drum is the same size as a washing machine rather than a tumble-drier, there is less room for the clothes to tumble and the result is not as good.

POINTS TO CONSIDER WHEN CHOOSING A WASHER-DRIER

- ◉ Washing programmes and features are generally the same as for washing machines, but because a drier is also incorporated there are generally fewer extra options.
- ◉ The drying cycles have two temperatures to correspond to fabric types.
- ◉ All washer-driers can carry out a continuous operation, washing followed by drying, provided you halve the capacity for washing.
- ◉ They can also be used as a washing machine only or a drier only.

Small Electrical Appliances

Here's what to consider when buying small electrical appliances, what to look for, and how to get the best out of your purchases.

- -

BREADMAKERS

If you love the taste and aroma of freshly baked bread, but do not have the time for kneading the dough, a breadmaker will do all the work for you. Just load the ingredients, close the lid and switch on – the machine will automatically mix, prove and bake the bread. It takes 3–4 hours to produce a light, white loaf with a good flavour, and around 3–5 hours for wholemeal. A loaf will also cost almost twice as much as a similar supermarket loaf though, but at least you'll have the advantage of knowing exactly what went into it, and the pleasure of eating freshly baked bread.

BREADMAKER FEATURES TO LOOK FOR

- **ADD EXTRA INGREDIENTS INDICATOR** Or a dispenser that automatically adds ingredients to dough at the right time – essential for making speciality breads with fruit and nuts.
- **CHOICE OF LOAF SIZE AND COLOUR** To make different types of loaf.
- **DELAY TIMER** So you can set the machine to come on at a predetermined time – what could be better than coming down in the morning to freshly baked bread?
- **EXTENDED BAKE** Cooks the loaf for longer if you like a particularly crisp crust.
- **VIEWING WINDOW** Lets you see how the loaf is progressing, but if there isn't one you can open the lid without spoiling the loaf.

Five breadmaker tips

1 Bread is best eaten within two or three days of baking.

2 It is best to start with the manufacturer's recipes supplied with the machine, until you get the hang of using it.

3 Always add the ingredients in the order described in the recipe.

4 Most breadmakers can also make cakes, rolls and even jam, so don't just limit yourself to bread loaves.

5 Use strong plain flour for best results – other types don't usually have a high enough gluten content to produce good results.

COFFEE MAKERS

There are many different types of domestic coffee-making equipment, and the choice depends on the type of coffee you prefer. Espresso, cappuccino and filter coffee can all be made successfully at home, and you can even grind your own coffee beans at home for the best flavour.

Espresso/cappuccino makers

Espresso is strong, dark and slightly bitter black coffee served in small-sized cups called demitasse. Cappuccino is espresso coffee to which milk, heated and aerated by steam, has been added. Often it has chocolate powder sprinkled on the top for a touch of added sweetness and flavour.

TEN TIPS FOR MAKING THE PERFECT CUP OF COFFEE

1 Arabica and Robusta are the main types of coffee bean used for espresso. Arabica tends to be milder and more aromatic, while blends of Arabica and Robusta have more body and a stronger flavour.

2 Use dark-roasted fine-ground coffees, allowing 7g/¼oz per cup – increasing the amount of coffee makes it thicker, not stronger. Press grounds down firmly into the filter to allow water to extract the full flavour.

3 Don't overpack the filter as this will make the coffee taste bitter.

4 To make a good cappuccino, use equal quantities of espresso and hot frothed milk.

5 Always use cold semi-skimmed milk for the best frothing results.

6 Use a metal jug taller than it is wide.

7 Don't let milk boil – stop heating once the jug is too hot to hold comfortably.

8 Once frothed, tap the jug down on to the worktop and swirl the milk until it becomes shiny and stiffens to form a dense foam.

9 Use coffee from vacuum-sealed packs and consume within two weeks of opening or instead use pre-measured 'pods'.

10 You can extend the life of freshly ground coffee by storing it in the fridge in a tightly sealed container.

Finely ground coffee is recommended to achieve the required strength. To make an authentic espresso with a 'crème' on the surface (a cream-coloured head) hot water has to be pushed through the finely ground coffee under high pressure. It is worth paying as much as you can afford if you want to make the kind of espresso/cappuccino served in coffee bars. Pump-operated models produce greater pressure, resulting in better-flavoured coffee. They also take less time to make their first cup of coffee. Machines that include a built-in grinder are less messy and allow you to produce freshly ground coffee every time. Some manufacturers' machines use 'pods' containing a pre-measured, perfect amount of coffee per cup – these are very convenient, but can work out quite expensive.

Models without the pump rely on steam pressure. They are half the price of pump-action machines but the coffee has less flavour and is more like filter coffee. The combination of steam and pressure extracts flavour that is left behind with a filter.

PUMP-ACTION ESPRESSO MACHINES Machines that have a pump produce the best results, but they are expensive.

STEAM-OPERATED (HOB-TYPE) Dispense only four cups before needing to be refilled, take longer to brew and have to be allowed to cool before you can refill them. This type of coffee maker doesn't froth milk, but if you want frothy milk for hot chocolate, you can buy gadgets that do the job quite well.

Electric filter coffee makers

Filter coffee isn't as strong as espresso. An electric element heats the water before passing it through a filter containing the ground coffee. The liquid then drips into a jug, keeping warm on a hotplate.

Filter machines use paper filters or permanent filters made from nylon, stainless steel or a metal mesh. As most standard-sized jugs can hold up to ten cups, and the hotplate keeps the coffee warm, filter machines are ideal for dinner parties, offices or occasions where larger quantities are required. Use medium-ground coffee.

POINTS TO CONSIDER WHEN CHOOSING FILTER COFFEE MAKERS

- An anti-drip device stops drips when the jug is removed.
- A filter holder that swivels out, making it easier to remove the filter and coffee grounds.
- A clear water-level indicator, so you know how many cups you are making. This is usually stated in small, demitasse cup sizes.
- Some filter machines have replaced the hotplate with a thermal jug to keep the coffee hot. A good idea if you want to serve your coffee away from the machine.

Budget choice: cafetières

You don't need to invest in elaborate hardware to make real coffee. The simplest way is to use a heat-resistant jug and make it in the same way as you'd make a pot of tea, pouring it through a strainer into cups. This is the principle of the cafetière method.

Using a cafetière is the easiest way of making delicious fresh coffee. It is a glass jug with a metal plunger that incorporates a stainless-steel mesh filter. This separates the grounds from the liquid as you push down the plunger. They come in a range of sizes with metal or plastic finishes. Choose a good-quality medium-ground coffee for use in cafetières.

POINTS TO CONSIDER WHEN CHOOSING CAFETIÈRES

- There are many makes and designs on the market. Cafetières with plastic holders are the cheapest option but are not as stable as metal ones.
- Sizes vary from 2- to 8-cup capacity.

ELECTRIC DEEP-FAT FRYERS

Because deep-fat frying heats oil to a very high temperature, safety is paramount when using this cooking method. An electric deep-fat fryer is safer and more convenient than a chip pan on the hob because it has a built-in thermostat, and frying with the lid on is cleaner because it prevents grease-laden steam and smells escaping. (Despite manufacturers' efforts, however, odours and grease still escape from fryers.)

Changing the oil

This needs to be done about every six uses, depending on the food you fry.

High-protein foods, such as meat and fish, will taint the oil faster. After frying, pour the oil through a filter to remove debris such as pieces

Tips for using cafetières

- Before making coffee, warm the glass jug with boiling water.
- To keep the coffee hot, wrap a cafetière warmer around the glass jug. Available from department stores.
- It is important to pre-rinse the filter with boiling water and take the filter apart and clean it after use. This improves the flavour.

of batter and crumbs. This can be quite difficult since fryers are unwieldy and heavy. If you are weak wristed look for a lighter-weight model. Other features to make emptying easier include a drain pipe or a removable reservoir, which makes lifting easier.

Look for a fryer with handles, as these are easier to lift. For convenience, some have a separate filter in the reservoir, which you can lift out, taking the crumbs with it.

POINTS TO CONSIDER WHEN CHOOSING A DEEP-FAT FRYER

⊙ Ease of cleaning.

⊙ Odour control.

⊙ To minimise the amount of airborne grease that escapes from the fryer with the steam, some manufacturers incorporate filters. The simplest of these are metal slats inside the lid. Linked in with some of these methods, the filters change colour when they need replacing (about every 30 uses). Other methods include:

- **CHARCOAL FILTERS** In the form of a cartridge which must be removed before washing.

- **CHARCOAL/FOAM FILTERS** Which must be removed with a screwdriver if you want to put it in the dishwasher, but can be left in place if washed in soapy water. Having to use a screwdriver is inconvenient.

⊙ To make washing-up easier, lids are detachable and some can go in the dishwasher.

OTHER FEATURES TO LOOK FOR

⊙ **DRAINING FOOD** With today's emphasis on healthier cooking, it is important that food is left to drain thoroughly. Make sure that you give it a good shake. Some models have a special shake facility, although this is not strictly necessary.

⊙ **TIMERS** Most models have a bell that sounds at the end of the cooking time – a useful feature. Some models ring once; other sound until switched off. A basket that is raised automatically once cooking is complete is useful.

⊙ **VIEWING WINDOW** A useful feature, as it allows you to see cooking in progress without having to take the lid off, which could be dangerous. Although the viewing window tends to get partially covered with condensation while in use, it's preferable to having no window at all.

⊙ **SAFETY** All the fryers should have

- Basket handles designed to lie flat when the fryer is in use, to prevent accidents.

- Cool walls, so the outside does not burn you if you touch it accidentally, even though it reaches a temperature of 50°C/122°F.

- Locking lids so that the fryer cannot be opened during frying or storage unless the open button is used. Oil can leak out if they are tipped over, but the mechanism will prevent a heavy spill. The better the seal, the longer the oil is likely to keep: about six uses.

FOOD PREPARATION MACHINES

All of this type of labour-saving kitchen equipment frees you from the time-consuming and repetitive tasks such as beating, whisking, puréeing and chopping.

Blenders

JUG

Useful for making smooth soups, mayonnaise, batter and milkshakes, and for chopping nuts, making breadcrumbs and crushing ice. Some blenders also have a mill attachment for grinding coffee beans. If possible, try out the blender before you buy – you will find that most are noisy to use and some have lids that are difficult to remove. Don't assume that a higher wattage automatically means a better blender. Measurements on the goblet are not always reliable either. For easier cleaning, look for a blender with a removable blade that is dishwasher-safe.

STICK

Electrically operated hand-held stick-style blenders with a small blade at the base. Useful for liquidising and puréeing foods. With care, some can also be used to process hot foods (look for one with a metal shaft). Some come with a range of attachments for all round food preparation.

Food processors

Their primary function is to chop, slice, grate, blend and purée.

Their secondary function is to mix cakes, knead bread, whisk egg whites and whip cream. Food processors are generally quite poor at tasks like mixing cakes and whisking egg whites, as they are unable to incorporate air into the mixture very well. Those that include a whisk attachment produce better results.

Liquidising in the main bowl is poor. It is better if there is a separate liquidiser attachment, which is fairly commonplace now. Most machines

---

FOOD PROCESSOR ATTACHMENTS TO LOOK OUT FOR

- ⊙ **DOUGH HOOK** An absolute must if you want to make your own bread.
- ⊙ **JUICE EXTRACTOR/CITRUS PRESS** Will save you buying a separate machine if you enjoy fresh juice.
- ⊙ **LIQUIDISER GOBLET** Useful if you want to make soups or prepare fresh baby foods because it processes to a smoother consistency than the standard processing bowl.
- ⊙ **MINI OR MIDI BOWLS** Fit inside the main bowl and are ideal for preparing herbs, nuts and baby food.
- ⊙ **VARIABLE SPEED SETTINGS** Some models have one speed designed to cope with all food preparation, but sometimes it is useful to have a slower speed to give you more control. Go for a model with a couple of speeds, plus a 'pulse' mode which gives short bursts at a high speed.
- ⊙ **WHISK ATTACHMENT** Balloon or rotary whisks produce a better aerated result when whisking cream, egg whites and sponges.

are supplied with a large bowl, grating and slicing discs (fine and coarse), a metal blade for chopping, a whisk for mixing and a spatula.

In general, the more you pay, the larger the capacity and more attachments you will get such as a dough tool and juice extractor.

Free-standing food mixers

A free-standing food mixer is the best type of food preparation machine for making cakes, pastries and breads – they take all the effort out of kneading dough and whisking egg whites. Less expensive models are less effective at combining ingredients as they use a different action to more expensive mixers – their bowls and whisks rotate, whereas on more expensive machines the attachment shaft rotates in a different direction from the beaters, resulting in a more effective beating action. There are also hand-held mixers available for about £20, which mix and whisk well, but are usually not very effective at kneading dough.

Ice cream makers

Ice cream makers allow you to concoct your own flavours and be sure the ice cream is additive-free. These machines make ice cream that is less fluffy than shop-bought varieties, but it has an equally good texture and consistency, and sometimes a far better flavour.

There are two types of ice cream maker: those you put in the freezer before use, and those that have their own electrically powered built-in chilling unit.

FREEZE-FIRST

These have an electrically powered paddle and a bowl with walls that contain a refrigerant. The bowl is put in the freezer for 8–18 hours before use, depending on the size. Although the insulated bowl keeps the refrigerant cold, it starts to defrost during mixing, so the ice cream becomes fairly soft and may need further freezing.

These machines are fairly cheap. Their main disadvantage is that the bowl needs to be re-frozen after each use so, for the more professional cook, it takes a long time to make a large quantity and you can't make ice cream on a whim because of the long amount of time required to pre-chill the bowl.

Tips for using ice cream makers

- For best results, chill the ingredients before use.
- Switch on the paddles before pouring in the ice cream mix.
- Mixtures containing a high percentage of alcohol, fat, gelatine or sugar take longer to freeze and remain softer.
- Use plastic or wooden utensils only when removing the ice cream mixture from the bowl.
- Clean the machine after use as bacteria grow rapidly in ice cream mix.
- Ice cream tastes best on the day it is made, but you can freeze it for up to a month.

SELF-CHILLING

Use a built-in chilling unit. You switch the machine on for five to ten minutes to chill the container before pouring in the mixture. Ice cream can be made in the built-in bowl and in the removable inner bowl, which is useful as it can be put straight into the freezer. To keep the removable bowl cold, you have to use your own cooling solution such as brine. These machines usually cost over £200, so are for the real enthusiast.

IRONS AND IRONING BOARDS

We spend a staggering 12 months of our lives ironing so it is worth choosing the best iron you can afford. However, with the huge range available, with increasingly sophisticated features, the choice can be bewildering.

Steam irons

These are the most versatile because they can be used as a dry or steam iron. They help take the drudgery out of ironing because they help remove creases quickly and more easily. The greater the steam output, the more efficient the crease removal. If stated on the packaging, look for at least 15g/¹⁄₂oz per minute.

Anti-scale features

Most irons use ordinary tap water. If you only iron occasionally, you don't need to worry too much about scale build-up, but if you are a frequent user or live in an area with particularly hard water, then look out for a clog-resistant model with features such as water filters and valves, which remove scale before it reaches the steam chamber.

POINTS TO CONSIDER WHEN CHOOSING A STEAM IRON

With the exception of safety features, all the extras make ironing easier and, in most cases, faster. Decide which ones are the most important to your style and type of ironing and consider if they are worth paying more for.

- ⊙ **WATER SPRAY** Most steam irons incorporate this feature. A fine mist or spray jet of water dampens the fabric just in front of the iron. Useful for very dry items, along seams and on stubborn creases.
- ⊙ **BOOST OF STEAM FOR DRY OR STEAM IRONING** The iron will emit an extra surge of steam, which will penetrate deeper into the fabric. Useful when pressing dry items, pleats and creases. This can cause water to drip from the soleplate and will use up the water tank more quickly. Continuous use will also lower the temperature of the soleplate.
- ⊙ **VARIABLE STEAM CONTROL** The output of steam can be adjusted from slight to maximum, according to the fabric type and temperature selected on the iron. Useful for steaming delicate fabrics such as silk.

- ⊙ **CONSTANT STEAM OUTPUT** Ensures a constant steam production and consistently good results until the tank is empty. Steam output decreases as the water level drops in the tank in irons without this feature.
- ⊙ **SAFETY FEATURES** Range from non-fray flex to devices that switch the iron off. All irons have a thermal cut-out that operates if the iron overheats when in use. Automatic cut-out turns the power off after a few minutes if the iron is left unattended; some will even bleep. Plastic flex, or flex that's attached by a ball joint for easy movement, to prevent wear and fraying.
- ⊙ **SELF-CLEANING FACILITY** Forces water and steam through holes in the soleplate to flush out any mineral and scale deposits.
- ⊙ **DETACHABLE WATER TANK** Makes it much easier to refill the iron with water.

Steam generator irons

These have a separate water tank, attached to the iron by its flex and a cord through which the steam passes. They are more expensive than traditional steam irons, but have a potentially longer life, especially in hard water areas. Steam generator irons are also lighter to use because the tank is separate and you don't have to carry the weight of the water. The large tank makes it possible to do a much larger pile of ironing without having to refill, but they are bulkier to store, and you will still need to descale the tank periodically.

SOLEPLATES

Originally chrome or aluminium, but many now have special finishes designed to reduce friction and speed up ironing.

- Nickel alloy polished with sapphires to strengthen the surface is one of the toughest and most scratch-resistant soleplates.
- Stainless steel: hardwearing and glides easily.
- Aluminium flecked with titanium: glides easily.
- Ceramic-coated metal: ribbed to improve crease removal, scratch and stain resistant.
- Non-stick finishes are easy to clean, but need extra care to avoid scratching the surface.

Ironing boards

The quality and performance of an ironing board is very price dependent. Lower-priced models tend to be smaller and less sturdy.

> **TIP**
> A flex holder keeps the flex off the board and costs only a few pounds. You can fix it on to the edge of your board.

POINTS TO CONSIDER WHEN CHOOSING AN IRONING BOARD

- Height is an important consideration, particularly for the elderly or those with back problems. Ideally the board should be adjustable between 78cm/31in and 90cm/35in. Set the height so that the iron handle is level with your elbow, or slightly below it. Alternatively, choose a board with angled legs, allowing room for a chair, so you can iron comfortably while seated.
- Longer boards are more convenient, so select one at least 1.5m/5ft long.
- Ensure the board cover fits well and is easy to remove. Ill-fitting covers soon wrinkle and impair ironing performance. Look for covers with sturdy ties or preferably elastic. Covers can be either padded cotton or metallic (milium). The metallic type will reflect the heat back into the fabric but become quite hot during use.

- An iron rest is a useful feature as it offers greater stability for siting the iron and reduces the temptation to rest the iron face down on the fabric cover. It is either fixed at the end of the board or is retractable.
- The shape of the board is an important consideration. A pointed end makes it easier to iron trousers but a wide tip speeds up ironing because of the larger surface area.
- To stop the board slipping, look for rubber covers on the end of the feet. Levelling feet may be useful if your floors are particularly uneven.
- If you use a powerful steam iron, choose a board with a metal mesh top. This allows steam to pass through the board and helps keep the ironing surface dry.
- A laundry rack attachment allows you to hang garments once they have been ironed.
- Detachable sleeve board.

JUICE EXTRACTORS

Unless you have a glut of fruit or vegetables, you may not save money by making your own freshly squeezed juice. The texture can also be thinner than shop-bought varieties, and the colour will be different – however, you will have the satisfaction of knowing exactly what has gone into your juice and being able to experiment with your own favourite flavour combinations. Choose a model with controls that are easy to use with one hand – you will need the other to add the fruit and push the plunger.

FIVE TIPS FOR MAKING PERFECT JUICE

1 Use fresh, well-ripened fruit and vegetables and always wash them very thoroughly before placing them in the juice extractor.

2 Avoid using very fibrous fruits such as rhubarb as they do not generate much juice and make the machine harder to clean.

3 Peel thick-skinned fruit and vegetables, such as melon, kiwi and beetroot. Roll up leaf vegetables tightly and stone fruit such as cherries and apricots.

4 Store fresh juice in an airtight container in the fridge with a little lemon juice added to help retain colours.

5 Homemade juice contains no preservatives so will not last as long as shop-bought. Drink it as soon as possible to get the maximum benefit of all those vitamins and minerals.

JUICE EXTRACTOR FEATURES TO LOOK FOR

⊙ **CENTRIFUGAL JUICERS** Use a circular filter basket with fine grating teeth to shred fruit/vegetables. When spun rapidly, centrifugal force separates juice from the skin, pulp and pips.

⊙ **DISHWASHER-SAFE COMPONENTS** Cleaning juicers can be a pain, especially if you don't do it straight away. Components that can go in the dishwasher will make cleaning up a far easier task.

⊙ **DRIP-STOP FEATURE** The spout is angled or can be tilted upwards to prevent juice dripping on to worksurface.

⊙ **ELECTRIC CITRUS PRESS** Attachment that looks like a traditional lemon juicer, but is quicker to use and extracts more juice – choose one of these if you are most likely to just be making citrus juices.

⊙ **JUICE-COLLECTING JUG** Separate jug that fits under the machine's spout for collecting juice.

⊙ **JUICE SPOUT** Directs juice straight into your glass.

⊙ **PRESS ON/OFF CONTROLS** Easier to use than dial controls.

⊙ **PULP COLLECTOR** Compartment where all the skin, pips and pulp are collected.

⊙ **WIDE FEED TUBE** Allows you to place larger items, such as whole apples, down the juicing chute and cuts down preparation times.

KETTLES

As they are used so often, kettles do need to be replaced quite frequently. The biggest cause of failure in kettles is limescale in water attaching itself to the heating element, as the layer of scale thickens, the time the kettle takes to boil increases. In the latest models, the heating element is concealed so that water does not have to come into contact with it. For rapid boiling, choose a kettle with a 'fast-boil' or 3kW heating element.

Non-electric kettles

These are enjoying a revival. They are not significantly slower in use than the electric ones, whether boiling a mug or a large volume of water. However, they do not have as many of the safety features of the electric variety such as locking lids, automatic switch-off and stay-cool walls.

TIP
To maintain efficiency it is still important to descale your kettle (see Kettles, page 231).

POINTS TO CONSIDER WHEN CHOOSING AN ELECTRIC KETTLE

- ⊙ On/off light.
- ⊙ On cordless kettles, look for a cord-storage facility on the power base. Only a minimal amount of cord needs to be visible between the power base and the wall, because the kettle is removed from the base once it has boiled.
- ⊙ Corded models should either have a short or coiled flex. This will ensure the flex never hangs over the worksurfaces to cause accidents. Look also for a 360° swivel base that allows the kettle to be replaced from any angle.
- ⊙ Other safety features to look for are a locking lid, cool-touch walls and an automatic thermal cut-out device to prevent the kettle boiling dry. A cool exterior is achieved on some models by using a double skin.
- ⊙ For extra stability, look for rubber feet on the base of the kettle or power base, which also makes it harder to pull along the worksurface.

- ⊙ For ease of use, choose a model with a wide spout so it can be filled from the tap without removing the lid.
- ⊙ A clear water-gauge down both sides enables both right- and left-handed users to see at a glance how full it is.
- ⊙ If you live in a hard water area, you may want to spend a little extra on a kettle with an integral filter. This acts like a tea strainer within the spout, stopping limescale being poured into your drink along with the water. This is increasingly important with more people making hot drinks directly in their mug rather than in a pot. It does not, however, stop limescale from developing.

PRESSURE COOKERS

A pressure cooker cooks more quickly than an ordinary saucepan and is useful for making stock, cooking root vegetables and pulses and tenderising tough cuts of meat. The pan is sealed and a weight is added to stop the steam escaping, so the water boils at a higher temperature, so reducing cooking time.

Stainless-steel pressure cookers are the most expensive, but they are hardwearing. Aluminium cookers are cheaper but they can discolour badly and are not dishwasher-safe. Both sorts can be used on all types of hobs, except induction, unless they have a special magnetic base.

PRESSURE COOKER FEATURES

- All pressure cookers have a safety valve that allows excess pressure to be released should the control valve become blocked. The valve is either pushed out or melted, but this should not happen if the cooker is used properly and the control valve is kept clear. This explains why such foods as dumplings should never be cooked in a pressure cooker, as the dough will rise and could block the safety outlets. Pressure cookers also have locking lugs that prevent the lid being removed when the cooker is being used under pressure.
- Pressure cookers usually have three pressure weights for a choice in cooking control: 2.25kg/5lb for blanching and steaming puddings, 4.5kg/10lb for jam making and 7kg/15lb for everyday, general cooking. Some models, however, have fixed pressure controls instead of individual weights.
- All pressure cookers come with a trivet and a separator basket so you can cook different foods at the same time using the divider.
- Some models have an automatic steam release which works in conjunction with a timer. The timer is set according to the length of cooking and then releases the steam automatically at the end of the cooking time. De-pressurising the cooker can either be done quickly or slowly depending on the type of food being cooked.
- Some models also have a useful 'rise and time' indicator or pressure-ready indicator to show that the cooker has reached the correct cooking temperature and that the temperature is being maintained. This helps to save energy and ensure consistent results.

Hi-dome pressure cookers tend to be aluminium and their extra height makes them especially suitable for making jams and pickles.

Cooking food by steam pressure

This principle has been known since about 1679 when Denis Papin, a French physician, invented the Papin Digester or 'Papin Pot'. This was a saucepan made of iron with a screw-on airtight lid and safety valve.

The first domestic pressure cooker was invented at the turn of the century in the United States, but they were not manufactured in the UK until 1947.

STEAMERS

Steaming is a healthy way to cook. It helps preserve vitamins and minerals in the food, and can be done without the use of any fats or cooking oils. Electric steamers have no great benefits over traditional stove-top steamers, but you may find the timer useful. Both share the basic design of a heated water chamber that produces steam, which cooks the food in the basket above. All tend to be tricky to clean and tend to take up a lot of space in a dishwasher.

STEAMER FEATURES TO LOOK FOR

- **BASKETS WITH REMOVABLE BASES** Bases that click out allow you to create a taller cooking basket and provide greater flexibility.
- **DELAY START** On electric steamers, allows you to programme the machine to come on at a predetermined time.
- **EXTERNAL WATER GAUGE** So you can see when more water needs to be added without having to lift the baskets off the water chamber.
- **EXTERNAL WATER INLET** Allow you to top-up the cooking water without having to lift the baskets.
- **JUICE COLLECTOR** Collects juices that seep out of foods; they can then be used in sauces and gravies.
- **RICE BASKET** Great for producing perfect, fluffy rice.
- **STACKABLE BASKETS** Look for at least three baskets to enable you to cook different types of foods at the same time.

TOASTERS

Toasters now offer a host of options from one-side and sandwich-toasting to roll and croissant warming. Look for safety features and avoid leaving the room while the toaster is in use.

IMPORTANT Never poke a knife into a toaster to remove an item – unplug the toaster and use a plastic spatula or tongs.

FEATURES TO LOOK FOR A TOASTER

- ⊙ **CANCEL** Lets you turn off the toaster mid-cycle.
- ⊙ **COOL WALLS** Keep the outside of the toaster cool enough to touch.
- ⊙ **DEFROST** Defrosts and toasts bread perfectly straight from the freezer.
- ⊙ **EXTRA LIFT** Pushes small slices and teacakes above the slots for safe removal.
- ⊙ **LONG TOASTING SLOT** Allows you to toast longer items such as baguettes.
- ⊙ **ONE-SIDED TOASTING** For bagels, teacakes and buns that need toasting on one side only.
- ⊙ **PAUSE** Allows you to pause toasting to see how brown your toast is – if its not done enough, pressing the toast back down within a set time will start the programme where it left off rather than starting a whole new toasting cycle.
- ⊙ **REHEAT** Warms toast that has cooled without extra browning.
- ⊙ **REMOVABLE CRUMB TRAY** For a mess-free worktop.
- ⊙ **SAFETY CUT-OUT** Turns the toaster off in case the pop-up does not work, or if bread jams inside.
- ⊙ **SINGLE SLICE SETTING** Saves energy when you just want to toast one slice.
- ⊙ **VARIABLE WIDTH SLOTS** Accommodates a wide range of thicknesses – from doorsteps to melba-type toast. Useful for bagels and muffins.
- ⊙ **WARMING RACK** Lets you heat items like rolls and croissants above the heat from the toaster.

VACUUM CLEANERS AND FLOOR POLISHERS

Vacuum cleaners

The latest vacuum cleaners are more efficient and compact than ever, and a far cry from the huge early models delivered by horse and cart. A carpet can hold up to three times its own weight in dust and grit. Carpets and upholstery wear because the dirt and grit trapped within them cuts through the fibres and destroys them. Choosing a good cleaner will make your furnishings last much longer. There are two main types of vacuum cleaner to choose from: cylinders and uprights. Some people find cylinders hard work, especially if they've always been used to an upright.

Traditionally, cylinder vacuum cleaners relied mostly on suction, while uprights had a rotating brush in the cleaning head, called a beater bar. These days, the distinction between the two is not so clear-cut – some cylinders now have a turbo brush attachment that mirrors the action of a beater bar, improving their performance, picking up pet hairs and raising carpet pile, while some uprights now allow you to switch off the beater bar (which can cause damage to wood floors, tiles and loop-pile carpets), so they function more like a cylinder.

Bag or bagless?

Deciding whether to choose a bagged or bagless cleaner is really up to the individual – there's not a lot of difference in cleaning ability. One of the obvious advantages of a bagless model is that you won't have to spend money on dustbags. However, the dust canisters in bagless models can be messy to empty and coming into contact with the collected dust does not help those with allergies.

POINTS TO CONSIDER WHEN CHOOSING A CYLINDER CLEANER

- Good manoeuvrability of cylinder with wheels that swivel.
- 360° swivel hose to prevent hose kinking.
- Anti-crush hose.
- Variable power control for different floor types and for upholstery, curtains and rugs.
- Tools on board for cleaning curtains, upholstery and crevices.
- Easy-to-use well-placed controls.
- Automatic flex rewind.
- Bag-full indicator.
- A parking-clip system for securing the hose when not in use.
- Telescopic extension tubes that allow you to adjust the height to suit.
- Metal tubes are more durable than plastic.
- Carpet beater (turbo brush) for heavy-duty cleaning.
- Filter-change indicator.
- Permanent or washable filters.

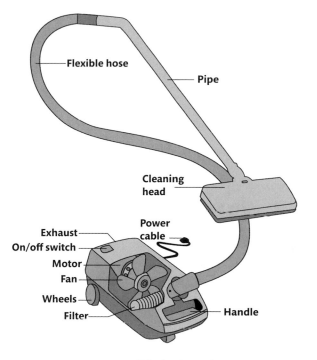

ABOVE Cylinder cleaner features

CYLINDER CLEANERS

Rely on suction power only to pick up dirt and therefore have a higher wattage than an upright.

- Easier to use for stair cleaning and more convenient for carrying.
- Light to use because only the cleaning head and hose are hand held.
- More manoeuvrable than an upright and easier for cleaning under beds and furniture.
- Most have on-board storage for attachments.
- Better on hard floors and short-pile carpets.
- Generally better than uprights at cleaning right up to the skirting board.
- Automatic cord rewind and bag full indicators are standard.
- The smaller the cylinder cleaner the more often you will have to change the bag or empty the dust canister.
- Useful as a second cleaner for upstairs.
- Useful for rooms congested with furniture.

Cyclone technology

Dyson revolutionised the world of vacuum cleaners in the 1980s with the introduction of the first bagless cleaner that utilised cyclone technology. Cyclone technology uses centrifugal force to filter dust and remove dirt from the airflow efficiently. Because there is nothing to obstruct airflow, Dyson machines don't clog or lose suction as the cylinder fills with dirt. Other manufacturers now also use similar technology.

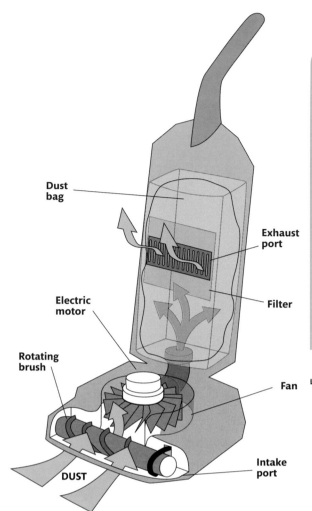

Dust
bag

Exhaust
port

Electric
motor

Filter

Rotating
brush

Fan   **LEFT** Upright cleaner features

Intake
port

DUST

POINTS TO CONSIDER WHEN CHOOSING AN UPRIGHT CLEANER

- ◉ Comfortable handle.
- ◉ Variable power control.
- ◉ On-board tool storage.
- ◉ Carpet height setting that can be adjusted to suit different carpet piles.
- ◉ Edge-to-edge cleaning.
- ◉ Easy-to-replace dust bag and filters or easy to empty canister.
- ◉ Bag-full indicator.
- ◉ Permanent or washable filters.

UPRIGHT CLEANERS

Use a combination of suction and the beating action of a rotating, motorised brush to loosen and remove dirt. The beater 'grooms' and helps to lift the carpet pile.

- ◉ Especially suitable for heavy traffic areas, where the beater helps to loosen deeply embedded grit and dirt that collects in the carpet pile.
- ◉ Heavier to use than a cylinder cleaner so look for a model at a weight you can manage comfortably.
- ◉ Most have carpet-pile adjustment, some of which adjust automatically, and bag-full indicators.
- ◉ Many have tools on board, including the hose, so are slightly heavier to push around.
- ◉ Generally not as good as a cylinder for cleaning right up to the skirting board so you may have to clean edges with the crevice tool.

WATTAGE

Don't be fooled into thinking that the higher the wattage the more efficient the cleaner. This isn't necessarily the case. The amount of dust and dirt a cleaner picks up depends not only on its wattage rating, but also on the air flow through the cleaner. Imagine trying to pick up a piece of paper with a

Filters

Filters help to trap dust and prevent it from being blown back into the room through the cleaner's exhaust. How much dust is retained depends on the cleaner's filtration system. Conventional vacuum cleaners have a filter efficiency of between 70 and 90 per cent. If you suffer from asthma or allergies, look for a vacuum cleaner with a filter efficiency of at least 95 per cent. These are known as HEPA or S-class filters and retain even the smallest of allergy-causing particles – but you'll still need to be careful when emptying the bag or dust canister.

Some vacuum cleaners have been awarded the British Allergy Foundation's (see Useful Organisations) 'Seal of Approval' and are particularly recommended for people with asthma or other allergic conditions.

OTHER TYPES OF VACUUM CLEANERS

- **BUILT-IN VACUUM SYSTEMS** The central power unit and dust collection bin are hidden away in a cupboard, garage or utility room. Connected to this is a series of suction pipes that carry the dust and grit to the bin, for emptying a couple of times a year. The pipes can be concealed under floorboards, run through the attic, concealed inside cupboards or under stairs, and emerge at convenient inlets on the walls (the discreet sockets look like electric points). A three- or four-bedroomed house might need only two. An extra-long flexible hose and cleaning tools connect to these inlets and are used like a conventional vacuum cleaner.

- **HAND-HELD VACUUM CLEANERS** Lightweight cleaners that are usually rechargeable. Range from 40–150 watts. Ideal for spot cleaning, stair cleaning and for cleaning car interiors. Some models are suitable for wet and dry jobs and can cope with small spills. Rechargeable cleaners are useful for cleaning areas away from a mains socket. They need to be charged for a number of hours initially, and usually provide about 20 minutes' operating time before needing to be recharged.

- **ROBOTS** The latest in vacuum cleaner technology, these small, usually disc-shaped machines use sensors to navigate themselves automatically around furniture and walls. They can be quite useful for cleaning large, unobstructed areas of floor, but are less effective at getting into tight corners, and no good for cleaning stairs.

- **STICK VACUUM CLEANERS** These portable, upright, broom-like cleaners are ideal for smaller homes. They are more lightweight and convenient to use than conventional vacuum cleaners, so are also good for people with disabilities such as arthritis. However, suction power tends to be more limited.

- **THREE-IN-ONE CLEANERS** These wash carpets and upholstery, sucking the moisture out as part of the process, as well as vacuuming.

drinking straw – it's fairly easy. But if the straw is kinked, it becomes much more difficult. So if the design of the piping inside the cleaner is poor, the cleaner can't utilise the wattage fully, no matter how high. Unfortunately, manufacturers don't quote airflow details so you have no way of knowing how well the cleaner will perform.

Floor polishers

If you want to polish parquet flooring, an electric floor polisher can save a lot of hard work and do an efficient job. Some models are suitable for scrubbing floors as well as shampooing carpets. A polisher has two or three rotary heads driven by an electric motor. Depending on the purpose, sets of stiff-bristled brushes, softer brushes or polishing buffers can be clipped on to the heads.

First brush or vacuum the floor to remove loose dirt and dust. Then clean the floor with a proprietary floor cleaner, preferably one that doesn't need to be rinsed. Some models have a tank to apply the cleaning solution automatically: a trigger releases the cleaning solution when required.

Use the stiff brushes to scrub the floor. A liquid wax should then be applied to the floor and polishing brushes work the wax into the floor. Depending on the degree of gloss you prefer, felt polishing or buffing pads are used to give shine.

Some polishers have a detergent tank that is fixed to the handle to convert the machine into a carpet shampooer.

Appliance Servicing and Warranties

Sales assistants often ask whether you would like to take out a service contract or extended warranty. These policies prolong the free 12-month cover provided by manufacturers but they are often an expensive way of covering an appliance, so consider some other options. Don't feel pressured at the point-of-sale. Ask how long you have to decide if you want the policy – it's usually 14 days after you have bought the item, which gives you time to check out other options. There is usually a 45 day cancellation period too, so all is not lost if you buy a retailer's warranty and then find a better deal elsewhere. Check also that you are not duplicating cover you have elsewhere, such as through your home contents insurance. If you buy a warranty online or over the telephone, you may be able to cancel under the Distance Selling Regulations 14 day cooling off period.

EXTENDED WARRANTIES

Bought at the time of purchase or within a specified time limit. Taking out an additional three to five-year warranty for parts or parts and labour is the norm, giving you a total of five years' cover. Many offer extra benefits beyond simple breakdown cover, such as accidental damage, theft or new-for-old replacement cover. All manufacturers and most electrical retailers sell extended warranties. There are large variations in price between brands. Insuring the same product but with different parties varies too: compare store costs with the manufacturer. But before you sign up, check exactly what it is giving that you don't already have through the manufacturer's free warranty. Check the warranty is backed by an insurance policy so you have more rights if things go wrong.

So why the difference?

- What's covered? Study the small print in the cover. Manufacturers tend to be more specific in what they cover than the retailers. Some retailers will include accidental damage, such as knobs knocked off and, for example with washing machines, items like coins from pockets and boning in bras getting outside the drum and stuck in the pump. They also offer same-day service, and new-for-old facilities if the machine is past redemption during its five-year life.
- Who does the work? Retailers may subcontract the work, whereas manufacturers have their own engineers.
- Cost of spares. Manufacturers' spare parts are made in their own factory, and supplied at cost to their own service engineers. Retailers are buying spare parts with a mark-up.
- Settling costs. With some store schemes you have to settle charges with the engineer and reclaim money from the insurers.
- Check you can take a warranty or agreement with you if you move.

Is it worth insuring appliances?

- Washing machines are far more likely to go wrong than fridge-freezers and microwaves.

- Encouragingly, appliances are getting more reliable. It is in the manufacturer's interests, as any design faults will become apparent in the first year when the machine is under warranty.

- Even if a product does break down you may be legally entitled to a repair or compensation, or it may be cheaper just to get the appliance repaired yourself.

If it goes wrong

If the machine is still under warranty when it goes wrong, it's quickest to contact the manufacturer's central office (given in instruction booklet), which will give you details of your local service centre. If it's an own-brand machine, go back to the retailer for help.

SERVICING AN APPLIANCE

If you have not taken out extended cover or a service agreement there are several ways to get the appliance fixed.

Local independent agent

Probably the least expensive option, because the repairers are within easy reach.

Independent agents tend to be more flexible with early and late appointments. The labour and call-out charge are usually charged together in a single fee.

Approach an agent who deals with a maximum of four manufacturers. It is more likely that he will be familiar with your appliance, that he will have attended the training sessions, will have the service manuals and carry the spare parts.

There are one or two points you need to watch:

⊙ Check the small print from your manufacturer. The five-year parts warranty is only valid if repairs have been undertaken by its recognised service engineers.

⊙ Cost of parts is at the discretion of the agent. A washing machine door seal and pump can be easily pirated. Bogus parts may wear more quickly, although you may be charged full price for them.

⊙ A manufacturer or retailer carrying out the repair will guarantee workmanship and parts. An independent may go out of business, so any guarantee given on repair will be useless. Some spare parts are more difficult to source and so an independent will have to send off for them to the relevant company's head office. Independent agents won't usually deal with own-brand appliances.

Manufacturers' engineers

Manufacturers' labour is charged in time slots: for example, for six minutes' work. Therefore a more complicated job may work out more expensive than using either a local independent retailer, or a service company where call-out and labour are combined in a single fee.

Servicing charged in narrower time bands will keep your costs down more than that in wider bands, such as half an hour.

Return to retailer

This will be necessary with own-brand machines. Retailers like Comet have established a full service back-up, since they are sole importers and the manufacturer has no manufacturing base in this country. Most retailers refer a main-brand service back to the manufacturer.

Service agreements

These are an expensive way of buying peace of mind if you compare the costs, quoted per annum, with a one-off call-out repair cost or extended warranty. They can be taken out on older appliances, but you will probably have to undergo an initial inspection visit first to have any necessary repairs carried out. Service agreements usually include an annual maintenance inspection; when, if something were seen to be amiss, it would theoretically be put right. Check the small print. If you are paying for this service, there should always be a machine provided for your use. Normally bought as a one-year renewal option, so they are easier to budget for. Manufacturers often see them as an opportunity for a repeat purchase.

Before calling out help

It's worth going back to the instruction book. Suggestions for maintenance include cleaning the inlet filters and the main pump filter on a washing machine; filters and spray arms on a dishwasher; and bag full, blockages in extension pipes and broken belts on vacuum cleaners. Following these simple steps may save you a considerable amount of money.

TIP
When calling out a service person, give some idea of the symptoms so that the engineer can bring appropriate spare parts.

Kitchen Essentials and Tableware

A well-equipped kitchen is one in which every item earns its keep on a regular or infrequent but essential basis, and does not stay unused. There is masses of choice in kitchen equipment, utensils and bakeware, so ask yourself the following points before buying:

- ⊙ Do I need it?
- ⊙ Will I use it?
- ⊙ Is it easy to clean/will it go in the dishwasher?
- ⊙ Is it easy to store?

A KITCHEN BASICS CHECKLIST

Opposite is a checklist, depending upon how much you cook and how often you entertain. For most people, entertaining is a small part of life, so it is better to have good-quality everyday items. There are four areas: cooking equipment, preparing, serving/entertaining and storage.
When choosing look for:

- ⊙ Quality and durability
- ⊙ Comfort in use
- ⊙ Ease of cleaning
- ⊙ Ease of storage
- ⊙ Cost.

CHOPPING BOARDS

The larger the board, the more convenient to use. Choose one that can be used on both sides. Colour-coded boards for foods such as raw meat and fish avoid cross-contamination of bacteria to foods that will not be cooked.

Marble and glass
Can be noisy, unyielding and will blunt cutting blades very quickly. Marble and glass slabs are more suitable as a cool surface for pastry making.

Plastic
Choose a polypropylene (PP) board – although more expensive than polyethylene (HDPE), they are more robust, resistant to staining and less likely to crack under stress. They can also withstand higher wash temperatures and so can go in the dishwasher.

Wood
Boards made from beech or other hardwoods are most durable. Ordinary wooden boards are usually made in sections that are glued together for extra stability. End-grain chopping boards or blocks are expensive, but

TIP
Chopping boards with edges that can be folded up make it easier to funnel chopped foods into your container of choice, or transfer waste into the dustbin.

Plastic versus wood

There are divided views on how hygienic wooden chopping boards are compared to plastic. Although wooden boards mustn't be soaked, as long as they are cleaned thoroughly and regularly and occasionally wiped over with a sterilising solution, they are not problematic. This also applies to plastic chopping boards. Bear in mind that polypropylene boards can be washed in the dishwasher, where the higher temperatures ensure thorough cleaning. Always replace a cracked, severely scored or stained board, whether it's made of wood or plastic.

The kitchen basics

COOKING EQUIPMENT

- Steamer
- Saucepans
- Large and small frying pans with lids
- Selection of casseroles with lids
- Roasting tin (with trivet) may be supplied as oven accessory
- Yorkshire pudding tin
- Flat tins
- Pie dishes
- Pudding basins
- Loaf tins
- Cake tins
- Baking sheets
- Ramekins
- Wire cooling racks
- Pan stands (to protect work surfaces from hot pans)
- Wooden spoons
- Fish slice
- Wooden and silicone spatulas
- Wok
- Skewers, wooden and metal

TIP
Tins give a crisper pastry base than china flan dishes.

TIP
Choose non-stick and silicone bakeware for easier release.

PREPARING

- Knives
- Knife sharpener
- Colander
- Sieves
- Chopping boards
- Kitchen scales
- Measuring spoons
- Measuring jugs
- Can opener
- Mixing bowls
- Cheese grater
- Pastry brush
- Rolling pin
- Ceramic baking beans (for baking pastry)
- Pastry cutters
- Garlic press
- Balloon whisk

TIP
Metal sieves are more durable than nylon.

TIP
Buy a double-sided measuring jug for right- and left-hand users.

TIP
Choose a sturdy box-type grater that has fine and coarse graters, and can also be used for citrus fruit.

- Potato peeler
- Kitchen scissors
- Kitchen tongs
- Palette knife
- Ladle
- Basting pipette
- Slotted spoon
- Potato masher/ricer
- Flexible spatula
- Lemon squeezer
- Meat mallet
- Funnel
- Minute timer
- Piping bag and nozzles
- Food processor
- Hand-held mixer
- Mini chopper

TIP
Basting pipette is also good for separating meat juices from fat.

TIP
Choose a meat mallet with a metal head for better food hygiene.

TIP
Choose large nylon or fabric icing bags and metal nozzles. Plastic nozzles are not very durable.

TIP
A hand-held mixer is better at incorporating air than a food processor: use for making cakes, whipping egg whites and cream.

SERVING AND ENTERTAINING

- Ice-cube trays
- Corkscrew
- Bottle opener
- Wine stoppers
- Wine cooler
- Heat-resistant plate mats
- Serving dishes and plates
- Glass dessert bowl for fruit salads, trifles etc.
- Citrus zester
- Hot tray
- Serving spoons
- Salad bowl and servers
- Bread basket
- Cream jugs
- Carving dish, knife and fork (with finger guard)
- Water jug

STORAGE

- Freezer bags and ties
- Freezer labels and pen
- Airtight containers for fridge/freezer
- Airtight containers for dried foods
- Airtight tins for cakes/biscuits

worth it because they are hardwearing and robust. Wooden boards usually can't go in the dishwasher.

CHOOSING COOKWARE

Pans

Before buying new pans, check that they are suitable for use on your hob. This information is usually available in the manufacturer's leaflets, or on the pan base.

ALUMINIUM

Available as non-stick coated, enamel coated (usually on exterior with a non-stick coating inside), hard anodised (see below), or cast aluminium – which looks like cast iron but has the weight and good heat conductivity of aluminium. Uncoated aluminium pans are not suitable for cooking acidic foods.

CAST IRON

Heats up slowly but retains heat well, so good for long, even cooking at a low heat. Cast iron rusts easily on its own, so pans usually have a non-stick interior coating or a thin protective layer of vitreous enamel. Uncoated cast iron is not dishwasher-safe. Very heavy; suitable for range cookers.

COPPER

Excellent heat conductivity. Good copper pans are very expensive but should last a lifetime. As copper reacts with certain foods, pans are normally lined with tin or stainless steel to act as a barrier – unlined copper pans should be kept for display only. Copper pans have to be cleaned periodically with a proprietary copper polish. Don't use them on a glass-topped hob unless they have a sandwich-base construction.

HARD-ANODISED ALUMINIUM

Distinguished by their steely grey or black colour. The surface has been electrochemically treated to produce a hard finish that will not chip, crack, peel or react with acidic foods. You can use metal utensils, although these can leave marks on the surface of the pan. These pans are not usually dishwasher-safe, but their surface is stick-resistant. Hard-anodised pans are reasonably lightweight and heat up rapidly, eliminating hot spots. Expensive, but perform and last well.

STAINLESS STEEL

Good-quality pans should last a lifetime, but they can be expensive. Food tends to stick, so you may have to use more oil. Stainless steel is a poor conductor of heat and is liable to have hot spots, so different materials such as copper or aluminium are usually incorporated into the base to improve conductivity – these are sandwiched between two layers of stainless steel. Cooking on a low heat also helps. Stainless steel is dishwasher-safe and food does not react with it. Overheating and minerals in water can cause a 'rainbow' effect, but a good stainless-steel cleaner will remove these.

Pan coatings

- Enamel: Usually applied to aluminium, cast-iron or steel pans. Price varies according to the metal underneath. Enamel pans generally do not pit, scratch easily or react with food. They can, however, chip if treated roughly. Heat distribution can be a problem with some pans – if the coating is too thin, food may stick and burn, so avoid very lightweight pans, which can also warp over a high heat.

- Non-stick: Ideal for frying, making sauces etc. A non-stick coating stops food sticking, reduces the need for additional fat and is easy to clean. Non-stick coatings are applied to most types of cookware, from aluminium and steel to cast iron and stainless steel. Choose the coating carefully as quality can vary – look out for branded coatings such as Teflon or Silverstone that come with their own guarantee. Do not use metal utensils or abrasive scourers as these can damage the finish.

COOKWARE FEATURES TO LOOK FOR

- ⊙ **DISHWASHER-SAFE** As a general rule, pans with plastic or stainless-steel handles or knobs are dishwasher-safe; most pans with wooden handles and knobs are not.
- ⊙ **FLAT BASE** Especially for electric cooking.
- ⊙ **OVEN-SAFE** Multi-purpose pans save time and storage space.
- ⊙ **POURING LIPS ON BOTH SIDES** Ideal for a household with both left- and right-handers.
- ⊙ **STAY-COOL HANDLES AND KNOBS** Handles should be a good length and not too narrow.
- ⊙ **WELL-FITTING LIDS** But free enough to allow steam to escape if there are no vents.
- ⊙ **WEIGHT** Make sure the pan will not be too heavy to lift when full.

CHOOSING A PAN TO SUIT YOUR COOKER OR HOB

- ⊙ **CERAMIC** All pans except copper, stainless steel with an exposed copper base and glass ceramic. Make sure the pan has a smooth, flat base to provide the best contact with the hob ring. Traditional cast-iron pans can be used, but be careful not to drag them across the hob.
- ⊙ **ELECTRIC RADIANT** All pans except copper.
- ⊙ **GAS** All pans. Lightweight pans are good as they use the controllability of gas to its full potential.
- ⊙ **HALOGEN** All pans except copper, stainless steel with exposed single-layer copper base and pans with reflective bases. Choose pans that have dull or dark bases – if the base is too bright and shiny, the thermal limiter may cut out to prevent the glass overheating.
- ⊙ **INDUCTION** The only suitable pans are ones made with a magnetic material in the base, such as cast iron or stainless steel.
- ⊙ **RANGE COOKERS** (e.g. Aga/Rayburn). Check with the manufacturer. As a general rule, heavy-based pans, such as cast iron, are best.
- ⊙ **SEALED PLATE** All pans except copper.

Woks

When selecting a wok, as with saucepans, you must consider the type of hob you have. All woks can be used on gas, but for glass-topped hobs, you must look for a smooth, flat base to provide good contact with the hob, as opposed to the traditional rounded base.

Traditional woks are made from uncoated carbon steel. Wash in warm water (without detergent), dry and then brush with a thin layer of vegetable oil to help to prevent rusting, as well as to season the wok.

If you don't feel you have the time or inclination for the preparation and maintenance needed with traditional carbon steel, choose a wok with a non-stick interior. These do not appeal to purists but they are easier to maintain.

Kitchen knives and sharpeners

No matter how many knives you have, there will be one or two favourites that you usually use for almost every task. What you choose depends upon whether you are prepared to sharpen knives. Generally, most professional knives need regular re-sharpening. So if you want a knife that stays sharp for years you may have to compromise on the quality of cutting.

CARBON OR STAINLESS STEEL?

Most knives today are made of stainless steel, which is resistant to rusting and harder than carbon steel, although purists swear by carbon steel, which can be easier to sharpen.

WHAT TO LOOK FOR IN A KNIFE

- ◉ A full tang – where the blade continues inside the handle to the end.
- ◉ A smooth heel to the blade, for safety.
- ◉ Evenly balanced weight between handle and blade. Check this by resting the knife across your fingers – it should remain level.
- ◉ The weight of the knife is a personal decision but professional cooks tend to prefer them heavier.
- ◉ Substantial handle with good grip.

KNIFE SHARPENERS

If you're going to invest in good knives it's vital that you keep them well sharpened. Get into the habit of sharpening them before use. The best way to sharpen a knife is to use a steel, but it requires practice to achieve the correct sharpening angle.

There are several ways of using a steel; find the most comfortable way for you. If you are right-handed, hold the steel horizontally in your left hand with the tip pointing slightly down. Holding the knife in your right hand, place the heel of the blade at the top of the steel at an angle of about 20 to 30°. Draw the knife down the steel, gradually pulling the knife away so that the tip of the knife ends at the tip of the steel. Repeat with the knife blade under the steel to sharpen the other side.

ABOVE How to check the balance of a knife

USING KNIVES

- ◉ Store knives separately, either in a divided cutlery tray or a knife block. Magnetic knife racks should be placed well out of range of young children.
- ◉ Don't leave knives soaking in the bottom of the washing-up bowl. It's easy to forget they are there – and it could damage the knife.
- ◉ Dry knives immediately after washing them.
- ◉ Use separate boards and knives for preparing raw and cooked foods.
- ◉ Be warned: cutting on to hard, unyielding surfaces like ceramic tiles or marble may be more hygienic than soft plastics or wood, but they blunt the blades more quickly.

THE RIGHT KNIFE FOR THE TASK

You don't need a drawer full of knives for different food preparation tasks, but a basic set should include at least these four:

- ⊙ **PARING KNIFE** For trimming, paring and decorating vegetables.
- ⊙ **COOK'S KNIFE (20–25cm/8–10in)** Versatile knife for chopping and slicing. The bigger it is the more control you have over cutting.
- ⊙ **BREAD KNIFE** Serrated to slice bread without tearing.
- ⊙ **FINELY SERRATED KNIFE** For slicing fruit such as tomatoes.

Dishwasher-safe?

Reputable brands come with care and use instructions. Generally, knives with plastic handles are dishwasher-safe and knives with wooden handles are not, unless they have been specially treated for dishwasher use. Don't leave knives in the dishwasher on a rinse-and-hold programme.

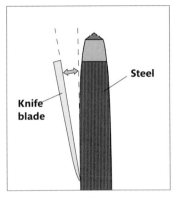

ABOVE Hold the knife at the correct angle to the steel, about 20–30°.

ABOVE Draw the knife down the steel until the tip of the knife ends at the tip of the steel.

ABOVE Repeat with the knife blade under the steel to sharpen the other side.

If you find that you tend to blunt a knife rather than sharpen it, you may find it easier to use a sharpener, which has angled slots to ensure that the blade is always held at the correct angle. However, these gadgets tend to wear out the knife blade faster and give a coarser edge compared to a steel.

Microwave cookware

It is not necessary to buy special microwave cookware. Many dishes in your kitchen cupboard are suitable for cooking and reheating.

To test their suitability, fill a heat-resistant measuring jug with 300ml/½ pint of cold water. Place it on the turntable alongside the dish to be tested. If the dish is large, stand the jug on top of the empty dish. Heat on full power for 1 minute. If the dish is suitable for the microwave, it will remain cool, while the water in the jug will begin to feel warm. If the testing dish feels warm, don't use it, as it's absorbing a lot of microwave energy that will not get through to the food.

GUIDE TO COOKING UTENSILS FOR MICROWAVE COOKING

CHINA AND CERAMICS
- Only use if heat resistant. If in doubt, do the water test (see page 75).
- Only use fine bone china for reheating for short periods – the change in temperature may crack the dish or craze its finish.
- Don't use dishes with any metallic trim.

HEATPROOF GLASS (E.G. PYREX)
- Can be used. Don't use delicate glass, which may crack with heat from food.

METAL CONTAINERS
- Unsuitable for most microwave-only models or microwaves with grills, but can be used in combination models when not in microwave-only mode. Always check with the manufacturer of the oven first.

PAPER
- Useful to prevent fatty foods spattering, and to stop foods like bread and pastries becoming soggy, but suitable for short cooking times only. Greaseproof and absorbent paper work well.
- Don't use waxed or plastic-coated containers as the coating can melt into food.

PLASTICS
- Most rigid plastics are suitable, but flexible ones tend not to be.
- Avoid using plastics to cook foods with a high fat or sugar content as the plastic may melt or distort.
- Plastic freezer bags can usually be used for short periods of defrosting.

POTTERY, EARTHENWARE AND STONEWARE
- Only suitable if completely glazed.

WICKER AND WOODEN BASKETS
- Wicker can be used for quick heating of items such as bread rolls, but will dry out if used too often or for too long.
- Don't use wooden dishes.

KITCHEN SCALES

Scale types

There are three types of kitchen scales.

TRADITIONAL BALANCE

Usually made of cast iron with separate weights. Limited weight range.

MECHANICAL

Numbered dial, usually in imperial and metric. Some types have a rotating weight gauge, which can be reset to zero enabling precise amounts of different ingredients to be added in an add-and-weigh style.

ELECTRONIC/ELECTRO-MECHANICAL

Electromechanical scales are no more accurate than their mechanical counterparts but have a digital readout. Fully electronic scales use a microchip and sensor to give a much more precise reading.

Most electronic scales have a versatile weight range and allow you to convert imperial to metric at the touch of a button. Others have memory facilities, automatic switch-off or a screen-save feature that switches the scales off if they're not touched for a couple of minutes, storing the weight in the memory until switched on again.

WATER FILTERS

If you are concerned about what's in your tap water you should contact your water supplier and ask for written details (they are legally obliged to tell you). The information you receive will tell you the quantities of particular substances present in your water and how much is permitted under EU regulations. Your water should meet certain regulations about what it may and may not contain, and in what quantities. It may be that there is nothing to worry about, in which case you don't need to buy a filter at all.

Filter types

Filters can either be plumbed into the mains supply or be separate, such as jug filters. With all types, you should follow the manufacturer's instructions for installation and use.

JUG FILTERS

Jug filters are designed to be portable, and have ion exchange units that reduce water hardness, as well as activated carbon filters to help improve the taste and appearance of the water. Once the water has been filtered of chlorine it has no defence against bacteria so you should use it within 24 hours.

PLUMBED-IN TYPES

If you find a jug filter too fiddly for your needs, and would prefer a more permanent solution, you may wish to consider a plumbed-in water filter. This is usually sited beneath the kitchen sink, and must have its own tap and a non-return valve to stop the filtered water getting back into the mains supply.

Waste Disposal and Recycling

A waste disposal unit is a very fast and convenient way to get rid of kitchen rubbish. It will deal with biodegradable matter such as vegetable peelings, tea bags and food leftovers which together amount to about a quarter of household waste.

WASTE DISPOSAL UNITS

Waste disposal units are installed under the sink. With the cold tap running, the waste is fed into a grinding chamber. Here it is thrown outwards, by centrifugal power, against a shredder attached to the inside wall of the chamber. The small particles of waste are then, with the aid of water, discharged into the sewage system.

A unit requires two connections to the plumbing system. The grinder receives the food waste through an opening in the bottom of the kitchen sink. The ground particles are discharged from the grinder, via a tail pipe, connected to the household drainage system. The electrical connection needed to power the unit is via a switch to an earthed outlet alongside the sink.

If you don't have a one-and-a-half sink, you may have to pay for a fitter to cut your existing sink and install the unit.

As well as being convenient, a waste disposal unit is also very hygienic, getting rid of food, which would normally begin to decompose and smell in an ordinary kitchen bin. It also helps to reduce the amount of rubbish in your own home. On the negative side, they do require quite a lot of water to work efficiently.

Waste disposal methods

There are two types of waste disposal unit: batch feed and continuous feed. The difference between them is the way the waste is fed and processed in the machine.

BATCH FEED

The unit is filled with waste, and the grinders will only start when the sink plug is put into place. The unit is therefore sealed, so there is no danger of getting fingers caught while in operation. You have to wait for the waste to be ground and flushed away before reloading.

CONTINUOUS FEED

The waste is fed in as and when you need to, which is ideal for larger families. You don't have to wait for the waste to be ground and flushed away before reloading. The main disadvantage, however, is that there is no cover on the unit, which could be dangerous, especially if inquisitive children are around.

REVERSE UNIT

To reduce wear and tear it is worth investing in a fully automatic reverse unit. This feature is available on both types of waste disposal unit. Unlike a single-direction model, it grinds in alternate directions each time it is used.

WASTE COMPACTORS

Unlike waste disposal units, compactors can deal with practically all household waste and require no special installation or wiring. They work by crushing waste, using an electrically powered ram inside the rubbish drawer. This lowers on to the rubbish, then returns to a raised position and shuts off automatically. This type of waste storage reduces household rubbish to one-twelfth of its original volume, saving space in the kitchen and numerous trips to the dustbin.

BIN SEPARATORS

These are an ideal way of storing rubbish suitable for recycling, such as glass, plastic, paper and metal. Free-standing separator systems can be stored anywhere in the house, or outdoors. Alternatively, built-in systems are installed under the sink unit. This is a more expensive option but it keeps the bin out of sight and saves space.

RECYCLING

Recycling helps the environment. Used materials can be converted into new products, reducing the need to consume precious, natural resources and lowering the amount of waste introduced into landfill. Using recycled materials in the manufacturing process also consumes less energy than is required to produce items from raw materials, and this helps to reduce greenhouse gas emissions. Currently, in the UK, recycling is estimated to save more than 18 million tonnes of CO_2 per year – the equivalent of taking 5 million cars off the road. However, we could be doing a lot more. A large percentage of households still throw away anything they consider rubbish into their ordinary bin – much of this waste can be recycled and should be disposed of separately to general household waste. Do your bit for the environment and look for ways you can reduce the waste you produce and to recycle more of it.

Waste disposal tips

- Be careful when emptying food into the waste disposal unit. It's easy for a spoon or other cutlery to accidentally fall in. This then jams the unit and damages the blades. If this does happen, it is essential that you turn the appliance off at the mains before you attempt to take the obstruction out.

- To avoid putting your hands in the plug hole, use a pair of long-handled pliers and a torch so you can see what you are doing.

- Even when all the food has been ground up, it is essential that you still keep the tap running for a few minutes. If you don't run sufficient water through, the pipes may become blocked.

Recycling facts: did you know?

* One recycled can saves enough energy to power a TV for three days.

* As much as 50 per cent of the waste in the average dustbin could be composted.

* 70 per cent less energy is required to recycle paper compared with making it from raw materials.

* Up to 80 per cent of the materials in a vehicle can be recycled.

* One recycled bottle would save enough energy to power a 60W light bulb for three hours.

Top five green tips for reducing waste

1 **RECYCLE ON YOUR DOORSTEP** Most councils now operate kerbside collection schemes which make it easy for you to dispose of recyclable items such as paper, glass, certain plastics and aluminium in an environmentally friendly manner. If you don't already have a special recycling container from your council, contact them and ask for one. Make sure you check which materials are covered by their scheme and put them out for collection on the appropriate day of the week. If you live in a rural area, or your council does not yet operate a kerbside scheme, you can find recycling banks in many areas across the UK where you can dispose of your recyclable waste safely and easily. To find out what you can recycle and where, go to www.recyclenow.com.

2 **FIND A NEW HOME FOR UNWANTED ITEMS** Rather than throw them away, contact your local council for details of charities or schemes in your area that can make use of unwanted furniture and other items. Alternatively, use your local Freecycle group (see Useful Organisations) to find your item a new owner – one man's junk is another man's treasure!

3 **REDUCE THE AMOUNT OF JUNK MAIL YOU RECEIVE** To do this, register with the Mailing Preference Service (see Useful Organisations) to stop addressed mail like credit card applications being sent to you. Advertisers will be given your details and told not to contact you with unsolicited mail. For unaddressed mail or letters addressed to the 'occupier', you will need to contact Royal Mail and the Direct Marketing Association (see Useful Organisations). Always be aware whenever you give your name and address to any business – make sure you tick the box that states you don't wish to be contacted about future promotions or your details to be passed on to other marketing agencies.

4 **RECYCLE FOOD WASTE BY USING IT FOR COMPOST** Home composting is a great way of minimising the amount of waste your household produces. It's very easy to do and will provide you with a great source of free fertiliser for the plants in your garden. For more information on what can and can't go into a composter, see Composters, pages 155–6.

5 **CONSIDER THE PACKAGING THAT COMES WITH YOUR PURCHASES** It is estimated that packaging costs account for roughly 16 per cent of the price of the products we buy. Not only is this an unnecessary expense, its also wasteful. When shopping, look for items that come loose, or packaged in simple, recyclable materials such as glass, aluminium and paper. Try to remember to bring your own reusable bags to carry purchases home, but if you forget, many supermarkets now offer in-store facilities where you can return your used plastic carrier bags for recycling.

RECYCLING SYMBOLS EXPLAINED

Numerous labels appear on packaging to advise consumers and promote environmental claims. To ensure these claims are accurate and help you also understand what they mean, a set of international standards have been developed known as the Green Claims Code. Use the guide below to help you make sense of the symbols you may see.

 GREEN DOT This does not have any environmental significance and means only that the producer has paid a fee towards the packaging recovery system in Germany.

 GLASS While most glass containers are recyclable, this symbol reminds consumers to recycle glass jars and bottles, either at bottle banks or, where available, through kerbside collection schemes.

 EUROPEAN ECO-LABEL Awarded to products that meet a set of stringent environmental and performance criteria. These criteria take into account all aspects of a product's life, from its production and use to its eventual disposal (cradle-to-grave approach).

 RECYCLABLE ALUMINIUM Can be taken to an aluminium recycling facility

 COMPOSTABLE Means you can put the packaging into your composter.

 RECYCLABLE STEEL Can be taken to a steel recycling facility

       PLASTICS Identifies the type of plastic: PET and HDPE bottles are recycled by the majority of local authorities.

 MOBIUS LOOP Usually found on cardboard; indicates the object is capable of being recycled.

 MOBIUS LOOP WITH PERCENTAGE Found on cardboard; shows the percentage of recycled material contained in the product.

 PAPER Paper or board made from a minimum of 75 per cent genuine waste paper and/or board fibre, no part of which should contain mill produced waste fibre.

Bathroom Fixtures and Fittings

A new bathroom adds an extra personal touch to your home. Consider the choice of colours, materials, fittings and positions in the room. The main limiting factors are permanent fittings such as windows, doors and plumbing connections. Some piping can be fairly easily moved or extended, but probably the greatest influence is the position of the toilet soil pipe.

PLANNING A BATHROOM

Consider the space available and the fittings required. Measure the room and mark the plan out on graph paper. NB: work in metric, as this is how bathroom fittings are always sold.

Remember to allow for manoeuvring, or the 'activity space', around the fitting (see illustration opposite). Space is needed for bending over fittings such as a basin, and climbing in and out of baths. Access for cleaning should also be considered. Some activity spaces can overlap (see opposite), as fittings are unlikely to be used at the same time.

Siting the toilet, bidet, basin and bath in line is an efficient way to run water pipes.

The final decision to make is the actual style and colour for the fittings. Light, pale shades and co-ordinates will give an illusion of space in small rooms. Dark colours give the impression of intimacy and warmth but show dirt easily.

Lighting should also be considered at this stage as artificial or natural light will affect the look of a bathroom.

Built-in units can be used to fill spaces. They provide useful storage space and help to tidy up corners that may be difficult to clean.

BATHS

The bath you choose depends upon the space available and your own taste. The standard bath is 1.7m (5ft 6in) long, but shorter baths and other shapes – such as oval and round baths, and corner baths – are also available. Contoured baths, usually made from acrylic, are shaped to trace the outline of the body, and water usage is slightly more economical. Shower baths are designed for both bathing and showering. They have an extra wide shower area for more comfortable showering.

All these baths have a rectangular outer frame, which usually has panels down the sides and ends. An embossed surface improves the grip and is safer, especially if the bath is to be used with a shower attachment.

Traditional Victorian-shaped baths are free-standing with feet and can still be obtained in cast iron – as pipe work will be on display, consider opting for decorative styles that will still look attractive in your bathroom.

RECOMMENDED ACTIVITY SPACES

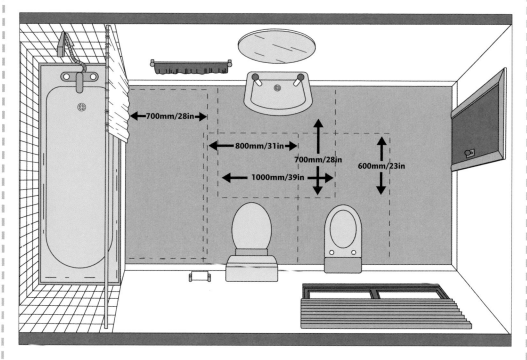

700mm/28in

800mm/31in

700mm/28in

600mm/23in

1000mm/39in

- ⊙ **BATH** 700mm/28in-wide standing area along the side.

- ⊙ **BASIN** 1,000mm/39in-wide area extending 700mm/28in from the front of the basin. Remember to allow space above for bending down over it. Don't fit a shelf or cupboard above a basin unit so that people using it will bang their head, or drop things into the sink.

- ⊙ **SHOWER** 700mm/28in standing space in front of the opening.

- ⊙ **TOILET AND BIDET** Allow a total width of 800mm/31in each, extending 600mm/24in back from the front edge of each. Less space is needed at the sides if they are placed next to each other. Bidets are designed to be used facing the taps, so knee room at the sides must be allowed.

A bath usually has taps positioned at the end of the bath, but some designs have them on the side or in the corner. There are two main kinds of bath material:

Acrylic
Lightweight, warm to the touch, and less slippery than metal. Acrylic is stain resistant, but will scratch easily. Light scratches can be removed using metal polish. Deep scratches may be removed by the manufacturer. The moulded acrylic is reinforced with fibreglass and mounted on a galvanised steel frame to give strength. A variety of shapes are available.

Enamelled
Pressed steel baths are coated with vitreous enamel and fired to give the hard finish. Cast-iron baths have a porcelain enamel (if you are installing a cast iron bath, make sure the bathroom floor can take the weight). Both types of enamel can be damaged by abrasive cleaners and some limescale removers.

Whirlpool baths

May also be called spa baths or jacuzzis, and are the most expensive types of baths. The jets and movement of the water massage the body, and can give relief to arthritic or rheumatic joints.

The number and position of the underwater jets can be varied, and along with different air and water pressures, different sorts of effects can be achieved. There are various options:

- Whirlpool jets recirculate the water and pump it through outlets along the bath.
- Spa baths pump air through holes in the base and back of the bath.
- Whirlpool spas pump a mixture of air and water round the bath.

Look out for self-draining features on recirculating water systems.

Some have a built-in sterilising system with a reservoir of cleaning chemicals, which needs to be kept topped up. Alternatively, a separate whirlpool cleaner can be purchased to disinfect the bath every two weeks. Baths fitted as whirlpools can be purchased new, or a system can be installed in your existing acrylic bath by the whirlpool manufacturer. The bath needs to be taken away to the factory for installation, but the only stipulation on design is that the bath needs to have a flat surface in which to fit the jet controls.

Before buying any type of whirlpool ask to listen to the pump working, as they can sometimes be noisy.

Check that the appliance is electrically safe and conforms to electrical standards. It should be protected by a residual current device (RCD) outside the bathroom.

WASH BASINS

Gone are the days when the only choice for a bathroom sink was vitreous china. Sinks are now available in a variety of materials, from traditional china to glass, wood and even copper. Your choice will depend on the style and size of your bathroom, and the needs of your family. Consider whether you require storage directly alongside the sink and how often the bathroom will be used – for example, a seldom used

SINK STYLES

- **PEDESTAL** As well as supporting the bowl the pedestal hides the pipes. The bowl is still usually fixed to the wall, so it is at a height of about 800mm/31in. Available in a variety of styles and shapes.
- **WALL MOUNTED AND PEDESTAL** Vary from large to small hand basins, which will fit into small cloakrooms. Because they are fixed to the wall the pipes may be exposed, although half pedestals may be fitted.
- **COUNTER TOP AND UNDER-COUNTER** The bowl is sunk to sit level or underneath the worktop, with a washstand or vanity unit supporting it. Cupboards underneath hide the pipework and provide tidy storage.
- **ABOVE COUNTER** The bowl sits above a worktop or vanity unit. Pipework may be exposed or concealed.

guest bathroom won't require as much counter or storage space, whereas in a master bathroom, you might want to consider installing multiple sinks side-by-side so that two people can get ready for work at the same time. For bathrooms that are used daily, choose a material that will wear well and is easy to keep clean.

TOILETS

A toilet is a vital part of everyday living – it's the most used fixture in the bathroom, so make sure you give some thought to which type you choose. Toilets usually consist of two main parts, the pan and the cistern, but a wide variety of styles and shapes are available. If you are looking for a traditional feel, then your choice will probably be focused on low and high-level systems, or for a more contemporary look, consider a back-to-wall, close-coupled or wall-hung model.

Types of flushing system

WASH-DOWN The simplest, most common mechanism. Water washes down from the cistern through the pan, and refills with the aid of a ball valve. The cheapest system, but can be inefficient and high-maintenance.

PUSH-FLUSH Becoming increasingly popular. They incorporate a cylinder of pressurised air inside the toilet tank to provide greater force to the flushing mechanism. This type of flush is more efficient than a 'wash-down' system, but is usually more expensive.

SHREDDING AND PUMPING UNIT This enables the toilet to be installed almost anywhere in the house. The discharge is shredded so that it can be pumped through a narrower pipe. Being smaller, the discharge pipe can be run behind the wall. An electrical connection is needed to operate the pump. They are an option for an additional toilet in the house. Permission must be obtained from the local authority before installation.

Green tip

Choose a 'dual-flush' toilet to help save water. This type of toilet offers a 'half-flush for liquid waste and a 'full-flush' for solid waste, letting you adjust the amount of water you use for lighter and heavier loads (only available with push-flush toilets).

Seat sizes

Toilet bowls come in either round or elongated models. Elongated models are generally around 5cm/2in longer, and provide a bit more surface area, so the seat is more comfortable. Rounds seats are smaller and better for tight spaces.

TOILET SIZES AND SHAPES

- ⊙ **CLOSE-COUPLE** The cistern sits on the pan to give the look of a single unit. The pan sits on a pedestal (floor-standing), but this can leave a space behind the toilet that is difficult to clean. Depending on the design, the cistern may be tall, narrow or short and can be operated with either a lever or push-button flush.

- ⊙ **LOW-LEVEL** The cistern is mounted a small way (about 935mm/37in) above the pan, connected with a small flush pipe.

- ⊙ **HIGH-LEVEL** The cistern is fixed on the wall high above the pan with a joining pipe. The cistern has a pull chain to flush the toilet.

- ⊙ **BACK-TO-THE-WALL** Floor-standing, but completely encloses the pipework so that it is flush with the wall behind. It has a neat appearance and a smooth finish for cleaning.

- ⊙ **WALL-HUNG** The pan and piping are enclosed and supported against the wall. The floor below is clear and easier to clean.

- ⊙ **CONCEALED CISTERN** The cistern is positioned with a unit or behind the wall with only the flush handle protruding. It may be fitted with a back-to-the-wall or wall-hung toilet pan.

BIDETS

A low-level wash basin made of vitreous china, like toilets and basins. Originally designed for personal hygiene, they are also used as a footbath in the UK. There are two main types, and they both need good, balanced water pressures in order to work effectively.

OVER-THE-RIM A mixer tap fills the bidet with hot and cold water, like a basin. The tap may have a swivel head to give directional water sprays. The over-the-rim is the most common type made by UK manufacturers.

BELOW-THE-RIM/BOX RIM More expensive, and looks more like a toilet. It is filled from under the rim.

Either type of bidet may also have an ascending spray or douche supply. The inlet nozzle is set in the base of the bowl giving an upward spray. High water pressure is needed for this type of bidet to be effective. Before buying a bidet, check that it conforms to your local water regulations. It may need special installation to meet backflow prevention requirements specified by the water company. Consulting a qualified plumber is recommended. Like toilets, bidets may be wall-hung or floor-standing. They are usually the same height as a toilet, and should be positioned as close to the toilet as possible.

TAPS

A variety of materials are used for taps and bathroom fittings. The most common are chrome or a gold-effect coating. Brass and coloured taps are also available coated with a coloured plastic finish.

The size, position and type of taps for baths, basins and bidets are restricted by the size and number of fitting holes. Choosing the right tap is important and can greatly influence the functionality of your bathroom as a whole. When choosing a tap, you need to consider the type of bath or basin you have and your water supply. Water systems

Ceramic disk technology

Look for taps that use ceramic disc technology – they are more expensive, but perform better and last longer, and what's more, you'll never have to change another washer again! However, they are unsuitable for very low-pressure water systems.

TAP STYLES

⊙ **PILLAR** These come as pairs for hot and cold water. The water enters the tap vertically, so they must be mounted on a level surface. They are generally small and neat with a twist top. Traditional styles have a cross-shaped handle.

⊙ **MIXER** Water is supplied via a central tap. A dual mixer supplies the hot and cold together but keeps the two separate within the tap. A true mixer combines the water as it goes through the tap and needs equal water pressures to be controlled accurately. Mixer taps may consist of a single unit with the taps connected on the same base as the spout. A three-piece unit has the controls and taps mounted on to the basin or bath separately. A bath/shower mixer has a diverter to send water to the attached shower head.

⊙ **SINGLE LEVER** As the name suggests, the tap is a single unit with a rotating control and lever. The flow of water is controlled by raising or lowering the lever, while the temperature is varied by rotating the control. This tap style requires only one fitting hole.

influence the performance of taps so you must be sure that the ones you select will work properly with your current water system. If you have a high pressure system then a low pressure tap will work fine, however, this is not the same vice versa, and a high pressure tap will not work with a low pressure system.

SHOWERS

The main factor affecting a choice of shower will be the type of water system in your house. If you're not sure which type of system you have, ask a plumber to investigate for you: see Fitting a Shower, page 88. If your hot and cold water are both supplied from a hot-water cylinder (in the airing cupboard) or a cold-water tank (in the loft) you can choose between a mixer shower (preferably thermostatic) and a power shower (a mixer shower with an extra pressure boost). If your house does not have a hot-water cylinder or constant hot water, you need an instantaneous electric shower. The cold water supply, direct from the mains, is heated by the shower as it is needed. An exception is for combination gas boilers (with constant gas-heated mains-pressure water), when you need a mixer shower. However, check first with your local gas company.

Instantaneous electric showers
Electric showers are the easiest to install in terms of compatibility with existing water systems, and can be used in most situations. They draw water directly from the mains supply and heat it as it is used for showering, so can be used at any time of day, and are a good choice if you don't have a lot of stored hot water. The disadvantages are that flow rate tends to be lower than showers that use the main water heating system, and will fluctuate between summer (when the incoming mains supply of water is warmer) and winter, when the colder incoming water requires more heating, making the flow is slower. To overcome this, look for a model with at least a 10kW output. Electric showers also require wiring from the shower unit to mains electricity by a qualified professional, so the installation costs will be more expensive.

Mixer showers
Mixer showers draw water from the hot water cylinder and cold-water tank. They are easy to install and require no electrical connections, but the cold-water tank needs to be several metres above the shower head to deliver sufficient water pressure – if the distance is less than 5m/16ft, you'll need to choose a model with a 'low pressure' valve to overcome the lack of water pressure. Mixers showers are ideal if you have an abundant supply of stored hot water. However, this type of system is likely to suffer from draw-off – water drawn elsewhere in the house, such as flushing a toilet or filling a basin, will cause the shower to run hot – therefore it's a good idea to choose a model with thermostatic controls (built-in stabilisers that ensure water stays at the same temperature). This will cost more, but will prevent you from being scalded if another cold-water tap is turned on when you are using the shower.

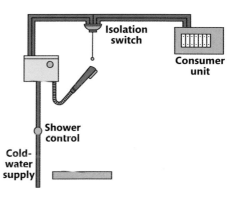

ABOVE Mixer shower

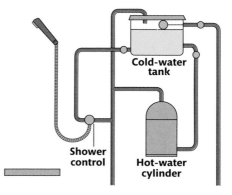

ABOVE Instantaneous shower

Power showers

These add a booster pump to a mixer to give a strong spray, and can be installed where there is insufficient pressure in the system (requiring only 7.5cm/3in head of pressure). A power pump can achieve as much as 9–27m/30–86ft head of pressure. The pressure and type of flow from the shower head can be varied to give effects such as a needle jet or soft foam-effect spray. The higher the wattage of the pump, the greater will be the flow. Power showers use a lot of water and you need a shower cabinet or fully tiled walls to prevent water damage.

Body-spray showers

In addition to an overhead shower, shower jets that spray water horizontally can be fitted on to the walls of the shower cubicle. They need to be fitted with a power shower, or a mixer shower with a pump, to have enough pressure to work. Body sprays can be like small fixed showerheads, or be direct jets from a vertical rail with holes along it. A diverter must be fitted to change the water between the shower and the body sprays.

Fitting a shower

The base of the cold-water tank needs to be at least 1m/3ft above the shower head for a mixer shower. This is described as a 'head of pressure' and the greater the distance, the greater the shower flow. If there isn't sufficient head of pressure – perhaps if you live in a flat – you will have to install a booster pump (see Power Showers, above). With an electric shower (supplied direct from the mains), the only way to increase the pressure is to buy one with a higher wattage, or a power shower.

Check that your water supply can cope with the type of shower you are considering. Showers with a high flow rate must not drain the water-storage system too quickly.

Foreign imported brands may not fit British plumbing systems. Check that the shower you are considering will fit, and complies with UK water regulations.

Cold-water tank
Shower control
Shower booster pump
Hot-water cylinder

ABOVE Power shower

WET ROOMS

The latest trend in bathroom design, a wet room is basically a super-stylish, contemporary shower room that does away with the shower screen and tray, and instead has an open, fully tiled shower area. Installing a wet room is strictly a job for professionals as the floor must be properly graded to channel water into a central drainage area, and the entire room must be tanked (waterproofed) before any tiles or other wall coverings are fitted. Underfloor heating is also a good idea because it helps dry out the large amount of shower water that will get sprayed directly on to the wet room floor.

◉ **BENEFITS** Wet rooms are a great way of making the best use of a small area – removing the bath and shower enclosures creates lots more space. They are also easier to clean, and if you opt for a wall-hung sink and toilet, cleaning is even easier.

◉ **DRAWBACKS** Cost is probably the main downside. The special requirements of a wet room mean you can expect to pay upwards of £6,500 for a proper installation. You'll also need to look out for wet towels and toilet roll caused by spray from the shower, and porous tiles (such as limestone) will need to be resealed every six months or so.

ENCLOSURES AND SCREENS

Surfaces need to be cleaned easily to prevent the build-up of limescale or mould. Whichever type you choose, the area around the shower needs to be protected from the water spray.

- **SHOWER CUBICLES** These may be built into a corner or alcove in the bathroom or other room, using two or three walls as part of the shower enclosure. Free-standing cubicles don't rely on any interior walls as frames but will need a wall to support the plumbing. The unit has four side panels and sometimes a top to contain water vapour. Usually they can be purchased as complete kits, including the shower tray. Different shaped trays, such as curved or triangular, can be purchased to fit into corners. For a neat edge with a tiled wall, look for a tray with a special tiling lip. Look for slip-resistant trays, but bear in mind that if the base is too rough it may be difficult to keep a clean appearance.

- **SHOWER TUBS** Larger than a regular shower cubicle, these are rather like a cross between a bath and rectangular shower tray 1,200mm/47in x 750mm/291/2 in x 545mm/21^{1}/2in. As well as a standing area under the shower there is a raised area for sitting towards the back of the tub.

- **SHOWER CURTAINS** The cheapest and simplest screening to put along a bath/shower, and can easily be pulled out of the way when the bath itself is needed. Mildew and a build-up of soapy deposits in the folds are the main problems associated with shower curtains. Look for PVC, which can be wiped clean, or washable nylon, polyester or cotton. Mildew-resistant curtains are sold impregnated with a fungicide. If you want a curtain to match the other furnishing in the bathroom, it can be hung with a waterproof curtain on the inside. Eyelets to use on homemade curtains are available from haberdashery stores.

- **SCREENS** Usually made from toughened plastic or rigid glass, these are a more permanent arrangement than a curtain. A single-panel fixed screen can fit to reach halfway along the side of the bath and may be fixed or hinged for easy access. Screens made from several hinged panels will fold flat to be kept out of the way, making getting in and out of the bath easier. For a completely enclosed bath, sliding panels on runners can be installed around all edges of the bath (or hinged along the bath length). For a rounded corner bath with a shower, curved screens are available with curved sliding panels. Check that the screen will make a good seal with the bath before purchasing, and bear in mind how practical it will be to keep clean: a smooth plastic inside and smooth seals between the screen and bath will make cleaning easier.

TYPES OF SHOWER HEADS

- **FIXED WALL MOUNTED** The hose to the shower head is concealed behind the wall. Only the actual head is fixed to the wall, but it can be pivoted to change the direction of the spray. Traditional fixed heads have a large circular head connected by rigid exposed pipes. You are not able to adjust the height of the shower.

- **SLIDE RAIL** The shower support is fitted on a wall-mounted slide rail, so that the height can be varied and the head can also be unclipped.

- **SPRAY VARIATIONS** The actual head will also affect the power and effect from the shower. They can give a variety of spray types. The greatest variation is on power showers, where a jet of water, a soft spray or a normal shower effect can be achieved.

- **SELF-CLEANING** Look for a shower head that is self-draining, so that no water is left in it to form limescale. Self-cleaning heads have internal plastic pins, which will protrude through the spray holes when not in use and keep them free from scale.

PROFESSIONAL ADVICE

Advice on your water system and appropriate installations can be obtained from a qualified plumber. Suitable local contacts can be obtained from the Institute of Plumbing (see Useful Organisations). All gas appliances and connections must be carried out by a plumber who is on the Gas Safe RegisterTM (see Useful Organisations).

BATHROOM ACCESSORIES

Wall brackets (grab rails)

Give extra support to the less stable. Can be mounted in shower cubicles, above baths, and can be incorporated into toilet-roll holders or towel rails.

Heated towel rails

There are two main types that can be installed in bathrooms. Before buying, consider the facilities for connecting to a water supply or electricity as necessary. Heated rails are primarily designed to dry and air towels, but if they are large enough, they can both dry towels and give off room heat. There are two main types:

ELECTRIC TOWEL RAILS Operated from an isolated switch positioned outside the bathroom.

HOT-WATER TOWEL RAILS Connected to the central heating so they come on when the bathroom is likely to be used. They are more efficient to run compared to an electric rail, as they automatically go on and off with the house heating.

BATHROOM VENTILATION

For rooms such as bathrooms, adequate ventilation must be installed in all new properties or extensions, but it is advisable to install ventilation in existing bath/shower rooms and toilets to prevent condensation and damp problems. For good ventilation, a bathroom needs six to eight air changes an hour. A fan should be installed which will extract at least 15 litres/3 gallons)/second (54 cu. m/1,900 cu. ft/hour) intermittently. All fans require electrical connection to drive them, and supervision of a qualified electrician may be required. There are two main types of fans, to suit different installation circumstances:

AXIAL FANS Should be fitted through a window or wall, because they are designed to move air over only short distances. To reach through a cavity wall, telescopic tubing is usually attached.

CENTRIFUGAL FANS Will move air over distances greater than 2m/6ft 6in. They can be fitted with flexible ducting to extract to the outside via the roof cavity, but remember that the greater the distance of the ducting, the less efficient the fan will be. A condensation trap may also be needed (see opposite).

Shower and bath accessories

- **FOLD-DOWN SEAT** For extra support and comfort for old and young.

- **SHOWER TIDY** Self-draining sets of shelves fixed to the wall or on to the slide rail.

- **GEL/SHAMPOO DISPENSER** Fitted on to the slide rail.

- **NON-SLIP BATH MATS** Plastic mats with suckers to improve grip in the bath. Always check that the mat is well suctioned on to the bath base or the whole mat may aquaplane. Stick-on grips can also be purchased as a permanent solution.

POINTS TO CONSIDER WHEN CHOOSING AN EXTRACTOR FAN

- ◉ Size of room and fan: see box below.
- ◉ Humidistat that automatically operates fan when humidity reaches a set level.
- ◉ Adjustable time selector for overrun (usually up to 20 minutes). The fan is connected to the light switch and will stay on for a set period of time after the light has been switched off.

- ◉ Back-draught shutters on the outside grill.
- ◉ Easy to clean parts, preferably removable grills.
- ◉ Pull cord to switch on and off.
- ◉ Dual speed for large bathrooms. The fan operates at full speed when the room is in use and a low speed during overrun on the timer.
- ◉ On small units, a manual boost speed facility.

Fitting an extractor fan

Always use a qualified electrician to install an extractor fan. To achieve the best efficiency the fan should be sited at the furthermost point from the source of replacement air, such as opposite the internal doorway. To comply with wiring regulations a bathroom fan must not be situated where it can be switched on or off by a person using a bath or shower A pull-cord switch is the safest option and the fan is often wired into this. For additional safety, an isolation switch outside the bathroom is also recommended.

WINDOW FITTING

A hole must be cut for the fan. It is advisable to have this cut in a new piece of glass by a professional glazier. If you have a hole put in an existing pane the stresses may crack it.

Check with the glazier that the weight of glass is appropriate to take the fan.

The fan will need to be fitted with a waterproof seal around the hole in the glass, following the manufacturer's instructions.

WALL FITTING

As well as the fan, a kit may be needed to fit the fan through the wall. Check that the selected position has no buried pipes or wires, or obstructions on the outside of the wall.

CEILING FITTING

Ventilation ducting will be needed to carry the air to the exterior via the roof cavity and an exterior grill.

If it is possible that condensation could run back towards the fan a condensation trap will be needed. The formation of condensation can be reduced by insulating the ducting in the roof space.

Check that the location and route of the ducting is not obscured.

WARNING
The extraction pipe must not be connected to a flue used for any other appliances other than electrically operated.

HOW TO CALCULATE THE SIZE OF EXTRACTOR FAN

To determine the size of extractor fan needed, the size of room must be considered.

1 Measure the size of the room in metres/feet: length x width x height = volume in cu. m/cu. ft.

2 Multiply the volume by the recommended air changes per hour (6–10 for bathrooms and toilets) = extract performance of the fan required (cu. m/cu. ft/hr).

3 Look for a fan with a performance as close to this as possible.

Beds

In an ideal world, beds should be changed every ten years, but in reality it's more likely to be every 15–20 years. For a piece of furniture that is expected to give over 36,000 hours of support to the entire body it's essential to choose a bed that matches your requirements exactly.

OUT WITH THE OLD?

If we could see inside an old bed we'd never settle for a second-hand one. A sagging mattress with a stained and badly frayed cover, warped or bent slats or springs you can feel through flattened fillings is a sure sign that it's past its prime. Most importantly, if it feels less comfortable than it used to and you're getting more nights of disturbed sleep than before, it's probably that the springs have weakened, giving less support. This can give rise to back problems and continual loss of sleep. To help people establish whether it is time to buy a new bed, the Sleep Council (see Useful Organisations) has devised a simple bed MOT (mattress obsolescence test), which they recommend should be done every year after the first three to five years after buying a new mattress.

BUYING A NEW BED

There are literally hundreds of types of bed to choose from, and making a decision can be quite overwhelming, so here are a few tips to help you make the right choice:

- Look out for the blue and white 'FR' label. All beds sold in the UK are required to meet fire safety regulations introduced in 1988 which require all foams to be combustion modified and the composite of springs, filling and cover in the mattress and base to be cigarette and match flame resistant.
- Make sure you try it out. At the end of the day it's up to you to decide whether it's comfortable. Lie on the bed, with your partner if it's a double, and stay there for as long as possible. Ask for a pillow so it is totally representative of the way you will sleep on it.
- Check the firmness of the bed by sliding your hand into the small of your back. If your hand becomes lodged the bed is too soft and if there is a distinct gap it's too hard. Make sure you can turn on to your side easily and that it isn't too hard on your shoulders and hips.
- As a general rule, the heavier you are, the firmer the mattress you will need. For partners of widely varying weights, it's possible to buy two different firmnesses of mattress that can be zipped together.
- Read the labels – you may be surprised how informative these can be. They'll detail the types of filling used for the mattress and the base.

Sleep Council MOT

- Is the bed ten years old or more?
- Do you ever wake up with neck or back aches?
- Is the mattress cover torn or stained?
- When lying in bed, do you feel springs or ridges beneath the surface?
- When moving in bed, do you hear creaks, crunches or other suspicious noises?
- Do you and your partner roll towards each other unintentionally?
- Is the bed too small to give an undistinct night's sleep?
- Is the divan or base uneven or sagging?
- Are the legs or castors worn out?
- Would it be embarrassing if neighbours saw the mattress without its covers?

If you answered 'yes' to three or more of the questions above, then you're not getting the best night's sleep. If you answered 'yes' to five or more questions, then it's time to buy a new bed!

Too hard

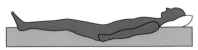

Too soft

Correct

LEFT The correct firmness of a bed is vital in getting a good night's sleep.

TIP
Avoid shopping for a new bed when you are tired: everything feels good then!

⊙ Spend as much as you can afford. There is no such thing as a cheap bed, only a lower-quality one. It's worth paying more for strong, durable springs, better stitching, hand tufting and firm handles, all of which contribute to longer-lasting performance. Sale buys are good value, but avoid discount stores unless selling well-known, genuinely labelled branded beds.

⊙ Buy a new base and mattress together. Even if the base still looks in good condition, it's likely to retain the imprint of the old mattress, which could affect the your comfort when the new mattress is installed on top of it.

⊙ A new bed will feel strange for a while; it will probably take about three weeks before you're used to it properly.

MATTRESSES

The first thing to consider is the mattress covering or 'ticking'. Manufacturer's choose the covering with care, as they are aware that this 'packaging' will influence consumer choice. However, remember that your mattress will spend most of the time covered by bedclothes, so don't be swayed too much by the design of the ticking. Look for closely woven ticking, especially on a tufted mattress (see below) where the cover must be tight to hold the tufts securely. Check that handles are strong and securely fixed. These bear the brunt of the weight when the mattress is turned. The mattress should be well finished off. Finishing methods include:

TUFTED The traditional method of finishing. Often found on top-quality mattresses. The mattress is punched through with cotton tapes or waxed threads with a tag left at each end. These are guarded by a cotton or wool-felt washer to prevent the tags pulling back into the mattress.

DEEP-STITCH QUILTING (DIAMOND SHAPED) Produces a smooth sleeping surface by stitching the top filling layers to the ticking. The quilted layer is then attached to the core of springs.

BED STATISTICS

STANDARD BED SIZES

Compact Single
75 x 190cm/2ft 6in x 6ft 3in

Popular Single
90 x 190cm/3ft x 6ft 3in

Standard Double
120 x 190cm/4ft x 6ft 3in

Popular Double
135 x 190cm/4ft 6in x 6ft 3in

Queen Size
150 x 200cm/5ft x 6ft 6in

King Size
180 x 200cm/6ft x 6ft 6in

Manufacturers are at last recognising that the population is becoming taller and producing more beds up to 200cm/6ft 6in long.

Average bed height
66–70cm/26–28in

MICRO OR MULTI-QUILTING Involves stitching or quilting the ticking to a thin layer of foam or polyester fibre. The stitch pattern stretches over the whole area of the cover. Under the quilted ticking the primary insulating upholstery is attached to the springs. This extends right to the edges of the mattress.

SMOOTH TOP Usually found on the cheaper ranges. Here the ticking is pulled tightly over the filling and there is no stitching to hold the filling layers in place. Over time, this is bound to move around.

Spring interior mattresses

This is the most popular type in the UK. Springs form the central core of the mattress and are the main support layer. The thickness of the wire and the number of springs determine the firmness of a mattress. A spring made from a 12-gauge wire is harder than a 15-gauge one. A pocketed-spring bed tends to use 15-gauge or higher because there are so many more springs offering extra support. Orthopaedic beds, on the other hand, use 12- to 14-gauge springs. In a top-of-the-range bed the number of springs used will be included in the sales literature or the cover label. A cheap, popular double will probably contain around 300 springs, whereas a bed at the luxury end of the market will contain over 2,500. There are three main types of spring mattress.

OPEN SPRINGING

The most common, and generally cheaper than pocket springs. Found in cheap to mid-priced beds. They consist of rows of waisted spring coils joined to adjacent springs by a continuous small-diameter spiral spring. The edge of the spring unit is strengthened by a heavy-gauge border rod at the top and bottom.

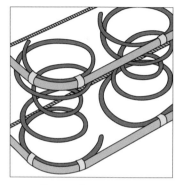

ABOVE Open spring

CONTINUOUS SPRINGING

A development of open-springing with one length of wire forming all the coils in the mattress, producing a three-dimensional knitted effect. The coiled unit is attached to helical wire springs and held within a metal border at the top and bottom. These tend to be in the middle price range.

POCKETED SPRINGING

Has cylindrical coils individually enclosed in fabric pockets made from calico, viscose or polyester. This allows them to work independently of each other and better contour to the shape of the sleeping person's body. These are generally in the middle to top end of the price range. The rows of springs can be joined in different ways:

ABOVE Continuous spring

CLIPPED POCKETED SPRINGS Are used fewer per bed than other types. Each encased spring is wire-clipped to its adjacent springs at four points, top and bottom.

HONEYCOMB POCKETED SPRINGS Have smaller coils and are crammed tightly into the frame. (There are over a thousand in a double mattress.) The coils are tied into position.

INDEPENDENT POCKETED SPRINGS Coils are neither clipped nor tied so they act independently when pressure is applied. An ideal choice for a double bed where the occupants are very different in weight.

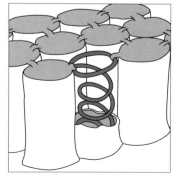

ABOVE Pocket spring

Although hidden, the upholstery filling contributes considerably to the comfort and support offered by a sprung mattress. Good-quality sprung mattresses will contain a number of layers (cotton felt, wool, coir, sisal or hair) on each side of the springs. The layers are built up, finishing with the comfort layer, which is generally polyester fibre, cotton or wool. Each have different advantages: polyester is non-allergenic, cotton is cool for summer while wool is warm for winter. Top-quality mattresses can contain up to 15kg/33lb of pure new lamb's wool. Basic materials include:

⊙ **COTTON FELT** Used for comfort and spring insulation.

⊙ **WOOL** Should be pure new wool, and is the luxury comfort ingredient.

⊙ **COIR OR SISAL** Usually worked into a jute or polypropylene mesh for easier handling.

⊙ **HAIR** Has a big role to play in the upholstery of a mattress. The curled hairs act like springs and are very strong when matted together forming a good resilient layer.

Non-sprung mattresses

There are three main types: foam, flotation (waterbed) and futon.

FOAM

Foam mattresses are made from layers of different densities of foam. The degree of support is determined by the density of the foam. Unfortunately this is difficult to determine, so always go to a reputable dealer where the beds are well labelled. Pay as much as you can afford. As a general rule, the heavier the mattress the better the comfort will be. Foams mattresses are particularly suitable for use with slatted bases and adjustable beds. They are also worth considering if you are an allergy sufferer because they do not contain animal-derived fillings and are bacteria static, which means they cannot support germs or mildew. They should always be well ventilated to allow them to 'breathe'. Compared to typical spring interior mattresses, they are light in weight, warm and don't need turning, so are often recommended for the elderly or disabled. Three main types of foam are used:

LATEX Made from rubber, which is superior and more expensive than polyurethane. Latex is durable and has natural elasticity, so recovers its shape very well when pressure is removed.

POLYURETHANE A synthetic, petroleum-based foam that is available in a variety of qualities and densities. It is the most widely used type and is very versatile.

VISCO-ELASTIC A special type of polyurethane foam (also known as memory foam) that has a unique feel – it responds to temperature and weight and will slowly take the shape of the body lying upon it. When body pressure is removed, it gradually returns to its original form. Available in a variety of qualities and densities. Tempur is the most well-known brand name in visco-elastic bedding, but other brands can offer equally good quality at lower prices.

Mattress care tips

⊙ To prolong the life of your mattress, turn it regularly to ensure even wear and tear.

⊙ Use a washable, protective cover to protect against stains.

⊙ Don't roll up or squash a mattress to transport it – this can cause permanent damage.

⊙ Don't make a habit of sitting on the edge of the mattress and try to prevent kids from bouncing on it too much!

⊙ Never soak a mattress – when dealing with stains, sponge gently using mild detergent and cold or warm water.

WATERBEDS (FLOTATION BEDS)

Modern waterbeds are a great improvement on the early models, but are still generally mistrusted and bear the brunt of many a joke. Surprisingly, they have a very long history, dating back some 3,500 years. During the Second World War they were widely used for treating badly burned patients. They offer a number of other benefits:

- The body sleeps in weightless suspension.
- The displacement of water takes up the shape of the body.
- There are no pressure points so sleep is less disturbed.
- Won't harbour dust mites: a typical bed can house over two million.
- Heated models are relaxing and particularly good for those suffering from rheumatism and arthritis. The gentle application of heat can help relax muscles and the spine.
- They don't sag or 'age' in the way a conventional bed does.
- Because of their support they are recommended for those with back problems and pregnant women.
- Don't need turning.

A waterbed consists of a vinyl mattress, like an envelope or series of cylinders filled with water. The degree of firmness depends on the amount of water and water motion controls within the mattress. The motion controls depend on the type of mattress you choose. These vary according to the type of obstructions, reducing the energy movement of the water, or movement inhibitors included in the mattress. The water inside contains special softeners, which keep the vinyl soft, and prevent the water from going sour by killing bacteria. This should be added every six months. You only need to change the water if you move house.

Installation tips

Most waterbeds are installed by the manufacturer or retailer in situ. However, because they come flat packed and are reasonably straightforward to put together, you could tackle this yourself. Filling the mattress can take time, particularly if your water pressure is low. If installed by professionals, they will bring along a pump to transfer water from your bath to the mattress at the correct temperature. If you do this yourself with a hosepipe from the sink then you need to alternate between hot and cold water.

DISPELLING WATERBED MYTHS

- A waterbed won't burst or leak even if the filler cap comes off. This is because it is a pressureless system. It is very rare for a waterbed to leak unless deliberately damaged.
- Even if the mattress is punctured the water will only leach out slowly into the bedding. The corners are reinforced and seams are strong. Mattresses are surrounded by a safety liner, so spillages are held inside this.
- It won't go crashing through the ceiling below, although it is heavier than a conventional bed. A double will be similar to eight people seated around a laden dining table. The tube beds are the lightest, and largest hard-sided beds are the heaviest. Most floors will take this weight because it is distributed over the whole area, not just on castors or legs.

- You won't feel seasick because the bed will only move when you do. There are no direct pressure points when you are sleeping, so you should find you turn over less.
- A waterbed isn't noisy, once all the air has been eliminated when installed. Like a radiator, some types may need 'bleeding' occasionally to remove the build-up of oxygen.
- Normal bedding can be used. If there is no mattress pad (a stitched-in quilted layer in addition to the mattress cover) use a blanket under the bottom sheet for comfort to absorb perspiration. Because the bed is heated to body temperature you will probably get away with a thinner duvet.

For more information about waterbeds, contact the British Waterbed Association (see Useful Organisations).

FUTONS

These have been the traditional form of bedding in Japan for centuries, used on the floor, then rolled up and stored during the day. They are made from layers of cotton or fibre wadding that moulds itself to the body. They need to be thin so the air can circulate properly, which in turn is the reason for their springiness. They can be used directly on the floor, but generally in the UK they are used with slatted bases. Often they are a good space-saving idea, used as a sofabed on a stacking slatted wood base, but are lower than conventional beds. They can have the following fillings:

COTTON Pure cotton is the usual filling. It offers the firmest support, allows skin to breathe and has good heat retention properties for the winter, while keeping you cool in the summer.

WOOL/COTTON Usually composed of 30 per cent wool and 70 per cent cotton. Compared to 100 per cent cotton it is softer to lie on, lighter in weight and springier. More expensive than cotton.

POLYESTER Futons made of 100 per cent polyester are soft, non-allergenic and washable.

BED BASES

Never mix and match mattresses and bases. They should always be bought together. An old base may look in reasonable condition but it's likely to have retained the sleeping pattern of the original mattress, so will not support the new one evenly. In some cases, unless the correct mattress and base are used together, you invalidate the guarantee. There are four types available.

Choosing a futon

A futon will feel very firm at first. Choose one in the same way you would a normal bed: lie on it and see if your back feels well supported. Check you can lie on your side comfortably without too many pressure points. Pay as much as you can afford if it is to be a permanent sleeping arrangement. Futons should last as long as a conventional divan bed, as long as you follow the manufacturer's instructions. Air regularly, as the futon will absorb body moisture during the night. Airing will ensure the filling remains fluffy. Occasionally, air it outside, or draped over two chairs in front of an open window. Turn the futon weekly, to prevent the filling from compacting. Only polyester-filled futons can be washed. Treat spills immediately: isolate the area and use a spot remover treatment on the cover. It's worth buying a removable cover for the futon, which can be laundered.

TYPES OF BASES AVAILABLE

⊙ **SPRUNG-EDGE BASES** Offer comfort right to the edge, and provide a luxurious sleeping area. They consist of an open coil sprung-mattress unit, which sits on top of a wooden platform. This acts as a giant shock absorber for a mattress, supporting it all over and increasing its durability. Often found on drawer-divan bases and with pocketed spring mattresses.

⊙ **FIRM-EDGE BASES** Lower than sprung edge. The support springs are held in the 'box' construction and held in place by webbing running from side to side, covered by upholstery. These are usually sold with an open-coil type mattress, and nowadays most common on divans with legs. Because the edges are hard you tend to sleep towards the middle and this is where it will give first. It also reduces your sleeping area.

⊙ **SOLID-TOP BASES** Have no springs, so are solid and firm with little give. They should be used with a specially constructed mattress; foam may be used rather than springs. The mattress and base must be ventilated to prevent the build-up of moisture from the mattress. These are the cheapest type of bed base, but make the mattress do all the work, thereby reducing its eventual durability.

⊙ **SLATTED BASES** Also very firm, and becoming increasingly popular especially with the fashion for pine furniture. (Wood frames help the bed look more like a piece of bedroom furniture with integrated head and foot boards.) The bases consist of wooden slats, generally about 10cm/4in apart, held over parallel support rails. Top of the range slatted bases have flexible fixings for extra 'give' compared with fixed slats. Initially a more expensive option, especially with adjustable sections. They don't wear like springs, so you only replace the mattress, unless the slats are badly bent. It is important to choose the correct mattress for a slatted base as recommended by its manufacturer.

ORTHOPAEDIC BEDS

These don't contain any miracle ingredients other than being firm. They will not cure a bad back. There is no standard definition of an orthopaedic bed, but it's generally accepted that such a bed is firmer than normal. The right bed should support your spine correctly, but also be comfortable. Your size and weight will determine what's best. Often, just getting a good new bed makes all the difference. Check first that it's not too firm for you, bearing in mind we toss and turn over 70 times in the night. A short-term solution, if you feel your bed is past its best, is to buy a bed board. This is placed under the mattress. They could, however, shorten the mattress's life because it provides an unyielding base.

MULTI-MECHANISM BEDS

These have adjustable head and leg sections, and are good for sufferers of high blood pressure or rheumatism, or for people who are bedridden; but they are expensive. They can be manually or automatically operated, and are easier for the less mobile to get in and out of.

BEDS FOR ELDERLY PEOPLE

Don't be guided into thinking it is not worth paying much because it doesn't need to last! It is important to choose a good-quality bed that's supportive with comfortable upholstery; wool would be the ideal.

- A firm bed is easier to sit up on than a soft one.
- Higher beds are easier to get in and out of.
- A firm-edged base may be more practical because they are often used for sitting on when dressing.

BEDS FOR BABIES

A small baby can sleep in a crib, Moses basket, carry cot or a cot. (Babies should not sleep in a baby nest. They can suffocate or get too hot.)

CRIB A crib is a small cot and may rock on a frame. Make sure the stand for the crib is firm.

MOSES BASKET A Moses basket is a woven basket, lined with fabric. They should conform to BS 7551 1992. The lining should be secure with no loose folds that could smother the baby. Handles should be long enough to meet together above the basket. Do not use these once the baby can move unaided.

COT When your baby gets older – about four months – he/she can sleep in a cot or cot bed. Look for British Standard BS 1753 when choosing a cot to ensure it is safe.

Bunk beds

- A good choice if your child is over five.
- Safety must be one of the prime considerations. Check they conform to the European Standard EN 747-1.
- The top of the mattress should be at least 10cm/4in below the guard rail for safety.
- There should be two guards on the top bunk.
- There should be no gaps in their structure more than 7.5cm/3in wide, except of course for access between the guards to the top bunk, which should be between 30–40cm/12–16in wide. It is illegal for anyone to sell new or second-hand bunks with gaps wider than this.
- There should not be any rough or sharp edges or points.
- The frame must be robust because children will use it as a climbing frame.
- The ladder should be firmly fixed and capable of supporting an adult's weight. Flat rungs are more comfortable to climb than rounded ones.
- A slatted base ensures that the bed maker doesn't get hair trapped in the wire mesh.

TIP
Don't position a cot near curtains or anything that might help your baby climb out. Keep away from blinds that could strangle.

WHAT TO LOOK FOR WHEN BUYING COTS

- When buying, check it's deep enough, so your baby can't climb out while still young. Most have bases that can be lowered as the child gets older. Initially, start on the highest setting (this saves bending). There should be at least 50cm/20in between the top of the mattress and the top of the cot. The overall size is about 120cm/47in x 60cm/24in.

- There should be no footholds in the sides or cut-outs where the baby could put feet, or trap arms, legs or head.

- Spaces between the bars should be between 2.5cm/1in and 6cm/2½in so that the baby cannot trap his/her head.

- If the cot has drop-down sides check the mechanism is secure and the baby should not be able to open it. Choose one where the sides do not come away completely, because if accidentally left down a child could roll off.

- If it has castors, check they are lockable.

- If you want extra storage space, some cots have roll-under drawers.

- If the cot is second-hand, make sure the fastening mechanism and the slats of the mattress base are all in good condition. Check side bars are not loose.

- The mattress should fit properly. Check it conforms to BS 1877 for safety, comfort and hygiene. The right side should be marked on the mattress or in the instructions. Often they have fabric on one side and PVC on the other. There shouldn't be a gap of more than 4cm/1½in anywhere round the mattress. Mattress types include foam with ventilation holes, which ensure a constant flow of air; natural fibre (often have a core of coconut fibres coated with waterproof latex and wrapped in cotton felt); springs are less common.

- Cot toys should not have strings longer than 30cm/12in, so they do not trap or strangle your baby. They should be firmly tied in position. Once the baby can pull himself up, remove toys that are strung across the cot as they could strangle him.

- A cot bed, which converts from cot to first bed by removing the sides, will last a child up to the age of six. They are useful for bridging the gap between cot and first proper bed.

CHILDREN'S BEDS

Children need proper support for a growing spine so don't be tempted to give them a second-hand bed that is already imprinted with someone else's sleeping pattern. However, it is not worth spending a lot because they should be changed more frequently than an adult's bed, ideally every four to five years. When the child is ready to leave the cot, he/she should be bought a new bed.

After a cot, a normal single may seem huge and frightening at first. Site the bed in a corner and position a low bookcase down the other side for added security.

Stacker beds, where one bed folds under the other, are useful when children have friends to stay. Choose a good-quality brand, even though only one is in constant use.

Novelty beds are fun, but you may find you are paying for the gimmick rather than support and comfort. Remember they'll soon outgrow them.

GUEST BEDS

Consider who will be using the bed, for how long and how often, and the space available. If you have room, a sofabed or single bed concealed underneath is the best option, especially if the bed will be used for more than a night or two at a time. It is important to realise, however, that most are shorter than standard beds. Futons and inflatable airbeds may be fine for children but are likely to be too low and unyielding for older people.

Sofabeds

Check the one you choose is comfortable both as a sofa and as a bed, and that you find it easy to convert.

BED Should be stable and not lift off the floor when you sit in the middle. Make sure you cannot feel the frame through the mattress and, if it's a double, that two people will not roll into the middle. Check the maximum weight load.

SOFA Upholstery, padding and cushions should be secure, with no gaps between arms and back. Check that patterns line up – inside and outside arms and arm strips should be symmetrical and central. Covers must fit well because creases accelerate wear and tear and collect dirt. Soil-retardant finishes and removable covers are desirable.

Concealed beds

A second bed is tucked under the main bed and metal legs raise it to the same height. Can be used as a single, twin or double. Suitable for frequent use for all ages.

Beds and storage

If you need extra cupboard space, storage divans are a good option. Choose between:

- Top-of-the-range models that have divan bases with springs. Different levels of support are available.
- Solid platform or slatted bases are more common. Use the manufacturer's recommended mattress.
- Ottoman-type storage beds hinge and open along one side or at the headboard end. A good solution if you haven't the space to pull out the drawers.

WHAT SORT OF SOFABED SHOULD YOU BUY?

Sofabeds convert from sofa to bed using one of the following mechanisms:

- **CLICK-CLACK/LENGTHWAYS FOLD** Box base of sofa supports metal frame and upholstery (foam or sprung) which doubles as a mattress. Frame opens out into the sleeping surface. Suitable for frequent use, but the bed is low, so may not be suitable for elderly or less mobile users.

- **PULL-OUT DRAWER** Front panel and seat of sofa pulls out like a drawer to form sleeping surface. Foam upholstery is reversed to become mattress. Sturdy but low. Suitable for occasional use.

- **THREE-FOLD** Seat cushions are removed and frame unfolds. Frame is metal, with a polypropylene or wire-mesh base, and high-density foam mattress. Suitable for occasional use and a good height, but the mattress is thin.

- **TWO-FOLD** Cushions are removed and mechanism unfolds. Bed frame is metal with a wire-mesh or wooden, slatted base plus webbing. Mattress can be foam or sprung. Fine for frequent use, especially if the mattress is sprung.

Choosing Bedding

There is a choice of bedding for every taste: from traditional blankets to high-tog duvets. Making an informed choice will help you achieve sweet dreams.

SHEETS AND PILLOWCASES

Bed linen can be made of a variety of different fibres, each of which have their pros and cons.

LINEN Cool and smooth to the touch, and durable, but you pay for the privilege. Often finished off with a corded hem or hem stitch. A strong but cheaper alternative is linen union, 60 per cent linen blended with 40 per cent cotton. Be warned: they are hard work to iron.

COTTON Tightly woven Egyptian cotton and cotton percale are the most common. Percale is in fact combed cotton, silky smooth and a similar weight to poplin. Cotton twill is a strong herringbone weave and slightly coarser.

FLANNELETTE SHEETS These are still available. Although they have an old-fashioned image their soft, fluffy surface can be comforting and warm in winter, as the raised surface traps air. Unlike cotton or poly-cotton they do not have a cold surface, so are pleasant to get in to on a cold night.

POLYESTER COTTON Usually a 50/50 blend, and probably the most popular type of bedding available, mainly due to its easy-care properties. If hung straight from the machine it doesn't really need ironing. Poly-cotton percale costs about 20 per cent more, but uses combed cotton for a silkier finish. Cotton-rich blends, 80 per cent cotton/20 per cent polyester, came into vogue with the trend back to natural fibres, but sacrifice some of the easy-care convenience.

Tips for using bed linen

- Protect pillows from greasy hair by using cotton under-pillowslips and lightly starching the top pillowslip.
- Fold straight from the tumble-drier or clothesline to cut down on ironing.
- Gently pull side edges while evenly damp to help pressing.
- Rotate clean bed linen.
- The airing cupboard isn't the best place for long-term storage, as constant warmth marks and discolours the fabrics. Instead, use strong polythene or blanket bags and keep in a cool, dry, well-ventilated place.

BUYING GUIDE

- Look for a strong tight weave. Hold a single layer up to the light to check its density.
- Matching sets work out cheaper than buying separate items.
- Check sheet sizes. Make sure there is enough to cover the mattress, its sides plus another 20cm/8in to tuck in.

- It's worth paying more for top-quality bedding – for comfort. All fabrics will pill (tiny balls of fibres appear on the surface, due to rubbing when you toss and turn) but it is less noticeable with pure natural fibres. The pill drops off during wear and laundering and you won't notice it. Pilling is more noticeable (and uncomfortable) on poly-cotton bedding: the cotton bobble is held on by the stronger synthetic fibre.

BLANKETS

Blankets are made in wool, cotton, cashmere, acrylic or thermolactyl chloride fibre, or a combination of these. Wool is the warmest. Blankets offer an advantage over duvets in that they can be removed or added to a bed as demanded by the temperature. On the other hand, they are less convenient when bed making and soon look a mess. Tog values are not given for blankets, but three good-quality blankets are roughly equivalent to a tog value of 13.5. Three blankets are needed on average, a combination of two cellular (open weave) and one solid (close weave) or vice versa. Cellular blankets are warmer than solid ones because air is easily trapped in the holes. Also, they are lighter than solid ones, giving more warmth for less weight. Blankets are good sale bargains, but check the finish and the correct size for your bed.

Underblankets

Although your mattress may be quite warm in itself, a greater feeling of all-round warmth and comfort can be achieved by putting a conventional blanket or underblanket on the mattress, under the bottom sheet. Make sure it is fixed securely to avoid rucking or wrinkling during the night.

If you use a duvet and find you need to add extra bedding on top use a blanket underneath the duvet instead. This prevents the duvet filling from compacting and does not impede air circulation.

DUVETS

Blankets are now generally out of favour, with most British people owning at least one duvet. Duvets provide warmth and comfort without being restrictive, and are more dust free than blankets. Early quilts were simply an envelope of fabric filled with a stuffing, but the filling was free to wander, leaving cold patches in one place and overfilled ones in another. Now a more sophisticated type of construction uses channels or pockets, which follow the way the body lies to keep the filling evenly distributed at all times. Look out for the label indicating that the duvet complies with BS 5335, i.e. it reaches set standards in both manufacture and performance.

Always measure your bed before you actually buy a duvet. The duvet should be wider by 35cm/14in for a single, 65cm/26in for a double, and 75cm/30in for a king-size bed. The length shouldn't be ess than the length of the bed, and if you're taller than 1.8m/6ft, look for a 220cm/7ft 2in duvet.

Tog ratings

Duvets are rated in togs, which is a measurement for warmth, not weight. The higher the tog rating, the warmer the duvet is; but it is not necessarily of a higher quality – or value for money.

If you live in a centrally heated house you'll probably find a 10.5 to 12 tog-rated duvet is fine. However, if you don't have central heating or live in a cold climate, look for a 13.5-tog duvet. Fifteen-tog duvets are available but are far too hot for most people. If your duvet is just right for

Electric blankets

When buying a blanket check it is BEAB approved (British Electrotechnical Approvals Board) and conforms to BSI Standards. It is illegal to sell an electric blanket without an overheating protection system. Follow the manufacturer's instructions for use. Most electric blankets have a thermostatic control that permits safe night use. Special features to look for include blankets with 'extra foot warmth panels, variable heat controls and pre-heat facility. All electric blankets should be returned to the manufacturer every three years for servicing. (See Electric Blankets, page 255.)

- **OVERBLANKETS** As a general rule, when using an overblanket, you shouldn't need other bedclothes apart from a light covering such as a bedspread. Do not put duvets or blankets over the top.

- **UNDERBLANKETS** These should not be used folded or creased, and must be tied securely to the mattress. On double beds, differing warmth levels can be obtained on each half of the bed to suit sleepers' requirements. Always switch off and unplug before getting into bed.

winter but you find yourself too hot in summer it's worth considering an all-seasons duvet. This gives you three options depending on the weather. They consist of a thick (around 9 tog) and thin (4.5 tog) duvet which can be used separately or joined together for extra warmth.

Fillings

The important part of a duvet is the air inside it and how the filling traps it. This air and moisture controls the temperature and the duvet's softness.

When choosing a filling you need to consider how quickly it compresses; how resilient and durable it is; how good is its insulating efficiency and breathability. The ideal duvet has a light and fluffy filling which traps warm air.

In general, the better the quality of the duvet the less filling is required, which means it has a light weight to volume ratio. For example, a 13.5-tog goose-down duvet (best quality) is not as heavy as a 10.5-tog polyester-filled one.

Down can absorb 11.5 per cent moisture given off by the body during the night; feathers can absorb 12.5 per cent, and wool 14 per cent.

This moisture is slowly evaporated off so there is no excessive or rapid loss of warmth from the body, leaving it feeling cold. However, with polyester, although the latest fibres have improved, there is a quick evaporation of moisture, which may lead to the body feeling chilly. As well, polyester quilts do not hug the body as effectively as natural fillings, so allow warm air to escape and cold draughts to enter.

Casings

Casings for naturally filled duvets must have a tight weave to prevent feathers and down from escaping. The fabric must also be able to breathe and allow free air circulation. Most are 100 per cent cotton and should be able to withstand washing without shrinking. Top-quality casings are made from fine Egyptian cotton. If you choose a polyester-cotton cover, it will shrink less, but will not be as absorbent, and therefore breathe as well.

Construction

Methods of construction vary depending on the quality and type of filling used.

STITCHED-THROUGH CHANNELS Generally used for synthetic duvets, it's the simplest and cheapest method. The cover is sewn all the way through the layers to hold the filling in place. However, this has the disadvantage that cold spots can occur along the lines of stitching.

INTERMITTENT STITCHING Patterns are stitched at regular intervals. If there is too much stitching there will be many cold spots, but insufficient stitching means the filling can move around.

DOUBLE CONSTRUCTION Duvets are made from two layers of channelled polyester, enclosed within the cover and stitched through only around the edges. This eliminates the danger of cold areas.

WALLED CHANNELS Often used with natural fillings. Inner walls are sewn between the two sides to form the channels. Unfortunately, the filling is free to move around and it tends to travel down the

---

TOG RATINGS

Summer
4.5, 6.0, 7.5

Mid-season
9.0, 10.5

Winter
12.0, 13.5, 15.0

The other half

If you and your partner feel the cold differently and can't agree on a tog rating for your duvet, John Lewis (see Manufacturers, Retailers and Service Providers) is able to make goose down duvets to order with a different tog rating in each half. They can also make duvets in non-standard sizes.

duvet. However, a useful feature in summer because you can shake the filling down.

WALLED POCKETS The duvet is divided into cassette or pocket-shaped sections, which keep the filling in place without thin cold spots. Often used for top-quality duvets.

PILLOWS

However good your mattress, you still need support for your head. A quick test to check if your pillow needs replacing is to lay it across your hand. If it droops over each side it is time to think about a new one.

CHOOSING DUVET FILLINGS

⊙ **DOWN** This is taken from ducks or geese, or is a mixture of the two. Down is a spherical plumule of thousands of soft fibres. Unlike feathers, which are used for flying, down traps the air at high altitude and low temperature with a minimum of weight.

The colour of the down (the feathers) doesn't make any difference to the quality, although white is usually marketed as a premium product. Duck down or feathers are a lower-priced alternative to goose down and feathers. As a general rule, the greater the proportion of feathers the cheaper and heavier the duvet will be. Always check the label carefully because the percentage of down to feathers does vary.

Choose pure down if you want a warm, light-weight duvet with excellent draping properties. However, it is expensive, because only 13g/$\frac{1}{2}$oz of down can be collected from each bird.

Down duvets are very durable: they will last up to four times longer than a polyester one.

⊙ **DOWN AND FEATHER** These mustn't contain less than 51 per cent down. This is a good alternative if you can't stretch to an all-down duvet. Still extremely light and warm.

Down and feathers cost more than synthetic fillings, but should last longer.

⊙ **FEATHER AND DOWN** These must contain a minimum of 15 per cent down. They will feel heavier than down and feather duvets so will suit you if you prefer a heavier weight of bed covering. However, they may also feel stiffer, depending on the type of feathers used. Some lower-quality duvets may contain chicken feathers that can be uncomfortably scratchy.

⊙ **OTHER NATURAL FILLINGS** Wool is becoming more common and other luxurious fillings include silk and cashmere. Wool tends to be slightly heavier and firmer than the others.

⊙ **SYNTHETIC FILLINGS** Usually made from layers of polyester fibres. They will not feel as light as natural fillings and don't mould round the body as well. However, they are quite fluffy and springy, and washable (although they could compress slightly after being washed).

They are generally cheaper than natural fillings and make a good choice for children because they are easily washable. Also, they are suitable for people who have an allergy to down and feathers.

Different qualities are available: the more you pay the better. Fillings are split into solid polyester fibres, and hollow fibres, which are a better quality. As the name implies, there is a gap in the middle of the fibres that holds air making a lighter filling without sacrificing any of the warmth.

Top-quality polyester fibres are siliconised, giving them the softest feel, and best imitating the softness of down.

- As a general rule, natural-filled pillows will mould to the shape of your head better than synthetic ones. Synthetic ones tend to give firmer support.
- Unbranded foam rubber or crumb fillings are the cheapest, but don't expect them to last more than two to three years.
- Latex is more resilient, retains its shape well, can be moulded to fit the contours of the head and is non-allergenic.
- Polyester filled, also non-allergenic, vary in quality and support. Give a firmer, flatter pillow.
- Some pillows contain hollow-fibre polyester that is fluffier than the ordinary type.
- Duck down and feather pillows offer the best support and recovery. Avoid poultry feathers as these are the least comfortable, although usually the cheapest.
- Tempur is a non-allergenic, visco-elastic, heat-sensitive material that has unique pressure-relieving qualities, allowing the head and neck to rest in a natural, tension-free position. It is becoming an increasingly popular choice of pillow material.

Quality is determined by the speed at which a pillow regains its original shape after being depressed. When purchasing, test natural-filled pillows by laying them flat on a surface and pressing firmly in the centre. When pressure is removed the dent should fill out quickly, regaining at least half of its original shape.

The degree of firmness is a personal choice and depends on the way you sleep. If you sleep on your side, choose a firm one; if on your back choose a medium one, and if on your stomach, a very soft pillow.

Coverings for natural-filled pillows are usually downproof sateen twill or cotton cambric. Synthetic fillings are usually enclosed in cotton or polyester-cotton covers. Check for strong seams.

NON-ALLERGENIC BEDS AND BEDDING

Doctors believe that 80 per cent of allergic asthma is irritated by house-dust mites. These microscopic creatures live on the dead skin cells that make up 80 per cent of household dust. Dust mites love the bedroom – moisture, heat and dead skin from your body provide them with the perfect living environment and obviously the older the bed, the more dust mites there will be. There are a number of steps you can take to help combat dust mite allergies in the bedroom. Choose a foam or polyester-fibre mattress. Alternatively, if you prefer natural materials, latex foam is a good choice. Waterbeds are also worth considering. Use allergen-proof protective covers on your mattress, and all duvets and pillows – these allow moisture through, but keep mites and droppings out. These types of covers are now widely available in department stores such as John Lewis or through specialist Internet/mail order suppliers. Covers should preferably be used on brand new items, but if this is not possible, air your existing mattress and launder pillows and duvets before covering them.

Tips for using pillows

- Plump up your pillows frequently to avoid the filling compacting.
- Follow care instructions. Laundering should be kept to a minimum as it can reduce the life of a pillow.
- Wash the pillow occasionally. Never dry clean, because of the fumes from the solvents used during the dry-cleaning process.
- Natural fillings tend to wash better than synthetic ones, which can become lumpy.

BEDDING FOR BABIES

Don't assume that babies are more susceptible to cold than they really are. It's just as dangerous to overdress them as to underdress. They do need to be warmly dressed in their first few weeks, but after this they are very good at keeping themselves warm. A young baby cannot kick off the covers if they are too hot. Feeling the baby's tummy is a good guide to how warm he or she is, even though the hands and feet may be cold. Research has shown that too high a temperature may be one of the contributory causes of cot death or Sudden Infant Death Syndrome (SIDS). Obviously, the bedding you use will affect your baby's temperature.

BLANKETS AND SHEETS These are best, because you can vary the combinations according to the baby's temperature (not the room temperature). Use a sheet to cover the mattress and one between the baby and blankets. Combine cellular and solid blankets according to the baby's needs. Avoid open-weave blankets as they can trap the baby's fingers.

COT DUVETS Use on their own with a duvet cover. These are marked with a tog rating, which is a measure of their insulating properties. A cot-size duvet is not recommended for babies under 12 months as they could suffocate.

COT QUILTS Unlike duvets, these don't need a separate cover and are designed for use with sheets and blankets. Use as many layers or combinations as are appropriate for your baby.

PILLOWS Not recommended for babies under 12 months because of the dangers of suffocation.

COT BUMPERS Useful to avoid draughts and bumps, but ensure they conform to British and European safety standards. Do not use once your baby can sit unaided as it could be used as a foothold to climb out of the cot. Ties should not be longer than 25cm/10in, should not fray, and must be securely sewn to the bumper and attached to the cot. Try to avoid your baby sleeping with his or her head against the bumper as this may prevent natural heat loss.

Tips to combat allergies

- Keep the bedroom well ventilated to keep the humidity down.
- Air the bed daily and wash bedding frequently at temperatures over 60°C/140°F.
- Avoid padded headboards, bedspreads and quilts as these make an ideal home for house dust mites.
- Vacuum your mattress regularly using the upholstery nozzle, remembering to keep the window open when cleaning or consider calling in a specialist mattress cleaning service, such as the Mattress Doctor (see Manufacturers, Retailers and Service Providers), who offer a three-step chemical-free process to remove dust mites and their contaminants.

TIPS TO HELP BABIES GET A BETTER NIGHT'S SLEEP

- Lie your baby on his or her back, unless your health professional advises otherwise.
- Don't prop your baby up with pillows or cushions.
- Check your baby isn't too hot or too cold by feeling his or her neck or body (not hands or feet). Use light-weight bedding in layers to which you can add or subtract.

- Position a room thermometer above the cot and check the temperature from time to time. A regular room temperature of 18°C (64°F) should be maintained.
- Don't use a duvet or pillow if your baby is under 12 months.
- Use quilts and coverlets with caution as their use may lead to overheating.

Soft Furnishings

Creating your individual style with soft furnishings can be an exciting process of experimentation: looking at different ways to combine colour, texture and form. Fabrics can be combined to create stunning effects, and often the simplest is the most dramatic.

For visual appeal, try plain fabrics with striped borders; look at different light effects; layer translucent fabrics with opaques; and try combining different weights and weaves. You can even design your own fabrics by making use of fabric paints and stencils on muslin or plain cotton.

FURNISHING FABRICS

When choosing fabrics, price and design are not the only factors you need to bear in mind. Consider:

- Which room they are to go in. Is it a feminine bedroom, an all-purpose family room or a utilitarian kitchen? Does the room face north/east, with little sun or south/west, with plenty of sun?
- How hardwearing the fabric needs to be.
- Draping characteristics and crease resistance.
- Resistance to fading and mildew.
- Ease of cleaning. Some areas (such as the kitchen) will require more frequent cleaning than others, so opt for washable fabric rather than dry clean only.
- If the fabric is to be used for upholstery it needs to be treated with fire retardant.

Buying fabric

- Have with you a sample of your wallpaper, plus colour charts and upholstery swatches for colour matching.
- Always try draping the fabric in the shop: you get a better idea of texture and effects of light on colours and patterns, and how translucent the fabric is.
- If the fabric is washable, allow for 10 per cent shrinkage, and wash the fabric at least twice before making up. Some fabrics may have been treated with a shrink-resistant finish. Check at point of purchase. Ready-made curtains include 5 per cent extra for shrinkage.
- Check the fabric is fade resistant. Curtains, for example, are constantly exposed to sunlight.
- Buy all the fabric you need for matching cushions etc., at the same time as your curtain fabric, as batch colours may vary.
- Don't skimp on the amount of fabric because this can spoil the draping effect. Curtains should be at least twice as wide as the window.

Buying tips for patterned fabric

- Check the pattern is printed correctly throughout the length you require.
- A pattern woven into the fabric rather than printed on is more likely to resist fading.
- Small or random patterning works out cheaper because you waste less matching pattern repeats.
- Hand-printed patterns are more irregular.
- Allow one pattern repeat for each drop or length.

- Traditionally, curtains have been full length (drop to 1cm/½ in above the floor) or sill length (leave 1cm/½ in short of the window sill to avoid dust and condensation). Currently, it is quite fashionable to have long curtains that trail on the ground by about 10cm/4in, for an opulent feel.

Fabric weight

Light-weights (cotton and poly-cottons) suit bathrooms and kitchens. In living rooms and bedrooms, use lining and interlining to improve the curtains' drape, insulation and light exclusion.

Hem weights help the curtains to hang properly. Sew weights into mitred corners and hem, or lay lead tape into the hem fold and secure it at intervals.

Heavier-weight fabrics and tighter weaves offer better insulation, but can be heavy to hang if lined. Check your curtain rail will support the weight.

Linings

These help the drape and general appearance of the main curtain fabric. They can be permanent or detachable. If they are stitched permanently in position it's wise to dry-clean the curtains. Otherwise the top fabric may shrink at a different rate than the lining, causing puckering.

Lining also protects a curtain from sunlight, which can fade and rot the fabric; dust and dirt; and condensation, which can cause brown staining.

Tips for using patterned fabric

- Centre the pattern for each width of curtain.
- Match up across the width.
- Parallel or horizontal lines need to be aligned with the walls and ceiling rather than the furniture.
- To check the direction of the pattern, look at the selvedge. There may be directional arrows to guide you; otherwise, in the case of flowers, think about the natural way they would grow.
- Even random patterning may have some order. Stand well back and check all the lines of the pattern.

TYPES OF FABRIC TO CHOOSE FROM

- **BROCADE** Woven with an embroidered, textured look. Made of silk, viscose or synthetic fibres.
- **CHINTZ** Tightly woven cotton with a shiny chemical glaze that drapes well. Don't hang in areas prone to dirt because the finish may wash off and fade. Once the glaze goes it cannot be replaced. Some companies will clean, rebuild existing chintz finish and rehang.
- **COTTON** Closer weaves are more hardwearing and crisp. Most cottons drape well, but fade and shrink unless specially treated. Cottons can almost always be washed, but may lose some body and colour.

   Treatments for crease resistance, flame proofing and stain repellency are often applied to cotton.
- **DUPION** Generally made from synthetic fibres, and because of its slubbed appearance, looks like wild silk. It frays badly, so allow extra for seams and hems and overlock raw edges soon after cutting.
- **GINGHAM** Identical on both sides so saves on lining, unless of course you want to add extra weight to improve the drape. Will shrink.
- **LINEN** Can be glazed or printed. Linen creases badly but can be treated to minimise this.
- **TAPESTRY** Light-weight tapestries drape better than heavy weights. Need regular vacuuming as they trap dust easily.
- **VELVET** Synthetic (Dralon) and cotton. Hang so that the pile runs down the length both to avoid the build-up of dust and to show off the sheen.

   The denser the pile the more durable they will be. They crease at first but will hang out after several weeks; do not hem until after this initial period.

   Dralon, unlike cotton velvet, is colour-fast to light and moisture, but it should never be ironed or the pile will be ruined.

Cotton sateen is the most common fabric, in cream or white, for deflecting the heat of sunlight. It is tightly woven and keeps its shape. Contrasting, fade-resistant coloured linings are available. These add depth of colour to the main curtain.

Don't line curtains that will need to be washed, such as those in kitchens and bathrooms, and nets and sheers.

THERMAL LININGS

With up to a quarter of heat escaping through the window it is surprising that most of us don't make the most of our curtains. A pair of thick or thermally lined curtains can be as effective as double glazing. All thermal linings work by reflecting heat back into a room, saving up to 17 per cent more heat than unlined curtains, and on the same principle keep the room cool in the summer. The reflective/coated side should be hung away from the window, with the reflective side facing into the room.

PROS
- ⊙ Protect fabric and upholstery from fading.
- ⊙ Dim the light coming into the room, but do not provide complete blackout.
- ⊙ Provide heat insulation.

CONS
- ⊙ Some types can be seen through light-weight and coarse-weave curtaining.

TIP
When sewing velvet seams, sandwich tissue paper between the two pile surfaces to prevent slipping.

Green tip
The following will save you money on your energy bills:

Make your curtains long, to rest on the floor or sill to create a seal. Place lead weights in the hem to keep the curtain anchored.
Make your curtains at least two widths of window.
Hang so the sides touch the wall. If possible, use adhesive Velcro to attach them to the wall.
Interline the curtain, or use a thermal lining.
Make linings detachable so they can be removed in the summer.
Beware of using net curtains on south-facing windows as they can deflect sunlight, which would be a valuable addition to your heating.
To preserve heat, close the curtains at night, an hour before it gets dark (even in unheated rooms).
✳ In winter, keep curtains closed in rooms you do not use and that do not get the sun.

BLACK-OUT LININGS

These have all the properties of thermal linings but are also impermeable to light. They are ideal for darkening children's rooms during light evenings in the summer, or for shift workers. They also act as a noise buffer, which is useful if you live in a noisy area. They are very heavy and do not drape as well as thermal linings because of their plastic-like feel.

Black-out linings are similar to acrylic thermal linings, but have more layers, technically known as 'passes'. To be termed a black-out the fabric must have a least three passes. Some brands are also treated with a flame-retardant finish.

Most must be dry-cleaned.

INTERLINING

This must be used between the main curtain and the normal lining. It gives body to the curtain, and makes it hang better, especially with very thin fabrics such as satin and silk. For insulation, interlining is comparable to thermal lining, but it is not opaque enough to act as a black-out.

If a curtain is interlined it must be dry-cleaned, even if the main fabric is washable.

There are various types and weights:

BUMP Coarsely woven brushed-cotton fabric similar in appearance to a blanket. It is very thick to sew, particularly at the top where the heading tape is sewn on.

DOMETTE Pure, brushed cotton, similar in appearance to a flannelette sheet. Is thinner than bump, so is easier to handle and sew.

RAISED INTERLINING A bonded fabric made from 90 per cent viscose and 10 per cent polyamide. It has all the advantages of the other two types but it is thinner, so much easier to handle.

STAIN-RESISTANT TREATMENTS

To help keep your soft furnishings in top condition it is worth having the fabrics specially treated for stain resistance, or to buy pre-treated upholstery or fabric. Stain-resistant treatments act like an invisible shield by preventing spilt liquids being absorbed before you've time to mop them up. You do still have to remove spills, but if you act quickly enough, permanent staining will be prevented. You'll also find the general grime from normal use is slower to build up.

When buying this sort of treatment, check the warranty being offered: some include the services of a professional cleaner. Before employing a cleaning firm or retailer offering this treatment, check they have undergone specialist training.

You can have existing furniture treated, but the protection will not be generally as good as when new fabrics are treated.

Two methods of treatment to look for:

Fluorochemicals

Form a protective layer that resists both oil and water-based stains. Spilt liquid forms droplets on the surface, giving you time to mop them up: about 10 minutes. The fabric is treated during manufacture, or in your

TIP
Black-out linings are easy to sew by machine and do not fray readily. They are very thick fabrics, so if you are sewing them by hand, make sure your needle goes all the way through the layers.

home by a licensed applicator. Pre-treated fabric offers better protection than most treatments in situ.

Copolymer resin

This coats or penetrates the fabric fibres, preventing spills from being absorbed. The resin is sprayed on to the finished fabric either in the shop or by a licensed cleaner in your home. Any spilt liquid is not absorbed for about 10 minutes.

For detailed advice on how to make curtains, see pages 339–43.

BLINDS

Blinds are ideal for small rooms because they do not take up much space. Large windows may need two or more blinds rather than one big one. Not all blinds block out the light, so check when choosing fabric and type. Most soft blinds are easy to make and kits are available.

Conservatory blinds

Essential to reduce heat and glare, unless the conservatory has reflective glass. Materials designed for conservatory use will withstand extremes of temperature and humidity without rotting or distorting, and include densely woven polyester, metal-coated acrylic and glass fibre finished with PVC. If funds are limited, just buy blinds for the roof. You can also use screens and tall plants to provide shade.

WHICH STYLE OF BLIND IS RIGHT FOR YOUR WINDOW?

⊙ **ROLLER BLINDS** Simple blinds which operate by means of a spring-loaded roller. Popular on windows that require shading from the sun. For a more elaborate effect use with front curtains in a sheer or delicate fabric.

⊙ **ROMAN BLINDS** These resemble roller blinds when hanging to their full drop but when raised, by a system of vertical cords at the back, they pleat into a series of neat horizontal folds.

⊙ **AUSTRIAN BLINDS** These look like a curtain but are pulled up from the bottom by a series of vertical cords. They are made longer than the required drop of the window, and this extra fabric ruches up from the bottom to form an elaborate swag-like effect.

⊙ **FESTOON BLINDS** Similar to Austrian blinds, but use more fabric because they are ruched all along the complete drop. Suitable fabrics include lace, voile or other soft fabrics to achieve the correct draping effect.

⊙ **VENETIAN BLINDS** A series of horizontal slats that can be made of plastic, wood or metal. They are operated by a cord system at the sides, which raises or lowers the slats. They can be totally raised to the top of the window in the day time. Good for providing shade. Simple but effective.

⊙ **VERTICAL LOUVRE BLINDS** Similar to Venetian blinds, but the slats are vertical. Can be drawn to one side like curtains. Often used in conservatories.

Buying Furniture

Don't be seduced just by the look of the furniture: appearances can be deceptive. Performance, durability, construction, safety and value for money are all equally important factors to consider when choosing furniture. It's worth waiting until you find exactly the right piece rather than buying something to 'make do' until you can afford something better.

THREE-PIECE SUITES

A suite is likely to be one of the major investments for your house or flat. It must look good, be comfortable, practical and hardwearing. Choose wisely; don't just be tempted by the colours and pattern. Consider:

Size

Is it right for your room? Too small and it will look lost, but too large and it will dominate the room and nothing else will fit in. In a large room a three-seater looks best, although the middle position is usually the last to be filled. Put a two-seater in a small room, so it won't dominate. With a two-seater you may have room for two sofas and a chair or one sofa and two chairs.

There should be about a 1m/3ft clearance at the front and sides of armchairs and settees. Although it seems obvious, check it will fit through the relevant doorways and up staircases.

Comfort

Sit in it for at least ten minutes. It should support your back and head and be easy to get in and out of.

The degree of firmness depends on the filling used. A foam cushion will be resilient and keep its shape, whereas a feather one will be very soft and need plumping up regularly. Modern furniture generally uses different layers of foam and polyester. Traditional fillings are hair, combined with spring seats and backs, and tend to be more expensive.

Back height and angle are important. Seating with a low back looks better in a small room, or if you want to position it away from walls, while high backs look grand in large living rooms.

Check you have good support for the base of your spine. It's personal preference whether you prefer to sit upright on a firm high back and head rest, or curled up on a squashy, low-backed sofa. However, you should be able to get out of the chair without having to use the arms for support.

Seat height

You should be able to rest your feet flat on the floor while sitting back in the chair. If the seat is too high your legs will dangle, putting pressure on the underside of your thighs. Too low and its difficult to get out of the seat. If the depth of the seat is too great it will put pressure on your calves and restrict circulation to your legs. You will also find you have to climb out of the seat, and you may tend to sit on the edge instead, therefore losing back support.

Style and design

Does it fit in with the other style of furniture in the room? Modern and period furniture generally don't mix. Remember gimmicky or trendy furniture will date within a few years.

Avoid buying unusual shapes because they will date more quickly. Bold and fussy patterns can be tiring on the eyes and restrict your choice of other soft furnishings and decor. They can also make your room look smaller.

Ease of cleaning

If you have children or pets it should be easy to clean. Alternatively, consider loose or permanent covers, and stain-resistant treatments.

Arm rests

One chair without arms can be useful, especially if you enjoy knitting etc.

Modular

Regaining popularity. Middle and end sections can be arranged to give greater flexibility, especially for seating a lot of people. Makes full use of corners, and useful if you move house, because it can be rearranged to suit.

Fabric type

A huge range is available, including both natural and synthetic fabrics. Check with the retailer as to the suitability for the purpose. The choice of fabric will affect the feel, look, durability and resistance to staining. The most expensive fabrics may not be the most durable, but will look and feel good.

CHOICE OF FABRICS AVAILABLE

- ⊙ **WOOL** Wears well but is quite expensive. Somewhat limited in style and colours. However, resists most staining well and is inherently flame and crease resistant.

- ⊙ **COTTON** Is quite durable but depends on the weave; opt for a closely woven cotton. Will show stains and burn marks. Can get cotton pile fabrics such as velvet and corduroy.

- ⊙ **LINEN UNION** A blend of cotton and linen, and is good for printed patterns. Linen, however, is not very resistant to abrasion.

- ⊙ **DRALON, OTHER ACRYLICS AND MODACRYLICS** (flame-retardant versions). Crease resistant. Choose the denser piles for greater durability. However, they show the dirt easily. Wide range of colours, patterns and textures.

- ⊙ **VISCOSE** Is quite durable but it does crease badly and shows dirt and stains.

- ⊙ **POLYPROPYLENE** Wears well and resists dirt and is easy to clean. It will melt if burnt.

- ⊙ **POLYAMIDE** Is crease resistant and resilient but shows the dirt.

- ⊙ **POLYESTER** Is similar to polyamide but is not as hardwearing.

Look at the weave. Textured fabric will snag more easily than a smooth, dense pile. A closely woven fabric should wear the best. Dark and patterned fabrics will show dirt less.

The fibre content of fabrics on furniture must be included by law; check labels. Most are blends so it can be difficult to assess their wear. Check there is a high proportion of hardwearing fabric, especially if textured. It might be worth buying one that has stain protection; discuss with your retailer.

Durability

The frame should be robust, with a little give, but a lot of movement indicates poor workmanship and cheap, ill-fitting components.

Sofabeds

See Sofabeds, page 100.

IN-STORE CHECKS

✔ Bounce lightly on the seat. You shouldn't be able to feel the support layer.

✔ Lean heavily against the back. You shouldn't be able to feel the springs or frame.

✔ Sit on the front edge of the seat. Again, you shouldn't be able to feel any part of the frame.

✔ Look at the overall finish, including in the hidden sections.

✔ Feel the cushions. Loose cushions should not flop when balanced across your palm. If too deeply padded, surfaces of the fabric will rub against each other when buckled under a person's weight. Constant abrasion will cause the pile to rub away.

✔ Put hands down the sides of cushions. There should be no hard lumps or bits of wood that will rub against the fabric and wear down the pile.

✔ Check buttoning, and that they don't irritate you when seated. Check that there are no large holes underneath the buttons.

✔ Ask sales staff about colour-fastness to light. Bright prints and patterns can fade in the sun.

✔ If buying leather, check on the swatches that the colour on the wrong side matches the top surface. There is a transparent finish, or lacquer, on leather, which is often coloured. The natural leather beneath may be a different colour, so if it gets scratched or worn a different colour may show through.

✔ If the wooden frames are on show check there are no knots, splits or cracks visible; joints smooth and a good fit; corner supports in the leg joints, especially the rear ones, as these take the most strain; well finished off.

✔ Check the flexibility of the frame by sitting on one end of the settee and get someone else to lean on the back of the settee at the other end. There should only be a slight 'give'.

✔ The back should be softer than the seat.

✔ If covers are too tight, wear will be more rapid. Bulky, softer styles with cushioning in areas of maximum body contact will last longer.

✔ Piping at ends of arms will probably wear quickly.

✔ Look out for the logo of The Furniture Ombusman (previously known as Qualitas). TFO was established to promote good standards throughout the furniture and floor-covering industries, and to provide efficient alternative dispute resolution. Companies affiliated to TFO provide consumers with additional assurances over service and excellence that reach further than their basic legal rights (see Useful Organisations).

Padding

Usually foam. Modern suites have to conform to fire regulations, but second-hand pieces might have been made before the new rules came into effect.

The thicker and denser the foam, the more resilient it will be. Check by feeling the cushions: they should be resilient and heavy.

The cover should fit tightly without being overstretched. Seams should be straight without any puckering.

WOODEN FURNITURE

The most popular woods are ash, oak, yew, beech, pine, rosewood, mahogany, teak, maple and walnut. All these woods can be stained darker, or given various opaque stains such as black, white, grey and even hints of pinks, blues and greens.

Solid timber has been considered to be better than a veneer, but that's not always the case. Cabinets and tables can be made completely of solid wood, but they are very expensive, and unless the quality is excellent there is always the danger of the wood cracking or splitting and twisting. Solid wood can change in an unstable environment, such as frequent changes in humidity, causing problems such as warping and loose-fitting drawers. Colours can change if exposed to excess sunlight. Chair and table frames are usually made of solid timber for strength, while panelling is another way of using solid timber, particularly for doors.

For horizontal surfaces, veneers – thin layers of wood peeled from logs and laid on a base of robust and stable chipboard or fibreboard – are the best and most common option. On top-quality furniture, edges are often lipped with strips of solid timber for extra protection.

With the huge range of finishes available, it's often difficult to distinguish between imitations and the real thing.

As well as wood, surface finishes include laminates, melamines, PVC and paper foils. Because of advancements in printing techniques, paper foils are no longer the cheap nasties of the 1970s. Other hard surfaces for furniture include metal, glass and marble.

The development of fibreboard (such as MDF), which is finer than chipboard and easier to cut, has brought many new shapes into furniture and also encouraged more painted and lacquered finishes.

Dining tables

- ⊙ Round tables are more sociable and seat more people without table legs getting in the way. However, they do reduce usable space by 25 per cent and work best in square rooms.
- ⊙ Rectangular tables look more formal and are a better choice for a long, narrow room. Allow about 50–60cm/20–24in of table edge per person. You also need about 1m/3ft all around the table for chair space, but you may get away with 45cm/18in at the least.
- ⊙ Choose an extending table to cater for different occasions. Gate-leg tables can fold down to a width below 30cm/12in and drop-flap tables can be as much as halved in size. Extension leaves can be added to round or square tables to make them oval or rectangular.

- ◉ Occasional tables: look for nesting ones to save space. Check that the finish matches the main furniture.
- ◉ Kitchen tables tend to be simpler but more robust because they take a lot of hard use. Ash is good because it is tough; pine is very popular; beech is good because it has a tight grain texture, and can double as a chopping board – but keep it scrupulously clean.

Dining chairs

Pay as much as you can afford; chairs without arms are cheaper. Chairs with arms may not go under the table and so take up more space. Check there is enough leg room: there should be about 10–12in/25–30cm between the chair seat and table top. Chairs with upright legs will save on space. Check they are a comfortable height for the table and offer good back support. Benches are good for rectangular tables. They take up less room in depth, and seat more people. Junk shops often have old church pews that are great for adding character to a room.

Cabinets and units

There is more to choose from than just a sideboard or wall units. As well, you must choose between free-standing pieces of furniture or fitted, modular systems. If furnishing a small room it may be more practical to opt for lots of flexible wall systems to house the stereo, TV, computers and children's play things, as well as glassware and ornaments.

Modular units are extremely versatile with various depths and widths of shelving and cupboards. However, solid walls of shelving and units will make your room look smaller and can be oppressive. Counteract this by including glass-fronted units and open shelving.

Take care if mixing traditional and modern styles of furniture.

Bedroom furniture

Furniture for bedrooms has advanced dramatically over the last decade, and because it is not generally on show, allows you to express your own individuality.

Fitted bedrooms can be full of ingenious storage areas like the kitchen, but remember you can't take them with you if you move. Free-standing ranges now have the fitted look, and are movable.

- ⊙ Bedroom furniture should be multi-functional, so choose built-in or free-standing modular units to maximise storage space.
- ⊙ Look out for fold-away furniture such as fold-down desks and tables.
- ⊙ Inexpensive white-wood furniture is ideal for children's rooms, and you can paint or stencil your own styles. Cover white melamine furniture with borders or stencils.
- ⊙ Small bedrooms can look cluttered with free-standing furniture.
- ⊙ Professionally fitted units can be expensive, but if you are a reasonably competent DIYer, try installing them yourself. You could just buy floor and ceiling tracks and slide the doors between them: the bedroom walls act as sides and back of the cupboard.
- ⊙ To make the most of space, fit cupboards over the entire height of the wall.
- ⊙ Free-standing furniture looks best in older houses with high ceilings and old mouldings.

BUYING CHECKS

- ✔ Test joints by pushing from the back.
- ✔ Check table and chair legs to see if they have been repaired: a trick is to repair any breaks quickly with metal brackets.
- ✔ Line up sets of chairs to see if they are the same height, and identical.
- ✔ Look for signs of woodworm: tiny holes that could be hidden under the rails and upholstery.
- ✔ Mahogany is the least expensive wood, then comes walnut, and rosewood is the most expensive.
- ✔ Sets of chairs are more valuable if they include a carver.
- ✔ Tables: check that the top and bottom go together and that the top is not warped.

BUYING FURNITURE SECOND-HAND

Buy either through auctions, antique shops, small ads in local papers. Online auction sites such as ebay (www.ebay.co.uk) are also a great way of finding second-hand furniture and other items, often at bargain prices. Remember though that what you buy will not come with the same guarantees as brand-new items and if buying online, you won't be able to check the condition before buying.

ARRANGING A ROOM

- ⊙ Don't cram too much in.
- ⊙ If there's no fireplace, create another focal point: often the TV, unfortunately.
- ⊙ Make a plan to help you make the most of all available space in the room.
- ⊙ A conventional settee may overwhelm a small sitting room so single chairs might work better.
- ⊙ As a general rule, there should be 90cm/3ft around each piece of furniture for walking around etc.
- ⊙ Traffic flow in a room is important: the more furniture, the less accessible.
- ⊙ Break up large rooms by dividing into sitting and working areas using a bookcase, screen etc.
- ⊙ If symmetrical, it is best to follow that formality and arrange the room accordingly.
- ⊙ Use furniture to disguise defects; e.g. put a bookcase over a door that's never used.

Lighting

Lighting is a necessity in the home, and used creatively, it can make a big difference to the way rooms look and feel. Good lighting gives a feeling of space, enhances decor and highlights areas of interest such as paintings and alcoves.

The most effective artificial lighting combines three forms, called general, accent and task.

TYPES OF LIGHTING

GENERAL Good background lighting is necessary for efficiency and safety, and can be supplemented by directional lighting, used as required.

ACCENT This provides highlights and shadows which make the room more interesting. It is also sometimes called 'mood' lighting.

TASK Task lighting needs to be bright enough for the job in hand, such as work at a desk, needlework or chopping food, but it must not provide any glare.

Working with inadequate light may lead to eyestrain, and the older we get the more light we need. Visually demanding tasks can be carried out beside a window during the day, but an additional light source is often necessary at night.

Daylight-simulation bulbs

Daylight-simulation bulbs are useful for task lighting. These blue bulbs show colours more correctly, and are therefore good for hobbies such as needlecraft and art. They are available in bayonet and screw fittings from large lighting retailers, needlecraft and art shops, or online from www.lightbulbs-direct.com.

Qualified electricians

To make sure that electrical work carried out in your home is safe and legal, use a qualified electrician, and ensure that work complies with Part P of the Building Regulations. To find a qualified electrician in your area, visit: www.findanelectrician.info.

The trade association for electrical contractors is the Electrical Contractors' Association; they will provide details of members (see www.eca.co.uk). The National Inspection Council for Electrical Installation Contracting carries out detailed inspections of electrical contractors and specifies compliance with national regulations. Contact for details of local NICEIC-registered Contractors (see www. niceic.org.uk). See Useful Organisations.

TYPES OF LIGHT FITTINGS

Select fittings for their light quality, and then their appearance.

Ceiling lights

Gives all-round lighting but needs accent and task lighting to enhance them. The shape and size of the shade determines the direction and spread of light.

Pendants

A variation of ceiling lighting with a rise-and-fall facility. Especially useful for people who can't climb to change a light bulb.

The amount of light depends on the height at which the pendant is hung, the type of bulb and the shade. A pendant should relate to the room size.

Wall lights

Give a decorative effect. They contribute to general lighting but also help illuminate particular objects.

Uplighters

Light the ceiling, and this light is then reflected back to provide soft gentle illumination. They are really a way to achieve accent lighting.

Uplighters are only suitable if the ceiling is in good condition, of a reasonable height and a pale colour. Don't use them if the ceiling is low or dark, as it will absorb the light, not reflect it. Ideal ceilings for uplighters are period ceilings, with wonderful, original mouldings or cornices.

Uplighters may be wall mounted, free standing, or suspended on a stem from the ceiling. They can be placed on the floor for a dramatic effect, behind large, bushy plants or in corners.

Downlights

Illuminate the carpet and furniture, and are usually recessed or semi-recessed into the ceilings. They achieve a clean, unfussy look and are useful for emphasising particular areas of a room.

Give thought to the reflector you choose: a gold reflector is wonderful for earthy tones and wood but not for pastel shades.

Make sure the beams of the downlights merge into each other so that you don't get pools of light. This will be dictated by the bulb and housing. For example, a bulb in a recessed fitting will be more concentrated than a bulb in a surface fitting.

Wall washers

Provide light like a downlight, but directional, to accent a wall or picture.

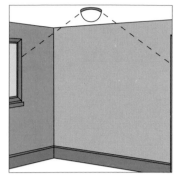

ABOVE Ceiling light

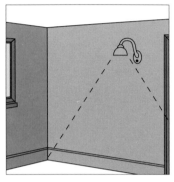

ABOVE Wall light

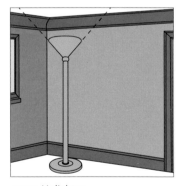

ABOVE Uplighter

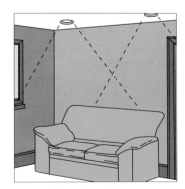

ABOVE Ceiling downlights

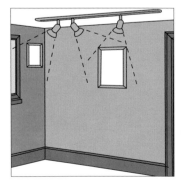

ABOVE Ceiling wall washer

Spotlights

Provide adjustable, directional lighting, with a dramatic effect.

Not all spotlights require a track mounting; they can be fixed directly on to the wall and ceiling or clipped on to shelves to accent areas or objects.

While most fittings obscure the bulb, some don't, so choose them carefully.

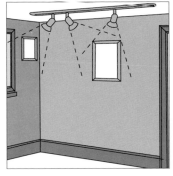

ABOVE Spotlights

ABOVE Strip lighting

Strip lighting

Used a lot in kitchens. It contributes to general, accent and task lighting. The source of light is usually concealed.

Standard lamps

A free-standing floor lamp that provides general or directional light depending on the shape of the shade. Provides a flexible source of light as it can be moved around. Standard lamps tend to be used in traditional settings, but there are modern equivalents.

Table lamps

Provide accent lighting and contribute to general lighting in a small area. Their light tends to be multi-directional.

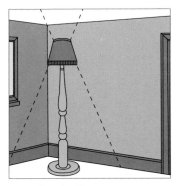

ABOVE Standard lamp

Desk lamps

The ultimate task lamps. They provide concentrated light in a particular area. An adjustable head allows you to alter the angle.

ABOVE Desk lamp

POINTS TO CONSIDER WHEN PLANNING LIGHTING

- ⊙ **PRACTICALITIES** E.g. can fittings be recessed into the ceiling?
- ⊙ **SPACE AND MOOD** How is the area used, what is its ambience; or is it multi-functional, so the lighting needs to be flexible?
- ⊙ **DESIGN AND COLOUR SCHEMES** Textures, walls, ceilings and curtains.
- ⊙ **SPECIAL FEATURES** E.g. fireplaces, paintings and alcoves.
- ⊙ **TYPES OF SWITCH** Would the installation of dual switches and dimmers be useful?
- ⊙ **LIGHT QUALITY** The quality of light required in a specific area, the type of fixture that will provide this, and whether it will look aesthetically pleasing.
- ⊙ **LOCATION OF SOCKETS AND SWITCHES** Traditionally, sockets are 46cm/18in and switches are 1.3m/51in above the floor.

TIP

If table or standard lamps provide general lighting, have them wired on the same electrical circuit. They can then be switched on together or dimmed simultaneously.

LIGHTING ROOM BY ROOM

Sitting room

Usually multi-functional, so flexibility is essential and you will probably need to combine the three types of lighting.

- ◉ Is it used mainly for entertaining, or as a family room?
- ◉ Are there formal paintings to be displayed or is it informal, for watching TV and reading?
- ◉ Any areas that need to be highlighted, such as the fireplace?

For general lighting, ceiling and table lamps are popular, but you could use track-mounted spotlights, or recessed downlights and uplighters combined with dimmer switches.

Table lamps provide a warm atmosphere and concentrated light, although for task lighting, such as reading or sewing, you will need a standard lamp or an angled table lamp. Don't forget to use accent lighting to highlight pictures or ornaments, by using uplighters or fluorescent or LED lamps concealed behind pelmets or shelves.

Dining room

Requires subtle yet plentiful lighting. You may wish to create different moods, such as a children's party versus dinner for two.

A pendant with a rise-and-fall mechanism is popular. You can raise it to lay the table and lower it for eating.

To add interest elsewhere, such as the fireplace or for necessity at the serving area, use spotlights, a downlight or wall lights.

Kitchen

Lighting needs to be functional and directed where it's needed to ensure safety and comfort.

There are three main work areas: the main worksurface, the cooker and the sink. All can be lit by task lighting, ideally controlled independently, so that you can darken and hide clutter in the sink area while you eat.

Use spotlights, on tracks or otherwise, to provide lighting. This means that light can be directed on to the cooker and worksurfaces or into cupboards, and eyeball downlighters can be rotated to direct light exactly where it is needed as well as bouncing light off the ceiling for overall illumination. Ceiling-mounted lights should be placed above the edge of any horizontal surface so that cabinets, shelves and the cook do not cast shadows on to the worksurface.

worksurfaces need localised task lighting. Fluorescent lights produce a bright light and do not cast shadows. worksurfaces can be reflective, so minimise glare by placing the light towards the front of the cabinet or shelf, using a baffle or cornice to cover the bulb, so that it does not shine directly on to the worksurface or into your eyes.

Hall

An area where you can be adventurous because you are not living in it. Wall or ceiling fittings are more practical than table lamps. Create an even level of gentle light; although you want to aim for some contrast otherwise

TIP

Watching TV in the dark tires your eyes so ensure there is low-level lighting behind the TV to soften the contrast.

Pendants over the dining table

A pendant should hang just above the head level of diners. With a large table you may need one in the centre and one at each end, possibly on different lighting circuits so that they can be used independently. If you are using several, fit them with dimmers.

Kitchen safety tips

- ● Never work in your own shadow.
- ● Make sure all worksurfaces are well lit.
- ● Avoid positioning lights where they may dazzle.
- ● Don't trail flexes over worktops or near water.

it can be uniformly dull. For example, highlight a table of ornaments with a spotlight.

Stairs

Safety is a priority. Aim for an even light, as contrasting brightness and darkness can be a hazard. The light above the stairs must be brighter than the hall light below so that the stair treads are well defined, and the risers are in the shadow. If you are installing a new staircase, consider fitting low-level stair lights.

If you have any dark corners, or a half landing, consider a downward-directed light to emphasise the change of level. Make sure the light does not shine into the eyes of someone using the stairs, as this could be hazardous.

Landing

Aim to provide an adequate light level while avoiding glare for those coming upstairs. A dimmer switch is useful when using the bathroom at night.

Bedroom

General lighting should be soft and gentle to create a relaxing atmosphere, but extra light is needed for reading and putting on make-up.

Ensure there is good lighting near mirrors. For this a pair of lights placed about 1m/3ft apart is ideal.

Bedside and dressing tables need extra thought. Choose wall lights or mini spots for bedside lights, as they don't take up space on the bedside table. They should be set above head level so that you can read easily but the light doesn't annoy your partner.

At the dressing table, the light needs to be in front of you to throw light on to your face. Put lights above the mirror, at either side, or ideally around three sides.

Light wardrobes and cupboards with a fluorescent tube placed inside the door so that light shines on the contents. A switch fitted to the door hinge brings the light on when the door opens and turns it off when closed.

Bathroom

As well as general lighting, task lighting is needed for shaving and applying make-up.

The mirror is often sited above the wash basin. Ideally, it should be lit on three sides with long incandescent tubes or lots of small low-wattage bulbs, or for a strong clear light install a fluorescent fitting with a diffuser, behind a valance or pelmet.

TYPES OF LIGHT BULB

In the UK, light bulbs come with either bayonet or screw fittings, in standard and small sizes. They cannot be interchanged, so make sure you buy the correct one.

To achieve the desired lighting effect the correct bulb must be chosen to go with the light fitting. The types available are incandescent or

Bathroom safety tips

- It should not be possible to touch any piece of electrical equipment while using the bath or shower.

- In Britain, only pull-cord switches are allowed inside the bathroom, and if a dimmer switch is used it has to be wired outside the door.

- The high level of moisture means that fittings have to be approved for damp locations, which inevitably limits the choice available.

- All bathroom light fittings should be either double insulated with no metal parts that can be touched, or properly earthed.

tungsten, tungsten halogen, halogen, fluorescent, compact fluorescent and LED. Incandescent lamps are being phased out as part of government energy-saving measures.

Tungsten filament

Once the most common type of bulb, they use more energy than tungsten halogen or fluorescent types. They are being phased out and will not be available in the UK from 2011.

Electricity heats the filament, a thin coiled tungsten wire, until it glows white hot. This is an inefficient means of lighting because most of the electricity goes into producing heat rather than light. This is why it is very important to use only the wattage recommended by the manufacturer of the shade, to avoid risk of melting or fire.

These bulbs cast a warm, slightly yellow light in all directions, although ultimately their direction is controlled by the shade or fitting.

Tungsten halogen

These combine a tungsten filament with a halogen gas. They produce a brilliant white light rather than the warmer light given out by simpler filament bulbs. The glass is closer to the filament so the bulbs are smaller, and the fittings are more compact.

Initially expensive they have, however, two to three times the life of a conventional bulb, and they are efficient to use. There are two types: mains voltage or low voltage.

Mains-voltage halogen lamp

The most popular, and easy to use. They are a direct replacement for ordinary bulbs of the same wattage, running at 240 volts, so they do not require a transformer.

Give a bright light, so choose one where the fitting keeps the bulb hidden. Ideal for display lighting with wall washers and downlights.

Low-voltage halogen lamp

The low voltage requires a transformer, which is usually built into the light fitting. The bulbs are filled with a combination of tungsten and halogen gases giving a very white light, much closer to real daylight than the more yellow tungsten lights.

This sort of bulb is ideal for spotlights because they give a really concentrated beam, and better sparkle in and around the light than the mains-voltage type.

Fluorescent

These are high-efficiency tubes, and are inexpensive to run. They give less shadow than tungsten because they are a more diffuse source of light. Ideal for kitchens, garages and work rooms.

In these tubes the electric current passes through an inert gas (such as neon) inside the glass tube, and makes a coating on the inside of the tube glow brightly, or fluoresce. This is more efficient than tungsten so it lasts longer. The light given out is usually bluer and harsher than tungsten, but the tube is cool to the touch.

Most fluorescent fittings are not compatible with dimmers.

TIP
When talking to professional electricians it may help to know that what we commonly call a bulb is called a lamp in the trade.

TIP
If you are out all day and like to leave an indoor light on so that you return to a brightly lit entrance then fit a timer to switch the light on at your usual homecoming time, to maximise energy saving.

Energy-saving bulbs

Energy-saving light bulbs use up to 80 per cent less electricity than a standard bulb to produce the same amount of light. Although they cost more than conventional types, you will save money because they last around ten times longer than standard bulbs. The Energy Saving Trust estimates that a single energy-saving bulb could save you around £40 before it needs replacing.

Early designs were cumbersome, slow to light and cold in tone, but today's bulbs are compact, take only a few seconds to warm up, and provide a warm white light that is very similar to a traditional incandescent bulb.

The most widely available energy-saving bulbs are compact fluorescents (see opposite), but the latest LED types (see page 126) are also energy-saving. Energy-saving bulbs have different wattages to conventional kinds. See the table below for equivalents:

WHAT WATTAGE?

Ordinary bulbs	Energy-saving equivalent
25W	5–7W
40W	8–9W
60W	11–14W
100W	20–23W
(Energy Saving Trust)	

SUITABILITY

A wide range of designs are available now, so you should be able to match most traditional styles, including natural daylight and outdoor types, and bulbs that work with dimmers. There is even a bulb that looks like an old-fashioned incandescent light bulb.

Low-voltage benefits

Apart from the green benefits, energy-saving bulbs have other advantages over the traditional incandescent type:

- They need changing less often. This is an advantage for fittings in hard-to-reach places like stairwells.
- They give out less heat than incandescent bulbs. This means that they are safer to use in an unattended security light, in a night light in a child's room, or with a delicate lampshade that could be damaged by heat.

Green tip

Unlike traditional bulbs, energy-saving types can be recycled, usually at household recycling banks or centres. Contact your local council for details of the nearest civic amenity site or look on www. recycle-more.co.uk.

WHAT TO LOOK FOR WHEN BUYING

- Make sure that the bulb you buy states that it is an energy-saving type: some bulbs labelled long-life will last longer than a conventional bulb but they don't save energy.
- Look for the Energy Saving Recommended logo. A light bulb with this logo has met the strict energy efficiency criteria set by the Energy Saving Trust

and has been independently tested by an independent accredited test house.

- If you have a dimmer fitting, then make sure that the bulb is compatible as some types are not suitable for use with a dimmer.
- If you are looking for outdoor bulbs, consider buying solar lights (see page 127).

LED

The latest type of bulb, these low-energy bulbs come on immediately, produce little or no heat, use only a fraction of the power of halogen lamps and are very long-lasting – an LED bulb can last around 100,000 hours. Although they are expensive, their longer lifespan makes up for this.

They are a good choice for low-level stair wash lights, lighting shelves and for uplighters. Recent colour change technology allows you to change colour at the touch of a button.

TYPES OF SWITCHES

Standard switches

These vary according to design and application. Standard, plate switches are available with various sizes of rocker control, and in plastic, wood or metal finishes. Architrave plate switches can be mounted on narrow door architraves.

Ceiling-mounted switches operated by a pull cord are usually used in bathrooms for safety, because wet hands could cause an electric shock.

Dimmer switches

These work by reducing the voltage passing through a bulb. This will not only cut down on the amount of electricity used, but also prolong the bulb's life. They are inexpensive to buy and provide an easy means of changing the mood of the room at the turn of a dial.

It is not advisable to install your own dimmer switch – it is much safer to call in an electrician. It is possible to wire them to all kinds of fittings from floor and table lights to ceiling and wall lights, but some fittings are not compatible with dimmers, so check first.

One- and two-way switching

A one-way switch means that the lights linked to the switch are controlled only from one switch position. A two-way switch is linked to a second switch to control the light. In most homes the commonest use of this is on the staircase, so lights can be switched on or off from either the bottom or top of the staircase, and on bedside wall lights.

GARDEN LIGHTING

With the advent of outdoor entertaining this form of lighting has become more in demand. Installing just a few lights will have a dramatic effect outside as a little light goes a long way. Lights can be mains voltage, low voltage or solar powered. Solar-powered lights are usually simple to install yourself. For wired lamps, consult an electrician for the best choice of lamp and voltage for the intended use, safety considerations and installation position.

Types of exterior lighting
LOW-VOLTAGE LIGHTS

These are clipped to a waterproof cable, which is attached to a transformer. This converts mains voltage (240 volts) to 12 or 24 volts so that if you accidentally cut through the cable with a mower, you will come

Remote control

New technology systems allow you to operate lighting, appliances, television, heating and door access from a single hand-held remote control. With some systems, you can even text commands from your mobile phone.

to no harm. The advantages of this type are that the cable need not be buried and it can be installed by a competent DIYer.

MAINS LIGHTING

Permanent garden lighting should have a separate circuit. It should have waterproof sockets, a PVC cable encased in a plastic conduit buried at least 50cm/20in deep, a current breaker (RCD) and a fuse. It should be installed by a qualified electrician.

The advantage of mains lighting systems is that you can have much more lighting than on a low-voltage system, for practical rather than decorative use.

LIGHTING AND THE ENVIRONMENT

If every household in the UK replaces just one tungsten bulb with an energy-saving light bulb (for use where light is needed for long periods each day), this country would save power equal to the output of one large power station. Tungsten halogen bulbs are being phased out to help cut down on carbon dioxide emissions, and so the use of energy-saving bulbs helps to reduce the threat of global warming.

Solar lighting

Solar panels absorb sunshine and convert it into electricity, which is stored in a battery. The advantage is that you have no installation or running costs, but many types will only give a decorative glow and efficiency depends upon the amount of sunshine absorbed. For brightness, look for types that use a fluorescent bulb or at least two LEDS.

Security lighting

See Security Lighting, pages 382–3.

Storage

It is not always possible to move to a larger house, so sometimes it's necessary to use the existing space in your current home in a better way.

It is easy to miss out on potential space by being too rigid in the way we use rooms. Just because the dining room has been there since you moved in, it might be better, particularly if you always eat in the kitchen, to free the room for other uses and replace it with a fold-away trestle and chairs.

Storage can nearly always be improved when required. Look for dead areas under beds, stairs, backs of doors, in alcoves, beneath the ceiling and under windows. Keep readily available only the things you use regularly; those 'might come in useful items' can go to the charity shop.

KITCHENS

Take a fresh look at your kitchen. There are usually several different ways of storing the same item: for example, by hanging, wall racks, shelves, cupboards above kitchen units etc. Nowadays, even budget kitchen units offer a good choice of storage systems.

Hanging space

⊙ Fix items, wherever possible, above the worksurface; remember you only use the front portion of the worktop for preparation. For example, magnetic knife racks, tools with a hanging hole in the handle, spice racks, extra narrow decorative shelves, racks and rails for mugs or spices can all be fixed to the wall.

⊙ Hanging rails, butchers' hooks and clothes airers can all be used for suspending kitchen clutter. Traditional cast-iron and pine self-assembly clothes airers save space.

IDEAS TO GET YOU STARTED

⊙ Think about which way your doors hang. Would hanging it around the other way make it possible to fit more furniture in the room?

⊙ Interior storage systems can be tailored to fit your exact needs.

⊙ To make space, use every square inch, adding shelves and cupboards to take the clutter.

⊙ Make an old-fashioned plate shelf. Fix it round the room or hall at picture-rail level to display old china.

⊙ Fix shelves across a dull window and put your plants there: they'll thrive in the sunlight. For more information about putting up shelves, see All About Shelves, pages 328–30.

- Ironing organisers hang both an iron and board on the back of a door or wall; or use a vacuum tool tidy.
- If worktop space is limited save space by wall mounting your microwave on brackets, available from DIY stores. Make sure you have a put-down area adjacent.

Drawers

- Use drawer space carefully. For example, a knife block on the worksurface saves drawer space; invest in deep drawers with shallow sides for saucepans. Usually double width, they allow you to see and reach contents easily.
- Drawers can get filled up with wasteful clutter unless the inserts are carefully chosen for the cutlery and tools required.
- Huge lift-out baskets allow you to fit more awkward items into drawers.

Miscellaneous

- A space-saving kitchen work station or trolley has wheels and consists of knife block, towel rail, chopping boards, cupboard storage and vegetable basket.
- Multi-pots and steamers are compact to store and can be used to cook many foods.
- Stackable cooling racks fold flat for easy storage.
- Use tiered mobile vegetable baskets, or floor-standing pan stands.
- Use a four-bar radiator airer to make the most of radiators.
- If the back door comes into the kitchen use a shoe rack, available in numerous designs, wall mounted or with wheels, horizontal or vertical in shape.

- Maximise the storage potential of a galley kitchen by fitting extra-deep base units.
- Fit units with sliding doors that won't obstruct a narrow passage.
- If your kitchen doubles as a dining room, look for folding tables, chairs or stools.
- If you want to maximise your cupboard space, many appliance manufacturers make narrower space-saving equipment 450mm/ 18in wide rather than the standard 600mm/24in wide. This applies particularly to cookers, dishwashers, fridges and freezers and some washing equipment.
- A wall-mounted drop-leaf table will provide useful extra worktop space when you need it.

HALLS

Old-fashioned cupboards under the stairs are fine for the vacuum cleaner but are not sufficiently organised for really efficient storage. Divide it into three separate cupboards, each with its own louvre door, for sports equipment, home office filing, outdoor shoes and wellies, small DIY equipment and spare light bulbs.

- Alternatively, open up the under-stairs space and fit the wall with shelves for books or games, or turn the area into a wine cellar with racks.
- Consider a wall-hung telephone and notice board.
- Fix coat hooks and/or make a cloak cupboard in the corner of the hall, behind the front door, if there is sufficient room. Sliding doors will save space.
- Fix slimline, pull-out shoe cabinets along the walls in the hallway-Ikea made a model that is just 18cm/7in deep.

ABOVE Storage in a hallway

LIVING ROOMS

The first decision is whether you want individual pieces of furniture, wall-mounted or free-standing storage systems. An integrated system can accommodate lots of different types of clutter.

- To save surface space mount your TV and speakers on brackets. They swivel to give adjustable angles and it prevents toddlers from fiddling with the knobs. If you have a flat-screen TV, then consider mounting it on the wall. Use the space freed up below for a cabinet in which you can store all your DVDs and videos.
- If you are short of a spare bedroom consider buying a sofabed for overnight guests (see page 100).
- Choose a dining room table with drop-down leaves or extending flaps.
- Choose coffee tables that have drawers or cabinet space where you can store the remote controls and TV magazines.
- Pull your sofa a few inches from the wall and put a shelf above to store paperbacks. You can also then use the space behind the sofa as a place to store items such as folding chairs.

An illusion of space

If you are still short of space, remember that by carefully choosing your colour and lighting scheme you will be able to create an illusion of more space. See Painting and Decorating, Colour and Design, page 304 and Lighting, page 119.

BEDROOMS

- Make the most of wardrobe space. There are numerous internal fitments to make better use of the space available. First, consider whether the clothes rail is unnecessarily high for your clothes, or are you more a separates person? Could you lower it and put shelves above or have two hanging rails?
- Use fixings on the backs of the doors, such as a tie bar.
- Add a bar hook over your existing rail to create additional space.
- Invest in heavy-duty clothes-storage covers with an extra-wide gusset, for ball gowns and evening dresses.
- Invest in multiple hangers, so that you can hang several skirts and trousers on one hanger.
- A shelf at the bottom of the wardrobe can store shoes both on and underneath it.
- If you have too many cupboards and not enough drawers you can buy wire basket racking systems in a variety of shapes and sizes.
- You can buy clothes and linen storage bags, which are usually transparent. They slide under the bed and store bulky items like sweaters when not in use.
- Use galvanised zinc or tough cardboard boxes and free-standing drawer units, some with carrying handles and wheels.
- Choose a bed with built-in storage drawers, for storing bulky items.
- Consider installing a wall bed from The London Wall Bed Company (see Manufacturers, Retailers and Service Providers).
- There is a design concept from Strachan (see Manufacturers, Retailers and Service Providers) called Convert-a-Room. It forms two rooms in one, converting from a fitted study to a fitted bedroom using a folding bed and a swivel-action dressing table that changes into a desk or work station.

Bathroom storage

- Open shelving and hooks solve some storage problems. Organise shelves in the bathroom or cloakroom: narrow glass ones for toiletries, wide wood or melamine for extra supplies and clean towels.
- A built-in vanity unit, or, even better, full-length fully fitted units from wall to wall will give you somewhere to house towels, toilet rolls and cleaning items.
- Utilise space underneath the bath for storing infrequently used items. It is relatively easy to fit a door or some kind of access on the bath panel.
- A wall-mounted shelf above the bath provides a handy place to store shampoos and shower gels.

CHILDREN'S ROOMS

The number of children's belongings expands rapidly, so any storage systems need to be adjustable.

- ⦿ Furniture needs to be adaptable so that you can rearrange and change it as necessary. Toys will give way to sports equipment, audio equipment or clothes.
- ⦿ For a teenager it will become more of a bed-sitting room than a bedroom. A bed-length bolster and cushions can turn a bed into a daytime sofa.
- ⦿ Colourful plastic boxes and baskets are useful for storing toys. Keep them on low-level shelving in the early years. Use different colours for different types of toys or to denote which toys are whose. They are more accessible than stacking boxes, and the shelves can be used for books and a stereo as they grow older.
- ⦿ Use broad, widely spaced shelves in children's rooms. Make sure they're too high to be climbed or sat on.
- ⦿ A wide shelf with strong brackets can serve as a desk in a study/bedroom.
- ⦿ Downward folding brackets from DIY stores can be used to create a desk surface at an angle of 45° and after use will fold away. Top with bookshelves.
- ⦿ A computer trolley holds all the essentials in the minimum space, and frees the desk space for hand-written homework and other activities.
- ⦿ Beds at a higher level above furniture saves space.
- ⦿ Stacking beds, where one of the beds rolls away under the main bed, saves space.
- ⦿ Foam beds fold into cube seating when not in use.
- ⦿ Small boxes hung on walls can store pens, pencils, crayons etc.
- ⦿ Keep clothing in a wardrobe with an adjustable hanging rail. Rather than buying your child a new wardrobe when they grow taller, you can simply raise the rail.

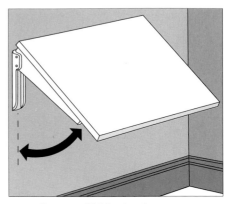

ABOVE Downward folding brackets can be used to create a foldaway desk

ATTICS

By adding flooring, access and running a light up into the attic you can make a large and useful storage area for infrequently used items like Christmas decorations and suitcases.

Make sure that the ladder used to gain access to the loft is firmly fixed: see Ladder Safety, pages 317 and 360.

STORAGE OF VALUABLE ITEMS

If you inherit something of value and don't want to display it, it is important to consult a conservator to make sure that you store it properly.

Outside storage

Storage efficiency outside the house in garages and sheds can be easily improved.

- ● Use lots of racking systems and hooks suspended from the ceiling.
- ● To store bikes out of the way and save floor space there are special bike hinges available from cycle, sports shops and department stores.
- ● Fit shelves to hold tools and DIY equipment.
- ● For gardening, choose multi tools which save space because you have one handle to which you can fit several heads. A fold-away wheelbarrow is compact to store.
- ● If your garage has a high apex roof, then consider getting it boarded out so you can use the area above your head for extra storage.

CAUSES OF DETERIORATION OF VALUABLE OBJECTS

⊙ **LIGHT** Is a source of energy and the chemical changes it causes cannot be reversed. Even weak light causes damage so lower the level by drawing curtains or covering items.

⊙ **HUMIDITY AND TEMPERATURE** Are closely related. We can take in drinks; objects can't. Central heating lowers the relative humidity. A humidity of 50 to 60 per cent is ideal for most objects. Too much humidity and you encourage mould growth; too little and paper becomes brittle and wood shrinks and cracks.

⊙ **CONDENSATION** Occurs when the temperature of a solid surface is lower than that of the air around it, so anything in contact with a surface like this will have water and dust deposited on it.

⊙ **LACK OF VENTILATION** Insufficient air is the best way of promoting mould growth. To prevent it, allow plenty of fresh air to circulate.

Finding expert help

⊙ Contact The Institute of Conservation (see Useful Organisations) for details of conservators of movable items such as paintings, stone, glass, metal, fabrics and furniture.

⊙ Contact your local art museum and ask for the conservation department or curator. He/she can put you in touch with trusted conservators.

⊙ Look for a regional conservation centre in your area.

⊙ There are specialist firms that store and transport valuable and precious pieces of fine art. Momart (see Manufacturers, Retailers and Service Providers) will keep the work of art wrapped and crated in a stable environment, which means controlling temperature, light and humidity. Each valuable object is different and requires different conditions. Ask about insurance and to see crated facilities.

Storing paintings

Don't clean gilded frames and don't touch the painting itself. If you have a painting in a frame, wrap and protect the whole thing. Don't wrap in household blankets and sheets; they are dusty. Buy some plastic sheet called Melinex from Conservation Resources (see Manufacturers, Retailers and Service Providers). It is almost impervious to moisture, and if the item should be knocked it will keep all the pieces together. Tape Melinex to itself only. Don't use tape on the picture. Then wrap it in bubble wrap, and use heavy card as packing. Check its condition at least once a year.

If you don't use Melinex, then acid-free tissue paper, which is widely available, is the next best option.

Any damp in a room will manifest itself throughout the floors and walls, so keep away from these where possible.

If you hang a picture, use cork spacers behind the picture to allow for ventilation by keeping the picture away from the wall. Make sure the cord is adequate. If you do anything to the picture, such as replace the cord, do it on a cushioned surface.

Questions to ask

● How are they qualified: in other words by apprenticeship or are they formally qualified?

● Do they have good references? Can you speak to other people who have used them?

● Can you see the studio?

● Are they adequately insured?

● Do they have a security system or alarm?

Storing carpets

It is essential that storage is dry and warm and not in a cold outhouse or shed.

Before storage make sure the carpet is dry to prevent mildew. Roll carpets and rugs; do not fold them.

If the carpet is dirty have it professionally cleaned. Ask for a beating and cleaning treatment. Ensure that all dirt and foreign substances are removed from the base of the carpet, and ask for the carpet to be dried and wrapped. Contact the National Carpet Cleaners Association (see Useful Organisations).

If storing in an attic, wrap in a plastic sleeve, but leave both ends open to allow ventilation. Unroll periodically to check its condition.

Some cleaning firms or furniture removers will store carpets. Contact the National Carpet Cleaners Association.

Storing wedding dresses

See Wedding Dresses, pages 264–5.

Storing books

Glass cabinets will protect books from dust and sunlight but adequate ventilation is still essential for preservation. Leaf through the books occasionally. Regular use stops books from smelling musty.

Books should be stored at a moderate temperature, 13–18°C/ 55–64°F, to prevent the paper drying out.

Store weighty tomes flat to stop the pages breaking away from the spine.

For professional help contact The Society of Bookbinders (see Useful Organisations).

Storing photographs

Buy albums or binders containing acid-free paper for photos you treasure. Use detachable corners, not glue to fix the photos in place.

Store negatives and old prints out of sunlight, at an even temperature, in polyester covers to prevent the photograph adhering to the surface and avoid bleaching of colours. Clear polyester sleeves are available from Secol (see Manufacturers, Retailers and Service Providers). They also have a specialised storage system, which can be used for photographs and negatives, documents and tickets.

Storing digital images

Most people store the bulk of their digital photographs on their computer's hard drive. Although this is a good option, it does have risks – if the computer crashes or becomes infected with a virus, all the images could be lost. Therefore, it is a good idea also to back up images as soon as they are transferred to the hard drive on to a separate CD or DVD. Make sure each CD or DVD is clearly labelled with details of the photographs, so you don't have to search through dozens to find a specific picture.

Storing possessions when moving house

See Storage, page 428.

Flooring

Flooring is the most hardworking area in the home so it must be functional to withstand abrasion, weight and spills, yet still be decorative. As well, the colour, texture and finish must blend in with the rest of the decor. Before you decide on the surface, think about what the flooring is to be laid over, that is, the sub-floor. This greatly affects the wear and appearance of the covering. The sub-floor must be dry, level, and without cracks, bumps or protruding nails. If it is uneven, damp or not very rigid, it is essential to deal with the problem before laying the new covering. Remove any residual bitumen backing or adhesive used for the previous flooring, because you could find that this works its way through the new flooring, particularly cork, linoleum or vinyl, causing discoloration. Some types of flooring, such as laminates and cork, require that a waterproof membrane or padded underlay be laid first. You can probably take care of minor problems yourself, but more severe faults are best left to professionals. Ask friends for recommendations, look online and in the Yellow Pages under flooring, flooring services and contractors. Obtain several quotes.

SUB-FLOORS

Wooden sub-floors

If it is uneven you may be able to sand out the bumps yourself with a floor sander, or better still cover with hardboard or plywood.

Use squares of hardboard (about 2.5mm/¹/₁₀in thick), which have been conditioned with water and stacked for 48 hours. Lay them textured side up. Alternatively, use sheets of 6mm/¹/₄in-thick primed plywood.

Secure using 25mm/1in rustproof nails, set at 10cm/4in intervals around the edge and every 15cm/6in across the middle of the room. Take care to avoid any cables or water pipes under the floorboards.

Quarry, terracotta, brick, stone or ceramic tiled flooring should not be laid over a suspended wood sub-floor because their weight would be too great.

Concrete sub-floors

To level out an uneven concrete floor use a ready-mixed self-levelling compound or screed, about 3mm/¹/₈in thick.

LAYING A NEW FLOOR

Never lay new flooring on top of an old one, as tread and wear patterns would soon be transferred. Some types of flooring can be laid by a competent DIYer, following the manufacturer's instructions, particularly tiles, carpet, vinyl, linoleum and cork. Laying sheet linoleum can be a

TIP
Plain, small patterns and light colours will give an effect of spaciousness.

problem because it isn't very flexible, and even sheet vinyl can be awkward because of the size.

Always use the correct adhesive or grouting. Some vinyl does not need to be stuck down: check when purchasing.

Hard flooring such as terracotta, quarry stone and ceramic tiles should be professionally fitted:

HARD FLOORING

Brick

Suitable for kitchens and dining areas, outhouses and conservatories.

Warm and rustic-looking, and available in many shades. Bricks are stain and grease resistant, non-slip and can be laid directly on to a damp-proof course. However, they can be hard and cold underfoot. Different patterns can be laid by positioning the bricks at different angles, e.g. herringbone style.

Ceramic tiles

Suitable for kitchens, bathrooms, hallways, and conservatories.

Hardwearing, hygienic and easy to clean, but cold, hard and noisy, and may crack or chip if anything heavy and rigid is dropped on them. They can be extremely slippery when wet so extra care should be taken in bathrooms and kitchens. Whether matt, glazed or unglazed, a huge range of colours, styles and patterns are available. When choosing, make sure the wear rating is suitable for the intended use – e.g. a minimum of PEI Grade 4 for heavy-duty areas, and Grade 3 for bathrooms. Can be fitted by a competent DIYer.

Cork

Suitable for kitchens, bathrooms and halls.

An excellent noise buffer, and warm and resilient underfoot. Cork tiles vary in thickness – the thicker and denser the better. Also available in strip laminate form. Ensure the tiles are thick enough to withstand sanding down if wear occurs, and avoid using thin cork wall tiles as a cheaper alternative. Don't forget to budget for a sealant unless ready sealed. Easy to lay.

Laminates

Suitable for most areas, but consider carefully before putting in a bathroom or kitchen.

Usually made from a wood composite base with a laminate surface that has been treated with an acrylic topcoat to increase resistance to wear and tear. Cheaper than wood, and available in a wide range of colours and designs – effects that imitate solid wood are most common. Look for boards that click together and do not require gluing. Laminates need to be laid on a sound, level base such as a concrete sub-floor (with acoustic boards on top) or at right angles to existing floorboards.

Leather

Suitable for bedrooms, livings rooms and hallways, but not kitchens and bathrooms.

Leather flooring is an increasingly popular choice. It looks beautiful, but tends to be rather expensive. Usually installed in tile form, leather is soft and quiet underfoot, hardwearing and easy to maintain. It develops a beautiful patina with age. Professional fitting is recommended.

Linoleum

Sold under the brand name Marmoleum in the UK, this is suitable for kitchens, bathrooms and conservatories.

Warm, quiet and hardwearing, and will resist dents, scratches and minor burns. Made from natural materials, including cork and linseed oil, it is inherently slip resistant and fade-proof, so ideal for a conservatory. It is also naturally antibacterial, so a good choice for allergy sufferers. Difficult to lay, so opt for professional fitting.

Marble

Suitable for most areas, but can be slippery in a bathroom or kitchen.

Marble has a wonderful coolness and is hardwearing and easy to clean. However, it can be noisy and hard underfoot. It's also very heavy, so check that your floor is strong is enough. Best fitted by a professional, and may need resealing from time to time.

Quarry and terracotta tiles

Suitable for kitchens, halls, conservatories and porches.

Quarry tiles are very hardwearing, but can be noisy and cold underfoot. Can be factory-made, hand-pressed or reclaimed. Appearance improves with age. Terracotta tiles are porous and need careful maintenance to keep them in tiptop condition – acrylic seals will maintain the natural colour of the tiles, while linseed oil will darken and change the colour during its life. Quarry tiles have a more regular appearance and are generally not sealed.

Slate

Suitable for halls, porches and conservatories.

British slate is quarried in Wales and Cornwall, African and Chinese slate is richly coloured, but expensive. Slate is hardwearing, easy to maintain and impervious to water, but cold and hard underfoot. A good range of colours and finishes include diamond sawn (with a smooth matt finish); riven (where the slate is naturally split leaving a textured surface); and fine rubbed (with a light sheen). Slip resistant, even when lightly polished. Very heavy, so check floor strength. Treat with a mixture of linseed oil and turpentine for extra lustre.

Stone (including limestone, travertine and granite)

Suitable for kitchens, halls and utility areas.

Extremely durable and hardwearing, and perfect for heavy traffic areas. Can be cold and noisy underfoot and very heavy, so floor strength must be checked before laying. Usually sold in tile form and should be professionally fitted for best results.

Terrazzo

Suitable for halls, porches, kitchens and bathrooms.

On your metal

Metal sheet flooring is suitable for bathrooms and kitchens

Extremely durable and practical. Metal sheet floors look funky and modern, but can be quite cold and uncomfortable to walk on in bare feet. While aluminium chequer-plate is the most usual choice, steel floor plate is also gaining popularity, but needs to be galvanised to prevent rusting. Look for sheeting with a thickness of at least 2–3mm/$^1/_{12}$–$^1/_8$ in.

TIP

Many types of hard flooring are cold to walk on, so consider installing underfloor heating before laying.

Made from marble chippings and dust set into cement, and is mottled rather than veined like real marble. Takes its colour from whatever type of marble has been used; a large range of colours is available. It looks smooth and elegant but is very expensive.

Vinyl

Suitable for kitchens and bathrooms, halls and playrooms.

The most versatile flooring available, vinyl imitates the appearance of natural flooring while retaining a softer, warmer feel. Available in sheet or tile form. Smooth surface is easy to clean, comfortable, hardwearing and reasonably stain resistant. Quick and easy to lay. Choose the thickest cushioned vinyl you can afford.

Wood

Suitable for throughout the house, with the exception of wet areas such as bathrooms.

Warm underfoot, hardwearing and easy to clean, and can be laid anywhere except in areas likely to get wet (moisture can cause it to warp). Ideal for people with dust allergies.

RENOVATING OLD FLOORBOARDS

Renovating old wooden floors is only worth the effort if they are in good condition. Hammer down protruding nails, fill in nail holes or gaps, and remove sharp edges or splinters. These can then be sanded, stained darker or bleached a lighter colour, and sealed or varnished.

When sanding down, use the sander along the length of the board, never across. Remove all traces of dust, and then wipe over with white spirit. Bleach, stain or paint.

TREATMENTS AND FINISHES FOR WOOD FLOORS

⊙ **LIGHTENING** Scrub with domestic bleach or a proprietary wood-lightening product and leave to dry. Repeat until the correct colour is achieved. Thoroughly wash the floor with water. Allow to dry. The wood grain may have expanded slightly due to the water: if so, sand it down before sealing.

⊙ **STAINING** A good range of colours is available, and they can be combined with a varnish. Choose either oil-, water- or spirit-based stains. Oil based tend to give a more even colour but are slower to dry. Apply with a clean dry cloth, along the grain. It's easier to concentrate on one floorboard at a time. Repeat until the required depth of colour is achieved. Dry, and then seal.

⊙ **SEALING** Use either wax or a polyurethane varnish.

⊙ **POLYURETHANE** These varnishes can darken and yellow the wood, but they are tough, water resistant and easy to maintain. Choose from gloss, satin and matt finishes. Gloss is the toughest, but shows up dust and marks easily. Apply across the grain, finishing with long brush strokes down the grain. Apply at least three coats in areas of heavy wear. Sand in between each coat to give the next one something to grip on to.

⊙ **WAX** Not as tough or water resistant as polyurethane varnishes and needs frequent retreating. Seal the floor with a floor sealer to prevent dirt penetrating the wood. Apply wax thinly with a soft cloth, leave, and then buff up the surface with a floor polisher. Polish with a soft cloth.

MAIN TYPES OF WOOD FLOORING AVAILABLE

- ⊙ **PARQUET** Solid blocks of hardwood either loose-laid or stuck to a level base. Parquet looks wonderful and lasts for years, but is very expensive.
- ⊙ **TONGUE AND GROOVE** Solid hardwood boards that can be sanded from time to time to keep them looking good. Lay them at right angles over existing boards or on a concrete sub-floor.
- ⊙ **ENGINEERED HARDWOOD FLOORING** Is a product made up of a core of hardwood, plywood or HDF and a top layer of hardwood veneer that is glued on the top surface. It has the natural characteristics of the selected wood species as opposed to the photographic layer used with laminate wood floors. Engineered wood flooring is designed to provide greater stability, particularly where moisture or heat might pose problems for solid hardwood floors. In addition to the top hardwood veneer, there are typically three or more core layers – the more layers, the better the stability. A quality engineered wood floor is very durable and will provide many years of wear.

CARPET AND NATURAL FIBRE COVERINGS

Thanks to advances in fibre technology, today's carpets are better value than ever before – a far cry from the 1950s when the choice available was restricted to either wool or nylon. Pay as much as you can afford, but do shop around as prices vary greatly between retailers. Check what you are getting for your money – ask for a breakdown of fitting and accessory costs, such as gripper rods, and whether extra is charged for taking up old carpets, removing doors etc. Make sure the carpet you choose is suitable for the intended area – stair and hall carpets need to be more hardwearing than bedroom ones. Most carpets are graded according to room suitability.

To check for durability, press your hand on the pile and see how long it takes to spring back into shape – the faster, the better. Most durable is short, dense pile and, if the construction is good (tufts close together and tightly woven), a combination of 80 per cent wool and 20 per cent nylon.

It is worth paying extra for professional fitting – a good fitter will ensure the floor below is properly prepared, that patterns and seams are correctly matched, pile is laid in the right direction and that the carpet is wrinkle-free and snug fitting.

Carpets
WOVEN CARPETS
Usually called Wilton or Axminster

AXMINSTER Named after the loom on which they are woven. Many colours can be used in the weaving and so they are often patterned. They can be natural, synthetic or a blend of fibres, with a short cut or shag pile (or a mixture of both).

WILTON Name is also derived from the loom they are woven on. The yarn is woven in a continuous strand so combination of colours is more limited. A maximum of five can be used. They have a close-textured pile that can be a smooth velvet finish or loops and twists. Can be natural, synthetic or a blend of fibres. Usually very expensive.

CARPET GRADES

Class 1: For light use, such as bedrooms.

Class 2: For medium, general use such as dining areas.

Class 3: For heavy use in halls, living rooms and stairs.

Class 4: For extra-heavy use.

BRUSSEL-TYPE CARPETS A Wilton with an uncut pile. Very hardwearing but without the velvety appearance and sheen of a cut pile.

TUFTED CARPETS

These are quicker to produce and form most of the UK market. Tufts are inserted into a pre-woven backing, anchored by latex or a polyvinyl compound and then another backing – usually hessian – is applied. Fibres are natural, synthetic or blended, which can be looped, cut or twisted. Available in a large range of widths, colours and textures.

Tufted carpets can have a secondary foam backing which acts as an underlay. This type of carpet is usually cheaper and less durable, and so is more suitable for bedrooms rather than heavy wear areas.

WHICH CARPET FIBRE IS SUITABLE FOR WHICH ROOM?

POLYAMIDE/NYLON About half of British-made tufted carpets have a nylon pile. Short-looped nylon pile is a good choice for kitchens, play areas and bathrooms. For heavy wear areas, look for a twisted-pile nylon carpet.

PROS
- ✔ Very strong fibre.
- ✔ Durable, and if the pile is dense will resist crushing.
- ✔ Keeps its colour well.
- ✔ Good economy choice.
- ✔ Rot resistant.

CONS
- ✘ Doesn't maintain its appearance well in low-density carpets (fewer tufts per square cm/in).
- ✘ The pile, once flattened, is difficult to restore.
- ✘ Cheap, untreated types can cause static shock.

POLYESTER A suitable choice for bedrooms.

PROS
- ✔ Reasonable resistance to abrasion.
- ✔ Does not fade easily.
- ✔ Warm feel.

CONS
- ✘ Cheap versions that haven't been treated are prone to soiling.
- ✘ Once the pile has been flattened it's difficult to restore.

POLYPROPYLENE Suitable for kitchens and bathrooms. About a quarter of British tufted carpets have a polypropylene pile or one that is blended with other fibres. Blends of 50 per cent wool and polypropylene are very popular, and if they have a good proportion of wool it helps to prevent the pile from flattening permanently.

PROS
- ✔ Good value.
- ✔ Non-absorbent and easy to clean.
- ✔ Withstands abrasion well.
- ✔ Colour-fast.
- ✔ Low in static.

CONS
- ✘ Traditionally harsh textured, but new ranges are softer.
- ✘ Will flatten more easily than wool so polypropylene is often used in low loop pile constructions (so the pile does not crush as easily).

WOOL Generally blended with 20 per cent nylon for greater resilience and durability. Suitable for heavy-duty areas. For maximum durability look for a short, dense pile.

PROS
- ✔ Good resistance to soiling and wear.
- ✔ Soft and comfortable.
- ✔ Good insulation properties.
- ✔ Does not burn readily.
- ✔ The pile does not easily flatten so retains its appearance well.

CONS
- ✘ Can rot if left wet.
- ✘ All wool is expensive, but you get what you pay for. A better option is to go for an 80/20 wool/nylon mix.

BONDED CARPETS

The carpet pile is held between two specially treated adhesive bases and is then sliced in two. This means that all the pile is on the carpet surface.

PILE TYPES

Density of pile is one of the most important factors in determining quality. The closer the tufts, the more hardwearing is the carpet.

LOOP PILE Consists of a series of small loops. Low loop piles are very hardwearing.

CUT PILE Cut off to form a flat, level surface to give its characteristic sheen and soft feel. Axminster carpets can only be cut pile.

VELVET A short, dense, cut pile which feels luxurious, but is susceptible to shading and shows up tread and furniture marks.

SHAG The longest cut pile.

CUT AND LOOP PILE A combination of the two constructions, creating a textured, sculptured effect.

BERBER Can be either a cut or loop pile (although traditionally is a wool, loop pile carpet), which has flecks of contrasting colour throughout.

TWIST PILE A tightly twisted cut pile. The greater the twist, the greater the durability and resistance to flattening.

CORD Woven carpet made from a mixture of yarns and very low loops, like corduroy. Very hardwearing but can be harsh to the touch.

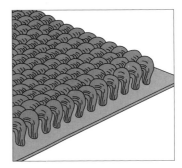

ABOVE Loop pile

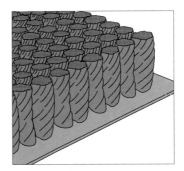

ABOVE Cut pile

Colour and design

◉ Ideally, choose your carpet before your other soft furnishings as it is the most expensive item and takes the most wear. Unfortunately, most of us choose it last and have to go for plain colours. Patterns disguise wear and soiling.

◉ Light colours make a room appear larger and more spacious, whereas dark colours can be oppressive. Choose warm colours for dull rooms with little light.

◉ Large patterns can dominate the room making the floor area seem smaller. Combine them with plain or textured fabrics for curtains and upholstery to balance the busy design. With directional patterns, it should be the right way up if you look at it from the door.

◉ Stripes can make a hall look longer and more narrow if laid lengthways.

◉ Primary-coloured rooms are hard to match with a carpet: use a contrast.

◉ When choosing your carpet shade, check against the colour of floor-length curtains, the door, and any strong colours showing from other rooms.

◉ If you have a pet, it's wise to choose a neutral shade, similar to your pet's coat.

◉ For a really elegant look, choose a carpet with a border. These are becoming increasingly popular, and you can mix and match styles. Borders give definition and detail to a room lacking any focal point. They are most effective if there is no furniture around the edge of the room, emphasising details like the fireplace, alcove or bay window.

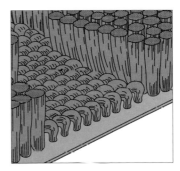

ABOVE Cut and loop pile

Underlay

Never underestimate the importance of a good underlay. Not only does it prolong the life of your carpet and prevent the penetration of dust from the floorboards, it also adds comfort and offers sound and heat insulation. There are several different types available:

Stain protectors

These are mainly applied to synthetic carpets because wool carpets have greater inherent stain-retarding properties.

Carpets can be treated in two ways:

❶ An overall soil-retardant finish acts as a shield to retard penetration of dirt and liquids.

❷ A stain-resistant finish reacts as stains occur and prevents the stains from being absorbed. Stain-resistant treatments do not provide total protection but they do give you time to blot up spills and thus help to prevent any permanent staining on the carpet.

Try to use a combination of both types of treatments. They can be applied in situ but they last longer if applied during manufacture. For expert information and advice on all aspects of carpet and upholstery cleaning, contact the National Carpet Cleaners' Association (NCCA) logo, which can be found on the carpet itself, or on the point-of-sale literature.

Natural-fibre floor coverings

Suitable for all dry areas.

These traditional coverings have been around since the days of the Ancient Egyptians but have become more popular in recent years as they provide a warm, muted background for many styles of room, contemporary or period. A wide range of weaves, colours and styles are available and they are hardwearing; and do not suffer from static.

Choose natural-fibre flooring with a latex backing for a total fitted look. The backing helps it to stay flat and keep its shape. Extra underlay will increase their comfort and insulation. It can be fitted or loose.

TYPES OF NATURAL-FIBRE FLOOR COVERINGS

- ◉ **COIR** Made from coconut husks, with a coarse texture. Suitable for most rooms, but too scratchy for areas where you might sit on the floor – e.g. in a playroom.
- ◉ **JUTE** Made from bark, yet soft underfoot. Suitable for bedrooms and other areas where wear is light. Treat with an anti-stain protector.
- ◉ **MIXED FIBRES** Combines the best qualities of natural flooring with the practicality of other fibres such as wool. Suitable for use anywhere in the house.

- ◉ **RUSH MATTING** A hardwearing flooring similar to seagrass. Rush fibres give a smooth, flat finish that wears well, but take care with furniture legs, castors and high heels.
- ◉ **SEAGRASS** Woven into herringbone or basketweave designs, it is hardwearing and ideal for hallways. Slightly slippery finish makes it unsuitable for stairways.
- ◉ **SISAL** Made from a cactus-like plant, it is tough and hardwearing. Suitable for busy areas such as living rooms, and hallways. Soft woven sisal is suitable for bedrooms.

FLOORING ROOM BY ROOM

Kitchens

Needs to be easy to clean, waterproof, tough, grease and spill resistant, non-slip and comfortable. Vinyl and linoleum are a good choice.

Lounge/living areas

Comfort and appearance are important. Flooring needs to be hardwearing, especially in areas in front of chairs and sofas.

Halls and landings

A very heavy wear area so if using carpet look for the corresponding BCMA label. To help prolong its life use scraper mats outside exterior doors and door mats inside.

Stairs

Very heavy wear area, especially the first step or two. Risers are kicked and edges scuffed over time. Flooring must be safe and durable.

If using carpet, avoid a pattern that disguises the stair edges: it may confuse young children and the elderly.

Foam-backed carpets wear quickly on stairs. Chunky, low-density loop-pile carpets are not the right choice either as the backing is exposed between the carpet tufts as it covers the nose (edge) of the tread.

Bedrooms

As we often walk about in bare feet, carpet is the best choice for comfort. A longer, more luxurious pile is suitable, but in children's rooms you want tough stain-resistant carpets.

Bathrooms

Flooring should be non-slip, rot resistant, comfortable and hygienic. Use cork with non-slip bath mats. Ceramic tiles look good but are cold, slippery and the grouting traps dirt; unglazed textured tiles are safer. Cushioned vinyl or rubber is a good choice.

Green tip

There are many good reasons why you should choose sustainable flooring. Traditional flooring industries use techniques and products that can be harmful to the environment, whether it be in energy-intensive and pollution-increasing methods, or in non-biodegradable waste which can poison the environment for decades after the flooring has been discarded. Many manufacturers are now trying to reduce this negative impact by promoting 'sustainable flooring' choices, so if you are concerned about the environment, here are a few suggestions to help you choose a new floor that will not only look beautiful, but also be more eco-friendly.

Firstly, think about more than just the main flooring surface – among the chief environmental offenders are petroleum products, particularly polypropylene, which is typically used in carpet underlay materials. Instead, go for felt (made from recycled materials) or 'crumb' rubber underlays (made from recycled tyres). To further increase environmental benefits, tack the underlay down with nails instead of using glue.

✳ **CARPET** Go for carpets made from natural fibres, such as wool, jute sisal and coir. It's also possible to buy recycled carpet, made from previously used materials such as plastic, cotton and nylon. Consider using carpet tiles – these can be moved around throughout their life, and worn individual tiles can be replaced rather than having to buy an entire new carpet. Carpets backed with a rubber and latex gel are preferable to traditional polypropylene backings.

✳ **WOOD** If you must go for solid wood flooring, then look for brands with Forest Stewardship Council certification. This means the wood has come from responsibly managed forests. Or you could opt for reclaimed wood, which often has more character than freshly sawn timber, and a beautiful, deep patina.

✳ **OTHER TYPES OF HARD FLOORING** Good sustainable choices include bamboo, cork, natural linoleum, and recycled glass, rubber and ceramic tiles. If you like stone floors, go for softer types like slate and sandstone. These are found closer to the earth's surface, so are easier to mine and require less energy and pollution-emitting extraction processes.

Home Office

If you want to work from home on a regular basis it is important to set aside home office space with room for computer equipment, printer, files, stationery and reference materials. Make sure that your contents insurance covers you for home working.

FINDING SPACE

A dedicated room is the ideal home office, but if you don't have a spare room try to allocate space on a landing or in a large hallway. You might want to consider a purpose-built garden studio, if you have space outside; these wooden chalet or cabin style buildings are not as expensive as building an extension and don't usually require planning permission.

If you need to site your office in the corner of a room that is used for other purposes, then choose a cupboard that enables you to shut away your office equipment at the end of a day, or use a screen to separate off the area. It is important that you can work without interruptions or noise, so if you are siting your office in a multi-purpose room, take this into account. For example, if you have children and they congregate in the living room to watch television after school, and you want to work in the late afternoon or evening, it might be better to convert a corner of a bedroom into your office.

When you are assessing a potential space, make sure that there are enough sockets for your computer, printer and other equipment. You will also need a telephone line and Internet access.

EQUIPMENT AND FURNITURE

Your work will go more smoothly if you take into account organisation, comfort and ease of use when furnishing your home office.

Desks

There is a wide range of styles available to suit any type of decor, from traditional wooden bureaus, to a simple shelf that folds away when not in use. Many modern desks are designed as workstations that take into account the needs of computer users.

Size is a key consideration. If you are going to use your office for the occasional day's home working and for managing household paperwork on your laptop then you don't need a large surface – you might even be able to manage without a designated desk and just use the kitchen table. However, if you are working at home on a daily basis, you will need a permanent workstation with sufficient space for your computer monitor and keyboard, printer, an area for writing, in and out trays, and containers with small supplies such as pens and paperclips.

If your desk doesn't have filing drawers built in, place your filing cabinet near your desk so that you can use it as you work, without getting

TIP
Think about cable management when choosing a new desk, as loose cables snaking over the floor can be a trip hazard. Look for desks with a hole in the worktop or with hollow legs that cables can be fed through.

Green tip
Think about making space for recycling – have separate bins for paper and toner cartridges near your desk.

up. This will encourage you to file things as you go along and not build up huge piles of paperwork awaiting filing.

Desk seating

If you are going to be working in your home office for long periods, you should invest in a well-designed, adjustable chair that supports your back and shoulders properly, and can be raised or lowered so that you can sit with your feet flat on the floor. If you have back problems, select an ergonomically designed model that is guaranteed to provide the correct lumbar and neck support.

Desk lighting

To avoid eyestrain, don't rely on overhead lighting alone. You will need a good desk light with an adjustable arm, placed so that it doesn't cast a shadow on your work.

Light from windows or a desk lamp can cause glare problems for your computer screen. When deciding where to site your desk, make sure you can position your screen with its back to the window, choose a desk lamp with a movable head so that you can set it at a suitable angle, and don't position any mirrors where they can create reflections on to the screen.

Other equipment

There are a few basic items of equipment every home office needs: a shredder, a calculator, a printer and stationery supplies. If you are working from home full-time you may also want a photocopier, a scanner and a fax machine; you can save space by buying a combination machine (printer/scanner/copier/fax).

Office equipment such as computers and photocopiers may have a detrimental effect on air quality, depleting the level of natural ions, which can make you feel stressed and exhausted. Install an ionizer and some green plants to redress the balance and help keep your energy levels high.

STORAGE AND FILING

Keep items you use every day to hand, on or near to your desk area. You will need shelves and a filing solution for things in regular use and somewhere free from damp to archive paperwork long-term.

There is a wide variety of storage furniture available, including pieces especially designed for the home office. You may want to repurpose furniture you already own, but if you are buying new items, then look for co-ordinated or modular pieces that will help create an uncluttered look.

If you don't have a great deal of paperwork some attractive box files you can store on a nearby shelf might be the answer. For a regularly used home office, filing cabinets are a compact solution. Look for heavy-duty ones designed for offices as the cheaper home alternatives are flimsy and won't stand up to everyday use. A set of open shelves that will hold box files and can be screened by a pull-down blind is an inexpensive alternative. If you are short of space, consider a moveable cabinet on castors that can fit under your desk when not in use.

TIP

A chair or a roll-out cabinet on wheels can be more versatile in a small space, but bear in mind that they are better suited to hard flooring.

Safety and security tips

Don't forget to take into account safety and security issues when planning your home office. If you have a garden studio office it is particularly important to make sure it is as secure as your main dwelling – it is likely to contain expensive computer equipment and could be an easy target for burglars. Fit window and door locks and install motion sensor lighting. Keep an inventory list of your equipment and make sure it is added to your contents insurance.

Ensure you take the following preventive measures:

- **ELECTRICITY** Consider whether you need to install extra sockets so you don't overload the existing sockets.

- **TRIP HAZARDS** Tidy away trailing wires.

- **POISONS** Keep glue, printer inks and toner securely locked away as they could harm children if ingested.

- **BOOKSHELVES** Make sure these are secured to the wall so that they can't topple over.

- **FIRE EXTINGUISHER** Ensure there is one to hand.

- **BACKING UP** Make sure you back up your important files and keep them in a separate place.

Home Entertainment

Technology is transforming how we access entertainment at home and getting it right is as important as choosing the decor.

- -

TVS

The digital revolution

All new televisions can receive a Freeview digital signal with up to 50 TV channels and 24 radio channels, paying only the BBC licence fee. You can also get free satellite TV with Freesat, or pay to receive additional channels from Sky (satellite), Virgin (cable) or BT (Freeview plus Internet). From 2012 only digital TV will be broadcast (earlier in some regions) – older TVs will require a Freeview box to get a picture. See www.freeview.co.uk for details.

Where to put it?

A modern flat screen TV is much more flexible than the old, chunky boxes. The corner of the room still has the advantage of being visible from a wider range of seating positions, so is probably best with a big family. But for elegance, a flat screen TV can be wall mounted, freeing up space and reducing clutter. Simple mounts fix the TV to the wall like a picture frame, while more expensive mounts 'float' the TV, meaning it can be adjusted for angle, or positioned in the corner of a room.

High definition

High definition (or HD) televisions have a clearer, more detailed picture and better sound than a standard TV. But ordinary programmes won't look any different – you need an HD source to watch. Blu-ray is the HD equivalent of DVD, while a number of broadcast services have HD channels. Sky has the most, followed by Virgin Media and Freesat.

Essential specifications

Check these when choosing a TV:

- **CONTRAST RATIO** The main difference between a cheap flat screen TV and a good one is the contrast ratio. A low contrast ratio gives dull, flat looking pictures. Look for a contrast ratio of 15,000:1 or more.

- **GOOD RANGE OF INPUTS** Look for at least two and preferably three HDMI (HD) sockets and two SCART (standard definition) sockets on your main TV.

CHOOSING A TV: LCD OR PLASMA?

- -

LCDS

- Available in a wider range of sizes.
- Greener – uses less energy.
- Better with close-up, high-resolution images, for example with games.
- Unlike plasma, won't burn in an image if left with the same picture for a long time.

PLASMA

- Cheaper for very large screens.
- Deeper blacks.
- Better when viewed at an extreme angle.

LED TVS

A few TVs have LED technology, which is a variant on LCD using a different backlight. LED TVs can be thinner than LCD, and often have better contrast and wider viewing angles, but are more expensive.

The standard Freeview system has HD channels in some areas from 2010, and across most of the country by 2012, but you will need a Freeview HD receiver.

High definition TVs come with two levels of specification. HD Ready is the basic. Full HD Ready (also called 1080p) displays higher quality images, which are noticeably better on screens over 37in. If financially practical, go for Full HD Ready to future proof your TV.

2010 saw the introduction of 3D TVs. These combine with expensive 'active shutter' glasses, controlled by the TV, to give the kind of three dimensional images available at the cinema for some movies. Programmes have to be broadcast in 3D to have any benefit: Sky launched a 3D channel in 2010, using their Sky HD+ box, while a few 3D movies are available on Blu-ray, from a standard Blu-ray player. This is liable to be something for the technology lover only for a good few years.

HOME CINEMA

Home cinema boosts TV sound quality and power, adding extra channels and usually incorporating a DVD or Blu-ray player. A typical system has two front speakers, two speakers behind the viewer and a centrally placed mono speaker for bass effects.

If you want cinema sound without the trailing wires, get a sound projector. Placed under the TV, these bounce sound off the walls, adjusting the balance until the effect is a convincing surround sound. Sound projectors are significantly more expensive than basic home cinema.

DVD, Blu-ray and TV recorders

DVD and Blu-ray have replaced tape as a way of watching pre-recorded movies and TV shows. DVD is still excellent quality, but Blu-ray adds high definition (HD) at a price – both players and the discs are more expensive.

For long-term storage, go for a DVD recorder, but for TV time shifting the best solution is the digital TV recorder (sometimes called a PVR). All the main digital broadcasters have recorders that are usually branded 'plus' – so Sky Plus, Freeview Plus etc.

A digital recorder stores many hours of recorded TV on a computer hard disc. Unlike video recorders, programming one is easy. It is just a matter of choosing a programme from an on-screen guide. Features vary, but most modern TV recorders can record a whole series with a push of a button, pause live TV, and record two programmes at a time.

Games consoles

Games consoles are an essential part of the home entertainment package for the young and young at heart. Main contenders are the Nintendo Wii, with unique motion-based controls and a lot of games for family and younger players, the Sony Playstation 3, with excellent graphics and a built-in Blu-ray player (the other consoles act as DVD players), and the Microsoft Xbox 360, which is often the dedicated gamer's choice. All the consoles have optional online connection to play games across the Internet, but this is more sophisticated with the Playstation and the Xbox. Bear in mind the cost of games as well as the console.

POINTS TO CONSIDER WHEN CHOOSING A SOUND SYSTEM

⊙ **POWER OUTPUT** The power output indicates not only how loud the system can go but how full a sound it produces. The bigger the better.

⊙ **BASS BOOST** Most modern sound systems have small speakers, so need all the help they can get with deep bass sounds. Some bass boost features are better than others: try before buying.

⊙ **INPUTS AND OUTPUTS** It is useful to be able to bring in a signal from a portable device (aux in), and a built-in iPod dock increases flexibility. Similarly, an auxiliary output socket and headphones socket give more output choice.

SOUND SYSTEMS AND IPOD DOCKS

For most home use a micro hi-fi, typically combining a CD player and a radio, is sufficient, though audio buffs still prefer a component system, where each part of the hi-fi is a separate box. If you own an iPod or MP3 player, consider an iPod/MP3 dock – this plays the music on your portable device through speakers big enough to produce a worthwhile sound. This way, your whole music library is available at the touch of button.

RADIOS

With radio available from many other sources – computers, digital TVs, iPod docks and hi-fis – the standalone radio is less in demand, but it can still find a place in the kitchen, bedroom or bathroom. The main decision is between DAB (Digital Audio Broadcasting) digital radio and conventional FM. FM is cheaper, and reception is stronger in some areas, but DAB gives a wider range of stations, has one touch tuning and will eventually replace FM, just as digital TV is replacing conventional TV. See www.getdigitalradio.com for more information. If you go for FM, look for RDS (Radio Data System), which displays the station names.

STREAMING AUDIO AND VIDEO

One further option is to stream sound or video. The audio or video is stored on your home computer, but can be listened to and watched elsewhere in the house. You can also buy a dedicated box to host the music and video on, but these are expensive. The most common setup is to have a small box attached to a hi-fi system that connects it to your computer through a wireless network. With this in place, and appropriate software on the computer, you can play any music files on the computer – your whole music library – wherever your hi-fi is in the house. It is like an iPod dock with no iPod required.

Equipment for Outdoor Spaces

Garden tools and furniture must cope with extremes of temperature, the stresses of digging etc., so a well-informed choice is very important.

GARDEN TOOLS

There is a mammoth difference between having the right tool for the job, and just making do. The more comfortable and easier it is to do the job, the more likely you are to do it and the more pleasurable it will be. In reality, it changes keeping the garden under control from a chore to working at leisure.

Digging tools

When choosing a conventional spade look for a head made from one piece of metal. Known as solid forged, this type is stronger than pressed steel, which is more likely to have weak joints. A longer socket also adds strength to a spade because it houses the weak point where the metal and wooden handle join.

Digging for a long period can cause backache. To avoid this, choose the weight of your spade carefully. The material used to make a spade will determine its weight.

The length of the shaft can vary by about 20cm/8in on different spades. Longer shafts mean less bending.

Spade handles can be D- or T-shaped; the choice is down to personal preference.

ERGONOMIC TOOLS

There are also ergonomically designed spades and other digging tools available, which do not look like conventional spades. They have been specially designed with a bend in the handle, so that the spade bends rather than your back. This gives more momentum when lifting. The handles are often longer. There is also a range of spades that

Avoiding back strain when digging

200,000 people suffer from backache due to gardening.

- Try to dig on a fine day. If the soil is wet it can be twice as heavy.
- Wear a good pair of boots with treads.
- Always keep warm.
- Do some loosening-up exercises before starting.
- Change jobs frequently.
- Don't dig for too long.
- Keep your back straight and bend at the knees.

STAINLESS-STEEL SPADES

Most tools are made from carbon steel, which is often coated to prolong its life. The coating wears off and so pitting and rusting occur, which impairs performance.

For a heavy clay soil, a stainless-steel tool makes digging much easier. The soil adheres less to the polished surface, so the spade does not get as heavy. The quality of the stainless steel can vary but generally these spades are much more expensive than those made of carbon steel.

TIP
When buying a spade, make sure it is equally comfortable when you are wearing gardening gloves.

CHOOSING GARDEN FURNITURE

- **CAST AND WROUGHT IRON** Cast and wrought iron are made from the same basic materials, but where cast iron is shaped using a mould, wrought iron is hammered into shape.

  Painted cast-iron furniture is usually based on traditional Victorian designs with table and chair sets (now copied in cast aluminium). The style of the furniture makes it quite rigid and not suitable for lounging in. It is usually painted white, green or black, and the paintwork will need annual maintenance.

  Cast iron is an expensive and rather impractical option for garden furniture and is hence not seen as frequently as other types. Unless you have your heart set on the real thing, it's more practical to look at cast-aluminium copies (see below).

  Wrought and cast iron are also used for the end supports of wooden benches. Look for durable hardwood slats as the bench is likely to be left out in all weathers.

  Iron is very heavy, so consider where the furniture will be positioned. It won't be appropriate if you want furniture you can move about, or if there is no firm surface to stand it on. The weight does, however, make it less likely to be lifted by a thief.

- **CAST ALUMINIUM** This looks like cast iron in traditional designs, but is much lighter and doesn't rust. It is also cheaper. Like cast iron, the designs are rigid and not comfortable for lounging.

- **SOLID WOOD** Durability and weather resistance varies depending on the type of wood used: Oak, Sweet Chestnut and Western Red Cedar are naturally resistant to rot, but prolonged damp spells will eventually lead to discoloration.

  Furniture from non-durable woods such as Ash, Beech, Elm, European Redwood, Pine and Spruce will need preserving and retreatment regularly. Similarly, painted wood will require regular maintenance to keep it in good condition. To reduce the risk of rotting, site furniture on concrete or gravel.

  Consider where the furniture will be positioned as solid wood can be heavy. For more portable wooden furniture consider folding slatted pine furniture, or casual seating such as directors' or deck chairs.

- **SYNTHETIC RESIN/INJECTION-MOULDED PLASTIC** Lightweight, durable and available in a variety of styles, synthetic resin is practical and comfortable. Good-quality furniture of this type is very resistant to moisture and deterioration due to chemicals.

  It is usually made in white, so look for UV-stabilised resin that shouldn't fade in the sun. Cheaper furniture will contain more chalk and yellow in the sunlight more quickly. Coloured styles will be less likely to show stains and signs of ageing.

  For convenience of moving or storage look for folding or stackable styles.

- **TUBULAR METAL** A practical, portable option. Its folding styles make storage simple. The tubular steel is either coated with zinc to prevent rusting or more commonly with polyester or epoxy resin (white or green) This feels like a plastic coating, is chip resistant and preserves the metal. The furniture should still be kept indoors to prevent the rivets rusting and making it look shabby.

  Choose between woven plastic or cloth seats and cushions.

- **CANE/WICKER** More suitable for attractive conservatory furniture that can be moved into the garden occasionally, rather than for heavy garden use. Available in cane, rattan, willow and bamboo.

  Look for makes that have been varnished or sealed, as they will then only need vacuuming and wiping with a damp cloth to remove dust.

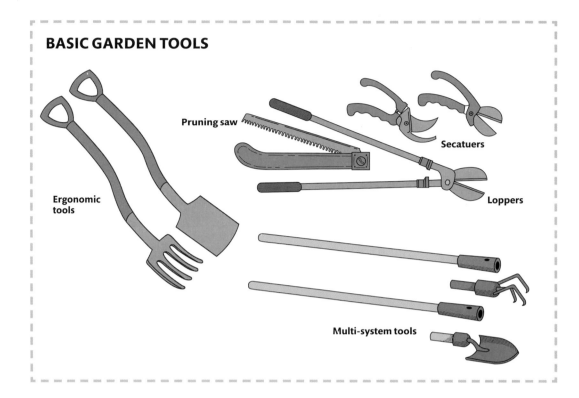

BASIC GARDEN TOOLS

Pruning saw

Secatuers

Ergonomic tools

Loppers

Multi-system tools

incorporates a stirrup design, which means you can put your foot in the middle of the spade and use your full weight to dig.

Hand tools

If you are buying hand tools for the first time choose multi-system tools, which use interchangeable heads with a choice of handles of different lengths. There is a range of telescopic handles: those for use while standing, or short handles.

Although they cost more than conventional tools initially, because of the multi-purpose function you only buy the handles once and then add whichever tool head you need. The essentials are a trowel and a three-pronged cultivator. They are also useful when storage space is limited.

Choose one with a firm click-fit attachment (like a seat belt) rather than a screw fitting. The screw fittings are fiddly and if soil gets into the fixing, locking the two pieces together could be a problem.

Short-handled tools are useful if working on rockeries or raised beds, or gardening from a seated or kneeling position rather than standing. They represent better value for children than some flimsy children's tools.

Electric tools

In a large garden, electric tools are ideal for cutting a big expanse of lawn or pruning a long hedge.

At first, electrically-powered tools had to be connected with a flex to a power point. In recent years, however, rechargeable battery-powered tools have become very popular. As they have no leads you can use the tools at the bottom of the garden away from a power point, and there is no danger of cutting through an electric flex. Battery-powered tools also tend to be quieter and lighter to hold. Most will operate for about 20 minutes before they need to be recharged. Lawnmowers, grass shears and hedge trimmers are all available as battery-powered models.

Safety and performance of electric tools have improved significantly in recent years. Before buying, always check for safety features. This is particularly important for hedge trimmers. All models should incorporate a lock-off switch with a two-step starting procedure, and a hand guard. When not in use always place a plastic cover over the blades.

Lawnmowers

BATTERY (CORDLESS) Ideal if the garden is an awkward shape as there is no mains cable to watch for. As flexible as petrol mowers, but easier to start and maintain. Not good for long grass and only about 45 minutes cutting time per charge.

LAWNMOWER FEATURES TO LOOK FOR

- **AUTOMATIC DRIVE SYSTEM** Similar to 'self-propelled', but you can control the speed of the mower to suit your own pace by adjusting the amount of pressure applied to the handle.
- **CABLE RESTRAINT** Special clip that slides across the handle frame, to keep the flex out of the way.
- **CUTTING HEIGHT** Lets you adjust the height of the cutting blade depending upon the length of the grass.
- **CUTTING WIDTH** Refers to blade width of the mower. A larger width is better for big gardens as you need to mow fewer lengths. Medium gardens need a cutting width of around 30cm/12in.
- **PLASTIC SAFETY BLADE** Cuts grass but, unlike metal, won't cut the electric cable if you run over it.

- **RECYCLER FACILITY** Instead of collecting grass in a grass box, grass is chopped and forced back into the lawn to 'feed' it.
- **ROTO-STOP** Allows you to empty the grass box while the engine is running, and lets you disengage the mower's blade so you can turn corners without scalping the lawn.
- **SAFETY KEY** Special overload protection fuse featured on cordless mowers. Mower will not work unless fitted.
- **SELF-PROPELLED** Mower is power-driven to make it easier to push and manoeuvre, but you cannot control the speed.
- **STRIPING FLAP** Works like a rear roller to produce 'bowling green' stripes on the lawn.

WHICH CUT IS BEST FOR YOUR LAWN?

- **CYLINDER** Series of rotating blades that cut grass with a scissor-like action against a fixed lower blade.

  RESULTS Gives a high-quality result with a traditional 'bowling green' finish, but needs a lot of maintenance.

- **HOVER** Single metal or plastic blade rotates horizontally at high speed. Fan beneath the hood creates an air cushion, making the mower 'hover' above grass.

  RESULTS Mowing in a straight line can be difficult, but the mower is light and easy to manoeuvre, especially across uneven areas.

- **ROTARY** Blade rotates horizontally at high speeds, cutting grass with a scythe-like action. Wheels raise the mower above the lawn and some have rollers to leave a traditional striped finish.

  RESULTS Gives a reasonable cut and good for all-purpose lawns and overgrown grass.

ELECTRIC Good for small to medium gardens as they are light-weight and need little maintenance. Best suited to square or rectangular gardens with no awkward areas, where mowing is no more than 60m/197ft from a power socket. Always plug an electric lawnmower in via an RCD (residual current device) to avoid the risk of electric shock should you accidentally cut through the cable.

PETROL Good choice for larger gardens as they do not need to be plugged in. Require more maintenance and are generally noisier and heavier than battery or electric mowers. Self-propelled petrol mowers make much lighter work of cutting grass.

Pruning tools

SECATEURS

There are two types of cutting action available: anvil and by-pass.

ANVIL Designed for heavier pruning. These work like a ratchet, cutting in two stages. First they grip and then they cut.

BY-PASS Use an action like scissors, and should be used for delicate pruning.

LOPPERS

Use these for thicker branches. They are similar to secateurs but have longer handles, giving you much greater leverage and reach.

PRUNING SAWS

Suitable for even heavier pruning work, they are a better choice for thicker branches with less intricate work.

They fold in half with a hinge in the centre and the sharp teeth enclosed.

POINTS TO CONSIDER WHEN CHOOSING PRUNING TOOLS

SECATEURS

⊙ A smooth action is essential. This is controlled by a spring, and buffers on the handle ends to stop jarring. These features become obvious after long periods of work.

⊙ Some manufacturers make right- and left-handed versions.

⊙ Some models have a rolling top handle so that as you squeeze the secateurs it rotates in the palm of your hand. This shifts the pressure around the palm of your hand, reducing the risk of blisters.

⊙ Secateurs usually have brightly coloured handles, to avoid losing them among cuttings or bushes.

LOPPERS

⊙ Like secateurs, these are available as by-pass or anvil construction.

⊙ Weight is an important consideration because loppers are usually used at shoulder level.

⊙ Loppers vary in length, so choose according to your height.

PRUNING SAWS

⊙ Check the balance and ease of opening.

⊙ Check the length of the blade, because it will be used for wood over 3cm/1$\frac{1}{4}$in thick. With a shorter blade you have greater control, but a longer blade gets the job done more quickly.

⊙ These saws are self-sharpening.

RAINWATER BUTTS

Investing in a rainwater butt to use on your garden can save a great deal of treated tap water. They can store run-off water from roofs of houses, greenhouses and sheds, fit neatly against walls and can be placed near vegetable beds to make watering easy. Water butts are easy to fit too:

- Select a drainpipe that is not in a prominent position with plenty of room to stand a butt nearby.
- Cut the downpipe at the desired height and fit a diverter to the water butt.
- Ensure the butt is on a water butt stand or firm base, preferably above the ground, so you can easily fit a watering can under the tap.
- A firm base is important otherwise, when the water butt is full, it could affect the angle of the diverters and cause them to overflow. It is best to purchase a conventional water butt stand.
- Make sure your water butt or any other collection vessel has a secure, childproof lid. As well as protecting children, it will also prevent debris and mosquitoes from entering.

COMPOSTERS

Composting is an excellent way to recycle kitchen and garden waste, and is very easy to do. If buying a composter, make sure it is well insulated. This is important because the bacteria that break down the matter require heat to work effectively. As compost can take two to three months to produce, it is a good idea to have two composters side by side.

What to put in your compost bin

PUT IN	WHAT TO AVOID
✔ Hair and fur	✖ Meat or fish
✔ Shredded paper	✖ Coal ash
✔ Straw and hay	✖ Animal waste
✔ Animal bedding and sawdust	✖ Nappies and used tissues
✔ Crushed eggshells	✖ Dairy products
✔ Grass and plant cuttings	✖ Cooked foods
✔ Raw fruit and vegetable trimmings	✖ Coloured or treated paper
✔ Teabags and coffee granules	✖ Chemically treated wood
✔ Horse manure	✖ Diseased plants
✔ Leaves	✖ Persistent weeds

For details on how you can compost even more of your household waste, see Green tip, page 156.

ABOVE Standard composter

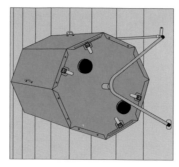

ABOVE Smartsoil composter

ABOVE Green Cone composter

FIVE WAYS TO MAKE THE BEST COMPOST

1 Start with a layer of tougher material to help drainage. Use a mix of tougher fibrous material, such as garden cuttings or prunings, and softer, wetter material such as garden waste and lawn mowings. Try to balance quantities of each or you'll get an uneven slow rot or a soggy mess. Add tougher material such as shredded cardboard if you have a lot of soft material.

2 Keep a square of old carpet on top, as well as the lid, until you've finished building up the compost heat. This helps to keep heat in.

3 Water occasionally to keep the heat moist.

4 Turn after four weeks, when the heap has cooled, to speed up and even out the rot.

5 Complete composting should take about two to three months if the tough material has first been shredded, otherwise the rotting down will take about six months. Speed it up by adding nitrogen-rich material (animal waste) or proprietary compost accelerator.

GARDEN SAFETY

See The Garden, pages 360–1 and Barbecues, page 361.

BARBECUES

Consider how often you will use the barbecue and what you will be cooking on it. If you are intending to cook large items, such as a whole chicken, choose a barbecue with a lid that will reflect heat back on to the food. Open barbecues without lids have a grill rack that sits over the heat source, and can be lowered and raised depending on the strength of the heat, and the food you are cooking. Open barbecues are suitable for cooking foods such as steaks, chops, sausages and burgers. With all types of barbecue, check that construction is sturdy and designed for stability.

Green tip

Most composting systems don't allow you to compost cooked food and meat products. However, the Swedish JK125 and JK270 domestic composters from SmartSoil Ltd (see Manufacturers, Retailers and Service Providers) will enable you turn ALL your kitchen waste into a nutritious soil-improving compost, meaning even less of your rubbish has to go to landfill.

A Green Cone or a Green Johanna system also allows you to compost all your food products. These unique systems use a combination of solar energy, oxygen and natural bacteria which digests all food waste, including cooked and uncooked meat, bones, fish, dairy, bread, pasta, vegetables and fruit into either its natural components of water and carbon dioxide with a minimal residue (Green Cone) or when garden waste is added, into a rich compost (Green Johanna). Both products are made using recycled materials. You can find more information at www.greencone.com (see Manufacturers, Retailers and Service Providers).

Disposable

A foil tray containing charcoal with a cooking grill. The charcoal is pre-soaked with lighter fluid to light instantly, and is ready to cook on in 10–15 minutes. The barbecue lasts for about one hour. A cooking grill supports food above the charcoal but you can't adjust the height to regulate cooking.

They are fun for picnics, but cooking space is limited, and you can't add extra charcoal to extend the cooking time. Care is needed in siting the barbecue and moving it after cooking, as it gets extremely hot underneath.

Portable

Small, and ideal for beginners. Portable barbecues tend to lack extras such as a wind shield, so are best used in a sheltered place.

Portables come in all sorts of shapes and sizes. Features to look for include a wind shield (some are a suitcase style with a lid), a grate to allow air flow under the coals, and folding legs. Without legs they are difficult to site; if there is no wall nearby you could find yourself cooking on the ground. The Hibachi style is compact and designed with a good air flow underneath the grate, and adjustable brackets for the food racks.

Consider how much you will be moving the barbecue. Look for a light-weight one made of aluminium as opposed to cast iron, if you will be carrying it far. Also consider how practical it is to carry around. Suitcase styles may appear convenient but are messy when you have to pack the legs back in with the greasy grill rack.

Open/brazier

Larger, open-sided barbecues, usually with a windshield into which the grill rack slots. Check these can have their height adjusted easily, so that food can be moved away from the hot coals for gentler cooking. Some barbecues have a spit or rotisserie, which also slots into the sides.

Lighting tips

- Always site on a level base. Some ventilation is needed to draw the fire and heat, so choose a spot that is neither too exposed nor too sheltered.
- Line the ash tray with aluminium foil, shiny side up, to reflect the heat and make the ashes easy to remove, but make small holes to allow ventilation.
- Pile a small quantity of charcoal in a pyramid shape, inserting a few fire lighters, or spray with barbecue lighter fluid or paste. Never use petrol, paraffin, methylated spirits or other flammable fluids.
- Light this pile, and as the heat begins to spread add more charcoal to the sides and top. Keep the pile small and to one side if you are only cooking for two.
- Light the fire about an hour before you intend to cook, to pre-heat the coals. Coals become covered with a grey ash, which may glow red in the dark. When the coals are fully covered with this ash and look cool, the cooking temperature has been reached. If you start cooking too soon, before the flames have subsided, you will end up with food that is overcooked on the outside, and uncooked in the centre.
- If the fire goes out, remove coals with tongs to a metal bucket and start everything afresh.
- Always have some means of extinguishing a fire at hand, such as a domestic fire extinguisher or fire blanket. Even sand will suffice.

Kettle/covered

Similar in size and variety to open barbecues, but with a dome to cover the food during cooking. Good for the more adventurous chef as they have more sophisticated options.

The dome concentrates the heat and keeps the moisture in the food. With the lid closed, large joints of meat can be oven roasted because the heat accumulates in the closed unit and enters the food from all sides. They can also be used open to barbecue food in the normal way.

Temperature is regulated by opening vents in the lid and fire bowl. Some have useful viewing windows.

Useful features are levers to adjust the height of the cooking racks, a motor-operated rotisserie, wheels and racks for food at the sides or underneath.

Gas

Range in size from large trolley styles to portable (but remember you'll need to carry the gas cylinder).

Contain lava rocks that are heated from beneath by gas burners. The heat is radiated from the hot rocks to give the same effect as burning coals. The gas allows easy control of the heat. They usually have a lid, and are on a trolley with wooden shelves. Gas barbecues are easy to light and heat up in only a couple of minutes.

They tend to be cleaner to maintain than other types because the rocks burn off the fats (rather like stay-clean oven liners) and don't need replacing for about five years.

Build your own

For a permanent barbecue look for a kit that includes an ash-pan, grate and cooking racks.

Alternatively, make your own with an old cooking tray or similar for an ash-pan, and an oven shelf for the grill. Remember to measure the ash-pan and grill before laying any bricks.

Choose a design with good ventilation from underneath, for example an open brick design.

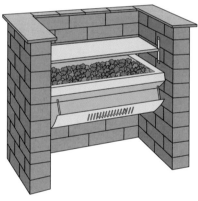

ABOVE Build your own barbecue

POINTS TO CONSIDER WHEN CHOOSING ALL BARBECUES

- ⊙ Ease of assembly.
- ⊙ Wheels for mobility.
- ⊙ Shelves and side racks for food.
- ⊙ Variety of grilling heights.
- ⊙ Tools supplied for cooking.
- ⊙ Storage space required when out of use.

Electric barbecues and grills

These use electric elements under a griddle. The same types of foods can be cooked, but they don't take on the same smoky flavour.

Check ease of cleaning: most can't be immersed in water because it would damage the electric elements.

Cooking on barbecues

- Brush grills with vegetable oil before cooking, to reduce food sticking to them, and make cleaning easier afterwards.
- For added flavour, marinate the meat, or scatter herbs or aromatic wood chips over the coals while cooking.
- To avoid charring the food on the outside, lift the grilling racks and cook for longer, or spread the coals further apart.
- Always use long-handled implements and barbecue gloves when cooking.
- A fine water spray is useful to damp down flames that flare up from dripping fat.

PATIO HEATERS

These can be either gas or log-burning. Gas models are cleaner and easier to light, and higher wattage models heat a wide area. However, their appearance and size can dominate a garden. Wood-burning models add more ambience, but can be smoky, take longer to light and give out less heat. Most heaters are flat packed for assembly and, as the average model has around 32 parts, can be quite tricky to put together.

After cooking

- Before storing or leaving the barbecue overnight make sure it is completely out and cold by extinguishing with water from a spray or covering with sand.
- Before storing for the winter, wipe clean metal parts with vegetable oil to prevent rust.
- Cover a permanently built barbecue with a plastic sheet to protect it from severe weather.
- Turn the gas supply off at the cylinder and store both the barbecue and cylinder outdoors in a well-ventilated garage or shed. Use a plug or cap to seal off the valve outlet of the gas cylinder, and make sure it is away from heat or ignition sources and combustible materials.

FIVE PATIO HEATER SAFETY TIPS

1 Look out for anti-tilt devices, which cuts the heater off if moved from an upright position, and never move a patio heater when alight.

2 Choose a model with a flame failure device that cuts off the gas if the heater goes out.

3 Patio heaters are for outdoor use only. The combustion products leaving the heater are very hot and could cause a fire inside a tent or marquee. Never position close to an awning, table umbrella or overhead trellis.

4 Stand the heater in a sheltered area to help prevent it blowing out. Most heaters can cope only with mild winds.

5 Never leave a patio heater unsupervised.

Green tip

Patio heaters are extremely unfriendly to the environment due to the amount of carbon emissions they produce. Before switching yours on, think carefully about whether you can achieve the same result by putting on some additional clothing!

Care and Maintenance

Keeping on top of household problems is a must: leaving things too long or getting caught out means you can face large and unnecessary repair bills. There are a number of simple ways you can avoid this: give your house regular check-ups both outside and in, learn how to cope with basic problems, and get to grips with a wide range of simple repair jobs. In this section you will find out how to do all this and more.

How the House Works

Before you can check that your house is running smoothly, you'll need to know how the systems inside it are designed and how they operate.

PLUMBING AND WATER HEATING

Cold-water supply

Cold water comes into the house via a high-pressure mains pipe. The supply is controlled by a stopcock, now called a stoptap, belonging to the water authority. You'll find it 60–90cm (2–3ft) underneath a square metal flap somewhere outside the house, usually in the front garden. If your home is very old, this may be the only stoptap, and in an emergency, you'll need to turn the water off here. Because it's so deep, a special tool is required.

Most homes have an internal stoptap as well, which can be used to shut off the water if a pipe bursts or the cistern overflows. This is usually in the kitchen, or a downstairs toilet or bathroom, close to where the mains supply enters the house, although occasionally you'll find it located in the airing cupboard.

TIP
The water board is responsible for the mains pipe on its side of the exterior stoptap; the house owner is responsible for anything to do with the plumbing that happens on the other side.

BELOW Plumbing and water supplies in the home

Diagram only – does not include requirements of water by-laws

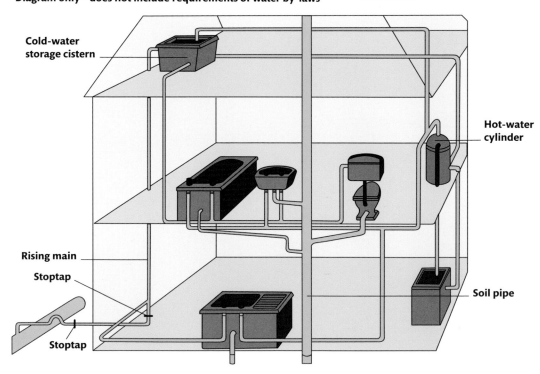

Cold-water storage cistern

Hot-water cylinder

Rising main

Stoptap

Soil pipe

Stoptap

DIRECT PLUMBING SYSTEMS

This type of system supplies all the cold taps in the house with water from the rising main, a continuation of the mains pipe. This goes all the way up the house to the cold-water storage cistern, a rectangular, open-top tank at the highest point of the house: in the roof space, loft or attic. As water is drawn from the cistern and the level drops, water from the rising main tops it up, and a float valve cuts off the incoming supply when the correct level is reached. Because all the cold taps in the house are connected to the rising main, the cold-water tank only supplies water to the hot-water cylinder.

INDIRECT PLUMBING SYSTEMS

Found in most houses. Only one cold tap, usually the one that supplies the kitchen sink, is connected directly to the mains. Drinking water should be drawn from this tap, because other taps, and toilets, will be fed with water from the cold-water storage cistern, which also sends water to the hot-water cylinder.

PIPEWORK AND VALVES There are three pipes leading from the cistern in an indirect plumbing system, two if the plumbing is direct.

❶ The overflow pipe prevents flooding if the cistern float valve fails, by directing water outside the house. Dripping from this pipe is a visible warning that the valve needs attention (see Dripping Overflow, page 208). Most modern cisterns' float valves have plastic floats that are virtually trouble-free. Older houses may still have copper balls for floats, which can spring a leak, and it's well worth replacing these with plastic ones before they give trouble.

❷ In indirect plumbing systems, another pipe serves the other cold taps in the house, lavatory cisterns, and appliances such as power showers and bidets.

❸ The third pipe feeds the hot-water cylinder, usually located in the airing cupboard.

The cold-water system also incorporates wheeled gate valves, which can be turned off to isolate the supply in an emergency. If you find that a stoptap or gate valve has seized, it's worth using some form of penetrating oil to free it. Don't use force if it won't budge, as this could fracture the capstan or wheel head, or even worse, break the valve.

How to cure an airlock

Air trapped in the pipes can interrupt the hot-water supply or bring it to a stop altogether. You can cure it, using pressure from the mains. Use a piece of hosepipe to connect the tap without water to the mains pipe, usually the cold-water tap at the kitchen sink. Turn both taps on and leave for a few minutes. Remove the hose from the affected tap and try it: it should run freely. If it doesn't, try the procedure again.

Cover up?

If the cistern is uncovered, it should be checked regularly to make sure it's not contaminated by birds, insects or other debris. It's worth covering it with a plastic top to make sure the water is clean and to stop particles damaging taps, valves and other components, but make sure the lid doesn't exclude air as well.

How to fix noisy pipes

Loud 'water hammer' noises indicate that plumbing components, in the tap or cistern, need replacing. In hard water areas, a knocking noise may also be caused by a build-up of limescale in the pipes. Consider a water softener to solve the problem, or try padding the pipe with a piece of foam until you can find the source of the trouble.

TIP
Lubricate stoptaps and gate valves with a thin oil and turn them off and on from time to time, to make sure they work if you need to cut off the supply in an emergency.

TIP
Buy a roll of waterproof mastic tape to keep for emergency plumbing repairs.

Most water pipes are made from plastic or copper, but you may also find stainless or galvanised steel. Very old houses may still have lead plumbing, which can be a health hazard. Contact your local water supplier for advice, and meanwhile, run the cold tap for several minutes before using the water for drinking or cooking. Additional, consider using a water filter whenever possible.

It is a good idea to inspect all pipework regularly. Though it's not possible to see concealed pipes, a quick check of the joints of those you can see is well worth the effort. Look for tell-tale signs such as moisture round joints, or discolouration of the pipework, walls or floors.

Although you are allowed to carry out straightforward repairs yourself, you must comply with water and electricity company requirements and building regulations when extending or installing a plumbing system. Contact your local authority building control officer for information.

Hot-water systems

Water heated by a boiler or immersion heater is stored in a hot-water cylinder, which usually ranges in size from 114–227 litres/25–50 gallons, though larger capacities are available. Cylinders need a thick lagging jacket made to BS 5615 (see Improving Energy Efficiency, pages 184–87). If you're replacing a hot-water cylinder, it's possible to buy one with a polyurethane shell for better insulation.

INDIRECT HOT-WATER SYSTEMS

Have a heat exchanger, or coiled pipe, inside the hot-water cylinder. Hot water from the boiler circulates inside the heat exchanger, which heats the cold water that surrounds it. The heat exchanger has its own small water tank in the loft, and a vent pipe, which takes steam and hot air back to this cistern.

DIRECT HOT-WATER SYSTEMS

Usually supplied by an electric immersion heater. Cheaper and easier to install than indirect hot-water systems, but won't supply central-heating radiators.

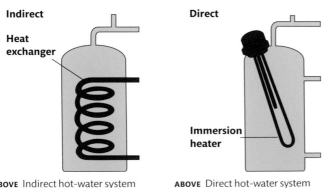

Indirect

Heat exchanger

Direct

Immersion heater

ABOVE Indirect hot-water system   ABOVE Direct hot-water system

Drainage systems

Rainwater always drains into downpipes outside the house so that the drains will not be flooded if there is a storm, but waste water and sewage may be taken away separately or together.

Pipe sizes

Pipe sizes are now metric: 15mm (½in), 22mm (¾in) and 28mm (1in). Because metric pipes are measured externally and imperial plumbing is measured internally, there may be a discrepancy in size, and problems can occur if you need to extend or repair an old system. Metric adaptors are available to make sure joints are tight, and you will need special adaptors when joining plastic pipes to metal.

Green tip

More and more houses, especially new ones, are being fitted with water meters, which means you pay for the amount you use. Make sure taps don't leak (see How to Mend Leaking Taps, pages 190–2). and turn them off properly. If you wish, you can have push taps fitted in cloakrooms or utility rooms, which turn themselves off after a predetermined interval. Modern toilet cisterns have a much reduced water capacity, making them just as efficient, but more economical. Look for dual-flow toilets that have a smaller flush for liquid waste, and a larger flush for solid waste.

OTHER FORMS OF WATER HEATING

⊙ **BACK BOILERS** So-called because they are incorporated into the back of a gas or coal fire. Their advantage is that they supply water to the hot-water cylinder, so you get hot water at the same time, but coal-fired models cannot supply hot water without lighting the fire.

⊙ **COMBINATION BOILERS** Provide both hot water and central heating, diverting water from the radiators when there's a demand for hot water. The advantage is that water is heated as required, so no hot-water tank is needed; the disadvantage is that the boiler may not be able to supply sufficient warmth and hot water simultaneously for a large family.

⊙ **GAS, COAL, OIL, OR WOOD-FUELLED COOKING RANGES** Such as those by Aga/Raeburn, can provide hot water as well as central heating and cooking facilities.

⊙ **IMMERSION HEATERS** Can be fitted to the hot-water cylinder, where there is no boiler, or for use when the boiler is turned off or if it breaks down. Immersion heaters are powered by electricity and work on the same principle as an element in an electric kettle.

⊙ **INSTANTANEOUS WATER HEATERS** Connected directly to the rising main, these heat water as you use it, so you are spared the expense of keeping it warm until it's needed. Powered by either gas or electricity, they can be fitted directly over a sink, but are only suitable for producing relatively small amounts of hot water. Gas heaters must not be fitted in bathrooms unless they have a balanced flue to make sure that harmful gases are extracted. Regular maintenance is also essential.

⊙ **ELECTRIC HEATERS** Available in 3kW sizes for basins; 7–9kW for showers. They must be carefully sited and installed to prevent any possibility of wet hands coming into contact with the electricity supply, which could cause an electric shock.

TWO-PIPE SYSTEMS

Found in older houses. Waste water from sinks, baths and basins is taken by pipes outside the house to a gully at ground level. This has a U bend to prevent smells and an underground pipe that empties into the main drain. Waste from toilets uses a separate soil pipe, connected directly to the drains.

SINGLE-STACK SYSTEMS

Have been standard for the past 40 years. With the possible exception of the kitchen sink, which may send water down a separate gully, and a downstairs toilet, which may have its own drain leading to a manhole (also called an inspection chamber), all waste water and sewage drains into a single soil pipe, which is often inside the house.

TIP
If you are thinking of buying a house that's not on mains drainage, have the cesspit or septic tank professionally checked to make sure it is in good order and that it is big enough for your family.

LEFT Drainage systems

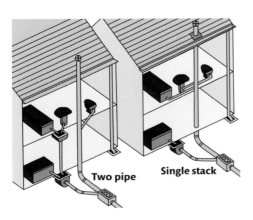

Two pipe   **Single stack**

Houses in towns are linked to mains drainage systems, but in the country, waste may be stored in a cesspit or a septic tank. Cesspits need emptying regularly, but septic tanks use bacteria to break down the sewage and disperse the waste underground. All the waste must be siphoned off via a filter system to drain on to the property.

ELECTRIC CIRCUITS

Electricity comes into the house via an armoured cable connected to a sealed cut-out unit, and like the meter it supplies, it is installed by the local electricity company. The domestic 'consumer unit' (still often called the fuse box), which incorporates a master on/off switch and fuses, or the more modern miniature circuit breakers, is also wired from the meter. Modern systems may have additional protection from a residual current device (RCD).

Miniature circuit breakers have a trip switch, which cuts off the supply if it is overloaded, and which can be reset later. There is usually one circuit breaker for each circuit.

Fuses are an intentionally 'weak link' in the system, designed to melt in the case of an overload and so protect the appliance and prevent any risk of fire. Fuses can be cartridges or one of three types of wired holder: a

TIP

If your system uses fuses, keep a supply of spare fuses or fuse wire and a torch handy, for emergency repairs. Always replace with the correct size fuse or fuse wire.

WHICH FUSE

Colour	power	purpose
White	5–6 amps	lighting
Grey	10 amps	light duty (e.g. lighting)
Blue	15–16 amps	standard immersion heater
Yellow	20 amps	storage heater
Red	30–32 amps	ring mains/shower unit
Orange	40 amps	cooker/shower
Green	45 amps	cooker/shower

Fuses up to 55 amps are available if required.

MEASURING ELECTRICITY

- ⊙ **ELECTRICITY SYSTEM** Measured in volts. The number of volts denotes the pressure at which the electricity is supplied: 240V in the UK (230V from 1995).
- ⊙ **APPLIANCES** Measured in watts, which assess power, 1,000 watts = 1 kilowatt (kW).
- ⊙ **FUSES** Measured in amps, which indicate the amount of electricity in the circuit.

bridge type with a raised plinth, where the fuse wire is held in place by a screw at each side; an asbestos mat with a small piece of asbestos beneath the fuse wire; or a protected tube, where the wire is concealed inside the holder.

Wiring systems

There are two main types of wiring systems for appliances in Britain today: the old-fashioned radial type (also used for cookers and other powerful appliances), and the modern ring main system, which is now standard.

RADIAL SYSTEMS

Are wired in series, one after the other, from the fusebox. Modern radial circuits are protected by a 20-amp fuse, for an area of up to 20sq m/ 215sq ft, or a 30-amp fuse, covering up to 50sq m/538sq ft.

Cookers and other appliances that make heavy demands on electricity, such as immersion heaters and electric showers, will also have their own circuits and fuses.

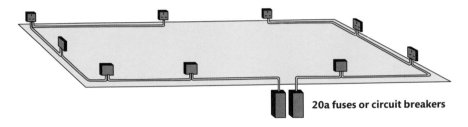

20a fuses or circuit breakers

ABOVE Radial system

RING MAIN CIRCUITS

This type of circuit has been standard since the late 1940s. A number of sockets – such as all those on one floor of a house – are linked in a central 'ring'. This ring can be broken into if you want to add extra sockets. There are usually two separate circuits on the ground floor, for the living rooms and for the kitchen. Each circuit covers up to 100sq m/1,076sq ft and supplies up to 7,000 watts.

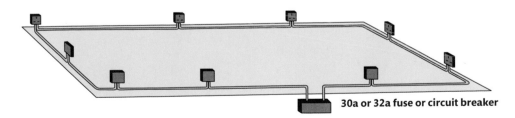

30a or 32a fuse or circuit breaker

ABOVE Ring main circuit

Lighting circuits

Most houses have two lighting circuits, each supplying about ten lighting points. There are two types:

JUNCTION BOX SYSTEMS Found in older houses, and use more cable. Each ceiling fitting or 'rose', and switch, is wired into a junction box, which is above the ceiling.

LOOP-IN OR THREE-PLATE LIGHTING Has one cable that supplies each ceiling rose. Switches are wired into the rose.

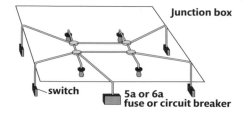

Junction box

switch

5a or 6a
fuse or circuit breaker

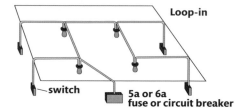

Loop-in

switch

5a or 6a
fuse or circuit breaker

ABOVE Lighting systems

HOW SAFE IS YOUR WIRING?

Wiring that is more than 25 years old may be dangerous because the rubber insulation that was used to protect the wiring until the 1960s may have perished. Signs of old wiring include:

- ⊙ An old fuse box, or a number of fuse boxes governing individual circuits.
- ⊙ Three-pin round sockets.
- ⊙ Frayed or perished flex and wiring.
- ⊙ Scorch marks around sockets and ceiling roses.
- ⊙ Fuses that blow constantly.

If you spot any of these, contact your local electricity board. An inspection costs from about £50 and it's a good idea to have the system tested every ten years by a qualified electrician. Modern three-pin square sockets don't always mean that your wiring is safe. The system may have been only partially updated and the wiring may still be a hazard.

Switch off safely

- ● Don't assume that if a light is turned off at the switch, the wires in the lamp holder will be dead. Always switch off the master switch at the mains before attempting any electrical repairs.
- ● To make absolutely certain that wires are not live, it's also worth investing in an electrician's screwdriver, which has a current tester at the end.

Always remember that according to Part P of the Government building regulations, most additional works in the home must be notified to Building Control. Failure to do this is against the law.

TIP
Do not use a dimmer switch to control a fluorescent light or a low-voltage light fitting.

Give Your House a Check-Up

You probably remember the last time your car was serviced, but do you recall the last time you gave your house a check-up? It's easy to ignore regular maintenance until things go wrong, and repairs can be expensive. That's why it's a good idea to keep an eye on the structure of the house and check it over twice a year, so you can cope with problems before they become emergencies. Look at it in late autumn before winter sets in, and again in the spring to check for damage done by bad weather. Here's what to do.

OUTSIDE

Roofs and guttering

Step into the street and take a good look at the roof. Use binoculars if necessary, because it's difficult to see damage here. (If you're on friendly terms with your neighbours, ask to look at the roof from their upstairs windows.)

Look for any loose or missing tiles or slates; damaged ridge tiles and crumbling mortar; cracked or crooked chimneys, and faulty flashings that seal chimneys; problems with bay windows, and extensions to the main roof. Try to peer into the 'valleys' if your house has two roofs or is built on different levels, because these are where water tends to collect and leaks often occur.

If the chimney smokes, consider fitting a cowl to prevent downdraughts. If you don't use the chimney at all, have the chimney pot capped to keep the weather out. (Have an airbrick set in the chimney above the roof-line.) If you decide to block up the fireplace, you'll need to fit an airbrick or ventilator to the wall to allow sufficient air to circulate, to prevent damp.

Look up and check that the gutters are secure and not broken or sagging. Patches of green slime may mean that there's a leaking downpipe, or that a blocked gutter needs attention (see Repairing Leaking Gutters and Downpipes, pages 206–7). The mould can then be wiped or brushed away and the wall can be treated with bleach solution.

Walls and vents

Walk round the house outside and make sure there's no earth piled against the damp-proof course, which runs round the walls about 15cm/6in above ground level; paths and terraces should be at least 15cm/6in below it. If it's obstructed, it won't work effectively and your home may be affected by damp.

Clean out the airbricks with a garden cane to make sure they're not blocked; they supply the ventilation beneath suspended floors, which is vital to protect them from rot.

TIP
Make sure the damp-proof course is clear all round your house, not just where the airbricks appear.

Check the walls. See if any rendering is cracked and in need of replacing. Use binoculars if necessary to check the mortar, to see if the walls need repointing. Large cracks need investigating, especially if you live on clay soil and they appear after a long, dry summer or a very wet winter, because they could be signs of subsidence. Tree roots can cause problems too. Look out for cracks near the corner of the house and diagonal cracks in the main walls running through the brick joints. Contact a chartered building surveyor or structural engineer, who will know if these are signs of normal movement or if subsidence could be the cause.

Woodwork

Take a look at all the woodwork: the bargeboards beneath the eaves, window sills and frames, decorative timbers, and outside doors, including garage doors. Look for cracked and rotting wood. Test gently with a screwdriver if possible. If the wood splinters or crumbles away, it needs replacing with a new strip, or an entire board, door or window if the rot is extensive. If you check it regularly, the damage should be limited and you can often treat affected areas with flexible frame sealant, as part of regular redecoration. See Exterior Painting, pages 314–7.

Check the windows to make sure that they're weather-tight, making a note to replace any crumbling putty or cracked panes (see Mending a Broken Window, pages 393–5). If the frames have shrunk away from the walls, scrape out the crumbling mortar with a screwdriver or filling knife and clean out with a brush. Dry the gap with a hot air gun, taking care not to melt the paintwork, and fill with exterior sealant when cool. Press into place and smooth down with a finger.

TIP

If you need a new damp-proof course, check that the company is a member of the Property Protection Association (see Useful Organisations), and find out what safeguards there are if the firm goes out of business.

Subsidence and your insurance policy

If your house is affected by subsidence, it may need underpinning and you may need to move out while work takes place. Check your buildings insurance policy to see if it covers the cost of renting a home elsewhere, as well as structural repairs.

INSIDE THE HOUSE

⊙ Go up into the loft and see if you can spot any obvious leaks or damage to the roof. It should be cool and airy. A gap of about 10mm/⅜in or airbricks at the eaves will allow the air to circulate. If there's insufficient ventilation, condensation may rot the timbers.

Make sure the storage cistern has adequate frost protection, and check for corrosion.

⊙ Check the interior woodwork for rot or pests, looking under the stairs and in cellars, where damage may go unnoticed.

Dry rot is a fungus that looks like cotton wool in its early stages and sprouts reddish brown growths as it advances. It eats into wood and can affect masonry too, causing serious structural damage. Specialist treatment is needed as soon as possible: contact the Wood Protection Association (see Useful Organisations).

Woodworm leaves small holes or heaps or trails of powdery dust. Small areas can be treated with woodworm fluid but serious infestation needs professional treatment.

Check all second-hand and antique furniture buys for woodworm before bringing them into the house. If they're left untreated, woodworm could spread from the furniture to the structural timbers.

⊙ Look out for damp. Penetrating damp, which seeps through the walls, usually appears in isolated patches, often well away from the floor. Rising damp can be detected by stains up to 90cm/3ft high on the walls, a tidemark of salts, and peeling wallpaper. The chief cause is a blocked or absent damp-proof course.

⊙ Consider the wiring. Mains wiring needs testing every ten years (see How Safe is your Wiring? page 168).

⊙ Subsidence can also be spotted inside the house. Cracks that occur inside as well as outside may be especially serious, but you should also look for walls that are out of true, tops of internal doors that are not level, and doors that stick. Contact a surveyor for advice.

Coping With Problems

Your house is designed to keep the weather out and warmth in, but to make sure it does so efficiently, you need to watch for the insidious damage caused by damp, woodworm and rot. Here's how to detect and treat them.

DAMP

Damp is a problem that affects more homes than almost any other; it is estimated that about 15 per cent of homes are damaged by it to some extent. As well as causing extensive harm to both the structure and furnishings, the mould it encourages can aggravate health problems such as asthma, so it's important to keep it under control.

The main causes of damp are penetrating damp, which seeps through the walls, rising damp from the ground, and condensation caused by warm, moist air inside the house, but don't forget that faults in the roof, or fractured pipes and water tanks can cause damp patches too. Stains on the ceiling that gradually increase in size may be traced to one of these, so it's worth searching for obvious causes before you investigate further.

You'll usually know if your home has a major problem with damp, but if you want to assess its extent precisely, you can buy a battery-operated damp meter from a DIY store. You can also contact a specialist damp-proofing company, but remember that it will have a vested interest in the problem.

Damp through walls

Penetrating damp means that the windows or walls of your house are not watertight, perhaps because you live in a very exposed part of the country in the north or west, or by the coast, where gales and heavy rain are frequent. Traditionally, many houses in these areas were low or single-storey designs, with small windows and thick, rendered walls for extra protection against bad weather.

Even if you don't live in the wilds, it's worth checking north and west-facing walls to make sure that the mortar or rendering is sound. Solid walls are more likely to be affected than cavity walls, which have the extra protection given by the double skin. Check the mortar first to see if the walls need repointing (see Repointing Bricks, page 207); if not, you can try applying a proprietary damp-proofing liquid – during dry weather – to see if that will cure the problem.

Cladding, rendering, and masonry paint certainly repel damp but they will also radically change the appearance of your house and need regular maintenance. Don't be tempted to use a completely water-resistant finish or a solvent-based paint, because any water trapped in the bricks will be forced inside the house itself and may then cause structural damage.

TIP
If a damp patch is caused by penetrating damp, it will usually be worse after heavy rain. To make sure that's the cause, soak the area with water from a garden hose, and then go inside to see if the damp patch enlarges.

OTHER REASONS FOR PENETRATING DAMP

- ⊙ **CAVITY WALLS** Where the ties between the inner and outer skin have been bridged, allowing damp to seep between the two. Ask a builder to investigate by removing a few bricks from the outer wall near the damp patch. Alternatively, contact a chartered building surveyor who can use a special, less disruptive boroscope to investigate the problem. If mortar has dropped on to the ties, extensive repairs may be needed, but a single blockage can be cleared relatively easily.
- ⊙ **CRACKED RENDERING** Which allows rain to penetrate but not evaporate. Isolated cracks can be stopped with an exterior filler but larger patches need professional treatment.
- ⊙ **LEAKING GUTTERS AND DOWNPIPES** See Repairing Leaking Gutters and Downpipes, pages 206–7.
- ⊙ **WINDOW SILLS WITHOUT A DRIP CHANNEL UNDERNEATH** This causes water to run down the walls. A blocked channel can cause similar problems (see Leaking Windows, page 211).
- ⊙ **CRACKS BETWEEN THE WINDOW FRAME AND THE WALL** To repair these, see Give Your House a Check-up, Outside, pages 169–70.

Damp from the ground

The damp-proof course is your first defence against rising damp, which is why it is so important to make sure it is kept clear. One sign of rising damp is a tidemark up to 90cm/3ft from the ground, caused by salts carried by moisture that rises up the walls. Older houses are more likely to be affected, because the mortar used in their construction is more permeable. The only way to cure rising damp is to make sure you have an effective damp-proof course, but it can be kept at bay by treating the interior walls: dry lining them with plasterboard, for example. The battens to which the plasterboard is attached should be treated with preservative and both wall and plasterboard treated with fungicide to prevent rot. Thermal plasterboard should be used, or sheets of polythene stapled to the battens. This will not stop rising damp, but it will prevent it from ruining your décor and furnishings. (You will need to provide ventilation between the wall and the plasterboard.)

TIP
If you have rising damp, examine the wall inside as well as out by removing the skirting by the damp patch. Check that the plaster stops short of the damp-proof course – it shouldn't cover it.

Condensation

The average family produces 20 litres/5 gallons of moisture a day by washing, cooking and simply by breathing. As home comforts, especially insulation and home heating, have steadily improved, this water vapour is trapped inside the house. The most obvious sign of condensation can be seen any winter morning on streaming mirrors and glass, but it does more than mist up windows. If condensation is extensive, it can lead to mould and damp, which ruin furnishings and cause structural damage, so prompt action is vital.

Condensation occurs when there's an imbalance between humidity, ventilation, and the temperature of the air and the surrounding surfaces. When warm, moist air comes into contact with a cold window or wall, it cools, and the water vapour condenses into drops on the surface. Unless the room is well-ventilated, this moisture can build up and cause rot. Older houses with open fires that create currents of air, and which also have high ceilings and low standards of insulation, may have frightening

TIP
If condensation is slight, try painting the wall with anti-condensation paint, which contains insulating particles.

PREVENTING CONDENSATION

- Make sure that walls are as well-insulated as possible. Solid walls are colder than cavity walls because they lack an inner 'skin', so consider covering them with expanded polystyrene, cork or panelling, or dry-lining them with thermal plasterboard (see Damp From the Ground, opposite) if condensation is a real problem. Cavity walls can be professionally insulated with material inserted between the two brick layers, or dry-lined with ordinary plasterboard.

- Try to avoid fitting cupboards, especially wardrobes, against a solid outside wall, or condensation may build up and you could find mould on your clothes. If this is the only practical site for a wardrobe, consider fitting louvre doors, which will allow the air to circulate in and out of it.

- Sometimes only small areas of wall are affected by condensation, often because a solid lintel or column forms a 'cold bridge' in an otherwise well-insulated wall. Although in theory you can deal with this by insulating the patch concerned, you will usually need to treat the whole wall if the result is to look acceptable.

- Consider double glazing to improve insulation at the windows. Double glazing with sealed units rather than secondary double glazing can drastically cut condensation on windows, but choose a naturally warm material for the frames, such as wood, uPVC, anodised aluminium or aluminium frames that contain a thermal 'break', to prevent moisture condensing when it comes into contact with a cold surround.

  If you decide to install double glazing, make sure the rest of the room is well insulated too, or the condensation may simply be moved on from the windows to the walls.

- Check the roof to make sure that the loft space is free from condensation, which can cause considerable damage here. Every surface on the floor of the loft should be insulated, including the loft hatch, and gaps around pipes except for the base of the cold-water tank. Ventilation spaces, or ventilators under the eaves, will encourage air circulation.

- Keep the house warm and don't allow the temperature to drop dramatically – a common cause of condensation. Turn the heating to low, rather than off, if the nights are very cold or if you go away during the winter, so the structure doesn't cool down completely. This can prevent pipes freezing, too.

- Keep moisture production to a minimum, by closing kitchen and bathroom doors when you're washing up or running a bath, and covering saucepans when cooking. Try to leave a window ajar if you have to dry clothes indoors and make sure your tumble-drier door is well sealed and that the drier is vented to the outside.

- Improve ventilation. Each living room should have at least three changes of air every hour. Install a ducted cooker hood, which takes smells and steam outdoors, or an extractor fan in the kitchen. Fit an extractor fan in the bathroom too, especially if you have a shower, which creates a lot of steam. Some fans will come on automatically when humidity reaches a certain level.

  Make sure the fan is the right capacity for the room and is sited in the right place. Kitchens need about 15 changes of air an hour, bathrooms about six (see Bathroom Ventilation, pages 90–1). The fan should be high on the wall, opposite the door if possible.

- Check that any airbricks are clear and that a fireplace, if blocked off, is fitted with an airbrick to prevent condensation in the flue.

  Efficient ventilation is essential for safety if you have gas or solid-fuel heating. To check, ask your Gas provider or branch of the Solid Fuel Association (see Useful Organisations).

fuel bills but are rarely affected by condensation unless they're allowed to become too cold. It's more of a problem in modern, energy-aware houses.

To find out if damp is caused by condensation, dry the damp patch with a hairdryer or fan heater and then stick foil to the wall with adhesive tape. Leave it for a week. If there's moisture on the back, it's probably caused by penetrating or rising damp. If it's wet on the surface, it's due to condensation.

If condensation is an intractable problem – in a holiday home, or a cellar or scullery, for example – consider using a dehumidifier, which extracts moisture from the air and collects it in a container, which has to be emptied periodically. Though dehumidifiers cost several hundred pounds to buy, running costs are low and they are very effective.

PROBLEMS WITH ROT

Dry rot

Dry rot is a fungus that flourishes in damp, poorly ventilated places that are often hidden from view. Look under stairs and floors, in cellars, beneath floorboards and behind skirting boards, though it can occur in other places too. It has long cottony strands, but as it proceeds, it can put out reddish-brown mushroom-like growths. These produce spores that look like brick dust, have a musty odour and crumbling, cube-like wood.

Don't close your eyes to them, because dry rot affects masonry as well as timber and is a serious structural threat. Contact the Property Protection Association (see Useful Organisations) for professional help.

All dry rot must be removed from brickwork and plaster; affected wood should be removed beyond any sign of infestation; and all wood treated with an approved fungicide. Contaminated bricks should be safely disposed of to prevent the rot spreading.

Wet rot

As its name suggests, wet rot attacks wood that's wet rather than damp. Like dry rot, it's a fungal infestation, but it's much easier to spot: look for dark, rotten wood that's split along the grain. Wet rot usually occurs outside, on fences, window sills, window frames and doors, all of which tend to rot at the base.

Regular decorating will keep wet rot at bay. If it occurs, cut away the damaged part and replace with timber treated with preservative. For small areas, you can use a wood repair system. The rot is removed and the wood treated with hardener, before being built up with filler. Preservative tablets are inserted to keep the wood sound.

HOUSEHOLD PESTS

Most household pests are destructive or unhygienic or both, and a few, such as woodworm, may pose a serious threat to the structure of your house.

Others, however, can affect your health: asthma or rhinitis may be irritated by the house dust mite; wasp or bee stings can cause serious reactions; food poisoning is caused by contamination from house flies or mice. Each year, many thousands of people receive hospital treatment for

TIP
An early sign of dry rot is cracked paintwork by window frames and skirtings or distorted skirting boards. Push a knife blade down and if the wood crumbles, call in a professional.

Health threat?

Local authorities may not charge to rid you of rats or other pests, which could cause a major threat to public health (a large-scale infestation of mice or cockroaches, for example). If you decide to use a commercial company, ring round for estimates before you commit yourself.

HOW TO PREVENT PESTS

- Keep food covered, preferably in sealed containers, or in the fridge. Rotate stocks so that older items are used first. Keep leftovers covered and never leave out overnight. Pet's food bowls are often overlooked, but can be a magnet for pests, so wash them regularly and remove from the floor at night.
- Wrap rubbish well and dispose of it in sealed sacks and animal-proof bins if possible, kept well away from windows.
- Clean sink wastes and drains regularly. Don't forget either to clean hard-to-reach areas, such as behind fridges and cookers.
- Stop up cracks and holes where pests may emerge, especially round pipes. Fit draught-proofing at the foot of doors, and consider fitting fly screens to windows.

- Clean up spills and crumbs as soon as they occur. Keep dishwashers loaded with dirty crockery closed to prevent food smells attracting pests.
- Vacuum carpets, mattresses and upholstery and move the furniture frequently.
- Look behind and inside cupboards, lofts and sheds regularly so pests can't breed undisturbed.
- Turn out lofts, larders and other kitchen cupboards from time to time, to get rid of stale food and unwanted papers and textiles. Always remove old bird's nests in attics as these can harbour many pests.
- Keep gutters and chimneys clear to prevent birds nesting and insects breeding.

accidents involving insects alone, so it's well worth making sure that they don't take refuge in your home.

As for larger pests, it's your legal duty as a householder to keep your home free from vermin and to contact the local authority's environmental health officer if the problem gets out of hand.

Ants

Ants love sweet, sugary things, so keep food covered, bottles wiped and plates and glasses rinsed clean. Don't ignore the problem, or you may find your home is overrun when the ants grow wings and swarm in late summer.

If you can find the nest, you may be able to solve the problem temporarily by pouring boiling water over it, but you'll need to use insecticide for a permanent solution.

Try to trace the ants to their source, and lay liquid bait, which the worker ants take back to the nest. For safety, if you have small children or animals, use a sealed tin trap, or use powders, spray or gel along the ant runs. An 'ant pen', used to draw a barrier round the house, can be a very helpful deterrent.

Bed bugs

Bed bugs are brown wingless insects about the size of a nail that move around by crawling or riding from place to place in clothing and luggage. They have become much more common in the UK in recent years, partly as a result of people travelling and using central heating more. They are found mostly in bedrooms and bites are usually the first sign. Infested rooms often have a slight almond odour. Treatment can be tricky, and removing the bugs you can see isn't enough, as they also like to hide behind pictures and loose wallpaper, skirting boards and in electrical

Green tip

For a traditional alternative to insecticides, you could try using cayenne pepper, cedar oil, or a mixture of one part borax or two parts sugar. To repel ants, plant strongly scented lavender, chives, spearmint and African marigolds by the back door. Smear entry points with petroleum jelly – ants don't like to cross any sticky surface. Use moats of water to protect food sources on the floor, such as pet bowls – add a small amount of detergent to prevent the ants using surface tension to float across the water.

fittings. Contact the pest control division of your local authority's environmental health department for advice on how to get rid of them permanently or use a specialist service provider such as Rentokil (see Manufacturers, Retailers and Service Providers).

Check areas such as behind pictures, loose wall coverings, headboards and bed bases for signs of infestation. Wash these areas with soapy water to remove bugs and their eggs. Close any cracks you find using silicon caulking or filler. Bed bugs are good climbers so prevent them gaining access to the host by standing beds away from walls and placing the legs in smooth metal jars or coating with petroleum jelly. Mattresses should be replaced or steam-cleaned, and bedding washed at temperatures exceeding 60°C/140°F (transport the mattress in a sealed bag to prevent cross-contamination). Bed bugs are sensitive to changes in temperature and start to die below 9°C/48°F and above 36°C/97°F, so raising or lowering the temperature in the infested areas to these levels will also help eliminate them. Diatomaceous earth (see Greener Pest Control Products, page 180) is the least toxic chemical solution.

Booklice

Booklice need damp to survive because they live on the mould that grows on the glue of bookbindings, damp cardboard, damp starchy food and moist plaster, leather or wood. To remove them, thoroughly dry and ventilate the surrounding area, discard affected food and wipe away all signs of mould. A powder or aerosol insecticide for crawling insects will destroy any remaining booklice.

Carpet beetles

Carpet beetle grubs, called 'woolly bears', are furry little bugs that thrive in centrally heated homes. They damage all woollen fabrics, from carpets to clothing, leaving holes similar to those made by clothes' moths.

Because the source of infestation is often an undiscovered birds' nest or feathers, it is worth searching the loft for signs of these before you try to eliminate grubs that have moved further down. Look for traces of damage in airing cupboards, wardrobes and chests where clothes and blankets are stored as well as under carpets and rugs.

Clean thoroughly if you spot signs of carpet beetle, taking care to remove any fluff, and launder or dry-clean any affected items. Vacuum carpets thoroughly and spray floorboards, cracks and the corners of cupboards with mothproofer or special carpet-beetle insecticide.

Cat fleas

Cat fleas are the most troublesome type of flea, because they are the ones most likely to transfer to humans and dogs. True dog fleas are comparatively rare; though dogs may well have fleas, they are usually cat fleas, which account for four out of five infestations. Cat fleas multiply fast in a hot summer (August and September are peak biting times) and they can survive for some time in carpets and furnishings.

To get rid of them, treat your cat or dog with a veterinary flea powder or shampoo. Wash pets' beds and burn old pet bedding, and launder any washable furnishings, such as cushions or bedding, they

Green tip

* Dust diatomaceous earth on to carpets and brush it into the pile. Leave for seven days before vacuuming to give it time to take effect. As an ongoing measure, place pheromone traps in airing cupboards and other common infestation sources to catch adult beetles (see Greener Pest Control Products, page 180).

* Groom your pet with a flea comb daily to remove adult fleas and fit a homemade herbal flea collar (see Greener Pest Control Products, page 180). Giving pets a dietary supplement of Vitamin B and garlic twice a week may also help. Dust carpets and other areas that fleas may be harbouring in with diatomaceous earth or a boric acid-based flea control product.

may have sat on. Vacuum carpets, mattresses and upholstery thoroughly and spray with flea killer; if this doesn't do the trick, you may have to shampoo furnishings too. It may be worth banning pets from bedrooms (and keeping the doors closed) to prevent fleas infesting beds and bedding if your pet is affected. Pet flea collars can help keep the problem at bay: ask your vet.

Cockroaches

Cockroaches can cause food poisoning so they should be eradicated as quickly as possible. They like warm, moist and often dirty places: behind boilers, by hot-water pipes and under sinks, and emerge at night in search of food, which they soil as they eat.

Clean out any areas where they may breed and treat with an insecticide for crawling insects. If they persist, call your local authority environmental health department, or a commercial pest-control company.

Flies

'Follow a fly for a day and you won't eat for a week' is a saying that still holds true today. House flies breed in rotting organic matter and the maggots hatch in about 24 hours, turning into adult flies within a week in high summer, when the life cycle starts all over again. Blowflies (blue- or greenbottles) lay their eggs on meat and take slightly longer to mature but are even more unpleasant.

Because flies transfer bacteria from their breeding ground to food, they are responsible for many cases of food poisoning. The easiest way to prevent them is to destroy any potential breeding sites, making sure rubbish is well covered and bins kept clean, taking care to clean up after pets, and covering food.

If you've no control over the source of infestation, keep windows on the sunny side of the house closed or fit fly screens to them. Fly papers impregnated with insecticide can help. Reserve fly spray for individual flies, as it should be used sparingly and not over exposed food or fish tanks. To stop flies buzzing at the windows, rub the panes with a little liquid paraffin.

House dust mites

The house dust mite is a major factor in allergies such as rhinitis and allergic asthma, and it is thought to aggravate eczema too. You can't eliminate it from your house because this microscopic creature is found in all textiles, especially pillows, mattresses and upholstery, where it lives on flakes of human skin and produces droppings, no bigger than a grain of pollen, that contain the cause of the problem. If affected, the first step may be to replace your mattress and pillow. Most mattresses are about 15 years old and many pillows about 12, so mould, mites and skin cells could account for one-tenth of their weight. It's also an idea to keep soft furnishings to a minimum, choosing synthetic fibres where possible, and fabrics (including bedding) that can be laundered at 60°C/140°F, which is hot enough to kill mites. If textiles are not washable, vacuum them regularly – mattresses, curtains and upholstery as well as carpets – using a machine with a HEPA filter (see Filters, page 66).

Green tip

Make your own cockroach traps using a slice of white bread placed in a jam jar coated on the inside with petroleum jelly – the cockroaches will fall in and can then be killed with boiling, soapy water.

TIP

Cluster flies are small flies that hibernate in roofs and attics, and they may return every year. Call in a professional contractor.

Green tip

Hanging bunches of mint or basil and growing strongly scented flowers such as marigolds and pelargoniums at the doors or window sills are all 'green' ways to deter flies.

TIP

Use a damp cloth when dusting to keep airborne dust to a minimum.

Because beds often harbour house mites, it may be worth investing in covers for pillowcases, mattresses and duvets made from a special, microporous fabric that keeps house mite debris in but still allows your body to breathe.

Other approaches include sprays to eradicate the mites or specialist mattress treatments offered by companies such as the Mattress Doctor and Servicemaster (see Manufacturers, Retailers and Service Providers).

Mice and rats

The mice that invade your home may be resident (House Mice) or merely taking refuge from hunger and cold (Field Mice), but both have the same unhygienic habits that spread disease. Because mice urinate to mark their territory, they contaminate food and can cause outbreaks of food poisoning; and because they are rodents they need to chew constantly, and are responsible for many fires when they bite through cables and wiring. Small dark droppings, shredded packaging, nests of paper and a sour smell are all signs of mice, and you may also hear them scuttling around at night.

Carefully block entrance holes and set traps. Traps should be placed in areas where there is evidence of rodent activity, and will be more effective if they are put inside tunnels or set directly alongside walls. Always use gloves when handling traps, as rodents tend to avoid anything with a human scent. They are also suspicious of changes in their environment, so for the first few days, provide bait (chocolate and bacon are good choices) but don't actually set the trap. Being able to take the food without harm at first lulls them into a false sense of security, and they will approach the traps with less caution, making successful capture more likely. For serious infestations, you should contact your local authority's environmental health officer, or a commercial pest-control contractor.

TIP
Consider getting a cat. While this won't guarantee your home will be rodent-free, it will certainly act as an effective, natural deterrent! If the infestation is bad, use a non-toxic cellulose-based rodenticide.

Mosquitoes

In Britain, the damage mosquitoes cause is limited to an unpleasant bite. They cause most trouble at dusk and at night, so you should wear insect repellent and cover arms and ankles outside after dark. Mosquitoes hibernate in dark, still sites such as sheds and hollow trees and breed in stagnant water. Cover water butts and consider adding a fountain to create movement in ornamental ponds. You also need to keep drains and gutters clear so they empty swiftly, and renew the water in birdbaths regularly.

Indoors, you can fit screens to windows or burn impregnated mosquito coils. These measures should be enough to cope with most cases of gnats and midges as well as mosquitoes, but if mosquitoes from marshland or rivers are a serious problem, contact your environmental health officer for professional help.

TIP
A few drops of paraffin on the surface of still water will stop mosquitoes breeding, by sealing the surface and depriving the mosquito larvae of oxygen.

Green tip
A traditional way to repel mosquitoes is to add a few drops of citronella oil to a saucer of water.

Moths

Adult moths don't damage clothes, but their larvae will eat any natural fibres, and leave holes in cotton, silk, wool and fur clothing and textiles. Moths prefer to live in dark areas, such as inside wardrobes, drawers and other storage areas. Most damage tends to occur to textiles soiled with perspiration and food, or items kept in storage, so clean items before storing and put them into airtight containers or sealed polythene. If evidence of infestation is found, empty out the area and vacuum thoroughly to remove lint and hairs. Clean thoroughly with hot, soapy water, paying particular attention to edges, cracks and crevices. Kill larvae in textiles by washing at the highest recommended temperature, or put in a plastic bag and place in the freezer overnight. Hang moth repellents in wardrobes and drawers, or spray affected areas with a homemade repellent of a few drops of lavender oil mixed with water.

Wasps

A particular nuisance in late summer, when the workers emerge from the nest. Foraging wasps can be kept at bay by fitting fly screens to windows, backed up with a wasp or flying-insect spray to kill those that find their way inside. Outdoors, it may be worth making a wasp trap by putting a little soft drink or a spoonful of jam, plus a little detergent, in a jam jar of water and partially covering the opening with paper to stop the wasps from getting out again. (Place it some distance away from where you are sitting, or they will be attracted to any food you eat and drink.)

Wasps' nests often need professional attention, especially if they are close to the house. Never try to remove a wasps' nest inside the house by yourself; call in your council or a commercial pest control company instead. You can buy proprietary wasp nest killer to deal with any nests that are further away, but take great care to protect yourself. Treat the nest at dusk when the wasps are inside, and cover yourself from head to foot, wearing a hat, gloves, boots and a scarf round your face. Leave the area as soon as you've applied the wasp killer; don't stay around to see what happens.

Weevils and other food beetles

A type of beetle with a long, pointed snout, around 3.5mm/$\frac{1}{7}$in long. Weevils arrive in your home in packets of food and go on to destroy other food stored in the same cupboard. They will be visible in foods, typically cereals, flour and pasta. Other tell-tale signs are piles of brownish dust, consisting of faeces and cast skins, appearing in or around food. They taint food with their droppings and urine, and certain species can cause a rash known as 'baker's itch'. Throw away affected food and other opened packets in the same cupboard. Empty the cupboard and wash and dry it thoroughly before refilling. Store food in tightly sealed glass, metal or tough plastic containers to prevent future infestations.

Woodworm

Woodworm is, in fact, infestation by any of three different insects: the furniture beetle, which is the most common and feeds on softwoods and adhesives, the death-watch beetle, which infests old timbers, and the house longhorn beetle, which is restricted to parts of south-east England.

Woodworm thrive in untreated wood, so preservative, varnish, paint and polish all act as a deterrent. The grubs cause most problems, by tunnelling through the wood as they feed, and you can often tell if your house is affected by active woodworm by looking for the powdery trails they leave, generally in spring and summer. Tiny, round exit holes

Wasp stings

If you are stung by a wasp, you can sooth the sting with vinegar, lavender oil (an aromatherapy oil), or 1 per cent hydrocortisone cream, available from pharmacies. Minor swelling can be treated with over-the-counter antihistamines, but you should call a doctor immediately if you are stung by a number of wasps, if you have ever had a severe reaction before, or if you begin to have symptoms that affect other parts of your body – such as hives ('nettle rash'), shortness of breath, redness or severe swelling – because wasp stings can sometimes cause life-threatening anaphylactic shock.

Greener pest control products

Most of us have to deal with unwanted house guests from time to time and the usual way to drive them out is using pesticides, insecticides and other chemicals. These may be effective, but aren't necessarily good for our own health or that of the planet, so here's our short guide to some of the more environmentally friendly alternatives that are available. You should be able to find most of them in good garden centres or chemists.

✱ **BORIC ACID/BORATE** An effective insecticide of low toxicity to humans and animals that is available from most chemists. Wear a mask while using boric acid to prevent inhalation and dust it into cracks and crevices that harbour insects.

✱ **CELLULOSE-BASED RODENTICIDES** These are formulated from natural plant extracts that disrupt the digestive system of rodents, causing them to become lethargic and die. They are completely non-toxic to humans and other animals, and completely biodegradable.

✱ **DIATOMACEOUS EARTH** A natural, inert product made from fossilised remains of a type of algae that can be used in place of toxic chemicals. It works by cutting through the exoskeleton of insects, so that moisture cannot be retained and the insect dies.

✱ **HERBAL FLEA COLLAR** Try this homemade flea-repelling collar as part of a non-toxic flea prevention programme. Soak a soft, untreated pet collar in a mixture of ½ teaspoon alcohol, one drop cedar wood oil, one drop lavender oil, one drop citronella oil, one drop thyme oil and the contents of four garlic capsules until saturated. Allow to dry, then fit onto your pet. The effects will last approximately one month.

✱ **INSECTICIDAL SOAPS** Commercial preparations based on soaps made from fatty acids are widely available in most gardening centres. They are less harmful than other insecticides, but effective only when wet and in direct contact with the pest.

✱ **NEEM OIL** Derived from a tropical Asian tree and has properties that are effective against many pests. It is non-toxic to the environment and is harmless to humans and animals.

✱ **PHEROMONE TRAPS** Use synthetic materials resembling sex attractants to lure male pests, and are usually very insect-specific. You can buy them at most garden centres.

✱ **SILICON DIOXIDE** A naturally occurring substance that works on a variety of pests (particularly cockroaches) by attacking their waterproof cuticle, leading to dehydration and death. Its toxic effects are so negligible it is even permitted for use as a food additive.

are made in wood by the adult beetles when they fly away, which remain after the infestation has been treated.

To prevent woodworm, check all second-hand furniture buys for signs of infestation before bringing them into the house, looking at the back and in the corners of drawers as well as at wood that is easily visible. Woodworm in furniture can be treated with a proprietary solution or aerosol, available from hardware shops, but specialist treatment is needed if the structural timbers in your home have been affected. Contact the Wood Protection Association (see Useful Organisations) for the address of an approved firm.

Ways to Keep Warm

Central heating is the most energy-efficient way to heat a home. This is because heat is supplied from a single source, such as a boiler, to every room, rather than relying on separate heaters to heat each room individually.

CENTRAL HEATING

There are two main types of central heating system: 'wet' or radiator systems (which are the most popular), and 'dry' warm-air systems.

Wet central heating
Uses a boiler to heat water, which is pumped through pipes to radiators or heaters and returns to the boiler where it is heated again. The advantages of wet central heating are that it can also be linked to a hot-water heating system and run by almost any fuel: gas, oil, liquefied petroleum gas (LPG), solid fuel or electricity.

BOILERS
The size of the boiler depends on the number of radiators it supplies, the hot-water supply, the standard of insulation in your home, the size and construction of your house and your pattern of heating usage. Electrically heated boilers don't need to be vented outside, but solid fuel boilers must have a chimney (if you rely on wood, the chimney should be swept monthly). Gas, oil or LPG boilers should be connected to a chimney or have a balanced flue, which draws in air and passes waste gases back through an outside wall. Gas and solid fuel can also be used with a back boiler, which is located behind an open fire or room heater.

In the UK, Building Regulations require that new and replacement boilers have to comply with energy efficiency standards (86 per cent for gas and 85 per cent for oil), and should be approved by the relevant organisation – British Standards or EU standards; the Heating Equipment Testing Approvals Scheme (HETAS); the Electricity Board; the Solid Fuel Association or OFTEC – and serviced regularly.

It is illegal and dangerous to install or service a gas appliance yourself. Work undertaken to install a new boiler (or a cooker that also supplies heating, such as an Aga or Raeburn etc.) requires Building Regulations approval because of the safety issues and the need for energy efficiency. This is generally achieved by employing an installer who is registered under an approved scheme.

RADIATORS
Radiators are usually made from pressed steel although some are alloy and older systems may have cast-iron radiators. Pressed steel has the advantage of being cheaper, lighter and quicker to heat up but will rust more quickly than cast iron, so leaks can be more common. Cast iron

TIP
Watch how long snow stays on your roof and on your neighbours' houses. Poorly insulated roofs become snow-free first, because the heat inside the house rises to melt it.

TIP
Make sure a corrosion inhibitor is added to the system, to prevent rust and scale and help stop leaks.

The right installer

- **Gas Safe** For a gas boiler and other gas-fired appliances (e.g. a gas cooker or gas fire): the installer should be Gas Safe Registered.

- **OFTEC** For an oil-fired boiler: the installer should be OFTEC registered.

- **HETAS** For a solid fuel fired boiler: the installer should be a member of HETAS.

HOW TO BLEED A RADIATOR.

If a radiator is colder at the top than the bottom, air in the system may be the problem. In conventional central heating systems, you can remove it by 'bleeding' the radiator with the radiator key usually supplied when the central heating was installed. If you've lost it, you can buy another from a DIY or hardware shop. This can't be done if you have a sealed system, where water is not automatically topped up, so you'll need to call in a heating engineer.

1 Switch off the heating system at the main switch.

2 Find the square-shaped bleed valve at the top corner of the radiator and insert the radiator key.

3 Turn the key slowly, anti-clockwise (about 90°) and use a rag or old towel underneath the valve to catch any water that escapes.

4 The air will hiss as it escapes. As soon as the hissing stops and water starts to spill out, turn the key clockwise to close the valve

TIP
Bleed radiators once or twice a year, because air can cause corrosion.

takes a long time (and a lot of fuel) to heat up, but retains the heat better.

Radiators can be single panels or double-panel designs, which give more heat and allow heat to circulate between the two panels as well as the surface; or panels with fins at the back for greater efficiency.

Warm-air heating

Usually runs on electricity, though some systems are still oil- or gas-fired. Most electric heating uses off-peak electricity that accumulates overnight, and is stored in an iron or other heat-retaining block. It is programmed to give out heat later in the day, and usually incorporates a convector heater running on full-price electricity to top it up during the day. Heating is either from separate storage heaters or, in flats and small houses, a single, central storage unit, with ducts or vents leading from it to the main rooms.

The chief problems are the lack of control (the heating is either on or off) and the fact that 'dry' heating systems cannot be used to heat water.

Electric underfloor heating, which used to be commonly fitted in flats, has fallen from favour because it is so expensive to run. It requires good insulation and to be effective, needs your neighbours to use it too.

Ducted warm-air heating, popular in the 1960s when energy was cheap, uses a conventional oil or gas boiler to heat the air and a blower or fan to push it along ducts in the floor and ceiling.

TIP
Make sure the filters, ducting and fan are cleaned regularly.

CONVECTOR HEATERS

Convector heaters produce warm air rather than radiant heat. They contain convoluted copper pipe surrounded by fins inside a casing, which has a grille at the top and bottom for warm air to pass through. They're also available as skirting board or as fan-assisted heaters, often fitted in draughty hallways or under kitchen units.

WHICH FUEL?

Fuel	Availability	Pros	Cons
Gas	Towns/suburbs	Versatile	Needs chimney/flue
Electricity	Almost everywhere	Clean; easy to install	Expensive for heating
LPG	Anywhere	Portable form of gas	Costly; needs flue/storage
Oil	Anywhere	Versatile	Can be costly and needs flue/storage
Solid fuel	Anywhere	Open fires	Can be economic but needs flue/storage/attention; may need to be smokeless

Central heating controls

Hot-water controls include thermostats or sensors connected to the hot-water cylinder, and boiler thermostats. Immersion heaters usually have a thermostat that can be altered to lower the water temperature, if you would like to cut costs.

Thermostats switch the boiler on and off to maintain the chosen temperature. They can be fitted on walls, usually in the living room or the hall, or as thermostatic radiator valves (TRVs) connected to individual radiators.

Room thermostats are relatively inflexible, because they can only react to the temperature where they are sited (usually in the hallway). Bedrooms may become unbearably hot as the boiler struggles to maintain the temperature set in the draughty hall, or you find yourself shivering, because a thermostat by a sunny window has switched the heating off.

In contrast, TRVs control the heat given out by each radiator, so you can fine-tune the system to provide the heat you require in each room. At least one radiator in the house should have a manual control or a bypass pipe, not a TRV, which should be left open when the heating is on, so the boiler and pump are not put under strain if heat to the other radiators is shut off.

Time switches and programmers control gas or oil-fired boilers, switching them on and off at pre-set intervals. The simplest versions switch on water and central heating together, twice a day, though you can override the setting manually if you want to. Modern devices allow you to control heating and hot water separately, while with electronic controls, you can programme the system on a day to day and hour basis.

Zone controls use thermostats linked to motorised valves that divert heat along particular pipes, so different parts (or zones) of the house – such as upstairs or downstairs – can be heated separately.

TIP
Look for a battery back up, so the timer won't need to be reset after a power cut.

INSULATION

Now that there's VAT on fuel in Britain, effective insulation is more important than ever. Here's what you can do to keep the heat high and fuel bills low.

Improving energy efficiency
INSULATE HOT-WATER CYLINDER AND PIPES

This is one of the most cost-effective steps you can take and one that's good for the environment too, because all insulation reduces power requirements and so helps reduce the carbon dioxide emissions that can damage the ozone layer.

A hot cylinder lagging jacket costs only a few pounds but it can cut heating costs by around £15 a year, so it should soon pay for itself. Look for a jacket made to BS 5615. It should be at least 80mm/3in thick, so if you have one thinner than this, it's well worth buying another to put on top. You can also fit a thermostat to regulate the temperature of the water in the cylinder.

Wrap up your hot-water pipes too, because they also lose precious heat. Concentrate on the hottest pipes and those in the coldest places, especially the pipes connecting the boiler and hot-water cylinder and those leading from the cylinder to the hot taps, even if it's just the initial 1m/3ft. This will help you save money on water if it's metered too, because you won't have to wait so long for the hot water to come through. Materials to use include pre-formed polyurethane foam, lagging, mineral wool or felt-strip, which are available in narrow-width rolls.

DRAUGHT-PROOF DOORS AND WINDOWS

It's important to distinguish between draughts and fresh air, because adequate ventilation is vital for health as well as comfort, especially if you use fuel-burning appliances such as a boiler or a gas or open fire. Unless they have a balanced flue, which means air is drawn in and vented outside the house, they need an air supply to burn effectively (remember the experiments with candles and oxygen at school?) and to take away the harmful gases, such as carbon monoxide, that are the by-products of combustion. For safety, there should be a permanent source of air, such as an airbrick, in the room.

A second line of defence would be to invest in a European Standard certified audible carbon monoxide alarm. These alarms monitor the levels of carbon monoxide in the home and will alert you if they are too high. However, they must not be regarded as a substitute for proper installation and maintenance of gas appliances by a Gas Safe Registered engineer.

To prevent condensation, don't draught-proof kitchen and bathroom windows. Instead, ensure the interior doors are well sealed and keep them closed, to prevent damp air causing problems elsewhere in the house.

Draughts provide fresh air where you don't want it. To exclude them, fit compressible draught excluders – brush strip, rubber or silicone rubber tubing – to window frames and brush strip to internal doors. External doors need tough, weather-resistant materials. Choose a brush type for outward opening doors; narrow if it fits close to the floor, longer bristles if the floor is uneven or worn.

You can have your home assessed for energy efficiency, and get valuable advice on how to cut fuel bills with the Government-approved Standard Assessment Procedure. This calculates the cost of heating your home and providing hot water, plus the heat systems and construction of the house, and comes up with an efficiency score of between 1 and 100; the average is between 35 and 49. There is an online carbon calculator from the National Energy Foundation and Energy Saving Trust (see Useful Organisations) to work out how much carbon you produce in your home, as well as in the car, and when you travel.

TIP
If you need a new hot-water cylinder, a popular choice is a cylinder that comes with pre-formed foam insulation.

TIP
A brush draught excluder in aluminium or PVC plastic holder is best if the door is warped.

WHICH DRAUGHT EXCLUDER?

- Brush pile seal is often self-adhesive but needs a clean surface or it can be difficult to fix firmly. For wood that is warped or uneven look for brush seal in a holder that can be nailed in place.
- Compressible rubber can be ribbed or tubular in shape. Usually self-adhesive but some tubular seals come in a holder that's nailed into place.
- Silicone rubber tubing may be self-adhesive or fixed with sealant and is very durable.
- Foam strip is self-adhesive and easy to apply but it's not very durable and can quickly deteriorate and become ineffective. Look for PVC or polyurethane foam with a wipe-clean finish to minimise these problems.
- Sealant from a tube is excellent for filling gaps permanently but won't help where you need to stop draughts around opening windows and doors.

You can also use brush draught excluder if the door opens inwards and there's a step up to it. If an inward-opening door is flush with the floor but the floor is uneven, look for a flexible flap that lifts when the door opens.

IMPROVE LOFT INSULATION

Twenty-five per cent of heat loss in houses occurs through the roof. Good loft insulation can cut heating costs by one-fifth and should pay for itself within three years. Even if you have some loft insulation, it may not be up to current standards, particularly if your home was built more than 20 years ago, so it's a good idea to check: a depth of 200mm/8in is now the recommended standard.

If you don't want to do the job yourself, you can hire a professional contractor, but it's relatively easy, if laborious, to install mineral wool loft blanket or loose-fill loft insulation (useful if access is awkward or the joists are irregularly spaced). Because the loft 'floor' is fragile and the materials used can irritate the lungs and skin, you need to follow the safety precautions below.

To fit it, first fill any cracks between joists, and gaps where pipes or cables pierce the ceiling with silicone rubber or foam sealant, which will

TIP
Don't forget the letter box. Cover it with twin-brush draught excluder or a sprung flap.

SAFETY PRECAUTIONS WHEN INSULATING A LOFT

- Wear clothes that cover you from head to toe, tucking trousers into socks and sleeves into gloves (choose smooth fabrics, not wool, so that fragments of insulation won't adhere to your clothes). Wash these clothes separately from the rest of the laundry.
- Put on a mask that complies with BS 6016/EN 149, rubber gloves and safety goggles.
- If you use a ladder to get into the loft, make sure it's tied securely in place. Use a properly secured extension light, not a torch or a candle.
- Use a board to stand on, wide enough to cover several joists.
- Never stand between the joists: you'll go straight through the ceiling.
- Open the bags of insulation in the loft, so particles don't spread outside.

prevent warm, moist air from below causing condensation. Then unroll the loft blanket or spread the loose-fill insulation between the joists. It's important to insulate the water tank and the pipes because the loft will be much colder once it's properly insulated. Don't insulate beneath the water tank because warm air from below helps stop the water from freezing. Use a loft blanket or a lagging jacket to insulate the sides of the water tank and insulate the cover to the tank too if you can. Don't forget to insulate the back of the loft hatch.

Make sure there's ventilation at the eaves, so that the roof timbers won't rot. You can use plastic eave ventilators or cut insulating blanket to a wedge shape at the ends. If you use loose-fill insulation, you may need to fit boards by the eaves to hold the insulating material in place.

While you're in the loft, take the opportunity to examine the timbers and wiring to see if they need attention.

INSULATING WALLS

More heat escapes through the walls than anywhere else in the house – up to half of the heat you pay for may be lost this way. Wall insulation can reduce this by two-thirds, but although you should notice an improvement in comfort immediately, it can take longer for fuel savings to cover the cost. Though cavity wall insulation may pay for itself in four years it can take up to 15 years for solid wall insulation to recoup its cost.

Solid walls, standard in older houses, can be insulated inside, by plasterboard attached to battens, creating a gap that can be filled with mineral wool. (See Damp, page 171). Alternatively, use thermal board fixed directly to the walls. As you may have to remove all mouldings, skirting and electrical points, this may be best left to professionals.

External insulation – rendering or cladding – may need planning permission and should be carried out by a specialist. Contact the External Wall Insulation Association for a list of members (see Useful Organisations).

Cavity-wall insulation must be carried out professionally, using chemical foam, mineral wool or polystyrene beads. Make sure the contractor you employ is registered with the British Standards Institute (for foam), or holds a British Board of Agrément certificate (mineral wool/polystyrene beads).

Window insulation

Double glazing has other benefits besides improved insulation, because it can reduce noise and condensation too. It can halve heat loss through the windows, but it's expensive and may alter the outward appearance of your home.

Employ a firm belonging to the Glass and Glazing Federation or the British Plastics Federation Windows Group (see Useful Organisations), which follows a code of practice, and ask three or more companies for a full quotation before committing yourself.

If you don't want to treat the whole house, concentrate on the rooms you use most and those with the largest windows. It's also worth considering replacing windows that are in poor condition with new sealed units (custom-made double-glazed windows).

Special cases

○ **FLAT ROOFS** Can be covered with pre-felted insulation slabs, topped with high quality roofing felt to create a 'warm roof deck'. Alternatively, you can call in a contractor to remove the ceiling or roof covering to install insulation underneath. Leave a 2.5cm/1in gap at the eaves when insulating a flat roof – more than you'd need for a sloping roof.

○ **LOFT CONVERSIONS** Usually have ceilings attached directly to the rafters. Professional treatment is best, because it may be necessary to remove either the ceiling or the roof.

How big a gap?

○ **SEALED UNIT** Made to BS 5713, 20mm/$^3/_4$ in gives the best heat savings.

○ **SECONDARY GLAZING** 200mm/8in provides the best sound insulation.

If you are good at DIY, you can install secondary glazing, which is used over existing windows. Kits contain frames made from aluminium or plastic, plus a draught-proof strip and glass.

Cheaper alternatives to glass include flexible plastic sheeting, which is taped in place, rigid plastic panels fixed with magnetic strip and plastic film, which is stretched across the pane and shrunk to fit using heat from a hairdryer. Though not attractive to look at, it shouldn't be noticeable when fixed properly and can improve safety as it will hold the glass together if the window breaks; worth considering if you have small children.

Make sure that there is always one window in every room you could escape from, in case of fire.

TIP
A 'low emissive' coating reflects heat back into the room and can further reduce heat loss.

Floor coverings

Fitted carpet helps stop the draughts that can account for 15 per cent of heat loss. Good quality underlay is important, especially if the floor beneath is made from concrete or tiles.

For a smooth floor, consider extra-thick cushioned vinyl, which contains a layer of foam, or cork tiles. If you're set on sanding the floorboards, fill gaps between boards with wedge-shaped off-cuts of wood or papier-mâché, stained to match the surround, and stop the gaps that appear along the skirting and the floor with flexible filler, or wooden moulding, tacked in place with panel pins.

If you have large areas of exposed boards, it's possible to insulate them from below, if you have access (from a cellar, for example), using loft blanket secured with netting, or polystyrene boards, between the joists. You can also insulate floorboards from above, by lifting the boards. You'll need to take the same precautions as you do when laying loft insulation (see pages 185–6), and you should take care not to cover any airbricks, so that there's adequate ventilation to the floor.

RENEWABLE ENERGY TECHNOLOGIES

There are numerous ways that homes can take advantage of renewable energy technologies. Some offer long-term paybacks but others, especially those like solar thermal panels, have come down in price and now offer a more realistic payback. The main renewable energy technologies available are:

Solar heating

Solar thermal panels can provide around 70 per cent of your hot water for free. The sun warms tubes mounted on a south facing roof – this heat helps warm water pipes to around 60°C/140°F (perfect for showers and baths), which is stored in a hot-water cylinder until it is needed.

COST £3,000–4,000, but Government grants can help with costs.
POTENTIAL SAVINGS Up to £400 per year depending on the fuel replaced.

Underfloor heating (UFH)

- A hot water underfloor heating system is more efficient to run than radiators, it provides luxurious invisible warmth and frees up wall space. If you're renovating a room it is the perfect heating solution for a greener home.

- Unlike traditional radiators that just heat the air, pipes under the floor concentrate the warmth where you sit or stand leaving your feet toasty and head slightly cooler – the ideal conditions for comfort.

- Radiators also require significantly higher temperatures to heat a room, while UFH needs around 45°C/113°F to work. This means the boiler needs to work less reducing running costs and saving CO_2. It also makes the system ideal for use with renewable technology such as ground and air heat pumps.

- Installation can be disruptive, but next time you're renovating a room, consider UFH. It works under almost all floor surfaces and because it takes up no wall space your furniture can be positioned anywhere you wish.

Solar PV panels

Photovoltaic panels convert sunlight into clean electricity and a 2.5kWp system (the peak output of the solar system) will provide around half a household's electricity needs – and it only needs daylight so can still generate power on a cloudy day. Depending on the system, if you generate more power than you use you could be sending the electricity company the bill.

COST From £5,000 per kWp, but Government grants can help with costs.
POTENTIAL SAVINGS Around £250 per year.

Wind turbine

Although technology is improving, roof-mounted turbines aren't big enough to generate significant amounts of power and urban wind speed is not consistent enough – but they are great for boats and small outbuildings that need just a limited amount of power.

To make real savings you'll need a 2.5–6kW mast-mounted turbine, and if you've got the space and sufficient wind speed, it can generate enough clean free electricity to power the whole house – and any you don't use you can sell back to the grid.

COST £11,000–19,000 (for a large version for homes and offices) but Government grants are available.
POTENTIAL SAVINGS With enough wind you may never have to pay another electricity bill.

Ground source heat pump (GSHP)

Pipes buried underground have liquid anti-freeze pumped along them at pressure. An electric heat pump converts the constant temperature (around 11°C/52°F) of the earth to 55°C/131°F – perfect for use with

Green tips

* Try looking for the items you require on Freecycle (www.uk.freecycle.org), a grass roots organisation that matches people who have things to get rid of with people who can use them. Freecycle aims to reduce unnecessary waste by keeping unwanted, but perfectly usable items, out of landfill sites – a highly commendable goal and better still, it's all completely free!

* Fix reflector foil behind radiators, to reflect heat back into the room.

* A large proportion of a home's energy consumption is due to heating. Set the room thermostat to no more than 21°C/70°F. Each degree below this temperature can save as much as 5 per cent on your heating energy.

* Fit a programmable thermostat to operate the boiler – this allows you to choose what times you want the heating to be on and what temperature it should reach while it is on. It will allow you to select different temperatures in your home at different times of the day and days of the week. It means you can save money and energy by not heating your home unnecessarily.

* Lower the thermostat on your hot-water cylinder. The temperature should not need to be more than 60°C/140°F and this is comfortable for most uses.

* Use a microwave instead of the hob for cooking vegetables. It saves money and they often taste better too.

* Appliances can account for about 20 per cent of a typical home's total energy bill, with the fridge being one of the biggest energy users. Getting rid of an old refrigerator or freezer could save you as much as £100 per year. If any of your appliances is more than ten years old, it might be worth replacing it with more energy-efficient models. Modern appliances can use up to 50 per cent less energy than those built ten or more years ago.

* Fill the oven completely, cooking an apple pie with the roast, batch baking or cooking several casseroles at once, to make the most of the heat.

* Choose a water-saving washing machine that sprays, rather than soaks the clothes. Results are just as good.

* Use a pressure cooker to save time and energy.

* Keep your freezer full and defrost it regularly.

* Descale appliances conscientiously, to cut running costs.

* Use a shower rather than a bath.

* Air-dry dishes instead of using your dishwasher's drying cycle (or use a tea-towel).

* Turn off/down the radiators in any unused rooms.

* Turn off the central heating in the summer (and get the boiler serviced).

* Defrost your fridge regularly to ensure it is energy-efficient.

* Turn off your computer and monitor when not in use. Don't forget the printer and other peripherals often left on standby.

---

underfloor heating. It is disruptive to install but if you have the space it can be twice as efficient as a traditional boiler.

COST 8–12kW system costs £6,000–12,000. Government grants are available.
POTENTIAL SAVINGS £400–1,000 per year.

Air source heat pumps

Air pumps extract the warmth in the air and convert it ready to be used in the home – either as warm air pumped through vents, or in underfloor heating. It is best suited to off-grid properties and is far easier to install than the similar GSHP.

COST 6kW system costs £7,000–10,000
POTENTIAL SAVINGS £300–800 per year.

Recommended websites

○ **HEATING HELPLINE**
www.heatinghelpline.org.uk/

○ **TRUSTMARK**
www.trustmark.org.uk/

○ **ENERGY SAVING TRUST**
www.energysavingtrust.org.uk/

A-Z of Household Repairs

Breakages and blockages don't need to spell disaster or expense. With a little basic knowledge, you can tackle minor repairs yourself without waiting for professional help.

BATHS, BASINS AND SINKS

Coping with blockages

Grease, hair, peelings and tea leaves are all common causes of blockages. To keep the waste pipes clear, keep them free from rubbish and fat, and pour down a little neat bleach occasionally. Flush the pipe with boiling water and washing soda once a week, opening the windows first to dispel fumes. If, despite your efforts, a blockage occurs, here's what to do.

If there's a partial blockage, and the water drains away slowly:

1 Pour a strong solution of washing soda (225g/8oz to 7 litres/1½ gallons of boiling water) down the blocked pipe.

2 Use a plunger to suck away the blockage. Cover the overflow outlet with a cloth and add enough water to cover the base of the plunger before pumping it up and down.

If these steps fail:

3 Use curtain wire to fish out hair and solid waste from the pipe.

4 Pour caustic soda or proprietary cleanser into the waste pipe, using as directed.

If the waste is completely blocked or other measures don't work:

5 Undo the U-shaped trap beneath the sink and put a bowl or bucket beneath it to catch the dirty water. Plastic traps can usually be unscrewed by hand, but if you have copper piping, you'll need to insert a piece of wood in the U-bend to hold the pipes steady, and undo the plug at the bottom with a spanner, turning it carefully anti-clockwise. Be prepared to probe with curtain wire or a wire coat-hanger to remove the blockage.

How to mend leaking taps

Dripping taps leave stains on baths and basins, and waste water.

If the tap is dripping from the spout, the leak is probably caused by a worn washer, which is relatively easy to replace.

1 Turn off the water supply to the tap, either at the stop valve on the pipe running to it, the gate valve in the loft or airing cupboard, or at the main stoptap. If you turn the water off at the stoptap, you'll need to drain the system before you start work, to stop water pouring out.

TIP
If you don't have a plunger you can improvise with a sponge on a stick, tied in place with a dishcloth.

TIP
You can also try clearing the waste with a wet-and-dry vacuum cleaner.

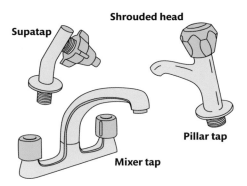

Supatap

Shrouded head

Pillar tap

Mixer tap

ABOVE Different types of taps

TIP

If a mixer tap is leaking, you'll need to replace the washers on each side.

That means turning all the taps on until they run dry and you may also have to switch off the immersion heater, or central heating boiler (if you have a 'wet' central heating system).

It isn't necessary to drain the system if:

⊙ The tap you're working on is a Supatap (reverse pressure tap), which turns off the water internally when the tap casing is removed. These taps were popular in the 1960s and are still found in some homes.

⊙ The tap is directly connected to the mains. This is usually (though not always) the cold-water tap in the kitchen.

❷ If the tap has a standard (capstan) head, loosen the little screw in the side, if there is one, and unscrew the top part of the casing beneath by twisting it anti-clockwise to reveal the tap head. If the casing is very stiff, wrap the tap with a thick cloth to protect the chrome plating and use an adjustable wrench for extra power

If the tap has a shrouded head, the head and casing form a single piece. There's no single way of removing it, so first look to see if there's a screw in the head (this is sometimes hidden by a flap that can be prised off). If there's no obvious way of removing the head, pull it to see if the head comes away. If it doesn't, turn the tap on full and carry on twisting to see if that works.

❸ Holding the tap firmly, unscrew the large nut inside with a spanner, turning it anti-clockwise (you may need to oil the nut first). This frees the 'headgear' that contains the washer.

Some modern taps don't contain washers but use stainless steel or ceramic discs instead. If this is the case, you'll need to call out a plumber.

❹ Detach the 'jumper' rod, which has a disc or nut at the base holding the washer in place. Prise off the disc to remove the washer, or oil the nut if necessary, and unscrew it with a spanner. Remove the old washer and examine it. If it's a conventional flat washer, you can use a standard replacement. If it has a special domed or curved shape, you may need to contact a specialist supplier. If you can't undo this nut, you can buy a new jumper complete with washer.

Look or feel inside the base of the tap to see if the 'seat', which the washer fits into, is worn and needs replacing.

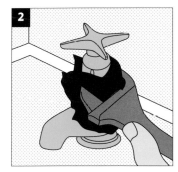

ABOVE How to mend leaking taps, step 2

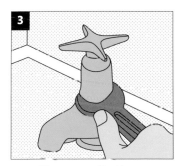

ABOVE How to mend leaking taps, step 3

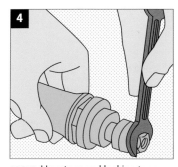

ABOVE How to mend leaking taps, step 4

REPLACING A WASHER ON A SUPATAP

1 Turn the tap full on and unscrew the nut at the top of the tap with a spanner in an anti-clockwise direction.

2 Remove the nozzle (the water will stop flowing as you do so), then turn it upside down and tap gently on a hard surface. The ribbed anti-splash unit to which the washer is attached should fall out.

3 In Supataps, the jumper and washer are designed as one unit. Pull them out and replace.

TIP

Put the plug in before you dismantle the tap, to stop any tiny screws disappearing, and protect the surface of the sink, bath or basin with an old towel.

While the tap is dismantled, check the small 'gland' nut and O-ring at the top of the spindle in a capstan head tap, or on the headgear assembly on a shrouded head tap. If the O-ring is worn, or the nut is loose, the tap is liable to leak from the top. Replace or tighten as necessary.

5 Fit the new tap washer. Standard sizes for sink and basin taps are 15mm/$\frac{1}{2}$in and 20mm/$\frac{3}{4}$in, and 25mm/1in for bath taps.

6 Put the tap back together and turn on the water supply.

Sealing gaps by the wall

It is important to make sure there's a watertight seal between the bath, sink or basin and the wall behind it, because dripping water seeping through the gap can cause rot or damage ceilings.

If the gap is quite large, you can use curved pieces of ceramic tile called ceramic quadrants behind ceramic basins or pressed steel for cast-iron baths. These are not suitable for plastic bathroom ware, which needs a flexible seal, such as plastic strip or extruded silicone. For small gaps, or to finish the strip along the bath when using ceramic quadrant, you will need silicone rubber sealant. To apply it:

1 Make sure surfaces are clean and dry.

2 Protect the wall and bath, sink or basin with masking tape.

3 Apply silicone rubber sealant into the gap and press down with a wet spatula if necessary. Remove the masking tape within five minutes and leave until completely dry (about 24 hours).

BLINDS

Hiding stains

Roller blinds are ideal for use above sinks and basins, but may become spattered with use. Stains usually mark the lower part of the blind, and if the drop is longer than the window requires, you can salvage the blind by detaching the fabric and turning it round, provided it's plain or has a non-directional pattern. Simply take down the blind, unpin it from the roller and remove the batten at the base. Cut away the damaged area and tack the new end to the roller. Make a new slot for the batten, replace and rehang the blind.

Disguising chips and scratches

- Chips in ceramic (china) basins and sinks can be repaired by sticking the piece back in place with epoxy resin adhesive, which is sold as separate tubes of glue and hardener.

- Allow the sink or basin to dry out completely and wipe the broken edges with methylated spirits to remove any trace of dirt or grease. Brush on the adhesive as instructed and replace the chip. Remove any excess glue when dry, using a safety blade. Any joins can be disguised with enamel paint.

- If the piece has fragmented or disappeared, apply layers of enamel paint, leaving each one to dry before applying the next, building the paint up until level with the surrounding surface.

- Enamel paint is useful for hairline cracks and crazing but shouldn't be used to cover large cracks, where bacteria could collect. If the damage is substantial, you'll need to replace the sink.

- Scratches and burns on plastic baths can be gently rubbed out with metal polish. First make sure the bath is dry and finish by buffing with a soft cloth.

Tightening a loose blind

If a roller blind is becoming difficult to rewind, you need to increase the tension. Pull the blind until partially closed, then unclip it and rewind by hand until fully wound. Replace, and repeat if necessary.

CARPETS

Repairing tears

From leftover scraps, cut out a piece of the same carpet a little larger than the torn area. Hold it firmly over the damaged area and use a sharp Stanley knife to carefully cut all the way through both the patch and the carpet underneath (to make a patch that will fit exactly into the removed piece of the main carpet). Make sure not to cut through the underlay. Apply double-sided carpet tape or adhesive to the patch and press it firmly into the space in the carpet. Leave to dry for several hours before walking on the patched area.

Scorch marks

If the mark is slight, you may be able to remove it by neatly trimming off the ends of the carpet tufts in the affected area. Lightly sponge the area with a mild detergent solution, then with plain water. Once it dries, you shouldn't be able to see the lower spot in the carpet.

CHINA

Hiding chips

You can repair chips in white china by mixing together epoxy resin and artists' powder paint, and coating with varnish to resemble glaze when dry. Alternatively, try building up the level with thin layers of enamel paint, allowing each to dry before you apply the next.

Mending broken china

Even china that has broken into several pieces can be mended successfully if you take care to glue it piece by piece. Although you should leave precious or antique china to the experts, it is worth repairing other items at home. Use epoxy resin adhesive for crockery, and super glue for purely decorative china that won't be washed. Once repaired, china is best kept as an ornament or for occasional use, because dirt can lodge in fine cracks and very hot water (in a dishwasher, for example) can soften the glue and make the piece disintegrate. Don't attempt to use a jug if you've mended the handle, because it may give way when lifted by the handle. Similarly don't try to mend anything used to contain hot liquids.

❶ Clean the fragments with liquid detergent, to remove all traces of grease and dirt. Rinse and allow to dry completely.
❷ Mix together the epoxy resin adhesive and hardener and brush sparingly along the broken edges of the two largest pieces. Press these together. Wipe the surface to remove excess adhesive. You can use a solvent such as methylated spirits or acetone, but avoid making contact with unglazed pottery.

WHICH ADHESIVE?

GENERAL PURPOSE GLUES (e.g. Bostik All Purpose Clear and Solvent-Free, Evo-Stik Household Adhesive, Evo-Stik Multi-Purpose Clear, Loctite Clear) provide a good, invisible bond, but shouldn't be used where strength is important (for handles, for example). Allow about 20 minutes to dry. Any surplus can be removed with acetone or nail varnish remover.

BEST FOR leather, paper, plastic, textiles, wood.

CONTACT ADHESIVES (e.g. Bostik Contact Adhesive and Evo-Stik Impact and Timebond) bond instantly and are heat and water resistant. Both solvent-based and solvent-free (water-based) types are available: choose solvent-based for metals, solvent-free for flexible plastic and polythene. Use in a well-ventilated room and remove solvent-based versions with oily nail varnish remover.

BEST FOR the same purposes as general purpose glues, plus pottery – but remember, the bond is instant.

EPOXY RESIN ADHESIVES (e.g. Araldite Rapid, Araldite Standard, Bostik Epoxy Adhesive) consist of two parts that are mixed together to form a bond. They are very strong, but though they are heat and water resistant, they won't stand up to frequent washing.

BEST FOR bonding items that don't fit neatly together (though the join will be visible), gluing metals and rigid plastics.

PVA (POLYVINYL ACETATE) OR WOOD ADHESIVES (e.g. Evo-Stik Wood Adhesive Resin 'W', Unibond PVA) are water-based adhesives that form a strong, permanent bond. Some can be stained or varnished and waterproof versions are available, but others should not be immersed in water. Remove any excess glue with methylated spirits.

BEST FOR carpet, cork, fabric, leather, paper and wood.

LATEX ADHESIVES (e.g. Copydex, Evo-Stik Fabric Adhesive) are rubber-based and will resist water, oil and steam. Special brands for children are also available. They take about 45 minutes to dry, after which any surplus glue can be removed with a knife.

BEST FOR flexible joins on carpets and textiles.

SUPER GLUE OR CYANOACRYLATE ADHESIVES (e.g. Bostik Super Glue 4, Evo-Stik and Loctite super glues, UHU Super Glue and Multi-Purpose Extra Strong Glue) form a very strong bond. Use gels for splintered surfaces, complex repairs, porous surfaces and working vertically as they are less likely to drip. Special releasing agents such as Bostik Skin Release Agent and Loctite Detach are available if the super glue adheres to the skin, but it's best to wear gloves when you use it to prevent this happening.

Best for: china, cork, fabric, jewellery, leather, metal and plastic.

You'll need to hold the china together as it dries, using elastic bands or masking tape, or by clamping it in a partly opened drawer. Ornaments and difficult shapes can be pressed into a piece of plasticine, or kept in place in a box of sand.

❸ Glue and fix the other sections in place in the same way.

❹ Leave for at least 24 hours to harden completely.

TIP
Number the pieces lightly in pencil, in order of gluing, and have a trial run at fitting them together.

CURTAINS

Tears in curtains

Rips needn't ruin your curtains. It's well worth trying to patch them, especially if they're made from expensive fabric, before you decide to throw them away.

LIGHT COTTONS, SILKS AND SYNTHETICS

Bring the edges of the tear together as closely as you can without puckering the fabric and sew as neatly as possibly to a matching offcut of fabric used to reinforce the back of the curtain. (Take this from a hem or seam if you have to, and patch the hidden area with plain fabric.)

SHEER, UNLINED FABRICS

Make a tiny seam to mend the tear. Rehang the curtains, pulling up the gathering tape different, if necessary, to hide the repair.

LACE, NETS AND LOOSELY WOVEN FABRICS

Either remove a few strands from a hidden area, or buy thread as close in texture and colour to the curtain material as possible, and weave carefully into the damaged area, working from behind. If you have snipped the curtain seam or hem, reinforce it with a patch.

DOORS

Damaged doors

If the joints of a panelled door have come loose, you'll need to clamp and glue them back in place.

❶ Take the door down and gently push the joints apart.
❷ Glue the joints and fix back in place. Hire a sash clamp or bind tightly with rope, to keep the door together as it dries.
❸ If necessary, strengthen the joints by drilling holes in the door at each joint and inserting small plugs of wood or dowels.
❹ Sand and repaint.

If a door is very bowed, you can help correct it by fixing an extra hinge, or by inserting wedges between the door and frame and leaving it shut tight for at least a week.

Doors that won't close

Doors that have warped or moved may not close because the two parts of the latch don't connect. If the door fits fairly well in the frame, you can unscrew the striking plate and move it to a better position.

Sometimes, doors won't stay shut because they're 'hinge-bound', which means that the hinge is set too deeply in the frame, or that the screws project, forcing the door open. To remedy this, either unscrew the hinge plate and pack the recess with offcuts of wood until the hinge is flush with the frame, or refix the screws. You may have to use smaller screws, and pack out the screw holes to fit them.

Dropped doors

Although doors often sag when the screws holding the hinges work loose, it's worth checking first to make sure that the hinges themselves are intact, or that there are sufficient hinges to support the door. If the existing hinges are suitable but need re-fixing, you'll need to fill the existing screw holes with wooden dowels and drill new holes, using longer screws if necessary to hold them firmly in place.

TIP
Make sure you fill the old screw holes for extra strength, before you reposition the striking plate.

CURING RATTLES AND SQUEAKS

⊙ **RATTLING DOORS** As long as the door still closes, you can often cure a rattling door by fixing a strip of wooden beading to the door frame, or using a draught-proofing strip. If the door frame itself has worked loose, you'll need to refix it to the wall using special frame-fixing wall plugs and screws, making sure you drill 6cm/2½ in into the wall, using a masonry bit.

⊙ **SQUEAKING DOORS** Ordinary hinges should be oiled from time to time to prevent doors sticking and squeaking. Move the door back and forth as you oil it so that the oil is worked into the hinge.

Rising butts, which lift the door over obstacles, can be lubricated with petroleum jelly. Remove the door before treating the hinge fixings.

Sticking doors

Wood swells when damp, which is why doors that open and close with ease in the summer may start to stick in autumn and winter.

❶ Tighten the hinges, which can work loose with time.
❷ If the door still sticks, rub the edges liberally with chalk, or slip carbon paper between the door and frame. Open and close the door several times. The places where the chalk rubs away the most, or the carbon paper leaves black marks, show where the problem occurs.
❸ Rub the problem areas with a candle to lubricate them.
❹ If this fails, sand or plane the door edge as necessary, leaving enough space to admit a knife blade all round.
❺ Where there is any bare wood, make sure you prime, sand the edge lightly, wipe with white spirit and repaint.

TIP
If you use a plane, work towards the centre where the wood is strongest, to avoid damaging the corners.

TIP
If the problem is at the bottom of the door, try opening and closing it over a piece of coarse sandpaper. This is easier than taking it off its hinges to treat it.

ELECTRICAL APPLIANCES

When appliances such as the oven, washing machine or vacuum cleaner won't work, carry out a few elementary checks on them. Here are some simple tests you can do before calling out an electrician or service engineer.

Make sure that there is in fact a problem. Check that the appliance is switched on at the socket and that any taps (to a washing machine or dishwasher) are also turned on. Check its fuse and flex, and renew if necessary. If the appliance still fails, try it in a different socket before taking it for repair.

The following advice applies only to the UK: in some countries, it is illegal to attempt any electrical repair unless you are a qualified electrician. For safety, always switch off and unplug an appliance before you examine it, unless instructed otherwise.

Check the small print from your manufacturer. A five-year parts guarantee is often only valid if repairs have been undertaken by a recognised service engineer.

Make sure that electrical repairs are carried out correctly. Electricity used carelessly can kill, or at least result in a shock or burn.

Cosmetic repairs on white goods

⦿ Touch up scratches on white appliances by wiping with white spirit and then painting with white enamel (such as Hammerite) applied with an artist's brush. Proprietary products are also available.

⦿ Use heat-resistant enamel for cookers and boilers.

Dishwasher

Dishwashers work wonders but they aren't miracle machines and won't cope with burnt saucepans or dried-on leftovers. To make the most of your dishwasher, scrape plates clean before stacking them and use the rinse programme if you don't want to run a full wash for some time.

Make sure that spray arms can swing freely and aren't impeded by tall or bulky dishes. From time to time, the spray arm may become clogged and the dishwasher won't operate properly. You can usually unscrew the arm and flush it clean under the tap.

To avoid a build-up of scale that can damage the machine, renew the salt for the water softener when the warning light shows that the level is low. Clean the filter after every use and wipe the door seal after every load or it may perish and leak. For best cleaning results, use the detergents and rinse-aid products that are recommended, in the correct amounts.

TIP
Before going away for any long period, clean out the dishwasher with proprietary dishwasher cleaner and leave its door slightly open so that air can circulate.

Electric fire

Fan heaters often pick up fluff, which interferes with the air flow through the heater and can cause overheating, so keep the grille clean and dust-free. If it does stop working, you can unscrew the grille and clean inside very gently with a soft brush.

Radiant fires need to be kept sparkling clean so they reflect the maximum amount of heat, but take care not to knock the bars or the ceramic mounts when wiping the fireback.

Fridge and freezer

These are among the most reliable kitchen appliances, partly because there's so little to go wrong in them. If a fridge or freezer suffers a major breakdown, the compressor may have stopped working, and you will have to decide whether it's worth repairing it or whether it's better to buy a new fridge or freezer. Don't attempt any repairs to the sealed unit yourself: call the service department or a refrigeration engineer.

TIP
Connect your fridge or freezer to an inaccessible electric point where it's not likely to be switched off accidentally.

IMPROVING EFFICIENCY

If the fridge or freezer is working but inefficient, try the following.

1. Don't allow ice to build up. Check that the thermostat is set correctly and defrost your freezer regularly. Most fridges are automatic defrost. If your fridge doesn't automatically defrost, even though it's supposed to, examine the hole at the back of the fridge and the channel where the water drains off to make sure they're not blocked. Clean out any debris. Ice shouldn't build up to more than 6mm/^{1}/$_4$in in the freezer compartment of a fridge or freezer.
2. Make sure there's sufficient ventilation at the back of the fridge or freezer and don't site either appliance next to a cooker or radiator as the heat will affect their efficiency. Allow an air gap of least 2cm/^{3}/$_4$in above the fridge or freezer, and at each side if they are beneath a worktop.
3. Clean the back of the fridge and dust the condenser. Dirt can prevent the motor running efficiently.
4. Check the seal round the door and replace if necessary. Warm air may lead to a build-up of ice as well as affecting temperature control.

TIP
Don't put warm food in the fridge. Cool it first by putting the container in a bowl of cold water.

DEFROSTING A FRIDGE OR FREEZER

- ⊙ Remove the fridge or freezer contents, wrapping frozen food in thick layers of newspaper and storing them close together or storing them in a cool-bag or a neighbour's freezer.
- ⊙ Switch off and unplug the fridge or freezer and leave the door open.
- ⊙ Push towels around the bottom of the fridge or freezer and use baking trays to catch the water. To speed up defrosting, place bowls of hot water inside and prise away large chunks of ice with a plastic kitchen tool, not a knife.

- ⊙ Wipe out the fridge or freezer and the shelves and compartments with dilute bicarbonate of soda (15ml/1 tbsp to 1 litre/1¾ pints water), applied with a clean cloth, and dry thoroughly.
- ⊙ Rub the freezer compartment or freezer with glycerine (from chemists) to prevent ice from sticking hard to the surface.
- ⊙ Switch on or use the fast-freeze setting. Allow a freezer to run for at least an hour before filling it.

Insert a sheet of paper between the seal and the fridge and close the door, then move the paper to different points. If it falls out, the seal may be worn.

Kettle

Kettles need regular descaling if they're to work efficiently and the water is to remain clear. Use a special descaling product – see page 231 – bring to the boil and leave overnight. Remember to rinse well and boil several times with clean water before using the boiled water for food or drink.

To maintain your kettle in good working order do not unplug by pulling the cord. On cordless kettles:

❶ Never allow the inlet pins to become wet.
❷ Don't use the kettle when the water level is below the minimum mark or above the maximum mark. If a kettle is overfilled there is a danger that boiling water may splash from the spout.
❸ Always close the lid before switching on the appliance otherwise the kettle will not switch off automatically.
❹ Do not force the kettle on to the base.

A boil-dry protection is a safety device to protect the kettle should it boil dry. If the kettle is left unattended while switched on with insufficient water or without the lid properly closed the kettle will cycle on and off to protect it from overheating. If this happens, switch off at the mains, allow the kettle to cool down for approximately five minutes.

Microwave oven

If your microwave is elderly or seems to take longer to heat food than it used to, it's worth carrying out a few simple checks. Do not attempt to carry out repairs yourself.

❶ Clean the microwave thoroughly to rid it of food particles, which attract microwave energy and can block up the air vents.
❷ Make sure the microwave is sited in a dry position, away from the sink or hob if possible, or steam may gradually corrode it.

Green tip

You can also use white vinegar and water to descale your kettle. Fill the kettle with a mixture of half vinegar/half water and leave it overnight. In the morning, the limescale will come off easily. Rinse thoroughly to remove any vinegary odours.

MICROWAVE CHECKLIST

Before calling out an engineer, check the following questions.

1 Does the oven lamp work?

2 Does the cooling fan work? (Put your hand over the rear ventilating opening.)

3 Does the turntable rotate?

4 At the end of your trial cook time is there a signal and does the indicator light go out?

5 Is your trial sample of water in a cup hot?

If the answer is no to any of these questions check the wall socket and fuse before calling out an engineer.

There is no need for a routine service as long as your oven is functioning properly. If you wish to have your microwave or combination oven checked you should have this carried out every three to five years, although this will be at your expense.

There are a number of microwave checking devices available. The results can be variable as the readings obtained are not always accurate.

Oven

To keep the linings clean and prevent the build-up of soil, make sure you use higher temperatures, over 200°C/392°F, periodically. Many oven doors can be removed for easier cleaning.

Clean the fan *in situ*. Wipe it gently using a cream cleaner. Do not exert pressure on the fan or you may damage it. If it becomes greasy you may have to remove the retaining nut to make cleaning easier.

If your oven goes wrong try the following:

❶ If the clock goes dead but the oven works, get in touch with the manufacturer.

❷ If the clock goes dead and neither oven seems to work, check the main fuse box.

❸ If the main oven does not work check that the oven is not set on automatic.

❹ If the main oven works but the small oven does not, check that the small oven has not been inadvertently put on to the grill symbol.

❺ If the main oven works but the light does not, contact the manufacturer for heat replacement bulbs and instructions. Remember to turn the oven off at the mains before replacing the bulb.

TV

Poor picture reception can ruin your enjoyment of a TV programme. Here are a few simple checks that can help you identify any problems with picture quality.

TIP
Several slices of lemon in a small bowl of cold water, cooked on full power for ten minutes, will soften food deposits so they're easily wiped away. Then wipe the interior dry.

TIP
Look at your neighbours' television aerials to see the way yours should face.

TV CHECKLIST

1 Check all cables and connections. If they seem sound, turn the TV on and lift the cable, running it slowly through your hands while you (or a helper) look at the screen. A sudden deterioration in picture quality may mean that the cable is faulty at that point and should be replaced.

2 Read your instruction book to make sure you have tuned in the channels correctly. With older sets, it's a matter of fiddling with the dial on the control panel and the pre-set buttons, but new

TVs are more sophisticated. Simply call up the tuning command on the handset or switch the set to tune, select a number, and set the television to search until it finds a strong signal. When you're satisfied with the reception, store it in the memory against the number of your choice.

3 Look outside to check that the aerial (or satellite dish, if pictures from this are unsatisfactory) is still in place and has not been blown off, knocked out of position or obstructed in some way.

Tumble-drier

Cleaning the filter every time you use the drier will keep drying times to a minimum and help save money.

Vented driers need an outlet through a window or cut in a wall to prevent steam collecting and condensation causing damage indoors. If you find the windows are steaming up, check that the hose hasn't split and that the connection is still secure.

If the load takes longer to dry than usual, make sure that the vent isn't blocked before you decide that the thermostat's at fault.

TIP
Make a temporary repair in a split hose with insulating tape.

Vacuum cleaner

Blockages make a vacuum cleaner slow to pick up and quick to overheat, and they're liable to occur when you are trying to clean up large amounts of dust or animal hair. To keep them to a minimum, change the bag or empty the cleaner when it is two-thirds full, and clean or replace any secondary filters.

If problems do occur, it helps to know how your style of vacuum cleaner works. In an upright, a belt links the motor to a roller, which has brushes on it. The brushes beat the dust out of the carpet and it is then sucked past the motor into the dust bag. In a cylinder, air is sucked through the hose inlet into the dust bag. Filters ensure that dust is not expelled in the exhaust air. These cleaners rely on suction only.

Wet and dry and three-in-one cleaners are very robust but should always be cleaned thoroughly after being used for mucky jobs and you should take care to use the detergent recommended, to prevent foam from damaging the motor.

If the blockage is near the inlet of an upright, you may need to take off the base plate to get at it. (You will also need to do this to remove the brush roll and replace the belt.) Check all the ducts and hoses at the same time, and clear if necessary, by fitting to the blowing end of the cleaner, or with a bent wire.

Uprights and cylinder cleaners with power heads have, as well as suction, motorised brushes to sweep up hairs and threads. Keep an eye on the brush to make sure it doesn't become jammed, and cut (don't pull) any threads that prevent it rotating.

TIP
Don't continue to use your vacuum cleaner if the sound it makes becomes noisier or high pitched. It's a warning that the brush roller may be stuck, the inlet blocked, or that the fan is vibrating.

WASHING MACHINE CHECKLIST

1 Check the hoses for kinks, which can affect drainage, and make sure the connections are sound.

2 Check the water pressure. On hot and cold fill machines, you can do this by switching to a hot wash (60°C/140°F or 95°C/203°F) programme. If the machine fails to fill or start washing within a few minutes, the water pressure may be inadequate.

3 Keep the dispenser drawer clean to prevent clogging with detergent or fabric conditioner.

4 Check the door seal regularly and replace it if it's split or worn.

5 Check that the machine is stable and level if it vibrates when you're washing a normal load. Don't overload or unbalance by washing heavy items alone. Add several light- or medium-weight articles for balance.

6 Empty pockets and close zips when washing clothes to prevent objects from damaging the drum. Check it from time to time.

Washing machine

Heat, water and constant motion put washing machines under terrific strain, so it's not surprising that they are among the domestic appliances most likely to go wrong. In many cases, faults need expert attention, but regular checks can make major problems less likely. Here's what to do:

If the machine fails to drain, it's worth looking for blockages before you take matters further. Empty the machine manually, check the outlet hose, filter and sump hose, if possible. Even a small item like a button can cause problems because it may act as a valve.

TIP
Wipe the inside of the door and the seal after using the machine to stop water collecting and leave the door open when the machine is not in use.

FLOORS

Most houses today have a solid ground floor, usually made from concrete, and suspended floors on the upper storeys, made from floorboards or sheets of chipboard or plywood, on timber joists. Older houses, built before the middle of the century, may have suspended floors throughout the house, with the exception of the kitchen and scullery. Whatever they're made from, they need to be kept in good repair and free from rot and damp, because problems in the sub-floor can affect the covering you put on top.

Damp floors

Damp can seep through solid floors and affect the floor covering you lay above, so it's vital to treat it. Remove the floor covering first so you can examine the sub-floor and see the extent of the damp: if it's severe, you'll need professional help. If the damp is limited, you can keep it at bay by installing a damp-proof membrane. The easiest way is to remove the skirting and seal the floor with dilute PVA adhesive, taken up the wall to the level of the damp-proof course; but you can also use bitumen, bituminous felt paper or adhesive, and polythene sheet, in the same way.

TIP
Quarry tiles and flagstones can resist a little damp, so they're ideal for use in old houses, basements, cellars, utility rooms and conservatories, which are rarely completely dry.

Levelling concrete floors
LARGE FAULTS

Hollows and dips in solid concrete floors are not only unsafe, but will cause extra wear on the floor covering laid on top, and thus ruin its appearance in a short time.

Large cracks and hollows are best filled with a mix of sharp sand and cement in a ration of 4:1, available from builders' merchants.

❶ To make a clean edge, tap round the damaged area with a hammer and chisel, wearing goggles to protect your eyes.
❷ Clean out the crack or dip, and coat with dilute PVA adhesive for a better bond. Leave to dry.
❸ Apply the mortar with a filling knife or trowel and smooth level.

SMALL FAULTS

Slopes, crazing and small dents can be treated with self-levelling compound.

❶ Make sure the floor is perfectly clean and free from grease before you start. Sweep and wash it well and allow to dry. Remove any resistant oil patches with white spirit, rubbed on with wire wool.
❷ Mix the self-levelling compound to a thick, creamy consistency.
❸ Starting at the corner furthest from the door, pour it over the floor, spreading it on with a trowel or steel float. Work backwards until the floor is completely covered.
❹ Leave to dry for about three hours.

LOOSE, GAPPY AND SQUEAKING FLOORBOARDS

Central heating is often the culprit here, because it makes timber dry out and shrink. Once gaps appear between floorboards, they may rub together and squeak.

◉ The simplest way to deal with the problem is to puff talcum powder (or a powder lubricant) between the boards.

◉ If only one or two boards are affected, try screwing the board to its neighbour, or to the nearest joist, taking care to avoid wires or pipes.

◉ Tiny gaps can be sealed with wood filler, and sanded level with the surround when dry.

◉ If there are numerous gaps, pack them with papier mâché (made from newspaper soaked in wallpaper paste and coloured to match the boards if they are stained or varnished), pushed well into the space between boards with a filling knife and sanded level when dry.

◉ Large gaps can be covered with wedges or fillets of wood coated with wood adhesive and coloured if necessary, then planed and sanded level with the floor.

◉ Use wood filler in the gaps formed where boards have shrunk away from the skirting. If there's a substantial gap, use quadrant (curved) moulding, attached to the skirting with panel pins every 15cm/6in.

◉ Very gappy boards need relaying or covering with plywood or hardboard, laid rough side up so that the texture acts as a key for any adhesive. Condition the sheets by sprinkling them with water on the textured side and stacking them on edge, in the room where they're to be laid, for a few days.

◉ If the floorboards sag substantially, lift those most affected with a wide bolster chisel or a spade. (Place a wedge of wood underneath to prevent the board springing back into place.) Examine the joists, and if they are broken or rotten, call in a builder.

Staircases

Strengthen stairs and stop them squeaking by screwing wedges of wood underneath the staircase, where the tread and risers meet. If you can't get under the stairs, use countersunk screws (which won't protrude above the level of the stair) to fix the tread to the riser just behind the nose of the stair.

Patching vinyl floors

It is always worth keeping a spare offcut of vinyl that has been used on a floor, in case the flooring is accidentally scorched or torn.

❶ Place the piece of new flooring over the damaged area and cut through both pieces with a sharp trimming (Stanley) knife, following the outline of the design if there is a tile motif or similar regular pattern. Lift and discard the damaged section.

❷ Clean the floor underneath thoroughly and allow it to dry.

❸ Stick down a new patch of flooring to fit. Use double-sized heavy-duty adhesive tape for loose-lay floors; or if the floor is stuck down, clean away any old adhesive and stick the patch in place with new adhesive.

FURNITURE

With a little work, a neglected piece of furniture or unpromising junk-shop buy can become a useful and attractive addition to your home. One advantage of rescuing old furniture is that it's very often made from solid wood, which is easier to restore and gives the best results. Badly damaged veneered pieces are rarely worth bothering with, unless they are intrinsically valuable.

First, examine the piece carefully. If you suspect you've bought a bargain-price antique, ask for a valuation and seek expert advice before doing more than dusting the piece. If you're confident that it's nothing special, check it for previous repairs, which may need replacing or removing.

Look for signs of woodworm: a powdery dust in drawers and corners, and pinholes in the wood itself. Treat the furniture with woodworm solution if necessary before you bring it indoors, or it may infest the rest of your home, which can be a serious hazard to the structural timbers.

Next, wipe the furniture with a detergent solution to remove the grime. If it has been treated with French polish or button polish the surface will almost inevitably be damaged and it's best to remove what's left by rubbing with methylated spirits.

If you want to remove old paint, try hand-sanding on small pieces or use a chemical stripper (gel or paste are best for intricate designs) before sanding with fine abrasive paper. Try not to use a hot air gun for this purpose because it may scorch the surface of the wood.

If there are only minor flaws, you can simply polish the piece, using a traditional wax polish, or varnish it. If it has been substantially patched and filled, it can be difficult to achieve a consistent finish and you may do better to stain it or give it a coat of paint.

For further details, see Paints for Woodwork, pages 304–5.

Vinyl floor tips

- Scrub gently with detergent and a brush or very fine wire wool until the new patch matches the surrounding floor, to 'age' it and make it less conspicuous.

- Stop loose-lay vinyl flooring lifting by sticking the edges with double-sided tape or clear household adhesive. Put a weight on top until the glue dries.

- You can lift a damaged vinyl floor by pressing with a hot iron over aluminium foil. The heat should soften the adhesive.

TIP
A cabinet scraper (a flexible sheet of steel held in both hands) removes a very thin layer of wood. The smooth finish then means furniture needs only minimal sanding.

First aid for furniture

LOOSE HINGES

Caused by screw holes growing too large. Unscrew the hinge and replace with thicker screws, or make the holes smaller by packing with wall plugs before replacing the hinge with the original screws.

LOOSE OR BROKEN CHAIR STRETCHERS

Need repairing or replacing for stability. If the stretcher is loose, fill the original holes to make them smaller before gluing and clamping the old stretcher in place. If the stretcher is broken, try to replace with one in a similar style. Architectural salvage depots often have a selection. Remove the old stretcher and if the holes are too small, drill them out, then plane the ends of the new stretcher to fit. If the holes are too large, fill as required.

Remove old glue from the stretcher holes before fitting the new stretcher. It's often animal glue, which is not compatible with modern adhesives and won't bond to them. Coat the ends of the stretcher and the holes with glue, fix in place and secure with clamps until dry.

STICKING DRAWERS

Often the result of damp, which makes the wood swell. Check the runners first to see if they are broken and need replacing. If they're intact, chalk the drawer edges, push the drawer shut as far as possible and then tug open. The areas rubbed clean of chalk will show you where it sticks. Sand or plane until the drawer closes easily, and spray the runners with furniture polish so the drawer opens and closes smoothly. Check the base of the drawer to see if it has split or warped and replace if necessary.

UNSTEADY TABLES AND CHAIRS

Often have loose joints, because the dowels that fix them have broken. Unscrew the block, drill out the holes and fit new dowels 6mm/^{1}/$_4$in shorter than the hole size. Cut a groove along the dowel with a safety blade, fill with wood glue and put back on the block before refixing.

WOBBLY CHAIRS

When caused by uneven legs, these can be levelled by cutting the legs to the length of the shortest, or building up the short one to match the rest. Glue and screw the extra piece in place so it's perfectly stable.

LOOSE CASTORS

Castors often become wobbly when the holes that house the screws that hold them on become enlarged. Try packing the screw holes with slivers of wood coated with woodworking glue, or move the castor so that it screws into an undamaged piece of wood. If the furniture legs are badly split, you may have to consider replacing the legs completely, or shortening them to reach sound, solid wood. Alternatively, you can try replacing all the castors with cup castors, which are screwed into the side rather than the base of the chair leg.

Torn upholstery

Torn upholstery needs patching for strength as well as looks.

Repairing cane chair seats

- Sagging cane seats can often be shrunk back using plain water. Wrap the chair frame in cling film to protect it and thoroughly wet the chair seat with cold water. Allow to dry and it should spring back into shape.

- To make sure the seat is thoroughly wet, soak a towel in water and leave it on the seat for a few hours.

- If a few strands of cane are broken, mend with pieces of cane available from craft shops. Soak the cane in cold water to make it supple. Study the broken strands to see how they are woven into the seat, and then remove one. Replace with a new strand, weaving it in to fit, and glue the ends in place under the frame. Repeat until all the broken strands have been replaced.

1. Carefully neaten the edges of the tear and remove loose threads.
2. Cut an offcut of fabric slightly larger than the tear.
3. Apply latex adhesive to the face of the patch and the underside of the torn fabric and leave until almost dry.
4. Slip the new patch underneath the tear, pulling the edges of the torn fabric together if possible. Press down and hold in place to form a firm bond.

If you don't have an offcut of fabric, try looking in department stores for a close match and ask for a sample. If all else fails, take a piece from a hidden area, remembering to patch that too with another fabric for strength.

GAS COOKERS

Repairs to gas cookers and fires should always be left to experts, but if your gas cooker won't light, check that the pilot light is still alight, or that the oven is not set to automatic. Erratic lighting may mean that the spark igniter or a burner is clogged and needs cleaning.

LIGHT FITTINGS

Fluorescent lights
Fluorescent light tubes last for years, but when they begin to flicker or blacken at the ends, they usually need replacing. To fit a new tube, pull one end of the tube away from the lampholder (you may need to turn it 45°) so that the pins come away from the socket and repeat at the other end to disconnect it. Reverse the procedure to fit the new tube.

Lampshades
If the binding that attaches the lampshade to the frame works loose, the shade will droop. This not only looks unattractive, but will continue to get worse as the weight of the shade exerts more pressure on what's left of the binding. Replace with new binding, glued into place with latex adhesive.

OUTDOOR REPAIRS

Clearing a blocked drain
If you've cleared the waste pipe of a sink or basin and the water still doesn't run away, if the toilet won't flush correctly or there's an unpleasant smell outside, it's likely that the drains outside are blocked. The drainage system in your house takes used water from baths and basins, and sewage, into pipes underground that can be examined via inspection chambers or manholes set along them at intervals.

Sometimes a blockage forms when leaves and debris clog up an open gully at the base of a pipe. This is usually easy to clear by lifting the grate and cleaning it, or by fishing out solid waste with a stick or bent wire. If the blockage is in the underground pipes, you will need to lift the manhole cover to clear it. You will need a set of drainage rods from a hire shop, stout rubber gloves and a strong stomach, because this is not a pleasant job, though it can save both time and expense.

TIP
When replacing buttons on deep buttoned upholstery, use a long mattress needle and keep the button in place with a knot.

TIP
If the lampshade fabric is torn, it may be worth making a new one, using the old covering as a pattern. Choose a light-weight but tightly woven, flame-resistant fabric and replace any lining at the same time.

TIP
Manhole covers are heavy, so get help if possible. Scrape away impacted earth with a knife and tilt the cover backwards, using the grips provided.

① Find the manhole closest to where you've detected the blockage and raise the lid. If the inspection chamber is full, the blockage is beyond the manhole. If it's empty, the blockage will be in the pipes between the manhole and the gulley close to the house.

② If you can't find the blockage, examine all the manholes on your property in turn. If they are all clear but you still have problems, ask the local authority 0to examine the drainage system in the road.

③ Once you've located the blockage, assemble the drainage rods, and wearing rubber gloves, push the rods down the manhole and into the drain, turning them from left to right. (Don't turn them the other way or they'll unscrew and you'll lose them.) Hook out and remove any solid waste and flush the pipes with a garden hose. When the pipe is clear, replace the manhole cover.

TIP
You can try shifting the blockage first with a burst from a garden hose turned on full, but don't persevere if it doesn't shift or flooding will add to your problems.

Repairing leaking gutters and downpipes

Blockages can make gutters sag and overflow. To prevent problems, check and clean the gutters annually, before winter sets in. Netting can be clipped over the guttering to prevent leaves or bird nests accumulating, but this will need checking too as anything that collects on the netting may make it sag into the gutter, causing the very sort of blockage it was intended to prevent.

If the gutter is sagging, check the brackets supporting it to see if there's sufficient slope: there should be a drop of at least 45mm/1½in towards the downpipe every 3m/10ft. If necessary, reposition the brackets. For a quick repair, insert a small wedge of wood beneath the gutter, inside the bracket.

CLEARING A BLOCKED GUTTER

① Block the downpipe with a rag so the debris doesn't cause a blockage in the pipe.

② Brush plastic guttering clean with a stiff bristled brush; use a wire brush for cast iron gutters.

③ Using a trowel, decant waste into a bucket suspended from the ladder by an S hook. Follow ladder safety tips (see Exterior Painting, page 314) and if necessary use a ladder 'standoff' (which supports the ladder but holds it away from the roof) for better access to the gutter.

④ Remove the rag from the downpipe and flush the system with water.

If the gutter leaks, loose joints or cracks may be responsible. Plastic guttering should be unclipped to see if the foam gasket needs replacing. Check the neighbouring joints at the same time and replace any gaskets that look worn.

CLEARING A BLOCKED DOWNPIPE

Cover the drain with a cloth and work from the top down and the bottom up, using a bent wire (a wire coat hanger will do) to fish out the blockage. Flush through with a hosepipe when clear. If that fails, you can unclip plastic downpipes or hire a special clearing tool with a screw action.

CAST-IRON GUTTERING

Cast iron guttering needs regular cleaning and painting to prevent rust, or it may crack. If leaks occur:

1 Clean the gutter thoroughly, blocking the downpipe with a rag to prevent blockages occurring further down.

2 Clean out the affected joint or crack with a screwdriver or a pointed trowel, and dry thoroughly.

3 Treat with a sealing compound, pressing it down well into the crack or joint.

If this doesn't solve the problem, call in a professional to replace a length of guttering or seal and re-bolt the joint, because cast iron is heavy to shift.

LEAKS IN DOWNPIPES

These can be traced by looking for signs of green mould on the walls near them. Plastic downpipe may need to be clipped back into position or wrapped in a self-adhesive flashing strip. This can also be used for cast-iron downpipes and painted to match the surround. Alternatively, coat cast-iron pipes with sealing compound (such as epoxy repair paste) and wrap the pipe with a glass-fibre strip while the paste is still damp. Overcoat with a second layer of compound and allow to dry before painting.

Repointing bricks

When the mortar between the bricks becomes loose and flaky, rain and snow can penetrate the wall and cause problems with damp. Although repointing a whole wall is best left to professionals, there's no reason why you shouldn't tackle small areas yourself using ready-mixed mortar.

New mortar can make the repointed area contrast with surrounding brickwork. Try tinting the mortar with colouring, available from builders' merchants, before it is applied, to blend in with the rest of the wall.

Roof repairs
TEMPORARY REPAIR TO A CRACKED TILE OR SLATE

If rainwater is coming in through a cracked tile or slate and you cannot get a replacement immediately, make a temporary repair to the slate itself, to reduce to a minimum the damage done by damp.

1. Raise the one or two tiles or slates that overlap on to the cracked one to give you better access. Prop them up with wooden wedges.
2. Use a wire brush to clean the surface round the crack.
3. Brush a coat of flashing-strip primer into and round the crack, painting a strip as wide as the flashing strip. The primer ensures a good bond between the tile or slate and the flashing strip.
4. Cut a piece of flashing strip with a sharp knife. Make it long enough to cover all of the crack.
5. Press the flashing strip into place and bed it well down into the primer. Run a small wallpaper seam roller over it to firm it down.

REPOINTING BRICKWORK

1 Clean out damaged mortar with a screwdriver or a hammer and chisel and clean the wall thoroughly with a wire brush.

2 Soak the bricks and existing mortar with water.

3 Mix the new mortar with water and push into the gaps with a pointing trowel, treating verticals before horizontals. Smooth away the excess.

4 Leave until it is almost dry, and brush thoroughly.

TIP

For a fine crack, just seal it with bituminous sealant (in an applicator gun). Using wooden wedges, prop up the tiles or slates that overlap the cracked one, brush out the crack and then inject sealant.

ROOF SAFETY

⊙ Set the ladder up at the correct angle: 1m/3ft away from the wall for every 4m/13ft up the wall. The top of the ladder should overlap the highest point and should be tied in place if possible. Secure at the base with a sandbag, or tie it to wooden pegs knocked into the ground. If the ground is soggy, place the ladder on a board to make sure it's secure.

⊙ Always move the ladder along the wall to keep within easy reach of the point where you are working.

⊙ Get someone to hold the ladder when you are ascending and descending and keep him/her within calling distance while you are working.

⊙ Have a safe place to put your tools such as a sturdy apron or a purpose-made belt.

⊙ Don't go on the roof without a roof ladder hooked over the ridge and reaching down to the eaves.

⊙ Take care not to drop anything. Have a sack or bucket hooked on to the roof ladder. Lower it with a rope.

REPLACING A ROOF TILE

Slates and tiles that are nailed in place are difficult to replace, but most roof tiles have nibs at the back that slip over a retaining batten and so are relatively easy to move.

❶ Carefully lift a few tiles in the course above the broken or missing
tile and wedge them with offcuts of wood so that they stay raised.

❷ With a large trowel, detach the broken tile from the batten that secures it to the roof, and remove it.

❸ Push the new tile into place, making sure it hooks securely over the retaining batten. (A loose tile can be replaced in the same way.)

❹ Remove wedges of wood beneath the top row of tiles.

TOILETS

Dripping overflow

A faulty ball valve or float can't control the flow of water from the tank to the lavatory cistern, and that means that water will drip through the overflow pipe. You can stop this temporarily by tying the float arm to a piece of wood laid across the top of the cistern, but you won't be able to flush the lavatory while this is in place. For a permanent repair, you'll need to replace the ball float or repair it.

Unblocking a toilet

See page 389.

REPAIRING A FLAT ROOF

Worn flat roofs often leak where rainwater collects in pools instead of draining away. A flat roof won't bear your weight, so cover it with boards or limit repairs to areas you can reach easily from a ladder or steps. (See Exterior Painting, Ladder Safety, page 317.) Don't work on anything higher than a garage or sun room unless you have scaffolding, professional spreader boards, and feel completely comfortable working at a considerable height.

1 Brush away the roof chippings and put to one side.

2 If the roofing felt is torn, clean out the crack. If it has bubbled, slit the bubble and pull back the flaps to let the interior dry out.

3 Apply a layer of felt 150mm/6in wide, loosely over the split. Apply a second layer 300mm/12in wide on top and bond them together with bitumen.

4 Leave to dry and apply again after 48 hours. Then replace any chippings.

REPLACING A BALL FLOAT

1 Turn off the water supply at the stop valve or main stoptap (see How to Mend Leaking Taps, pages 190–2) and drain the system, flushing the toilet to empty the cistern.

2 Take off the end of the valve to remove the float arm, using pliers if necessary.

3 Take the plug out of a narrow Portsmouth valve, then unscrew and remove the washer, or take out the plastic diaphragm from the wider diaphragm valve.

4 Clean out the inside of the valve.

5 Replace the new washer or diaphragm and reassemble the valve. Smear a little petroleum jelly inside the thread before screwing the valve back together to make it easier to dismantle next time.

6 The water level in the cistern should be about 2.5cm/1in lower than the overflow. To allow more water in, you'll need to raise the float; to lower the water level, you'll need to lower it. You should be able to adjust it if the float arm is attached to a diaphragm valve, but if it's attached to a Portsmouth valve, you'll probably need to remove the float arm and bend it into shape.

WALLS

Patching wallpaper

ORDINARY WALLPAPER

Wallpaper is best repaired with an irregular patch of paper torn into shape, which, surprisingly, makes a more discreet repair than a neat offcut.

1. Carefully tear away the ripped or stained patch of wallpaper in an irregular shape.
2. Take an offcut of wallpaper to fit the pattern of the damaged area and tear into shape to soften the edges.
3. Coat the back with wallpaper paste and press into place.
4. Wipe away any excess adhesive and make sure the edges lie flat by pressing with a clean cloth or a wallpaper seam roller.

VINYL WALLPAPER

If the patch is very difficult to match, or a vinyl wallcovering has been damaged, try the following method.

1. Place an offcut over the wall, covering the damaged area and matching the pattern.
2. Cut through both layers of wallpaper with a sharp trimming (Stanley) knife, to make an irregular shape.
3. Throw away the damaged piece and stick the new one into place.

Loose wall fixings

When properly fixed shelves and curtain poles should stay put indefinitely, but they may be pulled out of place if subjected to sudden pressure. Once the fixings have come loose, it's best to drill into a new area of wall if possible, because the filled patch may not be as strong. The existing holes can be filled and touched up with paint or patched with wallpaper.

If this is not possible, allow the filler to dry hard and drill more deeply, using longer wall plugs and screws than before. If the screws and plugs have merely worked loose, you can try packing the existing holes with some filling compound. For ways to fill cracks and chips in walls, see How to Fill Cracks, page 307.

WINDOWS

Leaking windows

Windows need regular maintenance to keep the weather out and heat in. As well as checking the frames and sills for rot, you need to replace crumbling putty around the glass panes, with the correct type for either timber or metal.

If the window sill is wood, it should have a drip groove so that rainwater runs off, away from the house. If this is missing, paint or stain a fillet of wood to match the sill and nail it to the underside of the sill, near the front, to keep the water away from the wall.

Mending a broken window

See pages 393–5.

REPLACING CRACKED TILES

To replace a cracked ceramic tile set in the middle of a wall or worktop:

1. Drill into the centre of the tile using a power drill fitted with a masonry bit. Wear safety glasses and gloves to protect yourself from tile chips.

2. Repeat until you have drilled several holes, then carefully chip away sections of the tile with a chisel and hammer, working outwards from the centre. Fix masking tape over the spot you want to drill, to stop the drill skidding on the slippery surface (useful also when you want to drill screw holes for towel rails or shelves on tiles).

3. Chisel away the old adhesive in the gap left by the old tile before spreading new adhesive on the back of the replacement tile. Press into place and regrout.

4. Crumbling grout can be removed, using a stiff brush plus a chisel if necessary, and replaced with new grouting, applied with a small sponge and worked in well. Wipe the surface with a damp cloth or sponge, and polish when dry.

3

Cleaning the Home

Your entire home needs regular attention to keep it hygienic and looking its best. In this section you will find out how to look after all sorts of household fixtures and fittings. Follow our tips and, with a bit of effort and planning, you will be able to keep everything in tiptop condition without having to spend every spare moment cleaning.

A-Z of Common Cleaning Materials

A quick glance down the aisles of any supermarket will reveal a bewildering array of cleaning potions, lotions and powders. You certainly don't need all of them. A few carefully chosen specialised products, along with some more general household cleaning materials, will do the job just as well. There is almost always a ready solution for any household cleaning problem, but before starting it is helpful to be aware of the most common cleaning materials and substances.

EVERYDAY ITEMS

Abrasives
Any material used to rub or abrade surface. Available in different degrees of fineness from metal polish cleaners to cream cleaners such as Cif. You can feel how abrasive a material is between your thumb and forefinger. When using an abrasive cleaner, follow the grain of whatever you are rubbing.

Alcohol
Dissolves grease and evaporates quickly, although not as effective as dry-cleaning fluids. As a solvent it is excellent for cleaning glass because it removes oils and waxes. Most commonly used is methylated spirits.

Ammonia
Ammonia is an alkaline gas dissolved in water. For household use, its strength varies from 5 to 15 per cent. It is great at cutting through grease and removing dirt from floors and walls. Can be used for stain removal as it is a mild bleach. Be careful, however: ammonia is poisonous.

Biological washing detergent
Great for many dirty jobs around the house, such as removing burnt-on food from saucepans, and brightening up dirty bathtubs.

Household bleach
This is a strong chlorine bleach and is usually made from sodium hypochlorite. It can range in concentration from about 5 per cent and has detergents and perfumes added. Bleach should be used with great care because it can weaken fabrics and fade colours.

Milton Sterilising Fluid (used for baby's bottles and equipment) is sodium hypochlorite at about 2 per cent concentration. For cleaning, it is used diluted 1 part to 4 parts water, and there is no need to rinse afterwards.

Important care using bleach
Never mix household (chlorine) bleach with ammonia. When mixed they release chlorine gas into the environment, a toxin so powerful and dangerous it was used as a chemical warfare agent during the Second World War. Exposure to chlorine gas can cause nausea, burning to the eyes, nose and throat, coughing, chest pain and difficulty with breathing. In extreme cases, it can even be fatal. As a general rule of thumb, it is never a good idea to mix cleaning products.

CLEANING EQUIPMENT ESSENTIALS

A well-equipped cleaning store cupboard will make life easier and should contain the following items:

- ⊙ **BROOM** Look for one with densely packed bristles to pick up more dirt and dust, and a handle that screws into the head so that it can be replaced easily if broken.
- ⊙ **COTTON HOUSE GLOVES** Perfect for cleaning the slats of Venetian blinds. Simply put on the gloves and run your fingers along the slats to pick up dust.
- ⊙ **CHAMOIS LEATHER** The best tool for polishing windows and leaving them smear-free.
- ⊙ **DISHCLOTHS** Plain white cotton dishcloths are indispensable for undertaking a vast array of household cleaning tasks.
- ⊙ **DUSTERS** Lambswool or feather dusters are best.
- ⊙ **DUSTPAN AND BRUSH** For dealing quickly with localised spills such as broken glass or upturned ashtrays.
- ⊙ **METAL SCOURING PADS** Must be moistened to get the benefit of the soap pellets inside. Designed for tough cleaning, but will rust if kept for more than one job.
- ⊙ **MICROFIBRE CLOTHS (E-CLOTHS)** Ideal when damp for cleaning glass, shower screens and mirrors.
- ⊙ **MICROFIBRE SURFACE MOPS** Great for picking up dust on floors in between washes.
- ⊙ **MOP AND BUCKET** Essential for keeping floors sparkling clean, but don't leave the mop sitting in stinky water!
- ⊙ **NYLON SCOURERS** Gentler than metal, but will still scratch delicate surfaces, so use with care.
- ⊙ **RUBBER GLOVES** Keep separate pairs of rubber gloves for bathroom and kitchen to avoid the transfer of germs from one room to another.
- ⊙ **TOILET BRUSH** A bathroom essential.
- ⊙ **TOOTHBRUSHES** Old toothbrushes are perfect for scrubbing nasty mould stains off grout and other hard-to-reach areas.

Hydrogen peroxide

A mild, slow-acting bleach safer for all fabrics, hydrogen peroxide has a different chemical composition to the hypochlorites. Its percentage strength varies. It is one of the slowest-acting bleaches and therefore the easiest to control. Available from chemists.

Methylated spirits

See alcohol, left.

Silicone polishes

Used in furniture and floor polishes. They act by lubricating the polish, making it easier to spread, so that an even film reflects light and appears glossy.

Silicone textile finishes give resistance to wear, water, weathering and stains because they form a film that acts as a barrier to make the surface more durable.

Solvents

Any substance used to dissolve another substance, such as grease, which attracts and holds dirt on to a surface. Water is the safest and best solvent. Try it first on all washable materials.

Alternatively, to dissolve and remove grease-based substances you need to choose a grease-based solvent (such as dry-cleaning fluids).

Turpentine

An oil-based solvent obtained from pine and fir trees. Used in certain paints, varnishes and waxes, and as an ingredient in furniture polishes and waxes. It will remove paint stains and grease. Flammable and poisonous.

Washing-up liquid

Not just for dishes! It is also good for stain removal and cleaning many household surfaces.

Greener alternatives

These days, we all worry about using too many chemicals in our homes, and the effect this might have on our health and the environment, so here are a few suggestions for greener alternatives to conventional cleaning products.

* **BICARBONATE OF SODA** No self-respecting domestic goddess should be without bicarbonate of soda, even if you never bake a cake. It has a myriad of uses around the home, and here are just a few. A scouring paste of half soda and half water is excellent for removing stubborn stains from kitchen worktops, sinks, cookers and saucepans. It is a great natural deodoriser and can be sprinkled on soft surfaces, poured down drains and placed in the fridge to help neutralise unpleasant odours. Bicarbonate of soda also boosts the performance of chlorine bleach in your laundry – follow the bleach manufacturer's instructions for dilution, then add an additional 2–3 tbsp bicarbonate of soda to the solution.

* **DISTILLED WHITE VINEGAR** Vinegar is a wonderful traditional remedy and is particularly good for removing limescale from a variety of surfaces. It is also a good odour absorber, and a few drops applied to clothing faded by perspiration will sometimes restore the colour. You can use it to buff windows to a streak-free shine. However, don't use it on gold-plated fittings or marble surfaces, because the acidity can cause damage.

* **LEMON JUICE** Lemon juice is a natural bleaching agent and is great for removing many stains, particularly those caused by rust. Half a cupful added to a wash load will also help brighten whites. Try removing food stains from chopping boards by rubbing them with lemon juice and leaving overnight.

* **WASHING SODA CRYSTALS** Washing soda or sodium carbonate has been used in the home for over 100 years. It is cheap, biodegradable, contains no enzymes, phosphates or bleach, and is effective for an enormous variety of household cleaning tasks, such as clearing blocked drains, getting rid of mildew from shower curtains, and removing stains from fabrics and surfaces. Don't confuse it with the much more unpleasant caustic soda.

SPECIALIST PRODUCTS

It helps to keep a few specialist products at hand in your cleaning store cupboard for dealing with specific tasks and particularly stubborn stains. Here are GHI's tried-and-tested favourites. You don't need all of them but do try to have two or three available.

All of these products should be readily available in most supermarkets, but if you have difficulty finding them, see Specialist Products.

SPECIALIST PRODUCTS AND THEIR USES

BISSELL OXYKIC	A spot-treatment carpet cleaner, which combines the power of oxygen and cleaning solvents and is effective on a large number of stains.
DE.SOLV.IT	A citrus-based spot-treatment stain remover spray, which is good for many types of stain, particularly greasy ones. Not recommended for use on silk.
ENZYME-BASED PRE-SOAKING AGENTS (SUCH AS BIOTEX)	These work by breaking down proteins and are effective on biological stains such as blood and egg. Don't use them on silk and wool, which are protein-based fibres themselves.
OXI-ACTION BLEACHING PRODUCTS (SUCH AS VANISH)	These are a good alternative to chlorine bleach. They are less toxic and gentler on delicate fabrics such as silk and wool. A scoop of powder added to the normal wash load will help brighten clothing.
STAIN DEVILS	These individually formulated, stain removers are suitable for use on most fabrics. Choose the one most suited to the stain type.
STICKY STUFF REMOVER	Excellent for dissolving traces left by sticky tape, labels and chewing gum.
WD-40	Not just for squeaky hinges! WD-40 has surprising uses as a cleaning agent. It is excellent for dissolving chewing gum and traces left by sticky labels and also works well on greasy stains, such as tar, lipstick and shoe polish. However, it can leave an oily mark on fabrics – to prevent this, rub liquid detergent into the affected area before washing as normal. Not suitable for use on silk.
WHITE WIZARD	Probably GHI's favourite wonder product! If you keep just one specialised stain removal product in your cleaning store cupboard, this is the one to go for. It is non-toxic, easy-to-use and brilliant for removing a wide range of stains from both hard surfaces and fabrics.
WINE AWAY	Another GHI favourite that does exactly what it says to red wine stains. It contains no phosphates or bleach, and is also effective on red ink and bloodstains.

Household Cleaning Schedule

Keeping your home clean can be a daunting task, but with all the labour-saving gadgets available these days, it is not nearly as difficult as it used to be. If you follow these helpful tips for putting in place a household cleaning schedule, you can make it even easier.

- -

DAILY TASKS

Taking a few minutes each day to do smaller chores will ensure things never get out of control. Here are five top tips for things to do on a daily basis.

1. Turning back the bed linen and allowing it to air each day while you get ready for work will help keep the bedroom fresh – leave a window open to help reduce humidity, but don't forget to close it before you leave the house.
2. Quickly wipe down bathtubs, sinks, taps and toilets after each use to keep them clean and sparkling at all times.
3. Wipe down kitchen counters and wash up after each meal – see the box below for the most efficient way to wash-up by hand. Soak dishcloths and scourers overnight in a solution of warm water with a few drops of bleach added to keep germs at bay.
4. Sweep or vacuum kitchen and bathroom floors.
5. At the end of each day, spend a few minutes clearing away clutter and returning items such as toys to their proper place, or dirty clothing to the laundry basket ready for washing.

THE MOST EFFICIENT WAY TO WASH-UP BY HAND

- -

- Scrape off as much food debris as possible and give each dish a quick rinse before stacking them to the side of the sink.
- Fill heavily soiled items, such as pans, with hot water and put them aside to soak.
- Make sure the sink is clean before you start. Using a plastic washing-up bowl requires less water and helps protect items from the sink's hard surfaces. If you don't have a double sink, the gap between the bowl and the sink means you can still use the hot tap for rinsing.
- Fill the bowl with hot soapy water and deal with dishes in the following order: glasses first, then lightly soiled dishes such as mugs, saucers and side plates. Next wash the large eating plates, followed by the cutlery. Do serving dishes, pans and roasting tins last. If necessary, change the washing water halfway through.
- Rinse each item in clean hot water as you go along and put it on a rack to drain.
- Using a clean tea-towel, dry each item and put it away.

WEEKLY TASKS

Some jobs don't need doing every day, but will soon mount up if you don't pay attention to them on at least a weekly basis. It is a good idea to allocate tasks to a particular day of the week, so you are never swamped with so many things to do it becomes overwhelming. Here are seven household chores for each day of the week.

1 Change all the bed linen. In hot weather periods, it may be necessary to do this twice weekly to keep things smelling fresh.

2 Do all the laundry (of course, large families may need to do washing more often). Either iron items immediately or put them away creased and just iron when you want to wear them – there are few things more depressing and unsightly than piles of ironing hanging around the house!

3 Spend half an hour or so dusting household surfaces. Dust from top to bottom to prevent resettling or use a vacuum cleaner attachment to suck up particles.

4 Vacuum all the carpets and floors in the house. Vacuuming on a weekly basis helps prevent the build-up of dust that can cause allergies and other respiratory problems.

5 Mop all hard floors, particularly those in high-traffic areas such as kitchens, bathrooms and hallways.

6 Give bathrooms a thorough clean, paying particular attention to germ-attracting areas such as taps, toilets, toilet brushes and toothbrush mugs.

7 Give a quick wipe down to those kitchen surfaces not attended to on a daily basis, in particular cupboard doors, shelves, splashbacks, and inside the cooker, microwave oven and fridge. Check the fridge for leftover food that is no longer edible and throw away. Rinse out and disinfect the kitchen rubbish bin.

MONTHLY CLEANING TASKS

Set aside one day of the month to dedicate to those tasks that need doing less often. Rope in family members to help and you'll get everything done in no time. Here are ten chores to consider for your monthly schedule.

1 Wash all the windows and mirrors in the house.

2 Vacuum hard-to-reach areas such as under beds and sofas, above doorframes, blinds and curtain rails, and cobwebs on ceilings and walls.

3 Polish woodwork, and metals such as silver and brass.

4 Wipe down door handles, light switches and walls to remove finger and scuff marks.

5 Turn mattresses and wash linens such as mattress covers and pillow protectors.

6 Give the oven a thorough clean inside and out.

7 Deep clean the fridge and while you're at it, defrost the freezer if necessary.

8 Clean lamps and other light fittings.

HOW TO CLEAN A FRIDGE THOROUGHLY

- ◉ Turn the fridge off and remove all the food, putting perishable items in a cool place.
- ◉ Run shelves and drawers through the dishwasher or clean in hot, soapy water.
- ◉ Pull out the fridge and wipe all interior and exterior surfaces to remove grease and marks, and dry with a soft cloth.
- ◉ Don't forget to clean inside the folds of the door seal – lots of crumbs and other debris collect there.
- ◉ While the fridge is away from the wall, vacuum up any dust that has settled on the condenser coil on the back – this helps it to work more efficiently.
- ◉ Place a bowl of bicarbonate of soda inside the fridge to absorb any unpleasant smells – this should be replaced each month.
- ◉ Return the fridge to its usual position and turn on again. Reload with the food.

9. Run a cycle of one cup of white vinegar through both your dishwasher and washing machine to help keep limescale at bay and pipes sparkling clean.
10. Spot clean any stains on carpets and other soft furnishings.

SPRING-CLEANING

This used to take place once warmer weather arrived and it was no longer necessary to heat the home with soot-producing coal fires. However, with the advent of central heating, the annual spring-clean has become somewhat redundant. Nevertheless, it is worth making the effort once a year to perform the following tasks to help ensure your home remains clean and clutter-free at all times.

1. Shampoo all the carpets in your home to give them a real deep clean.
2. Wash or dry-clean curtains, bedspreads, pillows and duvets.
3. Sort through wardrobes, cupboards and drawers and get rid of anything you no longer need or use.
4. Pull out heavy items such as cookers and dressers and clean the area behind them.
5. Spring is also a great time to get your outdoor areas prepared for summer entertaining. Clean patios, garden furniture and barbecues, and clear away any overgrown weeds and shrubbery. Ensure drains and gutters are unblocked and check exterior painting and retouch as necessary.

Green tip

Using Freecycle (www.uk.freecycle.org) is a great environmentally friendly way to find a new home for your discarded, but still usable items.

A-Z of Cleaning and Caring for Surfaces

The GHI regularly tests cleaning and stain removal remedies in response to a vast number of queries. In this section, you will find hundreds of tried and tested cleaning tips that will help you care for all manner of surfaces in your home. The products mentioned here are available from supermarkets, hardware stores and specialist shops, or by mail order.

BATHROOM FITTINGS

Baths

ACRYLIC Rinse bath after use to prevent water staining. Clean regularly with an all-purpose bathroom cleaner to prevent build-up of dirt and scum. For stubborn marks you can use a nylon scourer, but not an abrasive cleaner; warm soapy water and a cloth is ideal. In hard water areas, use a limescale cleaner; check the label before use to ensure it is suitable. Pay special attention to the areas around taps. Fine scratches can be gently scrubbed away with cream metal polish.

VITREOUS ENAMEL-COATED CAST IRON OR STEEL Clean as for acrylic baths, but use only products recommended by the Vitreous Enamel Association (see Useful Organisations), and use only a soft cloth. Products with anti-limescale ingredients may cause enamel to dull. Remove limescale with a solution of half white vinegar and half water, applied with a soft cloth to the area of limescale - avoid getting vinegar on other parts of the enamel. Rinse thoroughly and dry. If your bath is old, it may not be able to withstand modern cleaners, so test all products on a small area first.

WHIRLPOOL AND SPA BATHS Although most are self-draining, it is important to clean out scum left in pipework. Once a week, fill the bath with water and add a cleaning agent (the manufacturer's proprietary product or a cup of mild sterilising liquid, such as Milton). Allow to circulate for five minutes. Empty the bath, refill with clean water and circulate for a further five minutes to rinse.

Basins

Clean with an all-purpose bathroom cleaner and wipe with a damp cloth. Make sure the plughole is rinsed thoroughly as bathroom cleaners can damage the coating. Buff brass or gold-plated plugholes after use to prevent discolouration.

Bath resurfacing

If your enamel bath has become matt, or damaged by scale deposits and abrasives, you can have the surface professionally cleaned and polished. However, if damage is severe, you may need to have it completely resurfaced. Companies that offer resurfacing include Bath Renovations Ltd and Renubath Services Ltd (see Manufacturers, Retailers and Service Providers). For best results the bath should be completely removed and then resurfaced.

TIP

To remove mould on sealant, use a fungicidal spray, and respray regularly to prevent regrowth. Once sealant has gone black, mould is impossible to remove.

Showers

After showering, leave the door or curtain open to help prevent the humid atmosphere that encourages mould growth. Wipe down wet tiles with a plastic-bladed window wiper to prevent watermarks forming.

SHOWER TRAY

Clean with an all-purpose bathroom cleaner. If in a hard water area, use a limescale remover once a week.

SHOWER CURTAINS AND SCREENS

Nylon shower curtains can be removed and put into the washing machine – do this once a month to stop mildew and soap scum building up. Remove the curtain before the spin cycle and hang immediately so that creases can drop out. If the curtain is not machine-washable, clean it in a bathful of warm water containing a cup of biological detergent. Soak heavily stained curtains in a weak bleach solution to remove stains, rinse thoroughly or fabric could rot. Clean glass screens with a sponge and solution of water and white vinegar. On folding screens, pay particular attention to hinged areas, which can get very grubby if left unattended.

SHOWER HEADS

Descale using a liquid descaler and an old toothbrush. Steeping for two hours in a solution of half white vinegar and half water also removes scale.

GROUT

If grout between tiles becomes discoloured and dirty, apply a whitening product that contains a fungicide. Alternatively, clean with an old toothbrush dipped in a solution of one part bleach to four parts water.

Toilets

To keep the toilet bowl clean, use a toilet brush and bathroom cleaner with added disinfectant, or fit an in-cistern cleaner to release cleaner or bleach with every flush. Pay particular attention to the areas under the rim. Wipe down the outside of the bowl and the cistern with an all-purpose bathroom cleaner. Don't forget to do the toilet handle – people rarely clean their hands before flushing and this is an area that collects lots of bacteria. Neutralise odours by pouring a cup of washing soda crystals or bicarbonate of soda down the bowl once a week. Washing soda will also help to clear limescale from around the inside of the bowl. For heavy scale deposits, use a limescale remover with a thick, gel consistency.

Cleaning taps

- Products such as toothpaste can damage protective coatings on taps, particularly those with a gold or brass finish. Ideally, wipe taps and buff dry after every use.

- Clean regularly with a solution of washing-up liquid, rinse and dry. Do not use abrasive cleaners.

- To remove heavy limescale deposits, soak a cloth in descaler or white vinegar and wrap around the tap. Leave for a few hours. Rinse and dry thoroughly.

- Don't use descalers or vinegar on gold or brass-plated taps as they can permanently damage the finish.

CLEANING TOILET BRUSHES

Toilet brushes are a haven for all sorts of nasty bacteria, so make sure to clean yours at least once a week. Here's how:

1 Put the brush in the toilet bowl, pour some bleach into the water, then leave the brush to stand in it for a few minutes.

2 In the meantime, fill the brush container with hot, soapy water to which a few drops of bleach have been added. Swish it around and empty the dirty water away.

3 Flush clean water over the brush until all debris is removed, before returning it to the container.

BARBECUES

Always refer to the manufacturer's instructions if you still have them. Lining the ash pan with foil will make it easier to clean after use and also helps reflect heat up towards the food. Wiping the grill with cooking oil before use will also help prevent foods sticking during cooking.

CASINGS Wipe clean with washing-up liquid to remove grease marks. Don't use abrasive cleaners. If the paintwork starts to look shabby, touch up aluminium or enamel with heat-resistant metal paint.

GRILLS There are two main types: chrome-plated or porcelain-coated (which look black). Both types are easier to clean while still warm. Use a solution of washing-up liquid in warm water. Avoid using abrasive cleaners, which can damage the grill coating. Some grills can be put in the dishwasher.

GAS BARBECUES Disassemble and clean the burners every few months or so to prevent insects blocking the burner tubes and causing flashbacks. Volcanic rocks should be cleaned thoroughly at the end of each cooking session by turning the heat up to high for 5–10 minutes, then turning the rocks to expose the clean side. Replace rocks every five years or so, depending on how often you use your barbecue.

BASKETWARE

If stains cannot be removed with normal washing, try gentle bleaching, then revarnish if necessary. If a stain does not respond to bleaching, use a coloured polyurethane varnish to cover the stain.

BAMBOO Wipe clean with a solution of washing-up liquid, then dry with a soft cloth.

CANE Some types may have a light seal or varnish. Wipe down with water. For heavier soiling, you may need to use a washing-up liquid and water solution. Avoid using anything harsher, which may break through the seal and damage the cane underneath.

WILLOW Mainly used for hampers and similar baskets. Usually unsealed. Clean as for cane. Don't over-wet or leave to soak.

BLINDS (METAL AND WOOD)

BAMBOO Wipe with a solution of washing-up liquid; dry with a cloth.

VENETIAN Use a special dusting brush, available from hardware stores. Alternatively, wearing cotton gloves, run your hands along both sides of the slats. Metal blinds can also be taken down and soaked in the bath overnight in a solution of biological detergent and water.

BOOKS

Valuable books should be stored correctly to avoid damage. Don't let them slump on partly filled shelves. Invest in some book-ends. Large and heavy books, such as Bibles or atlases should be kept flat. Keep them in a cool room – too much heat can damage bindings and make adhesive brittle. Sunlight fades covers, and dampness can cause mildew and rot. Dust books thoroughly at least once a year. Dust them one at a time using a fine paintbrush. Holding the book closed, gently brush along the edges. Never bang the book as this can damage bindings. Once a year fan the pages of those books that are left undisturbed on your bookshelf.

CHANDELIERS

Always turn off the electricity before starting to clean. For occasional cleaning, use a dedicated proprietary cleaner – clean in situ by spraying on and allowing cleaner to run off along with the dirt. Protect the floor with polythene or old towels. For thorough cleaning, remove as much of the chandelier as possible from the light fitting. Wash using a solution of warm water and washing-up liquid, then pat dry with a lint-free cloth.

CHOPPING BOARDS

LAMINATED MELAMINE These boards, which usually have a picture on one side, are not dishwasher-proof and should never be soaked. Wipe over with a solution of washing-up liquid and dry immediately with a tea-towel.

PLASTIC Clean in hot, soapy water and dry thoroughly. If stained, soak overnight in a mild solution of bleach, then wash in hot, soapy water. Some plastic chopping boards can be washed in the dishwasher, which is the most hygienic method.

WOOD Rinse the board under very hot water. Never soak as the wood will swell, and can crack on drying. Leave to dry naturally, resting on one edge. Don't dry flat, which can cause warping, and also speed up the multiplication of bacteria. Once in a while, wipe over with antibacterial wipes or sanitising cleanser.

TIP
It is important to always replace a severely cracked, scored or stained chopping board, whatever material it is made from.

COFFEE MAKERS

CAFETIÈRES Remove plunger and unscrew rod from the filter assembly. Wash filter and glass beaker in hot, soapy water, or in the dishwasher if appropriate. Stains on bone china beakers can be removed by rubbing with bicarbonate of soda. Buff brass or chrome frames with a soft cloth.

ELECTRIC FILTERS Unplug and allow to cool before cleaning. Wash the filter holder and nylon filters by hand in warm, soapy water. Glass jugs can go in the dishwasher. Wipe the body of the machine with a damp cloth. Descale every 8–10 weeks in a hard water area, or every six months in areas of moderately hard water. Only use proprietary descalers that state they are suitable for coffee makers.

ESPRESSO/CAPPUCCINO MACHINES Descale as for filter machines, but never try to force open the lid of the water tank. Immediately after use, wait until pressure has subsided, and the lid comes off easily. Wash filter very carefully as coffee grains are extremely fine. Wash the steam nozzle thoroughly – most are removable and should be washed by hand. If the nozzle gets blocked, clean it out using a pin.

COOKING APPLIANCE CARE

- ⊙ **GAS HOBS** Some pan supports and spillage wells are dishwasher-safe. Otherwise use a suitable cream cleaner and a damp cloth. If possible, remove control knobs as dirt can quickly build up behind them. Clean the metal surround with a proprietary metal cleaner.

- ⊙ **GLASS-TOPPED HOBS (INCLUDING CERAMIC, HALOGEN AND INDUCTION)** Turn off the hob and make sure surfaces are cool before cleaning. A paper towel or damp cloth should remove light soiling, or use a specialist ceramic hob cleaner. Stubborn stains should be removed using a hob scraper. After cleaning, use a proprietary hob conditioner to protect glass. Sugar-based spills should always be dealt with immediately, otherwise they can crystallise and cause permanent pitting to the hob. To avoid scratches, always lift pans when moving them across the hob.

- ⊙ **SEALED PLATE HOBS** Make sure the hotplates are turned off. Clean using a nylon scourer and cream cleaner, rubbing in a circular pattern following the grooves on the hotplate. To avoid rusting and maintain colour, apply a proprietary hob conditioner after cleaning. Wear rubber gloves and use a strong cloth, as the steel plates have a rough texture. On reheating, the plates will smoke slightly and smell – this is normal.

- ⊙ **HOODS** Clean filters regularly – some hoods have indicator lights that indicate when filters need cleaning or replacing. Charcoal and paper filters are not washable and should be replaced regularly – charcoal every four months, paper every two months. Metal filters can be cleaned in a hot solution of washing-up liquid – leave for a few hours if really greasy to soften deposits. Some metal filters can also be washed in the dishwasher.

  For maximum efficiency, cooker hoods should be switched on 10–15 minutes before you start cooking and left running for a few minutes after you finish cooking.

- ⊙ **OVENS** Most modern ovens have stay-clean linings. Never attempt to clean these. To clean ordinary enamel linings and oven floor, use a proprietary oven cleaner, making sure it does not come into contact with stay-clean linings. Always wear rubber gloves and ensure the room is well ventilated. To make cleaning easier, place a bowl of water in the oven and heat on a high temperature for 20 minutes to help loosen dirt and grease. Wipe away any condensation with a cloth or paper towels. After cleaning, you can smear a thin paste of bicarbonate of soda and water on enamel linings – this dries to leave a protective layer that absorbs grease and makes the oven easier to clean next time.

- ⊙ **OVEN DOORS** Remove cooked-on deposits with a metal spatula or ceramic hob scraper, then use a spray-on oven cleaner. If the glass in the door is removable, soak it in a solution of biological washing powder.

- ⊙ **OVEN SHELVES** Clean in the dishwasher if possible. Remove racks before drying cycle, and chip off any residues with the back of a knife. Alternatively, soak the shelves in a hot biological washing detergent solution in the bath if the sink isn't big enough. Any remaining deposits can be removed using a mild abrasive cleaner.

COMPUTER EQUIPMENT

KEYBOARDS Unplug the computer from the mains before cleaning. Turn upside-down and shake to remove crumbs and dust. Gently work over the keyboard with the brush attachment of your vacuum cleaner, using a low suction setting. If necessary, wet a cloth in a mild washing-up liquid solution, wring it out well and wipe off any remaining dirt. Cotton buds are useful for getting in-between individual key crevices.

MONITORS Use screen wipes and sprays to polish off dirt and dust from the monitor.

CROCKERY

Most china can be put into the dishwasher, with the exception of hand-painted and antique pieces, and those with a metallic trim. If the china is labelled 'dishwasher-safe', use a detergent recommended by the china manufacturer. Load the dishwasher so that pieces are not touching one another to avoid the risk of chipping. For hand-washing, see The Most Efficient Way to Wash-up by Hand, page 216. Stains can be removed by soaking in a solution of biological washing detergent or bleach – rinse thoroughly before using again.

CUTLERY

STAINLESS STEEL Most stainless steel (except items with wooden and plastic handles) can be washed in the dishwasher, but rinse off food deposits first by hand, and remove as soon as the dishwasher cycle has ended to avoid pitting and rust marks developing. Never use the rinse and hold cycle for cutlery, especially not for knives, which are usually made of slightly less corrosion-resistant steel (in order to get a better cutting blade). Polish occasionally with a proprietary stainless-steel cleaner, such as Bar Keepers Friend. Wash thoroughly after polishing.

SILVER AND SILVER-PLATE It really is better to wash silver and silver-plate cutlery by hand (especially knives with silver handles), but if using the dishwasher is just too tempting, there are a few things you need to know to get the best results. Never mix stainless steel and silver or silver-plate cutlery in the same cycle – silver increases the risk of stainless steel corroding. Never allow undiluted dishwasher detergent to come into contact with silver cutlery as this can result in permanent staining of the surface. Many dishwasher manufacturers seem to be unaware of this and place the detergent dispenser directly above the cutlery tray! Remove and dry silver cutlery as soon as the dishwasher cycle has ended to avoid staining and pitting from salt residues.

DECANTERS AND CARAFES

To remove stains in the base, fill with a solution of warm water and biological detergent. Leave to soak. If the stain is stubborn, try adding two tablespoons of rice to the liquid and gently swirl it around, to help abrade and loosen the dirt. After cleaning, rinse the decanter thoroughly in warm water. Stand it upside-down in a wide-necked jug to drain and become completely dry before storing.

If the stopper is stuck, put on rubber gloves to protect your hands and help with gripping. Wrap a very hot, damp cloth around the neck of the decanter to expand the glass, then slowly dribble vegetable oil around the stopper. Wiggle and twist the stopper gently and it should come free. To avoid this problem reoccurring, store the decanter with a twist of clingfilm or muslin separating the stopper from the main body of the glass.

Removing stains from stainless steel

Hot grease can leave rainbow-coloured marks, and minerals in tap water can cause a white film if not dried thoroughly. Acidic foods such as vinegar may also cause staining – a proprietary stainless-steel cleaner will remove most marks.

TIP
To remove tea stains from teaspoons, soak them overnight in Bar Keepers Friend, or in a mug of hot water to which one teaspoon of biological detergent has been added. Rinse and wash thoroughly after soaking.

DEEP-FAT FRYERS

Lids of most deep-fat fryers are detachable, and some can be cleaned in the dishwasher. Clean the inside of the fryer every time the oil is changed (about every six uses). Once the oil has been emptied, clean the tank with a plastic scouring pad and washing-up liquid, taking care not to damage any non-stick coating. Wipe over the outside of the fryer with a damp cloth and non-abrasive cleaner after every use. Always store the fryer with the lid slightly ajar to allow air to circulate.

DISHWASHERS

Switch off the electricity supply before cleaning. Clean filters after each use. Spray arms should be cleaned in a solution of hot, soapy washing-up liquid – run water through the inlet of each spray arm to check holes are not blocked by food debris – use a needle to any remove limescale deposits. Wipe the exterior of the machine with a damp cloth and washing-up liquid solution. If the machine will not be used for some time, leave the door ajar to allow air to circulate and prevent unpleasant odours developing inside. If the dishwasher is not performing well, check that the baskets are not overloaded, the spray arms are not blocked, the correct detergent is being used, and that the filters are clean. Every now and again, use a specialist product designed to descale and freshen the machine – these are widely available in supermarkets.

DOORS

DOOR FURNITURE Clean hinges, handles and locks according to the type of metal they are made from (see Metals, pages 232–3).
UPVC Remove dirt using a proprietary frame and furniture cleaner to prevent permanent yellowing.
WOOD Wipe wood or painted wood with a damp cloth and solution of washing-up liquid. Avoid over-wetting.

DRIVEWAYS AND PATIOS

Remove the build-up of grime and algae with a high-pressure washer – take care, as these can remove pointing between paving stones. Alternatively, scrub using a stiff brush and specialist patio cleaner. Household bleach is a cheaper alternative. For heavy staining, use an acid-based cleaner. Products containing fungicide will help inhibit future regrowth of algae.

ELECTRIC FIRES

FAN HEATERS Keep the grille clean and free from dust. If the heater stops working, turn it off and unplug it, then unscrew the grille and clean inside very gently with a soft brush.
RADIANT FIRES These need to be kept sparkling clean so they reflect the maximum amount of heat, but take care not to knock the bars or the ceramic mounts when wiping the fireback.

Green tip

Don't pour discarded oil from deep-fat fryers down the sink – it is an environmental hazard as it can pollute waterways. Many local authorities have started to provide recycling facilities for used cooking oil, so check whether yours is one of them. If not, you can put small amounts into your composting bin or mix with seeds to make bird cake for feathered friends. Any leftover oil should be placed in a sealed container and put out with your regular rubbish collection.

Green tip

Running a cup of white vinegar through an empty cycle of your dishwasher once a month is a more environmentally friendly way to help keep limescale, odours and soap scum at bay.

Care with '3-in-1' dishwasher detergents

Even if you use the '3-in-1' dishwasher detergents that claim to deal with salt, rinse aid and detergent requirements, here at GHI we recommend you continue to keep your separate salt and rinse aid dispensers topped up. This is because the '3-in-1' types of products tend only to work effectively with the highest temperature dishwashing cycles, and are therefore not really suitable for use with lower temperature and 'eco' programmes.

EXTRACTOR FANS

Unplug at the mains. Remove the outer cover and wash in a warm solution of washing-up liquid. Rinse and dry. Wipe fan blades with a damp cloth wrung out in a solution of washing-up liquid – avoid getting them too wet and ensure they are dry before replacing the fan cover.

FIREPLACES

Where possible, refer to the manufacturer's cleaning instructions. Wear goggles to protect your eyes from flaking particles.

For cast- and wrought-iron, remove any surface dust by wiping with a soft cloth or using the brush attachment of your vacuum cleaner. Remove any rust with a wire brush or fine wire wool. Reblacken iron using Liberon Iron Paste. Work in sections, applying a small amount with a cloth, then buffing to a shine with a brush. Do not use water to clean uncoated iron as this will encourage rusting.

FLOORING

Vacuum or sweep hard floors regularly to avoid surface scratching by grit. If possible, follow the manufacturer's recommendations for sealants and polishes.

Wood
Sealed and unsealed wood floors need to be cleaned in different ways.

SEALED WOOD FLOORS Need only be swept and damp-mopped. Don't use too much water as wood swells. If you wish, apply an emulsion polish on top of the varnish, but remove after several applications using a proprietary wax remover. Don't apply wax polish to a sealed wood floor as it can make the floor very slippery and dangerous.

UNSEALED AND WAXED FLOORS Should be swept regularly and occasionally wax-polished. Use wax sparingly as too much will leave a tacky surface and attract dirt. Buff well. If worn patches appear in the surface, apply a non-slip floor polish. On waxed floors, polish and dirt builds up over time and the only way to clean them is to remove the wax and start again. Use a cloth moistened with white spirit. Let it soak in, and as the wax and dirt begin to dissolve, wipe away with crumpled newspaper. Scrub obstinate parts by hand, or with abrasive pads on a floor polisher. When polish has been removed, damp-mop with clean water. Allow to dry completely before applying new polish, working over small sections at a time. Don't varnish a waxed floor as it will not dry properly.

FOOD MIXERS AND PROCESSORS

Disconnect from the electrical supply before cleaning. Bowls, lids and feed chutes are usually dishwasher-safe, but it is better to wash blades by hand in a solution of hot, soapy water, using a soft kitchen brush rather than a cloth (to avoid cuts).

TIP
Use bicarbonate of soda and a damp cloth to get rid of shoe-heel marks.

TIP
For more stubborn stains, make a paste of two parts bicarbonate of soda and one part water and rub into the bowl using a nylon scourer, then wash and rinse as normal.

FLOORING TYPES: CLEANING AND CARE

- ⊙ **CERAMIC TILES** These need minimal maintenance – sweep and wash with a mild detergent solution. Rinse with clear water. Do not polish. Tile cleaning products are available at tile outlets. To clean dirty grouting, use a soft toothbrush dipped in a mild bleach solution, then rinse well. Specialist grout cleaning products can also be used.

- ⊙ **CORK** Wipe clean factory-sealed cork tiles with a damp mop, using a solution of washing-up liquid. To give an extra protective layer, especially in areas such as kitchens or bathrooms, apply an acrylic or polyurethane sealant. Never over-wet and take care not to damage the seal or protective coating by dragging appliances or furniture over tiles.

- ⊙ **LAMINATES** Vacuum, dust or wipe with a damp mop or cloth. Don't use soap-based detergents or other polishes, as they may leave a dull film on the floor, and avoid over-wetting. Don't use wax polish. To remove marks and stains, use a little dilute solution of water and vinegar. Never be tempted to use abrasive cleaners as these can scratch the floor's finish. Stubborn marks, such as shoe polish, can be removed with nail polish remover containing acetone. To protect the floor from scratching, put felt pads underneath furniture legs and castors.

- ⊙ **LINOLEUM** Sweep or vacuum surface to remove grit or dust. Clean with a damp mop and a solution of washing-up liquid. Use water sparingly and rinse after washing. Stubborn marks can be removed by rubbing lightly with a nylon pad and neat washing-up liquid. If you prefer a glossy finish, use an water-based emulsion polish twice yearly. Apply one thin coat at a time and allow to dry completely between coats. Do not use wax polish.

- ⊙ **QUARRY TILES** These should be swept and washed with a neutral detergent. Rinse with clear water. Do not polish. Quarry tiles do not require sealant or polish. To restore faded colour, use specialist products to remove polish.

- ⊙ **STONE (INCLUDING SLATE, FLAGSTONE, GRANITE AND MARBLE)** Stone should be protected with a resin sealant as it is susceptible to staining. To clean sealed stone, first vacuum thoroughly, then mop with a mild detergent solution. To remove grease or oil, use a proprietary spot stain remover suitable for stone.

- ⊙ **TERRACOTTA TILES** For the first year after installation, terracotta tiles mature. Most suppliers stock specialist cleaner, sealant and polish so make enquiries at the point of sale and use recommended products. Older floors may have traces of linseed oil on them, so in wet areas such as kitchens, bathrooms and utility rooms, use a specialist floor sealant that will not react with it, such as Liberon Floor Sealer. In dry areas, if you prefer a wax finish, apply a floor wax by Liberon. New floors are more absorbent, so to protect tiles from staining and water damage, apply several coats of sealant material.

- ⊙ **VINYL** Sweep with a soft brush or vacuum, then wipe over with a damp cloth or sponge, using a solution of detergent or floor cleaner. Rinse thoroughly after wiping. To remove scuff marks, use a cloth dipped in neat washing-up liquid or white spirit, then rinse off.

If stains from carrots or curry paste do not come off with normal washing, try wiping the bowl with a paper towel dipped in vegetable oil. Repeat if necessary, then wash in hot, soapy water to remove any greasy residues.

FREEZERS

Unplug the freezer before cleaning and freshening the inside with a solution of warm water and bicarbonate of soda (15ml/1tbsp to 1 litre/ 2 pints). Remove stains using neat bicarbonate of soda on a damp cloth. Clean outside with a solution of washing-up liquid, rinse and wipe dry. If your freezer has a drip pan at the back, clean this out too.

Defrosting

Many modern freezers are frost-free, but older freezers need to be defrosted when the frost is about 3–4cm (1–½in) thick. Remove all food and store in an icebox or other cool place, wrapped in newspaper. Speed up defrosting by placing containers of hot water in the freezer cabinet. Scrape off ice using a wooden spoon or spatula. Never use a knife or other sharp implement. When all ice has melted, wipe the freezer dry, replace food and switch on again. You can help prevent your freezer from developing ice too quickly by opening the door less often and closing it quickly – this is because water vapour in the air gets into the freezer whenever you open it and forms ice once it freezes. Freezers should run at a temperature of -18°C/-0.4°F.

TIP

Odours can be removed by wiping with a sterilising fluid, such as Milton and leaving the door open for as long as possible.

FRIDGES

Get into the habit of checking the contents of your fridge regularly. If you don't unpleasant things happen. Shelves become sticky and moulds can start appearing on forgotten-about food. At least once a week, check date labels and throw away anything past its sell-by date. To clean the fridge, unplug it first. Remove all the shelves and drawers – either run these through the dishwasher or wash in hot, soapy water. Wipe all the inside surfaces of the fridge with a damp cloth, and dry well with a soft, clean cloth. Clean the outside with a solution of washing-up liquid. Don't forget to plug the fridge back in. Periodically, dust the condenser coils at the back of the fridge.

Preventing fridge odours

To help prevent odours, keep strong-smelling foods in tightly sealed containers and place an open container of bicarbonate of soda at the back of the fridge, Replace with new soda every month. See How to Clean a Fridge Thoroughly, page 218.

FURNITURE

FRENCH POLISHED Dust regularly with a soft cloth. Remove sticky marks with a cloth wrung out in a warm, mild detergent solution, taking care not to over-wet. Dry thoroughly with a soft cloth. Use a wax polish occasionally and sparingly. Serious damage on valuable

POLISHES

There are three main types. You cannot mix them, i.e. solvent and water-based. If you start with one, you have to stick with it.

- ◉ **SOLID WAX POLISH** The old-fashioned, beeswax-type sold in a flat tin like shoe polish. It is solvent-based and suitable for unvarnished wooden floors and cork. Hard work to apply and has to be done by hand and buffed up to a shine – but produces the best results.
- ◉ **LIQUID WAX POLISH** A solvent-based liquid, sold in a tin with a screw-top opening. It can be applied with an electric floor polisher. Suitable for the same

floors as solid wax, and is easier to apply but may need more applications to get a similar finish. Has to be polished very well to get a good shine.

With both these types, the more buffing you do, the better the shine – the friction builds up heat, which drives off the solvent and leaves the wax gleaming.

- ◉ **WATER-BASED EMULSION POLISHES** Generally silicone polishes. These are easy to apply because they are usually self-shining. They are reasonably long lasting and claim to make the floor easier to clean because the gloss repels dirt.

items should be repaired professionally. Contact the British Antique Furniture Restorers' Association (see Useful Organisations) for recommendations.

LACQUERED Wipe with a damp duster. Apply a fine water-mist spray directly on to the duster to avoid over-wetting the wood. Wipe dry and buff with a soft, dry duster. Occasionally apply a good furniture polish to revive shine. Grease and finger marks can be removed with a damp cloth and a mild solution of soapflakes. Take care not to over-wet. Dry thoroughly with a soft cloth.

LLOYD LOOM Vacuum with a nozzle attachment. A small, stiff brush may help loosen dust. Wash down using a solution of washing-up liquid and a soft brush. Don't over-wet. Rinse and allow to dry out thoroughly.

MARBLE Wipe over with a solution of washing-up liquid. Polish once or twice a year with a proprietary marble polish to bring back shine. Stains may be treated with turpentine, although this may take several attempts. If any stain remains, cut a lemon in half and rub on the affected area, but only allow the lemon to remain in contact with the marble for a few moments (any longer can cause permanent acid damage), and rinse away all traces afterwards. Alternatively, try a proprietary cleaner such as Lithofin Oil-Ex and follow treatment with Lithofin Stain-Stop to protect marble from future accidents.

WAXED WOOD Dust regularly with a soft cloth. Remove sticky marks with a cloth wrung out in warm, mild detergent, taking care not to over-wet. Dry thoroughly with a soft cloth. Apply a wax polish once a year. Solid beeswax gives the best results, but requires a lot of elbow grease.

GARDEN FURNITURE

CANE Retain the manufacturer's cleaning instructions for reference. Most items only need vacuuming with an upholstery nozzle, or a wipe with a damp cloth to remove dust. Never leave cane furniture outdoors.

CAST ALUMINIUM Wipe clean with a solution of washing-up liquid. Touch up chipped paint with enamel metal paint (after rubbing any loose paint off with wire wool). Some manufacturers provide a touch-up kit.

CAST AND WROUGHT IRON Wearing protective goggles, rub down with wire wool and repaint with anti-rust primer and exterior metal paint.

SYNTHETIC RESIN Use a detergent solution and a plastic brush to clean. Remove stains with a mild solution of household bleach. Rinse well.

TUBULAR METAL Wash down plastic-coated furniture with a warm solution of washing-up liquid. Protect with a light application of wax polish. Store indoors.

WOOD Hardwoods such as teak, cedar, mahogany and oak do not usually need preserving. Wipe over with teak oil twice a year to help preserve colour. Softer woods, such as pine, ash, elm and beech need preserving. Apply a proprietary wood preservative, followed by a good varnish. To restore painted and varnished woods, rub down with fine sandpaper, then reapply the appropriate coating.

Green tip

You can make your own furniture polish using a mixture of two parts olive oil/one part natural lemon juice shaken up together in an empty spray bottle – this homemade polish smells wonderful and cuts through marks with ease, while also being kinder to the environment.

TIP
Lubricate hinged metal sections with household oil or WD-40 to keep then running smoothly and free of rust.

GLASSWARE

Glassware can become cloudy when washed in a dishwasher. This is because, over time the energetic action of the machine etches the glasses with tiny scratches, in which limescale can build up. The combination of these two factors causes the characteristic cloudiness. Unfortunately, if you have left it too long and the etching is very bad, the damage will be permanent, but you can try the following remedy. Check that rinse aid and salt levels are topped up, then try washing glasses using citric acid crystals (available from chemists). Fill the detergent dispenser with the citric acid and run the glasses through a normal wash, without any detergent. The citric acid acts as a limescale remover, and will descale the dishwasher at the same time. If this doesn't work, try soaking the glasses overnight in neat white vinegar, then rinse in cold water

It is always better to wash glassware (including lead crystal) by hand. Use warm water and washing-up liquid, then rinse in clean water. Dry with a soft linen cloth. If you must use the dishwasher, make sure it is always topped up with adequate rinse aid and salt, and remove glasses before the drying cycle starts – high temperatures accelerate the etching process. Alternatively, buy cheap glassware you won't mind replacing every couple of years. Don't store glasses stacked one inside the other as they can stick, and stand them with the drinking edge up – the top rim is the most delicate part and more prone to chipping.

GRIDDLE PANS

If using a cast-iron pan for the first time, wash it in soapy water beforehand, then rinse and dry thoroughly. Brush the pan with cooking oil, then heat slowly until the pan is very hot but not smoking. Leave to cool, and wipe out before use. After use, cool the pan completely before washing or soaking, making sure you remove any bits of cooked food. It is especially important to keep cast-iron pans clean – if debris builds up, the pan will start to smoke when you use it.

ICE CREAM MAKERS

Many recipes use raw eggs, so good hygiene is essential. Wash bowls with a hot washing-up liquid solution and always dry thoroughly with paper towels before use.

IRONS

Remove burnt-on or sticky deposits on the soleplate using a proprietary soleplate cleaner, making sure you work in a well-ventilated room as cleaners give off fumes. Alternatively, heat the iron on a warm setting and rub across a damp, loosely woven cloth or coarse towel held taut over the edge of the ironing board. Gentle use of a moistened nylon scourer will remove normal dirt.

Descaling irons

Always check the manufacturer's instructions before using any type of proprietary descaler – many irons are not suitable for such products. Built-in anti-scale devices should be replaced regularly.

JUICERS

Clean immediately after use to avoid fruit and vegetable pulp sticking and staining. Using a kitchen brush or the brush provided, clean all parts with hot, soapy water, taking care when handling the grating sieve, which has sharp edges. Wipe the motor housing with a damp cloth to remove spills. If the plastic has stained, use a damp cloth and mild solution of bleach or rub with vegetable oil on paper towels. Rinse well.

KETTLES

If the elements in your kettle are exposed rather than positioned behind a metal base plate, limescale build-up is one of the biggest causes of kettle element failure, so make sure to descale yours regularly. In hard water areas, this can be as often as every 4–6 weeks. Use a proprietary chemical descaler suitable for your kettle. Rinse the kettle thoroughly afterwards and boil up several times with fresh water after treatment. Use a kettle protector (available from hardware stores), a stainless-steel ball that attracts scale away from the element to help keep the problem at bay.

KITCHEN UNITS

Doors

COLOURED/WOOD EFFECT Wipe with a damp cloth and washing-up liquid solution, taking care not to over-wet the surface. Rub stains carefully with a slightly abrasive cream cleaner.

HIGH-GLOSS SURFACES These are easily scratched, so use a soft, damp cloth and make sure it is free from grit. Use neat washing-up liquid on stains, rubbing gently with a soft cloth, then rinsing and drying. Buff with a chamois leather to remove any water marks.

Green tip

Instead of using a chemical descaler, fill the kettle with a mixture of half white vinegar and half water and leave to soak overnight. In the morning, the limescale will come off easily. Rinse thoroughly to remove any lingering vinegary odours.

Cupboard interiors

Remove all items and wipe surfaces with a damp cloth and antibacterial cleaner or washing-up liquid solution. Replace items only when interiors are thoroughly dry. Take care not to soak exposed chipboard and around hinge joints where water can seep through to the chipboard below.

STAINLESS STEEL Wipe with a damp cloth and washing-up liquid solution to remove grease and marks. Buff dry with a soft cloth. For a streak-free finish, put a dab of baby oil on a clean cloth and rub down the whole surface. Never use abrasive products on stainless steel as it is easily scratched.

WOOD/WOOD VENEER Wipe with a damp cloth and washing-up liquid solution. Use neat washing-up liquid on stains, rubbing along the grain with a soft cloth.

LAMPSHADES

FABRIC Vacuum carefully using the soft brush attachment of your cleaner, reducing the suction strength to as low as possible. Spot treat stains with a solution of washing-up liquid at your peril – it might remove the surface finish and cause watermarks.

GLASS/PLASTIC Dust regularly or use a clean cloth and a solution of washing-up liquid.

PAPER/PARCHMENT Brush often with a feather duster. Avoid wetting.

RAFFIA/STRAW Vacuum using the soft brush attachment of your cleaner. Avoid wetting.

METALS

Always work in a well-ventilated room and protect worksurfaces with newspaper as some cleaners can leave marks on laminates and stainless-steel surfaces. Wear cotton or rubber gloves to prevent your hands getting messy and also to prevent grease from your hands getting on the polished metal. Use cotton buds or an old toothbrush to get into intricate areas.

Copper and brass

Wash in a warm solution of washing-up liquid, brush gently with a soft brush, then rinse and dry with a soft cloth. Polish in one of the following ways (see Copper and Brass Cleaning Techniques, right).

Lacquered items

These only need dusting and occasional washing in warm soapy water. If the lacquer wears away, remove with a proprietary paint remover, then polish brass or copper as above. Reapply transparent lacquer, such as Rustins Clear Metal Lacquer, or have the item professionally relacquered.

Pewter

About once a year, wash in warm, soapy water and dry well with a soft cloth. Never use harsh polish. If the pewter is heavily tarnished, use a proprietary silver polish (these are gentler than other metal polishes).

Silver

Silver is the metal most prone to tarnishing. Tarnishing is caused by hydrogen sulphide present in the atmosphere acting on the surface of silver. Several things encourage tarnishing, including certain foods, particularly acidic ones. Acid can also cause etching and pit marks. Cutlery is especially at risk, so always wash promptly after use. Use a warm solution

SILVER CLEANING TECHNIQUES

- ⊙ **CREAMS/LIQUIDS** Often recommended by manufacturers of fine silver services, these are ideal to clean medium tarnishing. Allow to dry to a fine, powdery deposit, then buff with a soft, dry cloth. Some require rinsing in water, so are ideal for cutlery, which needs cleaning after being polished anyway.
- ⊙ **FOAMING PASTES** These are ideal for cutlery, and for covering larger areas, such as platters, and are easy to use. The paste is applied with a damp sponge and lathers to a foam. Rinse in water and dry thoroughly.
- ⊙ **SPRAYS** Good for covering larger areas.
- ⊙ **WADDING** For heavier tarnishing. This is messy and requires elbow grease. Don't use too frequently as it is quite abrasive.
- ⊙ **DIPS** Not recommended by experts as they leave silver duller and with less lustre. Best for small items such as jewellery (but don't use on pearls, opals or coral). Only suitable for light tarnishing. Always follow the manufacturer's soaking times.
- ⊙ **DIY DIP** Line a plastic washing-up bowl with aluminium foil. Fill with very hot water and add a handful of washing soda crystals. Completely immerse tarnished silver, ensuring it is in contact with the foil. The aluminium and soda react with the tarnish to pull it off the silver without any effort! Don't immerse items for more than ten minutes and replace foil when it darkens.

of washing-up liquid. Rinse in hot water and dry immediately. When dusting, use impregnated silver polishing cloths and mitts, but don't rub too hard – silver is a very soft metal and a fine layer is removed every time items are polished. Over time, this damages fine detail and wears silver plate. To avoid scratching, use straight, even strokes and never rub crosswise or with a rotary movement.

IMPORTANT Never mix silver and stainless-steel cutlery in a dishwasher as the silver will turn black and do not allow dry dishwasher detergent to come into contact with silver items as black spots can appear. Remove and dry silver cutlery immediately after the dishwasher cycle has ended to avoid staining and pitting. For best results, wash by hand.

Silver-plate

Treat as for silver, but polish with less vigour as the plating is softer. Don't use dip solutions to clean silver-plate that is worn as they can attack the base metal, and never leave in the dip for more than ten seconds. Avoid using abrasive cleaners, such as wadding. Worn silver-plate can be resilvered, but this is quite expensive. For companies that offer a replating service, contact the British Cutlery and Silverware Association (see Useful Organisations).

MICROWAVE/COMBINATION OVENS

Always disconnect before cleaning. Models with an acrylic interior should be wiped out with a cloth and a hot solution of washing-up liquid. Never use anything abrasive. Some ovens with a stainless-steel interior can be cleaned with a normal oven spray cleaner, but spray on to a cloth first to avoid it getting into oven vents. Clean the glass plate regularly – they can usually go into the dishwasher.

Green tip

To remove microwave smells place lemon slices in a basin of cold water and heat uncovered on high to boiling point, then for a few minutes on medium so that steam passes through the vents. Wipe dry.

Green tip

For a more environmentally friendly window cleaner, mix one tablespoonful of white vinegar with 1 litre/2 pints of water in an empty spray bottle. Use as you would a proprietary glass cleaner.

MIRRORS

Use a microfibre cloth or proprietary glass cleaner and buff with a lint-free cloth or chamois leather. Don't let any liquid run between the glass and backing or under the frame as this could eventually cause spots on the silver surface behind the glass.

PAINTBRUSHES

Water-based paints need cleaning only in water and washing-up liquid. Oil-based paints require a proprietary paintbrush cleaner. If soaking is necessary, don't stand the brush directly on its bristles as this will splay and weaken them. When storing, slip a small elastic band over the bristles to hold them close together.

TIP

If you want to leave a brush overnight and continue painting the next day, wrap the bristles tightly in cling film. The paint in the brush stays wet so you don't have to clean it.

PAINTINGS

Cleaning and restoration should always be carried out by a qualified conservator. Contact the Institute of Conservation (see Useful Organisations) to find one in your area.

PANS

ALUMINIUM Always wash by hand, never in a dishwasher (it will discolour aluminium). If the pan develops a black tarnish, remove it by boiling up acidic foods, such as rhubarb or cut lemons in water. Wash the pan thoroughly afterwards.

CAST IRON Wash uncoated iron saucepans by hand, never in the dishwasher. Brush with a thin layer of cooking oil to prevent rusting.

COPPER Wash in a hot washing-up liquid solution. Polish as copper and brass (see page 232), washing the pan thoroughly afterwards.

ENAMELLED Wash in a hot solution of washing-up liquid and dry immediately to prevent a whitish film developing. Worn enamel may stain. Marks can be removed by boiling up a solution of biological washing powder in the pan, then cleaning as normal.

GLASS-CERAMIC As enamelled.

NON-STICK COATINGS Wash by hand or in the dishwasher. The non-stick coating may need to be lightly 'seasoned' by brushing the interior with cooking oil. Reseason after dishwashing. Remove tough marks with a nylon scourer and never use metal utensils on non-stick pans.

STAINLESS STEEL Wash by hand or in a dishwasher. If rainbow marks develop, remove them with a proprietary stainless-steel cleaner. Pans subjected to too high a heat may develop brown marks on the exterior – these should also come off with a proprietary stainless-steel cleaner.

Removing burnt-on deposits

For severely burnt-on deposits, bring the saucepan to the boil with a solution of 1 litre/2 pints of water and 15ml/1tbsp of biological washing powder (or a dishwasher tablet). Boil for ten minutes, repeat if necessary, then wash thoroughly.

RADIATORS

It is important to clean radiators, especially in winter, as heat carries dust up and spreads it over the paint and wallpaper above. Use a duster to

SINK TYPES: CLEANING AND CARE

⊙ **CERAMIC** As stainless steel. Restore whiteness to ceramic sinks by filling with cold water and adding a cup of bleach. Leave to soak, then rinse clean.

⊙ **COLOURED** As stainless steel. Don't leave tea, coffee and fruit juices to dry as they will leave stains. Soak stubborn stains in a solution of biological washing powder or well-diluted household bleach.

⊙ **COMPOSITES** Wipe down with a damp cloth and washing-up liquid. If limescale leaves marks, or the surface is stained, treat with Bar Keepers Friend, or remove with a scouring pad and bicarbonate of soda.

⊙ **ENAMEL** As stainless steel, but limescale removers are not recommended. To remove limescale, try using a plastic scourer, neat washing-up liquid and plenty of elbow grease or contact the Vitreous Enamel Association (see Useful Organisations). To avoid limescale building up, always dry the sink after use.

⊙ **STAINLESS STEEL** Wipe with a damp cloth and washing-up liquid solution or an antibacterial spray cleaner. For thorough cleaning, use a neat cream cleaner, rinse and dry. If you live in a hard water area, use a limescale cleaner once a week.

remove loose particles, then wipe with a damp cloth. Remember to cover the floor below while cleaning. Rinse thoroughly and dry with a soft cloth.

SINKS

Most manufacturers will send you care instructions for your sink. Many also sell their own specialist cleaning products. Don't overlook plugholes and overflows. Use a bottle brush to give them a regular cleaning. Lemon juice is good for removing rust stains from sinks. To prevent a build-up of grease in waste pipes, flush once a week with a washing soda solution (150g/5oz soda crystals to 500ml/18fl oz hot water).

TAPS

Chrome, plastic, gold and brass finishes should be cleaned regularly with a solution of washing-up liquid, rinsed and dried. Don't use abrasive cleaners. To remove limescale deposits, soak a cloth in a proprietary descaler or white vinegar and wrap it around the tap (although not for gold or brass finishes – the descaler can damage the metal coating). Don't leave for longer than the recommended time.

TUMBLE-DRIERS

Clean the filter after each use. Wipe exterior with a solution of washing-up liquid. Empty the water container in condenser-driers after every use.

VACUUM FLASKS

To prevent smells building up, store with the lid off, so air can circulate. If normal washing does not remove the smell of the last drink, fill the flask with warm water and pop in a couple of denture cleaning tablets or a few teaspoons of bicarbonate of soda. Leave to stand overnight, then wash in warm, soapy water and rinse thoroughly.

VASES

Remove white deposits on the inside of cut glass vases by filling the vase with malt vinegar and a handful of dry rice. Swill it around and leave overnight. Rinse with hot, soapy water. If this doesn't work, you could try a limescale remover designed for plastic kettles. Wear rubber gloves and apply neat, rubbing gently. Rinse immediately.

WALLS

Wall coverings can be delicate, particularly paper, so you should always test cleaning methods on an inconspicuous area first. Don't rub hard or you may damage the surface.

CERAMIC WALL TILES Wipe with a damp cloth and solution of washing-up liquid. Buff dry. Stains can be rubbed with neat washing-up liquid. To clean yellowing grouting, brush diluted bleach over the area or use a proprietary grout-whitening product.

PAINTWORK As for ceramic wall tiles. For heavy soiling, or to prepare the surface for repainting, use a sugar soap solution and rinse thoroughly.

WASHABLE/VINYL PAPER Sponge with a solution of washing-up liquid, taking care not to over-wet the surface.

TIP
Finger marks on wallpaper can sometimes be removed by rubbing the affected area gently with a balled-up piece of white bread.

WASHING MACHINES

Wipe out detergent drawers after each use to keep them free of soap build-up. Every couple of months, pull out the entire drawer and clean it thoroughly in hot, soapy water. While the drawer is out, wipe down the drawer recess with a damp cloth (unplug the machine first). Check and clean drain filters regularly – you'll be amazed by the amount of fluff that collects there. Inspect hoses for signs of wear or weakness. Most manufacturers recommend changing hoses every five years. Keep the exterior of the machine free of dust, which can be a fire hazard. Leaving the machine door slightly ajar when not in use will allow water to evaporate and help prevent mould developing on the rubber seal. Every now and again, run a maintenance wash to give the machine a good clean – set the programme at the highest possible temperature setting (60°C/140°F minimum), add powder or tablet detergent (liquids are no good as they do not contain bleach) and run the wash cycle with the machine empty. By doing this, you will help prolong the life of your machine.

WASTE BINS

Use a disinfectant spray or mild solution of bleach and a damp cloth for regular cleaning. If the bin is soiled and stained, soak in a mild solution of bleach, then wash out and rinse with clean water.

WASTE-DISPOSAL UNITS

A slice of lemon in the unit will help reduce smells. Avoid using any drain-cleaning chemicals as they may damage the unit.

WINDOWS

Take down net curtains and blinds to avoid damage. Remove ornaments from window sills. Avoid cleaning windows on a sunny day as the heat will make the glass dry too quickly and cause smears. Clean mildew off frames with an old rag dipped in fungicide. Use a proprietary window cleaner to wash the glass or make your own using 30ml/2tbsp ammonia mixed with 4 litres/7 pints water. For interior glass, use a weak solution of vinegar. Always use a lint-free cloth or chamois leather, or even crumpled newspaper to dry, for a streak-free finish. Alternatively, clean with a dampened microfibre cloth. Check exterior sills regularly for rot and immediately replace any crumbling putty around panes.

WORKTOPS

CERAMIC TILES Treat as laminates. Clean dirty grout with a toothbrush and weak bleach solution. Wipe over with a damp cloth and leave to dry.

LAMINATES AND MAN-MADE SOLID SURFACES Wipe down with washing-up liquid solution or use an all-purpose kitchen cleaner with an antibacterial agent. Remove stains with a cream cleaner, using a damp cloth. On textured surfaces, use a nylon bristle brush to get into the grain. Solvents will not damage laminates so stains such as felt-tip pen can be removed with white spirits or nail polish remover. Chips and scratches can be repaired with special laminate repairers and sealers. If you use solvents on man-made solid surfaces, always rinse them off thoroughly – prolonged contact can damage the surface. Cuts and scratches on man-made solid surfaces can be sanded away using medium-grade sandpaper, followed by fine grade. Buff well afterwards to restore shine.

NATURAL SOLID SURFACES (SUCH AS GRANITE) Treat as laminates. Pay particular attention to any joins in the surface. Wipe thoroughly with a soft cloth. This sort of surface is difficult to stain and neat washing-up liquid should be sufficient to remove marks.

STAINLESS STEEL To remove finger marks, put a dab of baby oil on a clean cloth and rub the whole surface, concentrating on marked areas. For thorough cleaning, wash stainless steel with a solution of washing-up liquid and buff dry with a soft cloth. Never use abrasive cleaning products on stainless steel as it is easily scratched.

Cleaning metal window screens

In erasable pencil, write a number on each window. Write a corresponding number on the screen before removing it from the window so you know which screen goes back where. Remove the screens and dust the mesh and frame with the soft brush attachment of your vacuum cleaner. Scrub both sides of the screen using a stiff brush dipped in detergent solution. Rinse using a shower attachment or the fine spray nozzle of a hosepipe. Leave to dry in a sunny spot before returning to the window.

Washday Wisdom

Laundry habits have changed dramatically over the past 20 years. Long gone is the tradition of washing on a Monday: wash-day blues can last all week, with some of us washing around five loads. Not only do we wash much smaller loads but also, with the increase in synthetic and man-made fabrics, gone is the boil wash and in many cases the pre-wash. As well, lower-temperature wash programmes are making new demands on detergents.

GETTING THE BEST OUT OF YOUR WASH

Whether washing by hand or machine, it is important to match the correct washing procedure to the type of fabric. Depending on how dirty your washing is, you need to consider water temperature, type of detergent, fabric and wash type, whether any special treatments are needed, and how you are going to dry and iron afterwards.

WHICH DETERGENT?

There are so many different detergent products, but do we really need all of them? The list below should help you decide which are best for you.

Powder versus liquid, gel or tablet detergent

These are all basically the same product, except that gels and liquids generally do not contain any bleach. Choose according to which you

---

MAIN DETERGENT TYPES

- ⊙ **BIOLOGICAL DETERGENT** Contains enzymes that boost cleaning power. It is the best choice for stain removal, but not suitable for prolonged use on protein-based fabrics, such as silk and wool.
- ⊙ **COLOUR-SAFE DETERGENT** Contains no bleach and has specially formulated colour protectors designed to help prevent clothes from fading when washed.
- ⊙ **DELICATES DETERGENT** Gentler than standard detergents, so more suitable for use on delicate fabrics, such as silk and wool. It does not contain enzymes, brighteners or bleaching agents.
- ⊙ **NON-BIOLOGICAL DETERGENT** Contains no enzymes and is thought to be less likely to irritate the skin. For this reason, it is also more likely to be free from added fragrances and colourings. However, the lack of enzymes means that it tends to be less effective at stain removal than biological detergent.

How is detergent different than soap ?

While soap and detergent basically perform the same function, they are not the same product. Detergents are synthetic products made from petroleum, while soap is made from natural fats. Detergents have better cleaning power and are easier to rinse away – they won't leave the familiar ring of 'scum' associated with soap. Another important point about soap is that it will 'set' tannin-based stains, such as tea, red wine and coffee – so if in doubt about the origin of a stain, it is always better to use a detergent.

OTHER INGREDIENTS THAT MAY BE FOUND IN DETERGENTS

- ⊙ **BLEACH** Helps keep items looking bright and removes stains caused by coloured materials.
- ⊙ **BUILDERS** These enhance cleaning action by deactivating the minerals that cause hard water.
- ⊙ **ENZYMES** Break down amino acids in protein-based stains, such as blood and egg, so the stain can be more easily removed.
- ⊙ **FABRIC CONDITIONERS** Reduce friction and static, reduce creasing and help give clothing a soft, fluffy feel.
- ⊙ **OPTICAL BRIGHTENERS** Used to improve the whiteness of fabrics. They work by reflecting light in such a way that the eye is tricked into thinking the washed clothing looks brighter.

- ⊙ **POLYMERS** Help to trap and hold dirt and dyes, and prevent them from being redeposited on clothing.
- ⊙ **PRESERVATIVES** Lengthen the product's shelf life.
- ⊙ **SOLVENTS** Prevent liquid detergents separating during storage.
- ⊙ **STABILISERS** Help maintain enzymes, bleach and suds-making ability, prolonging the product's shelf life.
- ⊙ **SURFACTANTS** Provide the primary cleaning action by improving the wetting ability of water, loosening and removing dirt, then dissolving, emulsifying or suspending it in the wash solution until it is rinsed away.

---

prefer. Powder is usually the cheapest, but is messier to use and you have to measure out the correct dosage yourself. Tablets save you the bother of measuring. Liquids and gels are more expensive, but handy for pre-treating stains and spots prior to washing. They are also less likely to leave those characteristic streaks caused by undissolved powder or tablet detergents. However, their lack of bleach means that bacteria is not killed and mould is more likely to build up on the rubber door seal of your washing machine. Overdosing with liquids and gels is also a common problem.

CHOOSING THE CORRECT WASH

Always read garment labels thoroughly before washing. These are designed to give you information about the fabric and how to care for it. The labels may not be immediately obvious, so look at the neck, hem or in a side seam. Furnishing fabrics often have the instructions printed on the selvedge, so keep a section back when sewing. If you find garments more comfortable without labels make sure you keep them safe so you can refer to them when necessary. The label should include details of:

Fibre content

This tells you exactly what the garment is made from – whether it's pure cotton or a blend, for example – and is a legal requirement. However, if there is less than 15 per cent of a fibre included it doesn't have to be listed as long as the bulk of fibres are. You may come across 'mixed fibres', which means mixed waste or reclaimed fibres have been used, which are difficult to analyse.

Washing and care instructions

Most garments in the UK have washing instructions as promoted and recommended by the HLCC (Home Laundering Consultative Council, www.care-labelling.co.uk, see Useful Organisations); see Understanding Laundry Symbols, opposite. These instructions include washing

Water temperature

It is vital to choose the correct water temperature because this can affect various aspects of wash results.

- ⊙ **COLOUR** Too high a temperature will cause fading of non-colourfast fabrics.
- ⊙ **CREASING** Many synthetic fabrics crease more when washed at high temperatures.
- ⊙ **CLEANING EFFICIENCY** Lower temperatures are less effective at removing some types of stain.
- ⊙ **ENERGY CONSUMPTION** Low temperature washes use less energy, so are kinder to the environment and work out cheaper too.
- ⊙ **FABRIC FINISHES** Easy-care finishes can be broken down by higher temperature washes.
- ⊙ **FIBRE TYPE AND CONSTRUCTION** Delicate fibres, such as wool or silk generally require lower temperature washing, while cottons and linens can take higher temperatures.

UNDERSTANDING LAUNDRY SYMBOLS

Always use the recommended care label advice to achieve the best results and help make your clothes look good and last longer. Labels on clothes should correspond with programmes on your washing machine.

As a general guide you can combine:

- All items without the bar symbol, and wash at the lowest quoted temperature.
- All items with the same bar symbol, and wash at the lowest quoted temperature.
- Wash labels with and without a bar, provided that you wash at the lowest temperature, but you must also reduce the washing action.

Always follow any special instructions shown on labels, particularly 'wash separately', which means what it says. Heavily soiled goods should be washed according to the care label, and not included in mixed loads.

THE SYMBOLS EXPLAINED

 Wash tub The washing process by machine or hand.

 Triangle Chlorine bleaching.

 Iron Ironing.

 Circle Dry-cleaning.

 Circle in Square Tumble-drying (after washing).

 St Andrew's Cross Do Not.

WASHING

 Cotton wash (no bar below)
A wash tub without a bar indicates that normal (maximum) washing conditions may be used at the appropriate temperature.

 Synthetics wash (single bar below)
A single bar beneath the wash tub indicates reduced (medium) washing conditions at the appropriate temperature.

 Wool wash (double underline below)
A double underline beneath the wash tub indicates much reduced (minimum) washing conditions, and is designed specifically for machine-washable wool products.

 Handwash only
Do not machine-wash.

 Do not wash

BLEACHING

Any bleach may be used.

Only oxygen bleach/non-chlorine bleach.

 Do not use bleach.

TUMBLE-DRYING

 May be tumble-dried.

 May be tumble-dried with high heat setting.

 May be tumble-dried with low heat setting.

 Do not tumble-dry.

DRY-CLEANING

Must be dry-cleaned. Letter within the circle and/or bar beneath circle indicates to dry-cleaner the solvent and process to be used.

Do not dry-clean

IRONING

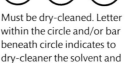

Iron at cool setting.

Iron at warm setting.

Iron at hot setting.

Do not iron.

recommendations, whether by hand or machine, suitability for certain treatments such as bleaching, plus drying and ironing procedures. Dry-cleaning instructions are also provided. As a general rule, the wash tub symbol represents washing, the triangle is about bleaching, the square is about drying, the iron about ironing and the circle about dry-cleaning.

PREPARING THE WASH LOAD

- Empty and turn all pockets outwards.
- Brush off any surplus mud, dust or fluff.
- Remove tissues from sleeves.
- Close zips and do up buttons.
- Make all repairs before you wash; washing will make damage worse.
- Turn pile fabrics, jeans and corduroy inside out.

SORTING THE LOAD

- Identify any items that must be washed separately.
- Sort out hand-wash only items.
- Group together items with the same wash symbol, but don't mix whites and non-colourfast fabrics.
- If you have to machine-wash mixed loads, always wash them according to the instructions for the most delicate fabric. Whites, however, will benefit from washing every few washes at their correct recommended temperature.

MACHINE-WASHING TIPS

- Before loading, shake items out, and load one at a time to reduce tangling.
- Load evenly with small items, then large, taking care not to over-fill.
- Follow care label instructions and do not over-dose with detergent, especially if washing small loads.
- If colours do run place the dyed item back in the washing machine and rewash.

Dosage

Overdosing can cause soap deposits and lint to form inside your washing machine, which can contribute to mould and bad smells. It can also plug filters and eventually lead to mechanical failure. For some high-efficiency (sensor) washing machines, overdosing can produce excessive suds and lead to overlong wash cycles as the machine tries to remove the soap, thus shortening the machine's life. To get the best results, it is important you pay attention to the manufacturer's dosing instructions according to level of soiling.

- **LIGHTLY SOILED** Generally means garments that are not worn next to the skin.
- **MEDIUM SOILED** Refers to items that are worn next to the skin (i.e. most clothing).
- **HEAVILY SOILED** Refers to items that are really mucky (such as tea-towels or dishcloths) or have been worn under physical duress and will be full of bodily fluids such as sweat etc. (such as sportswear)

For most everyday clothing, you will need to wash them as 'medium soiled'.

PRE-WASH SOAKING

- Use when items are very heavily soiled or stained.
- As a general rule, don't soak silk, wool, leather (including trimmings), elastanes, fabrics with special treatments such as flame retardancy, easy-care, non-colourfast dyes and items with metal fasteners.
- Soak in a plastic bucket or bath with plenty of water and check detergent is thoroughly dissolved before adding the clothes.
- Water should be cool for protein-based stains, such as egg, blood and milk; and hand hot for others.
- Allow to soak for several hours, or overnight for whites.
- For persistent marks, rub detergent or a stain-removal bar directly on to the stain.
- Treat collars and cuffs before washing. Dampen and rub liquid detergent along the marks. Leave for an hour and then scrub with an old toothbrush.
- To reduce colour run, soak the fabric in a solution of salt and water using 15ml/1tbsp of salt to 500ml/1 pint of water.

- ⊙ Wash tights and stockings in a pillowcase or cotton bag.
- ⊙ Don't leave damp items in the machine or clothes basket as mildew can develop.
- ⊙ To eliminate fluff, add 200ml/7fl oz/1 cup of white vinegar to the final rinse.

HAND-WASHING TIPS

- ⊙ Sort according to colour and temperature.
- ⊙ Make sure the detergent is thoroughly dissolved.
- ⊙ Rinse in cold water until free of scum. Add a little vinegar to the final rinse to remove all the scum.
- ⊙ Don't rub wool or it will pill. Gently squeeze the water through the fabric.

SPECIAL TREATMENTS

You may need to use special treatments for particular clothes or fabrics, such as starching shirts. Bleach or dye can be used to revamp clothes and prolong their life.

Bleaching
- ⊙ Always wear gloves.
- ⊙ Bleaches, particularly chlorine, should be diluted or they will rot fabric.
- ⊙ Do not bleach wool, silk, viscose, fabrics with special finishes, and deep colours.
- ⊙ Check the care label and try on a hidden area first.
- ⊙ Avoid bleaching damaged or discoloured items as they won't bleach evenly.
- ⊙ Rinse thoroughly or residual bleach will damage the fabric.
- ⊙ Check the container you use is colour-fast.

Starching
- ⊙ Mostly used for stiffening cotton or linen.
- ⊙ If you want a very stiff result, use a powdered starch. Vary the concentration depending on the application.
- ⊙ Liquid starches are easier to use.
- ⊙ Use a basin or bucket for powdered starches, rather than the washing machine.
- ⊙ Starch after washing, spin and finally rinse to remove excess starch.
- ⊙ Spray starches often contain silicones for easier ironing.

Dyeing
Home dyeing is an inexpensive way of adding a new lease of life to sad-looking clothes. However, it's not suitable for all fabrics and there are a few basic rules to bear in mind and choices to make.

MACHINE DYES: for natural fibres – cotton and linen – but not for silk, wool or viscose.
HAND DYES: for natural fibres, including wool and silk.

Green tips

In most households, the washing machine is used on a daily basis, but our desire for cleanliness can have a heavy environmental impact. Resources, such as water and electricity are consumed, detergents are discharged into the sewer system and the washing machine must be disposed of at the end of its useful life. Here are ten steps you can take to help make doing your laundry more environmentally friendly.

✱ **INVEST IN A NEW MACHINE** Most modern washing machines are now much kinder to the environment than older models. They do not require such high levels of water, due to increased overall washing performance; this not only saves you money on water bills if you are metered, but also means that less electricity is consumed, as there is less water to heat.

✱ **CONSIDER WHETHER YOU REALLY NEED TO WASH THE ITEM** We're not suggesting sacrificing hygiene, but do think carefully before just throwing clothing into the laundry basket. Most clothes do not need washing after every wear and will last longer if you don't wash them so often.

✱ **WASH ONLY FULL LOADS OF LAUNDRY** It is wasteful of both water and electricity to wash just a few items at a time. A full load will maximise your machine's energy efficiency.

✱ **WASH AT LOWER TEMPERATURES OR USE THE 'ECO' SETTING IF YOUR MACHINE HAS ONE** A 30°C rather than 40°C wash uses less energy and will get most clothes just as clean, especially with effective modern detergents.

✱ **USE COLOUR-SAFE DETERGENTS ON COLOURED ITEMS** These don't contain bleach and will help prolong the life of your clothing, meaning you have to throw it away less quickly.

✱ **USE AN ENVIRONMENTALLY FRIENDLY DETERGENT** Look for detergents that are biodegradable, contain no phosphates and are made from plant-based ingredients, rather than petroleum.

✱ **CONCENTRATED DETERGENTS** Use less packaging and have a smaller carbon footprint because more product can be shipped using less space and fuel.

✱ **IF YOUR MACHINE PERMITS, CHOOSE A COLD FINAL RINSE** Cold water gets rid of detergent just as effectively as hot water and uses less energy.

✱ **LET CLOTHES DRY NATURALLY, RATHER THAN USING A TUMBLE-DRIER** This is much kinder to the environment and nothing beats the smell of line-dried clothes.

✱ **DON'T IRON CLOTHING UNLESS YOU REALLY HAVE TO** Ironing isn't just one of our least favourite chores, it also consumes energy, so iron only those items that really need it. Hanging clothes up immediately after the cycle has finished will also help creases to drop out naturally.

MULTI-PURPOSE/UNIVERSAL DYES: for natural fibres and polyamide.
COLD-WATER DYES: for natural fibres, including wool and silk.

Remember you can't:

- ◉ Dye acrylics.
- ◉ Cover patterns with dye.
- ◉ Cover stains and marks with dye.
- ◉ Dye anything a perfect black.
- ◉ Remove colour from polyesters before dyeing them.

DRYING

First, spin dry the wash load, if possible, to remove any excess water. When spinning delicates, such as tights and stockings, place them in a pillowcase first. Otherwise wring them gently or roll them carefully in a towel to soak

TEN GOLDEN RULES FOR HOME DYEING

1 Wash and remove all stains so the fabrics will take the colour evenly.

2 You'll get better results if you remove the original colour first. Proprietary colour removers will strip non-colourfast dyes (natural fibres and some synthetics) to neutral.

3 Follow the manufacturer's recommended instructions carefully. Don't skimp on dye or else the colour won't match the colour card.

4 Wear gloves and wipe up spills immediately.

5 Machine dyeing will produce more even results than dyeing by hand, and is less messy.

6 Specialist machine dyes won't leave the drum of your machine dirty, but wipe any spills off the outside or window immediately. If using multi-purpose dyes in the machine you will need to dissolve the dye in a container beforehand and to clean the machine after use.

7 Smaller items, such as T-shirts and shirts, dye the best. Anything bulky or expensive should be professionally dyed.

8 If you have to dye over the original colour remember the basic rules: blue on yellow goes green, blue on pink equals mauve, red and yellow will make orange or red etc. For best results, dye within the same colour spectrum from pale to dark, for example pale blue to navy or black over grey. Add very dark blue dye to black dye to give a darker result.

9 Use a proprietary colour fixer, which helps to keep colours brighter after dyeing. Also stops dye bleeding on to other items.

10 Polyester does not dye well and blends containing this are pale and may be slightly mottled where the different fibres are. Obviously, the more polyester in the blend the paler the result will be.

up the water. Dry naturally wherever possible, rather than using tumble-driers – they are expensive to run and consume vast amounts of energy.

IRONING

All irons have at least three heat settings, each suitable for certain fabrics, depicted by one to three dots on the iron (see right).

Taking the stress out of ironing

◉ Always allow the iron to heat up thoroughly. This will give the thermostat time to settle down. Leave the iron for several minutes when changing temperatures as it does take time to adapt. This is particularly important when going from hot to cool.

◉ Start with the items needing the coolest settings, and work up to the hottest.

◉ If in doubt about temperature, start at the lowest and work your way up, ironing a small hidden area of the garment.

◉ When using a damp cloth you will need a higher temperature setting because the cloth will cool the soleplate.

◉ Move the garment away from you as you iron, supporting large items to avoid the fabric distorting.

◉ Use a plant sprayer to dampen really dry cottons and linen.

IRON SETTINGS

Cool ●
Acrylic, Silk, Polyamide, Acetate, Polyester

Warm ●●
Polyester blends, Wool

Hot ●●●
Cotton, Linen, Viscose, Denim

DRYING TIPS

LINE DRYING
DO
- ✔ Wipe the line before use.
- ✔ Line dry whites: the sunlight will bleach and freshen them.
- ✔ Hang pleated garments on a hanger.
- ✔ Hang drip-dry skirts by the waistband.
- ✔ Turn coloureds inside out to prevent fading.
- ✔ Fold sheets in half and hang by the hem.
- ✔ Hang striped garments vertically.

DON'T
- ✘ Dry silk, wool or polyamide outside because sunlight will cause them to yellow and weaken considerably.

FLAT DRYING
DO
- ✔ Flat dry knitted and jersey fabrics to avoid stretching.
- ✔ Pull into shape when damp.

DON'T
- ✘ Dry near a direct heat source such as a fire or radiator.

TUMBLE-DRYING
DO
- ✔ Make sure to always check care labels. Do not tumble-dry wool, knits, delicates and elastanes.
- ✔ Choose the correct heat setting for the type of fabric. Synthetics must be dried using the cool cycle or else the fibres could melt, crease or shrink.
- ✔ Tumble-dry harsh towels – it should soften them.
- ✔ Clean filters regularly.

DON'T
- ✘ Over-load, or drying will be patchy and uneven.
- ✘ Dry very large and small items together or results will be uneven.
- ✘ Over-dry, as the fibres can become brittle, more difficult to iron – and it's also a waste of energy.

Ironing tips

- ◉ Iron pile fabrics on the reverse side, on a thick cloth or towel, using minimum pressure.
- ◉ When ironing pleated items, tack the pleats down first; this will be quicker in the long run and will avoid double lines. Alternatively, hold pleats down with paper clips.
- ◉ If the fabric has a special finish, iron on the wrong side.
- ◉ To avoid shine, iron fabrics on the wrong side. Steam pressing with a damp cloth may remove slight shine.

Ironing specific items

- ○ **SHIRTS** start at the top and work down. Iron all the double sections first on the wrong side (collars, cuffs, front bands); then do shoulders and sleeves, back and front.
- ○ **SLEEVES** avoid creasing down the sleeve by inserting a rolled-up towel and ironing gently.
- ○ **TROUSERS (WITH A CENTRE CREASE)** iron pockets, waist; fold trousers lengthways so seams are in the middle and creases at outside edges. Repeat with other leg.
- ○ **BELTS** iron on the wrong side first.
- ○ **GATHERS** press on the reverse side, working with the point of the iron towards the gathers.
- ○ **HEMS** iron from the wrong side.
- ○ **SEAMS** press flat from the inside.
- ○ **SHEETS** fold lengthways twice.

⊙ **FABRIC HARSHNESS**

This applies particularly to towels.

CAUSE

Over-drying natural fibres.

Continual under-dosing with detergent, allowing mineral salts to build up.

Inadequate rinsing of the wash load.

CURE

For under-dosing, soak in a solution of water softener (e.g. Calgon) using 30ml/2tbsp of softener to 4 litres/7 pints of water. Also run the machine empty using the hottest programme with the recommended dose of detergent containing a bleaching agent to remove any calcium build-up within the washing machine.

For inadequate rinsing, wash the fabrics at as high a temperature as possible without any detergent. Add 200ml/7fl oz/1 cup of white vinegar to the drawer dispenser of the machine.

PREVENTION

Follow the manufacturer's pack recommendation for dosage. Increase this if the items are very heavily soiled.

If drying natural fibre garments on a radiator or in a tumble-drier, remove them before they are fully dry to prevent removal of natural moisture within the fibres. Over-drying will lead to harsh and brittle fibres.

⊙ **GREYING OF WHITE COTTONS**

CAUSE

Dirt and soiling removed during washing has re-deposited on to the clothes as a very thin uniform layer making whites appear slightly grey and coloureds dull. It occurs if insufficient detergent is used to suspend the soiling in the water.

CURE

Rewash using the maximum dose of detergent and wash temperature.

PREVENTION

Follow the manufacturer's recommended dosing instructions and wash programme. Don't overload the machine.

⊙ **PATCHY COLOUR STAINING**

CAUSE

Chemicals in the wash water. Light patches on bedding and nightwear can be caused by some skin creams and acne treatments. Neat, heavy-duty powders in direct contact with damp, non-colourfast fabric.

CURE

Rewashing may remove some types of staining. If the dyes have been affected the problem is permanent.

PREVENTION

Avoid fabrics touching offending chemicals or neat detergents.

⊙ **DYE TRANSFER FROM OTHER GARMENTS**

CAUSE

Non-colourfast items have been washed with paler items at too high a temperature. Excess dye from dark-coloured items has leached to other items in the wash load.

CURE

Rewash in as hot a wash as possible. It may be necessary to soak whites and colour-fast items in a proprietary colour-removing product.

PREVENTION

Sort your load carefully and test for colour-fastness (see Ten Golden Rules of Stain Removal, page 266). Always wash dark colours separately at first and do not use too high a temperature for non-colourfast items. Do not mix whites and coloured items.

⊙ **WHITE/GREY SPECKS OR STREAKS**

CAUSE

Hard water deposits that are present in the local water supply.

CURE

Rewash using maximum dosage of detergent. It may be necessary to soak the load in a water softener.

PREVENTION

Increase the dosage of detergent. In very hard water areas, carry out an idle wash periodically with just detergent and no load, to help reduce scale build-up.

EXCESSIVE CREASING

CAUSE

Incorrect wash programme, over-drying or overloading machine.

CURE

Reduce temperature, or wash with smaller loads. Use the specific synthetics programmes, which have reduced drum agitation and shorter spin cycles at lower speeds.

PREVENTION

Follow care labelling. Creasing of synthetics occurs if the washing and drying temperatures used are too high. Hang up items as soon as the wash cycle has finished.

SHRINKING AND FELTING OF WOOL

CAUSE

Washing temperatures too high, excessive agitation, and tumble-drying.

CURE

None. It is irreversible.

PREVENTION

Only machine-wash if the label states it is machine-washable. If in doubt, hand-wash. Never tumble-dry wool.

CLINGING AND RIDING UP OF SLIPS AND SKIRT LININGS

CAUSE

Build-up of static electricity in synthetic fibres.

CURE

Use fabric conditioner in the final rinse. Alternatively, use an antistatic spray before or while wearing the garment.

PREVENTION

Wear a natural fibre garment between two synthetic ones, e.g. a cotton slip between a polyester skirt and polyamide tights.

BOBBLING ON COTTON AND SOME SYNTHETIC BLENDS

CAUSE

Abrasion of the fibres from normal wear.

CURE

Pick off the bobbles by hand or with sticky tape. Alternatively, use a safety razor or specific de-fuzzing gadget.

PREVENTION

Difficult to prevent, but try washing garments inside out and use a fabric conditioner.

RUCKING OF COLLARS AND SHIRT FRONTS

CAUSE

Collars and bands have facings with layers of different sorts of fabrics to stiffen them. These can shrink at different rates when washed, causing puckering of the top fabric. Alternatively, using cotton thread to sew synthetic fabrics can cause puckering as the cotton shrinks.

CURE

This rucking or puckering may be irreversible. However, try steam ironing the garment while it is damp and carefully pulling the offending layers into shape.

PREVENTION

dry-clean items or wash them in cool water to avoid any shrinkage. If home dressmaking, ensure you don't over-stretch the facings when fitting and sewing them. Always match the thread content to the fabric.

- Don't iron over zips. Close the zip and iron lightly down each side of it, avoiding the teeth.
- Don't put clothes on immediately after ironing as it will encourage creasing.
- To remove bagginess, from skirt seats, for example, lay the baggy area flat and work from the outer edge of the bagginess towards the centre, pressing it repeatedly with a damp cloth, on the right side, until it flattens. Remove the cloth, place a piece of brown paper on the area and iron all over. This will absorb the moisture from the cloth and the shape will therefore hold better. Allow to cool.

DRY-CLEANING

Why dry-clean?
Always dry-clean items:

- If specified on their care label.
- If instructions are not available.
- With leather trim, pleated skirts, tailored wool suits, wool, jersey, hand-painted silk.
- Anything old, valuable or delicate.

Professional cleaners have the edge on stain removal because they have a whole range of cleaning solvents, which are not available on the domestic market. Choose a dry-cleaner that is a member of the Textile Services Association (see Useful Organisations). They should display a blue and white logo in their window with the current year's date on it (see below). These cleaners agree to observe a code of practice to guarantee high standards of service, and to protect you should anything go wrong.

Taking a garment to the cleaners
- Draw their attention to any specific stains or unusual fabrics.
- Avoid treating a stain yourself first, because this may fix it. However, if you have tried to remove it, inform the cleaner of the treatment.
- Remove unusual and ornate trimmings.
- Point out any dry-cleaning symbol, which is underlined because this tells the dry-cleaner that a special treatment is required.
- You may find that some stains, such as colourless spills that contain sugar, lemonade or alcohol, only show up after dry-cleaning because they have been brought out by the solvents used. These will need retreating.

TIP
Always air dry-cleaned items thoroughly before wearing to remove any toxic fumes.

IF THINGS GO WRONG

1 Make a formal complaint, in writing, to the manager of the company explaining the problem, keeping copies of all correspondence.

2 If you don't hear anything after ten days, or are not satisfied with the response, ask for help from your local Citizens Advice Bureau or Consumer Direct (see Useful Organisations).

3 If you don't seem to be getting anywhere, contact the Customer Adviser of the TSA (see Useful Organisations). If the cleaner is a member, the adviser will help sort out the problem. If the cleaner is not a member, the adviser will suggest your next step.

4 If the cleaner is not a member, under the terms laid out by the Office of Fair Trading, they still have a legal duty 'to provide their service with reasonable care and skill and in a reasonable time'. If this is not followed you are entitled to part or all of your money back.

Caring for Clothes

A little time taken to care for clothes is time well spent. The suggestions below will help to prolong their life and keep them looking their best.

CLOTHES CARE

- Always follow the care instructions found on clothes labels.
- Before you put clothes away give them a good brush down to remove any loose hairs and dust. Never put them away dirty. Clothes with stains – especially wool - attract destructive clothes' moths.
- Avoid wearing the same garment two days running. Fabrics need time to recover. Hang them up while still warm from the heat of the body, to help creases drop out.
- To help garments keep their shape close all zips and fasten buttons and hang or fold them away carefully.
- Don't fill the wardrobe too full, or clothes will crease and natural fibres cannot breathe. If short of space, only hang items you wear often.
- Pack summer clothes away in winter and vice versa.
- Wet clothes, such as swimsuits and sportswear, should be allowed to dry naturally before being put away.
- Don't allow clothes to become over-dirty; clean regularly.
- Repair hems and replace buttons etc., straight away.
- Cover hanging garments that are only occasionally worn with a plastic bin liner or dry-cleaning cover. This will protect them from dust and unwarranted creasing.
- Don't leave silk items in direct sunlight as they could fade.
- Line drawers with wallpaper or self-sticking plastic.

Clothes-care tips

SWIMSUITS After a swim don't just wring out your swimsuit. Rinse it thoroughly in tap water and then dry flat. Salt water, perspiration, suntan lotions or chlorine from swimming baths can rot the fibres. Wash by hand rather than the machine, and avoid wringing, tumble-drying and ironing especially if it has bra cups. Never leave damp swimwear in a plastic bag, for even a short time, or the fabric may rot.

TROUSERS Should be folded along the vertical crease line and stored on a solid coat-hanger (not wire).

SKIRTS Hang by loops on the waistband, or if storing don't fold pleated skirts. Instead, cut the feet and top off an old pair of tights, roll up the skirt lengthways and pull it through. Store flat.

SHIRTS Hang up on a coat-hanger, if possible, or store in a drawer. When folding, after fastening all the buttons, lay it face down. Turn both sides to the middle, with sleeves lying flat down the back. Turn the tail up about 8cm/3in and then take the bottom fold up to the collar.

Mothproofing

- Moths attack natural fibres, particularly wool. Synthetics are mothproof, but if blended with natural fibres they can be attacked.
- When storing clothes at the end of the season, make sure they are washed; then pack in plastic-lined cases or boxes, or hang in mothproof bags.
- Hang an insecticidal strip in the wardrobe or put moth-repellent crystals between blankets and woollens. Natural substances such as lavender and cedar wood are sometimes used to repel moths.

TIP
To avoid getting a crease across the legs of trousers, put a piece of cardboard or foam rubber along the coathanger bar.

KNITTED/WOOLLEN ITEMS Don't hang or they will stretch. Fold and put in a drawer. To fold place face down, fold one side and arm to the middle. Fold the arm back on itself and repeat with the other side. Fold in two, taking the top down to the bottom.

JACKETS Use a wooden coat-hanger that spans the width of the shoulder. Never hang by the loop as it will pull the shoulders out of shape.

SHOES Wipe wet shoes, stuff with newspaper or a shoe tree and dry away from direct heat.

HATS Stuff with tissue in boxes. Felt and velour hats need to be brushed, and if they become misshapen hold them in some steam, press them to shape again and let them cool supported by crumpled paper. Straw hats can be brushed and scrubbed with lemon juice and left in the sun if they become dingy.

TIES Hang over expanded curtain wire, or a wire coat-hanger hung on the inside of the wardrobe door.

BELTS Hang these by the buckles from hooks on the inside of the wardrobe door.

FLUFF OR HAIR Remove from clothes by dabbing with a piece of sticky tape. Wind a length round the back of your hand, sticky side out.

COAT-HANGERS Stop clothes falling off hangers by sticking a piece of foam rubber at each end.

BLACK ITEMS Store inside out to stop them from picking up fluff and dust.

STORING CLOTHES

- Before storing, launder or dry-clean. Make sure all items are completely dry.
- Don't iron clothes that are to be stored, or use starch, as these can weaken fibres and make them more prone to tearing along creases.
- Special items should be wrapped in acid-free tissue paper to help prevent creasing and provide further protection.
- Use cotton gloves to prevent potentially damaging bodily fluids transferring from your hands on to the garments.
- Avoid using ordinary cardboard or paper boxes; they aren't waterproof, chemicals can leach into your clothing and pests are attracted to the protein in the glue used to stick boxes together. For short-term storage, you can use plastic storage boxes, but make sure they are not completely airtight – the clothes need to breathe, not suffocate!
- For long-term storage of items such as wedding dresses (see page 264–5), the best option is a special acid-free storage box, available from stationers or archiving suppliers.
- Don't store items in direct contact with wood. All wood contains acids that can damage textiles over a long period of time.
- Place containers in a cool place, off the floor and away from damp, sunlight and direct or indirect heat.
- If items are being stored for longer than one season, take them out once or twice a year and refold them along different lines to prevent stress tears forming on creases. At this time, you should also inspect for any other damage that may have occurred.

Packing clothes

When going away, first make a list of the things you need to take with you: clothes, cosmetics, first aid kit etc.

- Collect together all items and discard non-essentials.
- Avoid over- and under-filling the case.
- Do up all fastenings on clothes before folding, and pack everything face down to minimise creasing.
- Place tissue paper between the folds.
- Place heavy items, such as shoes, books etc., at the bottom and fill gaps with underwear and socks.
- Pack heavy garments next, followed by woollens and breakables.
- Lay trousers with the waistband at one end of the case and the legs overhanging at the other. Pack shirts, sweaters etc., on top and then fold the legs over to reduce creasing.
- Finish off with dresses and blouses covered over with a towel or tissue paper. Fold dresses horizontally, as these folds drop out quicker than vertical ones.
- Unpack as soon as you can and hang creased garments in a steamy bathroom.

A–Z OF FABRIC CARE

If you want to keep your clothes and the soft furnishings around your home in pristine condition, it helps to know how best to look after them. Many an item has been ruined through lack of knowledge about the correct care of textiles. So, in this section you will find out how to treat just about every fabric under the sun.

Acetate
Man-made fibre often made into silk-like fabrics e.g. satin, taffeta, brocade and linings. Wash in warm water on a programme for delicates. Do not spin. Iron on cool. Avoid using acetone or vinegar to remove stains.

Acrylic
Often used for knitwear, as an alternative to wool or mixed with it. Hand-wash in warm water or use a low-temperature synthetics programme with a short spin. To reduce static, use fabric conditioner in the last rinse. Do not wring, and use a cool iron without steam. Pull back into shape while damp, and dry flat.

Blankets
Usually made from wool, but cotton and synthetics are available.

Blinds
AUSTRIAN/FESTOON Vacuum with the upholstery tool. Occasionally wash or dry-clean.
METAL BLINDS see Metals, page 232–3.
ROLLER Vacuum with the upholstery tool or use a soft brush. If spongeable, use an upholstery shampoo, but avoid over-wetting. Alternatively, try a proprietary blind cleaner, available from department stores or specialist curtain shops. Rehang while still damp. If it doesn't wind properly, re-ension by pulling down the blind halfway. Remove from the brackets and rewind by hand. Pull down and repeat if necessary.
VENETIAN Special brushes are available, or, alternatively, wearing cotton gloves, run your hands along both sides of the slats. Wash in the bath, avoiding immersing the operating mechanism, using a nylon scourer and a dilute detergent solution. Line the bath with a towel to prevent scratching. Rinse, shake off excess water and hang to dry.

Brocade
Heavy, stiff fabric with a raised pattern; often used for soft furnishings and upholstery. Made from cotton, silk, viscose or acetate. Dry-clean only.

Broderie Anglaise
Traditional open-work embroidered fabric or lace. Available in cotton or polyester cotton.

- Wash according to fabric type.
- Wash delicate pieces by hand or in a muslin bag in the machine to avoid other garments catching the embroidery.

Blanket care

- Rest blankets periodically to help prolong their life.
- When not in use, wash, clean, air and store sealed in a polythene bag in a cool cupboard, and avoid crushing. If you've forgotten to wash them and they've become infested with moths, see Moths, pages 178–9.
- Check the care label for cleaning details; most wool blankets should be dry-cleaned. Some laundries and dry-cleaners operate special blanket washing and cleaning services. Local addresses are available from the Textile Services Association (see Useful Organisations).
- Synthetic and cotton blankets can generally be machine-washed but always check the label first. Make sure the dry blanket will fit in your washing machine. If hand-washing, use the bath and remember the blanket will get heavier when wet and become bulky to handle.
- Dry naturally away from direct heat.

Calico

Plain, closely woven cotton. Generally unbleached and coarse. Wash as for cotton. To whiten unbleached calico, add a little white spirit to the first wash. Rinse thoroughly afterwards to remove the smell.

Cambric

Traditionally a fine linen from France but now generally cotton. Often used for table linen and handkerchiefs. Wash as for cotton. To crispen its texture, use a spray starch when ironing. Easier to iron when damp; use the steam setting.

Candlewick

Patterned, tufted fabric of cotton, nylon, polyester or viscose, used for bathmats, dressing gowns and bedspreads.

- ⊙ Wash according to fibre type.
- ⊙ Do not iron as this will flatten the pile.
- ⊙ Shake frequently to maintain the appearance of the pile.

Canvas

Stiff, coarse cotton used for strengthening tailored garments, and making tents, handbags and shoes. Sponge or scrub soiled areas with a stain-removal bar of household block soap. Rinse with cool water.

Carpets

Vacuum regularly to remove embedded dust and grit, which could damage the fibres, and keep the pile in good condition. Tackle stains and spills immediately. For all-over cleaning, see box opposite. For specific stains, see A–Z of Stain Removal, pages 271–99.

Chenille

Heavy fabric of cotton, viscose, wool or silk with soft velvety pile. Often used for furnishing. Wash according to fabric type or dry-clean.

Canvas shoe care

Some will withstand washing in the machine. Use a low-temperature synthetics programme. If they become muddy, allow the mud to dry before brushing off. Use an upholstery shampoo or proprietary cleaner for fabric shoes.

CARPET CLEANING

- ⊙ A manual or electric carpet shampooer (can be hired) dispenses dry-foam shampoo that forms a powder when dry absorbing dirt. This is then vacuumed away.
- ⊙ A steam cleaner sprays hot water and a cleansing agent under pressure into the carpet and then extracts it immediately together with any dirt.
- ⊙ For stubborn staining, it's worth having a carpet professionally cleaned. Choose a cleaner who is a member of the National Carpet Cleaners'

Association (NCCA). See Manufacturers, Retailers and Service Providers. Members have training in all the different techniques of carpet cleaning and will advise on the best cleaning method for your problem. However, do get several quotes and compare advice. If you have a problem with the cleaner, the NCCA has an arbitration scheme.

- ⊙ Raise the pile of crushed carpet by covering the area with a damp cloth. Apply a hot iron carefully. When dry, brush up to lift the pile.

Chiffon

Finely woven sheer fabric from cotton, silk or man-made fibres. Wash according to fibre type, or dry-clean. Handle with care and do not wring or spin. Iron gently while damp using a cool iron.

Chintz

Tightly woven cotton, generally with a flowery design used for furnishing fabrics. Some chintzes have a chemical glazed finish. Avoid using glazed chintz in any areas very prone to dirt because continual cleaning will remove the glaze. Dry-clean only. The finish can wash off and fade.

Corduroy

Cotton or synthetic-mix woven ribbed fabric. Used for garments and upholstery. Wash using a synthetics programme with minimum spin. If washing garments such as trousers, turn inside out. Iron on the reverse side, while damp, using the steam setting. Brush up the pile gently.

Cotton

A natural fibre fabric, which is available in different weights and qualities. Machine-washable, but may shrink or fade if washed at temperatures higher than 40°C. Iron while damp, using a steam setting.

Crepe de Chine

Light-weight, slippery fabric traditionally made from silk but now mostly from synthetics such as polyester. Hand-wash according to fibre type. Cold rinse and roll in a towel to remove moisture. Iron on a cool setting. If washing pure silk, soak in cold water first.

Curtains

The type of cleaning and treatment required depends on the type of fabric. Some can be washed; others must be dry-cleaned. Often, though, it is not just the fabric type but the weight and size, which will make washing impossible. Remember that whatever the fabric, dirty curtains will eventually rot and need to be replaced.

For care of net curtains see Net, page 258.

Damask

Heavy woven fabric with shiny thread. Silk, cotton, viscose or a combination. Used for table linen, soft furnishings and upholstery. Wash according to fibre type. Dry-clean heavier items.

Denim

Hardwearing, twilled cotton fabric. If not pre-shrunk, use a cool wash. Turn inside out and wash separately, as the colour runs even after several washes. Iron using the maximum or steam setting while still damp.

Dralon

Trade name for an acrylic-fibre, velvet-type, furnishing fabric.

◉ Brush or vacuum upholstery and soft furnishings regularly. Brush against the lay of the pile to raise it, then in the other direction.

Curtain care

- Brush down monthly using the upholstery nozzle of the vacuum cleaner or a soft, long-handled brush.

- Curtains should be thoroughly cleaned every few years.

- As a general rule the following fabrics should be dry-cleaned only: velvet, velours, chenilles, tapestries and brocades, all fabrics containing wool or silk, and all interlined curtains.

- Remove all hooks and curtain weights and loosen the heading tape. Let down the hem if the fabric is likely to shrink. Shake them first to remove dust.

- Soak curtains made of washable fabrics in cold water first. Then wash carefully, according to the type of fabric. Make sure, if hand-washing, that the detergent is thoroughly dissolved before putting the curtains in.

- Do not rub or wring. Rinse thoroughly. Squeeze out as much water as possible, or use a short spin.

- If machine-washing, use a programme specifically for delicates.

- Iron the curtains while they are still damp. Work lengthways, on the wrong side, stretching the fabrics gently to avoid puckering of the seams.

- Clean curtain tracks, windows and sills before rehanging.

- Curtains should be dry-cleaned at temperatures below 50°C/122°F. Do not iron, but hang immediately to avoid creasing.
- Do not over-wet Dralon upholstery, because this is often woven on to a cotton or cotton/synthetic backing, which could shrink and distort the surface.
- Clean using a dry-foam upholstery shampoo.
- Remove water-based stains by immediate and thorough blotting, followed by sponging with a weak solution of biological detergent. Work in the pile direction. Rinse and blot dry.
- For other stains, try acetone applied with cotton wool.
- If in doubt, have it professionally treated.
- Do not apply heat as the fibres will melt.

Duvets

These can have natural feather and down fillings, or polyester, e.g. hollowfibre.

Elastanes/Lycra

These are a synthetic alternative to rubber. They keep their elasticity well and resist attack from perspiration and suntan lotions. Often in blends with other fabrics, between 2 per cent and 20 per cent.

- Machine-wash at low temperatures using a delicates programme.
- Alternatively, hand-wash in warm water, rinse, and use a short spin or roll in a towel.
- Do not iron or tumble-dry.

LOOKING AFTER YOUR DUVET

- Should not require frequent cleaning.
- Air frequently in order to keep the filling fluffy and dry.
- Shake occasionally to redistribute the filling.
- Store in a cool place; on a spare bed is ideal, but if it must be put away, fold it loosely.
- Mop up spills immediately to avoid them soaking through the filling. If the casing has become stained, ease the filling away from that area and tie it off from the rest of the cover with an elastic band or string. Sponge this area first with cold water and then with a mild detergent solution. For stubborn marks, soak in a biological detergent solution.
- Unless specified, washing is recommended over dry-cleaning, whatever the filling. Before washing, check there are no holes or weak points in the casing. Repair and patch the casing where necessary.
- Use a launderette machine, unless you have a large capacity machine. Dose with one-third the usual amount of detergent.
- Wash children's smaller duvets using a wool programme with a short spin. Line dry or dry in a launderette-sized tumble-drier on the cool setting.
- Dry thoroughly and leave to air for a day.
- For companies offering commercial cleaning of duvets contact the Textile Services Association (see Useful Organisations).

Electric blankets

There are only a few companies who still manufacture under- and over-blankets. They carry out servicing and may offer cleaning services.

- Always check the manufacturer's instructions first.
- Some may be washable. Use a little washing-up liquid and water on a sponge, avoiding over-wetting.
- Dry completely. To freshen up, use a little talcum powder and then brush it away with a clothes brush. Never reuse the blanket until completely dry.
- Never have them dry-cleaned. The internal wires may be disturbed.
- Clean and service every three years.

Embroidery

Silks and wools used for this type of work are frequently not colour-fast. Check by pressing a wad of white cotton fabric against the stitches and ironing over it gently, in a hidden area.

- Dry-..clean if not colour-fast, otherwise hand-wash and treat as wool.
- If the piece is valuable, contact the Royal School of Needlework (see Manufacturers, Retailers and Service Providers), who offer a restoration service.

Felt

Thick, non-woven material made from matted wool fibres. Dry-clean, as it shrinks and is not always colour-fast.

Flannel

Woven wool or wool and cotton blend. Mainly used for suiting. Dry-clean tailored and expensive garments. Otherwise, treat as wool.

Fur

Includes natural and synthetic.

Gaberdine

Made from wool, cotton or either of these, blended with man-made fibres. The woven fabric has fine diagonal ribs. Often used for suits, coats, trousers etc. Dry-clean only.

Georgette

Fine, sheer fabric from cotton, silk, wool or man-made fibres.

- Dry-clean natural fabrics.
- Wash man-made fabrics according to fabric type.

Gingham

Checked or striped fabric typically made in bright colours and white, from cotton or polyester-cotton.

- Wash according to fibre type after testing for colour-fastness.
- Steam iron while damp.

Care of fur items

NATURAL

- Have cleaned regularly by a professional.
- Put expensive furs into cold storage during warm weather.
- Do not cover in polythene: store in a cotton bag in the wardrobe.
- Hangers should be padded.
- Allow air to circulate between the fur and other garments in the wardrobe.
- Shake before wearing.

SYNTHETIC

Made from polyamide, viscose, cotton, acrylic or polyester.

- Cotton and viscose should be dry-cleaned.
- Wash others as polyamide, and shake well before allowing to dry naturally.
- For light soiling, sponge the area with a warm solution of non-biological washing powder, rinse and towel dry.
- Brush straight-pile fabric while it is still damp. Curly pile should never be brushed while damp.
- Between washings, brush the pile with a medium to hard brush.

Goatskin

Rugs should be professionally cleaned because the hairs become brittle and break away from the base if washed. Coats are treated to avoid this.

Grosgrain

Fine, ribbed fabric of silk or man-made blends. Wash according to fibre type, or dry-clean.

Jersey

Stretchy knitted fabric of wool, silk, cotton or man-made fibres.

Lace

Cotton, polyester, polyamide or a combination.

- Wash according to fibre type.
- Use a gentle non-biological powder.
- If washing in a machine, first place in a muslin bag or a pillowcase.
- Iron while damp, on the wrong side, pulling to shape.

Leather
CHAMOIS

- Hand-wash in a warm soap-flake solution and squeeze in the water to release the dirt.
- Rinse once in a warm water solution to which 5ml/1tsp of olive oil has been added, to retain a soft texture.
- Squeeze out moisture and pull to shape.
- Hang to dry, away from direct heat. Scrunch up the leather during drying to maintain its flexibility.
- Store damp in a polythene bag.

LEATHER CLOTHING

Leather clothing described as washable can only be sponged, so do not immerse it in water.

- New or newly cleaned clothes should be treated with a water-proofing spray.
- A scarf around the neck will prevent grease marks on leather collars.
- All leather clothing should be professionally cleaned every three to four years, including retinting and reoiling. Contact the Textile Services Association for details (see Useful Organisations).
- Skins are stretched during manufacture so will contract with cleaning. These should stretch out when worn again but don't buy a very tight-fitting garment just in case.
- If it does get wet wipe over with a clean cloth and leave to dry.
- Remove surface soiling from washable leathers with a soapy sponge (use glycerine soap or soap flakes). Then wipe with a clean damp cloth and hang to dry.
- When not in use store in a cotton cover, not polythene, in a cupboard, using a padded hanger.
- Treat the garment occasionally with an application of hide food (see Leather Furniture Care, right).

Washing and ironing Jersey

- Wash according to fibre type or dry-clean.
- Short spin.
- Dry flat and pull to shape while wet.
- Steam iron on the reverse side to avoid the surface becoming shiny.

Antique lace care

- Wash by hand, using a mild detergent, which does not contain fluorescers, and dry flat.
- Delicate pieces should be pinned on to a padded board covered with cotton sheeting, sponged with a mild detergent solution and then rinsed with cold water.
- Precious items should be dry-cleaned; or consult the Royal School of Needlework (see Manufacturer's, Retailers and Service Providers).

LEATHER GLOVES

- Wash in a warm soap flake solution while on your hands. Rub together gently. Remove and allow to dry naturally.
- When nearly dry, pop them back on to restore their shape.
- Do not rinse doeskin gloves as the soap keeps them supple. After washing, press between two towels to remove excess moisture and dry naturally.

PATENT LEATHER

- If patent leather becomes very cold it will crack.
- Dust with a soft cloth and apply patent-leather dressing when looking dull and lifeless.
- If the item is only used occasionally, apply a thin layer of petroleum jelly or Vaseline all over and wipe off before use.
- Always use shoe trees or stuff with a wedge of paper.

REPTILE SKIN

- Dust shoes and handbags regularly.
- Occasionally, apply a special reptile dressing or hide food (see Leather Furniture Care, right), rubbing it in the direction of the scales.

SHOES AND HANDBAGS

- When new, apply a waterproof protector spray.
- Clean shoes regularly with recommended shoe polishes that will clean and maintain the dye colour. They will also cover scuff marks.
- If shoes get really wet, allow them to dry out at room temperature in a well-ventilated spot. Stuff them with paper to help retain the shape or use a shoe tree. Never dry in front of a radiator as it could crack the leather.
- Handbags need similar care, but less often. Do not use pigmented polishes as they will rub off on to clothing.
- To remove grease and oils from speciality leathers use a rubber adhesive that will absorb the grease. Coat the stain with a thin layer and leave on for 24 hours, then roll the adhesive off. Treat with hide food (see Leather Furniture Care, right).

Leather furniture care

Always check the manufacturer's care instructions first because some leather should not be wetted. Dust leather furniture regularly and give it an occasional application of hide food (available from specialist outlets or department stores) to prevent the leather from drying out and to protect against stains. Try to site furniture away from direct heat, such as radiators, which can encourage cracking. Remove all-over grime by wiping over with a soft damp cloth. For obvious staining have the item professionally cleaned.

Linen

Woven fabric from flax fibres. The sign of good linen is creasing.

- Hot wash and spin dry. Hang drying is preferable because it will remove some of the creasing.
- Some garments have special finishes applied to minimise creasing, and these should be dry-cleaned.
- Iron while still damp on the reverse side, to prevent shining. Use a hot steam iron.
- Stored table linen can become soiled along the crease marks. Rub a stain-removal bar along the dampened lines before washing.

Lycra

See Elastanes, page 254.

Mattresses

It is worth buying separate mattress covers that are removed for washing.

Metallic yarn

Includes lamé and woven brocade-type fabrics that contain a metallic thread. Dry-clean.

Milium

Metallic-coated fabric used for its insulating properties, particularly in curtain linings and ironing boards. If making curtains the metallic side should face inwards. Dry-clean.

Mohair

Light woven fabric made from hair of the Angora goat, often mixed with other fibres. Hand-wash and treat as wool.

Moire

Traditionally made from silk, but now often from synthetics. Heavy weights are used for furnishings and lighter weights for ball gowns.

- Watermarked surface is easily damaged by water, so dry-clean only.
- Do not use a steam iron.

Muslin

Open weave, loosely woven, sheer cotton.

- Hand-wash in warm water.
- Do not spin and dry flat.
- Iron carefully while damp with a medium setting.

Net

Loosely woven mesh fabric made from a variety of fibres such as polyester, cotton and polyamide. Mostly used for curtaining or underskirts.

Nubuck

Made from cow leather like suede but is buffed to a finer velvet pile.

- Use specialist nubuck and calf-leather cleaners that are solvent based, eliminating the need to brush as they evaporate.
- Do not use suede shampoos (which are water based) or brushes as they will damage the pile.

Nylon

See Polyamide, opposite.

Patent leather

See Leather, pages 256–7.

Percale

A finely woven cotton or cotton-polyester blend, often used in bedding. Can be glazed. Wash according to fibre type.

Mattress care

SPRING INTERIOR

- Turn over or swing round to reverse head and foot frequently when new, then quarterly after several months. This helps the filling to settle.
- Occasionally, brush the mattress and base to remove fluff and dust. Don't vacuum or it may dislodge the filling.

FOAM

- Foam mattresses with a layered construction should never be turned.
- Single-layered mattresses should be turned monthly.
- Use the crevice tool on the vacuum cleaner.

Washing net

- Wash net curtains frequently because they tend to hold on to dirt once soiled.
- Wash separately in hot water (but do not exceed the recommended washing and drying temperatures or they will become permanently creased), followed by a cold rinse.
- Use a proprietary whitener, for greying polyester, available from department or hardware stores. Alternatively, try soaking in biological detergent.
- Hand-wash dress net in warm water. Rinse, drip dry and iron with a cool iron.

Pillows

NATURAL FILLING

- Air regularly outside in summer.
- Do not have them dry-cleaned as it is difficult to remove all the toxic fumes from them.
- Can be washed in a washing machine. Check first that the machine will take the weight as pillows can be heavy when wet. Must be spin dried to remove as much moisture as possible.
- Dry thoroughly, or the pillow will start to smell and the feathers will be damaged. Hang outside and shake occasionally. It may take several days to dry.
- Air thoroughly before reusing.
- If possible, have them professionally cleaned. The feathers are removed and sterilised with ultraviolet light and the old pillowcase is replaced with a new one.

POLYESTER/HOLLOWFIBRE

- Machine-wash using the wool programme and about a third of the normal quantity of detergent.
- Spin, then tumble-dry.

FOAM

- Sponge in warm soapy water, about once a year.
- Rinse well and remove excess water with paper towel.
- Do not wring, and dry away from direct heat and sunlight.

Polyamide

Used to be known as nylon. Light-weight and non-absorbent man-made fibre; elastic and strong even when wet; flame resistant.

- Wash in hand hot water, or 40°C delicates programme; cold rinse, short spin and drip dry.
- It absorbs dye very easily, so wash separately from coloureds if possible.
- Whites become grey quickly, particularly if washed in water that is too hot.
- Wash pleated and delicate items after each use because once soiling occurs it is difficult to remove.
- Use fabric conditioner to reduce static.
- Do not bleach or expose to direct heat or sunlight.
- Inherently crease resistant, but if it does need ironing use a cool setting. Do not iron pleated nylon.

Polyester

Versatile synthetic fibre. Will not shrink, stretch, fade or crease. Often combined with cotton because of its easy-care properties.

Poplin

Closely woven cotton, viscose, silk or wool. Wash according to fibre type.

Polyester care

- Wash using the 40°C or 50°C synthetics programme with a short spin.
- Can be tumble-dried.
- Prone to static, so use a fabric conditioner in the final rinse.
- Grease stains are very difficult to remove from polyester so treat immediately by soaking in a biological powder.
- Do not wash over 50°C as it will crease badly when plunged into cold water.
- Whites have a tendency to grey or yellow.
- Cannot be home dyed successfully, but can be professionally treated.
- Hand-wash pleated items and drip dry.

PVC

Polyvinylchloride: a strong plastic material or coating. Used for upholstery, tablecloths, shower curtains etc.

- ⦿ Sponge marks off upholstery with warm water. Use a dilute solution of washing-up liquid for all-over soiling.
- ⦿ Where applicable, hand-wash in warm water and drip dry.
- ⦿ Do not apply heat as it will soften and melt.
- ⦿ Do not dry-clean.
- ⦿ Shoes should be wiped clean and dried away from direct heat.

Quilts

See Duvets, page 254.

Rainwear

Includes garments that are completely impermeable to slightly showerproof cotton coats.

- ⦿ Check care label as some items can be machine-washed.
- ⦿ Bulky items and those with protective finishes should be dry-cleaned only. Some dry-cleaners offer a reproofing service: contact the Textile Services Association (see Useful Organisations).
- ⦿ Rubberised macs such as riding coats should be scrubbed with a soft brush and detergent solution. Wipe with a damp cloth and dry with a towel.

Rush matting

Hand-plaited strips of rush that are sewn together.

- ⦿ Vacuum as regularly as carpet.
- ⦿ Treat stains with a solution of warm water and washing soda. Occasionally scrub over the matting with soap and warm water.
- ⦿ Lift occasionally and vacuum underneath.

Satin

Lustrous, smooth fabric with a short nap made from silk, cotton, polyester, polyamide or acetate. Used for dress fabrics, linings and lingerie.

- ⦿ Wash light-weight satins according to the fibre type.
- ⦿ Iron while still damp until dry, on the reverse side.
- ⦿ Acetate satin will spot if sprinkled with water so do not dry-clean.
- ⦿ Dry-lean heavier weights.

Seagrass matting

Seagrass is grown in paddy-like fields and needs a flooding of seawater during the crop cycle. It is spun into strands. It is naturally stain resistant and dye resistant so excellent for tough natural floor coverings.

- ⦿ Vacuum regularly.
- ⦿ Sponge up any spills.

Shantung

Originally a term for slubbed Chinese silk; now also made from acetate or polyamide. Wash according to fabric type.

Sheepskin

RUGS

- Can be washed at home if the wool pile is quite short.

Silk

Light-weight, resilient, luxury fibre made from the cocoon of the silk worm. Weakened by sunlight and perspiration.

- Dry-clean taffetas and brocades.
- Avoid biological detergents, heat and washing soda, which can damage silk fibres. Preferably, use a mild liquid detergent designed for hand-washing.
- Do not rub or wring the fabric or the fibres break and produce a white, chalky effect.
- Wash garments after each wear or perspiration stains may become impossible to remove.
- Have other stains professionally removed. However, for fatty stains try a detergent designed for coloureds that contains lipase.
- Iron while still damp with a warm iron. Do not use a steam iron on silks as the water will leave marks.
- Silk is not very colour-fast so after washing coloureds, to preserve the colour, soak the item in a solution of 10ml/2tsp vinegar to 3 litres/5 pints water after the final rinse. Leave for three minutes. Dry.
- Use the special detergents for coloureds with care because they weaken silk fibres.
- Printed silks should be dry-cleaned.
- Never hand-wash a garment labelled dry-clean only. Some silks have a resin applied to give texture and body that may watermark.
- Two-piece garments should be cleaned or washed together to avoid differential fading.
- Use a fabric conditioner in the final rinse to add softness.
- After rinsing, roll up in a clean dry towel and squeeze lightly to remove surplus water before ironing.

Sisal matting

Sisal is a fibre produced from the leaves of the *Agave sisalana* bush. It is soft and tough and available in a range of different weaves.

- Vacuum regularly except when wet or muddy.
- Lift occasionally to clean underneath.
- If necessary, clean very occasionally with a dry-foam shampoo, avoiding over-wetting.
- Dry naturally.
- Treat stains immediately as dried stains are difficult to remove. Some manufacturers will pre-treat with a stain inhibitor.

Sheepskin coat care

- Have professionally cleaned regularly.
- When new, or just after cleaning, apply a protective spray to help prevent marking.
- Wear a scarf around the neck to prevent grease marks. If these do occur the wool side can be freshened by using a dry shampoo for hair.
- To clean small areas of the skin use a suede cleaner. Test first.

Soft toys

- ⊙ Wash frequently to avoid permanent soiling.
- ⊙ Hand-wash using a mild detergent solution. Rinse thoroughly.
- ⊙ Wrap in a towel to soak up excess moisture, but avoid squeezing, to keep their shape.
- ⊙ Hang by the feet to dry and air.

Suede
CLOTHES

- ⊙ Washable suede does exist but is more expensive than ordinary suede.
- ⊙ Treat new or newly cleaned suede with a waterproof spray to prevent the colour rubbing off, and to provide a protective coating. Test first.
- ⊙ Dirty or rain-spotted suede should be wiped over with a clean damp cloth and allowed to dry naturally.
- ⊙ Brush up frequently with a wire brush or suede block.
- ⊙ Proprietary suede cleaning cloths or blocks are useful for removing soiling along wear creases.
- ⊙ For serious discoloration have the item professionally cleaned to restore both colour and oil.

Taffeta

Crisp, closely woven shiny material, made from a variety of fibres, including silk, acetate, viscose, polyester or polyamide.

- ⊙ Dry-clean.
- ⊙ Iron on the reverse side.

Tapestry

The Royal School of Needlework (see Manufacturers, Retailers and Service Providers) will restore valuable tapestry. Ring them for an appointment. Otherwise try the textile department of a museum.

Ties

Most are polyester, wool or silk.

- ⊙ Stains on these fabrics are quite difficult to remove without leaving a ring mark, so spray new ties with a fabric protector. Try on the back first and leave to dry before doing the front.
- ⊙ If stains do occur try a dry-cleaning spray, otherwise get professionally cleaned as laundering is rarely successful.
- ⊙ To iron, position the tie wrong side up on the ironing board. Make sure the interlining is lying flat.
- ⊙ Slip a cardboard shape inside the wide end of the tie so you press it without causing an imprint of the seam on the right side. Press over a damp cloth to avoid scorching.

Towelling

Looped pile fabric, usually made from cotton.

- ⊙ Machine-wash using a cotton programme.
- ⊙ Dark colours should be washed separately.

Suede shoe care

- ⊙ Treat new shoes with a protective suede spray.
- ⊙ Fading can be improved with an overall application of coloured suede dressing, generally available only in brown, navy, black and neutral.
- ⊙ When necessary, clean with a nailbrush and clean soapy water. Rinse and blot dry.
- ⊙ Proprietary cleaning products work well, but follow instructions carefully.
- ⊙ If they get wet allow them to dry naturally, then use a rubber or nylon suede brush to remove dust and raise the pile.
- ⊙ Scrape off mud while still wet and blot with a damp cloth.

- Nappies should be washed on a very hot wash. Add fabric conditioner to the final rinse.

Trainers

These are made from a multitude of materials, including plastic, leather, latex, canvas and other synthetic fabrics.

Tulle

Fine, sheer net-like fabric of silk, cotton, viscose, polyamide or other fibres. Used on evening and bridal wear.

- Dry-clean silk.
- For other fibres, hand-wash following the instructions for fibre type.
- If cotton tulle becomes limp, starch it in a weak starch solution, such as Dip, or use spray starch when ironing.
- Nylon and viscose tulle can be stiffened with a gum arabic solution available from health food stores.

Tweed

A woven woollen fabric available in different weights. Imitations are also made in polyester and acrylic. Dry-clean.

Upholstery

- Dust all upholstery thoroughly dusted every week, using the brush attachment (on pile fabrics) and crevice tool of the vacuum cleaner.
- Upholstery should be positioned away from sunlight to avoid fading.
- Removable cushions should be turned weekly to ensure they get even wear and soiling.
- Clean all upholstery before it becomes heavily soiled, following the manufacturer's advice.
- Loose covers should be washed or dry-cleaned according to the fabric type. Take care because they often shrink.
- If washed, place them back on the furniture before completely dry to reshape and prevent shrinkage.
- Iron while they are in position, using a cool iron on foam furniture.
- If covers cannot be removed, have them professionally cleaned or clean them with an upholstery shampoo and spotting kit. Try on hidden areas first.
- Avoid over-wetting, particularly on Dralon (see Dralon, pages 253–4).
- Always dry-clean chenilles, tapestries, velours, velvets and fabrics containing silk, wool or viscose.

LEATHER

See Leather Furniture Care, page 257.

Velour

Pile fabric similar to velvet usually made of acrylic but may be other man-made fibres, cotton or silk.

- Dry-clean or wash according to the fibre type.
- Iron with a cool iron on the reverse side of the fabric.

Training shoe care

- After use, check the sole for thorns and grit, which could penetrate and damage the mid-sole.
- Rinse off mud after use, using the back of an old knife in the tread. Pack with newspaper and let them dry naturally at room temperature.
- Clean according to the manufacturer's advice; only machine-wash if specifically recommended. Most should only be wiped over with a soft cloth soaked in a detergent solution.
- Don't leave shoes in bright sunshine or keep damp shoes in a bag.
- Remove the insole occasionally and wash it in warm soapy water. Rinse and dry naturally.

Velvet

Originally a silk or cotton cut-pile fabric. Now many velvets are made from viscose, polyamide, polyester etc.

Viscose

Also known as rayon, this is a cellulosic fibre made from the pulp of eucalyptus and spruce wood, which is then reacted with certain chemicals. It is used on its own, or in blends. Drapes well but creases easily so is sometimes treated with an easy-care finish.

- ◉ Wash with care at low temperatures because fibres are weak when wet. High temperatures will affect finish.
- ◉ To discourage creasing, use a short spin when washing, and do not wring.
- ◉ Iron on the steam setting while damp.

Viyella

Brand name for light-weight wool-and-cotton blend fabric.

- ◉ Hand-wash in hand-hot water.
- ◉ Do not spin; remove water by squeezing gently or rolling in a towel.
- ◉ Warm iron on the reverse side while damp.

Waxed jackets

Some brands can be cleaned by specialist companies, who will clean and rewax jackets, trousers, hoods and waistcoats.

Barbour branded jackets can be rewaxed, repaired and reproofed by the manufacturer. Barbour does not recommend dry-cleaning.

Wedding dresses

This information also applies to accessories such as the veil and other special, occasional clothes such as christening and ball gowns.

A wedding dress should be professionally dry-cleaned before storing. This should be done, even if the gown is not visibly dirty, since colourless stains such as alcohol, perfume and perspiration can develop and discolour as they react with the air. The discoloration cannot be removed.

For long-term storage, use an acid-reduced cardboard box and interleave the dress with acid-free tissue. These are available from stationers and archiving suppliers, although acid-free tissue is sometimes sold by department stores such as John Lewis. Unlike conventional tissue or cardboard, the acid-free has been specially treated and doesn't contain harmful chemicals.

Don't be tempted to use an ordinary cardboard box with acid-free tissue paper since the chemicals from the cardboard can still leach through the tissue.

Place the box in a cool cupboard, away from damp, indirect heat or sunlight. Inspect the gown every 18 months to two years, refolding the dress along slightly different lines to help prevent permanent creasing.

Velvet care

- ◉ Treat according to the fibre, or dry-clean.
- ◉ Curtains, particularly cotton velvet, should be lined as they fade readily in sunlight.
- ◉ Dry-clean curtains.
- ◉ Shake periodically while drying and smooth the pile with a soft cloth or velvet brush to restore the pile.
- ◉ Use steam to remove between-wear creases, e.g. hang over a bath of steamy water.
- ◉ Iron velvet with pile face down on a soft cloth or towel.

Storing wedding dresses

Never use ordinary plastic bags, PVC zip covers or cardboard boxes to store a wedding dress. Chemicals within these packaging materials can leach out over a period of time and cause the fabric to discolour. This reaction is accelerated if there is little air movement. Storing the dress in a wooden chest of drawers can have a similar effect. The yellow discoloration is permanent and cannot be removed.

FOLDING A WEDDING DRESS

- ⊙ If practical, detach bulky or stiff underskirts and store separately.
- ⊙ Line the base and sides of the box with overlapping layers of acid-free tissue.
- ⊙ Start from the hem and work upwards.
- ⊙ Fold in a concertina fashion, interleaving with layers of acid-free tissue.
- ⊙ Place rolled layers of tissue along each of the folds.
- ⊙ Insert tissue inside bodice, sleeves, shoulders and inside any bows.
- ⊙ Finish with layers of tissue and cover with lid.

VACUUM PACKING

Another option is to have the dress vacuum packed. Jeeves of Belgravia (see Manufacturers, Retailers and Service Providers) offer a vacuum-packing service. The process involves storing the gown in a polythene bag which has had all the air removed and replaced with nitrogen, a bit like shrink wrapping ham. This prevents the oxidisation of stains and discoloration. Vacuum packing should 'preserve' the gown for at least 25 years.

However, bear in mind that you won't be able to remove the dress, since once the seal is broken, the preserving properties will be lost. The other disadvantage is that leaving the dress in a fixed position for so long can cause permanent creasing.

Wool

Natural, versatile fibre used to manufacture woven fabrics and knitting yarns.

- ⊙ Wash with care as it is easily spoiled. Wool has a coating of scales, which work against each other if rubbed while wet, causing the fibres to shrink and felt. It stretches when wet but will never unfelt.
- ⊙ Only machine-wash if the label specifies that the item is machine-washable wool. If so, use the special woollens programme, which has reduced agitation and a very short spin.
- ⊙ Hand-wash in warm water using a gentle detergent. Do not rub, wring or twist. If your washing machine has the option for washing woollens, a very short spin will not harm the fabric.
- ⊙ Dry flat between two towels. Pull gently to the correct shape while still damp.
- ⊙ Never tumble-dry wool.
- ⊙ Oiled wool such as Guernsey sweaters should be washed in warm water using well dissolved soap flakes as detergents will remove the oil. They can be reoiled. Check with the manufacturer.
- ⊙ If you have washed a woollen garment and it has shrunk, sometimes a gentle wash in hair shampoo will soften the fibres and allow you to pull it back to shape.

All You Need to Know About Stains

In this section you will find detailed information on stain-removal methods and techniques, the four basic types of stain, and all the products you will need to remove them successfully

THE RULES OF STAIN REMOVAL

What makes a stain a stain? This may seem a strange question, but the truth is that the word 'stain' is over-used. A true stain occurs only when a chemical reaction takes place between the staining agent and the fibres of a fabric or surface, leaving a PERMANENT blemish or mark. Thankfully, this

TEN GOLDEN RULES OF STAIN REMOVAL

1 ACT QUICKLY The most important rule of stain removal. The faster you get to grips with an offending spill, the greater your chance of removing it. If a stain is allowed to dry you run a much greater risk of it becoming permanent, and in a few cases, you may even have to accept that the item cannot be saved.

2 BLOT THOROUGHLY With a water-based stain, remove as much as possible by blotting with white paper towels or a clean, white, cotton cloth. For very small stains, use cotton buds. Change the blotting material as soon as it becomes soiled. For a greasy stain, sprinkle with cornflour or talcum powder. Leave it to absorb the grease for a few minutes, then remove using a soft brush.

3 LIFT For more solid stains, gently scrape off lumpy bits with a blunt knife. On powdery dry stains, such as pollen, use sticky tape wrapped around your fingers to lift debris.

4 WORK FROM THE OUTSIDE INWARDS Always start at the edge of the stain and work towards the centre. That way, you will avoid spreading it and causing further damage.

5 TREAT FROM THE UNDERSIDE WHERE POSSIBLE The idea is to push the stain out rather than further in. When flushing with water, always run the water through from the 'wrong' side of the stain.

6 CHECK THE CARE LABEL Don't ruin a favourite item by panicking and throwing it straight into the washing machine, only to realise it's 'dry-clean only' and see it emerge from the machine small enough to fit a Barbie Doll! Read the care label (see Understanding Laundry Symbols, page 240).

7 READ THE INSTRUCTIONS This may seem obvious, but when using any stain-removing product, always follow the manufacturer's instructions. They are given for good reasons, so ignore them at your peril.

8 TEST FIRST Always test any stain remover on an inconspicuous area first to check for colour-fastness or other potential damage.

9 RINSE BEFORE WASHING If you have used any product to spot-treat a stain, be sure to rinse it out with plenty of cold water before washing the item. This will prevent any undesirable chemical reactions occurring between the product and detergent.

10 DRY NATURALLY After treating a stain, always allow the garment or fabric to dry naturally. Heat from a tumble-drier or iron can fix any remaining traces of the stain. If it's been allowed to dry naturally, you may still have a chance to remove the remnants with a second treatment.

is not the case with most of the spills, splashes and spots we generally think of as stains. In fact, with the correct approach and the right products, many 'stains' can be removed quite easily. You simply need a little bit of knowledge and understanding of how best to go about doing it! Without this information, your chances of success are much lower and you could even make the problem worse. In this section, you will find a simple explanation of the underlying principles of stain removal, as well as our Top 20 dos and don'ts.

FOUR BASIC PRINCIPLES

Understanding the four main principles involved in the successful removal of stains will help you to get better results, so here is the scientific bit!

1 Absorb it

The first thing to do is to lift off or soak up as much of the staining substance as possible from the fabric or surface, using absorbents such as talcum powder and paper towels.

... AND TEN THINGS YOU SHOULD NEVER DO!

1 DON'T USE HOT OR EVEN WARM WATER Flushing a fresh stain with hot water may seem like the obvious thing to do, but it can be disastrous. Hot water can permanently set some stains, particularly those with a protein base, such as blood. Always flush with cool water.

2 DON'T RUB FURIOUSLY Rubbing a stain frantically is likely to make it spread further, and may also damage the weave of the fabric. You'll have more success if you dab gently.

3 NEVER OVER-WET WITH STAIN REMOVER Light, repeated applications work much better than flooding a stain. This is particularly important on carpets and upholstery, which are awkward to rinse and get dry. Don't be surprised by the number of times you will need to repeat the process. Perseverance is the key!

4 NEVER WORK SOAP INTO FRESH STAINS Bar soap, soap flakes and detergents containing soap can set stains, particularly those that include tannin-based pigments, such as coffee, red wine and tea.

5 NEVER PUT SALT ON A RED WINE STAIN The salt may well absorb the liquid, but as with soap, it will also set tannin pigments permanently. The same principle applies to coffee, tea or cola and any other stain that contains tannin.

6 NEVER MIX STAIN-REMOVAL PRODUCTS Unless you're a chemistry boffin, it is a bad idea to mix different products. Chemicals can react together with very unpleasant consequences; particularly chlorine bleach with ammonia, which when combined, will create lethal chlorine gas.

7 DON'T USE ENZYME-BASED PRODUCTS ON SILK OR WOOL Both of these are protein fibres, and an enzymic product will have the same 'digesting' effect on them as it does on any protein-based stain – while this may be desirable on blood or eggs, it is less welcome on your favourite cashmere sweater!

8 NEVER USE CHLORINE BLEACH ON SILK OR WOOL These fabrics are too delicate to withstand the harsh effects of bleach. Bleach is also unsuitable for many synthetic fabrics. Check the care label (see Understanding Laundry Symbols, page 240).

9 NEVER TRY TO REMOVE STAINS FROM ANTIQUE FABRICS When baby vomits on your family's heirloom christening gown, don't try to remove the stains yourself. Antique fabric is particularly delicate and therefore treatment is best left to a professional.

10 DON'T GIVE UP Be patient. Some stains respond slowly and you may need to repeat procedures several times before you get results.

2 Dissolve it

Residue that can't be absorbed needs to be dissolved. However, different substances have differing solubility in solvents. For example, blackcurrant juice is soluble in water, while the curcumin colouring in turmeric requires an alcohol, such as methylated spirits, before it will dissolve. Therefore it is important to consider which solvent will be most effective on a particular stain.

3 Use a detergent

Greasy or fatty stains, such as gravy, will not dissolve in water. To get rid of the rest of the stain, use detergent. Detergents work by changing the surface tension of water so that it can flow more freely into the crevices of a fabric. Molecules in the detergent form a chemical link between the staining particles and the water. When the detergent is rinsed away, the water and stain are taken with it.

4 Use a chemical reaction

If principles 1–3 don't work, it is down to chemical reactivity, using agents such as bleach and enzymes. Bleach strips molecules of the electrons that give them colour, therefore making the stain invisible. Enzymes work by breaking down the bonds that hold the amino acids in proteins together. Separated, the amino acids are more soluble in water, so can be more easily rinsed away to remove the stain.

TYPES OF STAIN

Stain removal is an inevitable and troublesome part of caring for fabrics and surfaces. We've all thrown away a treasured item of clothing thinking that the red wine splashed down its front just isn't going to come out in the wash. To help prevent this happening over and over again, it is useful to have an understanding of the different types of stain that exist and how best to treat them. Some stains come out simply by rinsing in water, but you also need to know whether the water used should be cold or hot. Some stains require a solvent or detergent, while others might need bleaching or digesting by enzymes. This section will help you identify stain types and choose the most suitable way of dealing with each one.

The four main offenders

There are four main types of stain you need to be aware of: grease-based, pigment-based, protein-based and the more complex combination stains. Each requires a slightly different approach for successful removal.

GREASE-BASED STAINS

Grease-based stains are caused by items such as butter, cooking oil, mayonnaise, bacon fat, suntan lotion and face creams. They are not soluble in water and can be tricky to get rid of completely. As always, you'll have the most success if you act quickly.

THE RULES Gently scrape off any solid or lumpy parts of the stain with a blunt knife, and then soak up as much of the grease as you can with white paper towels. Lightly sprinkle the stain with talc or cornflour and allow to stand for a few minutes so that it can absorb the grease, then remove the powder with a soft brush. Any remaining grease must be dissolved, and for that you'll need an alcohol-based solvent such as methylated spirits. Gently dab at the stain with the solvent and allow it to evaporate. Then work a little liquid detergent into the stained area and leave for a few minutes. Machine-wash as normal on as high a temperature as the fabric allows.

PIGMENT- AND TANNIN-BASED STAINS

These stains are caused by coloured products and food. Examples are fruit juice, food colouring, coffee, perfume and grass. The stains are usually water-soluble (unless in combination with other substances), but can be difficult to remove if not treated immediately.

THE RULES Blot up as much of the stain as possible with white paper towels or a cloth, then flush or sponge with cold water containing a few drops of white vinegar, and blot again. If the stain still looks bad and the fabric allows it, pre-soak in a proprietary oxygen-based, colour-safe bleaching product for as long as is recommended by the manufacturer. Follow up by machine-washing with detergent at as high a temperature as the fabric allows. Dry naturally.

PROTEIN-BASED STAINS

Egg, vomit, blood and faeces are examples of protein-based stains. Although protein is quite straightforward to remove, it can coagulate and set into textile fibres at even relatively low temperatures, so the key thing is never to use very hot water.

THE RULES Lift off as much of the stain as possible, using a blunt knife and white paper towels. Soak the item in cold water. Adding a biological pre-soaking agent such as Biotex (see Specialist Products and Their Uses, page 215), will also help. This type of product contains enzymes that 'digest' proteins and break them down. Be careful though – certain fabrics, such as silk and wool, are protein fibres themselves and can be damaged by products containing enzymes. Always check

A warning about tannin

Certain types of pigment-based stains also contain tannin (e.g. red wine, tea, perfume, beer). For these stains, there is one very important rule to remember, and that is to never use salt (or, for that matter, ordinary bar soap). Both of these products can set a tannin stain permanently. So please, please, don't resort to that old wives' tale that suggests sprinkling salt on a red wine stain – it simply won't work!

BASIC TOOLS

To ensure you are ready for any stain emergency, always try to have the following top tools in your cupboard.

⊙ **BIOLOGICAL WASHING DETERGENT** This is excellent for removing many household stains from cotton fabrics simply by washing them at 40°C; it is also great for many other dirty jobs around the house, such as removing burnt-on food from saucepans and brightening up dirty bathtubs.

⊙ **BLUNT KNIFE** You will need one of these for gently dry-scraping off any solid or bulky part of a stain before treating it further. On delicate items, take care not to scratch or damage their surface.

⊙ **CHLORINE BLEACH** While it should always be used with discretion and kept well out of the reach of children, chlorine bleach is still one of the most useful pieces of kit in any stain-removing arsenal. It can restore white cottons to their original dazzling brightness and remove ugly mould on grout, as well as keeping your loo fresh and free of germs. Don't be without it!

⊙ **CLEAN TOOTHBRUSH AND NAILBRUSH** These are useful for brushing off talc or cornflour that has been used as an absorbent, sprinkled over an oily stain. Only use a soft brush that won't damage delicate fabrics. Old toothbrushes are also perfect for scrubbing nasty mould stains off grout.

⊙ **CORNFLOUR OR UNSCENTED TALC** Sprinkle on fatty and oily stains. The powder will absorb some of the grease and can then be removed with a soft brush.

⊙ **COTTON BUDS** Use these when a light touch is required or the stained area is very small. Dab gently at the stain to lift it.

⊙ **DETERGENT FOR DELICATES** Some fabrics are just too delicate to withstand normal biological detergents, so always keep a gentle detergent suitable for silk and wool.

⊙ **GLYCERINE** Glycerine is great for softening and loosening old stains. Dilute it with one to two parts of water and apply to the stain. Allow the item to soak for one hour before washing as normal. Glycerine is available from most chemists.

⊙ **ICE CUBES AND ICE PACKS** These are helpful for removing soft, sticky stains such as candle wax and chewing gum. Apply to the affected area (or if possible, place the entire item in the freezer) and leave until the solid part of the stain is brittle

enough to be picked or scraped off with a blunt knife.

⊙ **MEDICINE DROPPER** This can come in handy for targeting liquid stain removers on very small stains.

⊙ **METHYLATED SPIRITS** Methylated spirits is a good solvent, and can be used to dissolve greasy stains such as crayon and ballpoint pen; it is essential for curcumin-based stains such as curry and mustard. Use the colourless variety, and remember that it is flammable, so smoking is outlawed. Methylated spirits is not suitable for use on acetate fabrics, and you should be careful when using it on coloured items because it can dissolve some dyes – check for colour-fastness on an inconspicuous area first.

⊙ **NAIL POLISH REMOVER** The only thing that can remove a nail polish stain and even then when the stain is small. Don't use it on acetate fabrics though, as it can damage them.

⊙ **PAPER TOWELS AND CLOTHS** Use white paper towels or clean, white, lint-free cloths for blotting and soaking up moisture in water-based stains. Patterned or coloured towels and cloths could transfer dye and make the stain worse.

⊙ **SODA OR SPARKLING WATER** Pouring bubbly water on pigment-based spills such as red wine helps to force the stain out of the fabric fibres – handy for emergency action at a dinner party. However, only use makes that are low in salt, otherwise you may inadvertently end up setting the stain.

⊙ **STICKY TAPE OR SCOTCH TAPE** Sticky tape is ideal for lifting pollen particles off clothing and carpets. Gently pat the affected area with the tape to remove as much of the debris as possible. This method also works well for removing other dry debris, such as pet hair.

⊙ **WASHING-UP LIQUID** Not just for dishes! Many stains can be removed simply by working in washing-up liquid and rinsing with lots of water.

⊙ **WET WIPES** Not essential, but useful for getting rid of white deodorant marks on dark-coloured clothing.

⊙ **WHITE SPIRIT** A good solvent – use it for removing paint.

⊙ **WHITE VINEGAR** Good for removing water-based stains.

the manufacturer's instructions. After soaking, machine-wash at a temperature below 30°C.

COMBINATION STAINS

As the name suggests, these are stains that have more than one component. Good examples are gravy (protein and grease), ice cream (protein, grease and pigment), candle wax (pigment and grease), lipstick (pigment and grease) and crayon (pigment and grease). Unsurprisingly, they are complex to remove and you will have to adopt a two-step approach to deal with them.

THE RULES Treat the greasy or protein part of the stain first, following the rules given previously (see Grease-based Stains, page 268–9), right up to before the machine-washing process, then wash at as high a temperature as the fabric allows. Next, follow the instructions for treating pigment-based stains (see page 269).

TOOLS FOR THE JOB

The successful removal of most stains depends upon rapid treatment, so it's a good idea to keep a supply of the most useful stain-removal tools and products handy. See page 274 for a list of basic tools, and for a list of GHI's favourite specialist stain removers, and some environmentally friendly alternatives, see Specialist Products and Their Uses, page 215, and Greener Alternatives, page 214.

A–Z OF STAIN REMOVAL

In this section, you will find an alphabetical guide to individual stains that are likely to occur in your home, office and when you are out and about. Details on where to purchase any specialist products referred to can be found in the Directory at the back of the book.

Antiperspirant

Don't confuse fresh antiperspirant stains with the nastier, yellowy stains caused by perspiration – those build up over time and are much more difficult to remove. Marks left by antiperspirant normally wash out readily if dealt with quickly.

INSTANT REMEDY If you are wearing a sleeveless top and the dreaded marks have appeared, a quick swab with a baby wipe tissue will get rid of them.

GENERAL DIRECTIONS Before washing the garment, the one thing you need to do is to rinse the affected area under cool water. This will prevent chemicals in the antiperspirant being 'fixed' by hot water in the washing machine and causing a permanent stain. Incidentally, doing this to the underarm area of all clothing before washing it will also help to stop long-term perspiration stains from developing. Launder the garment according to fabric type.

STREAKY DEODORANT To avoid embarrassing streaks, always let your antiperspirant dry completely before you get dressed, particularly the

Mystery stains

When a mysterious murky splodge appears on one of your favourite items, how do you go about identifying and removing it? Smell, location and colour may give you a clue. Food and drink typically appear on the front of garments, while the smudge on the collar of a man's shirt may be lipstick! As a rule of thumb, begin with the stain-removal method least likely to cause damage. If the item is washable, start by soaking it in cold water. Next, try detergent and lukewarm water. If the stain remains, treat it with a solvent-based spot-treatment stain remover and wash again. The last resort is to soak the item in a solution of water and an oxygen-based, colour-safe bleaching product (or chlorine bleach for white cottons). And if all fails, give up and treat yourself to something new – you deserve it after so much effort!

gel and roll-on types. Don't use more product than necessary, it doesn't make it work better and will simply result in more being transferred to your clothes.

Avocado

The problem with an avocado stain is that if it is left it will oxidise and turn a nasty grey-black colour. Once this has happened, the stain is almost impossible to remove. Act quickly for the best chance of removal.

GENERAL DIRECTIONS Gently scrape the solids off with a blunt knife, taking care not to spread the stain.

CARPET Apply Bissell OxyKIC or White Wizard to the stain. Working from the outside inwards, gently soak up the stain with white paper towels or a clean, white, lint-free cloth. Don't drench the stain – it's better to make repeated small applications than to completely flood the area. Continue until the stain has disappeared. Rinse thoroughly with cold water and blot up as much water as possible with more paper towels. Leave to dry. If any traces remain, a complete carpet shampoo may do the trick.

WASHABLE FABRICS After scraping, dampen the mark with cool water and gently rub in a little washing-up liquid. Allow to stand for five minutes or so, then rinse with more cool water. For cotton, follow with a 40°C machine-wash, using biological detergent. For silk, follow with a 30°C machine-wash on the delicates cycle. For wool, follow with a 30°C machine-wash on the delicates cycle.

DRIED-ON STAINS Try treating with Dylon Stain Remover for Biological Stains before machine-washing as normal.

Ballpoint pen

We've all had a ballpoint that's leaked and left an angry splodge of ink on our clothing. This ink doesn't usually come out in the wash, and it can spread to other items, so always check clothing carefully before laundering. You might be able to get a small amount out, but it is difficult.

GENERAL DIRECTIONS Blot first with dry, white paper towels. For fabrics, place an absorbent pad under the stain. Follow the directions below for specific fabrics.

CARPET AND WASHABLE FABRICS Apply a cotton bud dipped in methylated spirits to the affected area. Don't over-wet. Dab the stain gently, trying not to spread the ink as it dissolves. Blot firmly with paper towels, moving to a clean area of both pad and towel frequently. Repeat until the colour has stopped lifting. Be prepared to make several applications. Flush with cold water, then gently rub White Wizard into any remaining traces, working it in well. Leave for a couple of minutes, then blot with dry paper towels. Press firmly and hold the towel on the mark for several seconds each time. Flush with water. If traces still remain on fabric, try spot-treating the area with Stain Devils for Ballpoint Ink & Felt Tip. Machine-wash at as high a temperature as the fabric allows.

LAST RESORT If there are still any signs of the ink, try soaking the item in an oxygen-based, colour-safe bleaching product. Follow the manufacturer's instructions and check the garment's care label first.

Banana

It may not look like much of a stain when it's fresh, but banana oxidises to a black colour when it's left. You then have little chance of removing it; so try to deal with the problem immediately.

GENERAL DIRECTIONS Gently scrape off the solids with a blunt knife, taking care not to spread the stain. For older, yellowed stains, try the methods below, but be prepared for limited success. Follow the directions below for specific fabrics.

CARPET Apply Bissell OxyKIC or White Wizard to the stain. Working from the outside inwards, gently soak up the stain with white paper towels or a clean, white, lint-free cloth. Don't drench the stain – it's better to make repeated small applications than to completely flood the area. Continue until the stain has completely disappeared. Rinse thoroughly with cold water and blot up as much water as possible with more paper towels. Leave to dry. If any traces remain, a complete carpet shampoo may be necessary.

WASHABLE FABRICS After scraping, dampen the mark and gently rub in a little washing-up liquid. Allow to stand for five minutes, then rinse with plenty of cool water. For cotton, follow with a 40°C machine-wash, using biological detergent. For silk, follow with a 30°C machine-wash on the delicates cycle. For wool, follow with a 30°C machine-wash on the delicates cycle.

Barbecue sauce

GENERAL DIRECTIONS Gently blot up as much of the sauce as possible using a blunt knife and white paper towels. Dab at, rather than rub, the stain. Follow the directions below for specific fabrics.

CARPET Spot-treat the affected area with Bissell OxyKIC and, working from the outside inwards, gently soak up the stain, using white paper towels or a clean, white, lint-free cloth. Repeat as necessary until the mark is removed. Be patient. Several applications may be required to get rid of it completely. Finish by blotting with cold water, then allow to dry naturally. If any traces remain, a complete carpet shampoo should do the trick.

WASHABLE FABRICS After blotting, rinse the stain under plenty of cold running water until no more colour is removed. For cotton, rub a small amount of liquid detergent into the stain and let it stand for five minutes. Follow with a 40°C machine-wash, using biological detergent. For silk, spot treat the stained area by blotting thoroughly with a baby wipe tissue and follow with a 30°C machine-wash on the delicates cycle. Allow to dry naturally. Barbecue sauce stains are especially tricky to remove from wool and to have any chance of removing them, you really need to treat the mark within 15 minutes of it occurring. After rinsing with cold water, cover the affected area with White Wizard and work it gently into the fabric. Use a damp cloth to lift as much of the stain as you can, moving to a clean area of the cloth regularly. Use several applications if necessary. Finish by working a small amount of delicates detergent into the stain, then wash at as high a temperature as the care label permits. Allow to dry naturally. If the stain is not completely removed, try soaking the item in an oxygen-based bleach suitable for wool, following the manufacturer's instructions and checking for colour-fastness first.

Beer

Even if you don't notice it until the next day, a beer stain is fairly easy to remove. Don't leave for too long , as the sugar in the beer caramelises, turning the stain darker brown and making it more difficult to remove.

GENERAL DIRECTIONS Use white paper towels or a clean, white, lint-free cloth to absorb as much of the stain as possible. Follow the directions below for specific fabrics.

CARPET Apply a proprietary carpet cleaner, such as Bissell OxyKIC and allow it to work for a few minutes. Blot with more paper towels. Repeat as necessary until the stain has disappeared. Rinse lightly with cold water, and blot as much moisture from the area as possible, again using white paper towels. Leave to dry. For old stains, try dabbing the area with a little methylated spirits.

WASHABLE FABRICS After blotting, gently rub in a mild detergent solution (15ml/1tbsp liquid detergent to a 250ml/9fl oz cup of water mixed with a few drops of white vinegar. Soak for a few minutes. For cotton, follow with a 40°C machine-wash, using biological detergent. For silk and wool, follow with a 30°C delicates machine-wash.

LINGERING ODOURS For carpets, dampen the affected area and sprinkle generously with bicarbonate of soda. Leave until dry and vacuum up. For fabrics, add a scoop of bicarbonate of soda to the wash load.

Beetroot

Beetroot stains are water-soluble and usually come out quite readily if they have not had time to dry.

GENERAL DIRECTIONS Gently scrape away any solid parts with a blunt knife. Use paper towels, or even white bread pressed on the stain, to absorb as much of the juice as possible. Flush with lots of cool water. Follow the directions below for specific fabrics.

CARPET Treat the stain with Bissell OxyKIC, following the manufacturer's instructions. You will probably find you need to make repeated applications, but keep going – the stain should come out eventually.

WASHABLE FABRICS Scrape, blot and flush with water as above. For cotton, follow with a 40°C machine-wash, using biological detergent. For silk, follow with a 30°C machine-wash on the delicates cycle. For wool, treat with Stain Devils for Tea, Red Wine, Fruit & Juice and follow with a 30°C machine-wash on the delicates cycle.

Handling beetroot

When preparing beetroot, avoid staining your hands by wearing disposable latex gloves. Peel beetroot after, rather than before, cooking to help limit the leaching of their juices. If you end up with stained hands or chopping boards, the marks will come off if rubbed with lemon juice.

Bicycle and car grease

Cycling is a great way to get around, but you need to keep it well oiled, and the grease forms a stain similar to that of shoe polish and contains both oils and pigment. Here's how to get rid of bicycle and car grease stains.

GENERAL DIRECTIONS Carefully scrape up any solid bits with a blunt knife. Follow the directions below for specific fabrics.

CARPET Squirt a few drops of WD-40 on the affected area, wait about 30 seconds, then blot with paper towels, moving to clean areas of the towel frequently. Work from the outside inwards, and use a delicate dabbing motion. You must be gentle, so that you do not push the stain deeper into the carpet or spread it. Repeat as necessary until no more of the stain is lifted. Remove remaining traces of colour with White Wizard. Apply the product to the mark and leave it for a minute or so, then blot with lightly dampened paper towels or a clean white cloth. Finish by dabbing the area with clean water to rinse it, then blot dry. Be prepared to make several applications before the stain is completely removed.

WASHABLE FABRICS If the stain is very small and faint, it may come out simply by rubbing in a little liquid detergent, then washing as normal. For larger, darker stains, try using the WD-40 method as described for carpet, followed by spot-treatment with Stain Devils for Grease, Lubricant & Paint to remove the greasy mark that WD-40 may leave. Machine-wash at as high a temperature as the fabric will allow.

Bird droppings

Always remove bird droppings from your car the instant that they appear. If they are left for more than a day or so, the acid in the droppings will eat into the top coat of paint and cause permanent damage. Be prepared: keep a bottle of spray cleaner and paper towels in the glove compartment.

GENERAL DIRECTIONS Gently scrape off as much dirt as possible with a blunt knife or paper towels. Follow the directions below for specific fabrics.

WASHABLE FABRICS The marks usually come out in a normal machine-wash. If they do not, try soaking the affected item in an oxygen-based, colour-safe bleaching product. Check the garment's care label first and follow the bleach manufacturer's instructions.

CANVAS AND AWNINGS Allow to dry thoroughly, then remove the dirt with a stiff brush. If marks remain, dip the brush in a solution of biological washing detergent and rub the affected area. Hose down and rinse well.

Blackcurrant and other berries

Blackcurrants and other berries leave pigment-based stains, which are soluble in water and usually easy to remove if you act quickly.

GENERAL DIRECTIONS Blot up as much of the stain as possible with white paper towels or a clean, white, lint-free cloth. Dab, rather than rub, at the stain. Follow the directions below for specific fabrics.

CARPET Cover the stain with White Wizard and, working from the outside inwards, gently soak up the stain, again using white paper towels or a clean, white, lint-free cloth. Don't be tempted to drench the area – it's better to make repeated small applications. Continue until the stain has completely disappeared. If traces still remain, a complete carpet shampoo may be necessary.

WASHABLE FABRICS After blotting, rinse the stain under plenty of cold running water. For cotton, follow immediately with a 40°C machine-wash, using biological detergent. For silk, treat with Stain Devils for Tea, Wine, Fruit & Juice, and follow with a 30°C machine-wash on the delicates cycle. Berry stains are tricky to remove from wool and the key is to act immediately. After rinsing with cold water, spray lightly with Wine Away until the stain turns blue. Blot again, and repeat this process until the stain has completely disappeared. Then wash at as high a temperature as the care label permits.

Blood

One of the most common stains, particularly for women. Don't panic, because blood is easy to remove if you treat it while it is still fresh. The most important thing to remember is that it is a protein-based stain and therefore must be treated at a low wash temperature. This stops the protein coagulating and setting the stain into the fabric.

GENERAL DIRECTIONS Gently blot up as much of the stain as possible with white paper towels or a clean, white, lint-free cloth. Dab, rather than rub, at the stain. Follow the directions below for specific fabrics.

CARPET Cover the stain with Wine Away and, working from the outside inwards, use white paper towels or a clean, white, lint-free cloth to absorb the stain. Make repeated small applications rather than soaking the area. Continue until the stain has gone. If traces remain, try covering the affected area with a paste of cornflour or un-pigmented meat tenderiser and water. Leave to dry, sponge off with cold water and repeat.

WASHABLE FABRICS Enzyme-based pre-soaking agents and biological detergents can be used, but are often unsuitable for use on silk and wool, so check the care label. For fresh blood, after blotting, rinse the stain under cold water. If the stain has dried, steep first in an enzyme-based, pre-soaking agent, or a washing soda crystal solution (for silk and cotton), then follow the instructions given for each fabric. For cotton, machine-wash at 40°C with biological detergent. For silk, machine-wash at 30°C on the delicates cycle. For wool, spray lightly with Wine Away until the stain turns blue. Blot again, and repeat this process until the stain has gone. Follow with a 30°C machine-wash on the delicates cycle.

Candle wax

Wax is usually quite straightforward to remove, depending on the colour of the candle. Follow our steps below to get the best results.

GENERAL DIRECTIONS The wax needs to be as hard as possible before you attempt to remove it – on carpets, cover the affected area with an ice pack or a bag of frozen peas; on fabrics, place the entire item in the freezer for an hour or so. Once the wax is brittle, you will be able to pick off most of it by hand or with a blunt knife. Follow the directions below for specific fabrics. If the wax has blown on to wallpaper try Sticky Stuff Remover after carrying out the steps above.

CARPET To remove the remaining wax deposits, place a sheet of white paper towel over the area and iron on a low heat. Don't let the iron touch the carpet pile or it may scorch and melt. Keep moving the paper around for maximum absorption, and continue until all the wax has been soaked up. Remove any resistant colour or stain with a few drops of methylated spirits (test first on an inconspicuous area, as it may discolour the carpet).

WASHABLE FABRICS Follow the directions for treating a carpet, but put an absorbent, white paper towel on both sides of the stain. If any colour remains, use methylated spirits on it, then machine-wash the item on as high a temperature as the fabric allows.

WOODEN SURFACES Chip away at the wax once it is hard, using your fingernail or a plastic spatula. Remove any remaining film with a duster, then polish as normal. If heat-marking has occurred, rub along the wood grain with a cream metal polish.

Carrot

Stains from orange vegetables, such as carrots, pumpkins and sweet potatoes, are caused by the pigment beta-carotene and can be tricky to remove. Here's what to do.

GENERAL DIRECTIONS Gently scrape up any solids with a blunt knife. Blot the area with white paper towels. Follow the directions below for specific fabrics.

CARPET Treat the stain with Bissell OxyKIC, following the manufacturer's instructions. You will probably need to make repeated applications, but the stain should come out eventually.

WASHABLE FABRICS Flush the affected area with cool water to remove as much of the stain as possible. Blot with white paper towels. For cotton, follow with a 40°C machine-wash, using biological detergent. For silk, follow with a 30°C machine-wash on the delicates cycle. Wool is tricky. If you act fast, washing at 30°C may work, but if the stain has dried, it probably won't come out. Repeated applications of Dylon Stain Remover for Biological Stains may just do the trick.

Chewing gum

GENERAL DIRECTIONS If possible, put the entire item in the freezer and leave until the gum is brittle enough to be picked off with a blunt knife. Otherwise, place an ice pack or bag of frozen peas over the gum until it hardens, and then pick off as much as possible. Follow the directions below for specific fabrics.

CARPET Use White Wizard or WD-40 to remove any remaining traces. Lightly cover the affected area, leave to work for a minute, then blot with paper towels to lift the gum. Rinse by blotting with damp white paper towels.

WASHABLE FABRICS For cotton, machine-wash at 40°C using biological detergent. For silk, spot treat the area with Stain Devils for Grease, Lubricant & Paint, following the manufacturer's instructions, then machine-wash at 30°C on the delicates cycle. For wool, spot-treat with Sticky Stuff Remover, following the manufacturer's instructions, then machine-wash at 30°C on the delicates cycle.

TIP
There is no solution that is 100 per cent effective of removing chewing gum in hair, but rubbing peanut butter or vegetable oil into the gum will help to soften it and make it easier to remove.

Chocolate

GENERAL DIRECTIONS Blot or gently scrape up deposits, using a blunt knife and white paper towels. Follow the directions below for specific fabrics.

CARPET Spot-treat the affected area with Bissell OxyKIC and gently soak up the stain with white paper towels. Repeat as necessary, and finish by lightly rinsing with water and blotting again to remove as much moisture as possible.

WASHABLE FABRICS For cotton, steep the item in a biological presoaking agent, such as Biotex, for 15–30 minutes. Gently rub the affected area every five minutes or so. Follow by machine-washing at 40°C with biological detergent. For silk and wool pre-soak as for cotton, but in a solution of washing soda crystals and water. Follow by machine-washing at 30°C on the delicates cycle.

TIP
Chocolate has a very low melting point, so putting it in the fridge to firm up before eating, will help avoid sticky fingers and consequent stains.

Coffee with milk

Coffee stains can be hard to shift. This is because the proteins in milk are affected by heat and liable to coagulate and set into fabrics such as wool, even at low temperatures (see Pigment- and tannin-based stains, page 269). For black coffee stains see Tea, pages 297–8.

GENERAL DIRECTIONS Gently blot up as much of the stain as possible with white paper towels or a clean, white, lint-free cloth. Dab, rather than rub, at the stain. Follow the directions below for specific fabrics.

CARPET Cover the stain with White Wizard and, working from the outside inwards, gently soak up the stain with white paper towels or a clean, white, lint-free cloth. Make repeated small applications rather than completely drenching the area. Continue until the stain has completely disappeared.

WASHABLE FABRICS After blotting, rinse the stain under plenty of cold running water. For cotton, follow immediately with a 40°C machine-wash, using biological detergent. For silk, treat with Stain Devils for Cooking Oil & Fat or for Tea, Red Wine, Fruit & Juice and follow with a 30°C machine-wash on the delicates cycle. If the item is wool, you'll need to act fast to prevent it being ruined. After rinsing with cold water, soak in a cool solution of washing soda crystals or a suitable pre-wash detergent. Then hand-wash in lukewarm water and allow to dry naturally. If this doesn't work, rewet the item and rub a little glycerine into the stain, then leave it to stand for approximately 30 minutes before hand-washing again as above.

Cola and other fizzy drinks

The main thing you need to know is that the sugar in these fizzy drinks will oxidise and cause the stain to darken over a period of time, making it more difficult to remove. So, as with all stains, the best thing to do is act immediately.

GENERAL DIRECTIONS Gently blot up as much of the stain as possible with white paper towels or a clean, white, lint-free cloth. Dab, rather than rub, at the stain. Follow the directions below for specific fabrics.

CARPET Cover the stain with Bissell OxyKIC and, working from the outside inwards, gently blot the stain with white paper towels or a clean, white, lint-free cloth. Make repeated small applications rather than completely soaking the area. Continue until the stain has completely disappeared.

WASHABLE FABRICS After blotting, rinse the stain under plenty of cold running water. For cotton, follow with a 40°C machine-wash, using biological detergent. For silk, follow with a 30°C machine-wash on the delicates cycle. For wool, follow with a 30°C machine-wash on the delicates cycle.

Coloured pencil and crayon

If the damage is limited to a small area, you should be able to get rid of it. Crayons usually contain waxy or oily parts and pigments. You need to deal with the greasy part first.

GENERAL DIRECTIONS Remove any solid bits by scraping gently with a blunt knife, and lifting the debris with sticky tape wrapped around your fingers. Follow the directions below for specific fabrics.

CARPET Put several layers of white paper towels on top of the stain and run a warm iron over them. The heat will melt the crayon and it will be absorbed by the towels. Move to a clean patch on the towels frequently. Dab methylated spirits or WD-40 on any remaining traces of colour. Finally, sponge the area with white paper towels dipped in a weak solution of detergent, flush with clear water, and blot with clean paper towels to dry.

WASHABLE FABRICS Place the stained area on a pad of white paper towels and spray it with WD-40. Let it stand for a few minutes, then turn the fabric over and spray the other side. Clean off as much of the crayon as you can with paper towels. Rub a small amount of liquid detergent into the stained area and machine-wash as normal on as high a temperature as the fabric allows. Remove any surviving traces by soaking the item in an oxygen-based, colour-safe bleaching product, according to the manufacturer's instructions. Check the garment's care label and test an inconspicuous area for colour-fastness first.

HEAT-SET STAINS IN TUMBLE-DRIER DRUM If a crayon left in the pocket of an item of clothing has inadvertently found its way into your tumble-drier and melted, you'll need to clean the drier's drum to make sure the crayon is not transferred all over your next load of laundry. Spray WD-40 on to a clean cloth and wipe around the drum to remove the mess. Follow by running a load of dry rags through a drying cycle to ensure the drum is clean. Repeat if necessary.

Correction fluid (e.g. Tipp-Ex)

Some brands of correction fluid are water-based and should come out with normal washing, but the ones with petroleum in them can cause problems. Dry-cleaning is recommended, but if you want to try yourself, here's what to do.

GENERAL DIRECTIONS Allow the product to dry and pick off as much of the deposit as possible, taking care not to snag the fabric. Dab the

---

Off the wall!

Coloured pencil and crayon can be removed from different wall surfaces and fittings in the following ways:

- **PAINTED WALLS** Rub the area with a lightly dampened cloth dipped in White Wizard, toothpaste or bicarbonate of soda. The slight abrasiveness will shift the crayon. Be very gentle to avoid damage.

- **VINYL WALLCOVERINGS, BEDHEADS AND RADIATORS** Wipe with a damp cloth. If necessary, apply a few drops of WD-40 to dissolve the crayon.

- **WALLPAPER** If the stain is small, you may be able to remove it by spraying lightly with WD-40 and wiping it with a cloth dipped in a weak solution of detergent. Be careful not to over-wet the paper and damage it.

affected area with paint remover or turpentine to help fade the mark. Flush with water, then treat with a citrus-based, spot treatment stain remover (such as De.Solv.It) according to the manufacturer's instructions. Follow the directions below for specific fabrics.

CARPET You may be able to remove the offending area by carefully snipping the tufts off the carpet.

WASHABLE FABRICS Machine-wash on as high a temperature as the fabric allows. Don't hold out too much hope though!

Curry

Stains from curry are usually caused by the pigment curcumin, which is found in turmeric. It is one of the toughest stains to remove and the best advice here is not to eat curry while wearing silk or wool. There's no foolproof way to get rid of a turmeric stain, but if you act quickly enough, the following suggestions might just do the trick.

GENERAL DIRECTIONS Use white paper towels to absorb as much of the stain as you can. Apply methylated spirits to the stained area and leave it for a short time. The mark will turn bright red initially, but don't be alarmed – this is quite normal. Blot with white paper towels to remove as much colour as possible, moving to a clean area of the towel regularly. Repeat this process until there is no further transfer of colour to the towels. Flush with cold water, then apply a mild detergent solution to the stained area. Allow this to soak in for a few minutes, then machine-wash the item as normal, at as high a temperature as the fabric allows. If traces still remain, you'll be pleased to hear that curcumin is unstable when exposed to light, and placing the affected item in direct sun for a few days will fade the stain further.

CARPET White Wizard is the proprietary product that is most effective for removing curry stains.

WORKTOPS AND OTHER SURFACES A slightly abrasive paste made from bicarbonate of soda and water works well on curry stains on hard surfaces.

Egg

Egg is a protein-based stain and needs to be treated at a low temperature so that it doesn't coagulate and set into the fabric. It is usually quite easy to remove.

GENERAL DIRECTIONS Gently scrape off any solid bits with a blunt knife, then blot up as much liquid as possible with white paper towels. Follow the directions below for specific fabrics.

CARPET Spot-treat with a proprietary carpet shampoo, then rinse with cold water and blot dry.

WASHABLE FABRICS After blotting, flush the affected area with lots of cold water. For cotton, follow by machine-washing at 40°C with biological detergent. If the stains are old, soak overnight in a solution of an enzyme-based stain remover and cold water. Machine-wash as normal. For silk and wool, rub a little mild detergent solution into the affected area, then wash at 30°C on the delicates cycle.

Excrement

Nappies are the most common offender, but you might also have a problem with an aged pet that is not quite as good at asking to go outside as he used to be. Excrement is a protein-based stain and not usually difficult to remove, providing you use a low wash temperature. As always, the main thing is to act fast. Wear rubber gloves to remove the poop and dispose of it down the toilet.

CARPET Blot with white paper towels dipped in a solution of bicarbonate of soda and water, to which you have added a few drops of disinfectant. Blot dry. If necessary, clean and deodorise the area with a proprietary pet stain remover (available from pet supply stores). Spray with a solution of one part white vinegar to five parts water, to deter your pet from returning to do his business on the same spot.

WASHABLE FABRICS Scrape away the deposit and blot dry. If it is not possible to remove the item for cleaning, isolate the stain by tying string tightly around the fabric and gathering it up. Rinse under cold running water. Sanitise by blotting with disinfectant solution or treat with a proprietary pet stain remover. Otherwise, machine-wash the item as normal.

STAINED NAPPIES AND UNDERWEAR Scrape away any deposits. Rinse promptly in cold water to minimise staining. Soak in a solution of bicarbonate of soda and water to help remove and deodorise stains. If possible, machine-wash with biological detergent – the enzymes are effective on the protein in excrement. To sanitise the garment, wash at a temperature of 60°C or above, but such a high temperature may mean you will be left with the stain.

Fake tan

Depending on the brand and length of time it has had to develop, fake tan can be impossible to remove, and many a bride has lived to regret that last-minute 'instant glow' which then transferred itself permanently to her beautiful wedding dress. If you're in luck and the brand is one of the less deadly types, try the following remedies, but don't hold out too much hope.

GENERAL DIRECTIONS Proprietary fake tan removers are available and although these are designed to remove product from the skin, it's worth trying them out on stained garments too, if all else fails. Just be careful before applying to check for colour-fastness on an inconspicuous area first. Follow the directions for specific fabrics.

WASHABLE FABRICS Often, a 40°C wash with biological detergent will get rid of marks on sheets and cotton clothing. For silk and wool, rub with a warm solution of washing-up liquid, followed by a 30°C wash.

Fats, grease and oils

Not as bad as you might think. The butter that dripped from your toast or the oil that spattered you from the frying pan will come out if you act quickly and use the right approach. The main thing to remember is not to sponge with cold water, as this can set the stain.

Applying fake tan

To avoid staining your clothes, always apply fake tan a few hours before you get dressed so it has time to dry properly. Wash your hands afterwards so you don't end up with brown 'nicotine-like' nails! For more even colour when applying fake tan, exfoliate your skin first.

GENERAL DIRECTIONS Sprinkle unscented talc or cornflour over the
stain to cover it. Leave for five minutes, and then remove with a soft
brush. If obvious signs of grease remain, try using white paper towels
to absorb more of it. Follow the directions below for specific fabrics.

CARPET Treat the affected area with White Wizard, then blot with lightly
dampened white paper towels. Leave to dry.

WASHABLE FABRICS For cotton, rub a little washing-up liquid into the
stain, then machine-wash immediately at 40°C with biological
detergent. For silk and wool, spot-treat with Stain Devils for Cooking
Oil & Fat, following the manufacturer's instructions. Then machine-
wash at as high a temperature as the garment allows, using a
detergent for delicates.

Felt-tip pen

Felt tip is difficult to remove, but if you are persistent and the stain is small,
you may be able to get it out.

GENERAL DIRECTIONS Blot first with dry white paper towels. For fabrics,
place an absorbent pad under the stain. Follow the directions below
for specific fabrics.

CARPET AND WASHABLE FABRICS Apply a cotton bud dipped in
methylated spirits to the affected area. Don't over-wet. Dab gently at
the stain, trying not to spread it too much as it is being dissolved. Blot
firmly with white paper towels, moving to a clean area of both pad
and towel frequently. Repeat until no further colour seems to be
lifting. Be prepared to make several applications. Flush with cold
water, then carefully rub White Wizard into any remaining traces,
working it in well. Leave for a couple of minutes, and blot again with
dry paper towels. Press the towel firmly against the mark for several
seconds each time. Blot with water. On fabric, if traces still remain, try
spot-treating the area with Stain Devils for Ballpoint Ink & Felt Tip.
Follow the manufacturer's instructions, then machine-wash at as high
a temperature as the fabric allows.

LAST RESORT If there are still any signs of the ink, try soaking the item in
an oxygen-based, colour-safe bleaching product. Follow the
manufacturer's instructions and check the garment's care label first.

Foundation

Foundation does usually come out of most materials, but as always,
deal with the stain as soon as possible and have the right removal product
to hand.

GENERAL DIRECTIONS Gently scrape off any solid residue with a blunt
knife. Follow the directions below for specific fabrics.

CARPET Apply White Wizard to the affected area. Leave it to work for a
few minutes, then use white paper towels to soak up the stain. Work
from the outside inwards to avoid spreading the stain. Repeat as
necessary. Finish by dabbing the area with a dampened paper towel
to rinse it, then blot dry.

WASHABLE FABRICS For cotton, spray the affected area lightly with
De.Solv.It, then follow the manufacturer's instructions. Repeat as

necessary, then machine-wash on as high a temperature as the fabric allows, using biological detergent. If the stain persists, try immersing in a biological pre-soaking agent before rewashing. For silk and wool, spot treat the stained area with Stain for Cooking Oil and Grease, according to the manufacturer's instructions. Wash at 30°C on the delicates cycle.

Glue

There are lots of different types of glue, so the treatment will depend on which type has caused the problem. If possible, follow the removal procedures given on the glue's packaging or contact the manufacturer for specific advice. Otherwise, try the methods below.

GENERAL DIRECTIONS Quickly and gently scrape off the glue with a blunt knife and white paper towels.

ALL-PURPOSE HOUSEHOLD ADHESIVE Dab the affected area with acetone (nail polish remover) until the glue has dissolved. Launder (where possible).

CONTACT ADHESIVE These harden on contact, so you must act fast. Treat as for all-purpose adhesives.

EPOXY RESIN This consists of a glue and a hardener. Once epoxy resin has hardened, it is almost impossible to remove. Use acetone (nail polish remover) or methylated spirits to remove it before it sets.

PAPER ADHESIVE AND LATEX GLUE Pick off the glue residue first. For carpets, dab the stain with a liquid detergent solution – do not over-wet. Rinse and blot dry. For fabrics, wash as normal.

Grass

Grass stains are mainly a mixture of chlorophyll and proteins, and it is the pigment in the chlorophyll that is hard to shift, particularly from delicate fabrics such as silk.

WASHABLE FABRICS For cotton, rub White Wizard into the affected area and blot with white paper towels to remove as much colour as you can. Reapply the product, then machine-wash at 40°C with biological detergent. You must act quickly to get a grass stain out of silk. Again, use White Wizard, following the directions for cotton, then machine-wash at 30°C on the delicates cycle. For wool, spot-treat the affected area with Stain Devils for Mud, Grass & Make-Up, according to the manufacturer's instructions. Follow by machine-washing the item at 30°C on the delicates cycle. You can also use White Wizard for grass stains on wool.

Gravy

Gravy is a combination stain, which contains mainly protein and grease. You need to deal with the greasy part of the stain first, and then use a low wash temperature so that the protein part does not coagulate and set into the fabric. As always, for best results you need to act fast.

GENERAL DIRECTIONS Gently scrape off as much residue as possible with a blunt knife. Apply a few drops of methylated spirits to the stain

Superglue removal

For carpets, sponge the area with warm, soapy water to dissolve the glue – you may have to do this several times. Do not over-wet. Blot afterwards to dry. If this doesn't work, try dabbing the area with nail polish remover, but test a hidden area of the carpet for colour-fastness first. For washable fabrics, dab with nail polish remover to dissolve the glue (having tested for colour-fastness), then machine-wash as normal.

TIP
For grass stains on white leather trainers or tennis shoes, try spraying the stained area with a few drops of WD-40 and wiping with a clean cloth.

and blot with white paper towels or a clean, white, lint-free cloth until no more of the stain appears to be transferring to the towels. Allow the solvent to evaporate completely. Follow the directions below for specific fabrics.

CARPET Apply White Wizard to the affected area and blot gently with a dampened white paper towel until the stain has been removed. Leave to dry.

WASHABLE FABRICS For cotton, after blotting with methylated spirits, put the item in a 40°C machine-wash with biological detergent. If the stain is large, work a few drops of liquid detergent into it before washing. For stubborn stains, try soaking the item in an enzyme-based pre-soaking agent before washing as normal. It can be tricky to remove gravy from silk. After blotting, rub a little detergent for delicates directly on the stain before machine-washing at 30°C on the delicates cycle. If the stain remains, take the item to a dry-cleaner, who may be able to remove it. For wool, after blotting, spot treat the stained area with Stain Devils for Cooking Oil & Fat (following the manufacturer's instructions), then wash at 30°C on the delicates cycle.

Ice cream

Ice cream is another combination stain. Most flavours contain grease, protein and pigment but despite this, ice cream is usually fairly easy to remove. Don't use a high wash temperature or you may set the protein part of the stain into the fabric.

GENERAL DIRECTIONS Gently scrape off as much ice cream as possible with a blunt knife, then blot with white paper towels. Follow the directions below for specific fabrics.

CARPET Spot-treat the affected area with a proprietary carpet shampoo such as Bissell OxyKIC. Rinse with cool water, and blot to dry.

WASHABLE FABRICS Rub a small amount of liquid detergent into the affected area, and leave to soak for a few minutes. For cotton, machine-wash at 40°C with biological detergent. For silk and wool, machine-wash at 30°C on the delicates cycle.

FLAVOURED ICE CREAM Some ice creams, such as chocolate or raspberry flavour, tend to be more highly coloured. If the removal methods described here don't completely remove the stain, try the techniques described for the individual foods.

Ink

Trying to explain how to remove ink is difficult because there are so many different types that it is impossible to provide one foolproof method. Your first port of call should be the manufacturer, who may be able to provide you with instructions specifically designed for the product. If so, follow these. Otherwise, the product many ink manufacturers seem to recommend is Amodex Ink and Stain Remover. If you can get hold of this, wait until you have it before trying to remove the stain – it claims to work as well on dry stains, and other methods used in the interim may reduce its effectiveness. Always follow the manufacturer's instructions. If you can't wait, the following tried-and-tested methods are the most likely to succeed. Unfortunately, 'permanent ink' usually means just that!

GENERAL DIRECTIONS Blot first with dry white paper towels. For fabrics, place an absorbent pad under the stain.

CARPET AND WASHABLE FABRICS Apply a cotton bud, dipped in methylated spirits, to the affected area. Don't over-wet. Dab the stain gently, trying not to spread it as it is being dissolved. Blot firmly with white paper towels, moving to a clean area of both bud and towel frequently. Repeat until no further colour seems to be lifting. Be prepared to make several applications. Flush with cold water, then rub White Wizard into any remaining traces, working it in well. Leave for a couple of minutes, and blot again with dry paper towels. Press the towel firmly against the mark for several seconds each time. Flush with water. On fabric, if traces still remain, try spot-treating the area with Stain Devils for Ballpoint Ink & Felt Tip, following the manufacturer's instructions, then machine-wash at as high a temperature as the fabric allows.

HOUSEHOLD SURFACES Rub away as much of the mark as you can with a sponge dipped in soapy water. If the stain persists, use a white paper towel dampened with methylated spirits, working from the outside inwards.

LEATHER Homeserve Furniture Care Kits can be used to remove ink and all sorts of other stains on leather furniture and clothing, see Specialist Products.

LAST RESORT If there are still any signs of the ink, try soaking the item in an oxygen-based, colour-safe bleaching solution. Follow the manufacturer's instructions and check the garment's care label first.

SPECIAL INSTRUCTIONS FOR RED INK If the above methods don't work, try spot-treating the affected area with Wine Away.

Jam

Jam and jelly stains are sugar- and pigment-based, so will usually be soluble in water. Some types are likely to contain tannins, so never use salt. Pigment stains are difficult to remove once they have had time to dry on fabric. You need to act immediately. If the removal methods described here don't completely remove the stain, try the techniques described for individual fruits.

GENERAL DIRECTIONS Gently scrape off as much residue as you can with a blunt knife. Follow the directions below for specific fabrics.

CARPET Use Bissell OxyKIC or White Wizard to spot-treat the affected area. Blot the stain with white paper towels or a clean, white, lint-free cloth. Rinse with cool water. Blot dry with white paper towels.

WASHABLE FABRICS Gently rub White Wizard into the affected area and leave for a few minutes. Blot up as much colour as you can with white paper towels. Flush the stain with lots of cool water. For cotton, machine-wash at 40°C with biological detergent. For silk and wool, machine-wash at 30°C on the delicates cycle.

Lipstick

Lipstick is a complex stain containing both grease and highly coloured pigments. You need to dissolve the greasy part first and then deal with the dye.

Inky fingers

Got inky fingers after a burst of artistic creativity? Try squeezing shampoo on to the affected area and lathering it up with a little water. Use a pumice stone to gently abrade the stained parts of your hands. Keep going until all the ink is removed, then rinse well under cool running water.

GENERAL DIRECTIONS Very gently, scrape off any lumpy bits with a blunt knife, being careful not to spread the stain.

CARPET Squirt a few drops of WD-40 on the affected area, wait 30 seconds, then blot with white paper towels, moving to clean areas of the towel frequently. Work from the outside inwards, and use a delicate dabbing motion. Be gentle to avoid pushing the stain deeper into the carpet or spreading it. Repeat until no more of the stain is lifted. Remove remaining traces of colour with White Wizard. Apply to the mark and leave for a minute or so, then blot with lightly dampened white paper towels or a clean, white, lint-free cloth. Dab with clean water to rinse, then blot dry. Repeat until stain is removed.

WASHABLE FABRICS On cotton, if the stain is small, it will often come out if you rub in a little liquid detergent and wash as normal. For larger or deep-coloured stains, pre-treat with De.Solv.It according to manufacturer's instructions and then machine-wash at 40°C with biological detergent. For silk, use the WD-40 method as described for carpet, followed by Stain Devils for Mud, Grass & Make-Up to remove the greasy mark that WD-40 may leave. Then machine-wash at 30°C on the delicates cycle. For wool, spot-treat with De.Solv.It, then wash at 30°C on the delicates cycle.

Mango

Mangoes are messy to eat, which is risky because the stain from their juice is lethal. It is virtually impossible to remove from wool, and you'll need perseverance to remove it from other fabrics.

GENERAL DIRECTIONS Gently scrape off any solid residue with a blunt knife. Follow the directions below for specific fabrics.

CARPET Use white paper towels to blot as much liquid as possible from the stain. Spot-treat with Bissell OxyKIC, following the manufacturer's instructions. You may need to make repeated applications.

WASHABLE FABRICS Flush the affected area with lots of cool water. Rub a little White Wizard into the stain and leave for five minutes. Blot with dry white paper towels to lift as much colour as possible. For cotton, follow by machine-washing at 40°C with a biological detergent. For silk and wool, follow by machine-washing at as hot a temperature as the fabric allows, using a detergent for delicates.

OTHER THINGS TO TRY If the stain still remains after the above treatment, try soaking the item in an oxygen-based, colour-safe bleaching product, such as Vanish. Always check the fabric care label first and test for colour-fastness.

Mascara

No matter how careful you are taking your make-up off at night, mascara always seems to leave dirty streaks on pillowcases and sheets. Don't worry, you should be able to remove it without too much trouble.

GENERAL DIRECTIONS Carefully scrape up any solids with a blunt knife or white paper towels. Follow the directions below for specific fabrics.

CARPET Spot-treat the affected area with Bissell OxyKIC, according to the manufacturer's instructions. Repeat as necessary until the stain has been removed. Rinse with cool water and blot with white paper towels to dry.

WASHABLE FABRICS Spot-treat with Stain Devils for Mud, Grass & Make-Up, following the manufacturer's instructions, then machine-wash at as high a temperature as the fabric permits. Allow to dry naturally.

Mayonnaise

Mayonnaise always seems to squirt out of the sides of sandwiches, no matter how delicately you bite into them. It makes a stain similar to grease and usually washes out very easily without any special treatment.

GENERAL DIRECTIONS Lift as much solid residue as possible with a blunt knife. Try not to spread the stain. Follow the directions below for specific fabrics.

CARPET White Wizard, applied to the affected area, works well. Cover the stain and blot with dry white paper towels until all traces are removed. Blot with a damp cloth to rinse and leave to dry.

WASHABLE FABRICS Rub a little White Wizard or liquid detergent into the affected area. For cotton, follow by machine-washing at 40°C with biological detergent. For silk and wool, follow by machine-washing at 30°C on the delicates cycle. If the stain has dried before washing, try applying a few drops of methylated spirits to the affected area and blotting with a white paper towel. Allow the solvent to evaporate, then rub a small amount of liquid detergent into the area before washing as normal.

Milk and cream

Milk and cream come out of most fabrics quite easily. This is mainly a protein stain (although cream also contains a certain amount of fat), so the water you use needs to be at a low temperature.

GENERAL DIRECTIONS Blot as much liquid from the stain as you can with white paper towels or a clean, white, lint-free cloth. Flush with lots of cool water. Follow the directions below for specific fabrics.

CARPET Spot-treat the affected area with a proprietary carpet cleaner, such as Bissell OxyKIC; you can also use White Wizard. Follow the manufacturer's instructions. Rinse with cool water and use white paper towels to blot dry – it is very important to lift as much moisture as possible, otherwise you may be left with a foul sour milk stench coming from the carpet. For lingering 'sour milk' odours, sprinkle bicarbonate of soda over the area and leave for a few hours before vacuuming. If that doesn't work, a specialised product designed for removing pet smells may do the trick.

WASHABLE FABRICS Rub a small amount of liquid clothes detergent into the stained area and leave for a few minutes. For cotton, follow by machine-washing at 40°C with biological detergent. For silk and wool, follow by machine-washing at 30°C on the delicates cycle.

Mould and mildew

Mould and mildew thrive in damp, humid conditions where there is inadequate ventilation. Stop them sprouting in the first place by keeping

TIP
If you've run out of eye make-up remover, wiping your lashes with baby oil on cotton wool will often remove mascara very effectively and stop it escaping on to your pillow at night.

the house dry and well aired. If certain parts suffer from high levels of condensation, consider buying a de-humidifier. If moulds and mildew do appear, here's how to tackle them.

For more information on dealing with mould on other surfaces, see A–Z of Cleaning and Caring for Surfaces, pages 219–37.

CARPET Brush or vacuum away spores and spray with a proprietary fungicide suitable for soft furnishings. Dab remaining marks with a mild disinfectant until they have been removed, then sponge with cold water to rinse.

WASHABLE FABRICS Normal washing should remove light stains when they are fresh. Treat stubborn stains on white fabric (except nylon and items with a 'do not bleach' symbol) by soaking in a solution of chlorine bleach (20ml/1½ tbsp bleach to 5 litres/9 pints water). Treat coloureds and non-bleachable whites with a stain remover such as Stain Devils for Tea, Red Wine, Fruit & Juice, following the manufacturer's instructions.

Mud

Mud can be as variable as the earth itself, and contains a mixture of soiling agents: clay, loam, proteins and pigments, even grease. Enzyme-based stain removers work well on the organic components in stubborn mud stains, but remember that you can't use them on silk and wool. Act fast, particularly with delicate fabrics, or you may have a permanent souvenir.

GENERAL DIRECTIONS Allow the mud to dry, then remove as much as possible by brushing or vacuuming the affected area. Follow the directions below for specific fabrics.

CARPET Apply White Wizard and allow it to work for a few minutes. Blot with lightly dampened white paper towels. Repeat as necessary until the stain has been removed. Rinse with clear water and blot dry.

WASHABLE FABRICS Often, the stain will come out of cotton simply by machine-washing it at 40°C with a biological detergent. For more stubborn stains, try a biological pre-soaking product. Follow the manufacturer's instructions, then wash the item as normal. For silk and wool, try rubbing a little washing-up liquid into the affected area before washing as normal. If this doesn't work, spot-treat with Stain Devils for Mud, Grass & Make-Up, according to the manufacturer's instructions, then wash as normal.

LAST RESORT Soak the item in an oxygen-based, colour-safe bleaching product. Follow the instructions given by the manufacturer and check the garment's care label first.

Mustard

A must on burgers and hot dogs, but not on your clothes. Unfortunately, once there, it's very difficult to remove. The colouring in mustard usually comes from curcumin, the culprit responsible for those fiendish yellow curry stains (see Curry, page 280).

GENERAL DIRECTIONS Gently scrape off any solid residue with a blunt knife. Dampen the affected area with a few drops of methylated spirits. The stain may turn dark red, but don't worry, this is normal. Blot up as much colour as you can with white paper towels. To avoid spreading the stain, use a delicate dabbing motion, and work from the outside inwards. Follow the directions below for specific fabrics.

CARPET Bissell OxyKIC and White Wizard are most effective on mustard stains. After blotting, apply either product to the stained area, following the manufacturer's instructions. Rinse as directed. Allow to dry naturally.

WASHABLE FABRICS Allow the methylated spirits to evaporate completely. Then spray the affected area on both sides with De.Solv.It. Leave for five minutes before blotting with a clean, white lint-free cloth. Reapply De.Solv.It and then wash the item according to fabric type. For cotton, follow by machine-washing at 40°C with biological detergent. For silk and wool, follow by machine-washing at 30°C on the delicates cycle.

IF THE MARKS PERSIST Try soaking the item in a colour-safe, oxygen-based bleaching product, but check the care label first. If all else fails, hang the item out in the sun for a few days. The pigment in mustard is unstable in light, so exposure to the sun will help to fade it.

Nail polish

If the nail polish has dried, you can forget it – it is virtually impossible to get out with any home treatment. Take the item to a dry-cleaner, who might be able to help. If the spill is tiny though, and you act while it is still wet, you may be in with a chance of removing it.

GENERAL DIRECTIONS Immediately dab the area with a cotton bud that has been very slightly dampened with nail polish remover, but do not use on acetate fabric. Repeat until no more colour comes off. Follow the directions below for specific fabrics.

CARPET If traces remain, you may be able to remove them by snipping off the tips of the carpet tufts in the affected area with scissors.

WASHABLE FABRICS Next, launder according to fabric type. Any remaining stain may be removable by bleaching. Check the care label first and test for colour-fastness.

STAINS ON HARD SURFACES Moisten a white paper towel with nail polish remover and gently dab over the stain until it is removed. Wipe over with a clean damp cloth and polish dry. Be careful on varnished surfaces as the polish remover may damage the finish.

WARNING Don't use nail polish remover on acetate fabrics.

Orange juice

A pigment-based stain that is soluble in water and should come out quite readily if you deal with it quickly.

GENERAL DIRECTIONS Blot up as much liquid as you can with white paper towels. Follow the directions below for specific fabrics.

CARPET Apply any proprietary carpet stain treatment, following the manufacturer's instructions. Leave to dry.

WASHABLE FABRICS After blotting, flush the affected area with cool water. For cotton, follow by machine-washing at 40°C with biological detergent. For silk and wool, follow by machine-washing at 30°C on the delicates cycle.

Paint

Some paints are more amenable than others to being removed. Just keep your fingers crossed that yours is one of the easy ones.

GENERAL DIRECTIONS If possible, refer to the paint manufacturer's instructions for removing stains and follow these. If there are no instructions and the paint is still wet, blot with white paper towels to remove as much of it as possible.

ACRYLIC PAINT Wash out with detergent and water. If the stain has dried, place an absorbent pad under it, if possible, and dab with white paper towels moistened with methylated spirits. Flush with cold water, then wash at as high a temperature as the fabric allows.

OIL-BASED PAINT Almost impossible to remove, but you can try holding an absorbent pad under the stain and dabbing it with white spirit. Afterwards, sponge with water (if on carpet) or machine-wash at as high a temperature as the fabric allows. If the stain remains, consult a dry-cleaner.

WATER-BASED PAINT Rinse out or flush fresh marks with cold water, then launder. Dried marks are difficult to remove, but treating with a proprietary paint remover may fade them.

Peach juice

Biting into a perfectly ripe, fresh peach is one of life's pleasures, but you should always have a napkin to hand to catch the drips. The pigment in the juice is a powerful staining agent and hard to remove unless it is dealt with immediately. However, it is water-based and if you act quickly, you should be able to get it out. Here's what to do.

GENERAL DIRECTIONS Gently blot up as much of the stain as possible using white paper towels or a clean, white, lint-free cloth. Dab, rather than rub, at the stain. Follow the directions below for specific fabrics.

CARPET Cover the stain with Bissell OxyKIC and, working from the outside inwards, gently soak up the mark with white paper towels or a clean, white, lint-free cloth. Don't drench the area – it's better to use repeated small applications. Continue until the stain has disappeared, then blot with cold water and allow to dry naturally. Follow with a complete carpet shampoo if necessary.

WASHABLE FABRICS After blotting, rinse the stain under plenty of cold running water until no more colour is removed. Work a small amount of liquid detergent into any remaining stained area and leave to stand for five minutes or so. For cotton, immediately follow with a 40°C machine-wash, using biological detergent. For silk and wool, follow with a 30°C machine-wash on the delicates cycle. Allow the item to dry naturally. If any traces of the stain remain, try soaking the item in an oxygen-based bleach. Follow the manufacturer's instructions and always test for colour-fastness first.

Perfume

Perfumes don't usually stain, but some contain ingredients that can discolour clothing. You won't notice a mark straight away, but it can darken with age. The best preventative measure is to allow perfume to dry completely before you get dressed.

If you do notice perfume marks, fresh ones usually come out with normal washing, but rinse the area with cold water first to stop the mark being 'set' by hot water in the washing machine. For old stains on washable fabrics, lubricate the stain with a solution of equal parts glycerine and water, leave to soak for up to an hour, then wash as normal. If that doesn't work, spot-treat the affected area with Stain Devils for Tea, Red Wine, Fruit & Juice according to the manufacturer's instructions, before rewashing.

Pollen

Lilies are probably the worst offender. They smell heavenly, but the mess made by their pollen is less appealing. You can get rid of it, but if it has landed on textiles, it is important to avoid pushing the powdery pollen deeper into the pile.

GENERAL DIRECTIONS Don't rub or wet the stain. Instead, gently pat the affected area with sticky tape wrapped around your fingers, or vacuum up the pollen using the crevice nozzle. Follow the directions below for specific fabrics.

CARPET Cover any remaining traces with White Wizard or 1001 Mousse for Carpets & Upholstery and blot with white paper towels. Rinse by dabbing with clean towels dampened with water, then blot dry.

WASHABLE FABRICS For cotton and wool, all you need to do after the sticky tape treatment is to machine-wash the item at as high a temperature as the fabric allows, using the appropriate programme. For silk, after removing the dry debris with sticky tape, spot-treat any remaining traces with Stain Devils for Mud, Grass & Make-Up, according to the manufacturer's instructions. Follow by machine-washing at 30ºC on the delicates cycle.

DELICATE REMOVAL You can use the sticky tape method to remove other powdery, delicate things such as spider webs and crumbs. It's also good for lifting pet hairs from fabrics.

Pomegranate juice

Unfortunately, that ruby-red juice is a super stainer. Unless you've spilt it on cotton that can be washed at a high temperature, be prepared for disappointment – it's almost impossible to remove.

GENERAL DIRECTIONS Your best chance of success is to try immersing the affected item in a biological pre-soaking agent before washing. (This is one instance where you can forget the advice about not using this type of product on silk and wool. The item will be ruined by the stain if you do nothing, so what have you got to lose?) If that doesn't work, soaking in a colour-safe, oxygen-based bleaching product may shift the stain. Don't hold out too much hope though – there's a reason why pomegranate juice has been used for centuries as a natural fabric dye!

Raspberry juice

Raspberry juice is almost impossible to remove once it dries, and can leave a permanent mark. However, it is a water-based stain and if you deal with it while it is still fresh (within 15 minutes or so of the stain occurring), you may be in with a chance. Act fast!

GENERAL DIRECTIONS Gently blot up as much of the stain as possible with white paper towels or a clean, white, lint-free cloth. Dab, rather than rub, the stain. Follow the directions below for specific fabrics.

CARPET Spot-treat the stain with Bissell OxyKIC, following the manufacturer's instructions. Use white paper towels or a clean, white, lint-free cloth to absorb the mark. Continue until the stain has disappeared. If traces still remain, a complete carpet shampoo may be necessary.

WASHABLE FABRICS After blotting, rinse the stain under cold running water until no further colour is removed. For cotton, rub a small amount of liquid detergent into the stain, preferably one that contains enzymes. Leave for five minutes. Immediately follow with a 40°C machine-wash, using biological detergent. For wool and silk, act immediately. After rinsing with cold water, spot-treat the area with any 'oxi-action' type product suitable for use on wool and silk. Follow the manufacturer's instructions, then machine-wash at as high a temperature as the care label permits.

PERSISTENT STAINS If the stain remains, soak the item in a solution of oxygen-based bleach and water. Follow the manufacturer's instructions and test for colour-fastness first.

Red wine

There are many myths surrounding the removal of red wine stains. The most common is the one about sprinkling salt on the stain – DON'T DO IT! Red wine stains contain tannin and can be set permanently by the application of salt.

GENERAL DIRECTIONS Blot up as much moisture as you can with white paper towels or a clean, white, lint-free cloth. Follow the directions below for specific fabrics.

CARPET Spray the area with Wine Away and leave for a few minutes. Blot with white paper towels to lift the stain. Repeat as necessary.

WASHABLE FABRICS Flush the stained area with cool water. Apply Wine Away and leave for a few minutes. The stain will turn blue first, then start disappearing. Blot to remove the remaining colour and repeat if necessary. Then machine-wash according to fabric type. For cotton, wash at 40°C with biological detergent. For silk and wool, wash at 30°C on the delicates cycle.

First aid for red wine stains

If the stain has occurred while you're out at dinner, and you can't treat it immediately, flush the affected area with sparkling water – the bubbles in the water will help push the stain out of the fabric. Then, when you get home, you can treat the mark properly with Wine Away.

Rust and iron mould

Rust is the common name for iron oxide, a substance that occurs when iron corrodes in the presence of oxygen and water. It often occurs when a lot of iron is present in the water supply. The resulting stain is a characteristic reddish-brown colour and can be difficult to remove. Try the methods opposite.

GENERAL DIRECTIONS The traditional way to deal with rust stains is to apply salt and lemon juice to the stain and leave it in the sun. Keep the stained area moistened with lemon juice until the mark disappears, then allow it to dry and brush away the salt. Or you can try the remedies below.

CARPET Use a solution of warm water and biological detergent (ten parts water to one part detergent), testing first on a hidden area. If the stain does not come out, try a stronger solution, but avoid over-wetting the carpet. Alternatively, try applying a mixture of lemon juice and salt to the stained area. This will help to fade it. Rinse or vacuum away the salt afterwards.

WASHABLE FABRICS Rust stains on clothes that have been through the washing machine are likely to be iron mould – a mould that develops if a rusty mark is left untreated. If your washing machine is old, it may be responsible – check for rust marks before and after clothes go in the wash. Wash clothes as normal to remove light marks. Treat heavily marked areas with a proprietary rust and iron mould remover. Follow the manufacturer's instructions and finish by washing at as high a temperature as the fabric allows. Iron mould is easily transferred from one garment to another, so be vigilant and treat affected clothes as soon as you spot them.

ENAMELLED BATHS MADE OF CAST IRON OR STEEL Rust stains can be reduced by rubbing with a paste of bicarbonate of soda and water – leave it on for one hour, then rinse off. Lemon juice and salt also work well. Rinse or vacuum away the salt afterwards.

CAUTION Never try to remove a rust stain with chlorine bleach – it will set the stain permanently.

Salt and watermarks on textiles

Rain and winter snow are usually the cause of these marks. Stains caused by salt and water can be hard to shift, so try to stop them appearing by waterproofing outdoor clothing regularly.

FABRICS Remove watermarks from viscose by wetting the whole garment to give a uniform finish. This is also worth trying on non-washable silk if the dry-cleaner can't help remove a mark: you've nothing to lose.

SUEDE OR LEATHER GARMENTS Let the item dry naturally at normal room temperature in a well-ventilated room. Brush out marks on suede and even out the colour with a suede brush. On leather, use a proprietary leather-cleaning product.

SUEDE OR LEATHER SHOES Moisten the stain and rub with a soft cloth, or try a proprietary cleaner. Then spray shoes with a water-repellent.

Semen

The joy of sex is not without a downside. Someone always gets the damp patch, and will probably have to clear up afterwards. Don't be caught out like Bill Clinton! Deal with a semen stain promptly and it won't come back to haunt you.

CARPET Semen stains in the carpet should come out easily by sponging the affected area with a cool water and detergent solution. Follow by

Outside the home

On concrete patios and driveways rust and iron mould marks appear when ferrous (iron-containing) materials come into contact with the concrete and leave traces that, when combined with oxygen and water, cause rust to form. A common culprit is garden fertiliser, which often contains iron. The best way to remove them is with a phosphoric acid-based specialist cleaning agent. These are available in most hardware stores. Phosphoric acid is toxic and can burn the skin and eyes, so be careful to follow the manufacturer's instructions to the letter, and always wear gloves and safety goggles. You should also avoid using stiff wire brushes because these can leave metal traces in the concrete that later cause rust to appear. Use a bristle brush instead.

rinsing, then blotting with dry white paper towels to remove as much moisture as possible. Leave to dry naturally. If any powdery, dry matter remains, use a soft brush to remove it.

WASHABLE FABRICS Fresh stains are usually removed easily by rinsing with cold water. It is important to use cold water because higher temperatures can coagulate the protein in semen and set it into the fabric fibres, causing a permanent stain. If the stains are old or crusted and on any fabric other than silk or wool, remove any dry matter first with a soft brush, then steep in an enzyme-based pre-soaking agent before laundering as normal. For old stains on silk and wool, make up a pre-soaking solution of water containing a detergent for delicates and leave to soak before washing as normal.

Shoe polish

GENERAL DIRECTIONS Carefully scrape up any solid bits with a blunt knife. Follow the directions below for specific fabrics.

CARPET Squirt a few drops of WD-40 on the affected area, wait 30 seconds, then blot with white paper towels, moving to clean areas of the towel frequently. Work from the outside inwards, and use a delicate dabbing motion. You must be gentle to avoid pushing the stain deeper in or spreading it. Repeat as necessary until no more of the stain is lifted. Remove remaining traces of colour with White Wizard. Apply and leave for a minute or so, then blot the stain with lightly dampened, white paper towels or a clean, white, lint-free cloth. Finish by dabbing the area with clean water to rinse it, then blot it dry. You may have to make several applications.

WASHABLE FABRICS A small stain on cotton will often come out simply by rubbing in a little liquid detergent and washing as normal. For larger stains, pre-treat with Stain Devils for Grease, Lubricant & Paint, according to the manufacturer's instructions, then wash at 40°C with biological detergent. Shoe polish is difficult to remove from silk, but try the WD-40 method as described for carpet, followed by Stain Devils for Cooking Oil & Fat to remove any greasy mark left by the WD-40. Machine-wash at 30°C on the delicates cycle. For wool, spot-treat with Stain Devils for Grease, Lubricant & Paint and wash at 30°C on the delicates cycle.

Soot

Barbecues, fires and smoke can all produce soot stains. Here are some remedies for removing them, but if you don't manage to fix the problem, some dry-cleaners offer special ozone treatments to remove smoke.

GENERAL DIRECTIONS Soot particles can be very fine and you may cause further damage by trying to brush them away. Instead, use the nozzle attachment of the vacuum cleaner to pick up the residue. Sprinkle talc over the area to absorb the stain – rub in lightly, then vacuum away the deposit. Follow the directions below for specific fabrics.

CARPET If stains remain, try spot-treating with a proprietary carpet stain remover such as Bissell OxyKIC. You may need to have the whole carpet professionally shampooed.

WASHABLE FABRICS After vacuuming up debris, machine-wash as normal at as high a temperature as the fabric allows. Keep the load small, so that clothing has plenty of room to move about, and don't use fabric conditioner until all odours have been removed, otherwise it will mask them. If the stain remains, carry on laundering the item until it disappears – you may have to rewash several times. Try not to let the item dry out between washes.

STUBBORN STAINS Soak garments overnight in a suitable pre-soak, or for 30 minutes in an oxygen-based, colour-safe bleaching solution, following the manufacturer's instructions. Check the garments' care labels first.

Soy sauce

Soy is basically a pigment stain (particularly the cheaper brands, which often add caramel colouring to darken the sauce) and comes out easily as long as you deal with it quickly.

GENERAL DIRECTIONS Use white paper towels to blot as much liquid as you can from the stain. Follow the directions below for specific fabrics.

CARPET Apply White Wizard to the stain. Allow to stand for a few minutes, then blot with lightly dampened white paper towels or a clean, white, lint-free cloth. Rinse to remove any remaining traces. Allow the carpet to dry.

WASHABLE FABRICS Flush the stained area with lots of cool water. This alone should get rid of most of it. Then gently rub White Wizard into any remaining stain and leave to stand for a few minutes. Blot with white paper towels, then machine-wash according to fabric type. For cotton, wash at 40°C with biological detergent. For silk and wool, wash at 30°C on the delicates cycle.

Sticky tape and labels

Manufacturers seem to stick labels all over their products and these can be terribly annoying to remove. Here's what to do!

Just spray the affected area with WD-40 or Sticky Stuff Remover and leave it for 30 seconds or so, then give it a wipe and the sticky stuff will usually come right off. Repeat if necessary. If the tape or sticker has been there for a long time, you might also need to make use of a plastic scraper to banish it once and for all. If the mark is on an item that is used for food or drink, such as glasses, pans etc., and you are uncomfortable using solvents on something you will be eating from, then try this more natural method instead. Make a paste of two parts bicarbonate of soda and one part water and apply it to the area. The abrasive action of the bicarbonate of soda is very effective for removing some types of sticky stuff.

Suncreen

Sunscreen and suntan lotion contain oils to make them moisture-resistant. If they get on clothes, they can be hard to remove and tend to get darker with age. Always let the product dry before getting dressed and wash your hands after applying lotion and before touching any clothing. If you do get a stain, you need to act fast.

For washable fabrics, gently scrape off any solid residue with a blunt knife. Spot-treat the affected area with De.Solv.It (not on silk) according to the manufacturer's instructions. Flush with cool water and rub a little liquid washing detergent into the affected area, then machine-wash on as high a temperature as the fabric allows. For silk, you can try using White Wizard on the stain before washing at 30°C on the delicates cycle.

Sweat

This is one situation where prevention really is better than cure, because the stains are really hard to shift. You can stop them appearing by rinsing affected areas with cold water, or by dabbing them with a little white vinegar, before each wash. Clean garments as soon as possible after wearing them. For older, yellowed stains, try the methods below, but be prepared for limited success.

NON-WASHABLE FABRICS For light soiling, dab with a solution of white vinegar (15ml/1tbsp vinegar to 250ml/9fl oz warm water) to help to clean and deodorise the area; however this may also cause watermarks. Dry-cleaning is a better option.

WASHABLE FABRICS For cotton, immerse in an enzyme-based pre-soaking agent. Scrub affected areas with a nailbrush, and then machine-wash with a biological detergent, adding an in-wash stain remover to the load. For stubborn stains, rub with a solution made up of half glycerine and half warm water, and leave for an hour before washing as previously described. Or, try using a nailbrush to work White Wizard into the affected areas before you put the garment into the machine. Unfortunately, nothing works very well on silk and wool, but with light staining, you may have some success with the glycerine or White Wizard methods described for cotton.

REMOVING ODOURS If odours remain even after washing, try soaking the offending garment for 30 minutes in a sink filled with cool water

---

SWEAT: OTHER THINGS TO TRY

If the suggestions above don't work, you can try these more unusual tips too.

- ☉ **ASPIRIN** Use this one on white cotton shirts. Take two soluble, white, uncoated aspirin and dissolve them in half a mugful of water. Apply to the stained area and leave to soak for a couple of hours. Rub a little liquid detergent into the stain, then wash as normal.

- ☉ **MEAT TENDERISER** Not as mad as you might think when you consider that perspiration is a protein-based stain and meat tenderiser works by breaking down proteins! Dampen the stained area with water and apply half a teaspoon of tenderiser powder. Allow to stand for 30 minutes, then wash as normal.

- ☉ **LEMON JUICE** Squeeze the juice from a lemon and add an equal amount of water to it. Apply to the stained area and scrub in well with a nailbrush. Place in a sunny area and allow to dry – the lemon juice and sunlight are both good bleaching agents and will help fade the stain. Follow by washing as normal.

- ☉ **STAY FRESH** Shower or bath daily, and use sweat guards or pads in the underarms of your clothes to prevent them from coming into contact with perspiration. These are usually available in department stores such as John Lewis, or good chemists.

containing 75–90ml/5–6tbsp of bicarbonate of soda. Wash again and allow to dry naturally.

Tar

Watch out for tar after roads have been resurfaced. It is very easy to end up traipsing it all over your house. Here's how to get rid of the sticky, black mess it leaves behind.

GENERAL DIRECTIONS Scrape carefully with a blunt knife to remove surface deposits. Follow the directions below for specific fabrics.

CARPET Tar that has hardened may need softening first with a solution made up of equal parts of water and glycerine. Leave for up to an hour, then rinse with clean water and blot well. Then use a proprietary carpet cleaner, such as Bissell OxyKIC, following the manufacturer's instructions.

WASHABLE FABRICS Hold an absorbent pad (such as a wad of white paper towels) over the stain and dab it from underneath with paper towels moistened with eucalyptus oil (available from chemists). WD-40 also works well. Move to a clean area of the pad and towels frequently. Repeat until no more of the stain transfers to the towels. Rub liquid detergent into the remnants of the stain, and machine-wash on as high a temperature as the fabric allows.

STUBBORN TRACES Soak the item in an oxygen-based, colour-safe bleaching product. Check the garment's care label first and always follow the manufacturer's instructions.

ON SURFACES Spray a little WD-40 on the affected area and leave for 30 seconds. Wipe away carefully with a clean, damp cloth.

Tea

Spilt your morning cuppa? Like coffee, tea is a tannin-based stain (see Pigment and tannin-based stains, page 269). Don't sprinkle salt on it as this can set it, and act fast (especially if the spill is on silk or wool) or the mark will be difficult to remove. If the tea has milk in it, don't use a high wash temperature as this may set the protein in the milk.

GENERAL DIRECTIONS Gently blot up as much of the stain as possible with white paper towels or a clean, white, lint-free cloth. Dab, rather than rub, at the stain. Follow the directions below for specific fabrics.

CARPET Cover the stain with White Wizard and, working from the outside inwards, dab with white paper towels or a clean, white, lint-free cloth to soak up the stain. Make repeated small applications rather than completely flooding the area. Continue until the stain has disappeared.

WASHABLE FABRICS After blotting, rinse the stain under plenty of cold running water. For cotton, follow immediately with a 40°C machine-wash, using biological detergent. For silk, treat with Stain Devils for Cooking Oil & Fat or for Tea, Red Wine, Fruit & Juice and follow with a 30°C machine-wash on the delicates cycle. With wool, you'll need to tackle the stain quickly to prevent the item being ruined. After rinsing with cold water, soak in a cool solution of washing soda crystals or a suitable pre-wash detergent. Then hand-wash in lukewarm water and allow to dry naturally. If this doesn't work, rewet the item and rub a little glycerine into the stain, then leave for about 30 minutes before hand-washing again as above.

Tomato-based soups and sauces

Tomato-based food stains are one of the worst to remove. They are complex products that contain proteins, fats and highly coloured pigments. If you don't attack this type of stain immediately, you can forget it! The only way you'll get the stain out is with scissors. However, if you get on the case straight away, you might just be in with a chance.

GENERAL DIRECTIONS Place an absorbent pad under the stain. Gently scrape off any solid parts with a blunt knife. Blot the stain with white paper towels to remove as much as possible. Apply a few drops of solvent, such as methylated spirits, and blot again, moving frequently to clean areas of the absorbent pad and changing the area of the paper towel as soon as it has colour on it. Repeat until no more of the stain is lifted with the towels. Let the solvent evaporate completely. If you are tackling a dry stain on the carpet or on washable fabric, soften it first by working in a solution of equal parts glycerine and water. Allow to stand for a few minutes, then rinse and follow the methods above according to fabric type.

CARPET After treating with solvent, cover the affected area with White Wizard and leave to work for a few minutes. Blot with white paper towels, then rinse with cool water and blot dry. If traces of the stain still remain, you may need to have the entire carpet cleaned professionally.

WASHABLE FABRICS After treating with solvent, apply a few drops of mild detergent solution, and work it into the stain. Leave for five minutes, then flush with lots of cool water. Follow by applying Stain Devils for Cooking Oil & Fat, according to the manufacturer's instructions. Finally, machine-wash according to fabric type. For cotton, wash at 40°C with biological detergent (you could also soak the item in an enzyme-based pre-soaking agent before washing). For silk and wool, wash at 30°C on the delicates cycle. As a last resort, soak the item in a colour-safe, oxygen-based bleaching product to remove any last traces of the stain. Check the fabric care label and test for colour-fastness on an inconspicuous area first.

PLASTIC FOOD CONTAINERS AND FOOD PROCESSOR BOWLS First try wiping all over the stained area with vegetable oil before washing as normal – if the stain is fresh, the oil will often lift out the colour. If this doesn't work, make a paste of two parts bicarbonate of soda and one part water and apply the paste to the stain. Rub in well with a nylon scrubber, then wash in soapy water and rinse as normal.

Urine

Why is it that cats always seem to find mattresses, sofas and other soft furnishings the most appealing receptacles for their offerings? Why can't they just use the kitty-tray lavatory you've so thoughtfully provided? It's a tough one, but with a bit of effort, you should be able to remove the stain, and the smell.

Keep plastic fantastic

Prevent tomato-based foods from staining plastic tubs and bowls by lightly coating the container with oil spray before adding the food. It's also a good idea to allow the food to cool to room temperature before storing it in plastic – heat contributes to the staining process.

CARPET Flush the affected area with cold water and blot with white paper towel until nearly dry. Sponge with a proprietary carpet cleaner, such as Bissell OxyKIC. Rinse well with cold water containing a few drops of disinfectant. Blot to dry.

MATTRESSES Hold the mattress on its side and sponge with a cold solution of washing-up liquid or upholstery shampoo. Wipe with cold water containing a few drops of disinfectant.

NON-WASHABLE FABRICS Remove fresh stains by sponging with a vinegar solution (15ml/1tbsp vinegar to 500ml/1 pint water). Dried stains should be cleaned professionally.

WASHABLE FABRICS Rinse the stained area with cold water, then soak overnight in a solution of biological detergent. Machine-wash as normal.

IF THE PONG PERSISTS The smell can be particularly difficult to get rid of. This is because the uric acid crystals and salts in cat urine are insoluble and bond tightly with any surface they land on, making them very resistant to regular household cleaning agents. If any type of moisture gets on the crystals, they are activated and release that 'tom cat' aroma – this also explains why the smell becomes particularly strong in humid weather conditions. The only way to completely get rid of the smell is with an enzyme-based cleaner designed specifically for pet urine. These usually also come with a special ultraviolet light torch that can show you exactly how far your pet has sprayed. There are lots of brands available – ask a vet or pet supply store which one they recommend.

CAUTION Never use ammonia to clean stains from cat urine – there is ammonia in cat urine, so cats will identify with the smell and go again.

Vomit

Vomit can be a problem: it's a complex stain containing acids, proteins, colours and other components (not to mention the awful smell), and you need to act quickly to ensure that it doesn't leave a lasting reminder.

CARPET Scoop up as much as possible and clean with a solution of bicarbonate of soda. Blot well with white paper towels or a white cloth. Spot-treat with a proprietary carpet cleaner such as Bissell OxyKIC. Follow the manufacturer's instructions and make repeat applications until the stain has cleared. Rinse with warm water containing a few drops of disinfectant. Blot well. If the odour persists, try sprinkling the area with bicarbonate of soda. Leave for a few hours, then vacuum up.

WASHABLE FABRICS Remove the deposit and rinse well, from the back of the stain, with cold water. Machine-wash as normal, using biological detergent if possible.

STUBBORN STAINS For cottons, try soaking in an enzyme-based pre-soaking agent. For silk and wool, soak in a solution of a suitable detergent for delicates. Always follow the manufacturer's instructions and check the garment's care label first.

TIP
If you have a 'leaky' toddler who's prone to night-time mishaps, consider investing in waterproof mattress covers that prevent urine from seeping through to the mattress below. That way, you'll just have the sheets to deal with!

Creative DIY in the Home

Making your own improvements to your home can be incredibly satisfying – as well as being a lot cheaper than calling in the professionals. In this section there are step by step instructions and a wealth of useful hints and tips on painting and wallpapering, tiling and shelving. There is also an overview of different types of window treatments and soft furnishings including a guide to making your own curtains.

Painting and Decorating

It's never been easier or more fun to do your own decorating. All you need is a little imagination and some basic know-how to transform your home, help protect it – and save money too.

WHICH PAINT?

Every year sees the introduction of new, sophisticated paint finishes, such as solid emulsion, one-step gloss, environmentally friendly, 'green' paints, and tough sheens for kitchens and bathrooms.

With all these different and confusing products on the market, it may be a relief to know that there are only two main types of house paint: water-based; and solvent-based, which is traditionally, if not always accurately, called oil-based paint.

Water-based paints include emulsion, quick-drying eggshell and water-based gloss, while solvent-based paints range from traditional eggshell and gloss to durable sheen finishes and specialist lacquers or paints for metal. Some paints may have added ingredients such as vinyl, acrylic or polyurethane – to make them more durable or to increase coverage – but that doesn't alter their basic composition.

Water-based paints are ideal for walls and water-based eggshell or gloss can be used for most interior woodwork. Solvent-based paints are perfect for areas of hard wear: exterior as well as interior wood, and metal.

TIP
Find out if a paint is water-based or solvent-based by reading the instructions given for thinning. If water is recommended, the paint will be water-based; if white spirit is advised, it's solvent-based.

PREPARATORY COATS

Primer

Primer seals absorbent surfaces and provides a key for the subsequent coats. Use it before painting bare timber, and when using gloss on bare metal. (Check the instructions to see if a special metal primer is required.) It's also possible to buy universal primer, for treating wood, plaster or metal.

TYPES OF PRIMER

⊙ **WATER-BASED PRIMER** (quick-drying primer or primer/undercoat) dries in around two hours. It is ideal for use indoors.

⊙ **SOLVENT-BASED PRIMER** can be used outside. In white or the traditional pink, it needs 12 hours to dry before you can apply undercoat.

⊙ **PLASTER PRIMER** (primer/sealer) and stabilising solutions are used for walls that are porous or liable to flake.

⊙ **ALUMINIUM PRIMER** is ideal for resinous woods. For added protection, apply two coats, thinning the first with 10 per cent white spirit.

Primer, undercoat and liquid gloss form the traditional three steps for painting wood but they are not always necessary today because you can buy combined primer/undercoat, which reduces the steps to two.

Undercoat

Undercoat provides a smooth, solid-coloured base for liquid gloss. It's a solvent-based paint that looks attractive in its own right, though the range of colours is limited. It tends to chip, so if using it without the top coat of gloss protect it with clear varnish.

TIP
For the best effect, buy the same brand of primer, undercoat and gloss. They're designed to be used together.

EMULSION PAINT

Emulsion is the first choice for walls. It is a water-based paint, and normally contains vinyl or acrylic resins, which makes it durable and easy to clean. It can be used on most sound, already painted surfaces.

If the area to be painted was previously covered with a different kind of paint, it may need some preparation. Sand gloss or eggshell surfaces lightly to provide a 'key' for the new coat. Strip varnish completely.

Old-fashioned treatments like distemper and whitewash must be washed off before you can start. You're unlikely to encounter these today but you'll know if you do because new paint won't adhere to them.

Emulsion paint can be applied directly to new plaster or plasterboard, but it's best to first apply a 'mist' coat diluted with water to improve coverage. Modern emulsion is quick drying: allow two to four hours between coats.

TIP
Use emulsion paint rather than solvent-based paint or wallpaper on new plaster. Emulsion allows water to pass through as the plaster dries out.

TYPES OF EMULSION

There is a range of different consistencies and finishes for a variety of purposes.

CONSISTENCIES

- ⊙ **ROLLER OR SOLID** emulsion paint (rather a misnomer, because it's more like cream cheese) is sold in trays for use with a roller. As it's virtually spatter-free, it's perfect for ceilings and stairwells but more expensive than buying paint in tins.
- ⊙ **'ONE-COAT'** emulsions are opaque enough to cover in a single application.
- ⊙ **FLEXIBLE** emulsion is designed to cover hairline cracks.

FINISHES

- ⊙ **MATT FINISH** gives a soft, velvety look, and is ideal for concealing flaws in plaster or uneven walls. (Shinier finishes reflect back more light highlighting any imperfections.) Like all vinyl emulsions it will wipe clean, but take care, because if you rub too hard it starts to shine.
- ⊙ **SILK FINISH** has a delicate sheen that can highlight patterns on textured wall coverings but may also emphasise flaws. The most durable type and good for rooms that are subject to a lot of moisture such as condensation.
- ⊙ **SOFT SHEEN** or satin is easier to clean than matt but is less shiny than silk finish.
- ⊙ **TEXTURED** emulsion gives a random rippled effect. Like flexible emulsion, it will conceal flawed plaster, though it won't cover wide cracks, and it can be difficult to remove.

PAINTS FOR WOODWORK

Gloss paints

Gloss paint is the traditional choice for wood and metalwork. Polyurethane gloss, an oil-based paint with added polyurethane resin, is one of the toughest finishes. All solvent-based gloss has a high shine but for a truly mirror-like finish, it is best to opt for the liquid gloss used over undercoat – a system favoured by professional decorators, especially for outside use. This is also extremely hardwearing and resistant to dirt. The one-coat non-drip formula designed for DIY use is much easier to apply, but sometimes brush marks are difficult to avoid. Self-undercoating gloss has added colour, and can be used directly over primer or existing paint.

Water-based acrylic gloss has more of a sheen than a shine. It's often recommended for use in children's rooms, because it is not toxic – completely lead and solvent free. Some acrylic gloss can be used outside, but check the tin before using it.

Eggshell paints

Eggshell is a versatile sheen finish usually sold for indoor woodwork, though it can also be used on walls for a uniform look.

TIP
As a general rule, the shinier the finish, the more hardwearing the paint.

TIP
Do not stir non-drip gloss as it will break down the consistency and ruin the finish. If it has been stirred, leave it for a while and the paint will become jelly-like again.

COLOUR AND DESIGN

- ◉ 'Warm' colours (red, yellow, orange) appear to bring surfaces closer. Use them for cool north- or east-facing rooms, high ceilings (especially effective if you continue the paint down to picture rail level), and the end wall in a long passage.
- ◉ 'Cool' colours (blue, green, lilac) make surfaces look further away. Use them in warm, south- and west-facing rooms and in small areas.
- ◉ Depth of colour can be used to modify the effect of warm and cool tones. Dark shades, which absorb light, seem to advance, while pastels, which reflect it, appear to recede.
- ◉ Lose unwanted features such as cupboards, radiators and pipes by painting them the same colour as the wall. If you want to highlight features, use a contrasting colour.

COLOUR AND ARTIFICIAL LIGHT

Artificial light can alter the effect of the colours you choose, so it's worth looking at samples at night as well as in daylight.

- ◉ Standard tungsten light bulbs emphasise red tones but reduce blue and green, making colours look yellower than by day.
- ◉ Fluorescent light can bring out blues and reduce shadows. Look for 'warm' fluorescents, which are closer to natural light.
- ◉ Halogen lamps have a bright white light and colours may look harsher.
- ◉ Reflected light is softer. Try using uplighters or spotlights that bounce light off the ceiling or wall.

PAINT COVERAGE AND DRYING TIMES

Coverage will vary with the brand and absorbency of the surface. Times depend on moderate, dry conditions

Type of paint	Area covered per litre	Touch dry	Recoatable
Matt vinyl emulsion	12–14 sq. m/129–151 sq. ft	2 hrs	4 hrs
Silk vinyl emulsion	12–14 sq. m/129–151 sq. ft	2 hrs	4 hrs
Soft sheen emulsion	13–15 sq. m/140–161 sq. ft	2 hrs	4 hrs
Solid emulsion	11–13 sq. m/118–140 sq. ft	2 hrs	4 hrs
One-coat emulsion	10 sq. m/108 sq. ft	2 hrs	4 hrs
Flexible emulsion	7–9 sq. m/75–97 sq. ft	2 hrs	4 hrs
Textured emulsion	5–7 sq. m/54–75 sq. ft	2 hrs	4 hrs
Water-based satin	14–16 sq. m/151–172 sq. ft	2 hrs	4 hrs
Eggshell **	15–17 sq. m/161–183 sq. ft	12 hrs	16 hrs
Liquid gloss	16–17 sq. m/172–183 sq. ft	12 hrs	16 hrs
Non-drip gloss	10–12 sq. m/108–129 sq. ft	1–3 hrs	5–6 hrs ***
Water-based gloss	14–16 sq. m/151–172 sq. ft	2 hrs	4 hrs
Self-undercoat gloss	10–12 sq. m/108–129 sq. ft	2 hrs	4 hrs
Undercoat	15–17 sq. m/161–183 sq. ft	8 hrs	12 hrs
Masonry paint	6–10 sq. m/65–108 sq. ft	1 hr	4 hrs

** Solvent-based

*** Normally only one coat required

SOLVENT-BASED

Traditional eggshell is solvent-based but because it can be difficult to apply, it's sometimes reformulated for domestic use and sold under another name: 'Satinwood' is one common example. Please note you can also buy water-based Satinwood (see below).

It has a rich sheen but is less shiny than gloss paint. It's ideal for metal, interior woodwork and walls in areas of hard wear or condensation, because it can virtually be scrubbed clean and seals the wall from damp. (Before painting bare plaster, apply a plaster primer.)

There are drawbacks, however, because it's expensive over a large area and the sheen will emphasise every possible irregularity in the wall. Traditional solvent-based eggshell can also produce troublesome fumes, but this is less of a problem now than it used to be with new, low-odour varieties.

WATER-BASED

Newer 'quick-drying', 'green' or 'kitchen and bathroom' eggshell paints are water-based and are effectively emulsions. It may be best to use water-based eggshell on walls, as it has less shine and doesn't give off fumes like solvent-based paints. Water-based eggshell is ideal for most purposes indoors, but shouldn't be used on wood outdoors.

Paint safety

- Solvent-based paint is flammable, so store it outside the house, but keep it protected from frost and damp.

- Fumes from solvent-based gloss and eggshell are unpleasant so make sure the room is cool and well ventilated before you start painting.

- Lead is no longer added to paint, although a tiny amount exists naturally in gloss, solvent-based primer and undercoat. If you want to avoid it entirely, use water-based paints.

PAINTS FOR SPECIAL PURPOSES

⊙ **ANTI-CONDENSATION PAINT** An emulsion that insulates the wall, reducing the contrast in temperature that can cause condensation. It may contain glass particles and usually has a fungicide to prevent mould. Recommended for use in kitchens and bathrooms.

⊙ **ANTI-DAMP AND ANTI-STAIN PAINT** Does not cure damp, but creates a thick synthetic barrier that prevents damp marks and stain marks (e.g. from felt-tip pens) from bleeding through to the surface. These paints are usually solvent-based.

⊙ **BITUMINOUS PAINT** Tar-based. It will waterproof concrete and metal gutters but should not be covered by any other paint.

⊙ **ENAMEL** A durable gloss available in smooth or hammered finishes and may contain metal particles. It is corrosion resistant and can be used on bare metal, though you may need to use a metal primer before applying it over existing paint. It is ideal for household appliances, painting over tiles, or on china and glass, but you will need heat-resistant enamel for cookers and fireplaces and a special enamel for baths. Enamel is expensive, which limits its use to small areas. Colours (such as hobby tins) are often bright, though the heat-resistant enamel sold for radiators is usually white or magnolia.

⊙ **FLAT OIL PAINT** Available from decorating specialists, is designed for use on walls, but because it is solvent-based, should be used over undercoat. It has a matt, velvety effect, but marks easily and is difficult to clean.

⊙ **FLOOR PAINT** Usually solvent-based, though some designed for indoor use may be emulsions. These are relatively non-slip and resist abrasion.

⊙ **LACQUER** A hard, gloss paint with a mirror-like shine. It's ideal for giving a colourful finish to doors, railings or furniture.

⊙ **MICROPOROUS PAINTS AND STAINS** For outside use. They are designed to flex with the timber, keeping damp out but allowing the wood to 'breathe', but they won't work as well on previously painted surfaces. No primer or undercoat is needed, but preservative is required on bare wood.

⊙ **MASONRY PAINT** A tough emulsion for outside walls, usually strengthened with nylon, chips of silica or sand, giving a textured effect.

⊙ **MATT BLACK PAINT** Used for beams and blackboards. It's a solvent-based paint with minimal shine.

⊙ **STOVE BLACK** Heat-resistant paint up to 200°C/392°F. Use it for grates and fire backs.

WOOD STAIN AND VARNISH

Wood stains

Wood stains designed for use indoors are more decorative than protective, so cover them with two or more coats of clear varnish. Some products offer a degree of protection, but will still need varnishing in areas of heavy wear, such as skirtings, chairs or tabletops.

Wood stains are designed to penetrate the wood and can only be removed with bleaching and sanding, so test the colour on an offcut or in an inconspicuous place before you start.

Stains for exterior use often contain a preservative to protect the timber and may not need varnishing. They include alternatives to creosote for use on rough-sawn wood such as fences and sheds, and mid-sheen finishes for planed wood on doors and window frames.

Varnish

Varnish provides a clear, protective coating for paints and stains. It's available in matt, satin (mid-sheen) or high gloss finishes and in liquid or non-drip consistency. (Liquid varnish is difficult to apply so non-drip is

TIP
Add a trace of white gloss paint to clear varnish, to stop it yellowing.

much better for beginners.) A solvent-based product, it may have acrylic or polyurethane substances added for extra durability.

Yacht varnish is one of the most weather resistant, but not all varnishes are suitable for use outside, or on floors, so check the label carefully before you buy.

Coloured varnish is available, usually in timber shades or occasionally in translucent tints, but when the top coat is chipped, the colour is removed too.

PREPARATION FOR PAINTING

Preparation is essential, because paint and paper won't adhere to flaking surfaces and can magnify, rather than disguise, any flaws beneath. As a rule of thumb, allow two-thirds of your time for preparation and one-third for decoration. Clear the room as much as possible, removing light fittings and carpets if you can, and cover what's left with dust sheets.

How to fill cracks

1. Open up small cracks with a putty knife or the end of a screwdriver to make them easier to fill.
2. Dampen with a small paintbrush dipped in water to clean out the crack and remove the dust.
3. Apply filler (available ready-mixed or in powder form) with a narrow-bladed filling knife, pushing it deeply into the crack so it fills it completely and leaving it raised above the level of the wall. (Deep cracks must be filled in layers, leaving each layer to dry before you add the next.)
4. When dry, sand the area down until it's flush with the wall and then wipe clean.

Choose a flexible sealant for cracks between walls and window or door frames, which may expand or contract. If you use ordinary filler, the crack may open again.

Walls

If the walls are in good condition, simply wash them with a detergent solution, rinse and allow to dry.

If the walls are damp, you'll need to find the cause and tackle it before you decorate. Then wash any mould away with a solution of one part bleach to four parts water, leave for two days, and rinse.

Lift off any patches of flaking plaster, fill dents and cracks, and sand until the repairs are level with the rest of the wall. Don't forget to sand any runs in old paintwork and lightly sand all over walls covered with eggshell or solvent-based paint to provide a 'key' for the next coat. Apply a stabilising solution to powdery plaster, plaster primer to new plaster if necessary, and allow to dry.

Woodwork

Remove all the door furniture (handles, finger plates and so on) and scrape old putty back from the window frames before you start.

If the paintwork is sound, simply sand the surface slightly to provide a key for the new coat, then clean with white spirit. Any blistered or flaking

TIP
Keep a pair of old shoes for the job, and leave them by the door of the room being painted when you finish. This will help prevent treading paint and dust through the house when you leave the room.

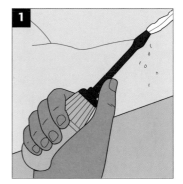

ABOVE How to fill cracks, step 1

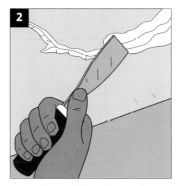

ABOVE How to fill cracks, step 3

ABOVE How to fill cracks, step 4

paint should be scraped back and sanded level with the surround.

New wood and bare patches must be primed before painting to seal the surface. This includes the bottom edge of new doors and any deep cracks.

Cracks should be stopped with flexible filler, but choose a wood filler and stain it to the shade you require if you intend to varnish natural wood.

Treat knots with knotting solution, to prevent resin seeping through and spoiling the new paint. If a knot does bleed through later, sand down to the bare wood, treat with the solution, and then prime before repainting.

STRIPPING WOOD

There are several ways of stripping old paint or varnish from wooden surfaces (see below).

Take care when stripping old paintwork. It may contain lead, which should not be released into the atmosphere. If the paint is very old and thick, take professional advice; otherwise use chemical stripper and always wear a mask.

If you don't fancy tackling stripping a door yourself, find a firm that will dip-strip it for you. The door is dipped in chemicals that remove all traces of paint particularly good if the door has intricate mouldings and it avoids risk of scorching.

PAINTING EQUIPMENT

Brushes

Brushes should have natural hog's-hair bristles, which pick up more paint than cheaper materials. Look for bristles that don't moult (run them through your hands a few times) and are tapered at the ends for a smooth finish – especially important when painting with eggshell and gloss.

Buy a range of widths (25, 50 and 75mm/1, 2 and 3in) for wood and metalwork, plus a 19mm/¾in angled cutting-in brush for painting the edge of the wall and a 12mm/½in brush for the glazing bars on windows.

TIP

Wash walls from the bottom up, to prevent dirty streaks running down and making the task more difficult.

Testing for damp

To find the cause of damp, tape a piece of aluminium foil over the patch and leave for a week. After this period, if the outer surface of the foil is wet, the cause is probably condensation. If the foil is moist on the underside, the cause might be rising damp (from a faulty damp-proof course) or penetrating damp, from walls that need repointing on the outside.

WOOD-STRIPPING METHODS

- ◉ **CHEMICAL WOOD STRIPPER** Comes in liquid form; or as a paste or gel, which are ideal for ornate or vertical surfaces such as chair legs or banisters. The process takes time (from 15 minutes to 8 hours) and may need repeating. They are quite expensive and more than one application is often necessary.

- ◉ **HEAT** Hot-air guns soften paint, making it easier to remove. Work from the bottom up to make the most of rising heat and move the gun backwards and forwards so you do not concentrate the heat in one area or you may burn the surface. Wear cotton gloves to protect your hands.

- ◉ **SANDING** Can be done by hand, or with an electric orbital or belt sander. Drills may have disc sander attachments, which are suitable for rough work but won't give a fine finish.

- ◉ **DRY STRIPPING** This is done with a shavehook (a small triangular, or combined straight and curved-edge scraper). You will also need a wide-bladed stripping knife to remove flaking paint. These tools are also useful to shift paint loosened by chemical or heat stripping.

If you want to paint the walls with a brush, choose a 100mm/4in wall brush, but make sure it is not too tiring to use.

WAYS WITH BRUSHES

- Hold a wide brush by the stock – the part that joins the bristles to the handle; hold a narrow one like a pencil.
- When dipping the brush into the paint, only cover half of the bristle area with emulsion, one-third with gloss. Remove the surplus by pressing the bristles against the side of the tin, not the rim, where paint may dry and lumps may fall into the tin, causing problems in the paint later.
- Tie a length of string tautly across the opening of a paint kettle or paint tin, so you can wipe excess paint off the brush as you lift it out of the paint.
- For easy cleaning of a brush used with solvent-based paints, drill a hole through the handle of the brush and push a long nail through. Suspend it in a jar of white spirit.
- When you take a break from painting, wrap brushes in clingfilm so they don't dry out.
- As soon as you stop for the day, clean brushes in detergent for water-based paints, or white spirit for solvent-based. (Check the manufacturer's instructions.) Pat dry with kitchen paper.
- Store flat, or hang from a hole in the handle. Use a rubber band to keep all the bristles together neatly.

Rollers

These are the best way to spread paint quickly over large areas. They vary in width from 175–300mm/7–12in and come with a single frame (with one end attached to the handle) or double (attached at both sides), and are used with a roller tray for holding the paint. A single-frame roller is easier to manipulate, especially in corners, but a double-frame roller helps you to exert even pressure – useful when painting ceilings or using an extension handle.

'PAINT POD' ROLLER SYSTEM

The 'Paint Pod' is a mains powered roller system about the size of a small cylinder vacuum cleaner. Paint is pumped from the container through a tube to the roller – the flow being controlled by a trigger on the roller handle. It features an integrated cleaning system that cleans both the roller and unit after use. Specially formulated Paint Pod Emulsion must be used. A compact version is now available.

Paint pads

Paint pads are easy to use but a fine finish can be difficult to achieve. They're available in sizes from an extra-wide 200mm/8in to a narrow 25mm/1in sash pad for windows. Like rollers, they are best for use on walls together with water-based paints.

Paint receptacles

Paint trays are sold with both rollers and paint pads. Most have ribs for removing excess paint.

TIP
Silicon carbide sanding paper can be used dry, or wet, to keep down dust. Wrap it round a sanding block – an offcut of wood will do – for ease of use.

TIP
Strain lumpy liquid paint through a stocking, or tie one loosely over the top of the tin to act as a filter when you dip in the brush.

ABOVE A length of string can be used to wipe excess paint off a brush

ABOVE A hole drilled through the handle with a nail pushed through is a good way to soak brushes in white spirit

A paint kettle is ideal for decanting liquid paint. Line it with foil to keep it clean and buy an old-fashioned 'S'-hook to hang it up on.

PAINTING A ROOM

Order of painting
The following steps are the most orderly way to paint a room, and will avoid any drips or spills of one colour or type of paint on another.

1 Paint the ceiling. If there is a ceiling rose or other mouldings, give them an initial coat of paint and complete after finishing the ceiling.

2 Paint the walls, working away from the light source.

3 Paint window frames, picture rails (if you have them), radiators and doors.

4 Paint the skirting.

Painting a ceiling
Working with your arms above your head can be tiring, so choose a roller or paint pad for fast coverage and, if you can find the colour you want, use solid emulsion (roller paint), which makes less mess. Using extension handles makes access easier but can also affect the way you control the roller. It may be better to work from a plank between two sets of step ladders, but make sure they are stable.

ORDER OF PAINTING
1 Paint a narrow strip around the perimeter of the ceiling where the roller won't reach, using a narrow 'cutting in' brush.

2 Paint a wider strip parallel to one edge with a wide brush, paint pad or roller, leaving a small gap.

3 When you come to the end of the run, reverse the direction and use the brush, pad or roller to fill in the gap. Go over it again lightly to blend in the paint if necessary.

4 Recharge with paint and start a new line, again leaving a small gap, and continue until the ceiling is complete.

Roller sleeves
There are three main types of roller sleeve:

- **LAMB'S WOOL** (real or synthetic) is good for use with most paints, especially matt emulsion. Use on rough or textured surfaces because the shaggy pile goes in the crevices.

- **MOHAIR SLEEVES** have a fine pile, and are ideal for smooth surfaces with eggshell, silk emulsion and solid emulsion paint.

- **FOAM ROLLERS** are good general-purpose rollers if a high finish is not important. They can be used on smooth and lightly textured surfaces. The foam deteriorates after several uses so will need replacing. Patterned foam rollers are available for use with textured coatings – only the raised area picks up paint. It can take practise to achieve professional results. Foam rollers are quite cheap but tend to spatter. You'll also find small rollers especially designed for painting behind radiators.

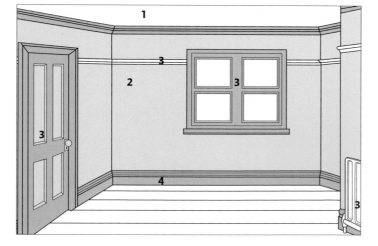

LEFT The correct order to paint a room

Painting windows

When protecting the glass with masking tape, let the paint overlap on to the glass by a millimetre to form a protective seal.

CASEMENT (SIDE OPENING) WINDOWS
❶ Paint any glazing bars on the fixed window.
❷ Paint the opening window except for the outside edge, which should match the exterior.
❸ Paint the window frame and sill.

SASH WINDOWS
❶ Open the window until the bottom sash and top sash overlap by about 20cm/8in.
❷ Paint the bottom of the top sash.
❸ Close the bottom sash and pull up the top sash so it's almost closed.
❹ Paint the rest of the top sash.
❺ Paint the bottom sash.
❻ Paint the frame, avoiding the sash cords.

Painting panelled doors
❶ Remove door 'furniture' (e.g. handles, knobs and key plates etc.).
❷ Paint the mouldings, if any.
❸ Paint the panels.
❹ Paint the vertical strips in the centre.
❺ Paint the horizontals.
❻ Paint the sides, edges and frame.

For the best effect, the outside edge of the door should match the paintwork of the room it opens into.

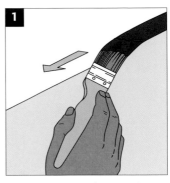

ABOVE Painting a ceiling, step 1

ABOVE Painting a ceiling, step 2

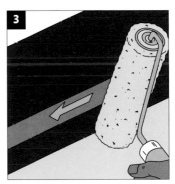

ABOVE Painting a ceiling, step 3

ABOVE Painting windows, casement

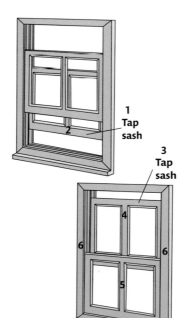

LEFT Painting windows, sash

PAINTING WOODWORK

When painting wood, brush along the grain. On a narrow area, a single movement will be enough to cover it, but with wide areas, apply paint in parallel bands, reloading the brush before painting each strip. Aim for a smooth flowing movement for even coverage. After painting the second band, paint across the grain to join the two strips. 'Lay off' with light strokes along the grain for a smooth finish. Use two coats of undercoat when covering a dark base – cheaper than an extra coat of gloss.

Make a 'tack rag' – a lint-free cloth moistened with a small amount of white spirit – to erase any mistakes.

VARNISHING WOODWORK

If covering a previously varnished or stained surface, sand and clean it. If varnishing bare wood or bare cork, apply a base coat thinned with 10 per cent white spirit.

Dip the brush into the tin of varnish so that half the bristle area is covered, and apply it along the grain, brushing out across the grain from the wet edge for even coverage. There's no pigment in varnish to disguise mistakes so take care to brush out overlaps and brush marks. Finish by brushing along the grain again with a single smooth stroke.

If more than one coat is needed, lightly sand with very fine abrasive paper when dry and clean with white spirit between each coat.

ABOVE Painting panelled doors

SPECIAL PAINT EFFECTS

Fashions in decorating are always changing. Plain walls will be popular one year, patterns the next. At present, the trend is towards plain walls, but decorative paint finishes have the advantage of camouflaging defects and adding interest without defined pattern. You can buy special textured rollers that add a design for you, but it's often just as easy to use traditional materials. Here's what to do.

Walls
COLOUR WASHING
This treatment gives a translucent finish.

Paint the wall with solvent-based eggshell (white will give a delicate effect) and leave to dry. For the top coat, mix 30 per cent transparent oil glaze with 50 per cent solvent-based eggshell and 20 per cent white spirit. If you want solid cover and a formal effect, use it straight; for a more casual, random effect, apply with a wall brush, moving it in all directions and leaving some areas uncovered to vary the depth of colour. Repeat when dry, covering the entire wall, still using criss-cross brush strokes.

You can protect the finish with a coat of polyurethane varnish in areas of hard wear but this will need to be removed when repainting.

A similar effect can be achieved with emulsion paint. Paint the wall and leave to dry, then apply two coats of emulsion thinned with water, following the instructions on the tin. Use a wall brush, not a roller, and apply the paint with a random movement.

BEST FOR Cottagey living rooms, dining rooms and bedrooms.

WHAT WENT WRONG?

You may encounter various problems while painting such as:

- **BLISTERS** Are often caused by painting damp wood. Allow the paint to harden, then prick the blister. If it's wet inside, you'll need to strip back and fill the grain before repainting.
- **CRAZING** Caused by applying a second coat before the first coat is dry. Leave to dry, then rub down and repaint.
- **CRATERING** Comes from too much damp in the atmosphere. Sand and repaint, keeping the room warm and dry.
- **FLAKING PAINT** Is caused by powdery or dirty walls underneath the new coat, or gloss paint that hasn't been sanded. Emulsion paint often flakes off woodwork and radiators, so rub it down and repaint with a coat of solvent-based eggshell or gloss.

- **RUNS** Come from overloading the brush. If there are only one or two, allow the paint to dry completely and then prick, rub down and touch in with a small paintbrush. Otherwise sand and start again.
- **SHOW THROUGH** Where what was originally underneath is still visible, needs an additional top coat (emulsion), or an undercoat plus a new top coat (gloss).
- **SPECKS AND STRAY BRISTLES** Can be avoided if both wall and paint are clean and you use quality brushes. Either sand down and start again or, in a small area, sand or pick out the pieces, rub with wet abrasive paper and touch in. This also works for insects that have been trapped in wet paint.
- **UNEVEN COVERAGE** May occur if you try to spread paint too thinly or fail to prime large patches of filler or bare plaster. These are more absorbent than the rest of the wall and so take in more paint than primed areas.

DRAGGING

This needs solvent-based eggshell for the base coat and a top coat made up of 70 per cent transparent oil glaze, 20 per cent eggshell and 10 per cent white spirit, which is applied in bands about an arm's length wide. After painting each band, a dragging brush is pulled through the paint from the top of the wall down, which creates the characteristic effect.

BEST FOR Formal living rooms, studies, halls and bedrooms.

SPONGING

An easy technique with emulsion paint, although solvent-based eggshell, which takes longer to dry, gives more time to create an effect. For the best results, use related colours, sponging the deeper colour over the paler one or vice versa. (Use three colours if you want a more elaborate effect.)

Pour a little paint into a saucer and apply with a natural sea sponge in a random direction, turning the sponge from time to time, until the wall is covered. You can use rags instead of a sponge if you prefer, choosing a textured cloth like stockinette or muslin for greater definition.

BEST FOR Bedrooms and bathrooms.

RAG ROLLING

This needs a base coat of solvent-based eggshell and a top coat made from 70 per cent transparent oil glaze, 20 per cent eggshell and 10 per cent white spirit. This is brushed on in vertical bands and rolled off with rags twisted into a sausage-shape, working from the top of the wall down.

BEST FOR Dining rooms and bedrooms.

STIPPLING

The subtlest way of producing broken colour. Paint the wall with solvent-based eggshell and, when dry, apply with a special stippling brush a top coat made from 70 per cent transparent oil glaze, 20 per cent eggshell and 10 per cent white spirit. Keep the bristles at right angles to the wall, and wipe them from time to time so they don't become clogged.

You can also stipple walls by painting narrow (50cm/20in) strips of the top coat from top to bottom and then removing colour by using a clean, dry stippling brush. For speed, pour the top coat into a roller tray and apply with a stiff brush.

BEST FOR All around the house.

STENCILLING

Stencilling can create attractive borders and decorative motifs. Cutting your own stencils takes practice, so it's easiest to use ready-made stencils, available from most DIY superstores and decorating shops (such as Laura Ashley) as well as specialist suppliers. Whatever you choose, start with relatively simple designs, especially if you're stencilling a border, which can be time-consuming. Add variety by reversing the stencil from time to time, but to avoid smudges, remember to wipe it clean before you turn it over.

Use a stubby stencil brush and dab colour into the stencil until the design is filled in. You can use a variety of paints, from standard emulsion or eggshell (use solvent-based on woodwork) to acrylic or spray paint; special crayons are also available.

BEST FOR Borders, ceiling decorations and motifs on furniture.

MURALS

Murals can be painted in sections using simple picture-book designs. Draw a grid over the original picture and number the squares, then draw a similar grid, the size of the finished mural, on the wall. Copy the outline of the design into each square, using chalk or soft pencil, then fill in, using one colour at a time and working from the top down. Rub off the grid marks when the mural is dry.

BEST FOR Passages and children's bedrooms.

EXTERIOR PAINTING

Paint helps protect your home from wind, rain and sun. That is why the outside needs redecorating about every four years, or more often if you live near the sea or in an industrial area. It's best to paint at the end of the summer, when wood has had a long period in which to dry out.

Choose bright, still days if you can, following the sun on the house so that the paint is dried, but avoid painting in full sunlight or when it's windy. It's dangerous to use a ladder in high winds, and paint splashes on walls, caused by wind, can be very difficult to remove.

Transparent oil glaze

- Also called scumble glaze, transparent oil glaze is essential for many paint treatments, especially those that take time to create, because it slows drying. It's available from specialist decorators and is often combined with solvent-based eggshell paint and white spirit as a top coat. A standard mix would be 70 per cent transparent oil glaze, 20 per cent eggshell and 10 per cent white spirit.

- Use solvent-based eggshell or acrylic emulsion paint in bathrooms for harder wear.

TIP
Fix the stencil in place with masking tape not Blu-Tack, which leaves a gap between the stencil and the wall, and may lead to runs.

SPECIAL PAINT EFFECTS FOR WOOD

BAMBOOING This decorative effect looks wonderful on turned wood as well as on bamboo furniture that has seen better days. Paint with three coats of yellow-brown solvent-based eggshell and mottle the top coat with a rag while the paint is still damp. When dry, draw circles of brown paint at intervals with a narrow brush. Paint a second, narrower and darker brown circle inside the first, followed by a final dark brown ring in the centre. You can also add the tiny spots and the V-shaped tail typical of natural bamboo.

BEST FOR Decorative pieces made from bamboo, cane or turned wood.

COLOUR RUBBING This gives a faded, weathered look. It involves brushing a milky glaze or a thin wash of water-based paint over the surface and then removing the excess before it dries, to highlight mouldings or emphasise the grain.

Alternatively, apply a base coat of solvent-based eggshell or wipe the bare wood with white spirit, and make a glaze from 75 per cent transparent oil glaze, 20 per cent solvent-based eggshell and 5 per cent white spirit. Brush this into the surface so that all the crevices are filled, and when it becomes tacky, rub along the grain with a soft cloth.

BEST FOR Doors, decorative fireplaces and floors (but not floors subject to hard wear).

LIMING Liming turns wood an attractive silvery grey and has been an especially popular finish for cupboard doors. Professionals use specialist products such as white shellac and liming wax, but you can achieve a similar look the following way.

Paint a base with white eggshell and leave to dry. Mix together 70 per cent transparent oil glaze, 20 per cent putty-coloured eggshell and 10 per cent white spirit. Brush this over the base coat, then tie a rag over a steel comb and drag over it from top to bottom. Finish by combing without a rag, using medium and fine combs. When dry, protect the finish with varnish, if needed.

To vary the look, comb the sides only and leave a darker panel in the centre, rippled with a rag to look like real wood. For a verdigris look, paint a coat of turquoise eggshell over grey and drag the surface while still wet. Or, for a characteristic limed finish, try colour rubbing along the grain with grey-white paint.

BEST FOR Floors and doors.

MARBLING Paint with off-white solvent-based eggshell and, when dry, add a top coat made from 30 per cent transparent oil glaze, 50 per cent bone colour eggshell and 20 per cent white spirit. Dab with a rag to soften the effect and, while still wet, trace in the marble 'veins' in dark grey, using an artist's paintbrush. Blur the lines with a special softening brush (or improvise with a rag) for a natural effect.

BEST FOR Table tops and floors.

WOODGRAINING A way to make chipboard and pine look like oak or mahogany. Give softwood and fibreboard a coat of wood filler thinned to the consistency of single cream, and sand when dry. Repeat this step, then paint with primer, undercoat and red-brown eggshell. (Make sure it is solvent-based.)

Mix several small batches of 60 per cent transparent oil glaze, 20 per cent eggshell and 20 per cent white spirit in progressively deeper shades of brown. Apply along the grain, starting with the lightest colour, using a comb or a special graining brush, and blur for a natural effect with a cloth or softening brush. Finish with button polish or polyurethane.

BEST FOR Small pieces of furniture, hand rails and panelling.

Order of painting

❶ Paint fascias, barge-boards and gutters.
❷ Paint walls in sections, starting in a corner and working from top to bottom.
❸ Paint downpipes.
❹ Paint windows and doors.

Painting wood and metal work

Use gloss paint or stains on wood and gloss on metal. It's important to make sure they are suitable for outdoor use. In most cases, this means using a solvent-based paint, which is more weather resistant. But although paint systems especially designed for exterior use may specify two coats of undercoat plus one of liquid gloss for maximum durability, it's often possible to use non-drip one-coat products too – check the recommendations on the tin. Start from the top and work down, placing a piece of board behind downpipes to protect the wall from the paint.

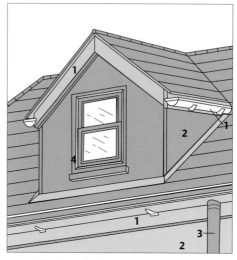

ABOVE Exterior painting

Painting walls

Before you start, wrap downpipes in polythene or newspaper to protect them from paint splatters and cover plants and paths with plastic sheeting. Start by 'cutting in' – painting a narrow strip – next to barge-boards, doors and windows. Change to a wide wall brush for small areas, a long-pile roller for large ones, and apply the masonry paint with a criss-cross

PREPARATION FOR PAINTING

- ◉ Tie back climbing plants.
- ◉ Check the state of the roof and guttering and repair any leaks.
- ◉ Check for rot on fascias and barge-boards beneath the eaves, windows, doors (especially the base) and decorative wood. Replace where necessary, or repair by scraping back to sound wood, removing flaking paint and filling any cracks with exterior stopper.
- ◉ If rendering is falling apart, cut it back until you reach the part that is sound, then clean it and patch with mortar. Large areas will need professional attention.
- ◉ Clean out defective pointing and fill large cracks with ready-mixed mortar, small ones with exterior filler.

- ◉ To remove dirt on painted walls, brush with a stiff brush from the top down. Treat mould with one part bleach to four of water. Leave for two days and then brush the mould away with a stiff brush. Apply stabilising solution to flaky patches.
- ◉ Replace any cracked window panes and leave for two weeks before painting the frame, because the putty needs time to harden. Fill gaps between the wall and window frame with flexible exterior filler.
- ◉ Scrape metal downpipes and gutters and clean with a wire brush to remove flaking paint. Apply anti-rust primer to any rusty patches that remain. Sand sound paintwork lightly to provide a key.
- ◉ Remove peeling paint from window frames and fill and prime where necessary.
- ◉ Strip peeling varnish to the bare wood, sand and apply a sealer coat of varnish thinned with white spirit.
- ◉ Clean, sand and dust off sound paintwork.

movement. Work from the top down in bands about an arm's length in width, and overlap each strip when you move on, for even coverage. Make sure you don't lean out too far when working at height.

LADDER SAFETY

Ladders should be placed at ground level 1m/3ft away from the wall for every 4m/13ft of height. The top of the ladder should overlap the highest point and should be tied in place if possible. Secure at the base with a sandbag, or tie it to wooden pegs knocked into the ground. If the ground is soggy, place the ladder on a board to make sure it's secure.

A tower platform, available from hire shops, makes exterior decorating easier if your house is large, but never climb down the side, which will unbalance it. Special designs are available for chalet bungalows, wide bay windows or houses that have roofs on several levels.

WALLPAPER

Wallpaper is the fastest way to add texture or a floor-to-ceiling pattern to a room. In addition to traditional wallpaper, you'll find paper-backed vinyl, relief papers designed as a base for paint, and a range of textiles from silk to grasscloth. Some are much easier to hang than others, so if you're a novice at wallpaper hanging, look for a medium-weight traditional wallpaper with a random design, which is unlikely to tear and won't need pattern matching. To avoid getting paint marks or splatters on the papered wall, make sure all the painting is completed before you paper.

ABOVE How to secure a ladder

Which wallpaper?

LINING PAPER Provides a smooth base for wallpaper or paint. It's available in several weights: light (for covering with paint), medium (suitable for most wallpaper) and heavy (for use beneath relief wallcoverings). Ideally it should be hung horizontally, so the joints don't coincide with those of the wallpaper on top.

TEXTURED WALLPAPERS Can act as a base for paint. These are less popular now but many types are still available including embossed designs, such as Anaglypta; high relief wallcoverings, which have a more pronounced design and are made from paper plus cotton or clay, or vinyl; and woodchip, used for disguising uneven plaster, made from sawdust and woodchips bonded on to paper.

TIP
Coat plaster walls with 'size' made from wallpaper paste (you'll find instructions on the packet) to make it easier to guide the wallpaper into place.

Wallpaper Design Tips

- Large patterns seem to reduce space, while small patterns on a light ground, which give a sense of 'looking through' the design, appear to increase it.
- Stripes look best on even walls and walls where a picture rail or cornice provides a break between the wall and ceiling.
- Small random patterns and textured designs may help disguise poor plaster.
- Create a focal point by having one feature papered wall and paint the others with co-ordinating coloured paint.

WALLPAPER SYMBOLS

Symbol	Meaning	Symbol	Meaning
~	Spongeable	🖌	Paste the wall
≈	Washable	→ ○	Free match
≋	Super-washable	→ ←	Straight match
▦	Scrubbable	→	Off-set match (half drop)
☀	Sufficient light fastness	50/25 cm	Design repeat distance off-set
☀	Good light fastness	∥	Duplex (layered)
↲	Strippable	⋙	Co-ordinated fabric available
↲	Peelable (leaves backing)	↑	Direction of hanging
⊔	Ready-pasted	↑↓	Reverse alternate lengths

PRINTED WALLCOVERINGS Range from expensive, untrimmed, hand-printed designs, to cheap wallcoverings when the pattern is printed direct on to paper. In between come papers with a coloured ground, and vinyl wallcoverings with a paper backing, which is left behind when the surface is stripped. Because the pattern is printed directly on to the vinyl layer, they're usually more water resistant than washable wallpapers, which have a clear coating.

TEXTILE WALLCOVERINGS Include paper-backed cork, hessian, grasscloth and silk, and flocked wallpapers, which are made from paper plus silk, cotton or wool, or vinyl and nylon. Because they're expensive, difficult to manipulate and liable to stain if adhesive comes into contact with the surface, all but the cheapest hessians and vinyl flocks should be professionally hung.

Preparation for wallpapering

Any lumps and bumps on the walls are likely to show through wallpaper just as they do through paint, so walls should be filled and sanded smooth. Old wallpaper should be stripped away because it's rarely a satisfactory surface for the new layer. Wrinkles will be repeated, colour may bleed through, and the weight of the new paper may pull it all away from the wall.

TIP
Make sure all the rolls of wallpaper have the same batch number, because colours may vary between printings.

TIP
Buy an extra roll of wallpaper and keep it for future repairs.

STRIPPING WALLPAPER

1 Vinyls and paper-backed wallpapers are often designed for dry stripping, which means they can be peeled away from the backing. Try lifting a corner and pulling upwards and outwards. The backing can be used as lining paper if it's in good condition, especially if you intend to paint over the top or want to cover it with heavy wallpaper.

2 To remove standard wallpaper, cover electric sockets and then wet the wallpaper with detergent solution, working from the top of the wall down so the water runs over the wallpaper, giving it a chance to penetrate. (Be careful not to overwet if you're working on plasterboard.)

3 If the wallpaper is coated or overpainted, you'll probably need to scrape the surface with a wire brush before wetting it to improve absorbency. Leave it to soak before you try to remove the wallpaper.

4 It's often worth hiring or buying a steam wallpaper stripper, which can speed things up if there are several layers of paper to remove.

5 Using a scraper with a wide blade, start at the seams and base. With luck, you'll be able to remove a sizeable strip of wallpaper, but try not to damage the wall beneath, as any chips will need to be filled.

6 When all the paper has been removed, finish by sanding lightly to remove any small pieces of paper still stuck to the walls.

Planning papering

Ideally you should start in a corner and work away from the light so that the joins between lengths are less noticeable. Before you start, it's worth marking where the joins will fall and adjusting your starting point if lengths meet in a prominent place. As a rule, where there are no special features, and unless you are left-handed, start at the wall to the right of the main window and work round the room.

However, if there is a chimney breast, paste the first length in the middle of it. Treat each half of the room separately, working towards the door and starting at the chimney breast again to paper the other side. This way, awkward joins can be minimised.

Wallpaper adhesives

- ⊙ Standard wallpaper paste (available as powder or ready-mixed) is suitable for light- and medium-weight wallpapers but heavy wallpaper needs a heavy-duty paste.
- ⊙ Vinyls and plastic-coated wallpapers need a fungicidal adhesive to prevent mould.

Equipment needed for hanging paper

- ⊙ Seam adhesive (for repairs).
- ⊙ Paper-hanger's brush.
- ⊙ Paper-hanger's shears.
- ⊙ Paste brush.
- ⊙ Pasting table.
- ⊙ Pencil.
- ⊙ Plumb bob and line.
- ⊙ Ruler or tape measure.
- ⊙ Seam roller (to press down wallpaper edges).
- ⊙ Wallpaper paste and bucket.

How to hang wallpaper

1 Using paper-hanger's shears, cut sufficient drops for about a wall at a time, adding 5–7.5cm/2–3in to the length of each drop to allow for trimming at the ceiling and skirting, and matching the pattern as you go. (If there's a substantial pattern repeat, drops will vary in length.)

2 Roll the lengths against the curl to flatten them and then turn them over so that the pasting side is uppermost.

3 Mix the paste as instructed and brush it down the centre of the wallpaper with a pasting brush. (Tie a taut string across the bucket to remove excess paste from the brush.) Brush the paste out from the centre, first away from you and then towards you, so that the edges are covered. Ready-pasted wallcovering simply needs soaking in

ABOVE How to hang wallpaper, step 1

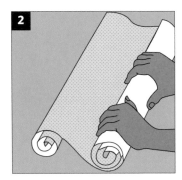

ABOVE How to hang wallpaper, step 2

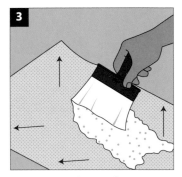

ABOVE How to hang wallpaper, step 3

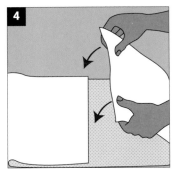

ABOVE How to hang wallpaper, step 4

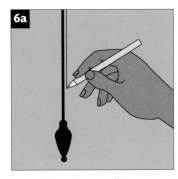

ABOVE How to hang wallpaper, step 6A

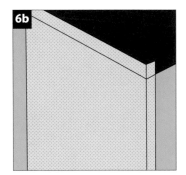

ABOVE How to hang wallpaper, step 6B

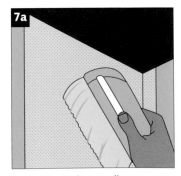

ABOVE How to hang wallpaper, step 7A

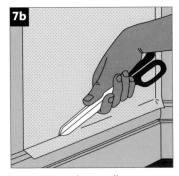

ABOVE How to hang wallpaper, step 7B

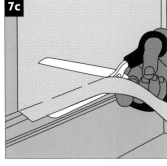

ABOVE How to hang wallpaper, step 7C

water in the trough provided and can be smoothed into place with a sponge. Apply seam adhesive to seams and edges if they have a tendency to lift.

4. Move the paper up and gently fold the paper over so the pasted surfaces meet. When you have pasted the whole drop, fold the other side so that the top and bottom meet in the centre. (When papering stairways and ceilings, you may have to concertina the paper to paste the longest lengths.)

5. Vinyls can be put up straight away but you should leave standard wallpaper to soak for five minutes and heavier relief designs for ten, so that the paper stretches and bubbles won't occur.

6. To make sure you hang the paper straight, find the vertical, using a plumb bob and line (a small weight on a string) as a guide (A). Mark a line 25mm/1in less than the wallpaper's width if you're starting at a corner (because you'll be turning this amount on to the adjacent wall) and hang the first piece of wallpaper, using this line as a guide, allowing about 70mm/2¾in to overlap on the ceiling and 25mm/1in to turn round the corner (B).

7. Manoeuvre the top half into place and smooth down with a paper-hanger's brush, pushing it well into the corner (A). Release the bottom half, lower gently and smooth into place. Mark a fold at skirting (B) and ceiling level with the shears and trim to fit (C).

8. Hang the next length so it butts tightly up to the first, because the paper will shrink as it dries. Leave for five minutes and then press into place with a seam roller.

Hanging lining paper

Hang lining paper horizontally, working from the top downwards and joining lengths edge to edge (butt-joining). Overlap by about 15–25mm/⅝–1in at the corners for a neat, strong finish and to take in any irregularities in the wall. Walls are rarely straight. You must do this or the paper may peel back from the wall where the edges meet.

TIP
Use a seam roller with care on relief wallpaper as it may crush the design.

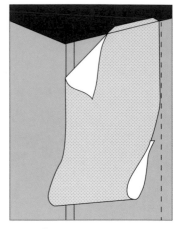

Pattern matching

- Straight-match wallpapers line up horizontally.
- Drop-match wallpapers require adjoining lengths to be moved up or down to match up.
- Random (free-match) designs don't need to be pattern matched.
- Pattern repeats can make a difference to the amount of wallpaper you need. Remember to allow extra when estimating quantity.

ABOVE Corners

Awkward areas

CEILINGS Paste the paper and fold into a concertina, then unfold as you press into place. Smooth down with a broom; this is best done by a partner walking behind you.

CORNERS Unless the gap between the previous length of paper and the corner of the room is very narrow, cut the last length on the wall so that it turns the corner by about 25mm/1in. Find the vertical on the new wall and hang the first length on that wall so that it covers the overlaps. External (convex) corners (on alcoves and chimney breasts, for example) may need a larger overlap to make sure seams don't coincide with the exposed corners, where they will undoubtedly tear.

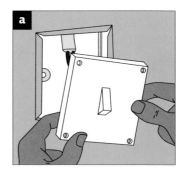

'Feather' relief papers to make the edge thinner by tearing the edge and press down with a seam roller to minimise bulk when overlapping a corner.

FIXINGS Insert matches to mark the site of screws or picture hangers and allow them to pierce through the wallpaper when you smooth it into place.

LIGHT SWITCHES Turn off the electricity and remove the switch cover (A). Hang the wallpaper over the switch and smooth into place. Cut away a square of wallpaper 6mm/¼in less than the size of the switch, then replace the cover, tucking in the edges. If the switch projects, cut an X shape in the paper across it and trim the wallpaper, leaving a small margin to overlap on to the sides of the cover (B). Always use this technique with foil wallcoverings, which conduct electricity and must not be tucked under the switch cover.

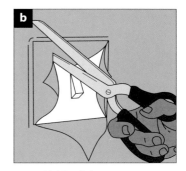

ABOVE Light switches

STAIRWAYS Start with the longest drop, marking the vertical by fixing a piece of chalked string from top to bottom of the stair well, and snapping it against the wall. Cut each length separately, matching the pattern and making sure that the length is sufficient to take in the angled skirting.

WINDOW SILLS Pull the paper over the corner of the sill and slit it before smoothing the paper into place.

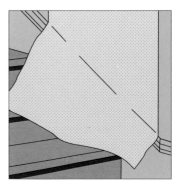

ABOVE Stairs

WHAT WENT WRONG?

⊙ **BUBBLES** These form if the wallpaper isn't pasted thoroughly or isn't given time to soak. They can also occur if the length isn't smoothed out properly. It's sometimes possible to slit air bubbles with a razor blade and paste the edges into place.

⊙ **DIRTY MARKS** Can usually be removed with a white eraser (use with care) or a piece of stale white bread.

⊙ **GAPS** Can appear if lengths are not pushed together or if the paper has been stretched too much when smoothed out and has shrunk back when dry.

⊙ **PEELING** Is often caused by damp. If it's not substantial, try lifting and repasting the edges with wallpaper paste or seam adhesive.

⊙ **TEARS** May not be noticeable if they're stuck down carefully.

HOW TO MITRE A BORDER

If you want to create a panelled look with wallpaper borders, you'll need to mitre the corners for a perfect right angle.

1 Find the right-hand vertical with a plumb bob and line and mark with a pencil, then paste a strip of border into place, allowing 25mm/1in more than the finished size.

2 Check the horizontal with a spirit level and smooth the border across the top of the panel into place, allowing another 25mm/1in overlap on the right-hand side.

3 Mitre the corner by placing a ruler across the diagonal from the outer to the inner edge and cut along this line with a trimming knife. Take off the surplus triangle on top, then peel back the horizontal border and remove the excess from beneath. Smooth the edges into place.

Borders

Borders are available in wallpaper or ready-pasted vinyl, but though pasting techniques may differ, they are cut and fixed in more or less the same way.

❶ Mark the position of the border lightly in pencil, using a spirit level to find the horizontal. Then step back and see how it looks to the eye. It's sometimes better to have a border that follows the walls or ceiling than one that emphasises irregularities.

❷ Cut the border and paste or soak it.

❸ Concertina the folds, matching pasted edge to pasted edge, and unwind carefully, smoothing into place as you go.

❹ Butt join ends, making sure the pattern matches, and press the margins down firmly.

TIP
For borders you will need the same equipment as for hanging wallpaper (see page 319), plus a spirit level.

Opening Up a Fireplace

There are very few rooms that don't look better when a previously filled chimney breast is opened and the fireplace restored. The fireplace is the natural focal point of the room and the decorative impact it makes is well worth the sacrifice of wall space, even in quite small rooms.

CHOOSING A STYLE OF FIREPLACE

Before you begin, look around for fireplaces that suit the style of your house. If you want an unusual design or one in a very small size, you may do best to look for authentic period pieces from specialists or architectural salvage firms. Alternatively, as grates and mantelpieces in good condition and a reasonable price can be difficult to find, you may find it easier to settle for a reproduction.

STEP-BY-STEP OPENING A FLUE

❶ Locate the chimney breast, which usually projects into the room but sometimes juts outside it. It may be covered by hardboard or plasterboard, which are simple to remove, or it may be bricked in.

❷ If the fireplace has been closed properly, you'll find an airbrick set into the wall to prevent damp. Insert the large chisel into the mortar surrounding it, and tap it with a hammer. Remove the airbrick carefully. If the fireplace has been filled with bricks and there is no airbrick, take out a few bricks about 30cm/12in from the floor.

❸ Light a candle and place it in the fireplace. If the flame is drawn upwards, the chimney is clear. If it goes out, ask a builder for advice.

❹ If the chimney is clear, unblock the opening, taking care not to damage the lintel across the top of the fireplace.

❺ Clean out the original fireplace and check that the fireback (which protects the wall from heat) is usable and not cracked, replacing it if necessary before you fit the new fireplace.

Equipment you will need

- ❍ Candle
- ❍ Hammer
- ❍ Bolster, or pointing chisel

TIP
For safety, have the chimney swept before you light the fire.

Wall Tiles

Tiles are waterproof, last for years and need little more care than a swift wipe over with detergent. They're ideal for walls that are likely to get wet or need protection from steam or grease, but because they last so long, it's worthwhile choosing colours and designs that won't date and will look good with a variety of colour schemes.

CHOOSING TILES

Most wall tiles are ceramic, though glass mirror tiles are available too. The most popular size is 152mm/6in square, though 100mm/4in square tiles and rectangular tiles (usually 200 x 100mm/8 x 4in, or 200 x 152mm/ 8 x 6in) hexagonal and Provençal shapes are also available.

Craftsman-made and continental tiles are often smaller and chunkier; that goes for borders and dados too and, as a result, it can be difficult to mix and match unless you're certain of the depth of the tiles you want to use. If you can't compare samples directly, it may be safer to choose all your tiles from the same range.

Types of tile

'UNIVERSAL' TILES Have at least two glazed edges so you can use them anywhere, turning the glazed edges to the outside when you reach the end of a run. Bevelled-edge universal tiles butt together leaving a space for the grout so you won't need to use spacers.

FIELD TILES Have unglazed edges for use in the centre of a panel. They may be self-spacing, with lugs on each side.

BORDER OR EDGE TILES Have one or two rounded edges, to finish the outside of a panel.

QUADRANT TILES Are narrow rounded strips, used to top standard tiles.

Equipment you will need

- Grout
- Hammer
- Metal rule
- Nails or tacks
- Notched tile-adhesive spreader (often supplied with the tile adhesive)
- Pincers for cutting random shapes (if necessary)
- Plastic tile spacers or matchsticks (if necessary)
- Sand paper (for stripping)
- Spirit level
- Sponge
- Tile adhesive
- Tile file
- Tungsten carbide tile cutter
- Wooden battens

Design tips

- Use a row of border tiles to create a frieze on a wall of plain tiles.
- Panels of patterned tiles can make long, high walls seem shorter.
- To show off the design on odd or antique tiles, set them into a window ledge.
- Tile well-used coffee tables for a water and heat-resistant finish.

TILING STEP BY STEP

❶ Wash down emulsion paint and sand solvent-painted surfaces to provide a key. Strip off all wallpaper before tiling.

❷ Work out where the cut tiles will fall. Have a 'dry run' and readjust if there are any very narrow pieces to cut at the end of a run. It's better to have two evenly cut tiles at each end.

❸ Measure the distance of one tile up from the skirting or worktop (A) and find the true horizontal with a spirit level (B). Mark with a pencil and nail or tack a slim wooden batten to the wall along this line.

❹ Check the vertical with a spirit level and fix a batten at the end of the last full row of tiles, to keep the tiles in line.

TIP

You can tile over old tiles if you rub down and seal with plaster primer to provide a key. You'll need a wooden strip or pieces of tile to conceal the double thickness at the top.

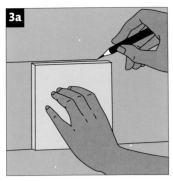

ABOVE Tiling, step 3A

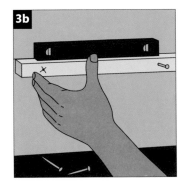

ABOVE Tiling, step 3B

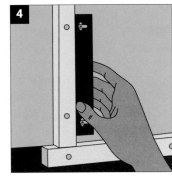

ABOVE Tiling, step 4

ABOVE Tiling, step 5

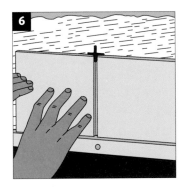

ABOVE Tiling, step 6

ABOVE Tiling, step 7A

ABOVE Tiling, step 7B

ABOVE Tiling, step 7C

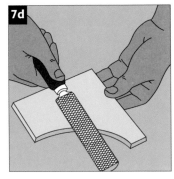

ABOVE Tiling, step 7D

5 Starting in the corner where the battens meet, spread tile adhesive on 1 sq. m/11 sq. ft of wall, combing with a notched spreader until even.

6 Press the tiles firmly into place without sliding them, inserting plastic spacers (to leave space for the grout) if necessary. Wipe off any adhesive on the surface of the tiles with a damp sponge as you go. Continue until all whole tiles have been fixed, checking the levels from time to time. Remove the battens when the adhesive is dry.

7 Now fix the cut tiles. Mark the cutting line on the tile and place it on a cutting board, right side up. Score through with a tungsten carbide cutter held against a metal rule (A). Place matchsticks or a pencil, depending on the tile's thickness, underneath the scored line and press firmly on each side. If you're lucky, the tile will snap evenly (B). For odd shapes, you will need to make a template and copy the shape on to the tile, nibbling away with pincers (C) and finishing with a tile file (D).

8 Fix cut tiles so that the smooth edge is next to the adjacent tile and the cut edge is next to the worktop or skirting.

9 When tiling is complete, leave the adhesive to harden as instructed on the packet. Waterproof adhesive takes longer to dry. Mix the grout (or buy ready-mixed) and spread it over the gaps with a sponge, pushing it in well and wiping away the excess with a clean damp sponge. Neaten with your finger or a lolly stick just before the grout sets.

10 When dry, wipe with a damp sponge to remove the last traces of grout, and polish the tiles with a soft cloth.

TIP
Use pincers rather than a tile cutter to cut away a very narrow strip at the edge of a tile.

TIP
Use flexible sealant between the tiles and bath or basin after you grout.

TIP
Don't rinse the sponges and cloths used for grouting under the tap. The grout residues may block the drain.

HOW MANY TILES WILL YOU NEED?

Measure the area you want to tile and divide by the size of the tiles or use this ready reckoner if you are using standard sizes. Add 10 per cent for breakages.

Area cm/in	10 x 10/4 x 4	15 x 15/6 x 6	10 x 20/4 x 8	30 x 12/12 x 5
Sq. m/sq. ft	Number of tiles			
1/11	100	44	50	12
2/21½	200	87	100	23
3/32	300	130	150	34
4/43	400	174	200	45
5/54	500	217	250	56
6/64½	600	260	300	67
7/75	700	303	350	78
8/86	800	347	400	89
9/97	900	390	450	100
10/108	1,000	433	500	111

Adhesive 1.5kg/3⅓ lb/1 litre per 1sq. m/11sq. ft

Grout 150g/5¼ oz per 1sq. m/11sq. ft

All About Shelves

Shelves are the most flexible form of storage. Once you can put up a shelf, you'll have mastered the basic techniques needed for hanging everything from paintings and mirrors to wall cupboards. It's easy when you know how, as long as you make sure the shelf is absolutely level and choose suitable wall fixings so the brackets are secure.

It's wise to start by hanging a single decorative shelf rather than a floor to ceiling fitment, and if you've never used a drill before, to practise on different surfaces first, such as brick and wood.

WHICH SHELF?

CHIPBOARD SHELVES Can be finished with a layer of plastic laminate, like that used for kitchen cupboards, or melamine, a spray coating available in wood effect or plain colours. Plastic laminate shrugs off water and stains but melamine is less durable. It protects against damp but is easily marked.

GLASS SHELVES Must be plate glass and should have ground edges for safety.

TIMBER SHELVES Range from unfinished pine, which you can paint, stain, varnish or polish, to expensive hardwoods. Most shelving for home use is made from softwoods, ready-cut or in lengths you can cut to size and then finish as you wish.

Shelf supports

Can be made from pieces of wood fixed each side of a narrow alcove, individual brackets, or slotted uprights, which allow you to vary the height of the shelves. You can also buy horizontal metal supports designed to support the shelf along its entire length, which are more discreet than brackets or uprights.

SPACE SAVERS

Shelves provide an easy answer to a host of storage problems. Here are a few ideas.

- Put a shelf at the bottom of a wardrobe and store shoes underneath.
- Fit shelves in a tall cupboard and use for storing toys and games.
- A wide shelf with strong brackets can serve as a desk in a study or bedroom. Top with some bookshelves.
- Fix shallow shelves to the inside of kitchen cupboard doors or at the back of the larder or broom cupboard for extra storage.
- Line an under-stairs cupboard with shelves to keep light bulbs, plugs, small items and tools handy.
- Hang narrow decorative shelves beneath kitchen wall cupboards, for mugs or spices.
- Fit broad, widely-spaced shelves in children's rooms and use them to store toys in large plastic crates. (Make sure they're too high to be climbed or sat on.)
- Fit shelves in the garage and garden shed to hold tools and DIY equipment.
- Organise shelves in the bathroom or cloakroom: narrow glass ones for toiletries, wide wood or melamine for extra supplies and clean towels.
- Make an old-fashioned plate shelf with a slot to keep plates upright. Fix it round the room at picture rail level, to show off old china.
- Fix glass shelves across a dull window and cover with sun-loving plants; they'll thrive in the light.

WALLS AND FIXINGS

Type of wall

It is important to work out what the wall is made from, because that decides the type of fixing you use and the stability of the shelves.

The dust from drilling is a guide to wall construction. Red dust indicates brick, which can take straightforward wallplugs. Grey powder is probably building blocks, which can also support conventional screw fixings. Black dust may mean breeze blocks, which need anchor fixings.

SOLID WALLS Are made from brick or building blocks. Most houses built before the First World War had solid exterior walls.

CAVITY WALLS Are made from two layers of brick or building blocks with a gap between for insulation. Houses built after the Second World War have exterior cavity walls.

BREEZE BLOCKS Were sometimes used for interior walls in houses built between the 1930s and 60s. Although solid, breeze blocks do crumble easily and need reinforcement to support heavy loads.

PLASTERBOARD Is used to line walls and for stud walls, made from plasterboard on a timber frame. (Stud walls are sometimes used as interior walls in recently converted flats, or where doors have been filled in, or in small added extensions.) You can tell if a wall is made from plasterboard because it sounds hollow when knocked. Unless the load is very light, you'll need to locate the timber supports underneath the plasterboard on stud walls, or provide timber reinforcement on the wall behind for strength.

LATH AND PLASTER WALLS Consist of plaster supported by a web of timber slats; found in period homes. You can usually detect this type of construction because most of these walls are very irregular.

PUTTING UP A SHELF STEP BY STEP

1 Plan the distance between the shelves. Make sure they're broad enough and far apart enough for your needs. The heavier the load, the more supports you will need. Make sure brackets are a minimum of 400mm/16in apart for bookshelves or when fitting glass shelves.

2 Check that the screws are the right size for the brackets and that the wallplugs and drill bit size are compatible.

3 Mark a line along the wall where the shelf will be, using a spirit level to check that it's straight (A). Hold the brackets in place and mark the screw holes (B), before checking the horizontal with a spirit level once more.

4 With a solid wall, use a masonry drill bit to make holes for the first bracket, about 4cm/1½in deep where marked. (Work slowly to make sure the drill doesn't overheat.) For breeze block or hollow plasterboard walls, use an ordinary drill bit the correct size for the fixing. When working on wood, use a bradawl to start the screw holes as that will stop the timber splitting.

To mark the drilling depth, twist a piece of masking tape round the drill bit marking off the first 4cm/1½in.

5 Push in the wallplugs until they are flush with the surface, and loosely

Which fixing?

If you're working on a solid wall, you can use standard wallplugs. Shelves fixed to timber uprights need strong screws, which are screwed straight into the wood. If you want to fix shelving to breeze block or hollow plasterboard walls, you'll also need cavity fixings (which open out when screwed in to provide support behind the wall) or stronger toggle bolts.

TIP
Use a cable detector to locate the uprights in lath and plaster walls: it will light up when passed over the nails used to fix the laths.

Equipment you will need

- Bradawl.
- Pencil.
- Power drill.
- Screwdriver.
- Shelves, brackets and fixings (including wallplugs if necessary).
- Spirit level.

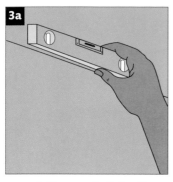

ABOVE Putting up a shelf, step 3A

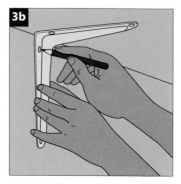

ABOVE Putting up a shelf, step 3B

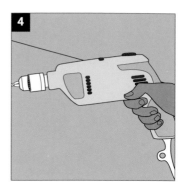

ABOVE Putting up a shelf, step 4

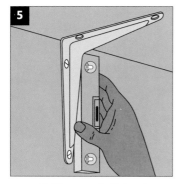

ABOVE Putting up a shelf, step 5

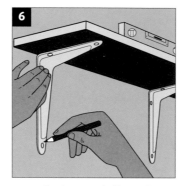

ABOVE Putting up a shelf, step 6

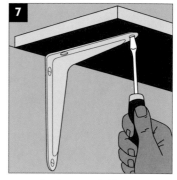

ABOVE Putting up a shelf, step 7

screw the bracket into place, keeping a check that it is vertical with a spirit level.

6 Repeat with the furthest bracket, and check both vertical and horizontal levels. Repeat until all the brackets are in place, carefully checking the levels each time, and making any adjustments necessary.

Drill and screw just one hole for each bracket, marking the others in pencil until you are sure the shelf will be level, to avoid making unnecessary holes in the wall.

7 Screw the brackets firmly in place on the wall and put up the shelf. Mark the position of the small retaining screws that secure the shelf to the bracket. Remove the shelf and make small 'pilot' holes in it with a bradawl before replacing the shelf on the brackets and screwing into place manually.

TIP
Rubbing screws with petroleum jelly makes them easier to remove later.

TIP
Make sure the screw is at least 6mm/$\frac{1}{4}$in shorter than the depth of the shelf, so it won't pierce the surface.

Mouldings

Mouldings balance a high ceiling and add a decorative finish to the wall. Traditional skirtings, picture rails and cornices are available if you need to replace the mouldings in your house. Many suppliers will match an existing moulding from an offcut.

WHICH MOULDING?

ARCHITRAVE Is the moulding that surrounds a door or window frame. Popular widths are 50, 63 and 75mm/2, 2½ and 3in.

CORNICES Are used where the wall and ceiling meet. Made from plaster or timber, they are often elaborate in style.

COVING Is the modern equivalent of cornice. Designs are usually simple, and it is made from easy-to-handle plaster or polystyrene.

DADO RAILS Timber mouldings fixed about 1m/3ft from the ground. Originally designed to protect the wall from knocks by furniture, now used to separate decorations, e.g. wallpaper above and paint below.

FRIEZE Describes the area between the picture rail and cornice.

PICTURE RAIL Is the timber moulding that runs round a wall above head height and has a special slot for picture hooks.

SKIRTING Protects the plaster at the base of the wall. Most skirtings are made from softwood, but hardwood designs are available.

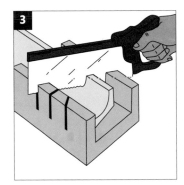

ABOVE Fitting coving, step 3

FITTING COVING STEP BY STEP

1 Remove any wallpaper or flaking paint from the top of the wall and make sure the plaster is clean and dry. Sand lightly to provide a key.

2 Measure the room, counting the corners, so you know how many angles you need to cut – both internal, such as in a recess, and external, where a chimney breast projects outwards.

3 Cut the lengths to the correct angle using a tenon saw and either a mitre box or a paper template. Smooth the edges by sanding lightly.

4 Apply adhesive generously to the reverse side and edges of the coving (A), and press into place (B). Use a clean cloth to wipe away any excess adhesive before it sets.

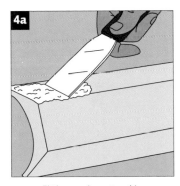

ABOVE Fitting coving, step 4A

Equipment you will need

- Coving adhesive
- Mitre box/paper template for cutting angles
- Sandpaper and sanding block
- Tape measure
- Tenon saw

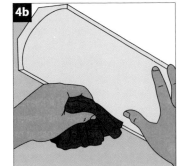

ABOVE Fitting coving, step 4B

Window Treatments

The last few years has seen a move away from heavily gathered, lined and interlined curtains hung from elaborate poles and festooned with pelmets and tiebacks to a more relaxed simple approach. However, there is still a huge variety of fabrics, headings, tracks and poles to choose from, and you are sure to find a style to suit your taste and your room. In fact, if there is a problem, it is that there's such a bewildering choice. Before you start shopping for material, jot down the effect you'd like to achieve and any considerations you should take into account.

QUESTIONS TO ASK YOURSELF

- How much natural light are you prepared to give up? Do you want to maximise or minimise the view?
- Are there any practical features that will influence the style that you choose? For example, is there a radiator or window seat beneath the window? Does the window pivot? Is it a dormer, or French doors? If the window abuts a wall or furniture, blinds let in more light than curtains. Alternatively, opt for a single drape, tied back at one side. If there is space for a pair of curtains have the finial at one side only. If there is a radiator beneath a window do not block it with heavy curtains. Fit a blind and fixed dress curtains on either side.
- What shape is the window, and do you want to alter it? A pelmet can help reduce the height of tall windows; long curtains can give importance to a small one. A square bay can be treated in several ways: as a single unit or with separate blinds or curtains. Tall windows can be elegant and generous: curtains should be floor length with a pelmet. Smaller windows should be simple; treatments like swags can be overpowering.
- How many windows are there in the room? Identical windows can be given the same treatment, while windows that are very different in size and shape can be treated individually. If they're slightly different, or oddly proportioned, it's often best to copy the treatment chosen for the largest window, or to curtain the entire wall, if the windows are next to each other.
- How much clearance is there between the top of the window and the ceiling? This will affect the type of track and heading. Curtain poles need space above and below to look effective. If space is very limited, you may need a ceiling-hung track.
- Is privacy important? If the room is overlooked, you may need to screen the window with sheers or blinds during the day, as well as having curtains that close at night.
- Do you need extra insulation? Full-length lined and interlined curtains, when closed, can help keep precious heat inside the room.

- Will you need to wash the curtains or blinds? Lined curtains should be dry-cleaned even if both inner and outer fabric are made from cotton, because if washed they're liable to shrink at different rates and the seams will pucker. If you want curtains for a kitchen, bathroom or family room, it may be best to choose detachable linings or unlined sheers. Fabric blinds are usually not washed, but roller blinds can often be wiped with a damp cloth.
- Would you prefer an architectural solution? Window coverings don't need to be fabric. Other coverings include shutters, wood-slat blinds and shelves.
- Does the window really need covering? Oriel, round, and stained-glass windows are often best left to speak for themselves. Skylights and high, narrow windows rarely need covering for privacy though you may want to screen out the light. Their proportions may need minimising rather than emphasising so if you want to cover them, it may be best to choose a simple treatment in a colour that blends with the walls.

Security matters

It is worth fitting simple locks to every window, but you may want to consider special blinds, security grilles or shutters for ground floor or basement windows, or if you live in a high risk area.

WHICH WINDOW?

The way a window opens and where it is positioned can affect the window covering you choose, especially if it projects inwards rather than outwards and needs blinds or curtains that pull clear of the pane. Here are the main types to consider.

CASEMENT WINDOWS Are side-opening. They usually have one fixed pane and one or two opening lights.

SASH OR DOUBLE-HUNG WINDOWS Are made in two parts that can be raised and lowered independently, worked by sash cords or a metal spiral balance.

WINDOW FRAMES

- **ALUMINIUM** Is popular for replacement windows, patio doors and double-glazed units. It can be coated as well as plain and is wiped clean easily but the cold metal may increase condensation. To prevent this, a plastic 'thermal break' is often provided in double-glazed windows, to improve insulation.
- **PLASTIC** Made from unplasticised polyvinyl chloride (uPVC) and reinforced with metal. They provide good insulation but should not be painted.

- **GALVANISED METAL** May be found in some older houses, but are rarely used today because their poor insulation can cause condensation and rot. They need careful maintenance to prevent them from rusting.
- **TIMBER** Provides good insulation, minimising condensation round the frame, but needs to be painted or stained regularly to prevent rot. Timber frames should be treated with preservative, and softwood should be thoroughly seasoned before building, to prevent warping later.

COMPLEX WINDOW SHAPES

⊙ **BAY WINDOWS** Extend the floor area of the room, letting in light on three sides. They can be square or angled, made from three separate windows, or a curved unit. You can cover a square bay with four curtains (two in the centre and one at each side); with three separate blinds; with a blind at the centre and show curtains on each side; or a single pair of curtains, provided you use track or poles that bend. You can also 'cut off' the bay by screening it with a pair of full-length curtains.

⊙ **BOW WINDOWS** Are curved windows set in a straight wall, and don't extend into the room in the same way as a bay. You can fit curtains or blinds to cut off the bow, or hang them from a curved track to emphasise the window's shape.

⊙ **DORMER WINDOWS** Project from the roof. There's usually only one window (though some dormers have windows in the side like a miniature bay), plus a broad shelf underneath. Though charming to look at, dormers may not let much light in, so shutters, simple blinds, or narrow curtains that pull right back from the pane, are often a good choice. Alternatively hinged portiere rods that swing out to lie flat against the adjacent wall during the day are an ideal solution for a small dormer window.

⊙ **FRENCH WINDOWS AND GARDEN DOORS** Need curtains that pull clear on either side so that the doors can open easily. Tie-backs or holdbacks that secure the curtains when the doors are open help keep soiling to a minimum.

⊙ **PICTURE WINDOWS AND PATIO DOORS** May take over most of the wall. In this case, it may be worth covering the entire wall, rather than the window alone, for the best effect.

TILTING WINDOWS Include pivoting designs, which turn through almost 180°; projecting windows, which push forward on metal struts; tilting designs which can be tipped ajar for ventilation and pull inwards or pivot to open fully; and louvre (jalousie) windows, made from horizontal glass slats. For privacy, attach net rods at both ends of the frame. The surround can be dressed using any style.

SLIDING WINDOWS Are usually patio doors, but small sliding windows are sometimes found in houses near the sea, where they're designed to resist buffeting by the wind.

SLOPING WINDOWS Use a roller blind with a side-winding mechanism, and anchor it at the lower edge. Alternatively, have wooden poles at both top and bottom of the window. Head the curtains at the top and the bottom and attach them to the poles.

RECESSED WINDOWS Curtains hung here can block out valuable light; fit blinds instead.

CURTAIN TRACKS AND POLES

Curtain poles are designed for show; curtain track is often best hidden by a heading or pelmet. But just to confuse matters, there are now a number of curtain tracks that are attractive in their own right and can even be mistaken for poles. Here's a basic guide.

TIP
Polish curtain poles from time to time with silicone polish so that the rings run up and down smoothly.

TIP
Metal curtain poles can be custom made to fit into bay windows.

Curtain poles

Poles are usually best for relatively short, straight runs, though it's possible to buy poles that bend to follow a bay. They are sold complete with fittings such as rings from which to hang the curtains, although it's usually possible to buy extra rings separately. For a simpler effect, the current trend is to have tie-top curtains, café-style slot headings or eyelets through which the pole is threaded.

Poles are usually made from wood – either stained or sprayed or left natural before painting – or metal. Metal poles, made from wrought iron, brass or chrome, can be quite decorative with stunning matching finials. Finials sit at the end of the pole and keep the last curtain ring in place. This can be removed if the window is close to a corner. Most are fixed to the wall, though ceiling fixing is sometimes possible. If space is limited, look for 'short reach' brackets, which fix the pole close to the wall.

The diameter of the pole is important. Long, lined curtains need substantial poles to bear the weight, although some metal poles will take a fair amount of weight – check with manufacturer when you buy. Slim wooden poles (under 25mm/1in thick) are best kept for short or sheer curtains. Long poles (over 2.4m/8ft) need a central support to prevent them sagging, and this can sometimes be used to join two lengths together. Larger poles may come ready corded, so the curtains don't need to be pulled by hand. It's possible to buy a draw rod, attached to the leading ring and concealed by the folds in the fabric to pull uncorded curtains.

In addition to conventional poles, there are also sprung rods that will fit inside a window recess. These include café rods for café curtains, and light-weight tension rods for lace curtains.

Curtain tracks

Curtain track can be fixed to walls or ceilings. The track is made from plastic, aluminium or steel and can be used with accessories such as cording sets (to open and close the curtains without handling them), a valance rail for fabric pelmets or a net curtain track.

It's important to buy track that's strong enough for the curtains, as long, lined curtains and fabrics like velvet need double the support required by light cotton curtains. Many brands of track are suitable for DIY use but the heavier metal curtain tracks may need to be installed by a professional, especially if the window is a difficult shape.

You may need a special type of track to fit a square bay window or to sweep each side of a bow window. Some types used by professional fitters will bend around 90°.

Before you buy a curtain track, check the tightest angle recommended by the manufacturer for bending it. Some tracks for DIY use won't bend enough to fit a square bay. If you like the look of curtain poles but need the flexibility of track, consider a track that combines the features of both.

PELMETS

Pelmets are an economical way of giving a decorative flourish to everyday curtains. They can disguise standard curtain heading, helping you make the most of a limited amount of fabric because basic heading tape

Fitting curtain track

Make sure the track is the right length before you start, Curtain track is either cut or telescoped to fit; poles are cut to size.

- **WALL FIXING** There's usually a concrete lintel above a window, so you will need to use a hammer drill and a masonry drill bit. (While it is possible to drill into a steel lintel, it is easier to hang curtains from the ceiling in this case.) Measure 5cm/2in above the window before you start to drill, and make sure the holes are at least 38mm/1½in deep so that you penetrate the wall beneath the plaster. If the plaster crumbles, try fixing a wooden batten to the lintel and screw the track to that. This will also cut down the number of holes drilled into the wall itself.

- **CEILING FIXING** It is very important to make sure the track is securely fixed into the timber joists above the ceiling plaster. You can locate them by tapping the ceiling: hollow areas will sound hollow and joists will sound duller. Then test with a bradawl, pushing through the plaster to find the wooden joists above. Or use a battery-operated joint and stud detector. If the joists run parallel to the curtain track, you will need to take up the floorboards in the room above and fit strips of wood between the joists. It may be easier to fit the track on the wall close to the ceiling

TIP
To prevent the gliders sticking, spray curtain track with silicone-based polish or a lubricant such as WD-40.

requires less material than more elaborate types; and they can cover basic curtain track. You can also use pelmets to correct the proportions of a room or window, because they can appear to reduce the height of a window if fitted over it, or increase the height if fitted above it.

At its simplest, a pelmet is a wooden box that can be painted to suit your room scheme or the colour of your curtains.

Box pelmets can also be covered with fabric, but it is more usual for fabric to be mounted on a stiffened backing (see below) and hung from a pelmet board or shelf.

Pelmets step by step

1 Make a paper pattern for the pelmet by drawing the design on to dressmaker's graph paper, remembering to include the width of the pelmet board, or 'returns', on each side: 10–15cm/4–6in.

2 Transfer the pelmet design on to a stiffener such as iron-on buckram, which is washable, or a product such as Pelmform (which comes with a range of pelmet patterns).

3 Cut the stiffener to shape. If you choose buckram, you will need to pad it with 'bump' (from haberdashery departments). Cut it to fit, joining lengths of bump with an overlapped, flat seam held in place with herringbone stitch.

4 Transfer the design to the fabric and lining and cut to shape, allowing a 2.5cm/1in margin all round. Notch any curves to ease the fabric.

5 Sew the edges of the lining under so that the lining is 5mm/¼in smaller all round than the pelmet stiffener.

6 If using Pelmform, fix the wrong side of the fabric to it. If using buckram and padding, lock-stitch the bump to the wrong side of the fabric. Then iron the buckram on to the padding. Iron the overlap of the fabric into place on the wrong side of the buckram or Pelmform.

7 Attach the soft side of the Velcro to the right side of the lining fabric along the top. Slipstitch the lining to the fabric overlap, so that it hides the raw edge.

8 Stitch, tack or glue any braid or fringing into place.

9 Tack or glue the hooked side of the Velcro to the top edge of the pelmet board, and attach the pelmet, making sure the two strips of Velcro line up and the pelmet is quite level.If the pelmet is large or heavy, you may need to use large drawing pins or upholstery tacks to keep it in place.

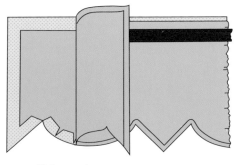

ABOVE Fitting a pelmet

Pelmet boards

These can be made from a standard 10cm/4in shelf or, for full-length curtains, a shelf 15cm/6in deep. Pelmet boards should be cut 5cm/2in wider each side than the curtain track, and fixed to the wall above the track with strong brackets.

Equipment you will need

- Dressmaker's graph paper.
- Fabric and lining.
- Pelmet board fixed in place.
- Iron-on buckram and bump interlining, or Pelmform.
- Tape measure.
- Touch-and-close (Velcro) fastener, same length as the pelmet board, or large drawing pins, or upholstery tacks.

TIP
Pelmets look best when their length (drop) is about one-sixth the total length of the curtains.

Soft Furnishings

Making your own curtains, cushions and coverings for furniture can be both creative and satisfying – as well as a way of saving money. The first piece of equipment you will need, however, is a good sewing machine.

CHOOSING A SEWING MACHINE

The latest machines bear little resemblance to Isaac Singer's traditional black and gold machine of the 1800s. Computer technology has brought the sewing machine industry back to life and unearthed myriad home-sewing possibilities.

Today's machines have sophisticated functions, which are easy to use, allowing you to concentrate on the work, not on the controls. They are becoming increasingly user-friendly, with built-in sewing advice, and the operating manual is becoming more of a design handbook than an instructor.

TYPES OF MACHINE
ELECTRONIC MACHINES
Electric sewing machines have a motor in the body of the machine, which drives the needle and the 'feed dog' that feeds the fabric through the machine. The motor is controlled by a foot pedal that usually offers a range of speeds – the harder you press with your foot, the faster you sew. Electronic machines offer greater needle penetration power, greater stitch control and allow you to maintain a constant sewing speed whatever the fabric thickness. They vary greatly in price but even the most basic models offer a good choice of stitches and sewing options.

OVERLOCKERS
Operated like conventional machines, but will overcast, seam and trim raw edges in one operation, to provide a neat professional finish. They will not replace a conventional machine, but are ideal for basic stitches for seams and seam finishes, stitching seams with built-in stretch (such as on knit fabrics), rolled hems and decorative flat-lock stitches.

Threading can be complicated as they can take from two to five threads, so an initial demonstration is essential.

Buying tactics
◉ Shop around. Mail order and Internet models may be cheaper, but remember you cannot try out the machines and after-sales service is more difficult to organise. Department stores and dealers will give you the best advice and after-sales service. All dealers who are members of the Sewing Machine Trade Association (SMTA; see Useful Organisations) will give the machine a pre-purchase check.

Computer machines

Controlled by a microprocessor that governs stitch selection, programming and memory functions, buttonhole formation and tension control. Stitches or patterns are selected either by:

- Push buttons and LED indication beside an image on the display panel.
- Numerical, digital selection by push button.
- Sensorised touch control panel.

Computerised machines have similar functions to traditional machines with some interesting extras. These include mirror-imaging (pattern can be turned over or reversed), visual stitch displays, memory banks, and the ability to elongate patterns. Stitch sequences can be built into a pattern and stored until recalled. The trend is towards total creativity: your own designs can be scanned into the machine's memory. Stitch selection is simplified because width, length and tension are automatically chosen. Some are able to download designs from the Internet when connected to a PC.

POINTS TO CONSIDER WHEN CHOOSING SEWING MACHINES

- Good selection of basic stitches and range of stitch lengths and widths. If you are a keen sewer pre-set widths or lengths can be restrictive unless they have a manual override.
- Look for clear colour-coded controls for easy selection of stitch, width and length.
- Most machines have a free-arm sewing area, for cuffs and sleeves plus an extension to convert to a flat-bed swing area – useful when sewing large items such as curtains.
- An integral accessory box within the body of the machine. These are getting more and more ingenious and handy.
- Auto-stop bobbin rewind is common to most machines to prevent the bobbin from over-filling.
- With some machines you can refill the bobbin without unthreading the machine.
- Transparent bobbin covers are useful so you can check how much bottom thread you have left, useful if you are about to start a long seam or intricate top-stitching.
- Check the machine has good height on the presser-foot lever, to give a little extra lift for fitting bulky fabric under or manoeuvring over thick seams.
- A range of needle positions ensures that the needle can be moved to various positions for straight stitching, stretch stitching, top stitching etc.

- Needle stop up/down. Useful to have needle that stops in down position for embroidery, appliqué top stitching.
- Good range of presser feet for buttonholing, overcasting, zips and hemming. Easy to clip on or press on. Many others are available as optional extras, e.g. 'walking feet' for sewing difficult fabrics such as velvet, which creeps, and sheer fabrics that slip. A walking foot or Teflon-coated foot will feed both top and bottom layers of material through the machine together, eliminating this problem. Some machines have this facility built in.
- If you are a keen dressmaker, a good buttonhole mechanism is essential. With the more basic machines you turn a control for each step of the buttonhole, whereas computer models will do this in one step; you don't have to turn the garment around halfway through the buttonhole. The size of the hole needed for the button can be programmed into the machine's memory to obtain a series of identical holes. Some machines will do differently shaped buttonholes, e.g. square or rounded ends.
- Auto lock-off automatically finishes off.
- Easy threading systems.
- Full rotary hook ensures smooth and jam-proof sewing.

- Consider the type of sewing you do. There is no point buying a hi-tech computer model just for occasional mending.
- Consider weight and size. How portable do you want the machine to be? Compact machines are much lighter but will have smaller dials and controls. They offer a smaller sewing area and may not be as stable when sewing heavier-weight fabrics.
- Try out several different machines. Take some fabric along with you (heavy-weight and sheer). Make sure you feel comfortable with the controls.
- Examine the stitch formation carefully, particularly the underside. Try satin stitching and buttonholes, often the most difficult to perfect.
- Check type of after-sales service available and the location of repair outlets.
- Some manufacturers run sewing schools – it's worth having instruction if buying a computer model or overlocker.

Second-hand machines

It may be worth buying a better-quality second-hand model rather than a cheap new one, but check the guarantees as these vary from dealer to dealer. Look out for older top-of-the-range models that keen sewers are replacing with new computerised models. Buy from a recognised dealer. (The SMTA will give you a list.)

HOW TO MAKE CURTAINS

Fabric quantity

1 Measure the width of the curtain track (see below).

2 Measure the length required.

SILL-LENGTH CURTAINS Either add 5–10cm/2–4in, or if the sill protrudes, deduct 1.5cm/⅝in so that they stop just above the sill.

RADIATOR-LENGTH CURTAINS measure to the top of the radiator and deduct 1.5cm/⅝in so the curtain will not touch the hot radiator.

FLOOR-LENGTH CURTAINS Measure from the top of the track to the floor and deduct 1.5cm/⅝in to stop the curtain from dragging and the hem from wearing.

HEM AND TOP TURNING Add an extra 15cm/6in to each length: this allows for 5cm/2in at the top and a double 5cm/2in hem at the bottom.

PATTERNED FABRIC Measure the repeat and add this amount to each length, except the first, to allow for matching.

3 Multiply this by the number of widths and you'll have the total length of fabric required.

Preparing the fabric

1 Straighten the raw edges along the grain of the fabric: snip about 2.5cm/1in into the selvedge at right angles to the edge. Tear or pull out a loose weft (widthways) thread from the snip to the opposite edge and cut along the resulting line.

2 Check the grain is straight by pulling on the bias until the fabric is smooth and flat and all the corners form right angles.

3 Press the fabric.

Cutting out fabric

- **PLAIN** Measure the length first, keeping the tape measure parallel to the selvedge. Mark the cutting line or pull a thread. Cut along the marked line.

  Cut all the lengths in the same way.

- **PATTERNED** Mark the bottom of the pattern with tailor's chalk. Make sure that after allowing for hem turnings the bottom of the pattern will lie on the hem edge. Trim off surplus fabric, then cut out as above.

  Reposition the uncut fabric next to the previous cut lengths so that the two match exactly. Repeat until all lengths are cut.

- **HALF WIDTHS** To cut half widths, fold one length in half lengthways, pinning selvedge to selvedge. Cut along the fold with sharp scissors.

HOW MUCH FABRIC DO I NEED?

1 Measure the width of the curtain track.

2 Multiply the width by the figure below that corresponds to the type of heading tape:

Standard gathered	1½
Tab top*	1½
Eyelet	1½
Pencil pleats	2½
Pinch pleats	2–2½
Triple pleats	2–2½
Smocked, goblet, Tudor ruff, box pleat	2–2¼

3 Divide this figure by the width of the fabric and this will give you the number of widths of fabric required.

* Allow fabric for the tabs: you should have a tab every 20cm/8in across curtain width. Cut fabric for tabs twice the width of tab required, plus 2cm/¾in seam allowance.

Unlined curtains

1. Cut away the selvedge at each side of all the widths. A tightly woven selvedge left attached to the material will cause the seams to pucker when the curtain is finished.
2. **PLAIN FABRICS** With right sides together, align two lengths, matching the raw edges. Pin and tack down one long side, allowing 1.5cm/⅝in seam allowance.
   PATTERNED FABRICS Match the pattern exactly before stitching. Work from the right side of the fabric, and tack the widths together.
3. Using matching thread, stitch all the tacked seams using flat seams. Support the fabric on a large table when sewing.
4. Turn in the side edges about 2cm/¾in and press. Turn up the hem about 5cm/2in and press.
5. To make mitred corners: make a mark or pin 10cm/4in up from the bottom, at the side edge. Measure 4cm/1½in along the bottom edge and mark or pin (A). Fold in the corner from the mark at the side and bottom edge to form an uneven angle. Press the corner (B).
6. Turn in the side seam again to form a double 2cm/¾in hem, and press. Turn up the hem edge again to form a double 5cm/2in hem and press. Pin and tack the side and hem edges.
7. Slipstitch the side and base hems.
8. With the wrong side facing, place the fabric flat and measure the length up from the hem edge. Turn over the excess at the top and press flat. Trim back to about 3cm/1¼in. On the wrong side, position the curtain tape on the folded top edge. Pin and tack.

Equipment you will need

- Curtain fabric.
- Heading tape.
- Curtain hooks.
- Sharp scissors.
- Pins, needles and thread.
- Tape measure.

TIP
Half widths should be attached to curtain on the outer edges.

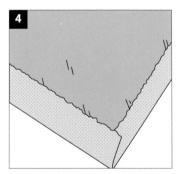

ABOVE How to make unlined curtains, step 4

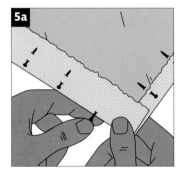

ABOVE How to make unlined curtains, step 5A

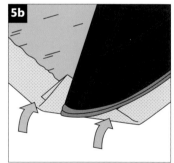

ABOVE How to make unlined curtains, step 5B

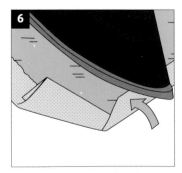

ABOVE How to make unlined curtains, step 6

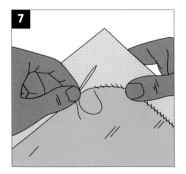

ABOVE How to make unlined curtains, step 7

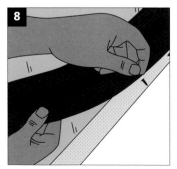

ABOVE How to make unlined curtains, step 8

SEWING HEADING TAPE

- Always sew the top and bottom edges of the tape in the same direction to avoid puckering.
- Always buy a little more tape than you need to allow for position of pleats.
- When buying deep heading tape, choose ones with three or four cords for pulling up, as this is easier and gives a more even result.
- When you've pulled up the cords, don't cut off the ends. Use a cord tidy, available from curtain shops or haberdashery departments, or wind up the excess, or make a cleat. You need to let out the cords when cleaning the curtain.
- Use five hooks to every 30cm/12in of tape for good support.
- To add body to sheer fabric insert Vilene or non-woven interfacing material along the length of the heading.

How to pull up curtain headings

- Knot the ends together securely.
- Anchor over a door handle or table leg so you have something sturdy to pull against.
- Pull evenly and slowly until the heading is gathered up.
- Triple pleats: pleat up the first pleat, and push along to the end, keeping space between the pleats flat.
- Adjust the heading to the correct width and tie up the excess cords.

Detachable lining

Calculate the quantity of fabric as for unlined curtains (see How Much Fabric Do I Need, page 339), but deduct about 2.5cm/1in from the length. The lining should be 1½–2 times the curtain track length.

1. Make as for unlined curtains, steps 1 to 7: see opposite.
2. Measure from the lining hem up and at the top turn under the excess to the wrong side and press. Cut back to about 1cm/½in. Place lining tape or narrow standard heading tape over the top, flush with the folded top edge. Pin, tack and sew in position.
3. To hold detachable linings in place either:
   - Stitch a 2.5cm/1in length of 5mm/½in-wide tape every 30cm/12in along the seam and inside edge of lining. Stitch a press stud to the free end of the tape. Stitch the opposite half of the stud to the top curtain.
   - Alternatively, stitch a length of touch-and-close (Velcro) fastening to the tape and the curtain.

Equipment you will need

- Lining fabric.
- Heading tape.
- Press studs and 5mm/¼in-wide tape or Tape and touch-and-close (Velcro) fastening.
- Scissors, threads, pins, tape measure etc.

Lined curtains

To calculate how much lining you need, measure as for unlined curtains and deduct 10cm/4in per fabric width.

1. Cut out curtain and lining as for unlined curtains, page 340, deducting 10cm/4in from the drop of the lining. Stitch the curtain widths together with flat seams taking 1.5cm/⅝in seam allowance. Repeat for the lining widths.

2. Main fabric: turn in 6.5cm/2½in down each side and press. Turn up 13cm/5in hem and press. Unfold. Mitre corners making single turnings.

3. If the fabric is very light, add curtain weights inside the hem. Slipstitch across mitres at each corner. Herringbone stitch down the sides and along the bottom hems.

4. With the wrong side of the curtain facing, lay it flat, and mark down the centre with pins. Draw in the centre line using tailor's chalk.

5. With wrong sides together, centre the lining over the main curtain material, with the raw edge of the lining level with the curtain top and bottom. Pin fabric and lining together along the centre line.

6. Using thread to match the curtain fabric lock stitch the fabrics together carefully. Begin at the top edge and end just above the curtain hem. Only pick up one thread from the main fabric so the stitches don't show through on the right side.

7. Tack lining to curtain at top. Trim lining level with curtain at sides. Turn in lining side edges by 2cm/¾in, turn up the base hem by 3cm/1¼in. Press and slipstitch the lining to the curtain along the sides and hem.

8. Turn in both top edges by 2cm/¾in. Press. Position heading tape on the curtain top, and stitch in place through all thicknesses. Pull up cords evenly and knot together.

Equipment you will need

- Curtain fabric.
- Lining fabric.
- Curtain weights (optional).
- Heading tape.
- Curtain hooks.
- Scissors, thread, pins, tape measure etc.

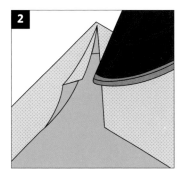

ABOVE How to make lined curtains, step 2

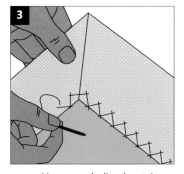

ABOVE How to make lined curtains, step 3

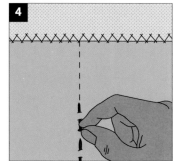

ABOVE How to make lined curtains, step 4

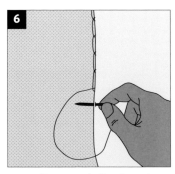

ABOVE How to make lined curtains, step 6

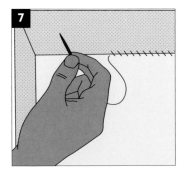

ABOVE How to make lined curtains, step 7

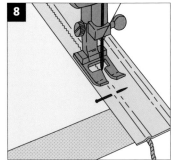

ABOVE How to make lined curtains, step 8

How to make tab top curtains

For a less formal look these are an ideal choice and can be made from any weight fabric. Tabs should be positioned at 20cm/8in intervals across the top of the curtain, with one at each end. Various styles are available such as button, pleated or gathered. These instructions are for unlined tab top curtains with both ends of the tab stitched into the top hem.

CALCULATING FABRIC REQUIREMENTS

1. Fit the pole to the window.
2. Measure the pole between the finials and multiply by 1.5 to give the required fullness. Divide this number by the width of the fabric – rounding up to the nearest whole number.
3. To calculate the length required, measure from the top of the pole to the required length. Deduct the length of the tabs, this should be the length from the top of the pole to 2.5cm/1in above the top of the window frame. Add 17.5cm/7in for seam allowances. Allow extra for pattern matching if required.
4. Work out how much fabric you will need by multiplying the number of widths by the cut length.
5. To work out how extra widths of fabric you will need for the tabs, decide on the number of tabs and multiply by the cut width of each one (finished chosen width x 2 plus 12mm/½in seam allowance). Divide by the width of the fabric and round up to next whole number.
6. To calculate the cut lengths of the tabs, take the finished length and double it and add 10cm/4in seam allowance.
7. Multiply the number of widths by the cut lengths.

MAKING THE TABS

1. Cut out the required number of tabs, each measuring the width and length as previously calculated above.
2. With right sides together, fold each piece in half widthways. Pin and stitch 6mm/¼in in from the raw edge down the length.
3. Turn right side out and press with the seam in the centre of one side.

MAKING THE CURTAINS

1. Cut the fabric to the required size, allowing 10cm/4in for side hems and adding 20cm/8in to the top and bottom hem allowances. If you are using more than one width join widths together with a 12mm/½in French seam, matching pattern where necessary.
2. Turn in a double 2.5cm/1in hem at each side and pin.
3. Turn up a double 7.5cm/3in hem at the lower edge and pin.
4. Mitre the corners.
5. Machine or handstitch all hems and press.
6. Turn down a double 2.5cm/1in hem at the top edge and pin.
7. Fold the tabs in half lengthways to make loops, with the seamed side innermost. Pin at 20cm/8in intervals along the top edge slipping the raw edges into the hem. Make sure you have a tab at each end and the rest are equally spaced and at right angles to top of curtain.
8. Stitch in position close to the top and bottom folds of the hem.
9. Repeat for both curtains.
10. Thread the pole through the tabs and hang the curtains.

TIP

As an alternative to tabs you could make holes in the top hem and add eyelets. Again these should be positioned every 20cm/8in. Eyelet tape is available rather than fixing individual eyelets.

TIP

The length and width of the tabs is up to you but make sure the top edge of the curtain covers the top of the window frame.

Safety and Security

Safety and security in the home is a priority for everyone. This section contains step-by-step instructions on how to administer first aid for a range of common household accidents, a room-by-room safety guide and an overview of home security, including locks, lighting and alarms. There is also a guide to managing household affairs, which will help to keep your home running economically and efficiently.

3

6

9

#

First Aid in the Home

Here you will find step by step instructions on how to apply first aid in an emergency, symptoms to look out for and when to call an ambulance.

- -

COMMON MISHAPS

Animal and human bites

- ⊙ Wash wound thoroughly with soapy water and rinse.
- ⊙ Dab dry and apply a clean, dry dressing.
- ⊙ If the wound is deep and or large, go to the Accident and Emergency Department of your local hospital as soon as possible, and check tetanus cover (i.e. when patient was last immunised).
- ⊙ Always report dog and wild animal bites to the police – while uncommon in the UK, rabies is very serious and potentially lethal.

Asthma attack

Call 999 if:

- ⊙ Patient is having a severe asthma attack that is worse than usual.
- ⊙ Attack is not relieved by their usual medication.
- ⊙ It is their first attack.

Bee and wasp stings

- ⊙ If the sting is still in the skin, brush or scrape it off with a fingernail or a blunt knife.
- ⊙ Do not use tweezers.
- ⊙ Do not squeeze skin; this can spread the venom.
- ⊙ Apply a cold compress or ice pack to relieve pain and reduce swelling.
- ⊙ Call 999 if the patient suffers a severe allergic reaction.

Bleeding

- ⊙ If possible, raise the wounded area.
- ⊙ Apply pressure to bleeding point with a pad of clean cloth.
- ⊙ Apply dressing and bandage firmly. If blood seeps through, put another bandage over the top (don't remove the first bandage). If blood comes through both bandages, remove both and reapply new bandage, ensuring it exerts pressure on the bleeding area.
- ⊙ Seek medical help.

Broken bones

Signs of a broken bone include:

- ⊙ Distortion, swelling and bruising at the site of the injury.
- ⊙ Pain and difficulty moving the injured part.
- ⊙ Send patient to the Accident and Emergency department of your local hospital if they exhibit either or both of the above.

Symptoms of severe allergic reactions

These may include:

- ● Swollen tongue or lips.
- ● Wheezing or shortness of breath.
- ● Rapidly spreading red rash.

Burns and scalds

- Cool area of burn or scald by holding it under a slow running cold tap, immersing in water or pouring cold water over the affected area. Keep the burnt area under water for a minimum of ten minutes, or until pain subsides.
- Gently remove rings, watches and belts from the patient before swelling occurs.
- After cooling, gently remove any clothing that is not sticking to the burnt area.
- If burn has been caused by chemicals, flood area with water for at least 20 minutes and, wearing protective gloves if available, gently remove contaminated clothing.
- If burn is not serious, apply a sterile dressing and secure with a bandage – do not use sticking plaster or ointment, or touch the burn with cotton wool or other fluffy material.

Send the patient to the Accident and Emergency Department of your local hospital if:

- The burn is bigger than the size of the victim's hand.
- The burn is on the face, arms, feet or genitals.
- The burn is on a child.

Choking
ADULTS (AND CHILDREN OVER 8 YEARS)

- Encourage patient to try and cough in order to remove the obstruction.
- Bend patient forward, and strike up to five times between the shoulder blades with the heel of your hand. Check mouth for obstruction.
- If this does not work, stand behind the patient, put one fist between his navel and breast bone and grasp the fist with your other hand. Pull sharply inwards and upwards up to five times (this technique is called abdominal thrust). Recheck mouth.
- If this does not work, repeat sequence three times, alternating five back slaps with five abdominal thrusts. You must always send the patient to hospital to get checked out if you have performed an abdominal thrust.
- If the patient loses consciousness, dial 999. Resuscitation might be required. Repeat steps 1–3 until help arrives.

CHILDREN (1–7 YEARS)

- Encourage the child to cough.
- Bend child forwards and give up to five slaps between the shoulder blades. Check mouth.
- If this does not work, stand or kneel behind child and give abdominal thrusts as for adult, but using less pressure.
- Dial 999 if this does not work. Repeat steps 1–2 until help arrives.

Cuts and Grazes

- Rinse with running water to clean dirt and grit.
- Dab dry and apply sterile dressing. Do not use creams or ointments.

First aid courses and kits

- Taking a recognised first aid course will equip you with the basic skills needed to deal with many common ailments. St John Ambulance holds first aid courses throughout the country. Call 08700 10 49 50 or visit the website at www.sja.org.uk for details.
- It is also advisable to keep a basic first aid kit handy in your home, so that you are always ready to deal with minor injuries and household mishaps. To order a first aid kit from St John Ambulance Supplies, call 020 7278 7888.

CHOKING IN INFANTS (0–1 YEAR)

1 Check mouth.

2 Lay infant face down along your forearm and slap firmly between the shoulder blades. Repeat up to five times. Check mouth and remove obstruction with one finger.

3 If this does not work, lay the infant on its back on your arm or lap.

4 Using two fingers, press down in middle of chest, one finger's width below nipple. Press sharply up to five times (this is called a chest thrust). You must always send the patient to hospital to get checked out if you have done a chest thrust.

5 Check again for obstruction, and remove if possible. Check mouth again.

6 Dial 999 if this does not work. Repeat steps 1–4 until help arrives.

- ⊙ Check tetanus cover (i.e. when patient was last immunised).
- ⊙ Get person to consult their GP if the cut oozes pus or is sore and inflamed.
- ⊙ Send patient to the Accident and Emergency Department of your local hospital if the cut is deep.

Electric shock
- ⊙ Look at the patient first, don't touch.
- ⊙ Check the power is off.
- ⊙ Once you are sure the patient is away from the source of electricity, check their breathing and circulation.
- ⊙ Resuscitation may be required.
- ⊙ Send patient to the Accident and Emergency Department of your local hospital.

Fainting
- ⊙ Get patient to lie down flat if not already on the ground and raise the legs.
- ⊙ Kneel down in front of them and support their raised legs by putting their ankles on your shoulder.
- ⊙ Make sure there is plenty of fresh air in the room – open windows if necessary.

Fits
Do not restrain patient, but try to prevent any injuries. Call 999 if:

- ⊙ The patient is fitting and is not known to be epileptic.
- ⊙ The patient is an epileptic and the fit is lasting longer than usual.

Minor wounds
- ⊙ Raise and support injured part if possible, and apply direct pressure to wound.
- ⊙ Protect wound with an adhesive plaster or sterile dressing.
- ⊙ Check tetanus cover (i.e. when patient was last immunised).

Send patient to the Accident and Emergency department of your local hospital if:
- ⊙ Any object is embedded in the wound. Do not remove it yourself.
- ⊙ Bleeding does not stop.

Nosebleeds
- ⊙ Get person to sit down and lean forward.
- ⊙ Ask them to breath through their mouth and squeeze the soft part of their nose for at least ten minutes.
- ⊙ Reassure and help them if necessary.
- ⊙ Send patient to the Accident and Emergency department of your local hospital if nosebleed is severe or lasts more than 30 minutes.

Poisoning or overdose
The effects of poisoning depend on the substance that has been swallowed, but signs and symptoms can include the following:

- Vomiting.
- Impaired consciousness.
- Pain or burning sensation.
- Empty containers in the vicinity.

Send casualty to the Accident and Emergency department of your local hospital but first try to discover what they have swallowed. Also be aware of the following:

- Send remains of poison with them, e.g. the bottle etc.
- Resuscitation may be required if the patient collapses.

Rash

- Send patient to the Accident and Emergency Department of your local hospital immediately if rash does not fade under pressure.
- Inform the Accident and Emergency Department of your local hospital of a possible diagnosis of meningitis.

Shock

- Loosen the patient's clothing and lay them down, raising their legs if possible.
- Keep the casualty warm by wrapping a blanket or coat around them; however, do not use hot water bottles or a heater to warm them.
- Moisten lips with water, but do not give patient a drink or anything to eat or smoke.
- Check and record the patient's breathing and pulse frequently.
- Reassure patient and make them comfortable.
- Seek medical attention if necessary by calling 999.

Splinters

- Clean area with soap and water.
- Sterilise a pair of tweezers by passing them through flame from a match or lighter, and allow to cool.
- Do not touch the ends of the tweezers, or wipe away soot.
- Holding tweezers as close as possible to skin, but without touching, grip end of splinter and gently pull out
- Carefully squeeze wound to encourage a little bleeding.
- Clean and dry the area and apply adhesive dressing.
- If the splinter breaks, go to the Accident and Emergency Department of your local hospital or your GP.

Sunburn and windburn

- Cover skin with light clothing or a towel.
- Remove patient to shaded area.
- Cool the affected area by sponging with cold water, and give sips of water.
- Do not break blisters.
- For mild burns, put on calamine lotion or an after-sun preparation.
- If burns are severe, seek medical aid.

Meningitis

Signs and symptoms of meningitis may include any of the following:

- High temperature.
- Vomiting.
- Severe headache.
- Neck stiffness.
- Joint or muscle pains.
- Drowsiness.
- Confusion.
- Dislike of bright lights.
- Seizures.
- Rash.

Home Safety

Accidents in the home are responsible for thousands of deaths each year, and at least three million people need medical attention for injuries sustained at home. Yet many of these injuries could easily be avoided with some common sense, safety measures and greater awareness of potential problems. Every household is different, so take a good look at your home, room by room and carry out a safety audit to see where the possible hazards lie.

KITCHEN

New kitchens

If you are planning a new kitchen, it is easy to get caught up with the overall look and the smart new appliances you would like to include, but don't forget to consider how practical and safe it will be. You'll need to consider layout, design and positioning of appliances carefully.

Inheriting a kitchen

If, on the other hand, you have inherited a kitchen, you may also be taking in potential problem areas, and it is important to be aware of badly planned or problematic fitted kitchens, particularly if you have young children. Ask yourself:

- Is the lighting adequate over worksurfaces?
- Are the plug sockets well positioned or will flexes trail near the sink or cooker?
- Are the edges of worktops or corners of tables sharp? Should you consider using covers for the tables?
- Is the kitchen ventilated adequately? Proper ventilation is vital, especially if you have gas appliances in the kitchen, and to provide a clean, airy environment.
- Are there unhygienic gaps in tiles on worksurfaces? Seal with waterproof sealant. Germs can be harboured in crevices.
- Is there safe storage for hazardous cleaning chemicals or medicines?
- Are there glass-fronted doors that would be safer with laminated glass?
- How even and ruck-free is the flooring?
- Have you inherited electrical appliances with unknown histories? Get them serviced.
- Did the previous owners install the kitchen themselves? Check how secure they are, especially wall units.
- How strong is the shelving? Don't overload shelves, and put heavy and fragile items in a low, but secure position. Make sure the shelves have shelf retainers to prevent them tipping forward if a heavy weight is placed at the front.

Medicines

- Always lock all medicines and chemicals away in a high cupboard, preferably in the kitchen where there are always more adults around than in a bathroom.

- Try to buy cleaning products and medicines in child-resistant containers.

- Never transfer gardening or cleaning liquids to squash bottles, in case children mistakenly think they are drinks.

- Don't take labels off anything; it may be potentially dangerous.

- If you have medicine left over, don't keep it or throw it in the dustbin. Take it back to a chemist where it can be destroyed.

HAZARDS IN THE KITCHEN

These are used every day and we often neglect to treat them with the respect they deserve.

COOKERS

- Don't leave saucepans unattended.
- Try to get into the habit of using the pan that best fits the size of hob ring available. If possible, use the rings at the back of the hob and remember to turn saucepan handles inward (so they don't hang over the edge of the cooker or get dangerously hot over another switched-on hob ring.
- Never fill the pan more than one-third full with oil, or two-thirds full when the food has been added.
- When cleaning, switch the cooker off at the wall panel. Don't be tempted to line any part of the cooker with kitchen foil to keep it clean – fat from foods may catch fire.

KETTLES

- If you have a corded kettle, buy a curly cord or check to see if you can wind spare flex underneath so that the kettle cannot be sited too near the front of the worksurface.
- Switch off and unplug at the wall socket before you fill or pour it.
- Fill with enough water to cover the element or base plate completely.
- If buying new, opt for a cordless kettle and site the power base near the back of the worksurface.

KITCHEN KNIVES

Don't keep sharp knives loose in the utensil drawer. Ideally, use a knife block at the back of the worksurface, or a wall rack (but don't overload it). Knives should also be washed separately from the rest of the cutlery to avoid bad cuts from hidden knives in soapy water.

TOASTERS

- Never use a knife to loosen bread stuck inside a toaster.
- Unplug the toaster and allow to cool, and only then use a wooden spatula to remove the bread.
- Don't disturb the heating elements – poking about with objects is likely to break them.
- Follow the manufacturer's instructions for removing loose breadcrumbs. Many models have removable crumb trays.

IRONS

- Fill a steam iron before you plug it in.
- Make sure the iron base is dry before using it.
- Fit a flex holder to the ironing board. Don't wrap the flex around a hot iron, and never leave an iron face down.
- If you are worried about leaving the iron after use, buy a model that automatically switches off if left in the ironing position after a few seconds.

BATHROOM

Many accidents take place in the bathroom. Inevitably, in an area where you are dealing with water and slippery surfaces there are a number of possible dangers.

- Baths should be filled with cold water first, then hot.
- Always use non-slip floor mats.
- Make sure the areas around your bath and sink are properly sealed with bath sealant. This can be a breeding ground for germs in a hot, wet environment, and the sealant will prevent damage to the room below and also prevent wet rot.
- Consider fitting an extra bath grip for elderly members of the family to assist them in getting in and out of the bath.
- There should be no electrical plugs in the bathroom, but if you live in a house which has not been rewired, watch out for this and get an electrician to advise you.

HOUSEHOLD CLEANING AGENTS

- **CAUSTIC SODA** This is a very strong alkali. If using caustic soda crystals, remember that they are corrosive and can burn the skin, so follow all the safety instructions on the can to the letter. Wear rubber gloves and avoid inhaling fumes. Always use in a well-ventilated room and if overcome by fumes, get to an open window as quickly as possible. For accidental splashes on the skin, rinse the affected area well under cold running water.

- **CHLORINE BLEACH** Always store bleach in a safe place. Don't be tempted to add it to any other household chemicals or proprietary cleaners to speed things up, as it may combine with the other ingredients to form toxic gases which can be extremely dangerous. If you spill any on your skin, wash the affected area immediately with plenty of cold water. If any is accidentally swallowed, drink plenty of water followed by plenty of milk, then contact a doctor immediately.

- **SOLVENTS (INCLUDING ACETONE AND TURPENTINE)** Keep all grease solvents well away from flames and sparks. Avoid inhaling fumes and vapours, and always work in a well-ventilated room. Avoid prolonged contact with the skin as it may make it feel dry. Keep well out of reach of children.

- **AMMONIA** This is a poison. Don't allow it to be taken internally and never open the bottle caps to smell the contents – the result can be most unpleasant. Avoid contact with the eyes, skin and clothing. Wear rubber gloves, always work in a well-ventilated area and store the bottle in a cool, dark place. If spilt on the skin, flush liberally with cold water. If ammonia is swallowed, make the person drink plenty of cold water and then contact a doctor immediately.

- All lights should be on pull cords, not switches.
- Make sure the shaver socket is situated well out of reach of children.
- Radiant heaters, towel rails and mirror lights must be fixed firmly to the wall. They should have permanent wiring (which means sockets) and pull-cord switches. Don't fix them above the bath or near a shower. Heaters must be out of reach of people using the bath and heaters with metal frames must be securely earthed and bonded to other metalwork in the bathroom. Have all work carried out by a qualified electrician.
- All shower heaters should have antiscald thermal cut-outs. If buying new, opt for thermostatic models that are designed to stabilise any temperature fluctuations while you're showering. Mechanical mixer showers are less expensive, but do not offer the same degree of temperature control and safety.
- If you have a gas water-heater in the bathroom, there should be adequate ventilation at all times.
- Hot-water thermostats should be set at 54°C/129°F.
- Always ensure that the radiators and towel rails are kept at a safe temperature.
- Install bath shower screens or curtains to reduce water escaping from the bath on to the bathroom floor.
- Take care not to leave medicines, cosmetics, household cleaners, razors and blades within reach of children.

- Never use loose rugs in the bathroom. All rugs should have safety grips.
- Never use a portable electric fire, hairdryer or other electrical equipment in the bathroom.

LIVING ROOM, STAIRS AND HALLWAY

TV and stereo
- Switch off when you are not using them and take the mains plug out of the supply socket.
- Never try to repair them yourself – call in a specialist.

Lighting
- Switch off light fittings before removing bulbs.
- To avoid causing a fire, do not use higher wattage bulbs than the makers recommend on shades and fittings.

Flooring and stairs
- Don't polish floors under loose rugs or carpets, or place them at the base of stairs.
- Ensure stair rods are securely fixed and the stair carpet is not loose.
- Check that banisters and railings are firm.
- Stick down loose tiles and sheet vinyl. Neaten off frayed carpet edges.
- Make sure lighting is adequate over the stairs.

WINDOWS

Each year, thousands of people in the UK are injured by glass in their homes. If you have young children, it may be worth considering safety glazing in fully glazed doors, door side panels, wet areas, low level glazing and glass in furniture. Glass in any window, whether it is double glazed or not, can be difficult to break. It is important to have at least one window wide enough to be used as an emergency exit in every room. With double glazing, always make sure the key to the window is at hand (put it on a hook on the wall beside the window, out of the reach of children).

Heating hazards
- Never hang things over a convector or storage heater.
- Don't place mirrors over fireplaces – it encourages people to stand too close to them.
- Portable heaters can start a fire if misused. When using, make sure the heater has a permanent safety guard and is clean and well maintained. Always turn them off before going to bed.
- If you have any heaters on time switches, keep them well clear of curtains and furnishings. Never fit time-switched or delay controls to an electric fire.
- Open fires cause thousands of house fires every year. Use a spark guard over the fire when you are not there to keep an eye on it. Don't forget to have the chimney swept each year.

WHICH SAFETY GLASS?

There are various types, so for guidance, go to an expert, such as a member of the Glass and Glazing Federation (see Useful Organisations). Use and look for glazing materials that meet BS 6206. As a general guideline:

- Toughened glass is up to five times stronger than ordinary glass so is difficult to break. When it does, it shatters into thousands of pieces, rather like a car windscreen.
- Plastic safety film can be stuck to one side of ordinary glass to hold the pieces together if the glass breaks.
- Laminated glass crazes but the pieces are held together by a strong, transparent interlayer, so minimising any injuries.

CLEANING UP BROKEN GLASS

- Always ensure you wear shoes for protection against shards of glass.
- Never pick up broken glass with your bare hands – this can result in pieces of glass sticking into your skin and these can be so tiny they are impossible to see and, therefore, to remove.
- Sweep the broken glass carefully into a dustpan, wrap it in several sheets of newspaper and throw out immediately.
- If the breakage is on a floor area, after carefully sweeping up the obvious glass as above, vacuum the entire area to remove any unseen shards of glass. It is best to replace the cleaner bag immediately to avoid any accidents at a later date when the possibility of glass in the bag has been forgotten.
- If the breakage was on a worksurface, sweep up as above, then wipe all around the area with a thick, damp pad of paper towel. This should then be discarded immediately.
- Rinse with a wet paper towel and wipe dry.

BEDROOMS

Hairdryers

Don't wrap the flex around the handle when you have finished with it and disconnect when not in use.

Smoking

Never smoke in bed due to the risk of fire.

CHILDREN

What may seem like a perfectly safe home can suddenly become an assault course of potential hazards once there are children in the house. Pinpointing the hazards can be difficult, particularly if your home is only invaded by small children occasionally, but accidents are a major health problem for children so it is important to try.

ELECTRIC BLANKETS

Electric blankets account for over 5,000 fires each year in our homes. Only use electric blankets that conform to the BEAB approval mark or relevant British Standard. Not all blankets can be left on all night: check the instructions. Overblankets are designed to be tucked in at the sides and bottom of the bed, without any of the heated area being folded under – always follow the manufacturer's instructions. Check the blanket regularly for wear, and have it serviced every two to three years. If your blanket or any part of the wiring shows any of these danger signs, you should have it checked or replaced:

- Fraying fabric.
- Scorch marks.
- Exposed elements.
- Creasing or folding.
- Soiling.
- Damp patches.
- Tie tapes damaged or missing.
- Worn flex.
- Loose connections.

Babies

Babies less than nine months old have limited mobility, and accidents frequently result from the perilous positions they are put in by others. Over half the accidents in this age group are from falls, such as rolling off furniture, or out of cots.

Toddlers

Toddlers often fall off and collide with furniture. They are also learning to climb stairs and are more likely to set off unaided. The increasingly mobile active child can come into contact with medicines and household chemicals, small, sharp or hot items and other household hazards. A high proportion of burning, poisoning and foreign body-type accidents occur among this age group.

Childproofing your home

Realistically no home can be 100 per cent childproof, but here are some ways you can make a child's environment a little safer. Don't worry if you cannot implement them all, but concentrate on those that are most applicable to your own children, depending on age and inclinations.

STAIRS

- Fit stair gates – there's little to beat the challenge of climbing the stairs. Barriers or gates should be fitted at both the top and bottom of the staircase. Look for one that conforms to BS 4125 as this ensures the spacing between the bars and the gap between the lower edge and the floor is much too small for a youngster to wriggle through. Buy a gate that can easily be opened with one hand.
- Install two-way light switches at the top and bottom of the stairway so you can light your way from either direction.
- Board up horizontal balcony rails so they cannot be used as a ladder.
- Never allow a child to play on or near stairs.
- Fix loose carpets and check that the carpet tacks are not poking through worn patches.
- Keep halls well lit and fit a dimmer switch on the landing light, to keep the light on low through the night in case your child wants to go to the toilet.

WINDOWS

Small children love climbing up to peer out of windows, but once up there, it is all too easy for them to topple out.

- Vertical window bars may save a toddler's life, but do make sure they can be removed in the event of a fire. Less conspicuous are window limiters, which only allow the window to be opened a small amount.
- Keep sash windows locked at the bottom.
- Don't put anything that a child can climb on to near a window.
- Check that patio doors, shower screens, glass tables and conservatories are all made from safety glass. If they are, they will be marked with BS 6206 or have the Kitemark. If not, replace them with laminated or toughened glass, or at least cover with window safety film.

Fire safety and fabrics

- If your upholstered furniture and bedding was made before the new fire safety regulations that first came into effect in 1988, consider improving their resistance to fire. If making loose covers for a sofa or armchair, look for match-resistant fabric (ask your fabric supplier for advice). Flame retardant sprays can be applied to fabrics, carpets and upholstery. These may not always be as effective as fire-resistance treatments that are applied by factory process. Check that the spray is suitable for furniture and follow the manufacturer's instructions carefully. Be warned: spray treatments that are not water resistant will simply wash out if liquids are spilled on the treated fabric.

- If having your furniture reupholstered, replacement covers and any material supplied in the course of the reupholstering service must now meet the fire-resistance requirements. You could also have the filling replaced with a fire-resistant one or use a fire-resistant interliner fitted between the new cover and the existing filling material to help protect the old filling in the event of a fire.

IN THE KITCHEN

Young children are at risk of serious injury from hot liquids and cooking fat. If a child is scalded, run cold water over the scald right away. Don't stop to remove clothing. Then get medical help for anything but the smallest incident.

- Always keep hot drinks well out of children's reach. Don't hold a baby when you are drinking. If you're passing a hot drink to someone else, make sure a child isn't underneath.
- Keep the kettle at the back of the worksurface out of reach of toddlers, and keep the lead as short as is practical.
- Knives and utensils must be locked away or stored well out of reach.
- Simple childproof locks should be fitted to kitchen cupboards and medicine cabinets.
- Try to cook on the back rings of the hob, and always remember to point pan handles inwards or towards the rear. Use a cooker guard to prevent toddlers pulling pans off the hob.
- An oven built-in above floor level ensures that at least one hot area is out of reach of children. If not, buy an oven door guard, which will at least diffuse some of the heat.
- Doors on washing machines, dishwashers and tumble-driers should be kept closed – don't forget that these doors too can get hot when the machine is in use.
- To prevent children fiddling with the controls on a washing machine or tumble-drier, get a control visor to cover them.
- Never store soft drinks and alcohol in the same cupboard.
- Choose drinks with child-resistant lids where possible.
- Keep aerosol cans well out of reach.
- Make sure bookcases and wall units are well-secured and cannot be pulled over or used as climbing frames.

IN THE LIVING ROOM

- Guards should be fitted to all fires and radiators. Check that there is at least 20cm/8in between the heat and the guard, otherwise the latter could get dangerously hot.
- Always extinguish cigarettes properly and empty ashtrays. Always keep cigarettes, lighters and matches out of reach.
- Consider fitting door slam protectors to stop little fingers being crushed.
- Rugs should be fitted with adhesive underlay.
- House plants should be checked for poison and possible allergic reactions.
- Consider fixing ornaments and movable objects in position with sticky pads or other fixings.
- Play pens are advisable for toddlers on those occasions when you simply cannot be in two places at once.
- Store any alcohol out of reach.

Electrical appliances

- Use child covers on electrical sockets and place furniture in front of sockets wherever possible.
- Use a residual current device for areas in which your children live and play. It will automatically cut off the power in a fraction of a second, before your child receives a serious shock. It plugs into the socket, and you then plug the appliance into it.
- Make the TV and sound system strictly out of bounds.
- Look for trailing flexes and clip them out of harm's way.
- Never leave a lamp without a bulb.

IN THE BATHROOM

- Try to ensure that the floor covering is water resistant without being slippery, and that any rugs have a non-slip backing. In the bath itself, a non-slip rubber mat will help prevent a child from slipping under water. Children can drown in just a few centimetres of water, so never leave them alone in the bath – even for one moment.
- Ensure that children cannot reach the lock on the bathroom or toilet door, so that they cannot lock themselves in.
- Baths should always be filled with cold water before hot. Mix the water well and test the temperature with your elbow before you put a baby in.
- If bathing a baby in the bath, check that the stand for the bath is solid and fits the bath well. If the bath is part of a changing unit, make sure that the mat or cover lifts off or slides away completely, and cannot drop down on to the baby while in the bath. Once a child can stand unaided, stop using the baby bath on a stand. Either use an adult bath or put the baby bath inside the adult bath.
- For toddlers who delight in flushing toys, shoes etc. down the toilet, buy a lid lock.

IN THE BEDROOM

- If the child has just graduated to his/her first grown-up bed, consider using a bed guard to stop them falling out.
- Non-toxic nursery paint should be used for children's rooms and furniture.
- Encourage children to be tidy and put toys away after use, to avoid tripping and falling over objects on the floor.
- Check that the wardrobe doors can be opened from the inside in case your child ever gets stuck.
- Don't leave medicines, cosmetics, nail scissors etc. within a small child's reach.
- Don't put under-fives in the top deck of a bunk bed.
- Changing units: Make sure the unit is stable when the drawers and cupboard are both open and closed. Make sure you can reach everything you need without leaving your baby alone on the unit.
- Cribs: Make sure the stand for the crib is firm and that swinging cribs can be locked into a resting position.
- Moses baskets: Make sure the fabric lining is stitched firmly into place and that there are no loose folds which could smother a baby.
- Cots and cot beds: Always put the side up when the baby is in the cot. Drop the mattress base to the lowest position as soon as your baby can sit up. Don't put the cot near curtains or anything that might help the baby climb out.
- As soon as the baby starts trying to climb out of the cot, either switch to a bed or leave the drop side down. Keep the bedroom door closed or put a gate across it so that he/she cannot get out of the room at night.
- Move beds and other furniture away from windows to stop children climbing on them and falling out.

Children's play equipment

- Check that outdoor play equipment is sturdy and well maintained.
- Paddling pools must always be emptied and ponds always covered when children are around. If you have a garden pond or swimming pool, fence it.
- Climbing frames or swings should be placed on a grassy surface or ground covered with bark chippings.
- Sand pits should always be covered when not in use to stop animals fouling in them.

GAS, ELECTRICITY AND FIRE

Most of us worry at one time or another whether we've unplugged the iron or switched off the gas cooker when we go out. But few people are aware of the full potential for accidents caused by the domestic services that we take so much for granted. Explosions caused by gas leaks don't just happen from leaving the cooker on accidentally – they are far more likely to be caused by appliances and central-heating systems that don't get regular servicing. Of course, the biggest fear is fire, but more people die without ever seeing any flames as they are overcome by smoke or toxic fumes first. Make sure all the family know the location of stoptaps, fuse-boxes, mains power switch, gas mains and what possible exit routes to use in case of fire.

Gas

- Have all gas appliances professionally installed and serviced. Make sure there is adequate ventilation at all times.
- Switch off instant water heaters before getting into the bath.
- Don't look for a gas leak with a naked flame and don't smoke near one. Open windows and phone the National Gas Emergency Service (see Useful Organisations).
- Always fill a paraffin heater outdoors and never while it is still burning.
- Gas installers who are registered by the Gas Safe Register must always be used for jobs involving gas appliances, by law.
- Install audible carbon monoxide (CO) detectors that will alert you in time to the presence of carbon monoxide gas that can be produced by unsafe gas appliances (see right). Carbon monoxide is deadly and can kill within minutes, but it has no smell or taste, so otherwise there is no way of detecting its presence. Detectors are available from DIY stores and usually cost around £20.
- For further advice on gas and electrical safety, see Gas and Electricity, pages 390–2.

Electricity
HOUSE WIRING

Faults in wiring cause many fires and some deaths in the UK each year. You should have your household wiring checked every five years. This may sound excessive, but the cost is a small price to pay for electrical safety. If your wiring circuits are more than 25 years old, or if your sockets are of the round, two-pin variety, you almost certainly need to replace them. Before checking or repairing wiring sockets, always turn off the power at the mains switch.

Get expert help for all repairs and wiring. If you think there may be a fault, immediately contact an electrical contractor who is approved by the National Inspection Council for Electrical Installation Contracting (see Useful Organisations). Always keep a torch or candles handy in case of a power cut.

Carbon monoxide (CO) detector criteria

Carbon monoxide detectors should:

- Comply with British Standard EN 50291 and have a British or European approval mark, such as a Kitemark. CO alarms usually have a battery life of up to five years.
- Be fitted in any room where there is a gas appliance. Read the manufacturer's instructions before installing the detector.
- Have an audible alarm. Don't use the 'black spot' detectors that change colour when carbon monoxide is present. They don't make any sound, and you need an alarm that will wake you up if you're asleep, or you may not be aware of early CO symptoms until it is too late.

Residual Current Devices (RCDs)

Residual current devices can be fitted by a professional at the mains supply where they offer protection throughout the home, or in a plug or socket suitable for portable equipment such as a lawnmower, drill or appliances which need an extension lead. The RCD can detect damage to the cable and other faults through change in current flow. It automatically disconnects the power, reducing the risk of electric shock, and warning you that there is a fault. RCDs must be fitted to any electrical supply expected to serve appliances outdoors.

PLUGS AND FLEXES

Faulty flexes cause many fires and injuries per year.

- ⊙ Always buy shatterproof plugs which are stronger than most.
- ⊙ Don't overload plug sockets. Use adaptors as little as possible. Ideally, you should use a separate socket for every appliance, but this is not always possible. If you regularly use two appliances from one point, consider getting a double socket fitted.
- ⊙ Make sure you are using the correct fuse for the appliance.

Fire

Never underrate the danger of fire. There are tens of thousands of accidental fires in the home each year, which kill hundreds and injure many thousands of people.

SMOKE ALARMS

Buying a smoke alarm could help save the lives of you and your family and save your home. Smoke alarms are self-contained units that detect fires and give a warning alarm. They are usually fitted to the ceiling, but can also be incorporated into a light fitting, and are powered either by battery or mains electricity. In a standard alarm, the battery will need to be replaced every 12 months. You should also test the battery once a week to ensure it is still working. Vacuum dust from inside the alarm regularly. Test the sensor annually by waving a smoking candle underneath it – the alarm should go off. Replace smoke alarms every ten years.

FIRE-FIGHTING EQUIPMENT

For most homes, a fire blanket in the kitchen and a multi-purpose dry powder, foam or water-type extinguisher in the hall are adequate. But it depends on the fire risks in your home and what you can afford. A multi-purpose dry powder or foam extinguisher in the garage, shed or car would complete the package. If in doubt about which type to have, contact your local fire brigade for advice.

SMOKE ALARM CRITERIA

Smoke alarms should:

- ⊙ Comply with BS 5446 and preferably carry the British Standard Kitemark.
- ⊙ Be placed within 7m/23ft of rooms where fires are likely to start and within 3m/10m of bedroom doors.
- ⊙ If wall mounted, be between 15–30cm/6–12in below the ceiling.
- ⊙ Be fixed in positions that allow easy maintenance, testing and cleaning.
- ⊙ Be sited well away from areas where steam, condensation or fumes could cause false alarms.
- ⊙ Be away from areas that get very cold or very hot.
- ⊙ If installing a mains-operated smoke alarm, it must comply with current wiring regulations. Always use a qualified electrician for installation.
- ⊙ There should be at least one smoke alarm on each floor of the home.

DIY SAFETY

One of the biggest causes of home accidents is the enthusiastic DIYer who overlooks essential precautions when using power tools, hazardous chemicals or even climbing a ladder.

- Never cut corners, always use the right tool for the job and keep tools in good working order.
- When drilling walls, avoid areas adjacent to power sockets and the area at right angles and vertically above them. Power cables are usually routed in these locations.
- Always take care of hands and wear gloves whenever possible.
- Always wear protective clothing – face masks, safety goggles, ear muffs or knee pads – when undertaking jobs which may be dangerous or harmful.
- Prepare yourself and your working area properly before you begin.
- Fuels, glue, cleaners, paints and lubricants all contain chemicals that can be harmful. Always follow the manufacturer's safety guidelines and instructions for use. Ensure that you have adequate ventilation.
- Use residual circuit devices when operating power tools.
- Put blade covers on knives and chisels when not using them.
- Keep children away from all DIY work.

Ladder safety

Falling off ladders and chairs is one of the most frequent DIY accidents.

- Always check ladders are suitable for the job.
- Use a special ladder tray that fits on to the ladder instead of carrying paint and tools.
- Never over-extend an extension ladder or exceed the recommended angle of a ladder.
- Use stabilising legs when using a ladder extension.
- Always wear a tool belt rather than carrying a whole handful.

THE GARDEN

The most obvious danger is the use of electrical equipment, such as mowers and hedge trimmers, but you must also consider barbecues and the plants themselves.

- Never use mains-powered electrical appliances outside when it's raining.
- When using mains-powered electrical appliances outside the home, wear rubber-soled shoes. Never mow the lawn or trim a hedge barefoot.

PLANTS AND GARDENING HAZARDS

- Think carefully before siting hazardous plants where they will be accessible to children or animals. If in doubt about certain plants, take a clipping along to your local garden centre (be sure to wear protective gloves) to get it identified.
- Rose bushes (and any other plants with thorns) should be well pruned.
- Dispose of broken or cracked plant pots.
- Always put away garden chemicals, such as fertilisers and weed killers, in a safe place.

- Be extremely careful of poisonous plants. The best known are Laburnum seeds, Yew berries and Foxgloves, but there are a number of other common plants with dangerous seeds or berries, such as Privet, Laurel, Rhododendron and Hydrangea. Teach your child never to eat seeds or berries from the garden.
- If your child has eaten parts of, or been poisoned by, an unknown plant, seek medical advice immediately. Don't make the affected person sick, and take a sample of the plant with you.

- Keep electrical cables behind you, and continually check that they are still behind you.
- All electrical equipment should be unplugged during cleaning or adjustment, and should be put away after use.

Outdoor glazing

Consider installing safety glazing in the conservatory, patio doors, at low levels, and in any balustrades. Contact the Glass and Glazing Federation for further advice and local member stockists (see Useful Organisations).

Barbecues

- Site these in a clear location away from fire hazards and children.
- Never sprinkle barbecue coals with flammable fluids.
- Always read the instructions and follow the recommended procedure for how to start or relight a barbecue safely. The quality of charcoal varies from brand to brand – the better the quality, the easier it will be to light and stay lit.

Outdoor wiring

- Use a single flex without joins and never work with wet or torn flex.
- Don't run power tools from a lamp socket. Have a proper, earthed socket fitted by a qualified electrician.
- If you use a socket to supply electricity to equipment outdoors, such as lawn-mowers or hedge-cutters, protect it with a residual current circuit breaker.
- Sockets installed outdoors must also be under cover, unless special weatherproof units in a waterproof box are used.

BARBECUE PROBLEMS

If your barbecue won't light, or the fire is flagging:

- Never use petrol, paraffin, methylated spirit or other flammable fuel to light or revive it.
- Do use special lighting fluid, pastes and fire lighters. Be sure they have totally burned away before you start cooking or they may taint the food with an unpleasant flavour.
- Add more charcoal, not fluid, to the sides of the barbecue.
- Try a different brand of charcoal.

- Try 'light the bag' instant-burn charcoal (place the whole bag in the barbecue bowl and light it).
- Buy a grill starter (a mini chimney that uses burning newspaper and the pull of air up the chimney to light the coals. Then pour the hot coals into the barbecue bowl).
- If the fire goes out, use tongs to place the coals in a steel bucket. Then start again with fresh charcoal.

Home Security

Every year, thousands of people suffer a burglary or break-in. The thought of a thief breaking into your home, picking through your personal belongings, and making off with the most valuable and resalable items is both unnerving and frightening. Yet, without turning your home into a fortress, you can employ a few simple precautions to make it less attractive – both to opportunists and to professional thieves.

DON'T MAKE THINGS EASY

Your greatest weapon against a burglar is time. The more barriers you place in front of him (such as fences, locked doors and windows) the less attractive your home will be. The chances are he'll give up and move on to the next house.

The area in which you live

Burglary isn't restricted to poor urban areas, although the chances of being burgled are greater in some areas of the country than others. There are, of course, centres of high risk but burglary is a national problem. Be prepared for house contents insurance to be affected by the level of crime in your area. You may not know whether you live in a high-risk area but your insurers certainly will! Before buying expensive locks etc., check with your insurer to see if he has any particular recommendations.

Planning home security

When considering home security measures, consider your lifestyle, what restrictions you are willing to impose on yourself and the practical aspects of any security devices.

BASIC SAFETY PRECAUTIONS

Often people could do more to protect their homes and possessions but are put off by the cost. But many homes lack even basic security precautions that cost little or nothing at all. Here are some initial steps:

- Don't leave doors and windows open.
- Use the locks already installed.
- Don't make it easy for the burglar: lock up tools and ladders.
- Don't 'advertise' the valuables you have.
- Don't advertise your absence.
- Ask neighbours to be vigilant (and do the same for their property in return).
- Ask your local crime prevention officer to visit your home and recommend ways to improve household security.

Neighbourhood watch

- Setting up a Neighbourhood/Home/Community Watch group can help reduce the level of crime and the fear of crime in a neighbourhood. They are not intended to encourage people to set up as a vigilante group, but just to be on the lookout for suspicious behaviour and to enhance the security of the members' own properties.

- If you are interested in setting up a scheme in your area, find out first whether others share your enthusiasm before approaching the police.

Encouraging burglars

Take a good look at your house from the outside, and consider whether any of these questions apply:

- Do you live in a quiet area?
- Is the house secluded or hidden from the road?
- Do you live in a poorly lit and neglected area?
- Could a burglar work unseen behind high walls and fences?
- Is there easy access to the rear, e.g. a footpath or a canal towpath?
- Do you have an open porch where a thief could hide?
- Does the house have side access, which would allow a burglar to work, unnoticed? Has the side passage been left unlocked?
- Are the locks on your external doors adequate?
- Is there a way through the garage to the house?
- Do you have valuables on display?
- Do you have a shed or garage containing tools, ladders, ropes etc, that the thief could use to break in?
- If you have a garage (or coal bunker) with access to your house, are the locks adequate?

All these features could encourage a burglar to target your home, and remedying them will make your house less vulnerable to theft.

THE LIVED-IN LOOK

It is easy for a thief to tell who's in and who isn't. The house may be in darkness, post left in the letter box or milk bottles left out on the doorstep. Over 80 per cent of burglaries occur when a house is empty, so try to keep your house looking occupied when you are out, and even when you're away on holiday.

- If going away, don't leave your car full of luggage overnight. Load it just before you leave. Lock everything in the boot or under the cover of the hatchback if you're trying to save time in the morning.
- Cancel the milk and papers.
- Keep curtains closed during the day will make it look as if no one is home. It is better to leave them open and get security lighting (see pages 366–7). If you have a large number of valuables, it may be worth considering an electric curtain-track system. You can programme it to open and close your curtains at pre-set times.
- Tell the local police station you'll be away.
- Mow the lawn before you go away.
- Buy a couple of automatic time switches for inside lights (from about £20). These can be used to turn on a light, TV or radio and help give the impression that you are in. They work at pre-set or random times.
- Don't announce that you're going away to a shop full of people. Only tell people who need to know.
- Don't leave valuable items like TVs, videos or stereos visible through windows.
- Don't have your home address showing on your luggage for the outward journey. Put this only on the inside of your cases.

Crime facts

- The average burglary takes place in daylight.
- On average, each of us will be burgled twice in our time as home owners.
- Once burgled, you may have a repeat visit a few weeks later when the thief has calculated that you have received an insurance payment and have replaced your TV and video etc.
- Most thefts are opportunist.
- Most burglaries take place between 2pm and 4pm on a weekday afternoon.
- Thieves are usually aged between 15 and 18 and live locally.
- On average, it takes two minutes for a burglar to go through your home.

HOW BURGLARS BREAK IN

Front door 25 per cent.

Rear/side door 23 per cent.

Rear/side window 43 per cent.

Front window 3 per cent.

Upper window 3 per cent.

TIP
Use Royal Mail's Keepsafe scheme when you go away on holiday. Under the scheme Royal Mail will hold all your mail until you return home up to a maximum of two months.

- If going out for an evening, leave a light on in a room, not the hall (many people leave the hall light on when they are out); and perhaps leave a radio playing.
- Ask a neighbour to keep an eye on the house, collect post and free newspapers left in the letter box, sweep up leaves, and even mow the lawn if you're going to be away longer than a fortnight. If they have two cars, perhaps one could be parked in your driveway. You can repay the favour by doing the same for them when they go away. Warn the key holding neighbour not to put your surname, address or even house number on your keys in case they fall into the wrong hands.
- A message recorded by a strange voice on your answering machine announcing that a guest is staying in the house while you are away will fool everyone except close friends. Never leave a message saying you have gone away.
- Just before setting off on holiday, it's worth spending a quiet couple of minutes on the doorstep to check you've done everything, and have taken all you need with you.

DOOR SECURITY

Doors are the obvious point of entry for a thief. In 30 per cent of burglaries, the burglar's life is made even easier by the owner leaving a door or window open.

Door locks

Look on the front face of the lock for a BS Kitemark, which ensures that the lock is of a reasonable quality.

If in doubt about the suitability of your existing locks, check with your local crime prevention officer or a locksmith who is a member of the Master Locksmiths Association (see Useful Organisations). Also find out from your insurance company whether the locks are adequate to meet their requirements.

When it comes to locks, most of us don't know our twin cylinders from our automatic deadlocks. Luckily, most lock manufacturers now put helpful advice on the packaging of their products to indicate which door it would be suitable for (front/back, internal/external).

There are basically two kinds of door locks:

MORTICE LOCKS (usually seen on back doors): Are sunk into the door so are more difficult to force out.

CYLINDER RIM LOCKS (usually used on front doors): Are screwed to the surface, which makes them easier to fit.

When you are buying a lock for an entry/exit door, look for a deadlock, which means the bolts lock into the extended position and can be opened only with a key. This means a thief can't smash a nearby panel, reach round and open the door from the inside, nor can he enter by a window and then leave by that door.

Don't forget that it's no use having a top quality lock if the door itself is of poor quality and can easily be forced. You can strengthen a door by

Home sitters

Leaving home for the pleasures of a holiday is often marred by the worry of burglary. Although you may be able to enlist neighbours to a degree, if you have pets or a conservatory full of precious plants, it may be worth considering a professional home sitter. Obviously you don't want just anyone living in your home, so be sure to choose a professional company that:

- Has been in business a reasonable length of time.
- Vets its home sitters/caretakers carefully and takes references.
- Is insured against any problems that might occur such as the home sitter having an accident, simply not being up to the task, or damage to the home.
- Provides full back-up for the home sitter so that if he/she falls ill, or has to leave the assignment, the company is still bound to honour the contract.
- For peace of mind and to ensure everything runs smoothly, meet the prospective home sitter/caretaker before the day you hand over the keys.

TIP
Never leave a spare key in a convenient hiding place. Burglars instinctively know where to look.

TIP
Change locks when move into a new house, as you don't know how many sets of keys may be around.

using a door-reinforcement kit, which includes two solid plates that bolt on to each side of the door around the lock area.

Front door

- ◉ The front door should be a minimum of 44mm/1¾in thick. Check this, especially if you live in a flat with a communal main door.
- ◉ It needs a high-security automatic deadlocking night latch with lockable internal knob or handle (to prevent entry by breaking glass and releasing the latch) and a five or seven-lever mortice deadlock (to BS 3621). These cost about £60. (A two-lever mortice lock isn't strong enough and should be used only on inside doors.)
- ◉ Fit a spyhole and a door chain.
- ◉ The letter box should be at least 40cm/15in away from the locks.
- ◉ Fit hinge bolts to reinforce the hinge side of the door.
- ◉ Check that the doorframe is fixed firmly to the brickwork and is strong enough to hold the lock in place.

Back door

Over 60 per cent of burglaries occur through the back door, so it needs particular attention.

- ◉ Fit a high-security two-bolt mortice lock, or ideally a five- or seven-lever lock (to BS 3621).
- ◉ Fit mortice bolts top and bottom.

Patio doors

Don't rely solely on factory-fitted locks for patio doors. These should be fitted with multi-point locks and an antilift device to stop a thief from lifting the door off. If the hinges are visible from the outside, the doors should have hinge bolts as well.

Glass-panelled doors

These should be fitted with laminated glass, which looks like ordinary glass, but is very hard to break. It may cost more than double the price of ordinary glass, but you should only have to put it in once.

Laminated glass is made of two or more layers of ordinary glass, bonded together with a strong, clear plastic interlayer. When attacked, the glass itself may break but the broken pieces will adhere to the interlayer and remain as a barrier. It's a good idea if there are many youngsters or vandals in the area, and it won't cause serious injury if you fall against it.

Laminated glass is available from members of the Glass and Glazing Federation (see Useful Organisations). Also, fit a cylinder rim lock with a lockage inside handle. If a thief breaks the glass to reach in, the door cannot be opened.

WINDOW SECURITY

The most common way for a burglar to break into your home is through a back window. If you're not sure about whether a window is large enough for a thief to climb through, the rough rule is if you can get your head through an opening, he can squeeze inside.

Identifying mortice locks

- ● To find out if you only have a two-lever lock (really too light-weight for the back door and only suitable for internal doors) look at the face plate in the edge of the door. This may be marked with the number of levers.
- ● If not, look at the key. If it looks cheap, or has very few notches in the bit of the key, then it is probably only a two- or three-lever lock.

Who's at the door?

Most callers are genuine, but we've all heard tales of burglars getting into people's homes by pretending to be the gas man or from the council. So it's sensible to be cautious. If you live alone, be especially careful to check the identity of unknown callers.

- ● Ask to see the identity card of meter readers or service men.
- ● For blind or partially sighted people, electricity, gas and water services can arrange for their staff to use an identifying code word.
- ● If callers claim to be from local services, ask them to wait, shut the door and ring the office to check.
- ● Call a neighbour or ask the visitor to come back when someone else is in.
- ● Don't keep a door chain on all the time, only put it on when someone calls, otherwise it may be difficult for others to get in in an emergency.
- ● Don't leave your handbag or wallet unattended in any room where a caller may need to enter. Stay with the caller and keep all other doors closed.

WINDOW SECURITY

- Fit window locks. Over 60 per cent of homes still do not have window locks. You can buy them for casement, skylight or sash types. Pay particular attention to ground-floor windows and those above flat roofs, near drainpipes or fire escapes.
- Glue the slats of louvre windows in place with epoxy resin, or fit them with special louvre locks.
- Consider replacing vulnerable downstairs windows with laminated glass.
- Install security grills on vulnerable windows, especially at the rear of the house. Many DIY stores and ironmongers sell decorative grills that can be attached to the wall quite easily with security screws.
- Shutters can be attached to the exterior wall, although they can be fitted on the interior if you do not want to change the appearance of your property. Both types are operated from the inside. They are usually aluminium or foam-filled aluminium, which also provides insulation. Contact the British Blind and Shutter Association for a list of local suppliers (see Useful Organisations).
- Even small windows, like casement windows, skylights or bathroom fanlights might need locks.
- Check the window frames are in good repair. There's no point having a good lock if the burglar can simply push in a rotten frame.
- Always have internal beading on double glazing: otherwise thieves can simply slit around the rubber seal and remove the whole window with a suction pad.
- If you live in a bungalow, for secure ventilation use window limiters/child safety locks. These limit the window opening to no more than 15°.
- Make sure there are no ladders left lying around and shut all windows – even small cloakroom ones – when you go out.

SECURITY FOR FLATS

- As the front door of an individual flat is often not as strong as the main, outside door, it's worth upgrading a thin door with a more solid one. And it needs as many locks and bolts as the main communal door.
- If a fire escape runs up the side or back of the flats, make sure nearby doors and windows are secure.
- Talk to other residents, or the landlord, about installing a door telephone entry system. Bear in mind, however, these aren't foolproof and you must use them sensibly. Don't let anyone in for another flat or hold open the door for a stranger whose arrival coincides with yours.

SECURITY LIGHTING

The more visible the burglar is when he is trying to break into your house, the less he will like it. It will also make him less sure about whether the house is occupied if you have security lighting coming on and off while the house is actually empty.

Plug-in timer controllers

These switch lights, radio, TV etc., on and off while you are away so that the house appears to be occupied. They are simple to install, not difficult to set and several of them can be used around the home and moved around wherever you need them. The most basic time switches simply plug into a socket outlet (like an adaptor) and then whatever you want the time switch to bring on – such as a lamp or TV – is plugged into it, to give the impression that you are home.

Electromechanical time switches are set by moving little markers or tappets around a dial. They operate, usually to the nearest 15 minutes, at the same time every day (or every week, with a seven-day timer) unless you move the tappets. Some switches will turn on at random within specified active periods. Electronic, programmable time switches can be set more accurately to the nearest minute. There may also be an option for setting different times each day.

Security wall switches

You can't fit a security light switch in place of a normal light switch to control a central room light, wall lights or an exterior porch light. It will normally be set so that it only brings on the light when it gets dark, but methods vary. There is a wide range of levels of sophistication.

- Simple photocalls, which turn lights on at dusk and off again at dawn.
- Switches that allow setting of the exact times at which lights will switch on and off.
- Switches that come on randomly.
- Switches that re-create the householder's own habits over a 24-hour period.

Outdoor security lights

If you live in a large property, it may be worth considering illuminating large areas such as a drive or lawn with mains-wired floodlighting. This will spread an even, practical light, ideal both for deterring burglars from shady corners, and for alfresco entertaining in the summer.

Alternatively, spotlighting may be more effective. Key areas to spotlight are over the front door, garage, shed, passages and any other obvious entry points.

Rather than having lights that stay on all night and require you to turn them on and off, consider installing passive infra-red lighting. This only works when someone approaches: a passive infra-red detector senses body heat and automatically operates a light (turning it off again after a few minutes). You can buy both integral lights, or separate lights and passive infra-red sensors.

SAFES

If you live in an area where burglary is common, a safe may be useful for small valuables and cash. Look for one that conforms to BS 7558. It's also worth checking with your insurer whether this will reduce your premium, and how much cover they will give for items in a safe.

Think carefully before buying second-hand (unless you are confident the safe has been reconditioned to BS 7582). If you move a house with an old safe, do not use it. Old safes may look secure, but the technology used will almost certainly be outdated, making them easy to break into. The most common types of safe used in the home are wall safes, which

Safety warning

- Unless you are competent at DIY, mains lighting should always be installed by a qualified electrician. There are strict safety standards for electrical installation to mains supply and you need a separate garden circuit with waterproof external plug sockets.

- For a list of electricians in your area ring the National Inspection Council for Electrical Installation Contracting, or the Electrical Contractors' Association (see Useful Organisations).

Tips for outdoor lighting

- Don't forget that outdoor lighting should have separate wiring from your household system with external plug sockets, and should incorporate a Residual Current Device (RCD), see page 358, and fuse. For installation, always use a qualified electrician.

- Mount light fittings high so no one can tamper with them and adjust the beam slightly off ground if you have cats or dogs, so they can't activate them accidentally.

- When positioning floodlighting or security lighting bear in mind that your neighbours may not want the night sky illuminated into the small hours. Be considerate.

can be set in brickwork or fixed to the wall, and floor safes, which are sited under the floorboards. You can buy small, free-standing safes but a thief may think you have something worth taking and decide to remove the whole safe.

It is important to ensure the safe is securely bolted to the floor or wall, and in a position where a thief would have difficulty prising it out. Have the safe professionally installed for maximum security. For a reputable company it's best to contact the Master Locksmiths Association (see Useful Organisations).

BURGLAR ALARMS

If after you've taken as many practical, physical and common sense measures as you can you still feel insecure, then it may be worth considering fitting a burglar alarm. This isn't a substitute for having good locks, but may be worth it if you live in an inner city or a secluded spot and have a lot of valuables. You will have to use it conscientiously, even if out for only a few minutes – the major danger time for burglaries.

Don't be rushed into a decision by the offer of a discount, or frightening stories of crime levels. You will need to discuss your security risks with a local crime prevention officer. Do not deal with doorstep salesmen of burglar alarms. You'll also need to think about who you would appoint as your key holders for occasions when you are away. You will have to give them – and your family – full instructions on using the system.

If installing a burglar alarm you should always inform the police and environmental health department.

Some insurance companies offer discounted premiums if you have an 'approved' burglar-alarm system. But think carefully before trying to get a reduction on this basis as it often involves you in regular maintenance checks by an approved company and, in the event of a burglary, if the alarm wasn't on you may have difficult claiming.

An 'approved' installer usually means one registered with the British Security Industry Association (the trade association) or the National Security Inspectorate (the industry inspectorate) – see Useful Organisations.

Don't expect any insurance discounts for DIY-installed alarms.

What system?

A burglar alarm consists of three main parts:

❶ The detection device.
❷ The control equipment. You should be able to set just part of the system, such as door, window and living room detectors at night when you are asleep.
❸ The signalling device/s.

Think of an alarm system as a stand-in for you: the detection devices are your eyes and ears, the control unit is your brain and the signalling device is your voice.

What will it cost?

● The cost of a professionally installed burglar alarm system will vary according to its level of sophistication. Installation charges, too, will reflect the type of house, its size, the number of entry points etc. Expect to pay, on average, £400–700 for the installation and £60–100 upwards per year for the maintenance.

● A DIY-installed system from your local DIY or hardware store will cost from £100, again depending on the complexity of the system. (See DIY Burglar Alarms, page 370 for further details.)

● To ensure you are charged the right price for the job, it is essential to obtain a minimum of three quotes from reputable installers before making your choice. Quotations are usually free and don't place you under any obligation. Remember, the cheapest installation is not necessarily the best option.

PROFESSIONAL ALARMS

⊙ Check that the system meets BS 4737.

⊙ Be suspicious of firms that offer you a ready-made package. For a burglar alarm to be really effective it needs to be tailored to your home and your particular needs. A professional installer should send someone to look at your home to determine what kind of lifestyle you lead so he can draw up the most appropriate form of protection before quoting. For instance, pets may cause a problem if allowed to run free in the area of movement detectors; or if you are elderly you may have visits from grandchildren who are attracted to personal-attack buttons placed at low level.

⊙ Don't forget to ask how much servicing and maintenance will cost and who pays if the system breaks down, or there is a false alarm.

⊙ You should also check that all equipment has a 12-month guarantee.

⊙ Establish which part of the system you own. Signalling devices are invariably rented from the company. If the control equipment is rented you will lose this if you change alarm companies.

POINTS TO REMEMBER INSTALLING ALARMS

⊙ Interfering signals from local police and taxis, etc., can prevent radio systems working properly, and some systems don't show this is happening.

⊙ Effective range of radio systems can be dramatically reduced by internal walls and floors, especially if reinforced with steel.

⊙ It is illegal to sell or advertise non-approved products. Certain radio frequencies have been allocated to these systems so that they don't interfere with the police, emergency services or cordless phones, etc. Talk to other alarm users and a couple of installers about the possibility of radio frequency interference if you happen to live near public services.

⊙ Look for BS 6707 on Intruder Alarm Systems for Consumer Installation.

⊙ Ensure that the control unit is accessible, but out of reach of young children and pets.

⊙ Make sure you can close windows and doors so they don't rattle or vibrate when there is heavy traffic or wind. Physical vibration may set off the burglar alarm.

⊙ If your system has an alarm clearly audible outside your home you should notify the local police station that you've installed an alarm within 48 hours of installation, and give them the names and addresses of at least two key holders. Show the key holders how to operate and silence the alarm The bell or siren should be set to cut out after 20 minutes.

⊙ Local authorities' environmental health officers have power to switch off alarms causing a noise nuisance. You may also be liable to a fine if you do not notify the police or key holders.

⊙ Rather than annoy your neighbours through noise, co-operate in looking after each other's property and taking notice if the alarm sounds, or suspicious activity takes place.

BE WARNED
Control panels and bell/siren boxes contain rechargeable batteries to keep the alarm working in the event of a power cut. These must be serviced regularly.

DETECTION DEVICES

These fall into two categories: fixed-point detectors and movement detectors.

FIXED POINT DETECTORS

Normally fitted to doors and windows and can be:

- ⊙ Switches that operate when a door or window is opened.
- ⊙ Vibration sensors, which can be fitted on walls, windows or doors to detect physical vibration.
- ⊙ Pressure sensors: hidden pressure pads that trigger the alarm when stepped on.

MOVEMENT DETECTORS

Normally fixed to the corner of a wall near the ceiling and can be:

- ⊙ Acoustic, to sense airborne vibrations such as the sound of breaking glass.
- ⊙ Passive infra-red, which react to a change in temperature as an intruder moves within a defined area.
- ⊙ Air-activated, which sense changes in air pressure caused when doors or windows are opened or broken.

THE CONTROL PANEL

This is the nerve centre of the alarm system and is usually situated in a cupboard or under the stairs. Once activated by any of the detection devices it sets off the bell/siren, or the central monitoring station.

SIGNALLING DEVICES

BELL ONLY This sort of system makes a noise when set off. These are designed to draw immediate attention to the break-in but rely on neighbours or passers-by to alert the police.

Bell-only systems are sometimes fitted with flashing lights fitted on the underside of the bell box. This gives a visual warning that the alarm has activated, which is useful for identification within a row of alarmed houses. The light will continue to flash even after the bell/sounder has cut out.

It's worth having a bell that sounds inside the house as well as out. This is important, as you may not be able to hear the outside bell: if you are in bed asleep, for example. It also stops a burglar from hearing what is going on outside, making him more vulnerable.

MONITORED SYSTEM When a monitored alarm is set off, it sends a coded message down the phone to a central monitoring station, which in turn calls the police or a nominated relative or friend. This system comprises a bell-only system with the addition of a digital communicator to link the alarm to the monitoring station. All the major alarm companies run their own continuously manned monitoring stations.

The police will accept calls signalled over the phone line from these types of system, provided the alarm company is approved. A list is available from crime prevention officers.

TIP

Remember that a highly visible alarm-bell box will provide a deterrent, and if your house is vulnerable to attack from the rear, it may be worth fitting a dummy bell box at the back. Buy spares at DIY stores.

DIY burglar alarms

- ● If you are a competent DIYer with experience in electrics, you will be able to fit your own system. Wire-free systems are the easiest to fit and should only take three or four hours, but you can also get DIY-wired alarms which are cheaper, but can take a day's work to install.

- ● In a wire-free system there are no wires between the detection devices and the control panel. Each device contains a small transmitting device that signals to a receiver in the control unit. Apart from simplicity of installation, the advantages of having a wire-free system are that you can also use the system to protect garages and a garden shed, and take it with you if you move house.

- ● Their main disadvantage is that the police won't accept call signals from them. Therefore they are restricted to local, audible signalling or signals to nearby friends or neighbours.

PERSONAL-ATTACK BUTTON You press a personal-attack button (usually situated by the bed with a second one by the front door) if you sense an intruder. These are deliberately operated by a push button and reset via a key. This device is used to activate the alarm at any time, whether the control unit is switched on or off.

NEW HOUSES

If you're buying a brand-new house, look for the builder's Secured by Design symbol. This is awarded to flats and houses that meet police standards for home security, which include substantial door locks, secure boundaries and limited access to the rear. Secured by Design is a police initiative involving builders and architects to improve the security of new and refurbished homes, see Useful Organisations.

Hot property

The most attractive items for burglars to steal are portable, high-value goods that can't be identified easily. If you mark your valuables, it will be harder for them to be sold and easier for the police to return them, if they're found.

- For absorbent surfaces, such as documents or fabrics, use a non-absorbent ultraviolet pen.
- For hard surfaces, such as plastic or metal, use a hard surface ultraviolet marker. Write in an inconspicuous place, as it's visible and can discolour some finishes.
- Etch your postcode, followed by the house number or the first two letters of the house name on to cameras and stereo equipment. Also make a record of serial numbers. Then if they are stolen and later found, the police can identify them and return them to you.
- Ask your local crime prevention officer for postcoded property warning stickers to display in the front and back windows of your house.
- Keep a list of valuable items with the make, model number and serial number.
- Hide holdalls and suitcases, as thieves find them handy for taking valuables away.
- Keep a note of your credit cards, cashpoint card, pension/allowance book, bank and building society account numbers and the companies' emergency telephone numbers so you can advise them of the loss immediately.
- It's a good idea to have colour photographs taken of jewellery, antiques, silver etc. that can't be properly marked. Without an accurate description of stolen items there is little hope of them being recovered (see Recovering Stolen Goods, page 373).
- Valuables should be stored in the bank when you go on holiday, and items of lesser value hidden away.

False alarms

- False alarms make up the vast majority of all alarm calls responded to by the police in England and Wales, wasting millions of pounds in lost police hours per year. If police are called out to false alarms at your property four times in a 12-month period, you may receive a warning letter from the local police. If the false calls reach seven in a year, the police may stop responding completely.

- It is not just the police who are inconvenienced by false alarms: it could cost you, the householder, dearly too. If your system has been installed by an approved engineer, the British Standard requires him to reset the system once it has been set off, accidentally or not, to prevent burglars cancelling the alarm. Your insurance cover and premium may also be affected if police cover is withdrawn. Find out what caused the false alarms and put it right. There's nothing guaranteed to annoy the neighbours more than an alarm bell continuously and needlessly going off.

HOUSE CONTENTS INSURANCE

There are over 100 insurers offering household insurance. All cover theft or attempted theft. Decide whether you want indemnity or new for old cover.

INDEMNITY Reduces the amount paid out, to allow for wear and tear, and depreciation.

NEW FOR OLD COVER Pays out the cost of replacing an old item with a new one, so is more expensive.

Contact at least one independent intermediary to find a variety of quotes. When you take out cover you will need to estimate the total, new replacement value of all your belongings (with the exception of linen and clothing. Nearly all policies make a deduction for wear and tear on these). Most insurers will now insist on you having certain minimum levels of security before they will give you cover. If you improve the security of your home above their minimum requirements, some insurers will give you a discount off your contents policy. For example, if you:

- Belong to a Neighbourhood Watch Scheme.
- Have locks approved to BS 3621 fitted to all front and back doors.
- Have an alarm system fitted and serviced by a member of the National Security Inspectorate (NSI), see Useful Organisations.

STRANGERS IN THE NIGHT

If you wake in the night and hear intruders, don't rush downstairs and confront them. Dial 999 immediately, if you can. Even if you can't give details, the police will respond. If you can't get to a phone, stay put until the thief has left and it's safe to move.

For the elderly or disabled who may not be able to reach a telephone during a break-in, a community alarm can be fitted. The alarms work as a normal telephone with the additional feature that they can automatically dial a control centre (run by local housing authorities, social services departments or commercial monitoring companies). It is triggered by pressing a button on the telephone or on a pendant around the neck. Contact your local housing authority, social services or Help the Aged.

STOPPING GARDEN THIEVES

Did you know that there is a 1 in 20 chance that something will be stolen from your garden in the next two years, whether it is powered tools, plants or ornaments? Garden tools are often used to assist the burglar breaking into the house, with ladders and garden spades and forks particularly helpful to your unwanted visitor.

Insurance tips

- Think carefully before installing an alarm. If you don't have it regularly serviced by a NSI-approved company and it wasn't switched on at the time of the burglary, you may invalidate your policy and be unable to make a claim.

- Fitting your own DIY kit alarm won't reduce an insurance premium.

- Check your policy for exclusion clauses. If you fit devices but don't use them, it may affect your cover.

- It's wise to check your policy for holiday cover. Leaving the house empty for over 30 days may restrict it.

- Policies often ask you to specify valuable items worth over £500.

- Check the policy covers garden items.

GARDEN SECURITY

- Put away all tools and equipment and ensure that all outside sheds and store cupboards are securely locked when not in use.
- Bring the tools inside if you do not have a garden shed or outbuilding.
- Install automatic security lighting outdoors (see Security Lighting, page 367).
- Use good-quality locks to secure your gates.
- If you have a burglar alarm, why not extend it to cover outbuildings and sheds?
- Photograph valuable garden plants or ornaments for identification if stolen.
- Postcode garden tools and equipment.
- Check that your household insurance policy covers theft from the garden and outbuildings.
- Use prickly plants to provide extra natural protection around your property. Suitable thorny defenders include Blue Spruce (dense blue, spiky needles), Creeping Juniper (thorny stem and foliage), Holly, Chinese Jujube (very spiny, pendulous branches), Firethorn (thorny stem), Juniper (prickly foliage), Blue Pine (spiky, needled stems).

RECOVERING STOLEN GOODS

If your home has been burgled, the chances of ever seeing your most valuable belongings again are, realistically, rare. If items are security marked the chances increase considerably, and if you have photographs and detailed descriptions of precious items, even better.

MALICIOUS PHONE CALLS

A harassing or malicious phone caller can make you feel unpleasantly vulnerable in your own home. To combat such calls, follow the procedures below.

- Call your telephone service provider for advice on what to do if you get one of these calls. (For BT, the department to call is the Malicious Calls Bureau on 0800 661 441) Such advice includes, for example: don't disclose your name, phone number or any other personal information, say nothing, walk away from the phone and gently hang up without saying anything after ten minutes.
- The operator can intercept all your calls (usually for about two weeks) or block certain numbers from getting through to you, or block calls coming from withheld numbers.
- Your telephone number can be changed.
- BT can organise Malicious Call Identification free of charge but only as part of a police investigation.

FURTHER INFORMATION

Further Information on crime prevention, a great deal of information is available from the Home Office (www.homeoffice.gov.uk).

And finally ... whatever security devices you fit, ensure they are simple enough for all the family to use every day.

Recovering antiques

If the stolen items are antiques, try contacting:

- **THE ANTIQUES TRADE GAZETTE** a weekly newspaper with a section on stolen goods, circulated to the antiques trade internationally (see Useful Organisations).

- **THE ART LOSS REGISTER** Any item worth over around £1,000 in value can be registered for £50, or you may take out an annual subscription for around £400 which permits you to register up to 25 stolen items. The information is kept on a permanent database of stolen art and antiques and checked against auction catalogue (see Useful Organisations).

Managing Household Affairs

Keeping track of the household budget, cutting down on spending and knowing where to find all th important financial, household and personal documents, are key to keeping a home running smoothly.

PLANNING THE FAMILY BUDGET

Budgeting wisely will help you make the most of your income and make sure that you end up in credit at the end of the month. You can find budget planners to download on the Internet or you could create your own list. Make sure that you include all your income and expenditure. Many planner lists only feature the basics, and it is surprising how much you can spend on essential occasional costs like dental visits or dry-cleaning. Once you have completed the plan, it's easier to identify areas where you can save – for example, if you buy your telephone, broadband and cable television separately you may save by switching to a bundled service.

Assessing your income

Your main income is likely to be from salary – your (and your partner's, if appropriate) net monthly income after tax and pension deductions. If bonuses or commission are a feature of your job, include them in your budget, but don't over-estimate them; you should make an allowance for the fact that these are not guaranteed. You may also have investment or rental income or benefit allowances that should be included.

Evaluating your expenditure

The best place to start to work out what you spend your money on is with your last three bank and credit card statements. They will list your standing orders, direct debits and regular spending such as supermarket visits.

It can help to think through your spending in groups: monthly costs and annual costs. Many annual costs, such as council tax, can be paid monthly by arrangement, and you can budget for annual costs like holidays by dividing the cost by 12 and setting money aside in a savings account every month. You may want to split the costs in each category into essential and discretionary to help you identify areas for potential savings.

Filing and tracking financial records

Just like a business, every household needs to keep financial records. An organised, accessible system will save you time and anxiety and make it easier for you to control your budget.

TIP
Make sure you are claiming all the allowances you are entitled to – to find out what you might be entitled to refer to money, tax and benefits at www.direct.gov.uk.

TIP
When you change utility supplier make sure you have cancelled the standing order or direct debit for the old service. Some companies may keep taking payments and you will then have to take time and effort to get a refund.

MONTHLY OUTGOINGS SHOULD INCLUDE

- ⊙ **HOME COSTS** Such as mortgage, council tax, water charges, electricity/gas, service charges for flats or a repairs contingency, and contents and buildings insurance.

- ⊙ **LIFE INSURANCE AND PENSION PAYMENTS** If you pay for your pension separately, not if it comes off your pay. You may also have an income protection plan that covers your mortgage if you lose your job through redundancy or ill health.

- ⊙ **LOANS AND CREDIT CARD REPAYMENTS** The credit card amount included here should be the cost of repaying your existing credit card debts, and not ongoing spending that you will pay off and that is accounted for elsewhere in the plan.

- ⊙ **FOOD AND HOUSEHOLD EXPENDITURE** As well as your food bills, this category should include cleaning products, stationery and basics such as shampoo and soap.

- ⊙ **COMMUNICATIONS** Services such as telephone (landline and mobile) and broadband.

- ⊙ **MOTORING** Car insurance, petrol, parking, repairs and other running costs. You may want to factor in a savings amount for car replacement.

- ⊙ **TRAVEL COSTS** Season tickets for any members of the family travelling to work or school on public transport.

- ⊙ **PROFESSIONAL COSTS** Such as subscriptions to a union or professional body and work-related journals.

- ⊙ **ENTERTAINMENT** Magazines and newspapers, cable or satellite subscription, theatre and cinema tickets.

- ⊙ **WELLBEING** Hairdresser, cosmetics, dental fees or plan, proprietary medicines, optician, fitness classes or gym subscription.

- ⊙ **CLOTHES AND SHOES** As well as a wardrobe budget, don't forget to include some money for tights, dry-cleaning and shoe repairs.

- ⊙ **GIVING** Gifts and cards, charity donations.

- ⊙ **EQUIPMENT REPAIR AND REPLACEMENT COSTS** You should factor in a sum for replacing household items that are beyond repair. If you can afford it, you will probably want to include an amount for updating and investing in new items, too. This includes things like refrigerators, TVs, and home computers.

- ⊙ **CLEANING OR GARDENING SERVICES** You may not employ a regular cleaner or gardener, but you may use occasional professional services such as carpet cleaning, drains maintenance or a tree surgeon.

PAPERS YOU NEED TO KEEP ... AND THOSE YOU DON'T

- ⊙ Keep receipts for expensive items in case you need to make an insurance claim. Shred receipts for consumables like food monthly, once you have checked the receipt against your credit card bill.

- ⊙ Financial documents: keep bank statements, utility, phone and council tax bills, payslips and official forms such as P60s, and credit card bills for the period defined by your tax status.

- ⊙ If you are employed, then keep interest statements from bank and building society savings accounts, share dividend vouchers, information relating to capital gains, costs and income from rental property, expenses receipts until the form for the year they apply to has been filed and accepted.

- ⊙ If you are self-employed you will need to keep your personal and business records for six years for tax purposes.

- ⊙ You can avoid accumulating paper by setting up online accounts with banks and suppliers. Just make sure that you print off any records you need for tax purposes as most such accounts only allow you to access a year's worth of past records.

ECONOMISING

Saving money shouldn't just be an emergency measure. Get into the habit of sensible economising on a regular basis and you will have money to spare for that rainy day or large purchase without taking on debt. Many economies are simply a matter of good organisation and investing a little time to make them will pay off almost immediately.

Simple savings

Look at your household budget and identify those areas where you can reduce costs without too much pain.

- Can you combine phone, mobile, broadband and TV for a cheaper deal?
- Look at money-saving websites, such as www.uswitch.com, every year to make sure that your deals on insurance and utilities are the best for your circumstances.
- Plan the week's meals and make a shopping list before you leave the house. You'll save money on impulse purchases and avoid buying more food than you need (it's estimated that the average household throws away more than 18 per cent of the food they buy untouched).
- If you have space to store products like lavatory paper and canned goods then consider buying in bulk either when on special offer or at your local supermarket or at a discount store.
- Clip coupons and make the most of loyalty schemes to maximise your discounts on everyday items.
- When the weather is dry, use an outdoor clothesline, rather than the tumble-drier; your laundry will smell fresh and you'll save on electricity.
- Ice cube trays are great for freezing small quantities of leftover liquid, such as stock or wine, or puréed foods, such as tomato paste, for cooking. You can also freeze leftover fresh herbs in a cube of water. When you are ready to use them in a soup or stew, simply add them to the pot.
- Set up a secret gift storage box and top it up with interesting things you find at sales or on holiday trips, as well as homemade presents, through the year. You will always have something to hand when you get an unexpected invitation, and you won't have to make expensive last-minute purchases before a birthday or Christmas.

Creditwise

If your budget is restricted because of expensive credit card debt, then focus on paying it off. The best way to do this is to look out for 0 per cent interest rate deals and move your credit card balances. Take the opportunity of the interest-free period to pay down your debt.

Alternatively, you may be able to get a personal loan at a lower rate. Once you have shifted your debt from the card make sure that you pay off your balance in full every month. If you have several cards, then reduce your collection to two and keep a close track of your balances.

Green tips

Take the old wartime 'make do and mend' slogan to heart and fight pressure on your budget by making your own gifts, clothes and children's toys. Turn the process into an enjoyable leisure activity; you'll find that crafting is a great way to relax. If you are concerned about the environment, you'll be gaining green points, too. You can even recycle things you already own or are about to throw away to save on materials.

For example:

* Use newspaper to wrap presents; bright ribbon will make it look stylish rather than cheapskate.
* Make a tote bag from an old pair of jeans – cut off the legs, sew up the bottom to form the body of the bag and make straps from the leg material.
* Turn a single woollen sock into a monkey puppet – wash it in the machine so that the fabric felts, embroider simple features on the foot face, stuff with toy filling and sew to secure.
* Use odd socks instead of a new duster to polish shoes. Not only will this save money, they are easier to use as you can slip them over your hand.

RUNNING YOUR HOME SMOOTHLY

A disorganised home will only add to stress levels. You'll save time in the long run if your household paperwork is well organised and the organisation system you choose is easy to operate. A day or two setting up an effective system will pay dividends.

Essential documents

Keep the following in a secure, accessible place. Take photocopies and store these elsewhere (in a safety deposit box or with a trusted relative) in case of fire or flood.

* Birth and marriage certificates.
* Passports.
* Driving licence (paper filing part).
* Share certificates.
* Wills.
* Property deeds (if not with the mortgage company).
* Educational certificates.
* Professional paperwork such as CRB (Criminal Records Bureau) clearance.

Household calendar

There are calendars available that enable you to fill in details for each member of the family in a separate column so that you can see everyone's daily commitments at a glance. You may also want to have a separate home planner folder that enables you to create a monthly schedule for household chores and file correspondence to action.

APPOINTMENTS Plan in regular appointments such as dental check-ups, haircuts, immunisations etc., at the start of the year.

SCHOOL Add end-of-term and half-term dates, training days, parent-teacher evenings, school concerts, games matches and the like. It might be helpful to have the days your children have sport lessons listed to remind you to get kit ready.

WORK Include any business trips and key deadlines that might affect other commitments.

BIRTHDAYS/ANNIVERSARIES Make a note of these on the family calendar. You may want to buy cards in advance and file them by month in your home planner.

HOUSEHOLD MAINTENANCE Use your home planner to remind you of chores like checking that the smoke detector is working, laundering soft furnishings or cleaning the tumble-drier vent.

Household phone book

Have a book by the phone with emergency and frequently used numbers so that you can find them easily. Your list should include:

- Immediate family.
- Close friends.
- Doctor.
- Dentist.
- Plumber.
- Electrician.
- Electricity and gas companies.
- Water company.
- Local council.
- Local police station.
- Local fire station.
- Children's schools.

You might want to add:
- Favourite local restaurants.
- Takeaway services.
- Computer support.
- Local delivery services such as newsagents, vegetable boxes etc.
- Painter and decorator.

Keeping track folder

It's a good idea to have a folder with contact details for insurance and credit card companies. At the front of the folder have a list of the dates when the following are due for renewal and the day of the month that payments are made.

Include sections for storing:
- Insurance policy documents and updates
- Subscriptions details
- Membership documents
- Credit card information and interest rate notices
- Personal loan initial terms, repayment schedule and yearly statements

> **TIP**
> You may want to store these numbers on your computer, too, but don't abandon the paper version as in the event of a computer crash or a power cut it will be needed.

- Road tax documents.
- Vehicle license registration.
- Car servicing and MOT records.

Household inventory

Preparing an inventory of furniture and fittings will be useful if you need to make an insurance claim in future. Keep it in a folder with receipts for major items.

Medical information folder

Set up a ring binder with record sheets, zipped pockets and tabbed dividers to file information for all the family. If one member of the family has chronic health issues you might want to consider creating a separate file for them that you can take to appointments. Start each person's section with a medical checklist:

- Birth details.
- Medications.
- Immunisations.
- Allergies and intolerances.
- National Health number.
- Phone number for GP registered with.

You may want to include further sheets recording appointments, dates and details of hospital stays, and copies of correspondence. Use zipped pockets to store insurance paperwork, doctor's and dentist's cards or contact details, test results and prescriptions. Make copies of your children's checklists and keep them in a pack to give to babysitters, and give a copy to your children's schools. Make sure you update the information regularly.

Product manual folder

Store all warranties and manuals in clear plastic sleeves in a folder. If you have a lot of appliances and electrical items you may want to create separate folders, sorted by room (kitchen, living area and bathroom). You may find it useful to store these folders in the appropriate room. Many products have online manuals you can download if you have lost the original.

Household Emergencies

We always hope that we will never have to deal with a household emergency. Keeping your fingers crossed is one way to deal with it but the best thing you can do is be prepared: know how your house works, take precautions, and be aware of some basic survival tips and you will be well on your way to surviving any crisis man or nature might throw at you.

Preparing for Emergencies

Knowing how to act in a household emergency is as much about understanding how your house works as staying cool in a crisis. In an emergency you probably won't have time to read the advice in this chapter, so read it now and try to memorise the main points. Emergencies can happen at any time to anyone, so as well as learning what to do yourself, teach your older children.

ESSENTIAL PHONE NUMBERS

First, it is a good idea to keep a list of essential numbers by the phone. Ideally, these should include:

- Family doctor.
- Nearest hospital with an accident and emergency unit.
- Plumber.
- Locksmith.
- Glazier.
- Electrician.
- Electricity company's emergency number.
- Local gas emergency number.
- Local builder.
- Local police station.
- Vet (if applicable).
- Your and your partner's work numbers.
- School and college numbers.
- Relatives or friends that the children can ring in an emergency.

While making a list of emergency umbers, include other useful family details , such as blood groups, medical card numbers, national insurance numbers and insurance policy numbers. Also list bank, building society and credit card numbers – and where to ring if they are lost or stolen.

FIRE

Take some time now to think carefully about how you and your family would escape from your house in a fire.

- Is there an alternative route down, as well as the stairs, in case they are blocked by fire?
- Is there a window in every room that could be used to climb out of?
- If you have double glazing, is the key kept by the window for easy unlocking?
- If you have secondary glazing, is there at least one window in each room that doesn't have it, which you could use to escape?

Choosing the right tradesmen

If choosing a tradesman for the first time, try to follow a personal recommendation from a neighbour, or at least choose a firm that is a member of a trade association that insists its members follow a code of practice, and that has a grievance procedure for customers to use should you need to complain, such as:

- Federation of Master Builders.
- Institute of Plumbing.
- Electrical Contractors' Association.
- National Inspection Council for Electrical Installation Contracting.
- Gas Safe Register.
- Glass and Glazing Federation.

(See Useful Organisations.)

Finally, hold regular, family fire practice and make sure the whole family knows what to do if there really is a fire.

FIRE AT NIGHT

If you were to wake up at night and notice the smell of smoke, here's what to do:

1 Wake everyone up (calmly, without causing panic).

2 Try to establish where the heart of the fire is and close the door to that room if you can. Don't open any door that feels warm to the touch. (Use the back of your hand to touch it.)

3 Use the stairs, if safe to do so, and get everyone out of the house. Call the fire brigade from a phone box, mobile or neighbour's house. Clearly state the address of the fire.

4 If the stairs are blocked, use an upstairs window as an escape route – if you can do so safely. Otherwise go to a front bedroom, close the door, block any openings such as vents or skylights, and seal up the gap along the bottom of the door with rolled up clothes or bedding.

5 Go to the window and try to attract the attention of someone outside. Shout and wave something brightly coloured (or pale, that will be seen in the dark).

6 Don't try to get out unless you are forced to. If the room starts to fill with smoke, try not to panic. Tie a handkerchief or scarf around your mouth and lean out of the window to breathe. If this isn't possible, crouch down near the floor (the heat and smoke will be less there).

7 Only as a last resort, jump. Drop bedding or cushions to the ground to break your fall, and lower yourself feet first from the window sill to reduce the drop.

FIRE-FIGHTING EQUIPMENT

KITCHEN Fire blanket. Make sure it conforms to BS 6575 and is at least 90 x 90cm/3 x 3ft in size.

HALL Multi-purpose dry powder, foam or water type extinguisher (conforming to BS 5423 or 6165 and the British Standard Kitemark). These would be adequate for most homes, but it depends on the fire risks in your home and what you can afford. A multi-purpose dry powder or foam extinguisher in the garage, shed or car would also be a good idea.

TIP
Fit a smoke alarm (to BS 5446) on every floor of the house. It can increase your chances of getting out in a fire by two or three times, giving you precious extra minutes. (See Smoke Alarms, page 359.)

TIP
Never store combustible materials, such as paint cans or solvents, under the stairs. They could give fuel to a fire and block your escape route.

WHAT KIND OF FIRE?

Different kinds of fires require different measures: that is, extinguisher, water etc.

Chip pan/frying pan fire

❶ Leave the pan where it is.

❷ Turn off the heat if it is safe to do so.

❸ Protecting your hands, place a damp cloth, a close fitting lid or a fire blanket over the pan to smother the flames.

❹ Allow the pan to cool for at least 30 minutes. (The fire can start again if the cover is removed too soon.)

Ideally, use a thermostatically controlled deep-fat fryer rather than an ordinary hob-top chip pan.

Furniture fires

Use a multi-purpose foam or a water fire extinguisher. Fires in upholstered furniture can spread very quickly and produce poisonous fumes. Do not tackle the fire if it is burning fiercely or if there is already thick smoke. Get out immediately, shut the door properly and call the fire brigade.

Electrical fitting and appliance fires

❶ If possible, turn off the power. (Pull out the plug or switch off the appliance at the mains.)

❷ Use a dry powder carbon dioxide extinguisher.

Don't use a water-based extinguisher unless the appliance is disconnected from the mains – but never use one on TV sets, even when they are unplugged.

Mains gas appliances fires

❶ Turn off the gas supply and wait until the gas flow stops.

❷ Call the fire brigade immediately and tell them that mains gas is involved.

❸ If the gas supply cannot be turned off, do not attempt to extinguish the burning gas jet, as this allows gas to escape and accumulate to explosive levels.

TACKLING A GAS LEAK

See Gas Leaks, page 390.

Clothes on fire

❶ Lay the victim down so the flames cannot reach the face.

❷ Douse the flames with water or any non-flammable liquid such as milk. Or smother the flames with a blanket or rug.

❸ If water isn't readily available, wrap the victim in a fire blanket or rug.

❹ Once the flames are out, check that there is no smouldering material.

❺ Get medical help immediately.

TIP
Never use water or any type of extinguisher to fight an oil fire. This is extremely dangerous.

TIP
Unplug TVs and computers and cover them with a damp blanket or a fire blanket to smother the fire. Don't use water.

Fire prevention

For further advice on fire protection in the home and how to choose and use a fire extinguisher contact your local fire safety officer. Alternatively, for general advice contact the Fire Protection Association. (See Useful Organisations.)

Floods and Severe Weather

Excessive water or wind, or both at once, can cause major headaches for the householder.

FLOODING

After fire, a flood is the most destructive element that can hit your home. If you live near a river, reservoir, the sea or a water main, get in touch with your local authority that will advise you on the kind of flood precautions you should take.

Ready supplies

It may be worthwhile having a supply of canned and dried food and bottled water in case you are cut off for any length of time. It may also be useful to buy a camping light, camping cooker and candles, as the first thing you'll have to do in a flood is turn off the mains electricity.

If you have room in a garage or shed, keep a stock of plastic bags filled with sand or soil to block off outside doors and airbricks.

Be prepared

Even if a downpour looks as though it is going to turn into a flood, you should have some time to prepare the house and your family.

- Block off outside doors and airbricks to try to keep water out of the house; place plastic carrier bags filled with soil against the outside faces of doors and airbricks.
- Turn off mains electricity, gas and water.
- Move your family, pets and what possessions you can (furniture, rugs etc.) to upper floors, or move out if in a bungalow.
- Take off downstairs internal doors, if possible. Severe flooding may damage them.
- Wait upstairs for the relief services to tell you what to do next.

Cleaning up after a flood

Let the emergency services pump as much water out of the house as possible before trying to return. Once inside, check damage very carefully.

- If water has got into the electrics, it could be dangerous and you should get the local electricity company to test it as soon as possible. All appliances should also be examined and tested at the same time.
- Call in the local gas suppliers to check the system and any appliances.
- Check with the water company on the state of the water supplies.
- You should be able to hire a pump to clear any remaining water from cellars, and then use a three-in-one vacuum cleaner to remove any final pools of water.

Flood survival tips

Get everyone to wrap up well, as the house may be cold, with no heating.

- Take an emergency supplies box with candles, a camping stove if you have one, canned food and bottled water etc.
- Flood water is almost certainly contaminated so don't use it for anything. Any cooking utensils that have been in the flood should be disinfected. Don't drink tap water until you hear from the local authority that it's all right to do so.

- Check the loft for any damage. It may need temporary repairs to stop the roof letting in even more water. An uncovered water cistern in the loft may be contaminated and so you'll need to drain it and clean it out. Throw out soaked loft insulation material.
- Remove furniture and lift floor coverings so you can hose walls and floors down. Scrub all affected surfaces thoroughly with strong disinfectant, as the flood water may have been contaminated with sewage.
- If you didn't get a chance to do this before the flood, take doors off their hinges and stack them flat so they can dry out without warping.
- Lift some floorboards so the underfloor area can dry out or be pumped out if necessary.
- Check that there is no water trapped underneath ground floors, in cellars or cavity walls. If water has got inside them, holes may have to be drilled from the outside to allow it to escape. Also check for trapped mud.
- Outside, make sure airbricks are free of debris. Unblock drains, clean out gulley gratings and rod the drains to clear them.
- Keep windows and doors open as often as possible (security permitting) to give good ventilation, even when the heating is on. Good ventilation is crucial. Your greatest enemy is rotting timber.
- At night, you could use a de-humidifier (which removes moisture from the air and collects it in a container which you then empty). When you think the structural and joinery timbers are dry, call in a surveyor to check the moisture content.
- If the wallpaper is ruined, strip it off to help speed up drying out. Leave cupboard doors open and keep furniture away from walls.
- If walls are very damp, it may be necessary to have some of the inside plaster removed to aid drying out.

It can take weeks for the walls and floors etc., of a house to dry out. A qualified surveyor will be able to tell you when the walls and structural timbers are dry and whether there has been any physical damage caused. It is a good idea to get the underfloor timbers inspected after about six months and again in a year's time, to check for rot.

Once the cleaning and drying is completed, get a qualified electrician to test the electrics for earth continuity and insulation resistance. Then ask him for an inspection certificate. Lookout for any signs of trouble in the electrics such as sizzling, cracking or buzzing. If either occur turn off the supply immediately. Have your electrics inspected every month for the first six after the initial test and at least twice again in the following six months.

MINOR FLOODS

If you suddenly find your home flooding with water:

1. Turn off the electricity at the mains.
2. Find out what is causing the flood (such as an overflowing bath, a leaking washing machine) and if possible, turn it off.
3. If this doesn't stop the flow of water, turn off the water at the mains (see Cold-water Supply, page 162).

Turning off your water supply

To turn a mains water stoptap off, turn it clockwise as far as it will go, like a tap. Check where your stoptap is now. It is probably under the kitchen sink. In older houses, it could be in the cellar, or possibly outside the house under a small metal flap. Twice a year, check the stoptap hasn't seized up and that you can turn it easily. If it is jammed, don't force it – turn off the one outside. If you don't know where that is ask your local water supplier.

4. Turn off the boiler, immersion heater, washing machine or anything that heats water.

5. If the flood is still in full flow, if possible, turn off the stoptap on the supply pipe from your cold-water cistern. If you cannot reach this easily, open cold taps and flush cisterns to empty the tank as quickly as possible. If water is coming from the hot-water system, turn off the stoptap adjacent to the hot-water cylinder (on its supply pipe).

STORMS

You can find out about any approaching strong winds or storms through the Meteorological Office, which operates a severe-weather warning service.

General precautions

Keep your property in good repair and pay particular attention to the state of the following:

- Roofs (particularly ridges, eaves etc.).
- Chimney stacks.
- Masonry boundary walls.
- Aerials and satellite dishes.
- Trees (particular those close to buildings and taller than the building).

If there is a severe weather warning

1. Move under cover anything that might blow about, getting damaged or causing damage, such as garden furniture, dustbins, bikes, children's toys. Take pets indoors.

2. Close and fasten doors and windows. (Don't forget the greenhouse, shed or garage.)

3. Park vehicles in a garage, if possible. If not, move your car away from the house, where it might be hit by falling debris.

4. Close and secure trap doors with bolts.

5. Stay indoors as much as possible. (Don't go out to repair damage while the storm is in progress.)

6. Open internal doors only as needed and close them behind you.

7. Move away from windows. Sleep downstairs if you have any large trees sited near the house. (It will also be less noisy and safer if you are not directly beneath the roof.)

8. Keep buckets handy to deal with any leaks in the roof and, possibly, heavy-duty polythene sheeting, tacks and a hammer to cover broken windows. Check also that you have candles, matches and a torch to hand, in case of a power cut.

The aftermath

After the storm, check the chimney stack and roof slopes as the wind may have lifted flashings, dislodged tiles and ripped down your roof-top aerial. If you have a flat roof, check it for torn felt. Check for unstable trees, walls and fences.

Notify your insurance company of any damage for which you might want to claim.

Drying out

- Once you have stopped the flood, assess the damage.

- If the ceiling plaster seems to be bulging downwards, under the weight of water from above, make a small hole with a skewer, screwdriver or knitting needle in the centre of the bulge, and put a bucket underneath to catch the water. This is important, otherwise the weight of water may bring the entire ceiling down.

- Wait to turn the power back on until any area with electrics in it has completely dried out. Check with a qualified electrician. You may be able to isolate the power and lighting circuits concerned by switching them off at your consumer unit (fuse box, see page 391), so you have power to the rest of the house.

- Stand mattresses and foam cushions on their edge as seepage is slower on a vertical surface. Take up wet carpeting and loose-laid flooring. Carpets should be professionally cleaned. Don't replace furniture and heavy appliances until the floor has dried out completely, which may take several weeks. (See Flooding, pages 385–6 for further advice.)

- Contact your insurance company (see Home Insurance, page 395).

Pipes and Drains

Knowing how to carry out some emergency repairs to pipework and drains could avert large-scale damage to your home and save money on plumbing bills.

FROZEN AND BURST PIPES

Freezing in winter and corrosion in the heating system often cause burst or frozen pipes. Don't panic. Disreputable plumbers thrive on this sort of problem but a burst pipe need not be a major disaster if you know how and where to turn off the water.

Burst pipes

❶ Turn off the water to the affected pipe quickly. For a burst on the mains-pressure pipes (such as in the kitchen, or an outside tap), turn off at the rising main (see Cold-water Supply, page 162). For bursts on low-pressure pipes fed from the tank in the loft (such as taps in a bathroom or guest room), turn off gate valves if they are fitted or turn off the rising main stoptap. Then open the hot and cold taps to empty all water from the affected pipes.

   If the burst is on the heating pipework, switch off the boiler and turn off the stoptap on the supply to the feed and expansion tank (if there is one) to stop it refilling. Then attach a length of hose to the lowest draincock on the system (such as from the washing machine) and take the other end to a drain outside (see Drainage Systems, pages 164–6). A draincock is fitted to parts of your plumbing system that cannot be drained via a tap, for example, the boiler. Open the draincock valve to empty the system.

❷ Now you have stemmed the flow of water, call in the plumber.

Frozen pipes

❶ Turn off your water at the mains, as above.

❷ If the freeze is on a heating pipe, turn off the boiler as above.

❸ Inspect the frozen pipes and try to find out whether they have burst. (You may see ice glistening in the pipe, or feel a split.) If it doesn't seem to have burst, very gently try to thaw it. Working back from the frozen tap, unwind any lagging and use a hairdryer, a warm air gun, a hot-water bottle or even hot cloths to thaw it. Never use a naked flame. Too much direct heat may cause the water in that section to boil and steam. Be patient.

❹ If the pipe has split, bind rags tightly around the leak, or plug it with something, and place a bucket underneath to catch the water as the pipe thaws.

❺ Call a qualified plumber.

❻ If possible, turn off the stoptap on the outlet to the cold-water tank. If it is a hot-water tap that has burst, turn off the stoptap controlling

TIP
Check your stoptap regularly by turning it off. This will help to stop it from scaling up.

TIP
Make sure you know where all the control valves and draincocks are in your plumbing.

TIP
If replacing a pipe, flexible plastic pipes will allow a certain amount of expansion and although the water will still freeze it won't necessarily burst the pipe.

the supply of water to the hot-water cistern. If escaping water cannot be controlled switch off the electrics at the mains, open all the cold taps and flush the cisterns in order to drain the system quickly. (Save some in the bath, jugs and bowls to use until the plumber comes.) Then wait until the area has dried out completely before switching the electricity back on. If you can, isolate that circuit and switch on the power to the rest of the house.

WATER AND ELECTRICITY

The greatest danger from a burst pipe is to the electrical system. If water gets into power and lighting circuits it can make the whole plumbing system live. If in any doubt at all about dampness, switch off the electricity and work by torchlight. Then call in a qualified electrician to test the system.

BLOCKED TOILET

Most households have toilets with a wash-down pan: when flushed, two streams of water come from each side of the rim. The water should leave the pan smoothly, not eddying like a whirlpool.

⊙ If the cistern is working properly but the bowl fails to clear, something is obstructing either the flush inlet or the toilet-pan outlet.

⊙ If the flush water rises almost to the pan rim then ebbs away very slowly, there is most likely a blockage in the pan outlet, or possibly in the drain it discharges into.

Unblocking a toilet

❶ Remove all visible waste. You may be able to clear it with a bent wire pushed round the bend. Wait until the water level has dropped and flush the toilet from a height with a bucket of water.

❷ If this doesn't work take the plunger and push it sharply on to the bottom of the pan to cover the outlet. Then pump the handle up and down two or three times.

❸ If this doesn't clear the pan, use a flexible drain auger (a plumber's snake) to probe the outlet and trap. If that doesn't work, you may need to call in a plumber or drain specialist to clear the underground drain. (See also Clearing a Blocked Drain, pages 205–6.)

❹ If when you flush the cistern, water is entering the pan poorly or unevenly, use a mirror to check the flushing rim. Probe the rim with your fingers for flakes of rust or debris from the cistern that may be obstructing the flush water.

BLOCKED WASTE PIPE

See Coping with Blockages, page 190.

Think ahead!

The most useful thing you can do to prevent internal flooding is to make sure that the cold-water pipes in your loft (and the top and side of the cold-water tank) are well insulated to prevent them freezing in winter. If you go away for a few days, leave the heating on low and prop the loft hatch open. If going for a longer period, drain down the plumbing system. This doesn't take very long and may save a great deal of aggravation on your return!

You will need

⊙ Plunger with long handle. (You may be able to use a mop or broom tied round with rags. Alternatively, stand on a stool and tip in a bucket of water in one go.)

⊙ Flexible drain auger (plumber's snake).

⊙ Bucket.

⊙ Rubber gloves.

⊙ Mirror.

Gas and Electricity

It is possible to fix minor problems with your gas and electrics yourself, but remember it is usually best to call in the professionals.

- -

GAS

Never carry out any DIY repairs to gas pipes, fittings or appliances. Gas installation and repairs should only be carried out by an installer registered with the Gas Safe Register.

Make sure everyone in the family knows how to turn off the gas supply at the mains. If you don't know where your gas tap is, ask your meter reader next time he calls. (It is usually a small level on the gas pipe near your meter.)

The gas mains

OFF Turn the lever until the notched line on the spindle points across the pipe. If your tap seems stiff, don't attempt to loosen it yourself: call your local gas service centre that will come and loosen it for you safely, free of charge.

ON Before turning the gas on again, make sure that all appliances and pilot lights are turned off. The gas tap is on when the notched line on the spindle points along the pipe. After turning the supply on, relight all pilot lights.

Gas leaks

If you smell gas:

- Turn off the mains gas tap (next to the gas meter).
- Put out all naked lights, don't smoke and don't operate any electrical equipment (including light switches and doorbells).
- Open doors and windows to increase ventilation.
- Ring the local gas board's 24-hour, 365 days-a-year emergency service: use your mobile phone. Look under Gas in the phone book.

After the gas leak has been dealt with and the gas supply is back on, don't forget to relight the pilot light.

Carbon monoxide (CO) poisoning

If any of your fuel-burning appliances (including gas central-heating boilers, water heaters, open fires and wood-burning stoves) use a flue, they must be kept clear. If the chimney or flue does get blocked, the waste gases could spill into the room, polluting the air you breathe with carbon monoxide. This could be fatal. Always ensure there is plenty of ventilation.If you notice any of the following signs on your gas appliances, stop using the appliance and contact your local gas office immediately.

Domestic gas and carbon monoxide detectors

GAS
Your sense of smell should tell you if there is a gas leak (which could lead to an explosion). But if you are worried about gas or have poor olfactory senses, consider having a gas detector installed (professionally, by wiring it directly to the mains). There are different types for natural and bottled gas, and each must be installed correctly: high on a wall to detect the lighter-than-air methane in natural gas, and low down for the heavier-than-air propane and butane in bottled gas.

CARBON MONOXIDE
A carbon-monoxide detector will tell you if you have a leaky flue (which could lead to you getting poisoned). You shouldn't rely on a gas or carbon monoxide detector to tell you if there is a leak. Carbon monoxide does not have a smell, so you will not be able to detect it unaided.

Follow the advice above if you are at all concerned about leaks. There is no substitute for making sure that all your gas appliances are properly maintained and serviced regularly.

- Is the outer case discoloured?
- Is the decoration around the appliance stained or discoloured?
- Does the appliance burn with a yellow or orange flame?
- Is there a strange smell when the appliance is on?
- Is the flue damaged or broken?

ELECTRICITY

Unless you are highly competent at DIY, never tinker with electrical wiring or carry out repairs, except for very minor matters such as mending fuses and fitting plugs.

Replacing a fuse wire

To replace the fuse or fuse wire, first switch off the main switch on the consumer unit (or it may be on a separate switch box nearby).

REWIRABLE FUSES

1. On a blown rewirable fuse you should be able to see the broken wire and scorch marks on the fuse carrier. If the fuse is one on which you cannot see the whole length of the fuse wire, pull gently on each end of the wire with the tip of a screwdriver to see if it is intact.
2. Loosen the two terminals holding the fuse and extract the broken pieces.
3. Wrap one end of a new length of wire (of the correct rating) clockwise round the terminal and tighten the screw on it. Then run the wire through the fuse carrier across to the other terminal, leaving it slightly slack, and attach it in the same way and cut off any surplus.
4. Replace the fuse carrier.
5. Refit the fuse-box cover and switch on the mains.

GETTING TO KNOW YOUR CONSUMER UNIT

This is the heart of your electrical installation, and every circuit in the house must pass through it. Go and take a look at it now, as these guidelines will then be easier to follow.

- Every unit has a large, main switch that can turn off all the power to your house. These switches are called RCCBs (residual current circuit breakers). On some units, the main switch will trip automatically if a serious fault occurs, as well as being operable manually.
- With some consumer units you can't remove the outer cover without first turning off the main switch. If yours is not like this, stick a label on the cover to remind you to switch off before exposing any of the elements inside the unit.

- With the main switch off and the cover removed, you can see how the unit is arranged. The cover must be replaced before the unit is switched on again – and remember that even when the unit is switched off, the cable connecting the meter to the main switch is still live, so take care.
- Look at the cables that feed the various circuits in the house (ideally they should all enter the consumer unit from the same direction) and should be labelled to tell you which area of electrics they cover.
- Each fuse covers a particular wiring circuit in the house. Check which has failed (lights, socket outlets etc.). If a faulty lamp or appliance is responsible, switch off the mains before replacing the fuse or closing a circuit breaker.

CARTRIDGE FUSES

1. Unscrew the fuse carrier.
2. Fit a new fuse of the correct rating.
3. Put together the carrier and screw tight.
4. Replace the fuse carrier and put back the consumer unit cover.
5. Switch on the main switch.

Minature circuit breakers

Instead of the usual fuse holders, you may have MCBs. These are amp-rated, like fuses, but instead of removing an MCB to isolate the circuit you merely operate a switch or button to switch it to off. When a fault occurs the circuit breaker switches to the off position automatically, so the faulty circuit is obvious.

1. Turn the main switch off.
2. Correct the cause of the fault.
3. Close the switch on the MCB to reset it. (There is no fuse to replace.)
4. Switch on the mains.

Residual current devices (RCDs)

If all the power to your house has gone off, it may be the residual current device (RCD) that has tripped. The RCD will operate quickly if there is an earth fault.

1. Correct the fault: unplug the faulty appliance or replace the light bulb.
2. Try to close the RCD.
3. If it opens again, switch off the mains, remove all the circuit fuses or breakers and replace or reset them one at a time until you find the faulty circuit.
4. Leave the faulty fuse or breaker out and ring an electrician, or ask your local electricity company for help.
5. Replace the cover before switching the electricity on again.

When will a fuse blow?

- When too many appliances are operated on a circuit the excessive demand for current will blow the fuse in that circuit.
- When current reroutes to earth because of a faulty appliance, the flow of current increases the circuit and blows the fuse. This is called short circuiting. Deal with the original fault before replacing the fuse.

Mains power cut

1. Organise light: make sure that you know where to find torches or candles and matches.
2. Ring your electricity company to report the problem and find out when you can expect a return of power.
3. Take care if using candles, putting them well out of reach of children. When the power comes back on again, make sure all candles are put out and that any appliances that you turned on before the power cut are not left on, such as a cooker, an iron or an electric blanket.
4. When the power comes back on reset electric clocks, for example, on central heating and cooker.

WHICH FUSE TO FIT?

Always fit a fuse of the correct rating for the job.

5 amp	Lighting circuits
15 amp or 20 amp	Immersion heater
30 amp	Socket outlets and average sized cooker
45 amp	Large cooker

Safety and fuses

- If a fuse continues to blow or the breaker keeps opening, don't fit a larger fuse. If in doubt, consult a competent electrician.

- If the RCD reopens, ring an electrician or your local electricity company. Don't try to repair the problem yourself.

For further advice on electricity in the home, visit your local electricity showroom for a range of practical leaflets.

Fridges and freezers

Leave the fridge and freezer switched on. Check that the fridge drip tray is in position and keep the fridge door closed. Don't open your freezer; its contents will remain frozen for about eight hours. The more food inside, the longer the contents will keep without thawing. Food that has started to thaw shouldn't be refrozen. To save uncooked but thawed meats and vegetables, make them into pies or casseroles etc., and then refreeze them.

Burglars, Intruders and Insurance Claims

Here you will find advice about what to do in the event of a break-in at your home.

BURGLARY

If you find you have been burgled, call the police immediately. While waiting for them to arrive, don't move or touch anything except to minimise any damage. Check whether valuables have been stolen so you can give their details to the police when they arrive.

If you arrive home and think a burglar is still inside your house (due to an open door or window) don't go inside. Go to a neighbour's house or phone box or use a mobile phone and ring the police, then keep a discreet watch so you can give the police a description of anyone leaving.

Coming home to a burglar
If you arrive home to find an intruder in the house with you:

- Ask calmly what they want.
- Don't get angry or attempt to prevent them from leaving: they may get violent.
- Try to remember what they look like in as much detail as possible.
- Call the police as soon as they have gone.

If you suspect a prowler
If you hear a noise as though someone is in the house, or someone is trying to break in:

- Switch the lights on and make plenty of noise. Most burglars will flee immediately.
- Stay upstairs or out of the way, call the police if you have a bedroom/extension phone, and find something you can use as a weapon to defend yourself – but don't go in search of them.
- As soon as you hear the intruder leave, try to see what they look like and what they are wearing, which way they go and whether they have a car or van. Then ring the police.

MENDING A BROKEN WINDOW

A broken window is both a safety and a security risk and should be dealt with as soon as possible. It's not a difficult job to tackle yourself as long as you have or can borrow the right tools.

TIP
If you get a good look at an intruder, try to memorise details to help the police: age, sex, height, build, skin colour, hairstyle and colour, facial characteristics, clothing. For vehicles, note the type, model, colour and registration number.

If the window is hard to reach, it's safer to remove the frame and work on it at ground level. Make sure you protect your hands with strong gloves and wear safety goggles.

There are two methods for fixing glass into a wood frame. With wood beading, you simply lever off the beading, replace the glass in mastic (sealant) and refix the beading. The method using putty is explained below, and applies equally to wooden and metal-framed windows.

TIP
If the window is only cracked, stick tape over it in a criss-cross pattern to contain fragments and then tap out the pieces from the outside with a hammer.

ABOVE Mending a broken window, step 1

ABOVE Mending a broken window, step 2

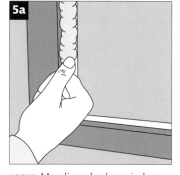

ABOVE Mending a broken window, step 5A

ABOVE Mending a broken window, step 5B

ABOVE Mending a broken window, step 6

ABOVE Mending a broken window, step 7

1. Carefully remove all the loose glass and dispose of it safely (wrapped in newspaper).
2. Hack out the old putty and any remaining bits of glass from the rebate (the groove where the glass sits) with a chisel.
3. Brush out dust and loose bits of putty from the rebate and apply a coat of wood or metal primer to the rebate.
4. Measure up for the new glass. Check that the rebate is square by measuring all four sides, and use the smaller measurement in each case. Subtract 3mm/⅛in from each measurement to allow for clearance. Then order the pane and appropriate putty from your glass merchant. If in doubt, cut a paper pattern and take this to your glass merchant.
5. Put a layer of putty in a thinnish bead all around the rebate (∧), rest the bottom edge of the pane in the rebate and push it gently and firmly into place, pressing round the edge rather than in the centre of the pane to compress the putty evenly (B).
6. To hold the glass in, tap glazing nails in the rebate, at about 12–15cm/4½–6in intervals in a wooden frame, or use glazing clips in a metal one. Trim away excess putty from the inside of the frame with the putty knife.
7. Finish off with a layer of putty around the outside of the frame. Wet the blade of the putty knife to prevent it from sticking, and shape off at an angle. Finish off by trimming away the bedding putty where necessary and cleaning off the putty marks with methylated spirits.
8. Allow the putty to dry for two weeks before painting.

TIP

With metal frames, the glass will have been held in by small clips. Take these out carefully with pincers as you uncover them, mark the hole positions on the frame and save them for later.

HOME INSURANCE: MAKING A CLAIM

If, unfortunately, you have to make a claim on your home insurance, here is how to make the process as smooth and fast as possible.

- ◉ Read your policy carefully. Does it cover the cause of the damage or loss? Should you claim under 'buildings' or 'contents'? Some policies cover both.
- ◉ Ring your insurer and ask for a claim form, quoting your policy number. Don't forget to quote the number on any correspondence as well, and keep copies.
- ◉ If temporary emergency repairs are needed, arrange these immediately and let your insurer know. The cost may form part of your overall claim, so keep all the bills and any damaged items as the insurers will probably want to see them. Take photos if necessary.
- ◉ Some insurers offer a 24-hour emergency helpline, which can give details of local tradespeople.
- ◉ While waiting to receive a claim form, get repair estimates from at least two specialist contractors, list all items lost or damaged, and find the original receipts if you can. If you can't, estimate their current value and check the price of replacements. Remember that some policies offer replacement as if the items had been new, while others take wear and tear into account.
- ◉ Complete the claim form and return it quickly, with any estimates, receipts and valuations you can find to support your case.
- ◉ The insurers will either pay your claim, or arrange for their claims inspector to call on you, or send a loss adjuster to assess the loss or damage.

Moving House

One of the most stressful events in our lives, moving house is fraught with difficulty. While this section cannot guarantee a hassle-free property purchase, it will at least provide all the information you need to be clued-up about buying a home: the costs involved, getting a mortgage and house hunting. There is also a wealth of practical advice on selling a property, and finally a detailed overview of the big day itself: the move.

Buying a home

There's nothing quite like the excitement of stepping over the threshold into your new home. But with months of house hunting, arranging a mortgage, negotiating a price and carrying out the move, few would deny how stressful the whole process can be.

Buying a house is probably the most complicated and costly purchase you will ever have to make. Whether the move is to accommodate a family, a change in financial position, or a new job, it takes weeks of planning, costs thousands of pounds and results in a very large commitment for 20–25 years. Yet, with careful planning and a basic understanding of the processes involved, you can make the whole operation run relatively smoothly. The following pages will show you how best to approach the entire undertaking.

ARRANGING A MORTGAGE

One of the first steps for most people when buying a new house is to approach a building society, bank or other lending institution to find out how much, in principle, you can borrow. You'll find it useful to get a mortgage certificate from your lender. This will tell anyone considering selling to you that (subject to a valuation and status – see pages 420 and 408 respectively), you are guaranteed a mortgage up to a certain sum. It will reassure people that you are a serious buyer.

HOW MUCH CAN YOU AFFORD?

Before you decide on the price range for possible properties, consider what you spend on all your other regular commitments. Use our checklist to help organise your monthly budget:

MONTHLY INCOME

Take-home pay (after tax)	£
Partner's take-home pay (after tax)	£
Other regular income, e.g. investment	£
Total	**£**

MONTHLY OUTGOINGS

Present mortgage/rent	£
Second mortgage repayments (if applicable)	£
Home repairs/maintenance	£
Other loans and repayments	£
Credit-card repayments	£
Council Tax	£
Endowment/life assurance premiums	£
Food/drink	£
Clothing	£
Services (e.g. electricity, gas, telephone, broadband)	£
Petrol/car maintenance	£
Car insurance/road tax	£
Savings	£
Social life	£
Travel expenses	£
TV licence/rental/subscription	£
Total	**£**

A mortgage adviser will be able to give you an idea of how much you could borrow, based on your income/s (see page 407). Add your own savings to this and you'll have a rough guide to the price range of properties open to you. It is also useful to take into account the other costs involved in house purchase: fees for valuation, survey, legal expenses, Stamp Duty, Land Registry and removal expenses (see pages 404–5).

WHERE TO BUY

You probably have a reasonable idea already of the area in which you want to live, and the sort of house you're looking for, but it's worth bearing in mind the differences between town and country, and flats and houses, that may not at first be obvious.

HOUSE OR FLAT

If you were previously in rented accommodation and are now buying your own flat, consider:

- Maintenance costs and buildings insurance. If the freehold of the building is owned by a separate freeholder, these will probably be handled by a managing agent who will charge a management fee, as well as passing on the costs of insuring and running the communal areas of the building. If the freehold is controlled by the flat-owners' own management company, you will have to deal collectively with these items.
- Organisation of cleaning communal areas, gardening etc.
- Terms of the lease e.g. restrictions on pets, parties, noise after 11pm etc.

TOWN OR COUNTRY?

If you are moving into the countryside, you will need to take the following factors into account:

- Usually less crime in country areas, so insurance rates are lower for home contents and car security.
- Reduced accessibility in the winter if the weather turns bad or there are problems with public transport.
- Better outdoor leisure facilities.
- Greater variety of housing and generally more space for your money.
- Health and welfare facilities are spread more thinly due to a sparser population.
- Greater distance from the nearest school/hospital/shops.

Likewise, if you are moving to a town or city, consider:

- More frequent and more accessible public transport.
- Larger, more convenient shops.
- Better indoor leisure facilities
- Higher house prices, especially near schools with good league table ratings.
- Larger insurance premiums. For example, for the contents of a three-bedroom house, insurance cover has been quoted as five times more expensive in London than in a Dorset village. Similarly, car insurance in London was nearly 50 per cent more expensive than in the country.

If you are moving from a house to a flat, you need to consider:
- ⊙ You may need less furniture.
- ⊙ Close neighbours within the building may need more consideration.
- ⊙ Maintenance costs and buildings insurance, see above.
- ⊙ Terms of the lease, see above.

If you are moving from a flat to a house, consider:
- ⊙ The additional expense of furnishing.
- ⊙ Higher heating costs.
- ⊙ Having a garden for the first time, which may entail extra expense of tools and plants.
- ⊙ More housework.
- ⊙ Higher maintenance and repair costs.
- ⊙ Sole responsibility for insuring the building.

NEW OR OLD

New build houses

Over the last few years, brand-new homes have become increasingly popular with house-buyers. They save on repair and maintenance (at least for the first few years) and are becoming increasingly energy efficient: new homes use much less energy than homes built in the 1980s or earlier. Most house builders offer you a choice of colour schemes, fixtures and fittings, so you shouldn't have the costs of redecorating to suit your own taste.

Disadvantages include some teething problems, such as plaster cracks, for the first couple of years. And if you decide to move again within one or two years, it is unlikely that you would be able to sell at the same price as you paid for the house.

Mortgage lenders require a structural warranty. Check that your builder is offering, and is entitled to offer, a warranty before exchanging contracts on a new home. The National House Building Council (NHBC) runs the Buildmark structural warranty scheme, which covers new houses for ten years. A few insurance companies offer alternative building defects insurance schemes.

Old houses

Buying an old, run-down property for a song and renovating it isn't a job that appeals to everyone. It can, however, be extremely rewarding if you have the time, patience and dedication to follow the job through. Just getting the right planning permission and any improvement grants on offer could take up to a year before building work can start.

Self-build houses

Every year, an increasing number of people design or build their own house. It is a way to get a home designed exactly to your specifications, such as a traditional structure but with all the modern fixtures and fittings, or an environmentally friendly structure.

Self-build doesn't necessarily mean you do all the work yourself. You don't have to be a master builder to create the home of your

Renovation and adaptation grants

- ● It's always worth checking whether you are entitled to any financial help with modernising and renovation, or adapting your home if you are disabled. Local authorities administer and give improvement or renovation grants. Grants are means-tested.

- ● Living in a listed building or in a conservation area can be a boon or a blight. English Heritage, Cadw in Wales, the Northern Ireland Environmental Agency and Historic Scotland compile lists of buildings of special architectural or historic interest. This means that you cannot alter or extend the property in any way that would affect its character, without getting permission from the local planning authority. If you are moving into a conservation area, be aware that there are restrictions on alterations to houses.

- ● You can check whether a house is in a conservation area, or is a listed building, by contacting the local authority. Do this before buying a house if you have any big ideas about changing things, such as installing double glazing or a conservatory at the back. On the positive side, your listed building may be eligible for a local authority grant if it is in need of structural repair, or to retain certain aspects of architectural interest.

OPTIONS FOR SELF-BUILD

- Employ an architect to do the design, specifications, and oversee the work. His fee will be around 10 per cent of the overall cost.

- Go straight to a builder, who can advise on the project and do the work. Make sure he is registered with the National House Building Council (NHBC). These mean the house is built to specific standards and provide a means of redress should there be any problems in the future.

- Get a self-build 'package'. More than 70 companies specialise in mid to top-quality house packages, including eco-home options. They will help you estimate your budget, assist in co-ordinating the project and recommend builders and subcontractors.

- Organise everything yourself, and use a design consultant for as much or little as required. (If the designer is not subject to The Royal Institute of British Architects or Architects' Registration Board, check that he/she has professional indemnity insurance.)

- Choosing your own subcontractors and doing some work yourself can save 20–25 per cent of the cost, but could be problematic if you need an NHBC warranty for a mortgage. Bear in mind that if you plan to sell within ten years, your buyers may have difficulty getting a mortgage.

dreams. There are a variety of options enabling you to do as little or as much of the work yourself as you choose. Whichever option you choose, be prepared to spend at least nine months on the project.

FINANCIAL CONSIDERATIONS

First, you must have the land on which to put your house. You'll need to shop around for a lending institution that will give you a mortgage to buy land. For land, try public exhibitions or estate agents. For further help you can subscribe to a self-build plot-finding search service such as Plotsearch (www.buildstore.co.uk/findingland). Plots with buildings due for demolition are also suitable. Talk to the local building inspectorate before purchase because some ground requires expensive foundations.

It is possible to get a mortgage for a self-build project, provided you meet the lender's conditions, such as using a builder who is NHBC registered.

When dealing with builders, always get several quotes, so that you can get the best deal for your available money. If a builder is given the entire contract, he can zero-rate the VAT, and therefore need not charge you VAT at all. Check this before work starts. Once work has begun, don't hand over large amounts of money without checking progress. Keep back most of the builder's payment until an architect or surveyor has checked the work.

With all self-build projects, you must be covered by public and employers' liability, and site or contract works insurance.

Finally, you will also need a solicitor to check planning permission, searches, availability of electricity, gas and water, and to apply for a building-regulations certificate.

Planning permission

To find out what, if any, planning permission you need for the work you would like to do, such as extensions or structural alterations, ask the planning department and the environmental health department of the local authority for advice. Conservation officers working for district or county councils can also sometimes help with general advice.

Renting a House or Flat

Although most people aspire to owning their own home, and historically home-owning has proved to be a good investment, in some circumstances renting can be a better option. Rental is also a useful short-term option if you have sold your house and have not found a new property to buy.

PROS AND CONS

Advantages
- ⊙ No unexpected repair bills.
- ⊙ Flexible if you need to move frequently for your job.
- ⊙ In some areas you may be able to rent a property you could not afford to buy.
- ⊙ Rental deposits are usually much lower than the deposit you need for a home purchase.
- ⊙ You can try out a new area without making a big financial commitment.

Disadvantages
- ⊙ You may have to move out at a month's notice if the landlord requires.
- ⊙ You may not be able to decorate to your own taste.
- ⊙ Costs are likely to increase annually and in time will compare unfavourably with a mortgage taken out at the same time.

FURNISHED OR PART FURNISHED

If you choose to rent a property that is already furnished, you can move straight in. The cost of moving personal possessions will be much lower than a home move that includes furniture. Part furnished properties often include all basic furniture except for beds (many people prefer to use their own beds). When you move out, you will be liable for any damage to the items in the property.

Unfurnished
There is little (or sometimes no) difference in price between a furnished and unfurnished property. However, unfurnished properties will allow you to choose furniture to your taste and take it with you. They are useful if you already own furniture as this saves the cost of storage.

Make sure that your letting agent is signed up to a professional body such as Association of Residential Letting Agents or the National Association of Estate Agents. Check that your deposit is held in a Tenancy Deposit Scheme that provides access to an independent adjudicator who will mediate and settle any disputes.

The Cost of Moving House

The expense of moving house, or setting up home for the first time, can seem enormous. Taking into account a deposit, legal fees and other charges, it costs much more than it initially appears just to get the keys of your new home.

For example, to buy a £250,000 home, you would need to pay out approximately £30,000, as well as repaying the mortgage itself.

WHAT CAN YOU AFFORD?

To give yourself a rough guide on the maximum that you can realistically afford to spend on a new house, add together all the following amounts:

1 The likely net proceeds from the sale of your present home, after repaying your present mortgage. (Find out what other similar properties in your area are selling for or use an estate agent's valuation as a guide to what your home is worth.)

2 The maximum mortgage you can comfortably afford (see pages 407–8).

3 Any other available capital or savings that could swell the amount available.

Then deduct:

1 The cost of selling through an estate agent, who will charge from 1.5–3 per cent of the sale price, plus VAT (see page 403–4).

2 The cost of solicitor's or licensed conveyancer's fees for selling your old home.

3 The cost of buying a new property: valuation fee, survey fee, legal expenses, stamp duty, Land Registry fee, removal expenses and VAT.

4 The cost of essential repairs, redecoration and improvements to the new house.

FEES TO PAY

The various fees that are involved in house buying are considerable, and must be taken into account when planning your purchase. They are as follows:

Legal fees

Solicitors and, in England and Wales, licensed conveyancers, can charge what they choose. The cost is based on the complexity of the transaction (i.e. the skill, number of hours, and the number and importance of documents) plus other local factors, such as the place and circumstances of the conveyancing, and whether the land is registered or unregistered.

Finding a deposit

- You may be asked for a deposit of around 10 per cent of the purchase price to put down on the house when you exchange contracts.

- If you don't have enough for the deposit in ready money, you may be able to get a bridging loan from your bank, but they can be extremely expensive. It would have to be repaid on completion of the sale of your present house.

- If you are selling a property, it may be possible to use your sale deposit towards your purchase deposit.

If you don't already have a solicitor or conveyancer in mind, get estimates from several before choosing one. The Law Society website (www.lawsociety.org.uk) has a searchable list of solicitors' practices by location and area of law. The Council for Licensed Conveyancers website (www.conveyancer.org.uk) lists its members (who specialise solely in house purchase and sale transactions). Many solicitors and conveyancers charge a fixed fee plus disbursements (stamp duty, local authority searches, Land Registry fee) for all the work involved. As a rough guide, allow up to 1 per cent of the home purchase price (plus VAT).

Selling your present home

You will probably need an estate agent to sell your current property. Most charge a fee of between 1 and 3 per cent of the selling price (plus VAT). (See Selling Your Home, pages 423–4.)

Alternatively, if you decide to sell privately, you must allow for your own advertising costs (see page 425).

There may be a mortgage redemption charge if you already have a mortgage on your existing property. This is a penalty for repaying it within a short period (e.g. less than four years), and may be up to three months' interest and/or administration or legal fees.

Stamp Duty

This is a statutory 1 per cent tax on property purchases. It only applies to purchases of over £125,000, but it is charged on the whole amount once this threshold is passed; e.g. on a house costing £125,000, the Stamp Duty is nil. But a house at £125,001 would cost £1,250 in Stamp Duty.

Currently Stamp Duty for first-time buyers on properties between £125,000 and £250,000 is zero. See www.hmrc.gov.uk for further details.

Local authority searches

These fees are payable to the local authority for information about, for example, planning in the area and is about £100–300.

Other search fees

This includes a range of possible searches, from company to mining searches, but not all are applicable to every transaction. Check with your solicitor what will be needed and ask them to give you an idea of the cost.

Lender's legal fees

Usually your solicitor will act for the lender as well as for you. His/her fee for the purchase will include all the work on the mortgage. You should check the costs of this with your solicitor. A few lenders require their own solicitors to act for them. You may have to pay their fees (in addition to your own solicitor's fees for acting on your side of the mortgage) and for this your solicitor may make a separate, additional charge.

Valuation fee

This pays for the lender's surveyor's valuation, and is based on the price of the house. It varies according to the lender's arrangements with the valuers. Add on approximately £300 (plus VAT) as an estimate.

Stamp duty rates

The following table shows what is payable on amounts over £125,000:

Purchase Price (£)	Duty (£)
125,001–250,000	1 per cent
250,001–500,000	3 per cent
500,001 and above	4 per cent

Land Registry fee

This has to be paid on all purchases on a scale related to the purchase price.

Value (£)	Fee (£)
100,000–200,000	200
200,001–500,000	280
500,001–1 million	550
1 million and above	920

Top-up loan

This may be needed if you are unable to raise enough money from your lender to cover the whole cost of the purchase (see Top-up Loan, page 408).

Mortgage indemnity policy

After the deposit, this is likely to be the biggest cost. It is a one-off charge the lender uses to buy an insurance policy if your loan is over 75 per cent of the property's value. It compensates the lender if they have to repossess your home and are unable to sell it for enough to clear the loan and any arrears. This may be added to your mortgage, or paid separately, depending on your lender. The cost can vary from lender to lender, so if you need a 90 or 95 per cent mortgage, you should also take into account the cost of mortgage indemnity when comparing the different mortgage quotations.

Mortgage arrangement fee

This is payable on almost all fixed-rate mortgages. Costs vary depending on the type of mortgage and are usually a percentage of the loan amount, ranging form 0.5–1.5 per cent.

Survey fee

It is wise to allow for more than one survey during house hunting, as you may find a property that fills all your criteria, but is structurally unsound. If this happens, you will have to keep looking, and eventually pay for another survey on a different building.

Most building societies offer you the choice of a full structural building survey, a Home Buyer's Survey and Valuation, or just a valuation. It is important to have at least a Home Buyer's report, which should highlight any major defects in the property. A valuation is just that: it will highlight only significant defects such as would affect the value of the property.

For a full survey, allow from £500–1,500 (plus VAT). The cost relates to the size, value of the property, and amount of time spent by the surveyor. Get a quotation before instructing the surveyor. There could be a reduction if it is combined with a valuation.

If buying an old property, budget for possible extra charges in case tests by specialist firms (such as for wood rot) are needed.

Insurance

For a freehold property, the first premium for building insurance is payable in advance. Ring your insurance broker for a quotation. You may also wish to consider contents insurance. Combining contents and insurance cover in one policy can save money.

Removal expenses

Will you be using a professional removal firm or hiring a van? Either way, get at least three quotations, and arrange insurance cover for your possessions while in transit. If hiring a van, budget for packing materials, petrol for several journeys, plus food and refreshment for your helpers. If your possessions are going into storage for a period of time, budget for this too. (See Storage, page 428).

Bridging loan

If such a loan is required, interest on it will be charged at a significant percentage above the current bank base rate. The actual percentage will depend on prevailing interest rates and whether your loan is open (you have found a property but have not sold yours yet) or closed (you have exchanged contracts but completion dates differ).

CHECKLIST OF MOVING EXPENSES

Advertisements (if DIY selling)	£	Removal insurance cover	£
Bridging loan	£	Services disconnection	£
Building insurance premium	£	Services reconnection	£
Carpet laying	£	Solicitor's/conveyancer's fees	£
Contents insurance premium	£	Specialist structural tests	£
Estate agent's fee	£	Stamp Duty	£
Land Registry fee	£	Storage	£
Lender's legal fee	£	Structural survey	£
Local authority searches	£	Top-up loan charges	£
Mail redirection	£	Valuation fee	£
Mortgage arrangement fee	£	Van hire	£
Mortgage indemnity policy	£	Other	£
Mortgage redemption penalty (if relevant)	£		
Removal company	£	**Total**	£

Services

Check if you need to arrange the following:

GAS Disconnection charges at your old home and reconnection at the new one.

ELECTRICITY Disconnections and reconnection charges, inspections, tests or installing additional circuits.

TELEPHONE You may have to pay for the installation of a phone at your new home or for taking over the existing line if disconnected. (There is no connection charge if a line remains unbroken between one owner and another.)

BROADBAND Service switch.

MAIL Redirection of letters.

WATER Inform your supplier about your change of address and whether you will be moving within or out of the region. If you are moving to a new region you will need to contact your new supplier. The relevant forms can be complete online.

PLUMBER Disconnection and reconnection of a washing machine or dishwasher.

Repairs and redecoration expenses

As well as the expense of the move itself, also consider the cost of any immediate repairs, improvements or redecoration.

If you are buying a brand new house you will have an initial outlay on many items that would be considered fixtures in a second-hand property, such as kitchen units and curtain rails, but you probably won't have the cost of decoration and carpets.

Getting a Mortgage

One of the first steps for most people, when buying a new house, is to approach a building society, bank or other lending institution to find out how much can be borrowed. Visit several lenders to discuss a loan and their terms because they each have different lending criteria.

When you have decided which lender to use, ask them to give you a mortgage certificate. This will show that you are guaranteed a mortgage up to a certain amount (subject to valuation and status – see pages 420 and 408) and will be useful when house-hunting to show you are a serious buyer.

WHAT IS A MORTGAGE?

A mortgage is any loan that is secured on property, whether it is the home you wish to buy or, in the case of a remortgage, the property you are living in.

The usual term of the loan is 20 or 25 years, but it can be longer. Lenders may insist that a mortgage is paid off by the time you reach retirement age – but many now offer shorter-term loans for retired people (see Home-Income Plans, page 411). If the loan is not repaid, the lender has the right to repossess and sell the property.

HOW MUCH CAN YOU BORROW?

A mortgage adviser will be able to give an approximate loan figure. This may differ slightly between lenders, but the calculations are based on your income. If you are in employment, your gross income before tax, forms the basis of calculations. If you are self employed, your net income (that is, gross income minus the expenses of running your business) is used for calculations.

In general, if you are single, you might be allowed to borrow between 2½ and 4 times your basic annual income. If you are a couple who are both earning, you would usually be able to borrow up to four times your joint income. Take note that mortgage lenders don't usually take into account any overtime or bonuses. Some lenders will be more flexible if you are able to put down a big deposit.

Check your finances carefully. Just because the lender is prepared to give you a mortgage of a certain size, don't automatically assume that you can afford it. Lenders work on averages, but you need to take into account any heavy or long-term financial commitments, such as the cost of equipping your new home, your family and travel costs. (See The Cost of Moving House, pages 403–6.) Before making a firm commitment to lend you any money, the lender will want to make sure you can keep up the repayments and that the house you want to buy is worth enough to cover the loan if you default on your repayments. When you make your formal

A ROUGH GUIDE TO MORTGAGE BORROWING

1. Kate is single, and earns £20,000 per year. Her lender is prepared to let her borrow three times her salary. So she can borrow:
3 x £20,000 = £60,000

2. Mr and Mrs Brown want to take out a joint mortgage. He earns £25,000 per year and she earns £22,000 per year. Assuming that their lender is prepared to let them borrow four times their joint income, the amount they can borrow is:
4 x £47,000 = £188,000

mortgage application the lender will make certain 'status enquiries', such as seeking confirmation of your salary from your employer and getting details of your existing mortgage account. He/she will also consult a credit reference agency and have a valuation carried out on the property.

The deposit

The lender will probably expect a deposit of 5 per cent or more.

A 95 per cent loan doesn't automatically equal 95 per cent of the purchase price. The lender will be letting you have 95 per cent of the value that the lender believes your house is worth – which may not be the same sum. For example, if you agree to buy a home for £200,000 on a 95 per cent loan, you should be able to borrow £190,000 with a deposit of £10,000 covering the rest. If the house is only valued at £180,000 then a 95 per cent loan will only give you £171,000, and you will have to find the rest yourself, i.e. £29,000.

If the valuation is considerably lower than the buyer's asking price, it may be worth trying to negotiate a price reduction with the buyer.

Interest rates

The size of the monthly mortgage payment will depend on the sum you borrow, the length of the mortgage and the current rate of interest. You'll find the initial rate of interest and monthly repayments set out clearly in your mortgage offer.

After that, any changes in the interest rate will be reflected in your mortgage payments, unless you have a fixed-interest agreement (also called a fixed-rate mortgage) where the interest rate, and therefore your payments, stay the same for a fixed period. Some lenders adjust the amount you pay on an annual basis so that changes that occur during the year take effect when calculating the following year's repayments. With any mortgage, you will be notified of any change in the level of your repayments.

MAKING A FORMAL APPLICATION

Once you have found a suitable property, you will have to apply formally for the mortgage and pay for the lender to value the property. If the lender decides not to give you a loan as a result of the valuation, you will not get the valuation fee back.

When the valuation has been done and the status enquiries are complete, the lenders will let you know whether they are prepared to lend, how much and on what terms (for example, not letting it out or altering the property without the permission of the lender).

Top-up loan

You may be able to get a top-up loan from an insurance company or bank if the sum that the lender is prepared to grant you falls short of what you need to borrow. The first lender will normally have to give permission. You may have to pay a higher interest rate on the top-up loan than on the main mortgage, and may have to take out an additional insurance policy to cover it.

Mortgage indemnity policy

If lenders are prepared to lend you more than 75 per cent of a property's value they will require that you pay for them to take out a mortgage indemnity policy. This guarantees to pay the lender the outstanding balance of the loan if the home has to be repossessed and sold for less than the amount of the mortgage.

BE WARNED

It can be expensive to take out such a policy and it usually payable in a lump sum up front, although in some cases it may be added to the mortgage loan.

TYPES OF MORTGAGE

With all mortgages, you have to pay back the money borrowed (the capital) and something towards the cost of borrowing the money (the interest). There are two main methods:

REPAYMENT MORTGAGE Every month you pay back some of the capital, plus interest on the outstanding loan.

INTEREST-ONLY MORTGAGE Each month you pay just the interest to your lender, and make a separate payment into a savings plan that is eventually used to pay off the mortgage. These mortgages may not be available on loans of more than 75 per cent of the property's value.

Be wary about taking out an interest-only mortgage without having a suitable savings plan alongside it. This may seem like a nice, cheap option, but you may come unstuck eventually. The longer you wait to set one up the more you'll have to pay to ensure that you can pay off the capital at the end of the term. Lenders may require that you show you have a proven plan in place.

Repayment mortgage

You pay a monthly instalment to the lender that is made up of the interest on the loan and some of the capital. The longer the term of the loan, the less capital you pay in the early years. Initially, most of the monthly payment will be paying off the interest, but as the years pass more will go towards capital repayments.

PROS
- The cost of the mortgage is not related to your age or health.
- If times are hard, you can often extend the term to reduce monthly payments.
- Your loan is guaranteed to be paid off at the end of the term.
- You reduce the amount you have borrowed with regular payment.

CONS
- It can work out more expensive than an interest-only mortgage with savings plan scheme, if the mortgage rates are lower or you move frequently.
- If you are buying a home with a partner, have a family or other financial dependants to think about, you will need to take out separate life assurance to run alongside the loan so that the mortgage would be repaid if you or your partner should die. This is called mortgage protection insurance.

Interest-only mortgages

You pay the interest only to the lender and simultaneously you pay a monthly premium into an insurance company's savings plan, which eventually pays off the capital sum of the mortgage. The savings plans fall into three main groups: endowment policies, pension plans or personal equity plans.

Turned down?

- If your mortgage application is turned down, it may be worth trying another lender with different lender criteria. You could also enlist the help of a mortgage broker, who is not linked to any one lending institution and may have a better idea which companies are more likely to give you a loan.

- If the lender has received a bad report about your financial background from a credit-reference agency, you should ask the lender for the address of the agency concerned. The large agencies keep computer records on every address in the UK.

- You can obtain a copy of your file from the agency. You will usually be charged a nominal fee of a few pounds. If the facts are incorrect you can ask the agency to change them. If the company refuses to change your details or allow you to include a correction, complain to The Office of Fair Trading (see Useful Organisations).

- If the lender is experiencing a shortage of funds, they may be prepared to commit themselves to granting your mortgage in the near future.

LOW-COST ENDOWMENT

In this type of savings plan the insurance company makes assumptions about the future rates of return on investment. If those assumptions are accurate, the mortgage will be repaid in full, and there may even be some money left over. If the returns are not as high, then there may be a shortfall, which you would have to repay. Because of stock market conditions, many existing policies are unlikely to pay out the sum estimated at the time they were taken out. Alternatively, you could take out a full endowment policy, which guarantees to repay the loan at the end of the term. This is much more expensive.

PROS

⊙ The savings plan may repay your loan early.
⊙ Life assurance is included automatically.
⊙ You can move home and take the existing endowment policy with you, rather than taking out a completely new mortgage, as with a repayment mortgage.
　　For example, you buy a house for £200,000 with an endowment policy for £180,000 over 25 years. In ten years' time you sell up and buy a new house for £300,000, taking your existing policy with you and topping it up with another policy for £100,000. After 15 years of the new mortgage the first policy will mature and pay off £180,000 of the mortgage. You will be left with the balance, £100,000 to pay off over the next ten years.

CONS

⊙ The minimum term of the mortgage is usually ten years.
⊙ A new mortgage lender may not accept an existing endowment policy.
⊙ If you cash in the policy in the early years it won't be worth much.
⊙ The amount of the original loan remains the same throughout the mortgage term, so the interest payments remain the same.
⊙ With a low-cost endowment, there's no guarantee that the loan will be repaid at the end of the term.

PENSION MORTGAGES

You pay interest on the whole amount borrowed throughout the term of the loan. In addition, you pay regular premiums to a pension plan. When you start drawing your pension, part of it can be taken as a lump sum and used to pay off the mortgage, while the remainder provides a regular pension.
　　Pension mortgages are most suitable for people who have, or are eligible for, a personal pension plan: that is, people who are self employed and those not in occupational pension schemes.

PROS

⊙ Tax relief on contributions, especially for high earners.
⊙ The fund grows tax free.
⊙ Low-cost life cover can usually be included within the pension plan; these contributions also gain full tax relief.

Mortgages on new homes

o If you are buying a house in the process of construction, you will not receive all the money you are borrowing at once. The payments will be made at various stages, and most building societies or other lenders will not release the final loan until all the work is complete.

o You will also find that lenders normally only lend on a new house built under the supervision of an architect or surveyor employed solely by the buyer, or by an NHBC-registered builder.

o If you are commissioning a house to be built, most building societies or other lenders will not release any money until the ground floor of the house is complete (or, if a bungalow, once you get to the roof stage). They will then send a valuer to inspect the work. The next instalment will be made when the second floor of the property has been completed and inspected. A final payment will be made when the property is complete and has been inspected. You will be charged a fee for each inspection.

CONS

- As you are using part of your pension fund to repay your mortgage loan, the sum available for your pension will be smaller.
- The loan is not designed to be repaid until retirement, and it remains the same throughout the mortgage term.
- You can only pay off the capital when you are eligible to take the pension lump sum, so if you are 25 and due to retire at 65 your mortgage would run for 40 years (unless you remortgage to a different product).

SAVINGS PLAN MORTGAGES

Here you pay to the lender interest only on the loan, and also make contributions to a tax-efficient savings plan, such as an ISA, that builds up tax free over the years. This should provide a lump sum to pay off the loan.

PROS

- The main advantage is that it's a tax-efficient way of building up a fund to pay off the mortgage.
- Suits high-rate taxpayers.

CONS

- ISAs may be invested in company shares, often via unit trusts, so there is no guarantee that there will be enough to repay the mortgage at the end of the term (as the value of shares and unit trusts can go down or up).
- There is a maximum annual contribution permitted.
- No built-in life cover.

Equity release or home-income plans

Equity release or home-income plans, sometimes called mortgage annuity schemes, are arrangements made with financial institutions through which older homeowners (over retirement age) can raise an annual income for life from the capital value of their home, while still remaining the owner. The interest payable on the loan has to be deducted from the annuity and because of this many people are disappointed to find that the extra income is not as much as they hoped it would be. The loan is repaid when the homeowner dies or sells the property.

Get independent financial and legal advice before making any commitment to such a plan, and look for companies who are part of the Safe Home Income Plan (SHIP) campaign.

TIP

A home income plan may not be worthwhile if you are receiving a means-tested social security benefit, as the income from the plan could jeopardise the benefit.

INSURANCE AND REGULATION

Anyone can adopt the title of mortgage broker or insurance consultant, whereas to be called an insurance broker you have to be registered with the Institute of Insurance Brokers. Along with other financial services, insurance is regulated by the Financial Services Authority.

Getting good mortgage advice

There are well over 200 institutions in the mortgage market so take some time to shop around. Make sure you know what sort of loan you are being offered; check the costs involved; find out whether life assurance is included or not. Study the literature from different building societies, banks, insurance companies and other financial institutions. An adviser who has a computerised mortgage database will be able to find the best deal for you quickly.

Under the Financial Services Act, companies that sell endowments and pension plans have to be authorised to carry out their business, and have to abide by a set of rules. One important feature of these rules is that the company has to make it clear whether it is giving completely independent advice to its customers, or whether it is tied to selling one company's products. (If so, look for a sign in the window or on their website stating this.)

Comparing quotes

When calculating how much you can afford to pay each month, remember that mortgage interest rates fluctuate. A change in interest rates can make a substantial difference to your monthly outgoings.

It isn't easy to compare like with like between mortgage quotations. They all have to show the Annual Percentage Rate (APR) in their printed information. This tells you the true cost of your mortgage but spreads all the upfront charges involved in buying a house (such as arrangement fees, valuation and legal fees) across the term of the loan (usually 25 years). In reality, few mortgages last as long as this so the up-front fees have to be spread over a much shorter term than the APR calculation implies. So the best way to compare costs is to ask for a written quotation that clearly shows how much you will have to pay each month and details all the initial charges.

Also, you can compare current interest rates and conditions for mortgages in specialist mortgage magazines and online at price comparison websites.

PROBLEMS WITH MORTGAGE PAYMENTS

If you find that you cannot keep up your mortgage payments, do not assume that you will automatically lose your home. Ask your mortgage adviser for advice. With a repayment mortgage, the lender may agree to extending the term of a mortgage possibly by up to 35 or 40 years; or to you paying only the interest for a short period. There is less flexibility with an endowment mortgage, but you may be able to extend the term of the loan, and so reduce the amount you have to pay each month.

If you are out of work, or too ill to work and eligible for income support, the Department for Work and Pensions may pay the interest on your mortgage for you. Ask for details at your unemployment office or Jobcentre.

Some lenders offer insurance policies that pay the mortgage payments if you are unable to earn because of illness or unemployment. These policies aren't cheap, so the wider the circumstances in which you are eligible to claim, the better.

Read the contract carefully. Many policies will only pay out for a fixed period (e.g. one year) and the money paid under the policy will also be taken into account if you are claiming means-tested state benefit.

Mortgage brokers

- Mortgage brokers make arrangements for you to borrow from someone else. If mortgages are not in short supply, or you want to buy a fairly ordinary house with an average sort of mortgage, there is little point in paying a broker. Go straight to a lender. But if you are hoping to buy an unusual house, or one which most lenders aren't too keen on (for example, a flat combined with shop), or if you want a very large loan, are self-employed, or a significant portion of your income is derived form commission or bonuses, or mortgages are in short supply, a broker could be useful.

- A good broker should give you a choice of mortgages to suit your circumstances. Get written quotations setting out all the payments involved and study the figures carefully.

- If a broker offers you a repayment mortgage you will usually have to pay an arrangement fee. This can be a fixed amount or a percentage of the loan. If you are offered a mortgage attached to a savings plan (e.g. endowment or pension) you should not have to pay a fee as the broker will get commission from the insurance company that provides the savings policy.

BE WARNED
Some brokers may charge if you lapse the policy before a certain time has elapsed, e.g. four years.

MORTGAGE INTEREST RATES

- ⊙ **VARIABLE** Most people have a mortgage with a variable rate of interest, which reflects the general ups and downs of the interest rates in the economy. This means that when bank interest rates go up and down, so do your mortgage repayments. Your lender will always notify you of a change in advance.

- ⊙ **FIXED-RATE** Alternatively, it may help you to budget more effectively if you opt for a fixed-rate mortgage. This gives you a guaranteed rate of interest for an agreed period of time, usually between three and five years.

    However, with a fixed-rate loan you are, in effect, gambling on future interest rates. At best, it guarantees that payments won't rise, but at worst, it may leave you paying over the odds if the interest rates fall. This type of mortgage can be expensive, too, if you want to switch to a different type of loan or repay the mortgage early.

- ⊙ **CAPPED** Similar to a fixed-rate loan but you have a ceiling above which the interest on your loan will not rise for a set period.

- ⊙ **TRACKER** A variable loan that follows the Bank of England base rate and is set to cost a fixed percentage more than this rate. A tracker will change as soon as the rate changes.

- ⊙ **LOW START OR DEFERRED RATE** These mortgages allow you to pay less interest each month than is actually being charged on your loan. The difference between what you pay and what you are charged is then added to the outstanding capital. With the low-start version the reduction is phased out over several years, while the deferred type the reduction is in place for a set time, e.g. three years, and then changes dramatically.

- ⊙ **DISCOUNTED** Discounted rates are often used to entice first-time buyers to place their business with a particular lender. With this, a percentage discount is offered off the current mortgage rate for a specified period, e.g., a 2 per cent discount on the standard rate for a year. A discount can substantially reduce outgoings for a short period, but the increase at the end of the discount period can take you by surprise.

    Look out for early redemption penalties. Some lenders make a special charge if you want to pay your mortgage off early. It can be as much as three months' extra interest.

- ⊙ **FLEXIBLE** These mortgages allow you to make over- and underpayments, take payment holidays, and offset current and savings account balances against your loan to help you repay your mortgage early.

Home repossession

There are government schemes in place to help home owners delay or avoid repossession. Contact your Citizens Advice Bureau for details as soon as you get into financial difficulty.

House Hunting

Looking for the home of your dreams can involve weeks of hunting which may at times be exhausting and demoralising, trailing round estate agents and viewing disappointing and unsuitable properties. So, take a deep breath ... and be prepared to use all available methods: visiting estate agents, online searches using the Internet, looking at advertisements in property magazines and newspapers, driving round the area, and even word of mouth.

ESTATE AGENTS

Look for local estate agents' names in the local paper, on the Internet, or in a local directory. Most in England and Wales are members of professional associations such as the National Association of Estate Agents and the Royal Institution of Chartered Surveyors.

MOVING FAR?

If you are planning to move into a completely new area, too far away for any regular on-the-spot house hunting, it's worth getting your name on the mailing lists of the estate agents in the locality. Call on an agent in your home town and ask if he or she has any contact with fellow agents in the other area. He/she may have the Estates Gazette, which publishes a monthly regional directory of agents.

Also contact the National Association of Estate Agents' national Homelink Service, which provides a national network of estate agents. If you want to buy or sell a property in a different area it helps you to do it from a distance. You deal with your local estate agent, who will liaise with the estate agent in the area on your behalf. There is no charge for this service. (See www.naea.co.uk.)

There are a number of agencies that offer a national relocation service. These can take on much of the groundwork for you, from viewing properties and negotiating the price. They may even help you choose the children's schools. Expect to pay from around 1 per cent of the house purchase price. (Some charge a registration fee from about £500, which may be deductible from the final payment.) These agencies advertise in the national press and may be members of the Association of Relocation Professionals.

SOLICITORS IN SCOTLAND

In Scotland, more properties are sold by solicitors than by estate agents. Solicitors' property centres are run on a co-operative basis, and are usually situated in shopping areas to provide details of all properties being sold by local solicitors. The property centres are often part of chains owned by UK

Getting the best from an estate agent

- At first, be prepared to spend time calling in or ringing up regularly in order to establish a good relationship with the agent. Ask to be put on the mailing list.

- If it is a seller's market, property may be bought up so quickly that the agent barely has time to print the particulars or put up a 'For Sale' board outside the house, so go straight to the agent's office and leave your name and your requirements.

insurance companies or building societies. You will find listings online: www.sspc.co.uk; Scotland's largest property website.

For further information see Buying in Scotland, pages 422–3.

AUCTION

The requirements for buying or selling at auction are somewhat different from ordinary sales. You must be aware of these before committing yourself in a sale room.

Selling

If the estate agent finds it difficult to value your house because it is so unusual, or there is nothing similar to compare it to locally, he/she may suggest that the best way of getting the best price is at auction. The actual cost of selling is more expensive by auction, but you may get this back through a better sale price.

The estate agent will prepare detailed particulars, or a brochure, and extensive advertising. Prospective buyers will want to have surveys and valuations carried out before the auction, and you will need to be accommodating about these. The agent will help you to decide what the reserve price should be.

Buying

Usually, the seller gains more benefit by going to auction than the buyer. Repossessed homes, or properties being sold by the executors after the death of the owner, often come to auction.

If you find that a property in which you are interested is going to auction, check immediately whether it must definitely go to auction, or if offers might be accepted beforehand.

Buying at auction is quite different to the normal method of sale, 'by private treaty' as it is known. By the day of the auction you must have carried out all the usual preparation work up to exchange of contracts on the property (see page 422).

You should have viewed the property, had a valuation survey carried out, raised a mortgage and had your solicitor carry out all the usual conveyancing. You will also probably be competing with other interested parties for the property. It's important to fix yourself a maximum price and stick to it at all costs. If your bid is accepted, you will be expected to exchange contracts there and then with the auctioneer, and pay at least 10 per cent of the purchase price. You will have vacant possession usually within 28 days after the auction.

THE RIGHT PROPERTY

Once you have found a property you want to see, make an appointment to view it as soon as possible, preferably with your partner, a friend, or a relative to give you a second opinion. Before you go to see it, make up a short checklist of things that are important to you, such as number of bathrooms, whether it has a garage etc. Take a pen and paper and measuring tape with you, and the agent's particulars, so you can check the dimensions of the rooms.

Advertisements

- Find out which day the local newspaper devotes to property advertising. The paper will usually carry notices with details of property developments, and lists of recently granted planning permission may appear with the names of builders and developers. The local authority planning officer and building control officer know about future developments. There are also some monthly magazines, which contain information on new estates being built and have regular articles on different areas of the country.

- If looking for a newly built house, ask local builders or national companies whether they have any future plans for putting up houses in the area. Ask local estate agents not only for details of houses being built or just completed, but also about any plans for the building of future estates.

SELECTING A PROPERTY

Here is a checklist for the kind of details you'll need to help you make an informed decision about a property:

LOCATION

- ⊙ How heavy is the traffic?
- ⊙ Is it near a school with a good league rating, shops, police station, hospital, sports ground?
- ⊙ Are traffic lights, road junctions, bends, hills, etc. close by?
- ⊙ Do you share gateways, drives, hedges etc. with neighbours?
- ⊙ How secluded is the house? Are there footpaths or rights of way across your land?
- ⊙ Do cars regularly park outside on weekdays?
- ⊙ Do trains/planes pass within unpleasant hearing distance?

ACCOMMODATION

Does it have the right number of bedrooms, bathrooms, a large enough kitchen, separate toilets etc?

STRUCTURE

Obviously, if you like the property and decide to put in an offer, a professional survey will have to be carried out. But try to get as good an impression as you can of the structural condition of the building when you visit it. If there is a great deal to be done, the cost of repairs may not justify the cost of the house. You could save yourself a survey fee. It's worth conducting your own 'mini MOT':

- ⊙ Ask which way the property faces. A north-facing living room or kitchen is likely to be cold and gloomy if it gets no sun at any time of the day.
- ⊙ If the house is less than ten years old, ask whether it has a National House Building Council Buildmark Guarantee and, if so, how long is left on it.
- ⊙ Look for flaking outside brickwork, cracks, crumbling pointing etc.
- ⊙ 15cm/6in above ground level, look for the damp-proof course.
- ⊙ Look out for damp patches on ceilings and walls, which may indicate a leaking roof, broken rainwater pipe or gutter, or perished pointing to the brickwork. Areas of lighter wallpaper or tide marks above the skirting boards may indicate rising damp.
- ⊙ Timber defects: Are the floors springy? Be wary if the carpets or vinyl are firmly fixed down so inspection is difficult. Get your surveyor to check this out carefully.

Try to imagine your own decorations/furnishings/family/dogs in the house. Take your time when looking round – it's a big decision that you will live with for a long time.

House hunting and the weather

Most houses look at their best when it's warm and sunny, so bear this in mind if house hunting in the summer. If you like the look of a property on a cold, wet, winter's day, there's a good chance you won't be making a rash choice. Also, in cold weather the heating will probably be on, so you can judge for yourself how efficient it is.

- ⊙ Open and close doors and windows to see if they stick.
- ⊙ Dry and wet rot: If the house is old, ask about any timber treatments or damp courses which may have been inserted, how long ago and what guarantees go with them. The present owner may even insure against such defects. Wood preservation wasn't standard until the early 1970s.
- ⊙ Subsidence has become a common problem, particularly in the

Rotten problems

- ● **DRY ROT** Look for cube-shaped cracking in the structural timbers, and in advanced stages, matted greyish-white strings, rusty red spores, pancake-like fungus and a mushroomy smell.
- ● **WET ROT** Check the basements and along bases of exterior doors, sills and window frames. Look for brittle wood with dark brown or black strands of fungus.

WHAT TO CHECK IN A FLAT

- ◉ **SOUNDPROOFING** Tap the walls to establish how thick they are. Establish whether there is soundproofing between floors, especially if the floors are stripped boards. Try to make your visit on a weekday evening when neighbours are most likely to be in, to assess noise levels.
- ◉ **LIGHT** If it is a basement flat, how much natural light can you expect on a dull day? Is there on-street parking, and if so, will the windows be obstructed?

- ◉ **GENERAL CONDITION** Take a good look at the general condition of the property. You may be liable for major repairs if it hasn't been properly maintained in the past.
- ◉ **OUTSIDE FACILITIES** Check the facilities for storage/dustbins/drying clothes/car-parking.

southeast. Look for cracks in the main supporting walls, running diagonally through brick joints; walls that are obviously out of plumb; the tops of internal door linings that are not level and doors that stick in their frames.

- ◉ General décor: in what state are the doors, window frames, plasterwork, skirting boards and staircases?

Fixtures and fittings

Does the vendor intend to leave the carpets, curtains and light fittings etc? Make sure all extra items that you see on your tour are included in the contract.

Light fittings, curtain rails, bathroom fitments, fitted bookcases, plants in the garden etc., are often disputed. Look for a solicitor using The Law Society's TransAction Scheme. It is designed to make clear exactly what is included in the purchase price. The seller is provided with a complete list of items and must indicate on it what is and what is not included

Services

HEATING Ask the owners about the past year's fuel consumption and heating costs. Ask if the loft is properly insulated; and if the cavity walls have been insulated by foam or other fillings, by whom.

WATER SUPPLY Is it on direct mains water? Check that both hot and cold-water taps run clean. Discoloration could indicate a rusting storage tank and pipework. Ask how hard or soft the water is. If it's very hard, you may need to consider water-softening measures in your central heating and water systems to stop the pipes from furring up. If the water is naturally soft, it shouldn't be a problem as long as the water pipework isn't lead. Most lead plumbing has been replaced now.

COUNCIL TAX How much is it?

ELECTRICITY How old is the wiring? Anything older than 25 years will definitely need replacing. Newer wiring systems will have a consumer unit (a box of miniature circuit breakers which don't blow) instead of an old-fashioned box of fuses.

Buyer's and seller's markets

There are times when it is easier to sell than to buy (a seller's market) and times when the reverse is true (a buyer's market).

- ◉ **A SELLER'S MARKET** Occurs when more people want to buy than there are properties, and when loan finance is comparatively easy to obtain. At these times you will probably be able to sell your property within a few weeks at a good price.

- ◉ **A BUYER'S MARKET** Is when there are more properties than prospective purchasers, and loan finance may be difficult to obtain or interest rates high. It may take a long time before you find a purchaser prepared to pay the price you want.

DRAINAGE Is the house connected to mains drainage or is there a septic tank or cesspool?

PARKING
- ⊙ Is there a garage, and is it big enough?
- ⊙ Is there parking for more than one car?
- ⊙ Street parking – Is this restricted? Does the local authority charge for resident's parking permits?

Vacant possession

When could you move in?

Taking a second look

If you are still interested in the property, it is essential to go back again to see it at a different time of the day, on a different day of the week and in different weather conditions if possible. It is easy to gloss over the faults in your enthusiasm and a second look will ensure you've covered all the points on the checklist above.

THE MECHANICS OF BUYING

Once you have chosen your property, there is a series of steps that must be followed.

1 Consider making an offer Once you have seen the house you like, you will be considering putting in an offer. Now, you need to ask yourself about the likely changes it would make to your standard of living and outgoings:

- ⊙ What is the house going to cost in monthly mortgage payments?
- ⊙ How will the mortgage affect your life insurance premiums (if payable on endowment or a mortgage-protection policy)?
- ⊙ House contents insurance: is the premium higher for this area than where you are currently living? Ask your insurers for a quotation on the new property.
- ⊙ Fuel consumption and travel costs: how much will it cost to get to work/the children to school. Will you need a second car?
- ⊙ Will you have to spend out on redecoration or is the decor 'liveable'?

2 Find a solicitor If you are ready to put in an offer and haven't yet found a solicitor, now is the time to choose one. In England and Wales, you will also have the choice of going to a licensed conveyancer who specialises in house purchase transactions. Tell them about the offer.

Conveyancing is covered in more detail in Legal Matters, see page 435, but in essence your solicitor or conveyancer will:

- ⊙ Advise you on the draft contract.
- ⊙ Explain the details of the mortgage deed.
- ⊙ Check that there are no developments planned (such as a road widening scheme) that might adversely affect the value of the property under consideration.

BUYING A FLAT

- Is it leasehold or freehold? If leasehold, ask the current owner or estate agent who handles the general administration and maintenance of the building, and how much times is left on the lease
  In Scotland, leasehold as such doesn't exist. Responsibility for repairs, the proportion of costs to be borne by each owner and the rights of owners to instruct repairs are dealt with in the title deeds of the property.
- Find out what ground rent is payable.
- Get an idea of the annual maintenance charges for repair or redecoration. Is there any major expenditure to come?

- If the flat comes with a share of the freehold, there will still be these common bills to pay, but they will be the joint responsibility of all the flat owners. Ask to see the lease and find out how the bills are divided between the flats.
- In the case of converted and freehold flats, check with your mortgage lender before proceeding too far towards buying to see whether they will accept such properties.
- Are there any restrictions in the lease such as hanging out washing, making a noise after 11pm, keeping pets or having parties?

- Go through the title documents to ensure that proper title to the property is obtained.
- Check restrictions on the way the property is used, compliance with building regulations and planning legislation.
- Check legal aspects of facilities, such as sewers serving the property.
- Arrange the exchange of contracts.
- Arrange for completion, when the balance of the mortgage is paid to the seller and the buyer moves into the property.

3 Make an offer Make sure you have a clear understanding of exactly what the property includes and that the particulars are all correct. Put your offer in quickly, either direct to the seller if being sold privately, or to the seller's estate agent. Don't forget to take into account how much you can afford, the state of the property market (i.e. whether you have any bargaining power) and how much you are prepared to raise your offer. Let the estate agent or vendor know if you:

- Are a cash buyer.
- Already have a buyer for your own property.
- Have a mortgage certificate guaranteeing the offer of a loan.

Any of these will make your offer much more attractive to the seller.

Be prepared: you may be asked to pay a small holding deposit as a token of your interest. This deposit isn't binding in law so if you are unwilling to pay it it shouldn't jeopardise your chances of buying. If you do pay it, get a receipt saying 'subject to contract and survey'. If the sale falls through before contracts are exchanged, that money has to be returned.

Once you have put in your offer you will be asked for the details of your solicitor or conveyancer. The average period, from putting in your offer to the date when the keys are handed over, is about 12–16 weeks, but this can vary considerably.

Problems with solicitors

If you experience any disputes with your solicitor, you can use the Law Society's Arbitration Scheme. For problems with a licensed conveyancer turn to the Council for Licensed Conveyancers (see Useful Organisations).

4 **Sell your current house** Put your own house on the market if you haven't already done so. (See Selling Your Home, pages 423–6.)

5 **Confirm your offer** Confirm your offer in writing 'subject to contract and to survey' either direct to the seller or to his/her estate agent. Liaise with your solicitor or conveyancer over this.

You may have to wait some time for the offer to be considered by the seller, or you may have to put in a new offer. If you are lucky, your offer may be accepted straight away. If so, the house is 'under offer', and you can ask the seller not to take offers from any other potential buyers – but he or she is under no obligation to do so. While the sellers may not look like the kind of people to accept a higher offer after accepting yours, it may well be the estate agent who is keen to get as much for the property as possible. 'Lock-out' agreements are now used by some solicitors, where both sides agree in writing not to withdraw from the offer. The seller agrees not to deal with anyone else for a fixed period, and the buyer agrees to take active steps to proceed with the purchase.

The time between making an offer and exchanging contracts is always an anxious one, as in England and Wales, simply making an offer and having it accepted isn't legally binding on either side.

6 **Make a formal mortgage application** Return the mortgage application form to the lender with the fee for valuation. The lender will require considerable information about the house (most of which can be obtained from the particulars provided by the estate agent or seller) and also about you, the borrower.

7 **The valuation** In order to check the value of a property, the lender will commission a qualified valuer to inspect it. You will be expected to pay for this even if you don't subsequently buy the property. There is no set scale of fees for valuation, but an average fee would be in the region of about £300. Ask the lender for an exact figure.

The valuation assesses whether the condition and value of the house is adequate security for the loan. If the building society feels the house is worth less than the purchase price, the proportion that will be lent may be calculated on the valuation price, not the purchase price.

For a lender's valuation, the valuer takes into account factors such as the age, and type of property; its fixtures and features, construction, general state of repair and amenities. It will provide some idea of the condition of the 'visible' parts of the property. The lender is not legally bound to disclose the contents of the report, but may recommend that certain work is done, such as repointing a chimney or putting in a damp-proof course, before the loan is given. He/she may even recommend that an amount of the loan is withheld until the work has been carried out.

8 **Get a survey** The lender's valuation is no substitute for a full structural survey on the property. Only about 20 per cent of buyers arrange even a House Buyer's report, and the result is that around 4 per cent of house purchases involve a property with a defect such as subsidence and dry rot.

General house-buying tips

- Keep all the paperwork to do with your house transactions together in a file. Keep a copy of every letter you send and take a note of every conversation relating to the buying or selling transaction. Note the date, time, who you spoke to and what was said.

- Keep a record of financial details and all the money you spend.

- If possible, type letters and documents and use email or a fax machine to speed up the process. Make sure that you print off hard copies of your emails. Send any important communications by registered post.

- Stay in regular contact with your solicitor.

TYPES OF SURVEY

FULL STRUCTURAL/BUILDING SURVEY

If the property is old, or clearly in need of repair, or you are contemplating alterations such as extensions, you should definitely commission a full structural/building survey. There is no scale of fees for structural surveys. Costs depend on the property's size and age, but typically are £500–1500. It's expensive, but it can be invaluable to ensure that there are no major structural faults that may prove expensive to repair. It will also tell you in detail about minor defects, which in the long run, you can't ignore.

An inspection lasts several hours and provides a detailed examination and report of all visible parts of the building, including testing walls for dampness and timber for damage. It is important to discuss with your surveyor exactly what is to be covered in the survey before he or she proceeds.

HOME BUYER'S SURVEY AND VALUATION

The Royal Institution of Chartered Surveyors (RICS) offer the Home Buyer's Survey and Valuation (HBSV), which is less detailed than a full structural survey but is more than a valuation. Buyers are advised to commission this type of independent survey at the very least. It will tell you about:

- The general condition of the property.
- Any factors likely to affect materially the value of the property.
- The true, current value of the property in the open market.
- The estimated reinstatement cost for insurance purposes. This is the cost of rebuilding the house if it burns down.

The HBSV is suitable and sufficient for most purchases of second-hand property. If a problem is spotted, you can then arrange a more detailed examination with the agreement of the existing owner.

For more advice on the different surveys available, visit the RICS website: www.rics.org.

You can organise the survey yourself, or in most cases get the building society's surveyor to do your survey at the same time as the valuation. This may reduce the overall fees for both survey and valuation slightly.

Tell the surveyor as much as you know about the house and its history, and any plans you have for changing the structure, such as knocking down walls, opening up fireplaces or building an extension. Of course, it will be easier for your surveyor to be thorough if the house is empty (and therefore floorboards etc. accessible). If it's still occupied try to get an idea how much prodding and upheaval the owners are prepared to put up with, as they may already have had to put up with other prospective buyers' surveys.

Alternatively, you will need to find a qualified surveyor to carry out the work for you. Contact the Royal Institution of Chartered Surveyors for names of any of their members in your area. Otherwise, get a recommendation from a friend.

The surveyor may recommend that you have specialist tests carried out if the property is of a particular age. He may also recommend specialist treatment such as damp proofing is carried out. Get at least three estimates and then bear this in mind: you may want to offer less to take into account the work needed.

9 Exchange contracts for sale and purchase

Now you are legally committed to buying. You will have to pay a deposit of 5–10 per cent, and arrange a completion date. Ensure that any life policy runs from the date you exchange contracts. Also arrange buildings and contents cover from this date.

10 Completion

This is when you pay the balance of the purchase price, and in return you get the keys and title deeds (usually done via the solicitors). Your mortgage lender is then sent the deeds.

BUYING IN SCOTLAND

The buying and selling process is rather different in Scotland than England or Wales. There are two major advantages of the system in Scotland:

❶ It avoids the difficulties of delays resulting from 'chains'. (These can arise under the English and Welsh system if one sale is delayed, thereby affecting a whole series of transactions.)

❷ Formal offers are legally binding, so you cannot be gazumped (where someone offers more for the property) or gazundered (where someone can act more quickly on the transaction than you can).

If you are thinking of buying a property in Scotland, you should seek advice from your legal adviser before you take any steps at all.

SELLING YOUR HOME

If you already own a home, you'll know that the first step to finding your new home is to get a good idea of your current property's value and then put it on the market.

It's also a good idea, at this stage, to make a list of the items you are prepared to leave (such as carpets, curtains, a washing machine), then to include the cost of buying new items in the calculations for your new property.

TIP
If your appliances are built-in or plumbed in, it can be more cost-effective to leave old appliances and buy new.

Using an estate agent

The estate agent's role is to value your property in line with others of a similar nature in your area, advise on how to prepare the house for sale, handle enquiries and receive offers on your behalf. He or she should guide you through all aspects of your sale and have a good relationship with other professionals such as banks and building society managers, mortgage advisers, solicitors and accountants. The estate agent's fee is usually about 1 to 3 per cent of the selling price, plus VAT.

Ideally, go to an estate agent who has been recommended to you or in whom you already have confidence. Since the implementation of the Estate Agents Act 1979, the industry has had to clean up its act. It is, however, still permissible for anybody to set up as an estate agent without training. So ask if the estate agent of your choice is a member of a professional body. There is also an ombudsman to deal with complaints. The Properties Misdescription Act also curbs the natural tendency towards flowery descriptions, such as 'bijou' when they mean cramped.

THE SCOTTISH SYSTEM

This is the basic process:

1 Even before you have found a house, you should establish your eligibility for a mortgage on the intended type of property.

2 When you have found a house you like, tell your solicitor. He will then notify the seller's solicitor or estate agent of your interest.

3 The survey is usually carried out before you make a formal offer for a property.

4 If the survey report is favourable, make a written offer (with a time limit for acceptance) to buy the property through your solicitor. This is a formal document specifying all the conditions on which you are willing to buy the property right down to when you want to move in and what extras you want to buy (such as carpets, curtains or cooker). If your offer is accepted, it is a binding contract under Scottish Law and you will not have an opportunity for second thoughts. You may be penalised if you do break the contract.

5 If there is more than one interested party, there will be a closing date by which all interested parties must have made their offer. The highest offer is normally the one accepted, but the seller may take other factors into consideration such as the moving date. (The offer will be subject, among other things, to local authority and property searches. If they disclose anything adverse, you can withdraw your offer or renegotiate the price.)

6 Usually, the seller's solicitor will tell your solicitor if the offer has been accepted with any modifications to the terms of your offer, such as the date of entry. These written modifications along with the offer are called 'the Missives'. This bargaining process should only take a few days. From the date of signing the Missives to the date on which you get the key is a matter of negotiation.

7 Your solicitor will then start the conveyancing procedure and you must formalise your mortgage arrangements.

8 On the date of settlement, the money for the full price will be handed over in return for the title deeds and the keys.

If you don't have a particular firm in mind, look for estate agents who are members of The National Association of Estate Agents (or RICS, or the Incorporated Society of Valuers and Auctioneers). The NAEA insists on a certain level of training for its members, has a code of practice and a grievance procedure for dissatisfied customers.

Ask at least three estate agents to value your house (this is usually free of charge) and get an idea of how long they think it will take to sell. Choose one that will co-ordinate your sale carefully, not just the one that offers the highest valuation or the lowest fees.

DIY selling

If you are prepared to organise advertising and viewing of your home yourself, you could save an estate agent's fee. On a property worth £200,000, this could be as much as £6,000. Around 5 per cent of homes in the UK are sold successfully in this way. As long as you don't hand over sole selling rights, you could even try to sell private as well as having an estate agent working on your behalf. However, selling privately involves effort, and depends on a number of factors:

- ⊙ You. Are you resilient enough to put up with derogatory comments about your home, or insultingly low offers?
- ⊙ The time you have available to organise appointments and show viewers round.
- ⊙ The area in which you live, i.e. sought after or run down.
- ⊙ Market conditions, i.e. buyer's or seller's market. In a seller's market it may be easy to find buyers, but in a buyer's market you may well need help to access potential buyers.
- ⊙ The type of property you are selling. It is probably easier to sell DIY at the lower end of the market.

Selling in Scotland

If you are selling a house in Scotland you may be familiar with the Scottish system already, where more properties are sold by solicitors than estate agents (see Buying in Scotland, pages 422–3).

First, you should contact your solicitor before putting your house on the market, to give him/her time to get your title deeds in good order, and get local authority searches under way.

You can advertise your house for sale either using a solicitor, which is the usual way; using an estate agent; or by doing it yourself.

The first thing to decide is when you are going to sell, how much you want for the property and what items you are prepared to leave behind. In Scotland it is normal to advertise at 'offers over' a certain figure, in anticipation of receiving a higher bid.

It is usual for any interested parties, whom you may have shown round your house, to tell their solicitor that they are interested. They will then notify your solicitor. You should then not sell to anyone without giving everyone who has notified an interest to you, your solicitor, or your estate agent, an opportunity of making an offer.

Noting interest is usually followed by a visit from the surveyors of interested parties. If the reports are favourable they will probably be followed by an offer, which will be made in writing by the buyer's solicitors.

Sole or joint selling rights

You can instruct more than one estate agent to sell your property. If you ask just one, he/she may reduce his fee, say to 1 per cent. Don't give them sole selling rights, as you will have to pay them commission even if you sell privately without their help. Joint sole agency is more usual. Two agents take the property on their books and split the commission, say 1.5 per cent each, whoever arranges the sale.

Sell safely

Take into account security when showing potential buyers around your home. Make sure you take contact details when you make an appointment and ring back to check that the number is genuine. Arrange to have a friend with you if you are alone and concerned about personal safety.

The offer – usually the highest is accepted – will form the basis of the sale contract and will usually contain a large number of conditions.

Sometimes a number of letters are required to adjust the details for your and the purchaser's contractual obligations. Only once all the conditions are agreed is there a binding contract. The offer and letters are known as 'the Missives'.

When more than one person wants to make an offer for your property it will be appropriate for your solicitor to fix a closing date for offers.

For more details, see the Law Society of Scotland website: www.lawscot.org.uk.

REMOVALS

Once you have exchanged contracts and been given a moving date, there's no time to lose in preparing for the big day.

Professional removers

If using a professional removal company, start selecting one well in advance. Ask friends and neighbours to recommend firms or contact the British Association of Removers (www.bar.co.uk) for firms in your area. Alternatively, your local estate agent may well be able to recommend someone. You may stand a better chance of getting the firm you want

SELLING TIPS

Everyone knows a few tricks of the trade when it comes to making a house seem instantly more appealing to prospective purchasers. But there's more to it than simply putting out cut flowers in the sitting room and wafting the aroma of freshly brewed coffee around the house.

DO

✔ Tidy up any peeling wallpaper and repair damaged paintwork.

✔ Fix any dripping taps and replace broken light bulbs.

✔ Deal with sticking windows and doors.

✔ Keep halls and stairways clear.

✔ Kitchens and bathrooms sell houses more than any other rooms in the house. Keep them neat and clean.

✔ Tidy fitted cupboards, basement and attic.

✔ Clean windows.

DON'T

✘ Have too many people present. Potential buyers always feel like intruders and wish to respect your privacy. Try not to hurry them through the house.

✘ Arouse suspicion with last-minute redecoration or tell-tale fresh paint smells.

✘ Apologise for your home. By doing so you might suggest problems that don't actually exist.

PRIOR TO A VISIT

+ Keep the front of the house clean and tidy: lawns trimmed, flower beds cultivated and free of rubbish and clutter.

+ In bad weather, be sure that paths and steps are free from snow and ice.

+ Keep the driveway clear and the gates open with adequate room for the visitors to park easily.

+ At night, turn on a porch or hall light to welcome them.

+ Make sure the house number or name can be seen from the road, and if you have a doorbell, make sure it works.

+ Keep pets under control and quiet, or out of the house.

+ Turn off the radio, TV or stereo so buyers aren't distracted.

+ If your buyer seems interested, offer to answer their questions but then let them look at their leisure.

+ Have an idea of the latest gas/electricity/water bill, in case they ask.

on the day you want if you pick a day in the middle of the month, as this is when they are usually least busy.

Get two or three estimates based on a thorough inspection of your entire house, garden and belongings. Point out anything that may need special packing such as an antique clock, computer equipment, or the freezer. Don't forget to include the loft, garage or shed in the grand tour, and remember to mention any items that need to be picked up from somewhere else. Also tell them what to expect in terms of access at the new house. (Break it to them gently if you're moving into a fifth-floor flat with no lift.)

When you accept an estimate you are expected to give a firm date for the job. It's a good idea to confirm in writing any special packaging arrangements. You'll also need to consider extending your insurance cover for the move.

PACKING HINTS

- You may be able to hire packing cases along with a van. If not, collect some heavy-duty boxes from the local supermarket: arrange to call when they have had an unpacking session. Alternatively, you can buy packing kits online or from stores like Argos.
- Collect old newspapers and bubble wrap for packing.
- For moving TVs and computers etc., ask a local electrical retailer if they have any cartons with leftover polystyrene shavings.
- Don't fill boxes too full otherwise they become impossible to lift. Boxes of books should be no more than half full if you intend to lift them off the ground.
- When packing china and glass, make a thick bottom layer of crumpled newspaper. Put heavier items at the bottom. Wrap large items individually and put other items round them with plenty of crumpled newspaper or bubble wrap.

- Put vases in plastic bags before wrapping in newspaper so you don't have to wash them when you unpack.
- Label boxes as you pack by content, by room and with any other useful details such as non-essentials, or in order of unpacking.
- Remember that the order in which you load the van will be the reverse of how you unload it. Items you will want to unpack first e.g. carpets, should go in last.
- Lift heavy items with your knees bent and your back straight to avoid strain.
- Don't forget to keep your emergency box (see page 430) accessible in your car.

DIY removal

It may be worth considering doing the removal yourself if you are a first-time buyer, or moving out of furnished rented accommodation, or simply have few heavy belongings and plenty of muscle to help. It will also be considerably cheaper. But don't attempt it otherwise, as the process can be totally exhausting, even with a removal firm who can pack more carefully and move furniture much more quickly than you.

You'll need to hire a large van for the duration of the move. You can drive up to a 7,500kg/7½ ton vehicle with a standard driving licence, but you have to be over 25 years to satisfy most hire firms. Choose a hire company that is a member of the British Vehicle Rental and Leasing Association (see www.bvlra.co.uk). Once you know the capacity of the van, you will need to estimate what loads it will take and therefore how many journeys you will have to make. Check whether you can hire it just one way.

If you are doing the removing yourself, allow plenty of time in advance for packing. You will need packing cases, rope or webbing to secure items in the van, and blankets or other protection for polished surfaces.

Many firms don't include contents insurance for the moving of your goods and chattels. Those that do usually offer a fairly low threshold of around £10,000. Otherwise it may be sensible to organise your own.

Storage

If you cannot move straight into your new home, you may have to put your belongings into storage for a while. Many removal firms have their

Damaged goods

Removal firms don't generally accept responsibility for damage to any items which have not been packed by them, and nor do their insurers. So check before you start packing. Watch out for the 'pairs and sets clause', which means that the insurers will not pay the costs of replacing any undamaged item forming part of a set such as a dinner service when replacements cannot be found.

own storage facilities. Look in the telephone directory or ask the British Association of Removers (see Useful Organisations) for a list of its members. Always get more than one estimate, and compare costs. Storage firms accept the whole contents of a house with the exception of perishable or flammable goods. Non-perishable food items will be accepted if they are packed carefully, in order to discourage attack by vermin.

Stored goods are usually packed into sealed containers at your home and the containers are stored untouched in a warehouse until you need them again. This way there is less risk of damage in transit or warehousing, there is greater protection from dirt, and a lower possibility of loss.

The storage firm or your own household insurers can arrange cover for house contents during storage. Make sure it is a sufficient sum and covers all risks.

It is expensive to retrieve items once they are in storage. Attach 'keep forward labels' to items you may want in advance so they can be kept reasonably accessible.

PREPARING TO MOVE

Up to a month in advance

❶ Get removal firms' estimates and/or quotations for van-hire charges. Choose the firm, or van company, and confirm arrangements in writing with your down payment. Check the quotation. Usually, your mover will take down curtains/blinds and lift carpets if asked – but will not put them up again or lay fitted carpeting.

❷ If doing the move yourself, book strong friends and family early for help with the packing, cleaning and moving.

❸ Services: Arrange for electricity, gas (and if applicable, water) meters to be read at your old address. At the same time, arrange for the cooker, washing machine and dishwasher to be disconnected.

❹ About two weeks before moving in, contact the various services – electricity, gas and water – about your moving date so that they can connect supplies. Ask the previous owner not to disconnect the services when they leave.

❺ Telephone: Arrange for a final bill to be made up to the day on which you move out of the old property. If new occupants don't want the phone, arrange for disconnection.
Make sure that the line to your new home is not disconnected, or if a new line is required, arrange for installation as early as possible since there may be a delay. Now's the time to think about also getting extra sockets installed.

❻ Media: Arrange for Internet and satellite services to be transferred to the new property or cancel the old services and arrange new ones.

❼ Get change-of-address cards, and fill in a mail redirection form, available from any post office. The postal service can redirect y our mail for up to a year after the move, but you must give seven days' notice before the date you want the redirection to start.

❽ Notify the National TV Licence Records Office in Bristol of your change of address.

STORAGE GUIDELINES

Use the following as a guide for containers:

2-bedroom semi or terrace
= 2–3 containers

3-bedroom semi or terrace
= 3–4 containers

3 bedroom detached
= 4–6 containers

TIP
Storage firms recommend that you clean your carpets before putting them into store. Damage from moths can be a problem during storage. Wash then treat woollen clothes and blankets with a moth-deterrent spray.

9. You may want to transfer your bank account to your new area. The bank may require a formal letter, or a new form, asking for the transfer to be made on a certain date.

10. If you hire appliances such as a TV, DVD recorder or washing machine, check with the rental firm whether you can take them with you to your new home. This is worth doing if you have been paying a reduced rent for an older appliance. Otherwise turn it in and take out a new contract locally.

11. Arrange buildings and contents insurance at the new house from the date of moving, and contents insurance during removal.

12. Locate your nearest household refuse site and start sorting and throwing things out. Buy plenty of strong black sacks, and check with charity shops exactly what they will and won't take. Then tackle hoarding places, such as a loft or garage, as early as possible.

13. If doing your own removal, arrange to use boxes from a local supermarket.

14. Book overnight accommodation for the night after the move, if necessary.

15. Arrange for children and pets to stay with friends or relatives during the move.

One week ahead

1. Plan in advance roughly where the furniture – or at least the heavier items – will be placed. Better still, make a room-by-room plan and mark the furniture with coloured stickers to represent different rooms. This will help you work out if you have room for everything, and will give you something to pass on to the removal men on the day.

2. Send off change-of-address cards, and let the following people know about the change of address (see box right). Many companies will have an area on their website that allows you to make updates online.

3. Cancel deliveries to your old address such as newspapers, vegetable boxes and settle accounts. Rearrange at the new house.

4. Put valuables and documents in a safe place.

5. Clarify parking arrangements: Tell police or the local authority about the move, purchase permits if required and if necessary ask about getting the space outside your house coned off until the removal lorry has arrived. You need about 15m/50ft of parking for one large moving truck.

6. Check self-drive van arrangements.

7. Double-check the arrangements and timings for meter readings, disconnection and connection of electricity and gas.

8. Double-check with seller or buyer about leaving off or on electricity, water and heating, plus where to leave old keys and collect new.

9. To make life easier for the removers, put crockery and glass ready on a level surface ready for packing; leave drawers unlocked.

10. Dismantle modular furniture (which isn't usually covered by insurance). Remember that your insurance will not cover items you have packed yourself so think carefully about what you should leave to the removal men.

TIP

If you are moving to a new address within the same telephone exchange area, it is usually possible to take your existing number with you, but there may be a charge for doing so.

Notifying your move

- Car breakdown company.
- Bank/building society.
- Children's schools.
- Credit and charge-card companies.
- Doctor/dentist/optician.
- Employer.
- Current employer and previous employer's pension fund.
- Hire-purchase/TV rental company.
- Inland Revenue (notify Inspector of Taxes).
- Insurance company for policies on car, house, life, private health etc.
- Magazine subscriptions.
- National Insurance (notify the Department for Work and Pensions).
- Pension/benefit book (notify the Department for Work and Pensions).
- Professional bodies
- TV Licence records office (via Post Office).
- Vehicle registration and driving licence (notify DVLC, Swansea; this is a legal requirement).
- Vet.
- Local council.
- Loan companies.
- Investment companies.

⑪ Run down food stocks in your deep freeze so that as little as possible is left. (The removal men are not responsible for the contents.) Don't pack your cool box – set it aside to take remaining contents of refrigerator and freezer.

The day before

If you have a long journey or a lot of possessions the removal company may start packing in advance.

❶ To ensure your move out of the old and into the new house runs smoothly, it's a good idea to prepare two boxes of useful items, to take directly with you (see box right).

❷ Pack overnight case if necessary.

❸ Defrost fridge.

❹ Get supply of cash for tips and meals.

❺ Leave out vacuum cleaner, broom, cleaning equipment and plenty of black sacks for last-minute rubbish.

❻ Keep phone numbers for service companies handy in case of problems.

Completion and handover of keys

Your solicitor or conveyancer will have dealt with the legal and financial side of completion. Normally, the keys are not released until the purchase money has reached the seller's solicitor. The seller should give keys to the solicitor, who will give them to your solicitor and then to you. It may be more convenient for the keys to be handed over by the estate agent. The seller's solicitor will authorise this as soon as completion has taken place.

Moving day

❶ Don't leave your handbag, wallet or any valuables lying around either house on moving day. Keep your bank card and some cash handy.

❷ Strip and pack bedding in labelled sacks.

❸ Clear kitchen of foodstuffs.

❹ The meters should be read and services disconnected.

❺ When the removal company arrives, show the foreman around and explain your labelling system. Check that any special requests have been noted. If the men are doing all the packaging and loading keep out of their way.

❻ Check that the heating system and mains water has been left on or off, depending on the arrangements made with the new owner.

❼ Leave all the keys labelled.

❽ Make sure the removal men know exactly where they are taking your belongings. Ideally, give them a map, the postcode for their GPS, and contact phone numbers (mobile and landline).

❾ Send someone on ahead to let the removal men in and start directing the proceedings.

Items to take with you

- **BOX ONE** For the kitchen, containing: kettle, tea-bags, coffee, milk, sugar, cold drinks (if summer), biscuits, mugs, spoons, plates, knives, cleaning cloth, towel, can opener, toilet paper, pain killers, plasters, antiseptic wipes, hand sanitiser, note-pad and pen, corkscrew and change.

- **BOX TWO** For the car, containing: emergency tool-kit, mobile phone charger, screwdrivers, pliers, adjustable spanner, nails, hammer, screws, fuses, fuse wire, tape, string, light bulbs, plugs, adaptors and torch.

At the new home

❶ Stick your plan for rooms, if you have one, in a prominent place. Alternatively, you may prefer to stand there yourself and direct the men as they unload each item of furniture.

❷ After all your possessions have been unloaded and the job finished, the removal men will expect a tip (about £5–10 per man is usual). If you aren't satisfied, say so now, otherwise any claim you make later may prove to be a problem. You may be asked to sign a discharge document that the job is completed. Write on this any reservations you have about the work. If you have not yet inspected your belongings, sign as 'unexamined'.

❸ Make up beds and find towels and soap.

❹ Ring the local council to find out the day for refuse collection, local recycling practices, and the location of your nearest household waste site. (There's bound to be rubbish when unpacking is finished.)

❺ You may want to have a good clean of the house before you unpack. But be warned, the time limit within which a claim for removal damage must be made, in writing, both to the insurers and the removal company, may be as little as three days after delivery.

Nevertheless, on the removal day, don't attempt to unpack everything immediately. Just sort out the essentials, and celebrate being in your new home.

After the move

❶ Have locks of outer doors changed.

❷ Fit key-operated window locks if they are not already in place.

❸ Check if your insurer recommends specific types of lock or offers any discounts if certain brands are installed. In general, when buying new locks, look for the British Standards Kitemark on the front face of the lock or on the packaging. For further advice on security see Home Security, pages 362–73.

Useful Information

Legal Matters

INTRODUCTION

The purpose of this section is to give you a guide to the law and explain your rights as they affect your acquisition of your home and your enjoyment of it. It is not intended as a substitute for taking legal advice, if you have a serious legal problem, or if you are about to enter into some important legal transaction. This is how the law affects you, and is aimed at encouraging you to be more confident in consulting a professional expert if it becomes necessary. It may also help you to understand the advice you are given.

Every attempt is made to give you an accurate outline of the law (as it stands on the 10 January 2010). But the law on many subjects is complex, and many detailed provisions and exceptions apply to particular situations. Furthermore, the law is subject to constant changes as a result of Acts of Parliament and court cases where judges interpret those Acts, and the law in Scotland and Northern Ireland often differs from that in force in England and Wales.

You should not, therefore, use this outline of the law as if it is tailor-made to deal with your own particular case, and no liability can attach to the author or publisher of this work if you do.

If you are in doubt about whether or not to enter into a transaction, or whether or not to bring or defend a case against another party, you are strongly advised to seek professional legal help.

BUYING A FLAT OR HOUSE

EMPLOYING A SOLICITOR

Once you have chosen the home of your dreams and your offer has been accepted, you must decide who should be responsible for carrying out the legal side of the transaction.

It is perfectly possible to do the conveyancing yourself. Buying freehold property is less intimidating that leasehold. Either way you will have to do a great deal of homework. If you get it right it will save you the cost of employing someone – about several hundred

> ### How do I find a professional?
>
> You can search online for solicitors at www.lawsociety.org.uk/choosingandusing/findasolicitor.law and for licensed conveyancers at www.conveyancer.org.uk.
>
> The Law Society and the Council for Licensed Conveyancers have complete lists of professionals for any given area (see Useful Organisations) and your local library should also have a directory of local practitioners.

pounds or even a four figure sum. However, if some complication arises, or you get it wrong, it could cost you a great deal more with only yourself to blame.

The information set out in this section is not intended to be a guide to do-it-yourself conveyancing. It may, however, help you when dealing with a professional to have some idea what is being discussed and what is involved.

It has also to be said that solicitors prefer to deal with other solicitors, and although they will, of course, co-operate with a person conducting his or her own affairs, the whole operation runs more smoothly between professionals. Since buying a home is probably the biggest transaction you will ever make, you will probably not wish to add to your headaches by doing your own conveyancing.

Most people, therefore, employ a solicitor or a licensed conveyancer. If you do not already know of one don't hesitate to shop around in the same way as you would to find a plumber or builder. Try and get a friend to recommend a local practitioner, and, don't worry about walking off the street into a local office and enquire about conveyancing. See How Do I Find a Professional?, above.

Advantages of employing a solicitor
One advantage is that he or she may be accepted by the building society or bank to deal on their behalf with the mortgage. Quite apart from his or her knowledge and experience of the procedure, items such as the transfer of funds can be dealt with more easily by him or her.

Licensed conveyancers

For many years, solicitors have faced competition from licensed conveyancers, who are also trained to take care of the legal aspects of buying and selling property. The purpose of licensing such people, who do not need to be trained in other aspects of the law, was to provide a cheaper alternative service. The effect has been to encourage solicitors to reduce their prices.

Can I afford a professional?

Before you employ either a solicitor or a licensed conveyancer to undertake the legal work for you, make sure you ask for an estimate of the cost involved. Most will take on the conveyancing of freehold and straightforward leasehold properties for a fixed fee. Otherwise you'll be quoted an hourly rate. The amount charged by different people varies considerably, and unless you happen to know a solicitor well, it is worth getting two or three quotations.

TIP: There is no such thing as legal aid for conveyancing – you have to pay the costs yourself.

What will the professional do?

The first job of a solicitor or conveyancer is to ensure that the property belongs to the seller: that is, that it is really his or hers to sell. It is vital to make sure that it is not subject to rights owned by others. For example, there could be tenants who have the right to stay in the property. Or a property apparently owned by one person could be subject to the rights of an estranged partner. It could even be subject to a mortgage that cannot be paid off, or there may be some other legal charge on the property.

In addition, the solicitor will have to check to see what rights anybody else has in relation to the property, and what local plans there are which might affect it. He also has to make enquiries about the property from the sellers, and ascertain what is included in the sale. Most of this will usually be done before you enter into a binding contract.

How can I be sure the property will be mine?

The most fundamental task is to establish title to the property. Nowadays, most properties are registered with the name of the owner at the Land Registry (see Useful Organisations). This means that there is a State guarantee that the person whose name is registered there is the owner of the property. When you complete the purchase, your own name will be recorded at the Land Registry as owner.

The Land Registry keeps a record that includes a description and plan of the property, the name and address of the owner, and details of any mortgage outstanding on it.

Despite the scheme for compulsory registration of any conveyance, although becoming less and less common some properties which have been in the same ownership for a considerable time are still unregistered. Where this occurs, title has to be proved by establishing an unbroken chain of ownership for at least 15 years by having the deeds by which the property was conveyed each time. The idea is that each previous purchaser prior to that will have investigated the title for him- or herself. You have to go back to the last sale before 15 years ago. The last sale more than 15 years ago may have been a very long time ago. Thus, some of the deeds produced may be quite old and will simply be a bundle of deeds, which form a record of previous sales, mortgages and other dealings with the land. If the land is mortgaged, the lender normally holds the deeds as security for their loan.

Where the property is unregistered the Land Charges Department at the Land Registry will have details of any charges on the property. Although a different body to the Land Registry you can contact the Department via the website – www.landregistry.gov.uk.

TIP: A record is kept at the Land Charges Registry of any charge against unregistered property, for example security for a loan, or an interest of a wife in the matrimonial home where she is not actually a part owner.

What is meant by 'enquiries'?

Pre-contract enquiries are where you, or more likely your chosen professional, try to get relevant information about the property from the seller. Until recently these enquiries were in the form of a standard, printed form with some additions relevant to the particular property. They required the seller to give answers, as far as they could, about the condition of the property, any guarantees which there may be with it, any rights which neighbours may have, including any disputes with neighbours.

The answers to these enquiries did not often add much to the buyer's level of knowledge as they tended to be of the nature 'not so far as is known to the vendor' or 'ask your surveyor' or 'ask the local authority'.

Energy Performance Certificate

Whilst 'Home Information Packs' have been suspended, it is still the seller's responsibility to commission an Energy Performance Certificate. The EPC must be commissioned by the time the property is put up for sale, and provided to potential buyers as soon as possible. Trading Standards Officers will charge a fixed penalty fee of £200 if an EPC is not available at some point during the sale. Visit www.communities.gov.uk/housing/ for detailed and up to date advice.

Freehold or leasehold: the difference
FREEHOLD

The property will belong to you and your heirs absolutely for all time, or until it is sold. Although there could be rights of way over the land, e.g. a footpath, no one else can claim rights of ownership over it. You own both the land and the building.

LEASEHOLD

You may have bought the building (or part of it, as with a flat) but the freeholder still owns the land on which it stands. You will therefore have to pay ground rent upon it. The interest you have in the land is for a fixed term only.

Historically, this meant that after the lease had expired, the land, and with it anything built upon it, reverted to the owner of the freehold, and you were left with nothing. In the case of a long lease, this may be a long time in the future. Many leases were granted for 99 years or longer. But it meant that it was an asset with a diminishing value as the lease drew to an end. For that reason, building societies were reluctant to lend on leasehold property unless the lease still had a very long time to run: perhaps 25 years or more after the end of the mortgage period, which could mean a total of 50 years or more.

Nowadays, the law provides a remedy for this situation by creating a right to buy the freehold or extend the lease. Even if you do neither of these, the tenancy no longer automatically comes to an end. It will continue on a periodic basis until the freeholder takes action to bring it to an end.

If the property is a flat, it is almost certainly leasehold, although you may also own a share of the freehold along with some or all the other flat owners (see opposite). When a developer builds a block of flats, he will grant a lease for each of the individual flats. These may be bought and sold many times, but the freehold remains vested in the developer or is sold to an individual or company as an investment. That person or company is then entitled to collect the rents and is responsible for keeping the whole block in a good state of repair and decoration. This is a service for which they will make a charge.

TIP: It is usually in your interest to buy the freehold or extend the lease, if you can.

How can I buy the freehold or extend the lease?
HOUSES

If your home is a leasehold house, you have a right to extend the lease, or buy the freehold. If you and your home fulfil certain qualifications, you can insist on buying the freehold, even if the owner of it does not agree.

This applies if you have a long lease and have lived in your house for three years or more. Even then it only applies to leases lasting longer than 21 years, and only if the rent is no more than two thirds of the

Buying the freehold

In order to set the process in motion, you must serve notice on the landlord. You will have to pay a deposit, since you are liable for the landlord's costs of valuation, and legal fees. When you learn the cost of enfranchisement, (the cost of purchasing the freehold) you may withdraw, but may not serve notice again for another five years.

The method of calculating the value of the freehold is complicated and depends upon the value of the property. The value is based on the market rate for the freehold bearing in mind that there is a tenant living in the house.

Further information can be obtained from a booklet entitled *Residential Long Leaseholders – A Guide to Your Rights and Responsibilities* (Department for Communities and Local Government) (www.communities.gov.uk/publications/housing/booklet).

If the lease reserves a right of re-entry for breach of covenant to pay rent, the landlord may elect to forfeit the lease. The right of re-entry does not mean, however, that he can simply walk in and take over. It means that he may apply to the county court for an order that he should recover possession of the property, in which event your rights will come to an end. However, you can avoid this so long as you pay the money to the court at least five days before the hearing. Even if the court orders possession, it will not take effect for at least four weeks, and again you can obtain 'relief' from the forfeiture if you pay the money owing to the court. The court can extend this period in an appropriate case, and is likely to do so if you are making a realistic attempt to pay off the arrears.

OTHER PARTS OF THE LEASE

The lease will also show what restrictions are placed on the use of the property. For example, can it be used for business purposes as well as for a dwelling? Without an express restriction on use, the tenant may use the property for any lawful purpose subject to the requirements of planning permission.

The lease will also specify whether the property may be sub-let in whole or in part. For example, if you have a five-year lease, but are posted abroad for a year, could you let the property while you are away? Even if the lease prohibits it, would you be able to do so with the landlord's consent in writing? If the lease says you can do it with his consent, that consent may not be unreasonably withheld. Otherwise you may wish to rent out a room in order to help to pay the rent. You should check to see if the lease prohibits this altogether, or only prohibits it without the landlord's consent.

TIP: If you wish to do something forbidden by the lease, ask the landlord's permission; if your request is reasonable it will probably be granted. If the lease requires consent it may have to be granted. You must ask first, though, because otherwise, you may find yourself forfeiting the lease.

Responsibilities

The lease also sets out the responsibilities of the landlord and the tenant. It shows who is responsible for carrying out internal or external repairs or decoration. Once again, the law imposes obligations of its own.

Under the Housing Act 1985, the landlord has repairing obligations where the lease is for a term of less than seven years. He must keep in proper repair the structure and exterior of the building. This includes the drains, gutters and external pipes as well as walls, chimneys and roof.

Where the lease is for a flat, contained in only part of the building, and the landlord maintains control of the common parts, he is obliged to maintain those parts and any installation that is placed there, e.g. a boiler, which is in the part of the building controlled by him.

On the long lease of a house it is normal for the tenant expressly to undertake the obligation to keep the property in proper repair. Where the property consists of a flat in a block, usually the landlord undertakes the structural and external repairs and charges each tenant for doing so, usually with a fee or commission for his own services in making the necessary arrangements.

TIP: If you want the landlord to carry out the repairs for which he is responsible, you must inform him by letter that the repair is needed; he is under no obligation to carry out repairs he did not know had become necessary.

Does the landlord have the right to visit my home?

As we have already seen, when you rent a property you pay for the exclusive right to occupy it. But the landlord will probably have reserved certain specific rights to himself.

The rights of the landlord should be set out in the lease. This usually provides for entry by the landlord for the purpose of carrying out his duties to keep the property in good repair. Even if not specifically reserved, he has the implied right to enter for the limited purpose of carrying out work, which he has an obligation to do. Normally, he will also reserve the right to enter to inspect the property to make sure you have also fulfilled any duties you may have, but can only do so at reasonable times and on giving reasonable notice.

If you refuse to let him in, he may obtain a court order. You would also be in breach of the terms of the lease, and this may result in him obtaining possession of the property.

Can the landlord make my life difficult?

It is a criminal offence if a landlord, or anyone acting on his behalf, acts in a way that is likely to interfere with the peace or comfort of the residential occupier or members of his household. It is also an offence if he persistently withdraws or withholds services. So, if your landlord cuts off your electricity, and leaves you without light and heat, he is committing a criminal offence for which he can be taken to court and fined, or in a bad case, even sent to prison.

Since he is not entitled to force you out, you can sue him if he tries. You can sue him for breach of his obligation to allow you enjoyment of the property, or for creating a nuisance, or for trespass to the property itself. You can also ask for a court order (injunction), to stop him harassing you. If he succeeds in forcing you out of your home, the damages may be substantial. You may have to pay more to find accommodation elsewhere, particularly if the amount of your rent was limited to a registered figure. The landlord, meanwhile, will have made a gain by having vacant possession of his property.

To offset this, you can claim his profit. This is the increase in the value of his interest in the property by virtue of acquiring vacant possession.

Can he break in?

The landlord is not entitled to break in, and is committing a crime if he does. It is a criminal offence for a landlord to use or threaten violence for the purposes of securing entry into any premises, providing that to his knowledge a person opposed to his entry is on the premises.

Is my right to stay protected by law?

As we have seen, many kinds of tenancy are subject to Acts of Parliament. When the lease expires, or when the notice to quite expires, you still have the right to remain there. If the landlord wishes you to

leave he must serve on you a notice to quit. This gives you a specified time in which to leave but is only valid if this is at least four weeks.

A notice to quit, however, does not entitle the landlord physically to eject you. In order to do that he must first obtain a court order. This allows you a right to attend the hearing and put your own case forward. It is not enough, however, simply to say he has no grounds to eject you. Unless you are protected by the Rent Acts he can serve notice at will.

When is a tenancy protected?

For a tenant to be protected from eviction, certain conditions must apply. First, the property must be within the financial limits. Only very expensive properties are outside them.

Second, the landlord must be a private individual or company, not the local council, or the Crown, or in some cases housing associations, or colleges.

Third, the protection does not apply to furnished property. In order to be furnished the furniture must be substantial, not just a nominal couple of chairs.

Nor is protection offered in the case of a holiday let, or a let where the provision of services, such as meals, are an important part of what is being paid for.

In past years, because of the protection accorded to tenants, many people became reluctant to let out property and the stock, particularly of unfurnished homes, to rent on the market was diminished. This in turn led to high rents being charged. As a result 'shorthold tenancies' were created. A property let for two years or less is not subject to the Rent Acts. If the lease is extended or repeated, the Acts then start to apply.

Even when a property is protected, the landlord can regain possession in certain circumstances. For example, he can do so if you default in paying the rent, unless at a court hearing you persuade the court that you will pay within a specified time. The same applies if you are in breach of one of the other conditions of the lease.

Supposing a tenant is damaging the property, or removing items that form a part of it, or causing a nuisance to neighbours. This would entitle the landlord to have him evicted. He can also do so if he can offer the tenant suitable accommodation elsewhere, or in certain circumstances, if he wants the property back in order to make a home for himself, or for a relative.

If you are an owner-occupier who has been posted abroad for a spell, or who has to give up your home for a temporary period for some other reason, and this is made known to the tenant, you can recover the property on your return. Thus renting out your home may be a useful source of income in the meantime, and even enable you to pay the rent on your own temporary accommodation; and you can be sure of getting your home back on your return.

COUNCIL TENANTS

Security
WHAT RIGHT DO I HAVE TO STAY IN MY HOUSE OR FLAT?
Tenants of a dwelling house have a secure tenancy where the landlord is a local authority or other public body, and certain conditions apply. The house must be let as a separate dwelling and must be the tenant's only or principal home. Long tenancies, that is those for over 21 years, do not qualify as secure tenancies, nor do lettings to students.

A secure tenancy means that when the term of the tenancy runs out, a periodic tenancy takes its place: that is, a tenancy from week to week or month to month, on more or less the same terms as before.

A secure tenancy lasts for life, unless determined (i.e. brought to an end) by an order of the court. Such an order will only be made in limited circumstances. Examples are as a result of a breach of the terms under which the tenancy is held, such as non-payment of rent, or some bad behaviour on the part of the tenant. The tenancy can also be determined where the accommodation is inappropriate, that is, overcrowded or larger than is necessary, and alternative accommodation will be available for the tenant elsewhere.

So unless the council is offering you alternative accommodation for some good reason, you may stay in your council home so long as you have kept up payment of the rent, and have not behaved in some outrageous way, annoying the neighbours.

SUPPOSING I DIE, WOULD MY GROWN-UP SON BE ABLE TO TAKE OVER THE TENANCY?
Even after the death of the tenant, the tenancy may be passed on to the tenant's husband or wife, or another member of the family occupying the house as his only or principal home. He will then have the benefit of the secure tenancy. So long as your son actually lives there, and needs the property for his own accommodation and perhaps that of his family, he acquires the same rights as you had.

Right to buy
CAN I BUY THE COUNCIL HOUSE I HAVE LIVED IN FOR THE LAST TEN YEARS?
Where there is a secure tenancy, the Housing Act 1985 gave the tenant the right to buy the property from the council. This right applies where the tenant has occupied the dwelling for at least two years. If the property is a house, he may usually acquire the freehold (see Freehold or Leasehold: the Difference, pages 436–7). Where it is a flat, the tenant may acquire a long lease, for up to 125 years.

HOW MUCH WILL IT COST?
Where a council tenant exercises the right to buy the home in which he lives, the price is determined by the local council's valuer, and in the event of any dispute over the price it may be put to the district valuer to decide. He works out a figure based on the market value, assuming the house is sold with vacant possession, that is, without a sitting tenant. But the tenant does not pay the full market price. He gets a discount of between 32 per cent and 60 per cent of the market value depending on the length of time that he has been a secure tenant. So the price you pay will be less than the real value and will depend on how long you have lived there.

HOW WILL I PAY FOR IT?
On buying the property, the tenant is also entitled to borrow money to pay for it by creating a mortgage on the property. (See Getting a Mortgage, pages 407–13.) As the property is worth substantially more than the purchase price, you may be able to buy it without having to produce any large lump sum. You will simply be making repayments on the mortgage loan instead of paying rent.

RESPONSIBILITY TO VISITORS

INJURIES

Am I responsible if a visitor is injured?
Every occupier of property, whether as an owner or tenant, has a duty of care towards those who visit. The duty is to take reasonable steps to ensure visitors' safety. If you fail in this duty you may find yourself liable to pay compensation if someone is injured.

Thus if your visitor breaks his leg due to a loose floorboard on the landing, or a loose tile falls and hits her on the head, you may find yourself liable to pay for the damage resulting from the injury, including pain, suffering and loss of earnings.

HOW WOULD I PAY FOR INJURIES?

Because damages for injuries can be very substantial, they are covered by standard insurance policies under your cover for third party loss. Although there is no legal liability to have this cover it is obviously wise to do so.

The need to take out such insurance lies with the occupier rather than the owner of property. This means that even if you are only renting the property you still owe a duty of care to your visitors and can be sued if you do not fulfil it. For this reason, the liability of an occupier of property is usually covered by household contents insurance, which you would be sensible to have, whether you are a tenant or owner-occupier.

The owner, on the other hand, is liable to compensate a person who is injured as a result of a failure on his part to do the repairs for which he is responsible under the lease. So he who is bound to ensure that the drains and gutters are in good repair will be liable if a piece of guttering detaches itself and hits the milkman on the head. For this reason, buildings insurance, normally taken out by the owner, should cover the liability of the owner of the property to others. Again it is not compulsory to have buildings insurance, but if you are borrowing money on a mortgage, the lenders will insist on your having cover.

TIP: If you are the owner of a building, whether you live in it or not, make sure you have buildings insurance cover: if you are the occupier of a building, whether you own it or not, make sure you have contents insurance; make sure in both cases that they cover you for liability to third parties.

To whom does my responsibility extend?

Your liability to compensate your visitors extends to their property as well as to their persons. For example, if your guest's clothes are ruined in a flood resulting from your faulty plumbing, he will be able to claim against you. Again, damage to your visitor's possessions should be covered by your insurance.

The responsibility for your visitors applies whether they are guests who are staying in the spare bedroom for the week or have just dropped in for a cup of tea. It applies equally to anyone who is lawfully on the premises, such as those who come there to work, like plumbers or electricians, and those who come to read the meters. Even those who get no further than the front garden are included, such as postmen and milkmen. It also extends to those who have an implied right to be there such as salesmen and people collecting for charity. You can forbid such people to enter by putting a notice on the gate, and they then become trespassers if they proceed.

TRESPASSERS

It may go against the grain, but you even have a duty of care towards trespassers, so long as you can foresee that they are likely to be present. This would apply equally to someone walking across your garden, or to a group of squatters who have occupied your house. You are only under a duty to avoid taking positive steps to harm them. You do not have to protect them against existing features of your property, which may happen to pose a potential hazard. So you are not liable to pay compensation for injury to a hiker who, much to your surprise, decides to take a shortcut across your land and falls into a ditch. But you are liable if you set a hidden trap – even if the injury is to a burglar. You should have foreseen that he is likely to be injured.

There is a special duty towards children whom you know are likely to be affected by danger. While you might meet your duty towards adults by putting up a notice saying 'danger, deep water', children cannot be expected to read or to have a high degree of common sense. So you may find yourself liable if a child falls in your pond, if you know that children are accustomed to play in your garden, even if they are trespassers there. You can fulfil your duty if you take reasonable steps either to safeguard them, or alternatively to keep them out.

'Trespassers will be prosecuted'

No they won't, at least not at the moment. The word 'prosecute' applies to cases where a criminal offence has been committed. Although you'll often see this sign on land, it is not a criminal offence to trespass on someone else's property. Consequently trespassers cannot be prosecuted, at any rate not for trespassing. Of course, if they steal your possessions while they are there, or commit criminal damage to the windows or front door in order to gain access, they could be prosecuted for that. Changes in the law of trespass have, however, been proposed, and may be made soon.

What happens if my dog bites the postman?

If the injury had been caused by your pet tiger, you would be liable for it as the keeper, as your pet would belong to a dangerous species. In the case of a dog, the species as a whole is not dangerous; you are only liable if the injury caused by the dog was likely as a result of some unusual characteristics of which you were aware. Thus, if you knew perfectly well that the dog was liable to bite a stranger walking up the path, and allowed it out nevertheless, you would have to pay compensation.

There are helpful leaflets available from the Department for the Environment (DEFRA) on your responsibility for dogs – www.defra.gov.uk/wildlife-pets/pets/dangerous/index.htm.

It is an offence to use a guard dog to protect your property unless the dog is under the control of a capable handler, or unless the dog is secured so that it can't roam freely about the premises.

In civil law you can sue a trespasser, but you will only be able to claim anything more than nominal damages by way of compensation if he has damaged your property. If you are annoyed by someone regularly trespassing on your property, you might be able to get an injunction to stop him or her from entering.

May I harm a burglar?

Never, although in a few very special circumstances you may have a defence to any criminal prosecution if you do. The rules of self-defence apply. This means that a person is entitled to use reasonable force to defend himself if he is either attacked or put in fear of an immediate attack. Of course, what is reasonable has to be seen in the context of what is happening. A person may easily be put in fear of attack by the discovery in the middle of the night of an intruder who did not in fact intend to harm him. Unless you are an expert in unarmed combat, however, it would be better to avoid violence and if possible make a telephone call to the police.

How can I get rid of squatters?

Imagine returning from holiday to find that squatters have taken over your home. Perhaps they have established themselves and are living there as if it is their own home. You are permitted to use reasonable force to protect your property and to eject a trespasser. But as force is best avoided, how can the law help? Again, if they have damaged your property in order to gain entry, or even, for example, by drawing on the walls, they have committed a criminal offence, and you could ask the police to arrest them. Likewise if they have stolen your food from the freezer.

But there are special criminal offences associated with trespassing. It is an arrestable offence to remain on property when asked to leave by the owner. So if you ask them to go, giving them a reasonable time to gather their things together, and they refuse, you can get the police to arrest them. The police, on the other hand, would be reluctant to be involved in a civil dispute. In other words, if the squatters claim to be there as of right as tenants or licensees, you may have to go to the civil court in order to obtain an order for possession of the property.

GOING TO COURT

In order to obtain such an order you must go to the county court and issue what is called an 'originating application'. If you do not have a solicitor, the court staff will help. You also have to swear an affidavit, a sworn statement about your interest in the property. This could be as owner, or tenant; the important point is that you are entitled to immediate possession. You also have to say how it came about that the land was occupied without either your permission or consent.

Assuming that you do not know the names of the illegal occupiers, you should also say this. If you do know any of their names they must be named in the action. A copy of the application, specifying the date for hearing the case, must be delivered to the squatters personally. Alternatively, if their names are not known, the documents can be served by attaching them to the front door, and by putting them through the letter box in a sealed transparent envelope addressed to 'the occupiers'. Another method is to attach such envelopes to stakes placed in the ground at conspicuous parts of the occupied property.

The date fixed for the hearing must be at least five days after the day of service, including weekends. In cases of urgency, with the leave of the court, the date may be earlier. Anyone in occupation of the property who wishes to be heard may apply to become a party to the proceedings.

At the hearing, once your case has been proved by the affidavit, the court will make an order that you shall recover possession. Because the initial entry on to your property was illegal, the order is to take effect immediately. The bailiff will go to the property and evict anyone he finds there, whether parties to the proceedings or not, and hand possession of the premises to you.

IF THE SQUATTERS CHANGED THE LOCKS, CAN I STILL GET BACK IN?

As a displaced residential person, you are free to break into your own home or one you rent, so long as you do so peacefully, that is, not as part of a violent act against the squatters. So you can go in to see to your own affairs, and rescue your belongings, or even to resume occupation.

DIFFICULT NEIGHBOURS

Disputes between neighbours are particularly likely to cause frustration and strife. Once a problem has arisen, it is impossible to walk away from it, and complaining about it often seems to aggravate the matter.

NOISE

Different ways of life often result in noise being made at inconvenient times. People have different ideas about what constitutes a reasonable level of music. Where people live in close proximity, in terraced houses or flats, thin walls mean that the problem can be especially acute.

Although the courts can sometimes find a remedy for the particular problem, there can never be a remedy for the ill-feeling which can arise, and which is likely to be exacerbated by going to court. If, therefore, the matter can be settled amicably it is far better than invoking the law. Your neighbour may not have realised how the powerful bass of his stereo carries into the flat upstairs, or that his late night do-it-yourself activities coincide with your bedtime.

Can I stop my neighbour playing music in the early hours?

If speaking to your neighbour about this problem does not produce results, the next step is to keep a proper record of what took place. This can take the form of a diary, but it should set out the nature of the nuisance and record the times and dates when it occurred.

It may be that if you show this to the neighbour it will dawn on him that his activities really are disturbing you, and take steps to curb them of his own accord. If not, it will provide valuable material from which you will be able to give evidence in support of your complaint.

It would also be helpful if you could get somebody else to be present on occasions when the noise is noticeable, since noise levels are difficult to establish without a scientific instrument, and may seem louder to some than to others.

Once you have your evidence, you can take your neighbour to court by issuing a summons in your local county court, asking for compensation in the form of damages, and seeking an injunction, ordering him to stop the noise. Be warned, however, that the process may be lengthy, and any compensation is likely to be small.

Instead of suing your neighbour in the county court, where the case is tried by a judge, you could enlist the support of the Environmental Health Officers at your local council. They can issue warnings and on-the-spot fines to noisy neighbours who carry on dispite a warning. They will monitor the noise, which will make the evidence much more effective. If they take the view that there is a nuisance, they will serve an abatement order, to prohibit or restrict the noise. If this is disobeyed, your neighbour could be fined up to £5,000 and £500 a day if the nuisance continues. This will not get compensation for you but the procedure here is likely to be quicker and also cheaper, especially if you lose the case.

What other sort of noise is considered a nuisance?

Any type of noise is capable of constituting a nuisance. So a dog persistently barking, an alarm that seems to be always ringing and continual hammering are all examples of a nuisance, which could result in a court case. It is all a question of what is reasonable in the circumstances. This depends not only on the level of the sound and the time of day, but also the area. What may be considered a nuisance in a quiet residential area is not necessarily so in a noisy industrial estate where there happen to be a few houses.

Can I insist on peace during my afternoon nap?

You cannot expect the neighbours to cope with your 'unusual' habits. Thus, if you sleep in the afternoon either because you need the extra sleep or because you work at nights, you will have no complaint in law unless the noise is sufficient to disturb people who are awake during normal hours.

What about building work?
The same applies; it is all a question of what is reasonable. If repairs or alterations are being carried out on a nearby property, it is bound to create some disturbance. But you may have a case if it goes on late into the night or continues on Sunday. Many works will need planning permission. Check with your local council. Permission will usually have time restrictions so the work can't go on into the evening or on Sundays, say.

What about Anti-social Behaviour Orders?
ASBOs (Anti-social Behaviour Orders) received a lot of media coverage when they were introduced a few years ago. Anti-social behaviour includes noisy neighbours, vandalism, litter, abandoned cars, intimidation by groups, and many other activities. If you are affected by anti-social behaviour you should contact your local anti-social behaviour co-ordinator at the local council. If the activity is bad enough, although you can't apply for an ASBO yourself, you can get involved by collecting evidence and helping the co-ordinator to monitor breaches and act as a witness in applying for court orders.

OTHER NUISANCES

It is not only noise that can constitute a nuisance. Smells, smoke and vibration could also amount to a nuisance. The smoke from an occasional bonfire is not likely to be regarded as such however. Noisy children generally do not qualify, although you may think they are sometimes a nuisance in non-legal terms.

Supposing a neighbour's water floods my house?
If anything is permitted to escape from your neighbour's house, which is likely to cause damage, you can claim compensation from him or her for the damage caused. Thus if his pipe bursts or bath overflows, and water penetrates your home causing damage to the carpets and decorations, you can make him pay for it.

Can I make my neighbour tidy up his garden?
If you take the trouble to keep a tidy garden it is annoying to have an eyesore next door. There is no law against untidiness, however. There may be covenants with the land, for example where you both agree to do or not to do certain things in relation to your property. Unless he is disobeying mutual covenants as to the state of the properties it is unlikely that you have a remedy, except in an extreme case. You could report the matter to the local council. If there is a pile of rubbish in the garden that is attracting mice and rats, the environmental health officer may insist on its removal. Or the council may take steps under its powers to preserve the amenity of the area if the mess is very visible to the public.

Can I stop trees or fences from blocking the sun?
There is no general right to light, and in particular no right to have the sun on your garden. So whether it is blocked by a fast-growing tree, or by a fence or wall that has just been erected, you have no automatic right to complain. There may be express covenants that have to be obeyed by the owners of all the properties on a particular estate, restricting the height

---

Problems with trees

Your neighbour has no right to encroach upon your territory with his trees, so you are entitled to chop off any branches that overhang your own garden or any roots that project into it from under the fence. If you do, however, he is entitled to whatever you have cut off, since even though it was growing on your side, it is still owned by him.

For example, you may not pick your neighbour's apples and keep them, or even shake the branch causing them to fall, although you may keep those that fall naturally to the ground.

If your neighbour's tree is causing serious problems, say because the roots are affecting your foundations or penetrating your drains, he or she is responsible for the damage. You would therefore be entitled to claim compensation. As your buildings insurance policy should cover this sort of damage it is easier to claim under this and let the insurance company make the appropriate claim. It is likely that he/she too is insured to cover this sort of damage.

A tree subject to a preservation order may not be lopped without permission from the local authority, whether it is yours or your neighbour's. You could be subject to a fine if you do interfere with it. Likewise if you live in a conservation area.

of fences. They are also the subject of the planning laws (see Alterations and Extensions, opposite). This does not apply to trees.

You can acquire the right to light to a particular window or, for example, to a greenhouse by having enjoyed it continuously for 20 years or more. This is a right to have a reasonable amount of light, not necessarily direct sunlight, and anyway you cannot complain if it is blocked by a tree or bush.

Who is responsible for the fence?

Often, the answer to this is clear from the deeds of a house, or the lease in the case of a leasehold property.

Generally, you are responsible for any fences wholly on your own property. Sometimes there are party walls and fences. Then both sides are responsible. If the fence marks the boundary, there is a presumption that the party responsible is the one on whose side the fence posts are. This is rather anomalous as it probably means you have to go next door in order to repair it.

How do I stop people next door taking some of my land?

Boundary disputes are frequently the source of trouble between neighbours. Although you might expect the Land Registry entry, or the deeds of a property to show exactly where the boundaries are, they are often not sufficiently detailed to do so. Furthermore, existing fencing is not always a reliable guide. It may have been put where someone once thought the boundary lay. Or it may have been built on the owner's land. Or it may even have been built on someone else's land in order to annex some of that property. If you treat land as your own for over 12 years (ten in Scotland) e.g. by occupying it, or enclosing it with a fence, and the owner has not claimed it back, the land becomes yours.

If you do have a dispute that cannot be resolved in any other way you can bring an action in your local county court, but this can be complicated, lengthy and expensive.

Can I stop a neighbour parking in front of my house?

You have no rights to the road outside your house. Even if you have parked there for years, you cannot stop your new neighbour from parking his car there. However, he may not park in such a way as to block the entrance to your drive or garage. Call the police or contact the local council if this happens regularly.

Another common problem occurs when neighbours opposite park outside their own house in such a position as to make it awkward to manoeuvre your own car into your driveway. However, unless they are actually obstructing your entrance you would have no grounds to complain.

ALTERATIONS & EXTENSIONS

Normally, you have to apply for planning permission from the local planning authority to erect or enlarge a building. In many cases, the enlargement, improvement or other alteration of a dwelling house is what is called 'permitted development'. This means that you can go ahead without obtaining planning permission. This does not necessarily apply to certain areas, including those designated as conservation areas, or areas of outstanding natural beauty. These are specially protected.

If you live in a listed property or in a conservation area there will be restrictions on the work you can do. Always check with the local council first.

INTERNAL ALTERATIONS

In general, any maintenance, improvement or alterations, which affect only the interior of a building and which do not affect the outside appearance, are not regarded as a 'development' at all, and therefore planning permission is not required.

If the alteration is structural, you will still require building consent, but this is simply to make sure that the alteration is properly carried out.

If the alteration is to a kitchen or bathroom it may affect drainage or sewerage. Then the local authority should be consulted.

Can I knock down a wall between two rooms?

As there is nothing to stop you making internal alterations that do not affect the outside appearance of the house, you may join two rooms into one by knocking down the dividing wall. Before embarking on a structural alteration, however, notice should be given to the building inspector at the local authority. This should be given by the builder, or by you if you are doing the job yourself or are employing direct labour.

The building inspector will visit the site and make whatever requirements he thinks fit to ensure compliance with the Building Regulations and good building practice. If you are knocking down a wall this may involve the need to use an RSJ (or steel beam) of a particular size to support the floor above. If you are building a wall it may involve providing foundations of a certain depth. If you are installing a new boiler, the building regulations may involve lining a chimney.

Do I need planning permission for a loft conversion?

In general, you do not need planning permission in order to convert your loft into living space, even if you have to alter the roof, for instance by putting in dormer windows, in order to do so.

This type of conversion will add to the amount of living space afforded by the house. The amount by which you can increase the cubic capacity is limited, just as it is with any other extension, but slightly more stringent limitations on the increase in size apply. Again, you must not raise the roof level above its original height. Although you may put in dormer windows in the back or side of the roof, you may not do anything which projects beyond the slope of the roof on the side facing the road. You would only be able to put in a skylight there. You must not alter the roof to such an extent that it results in a material alteration to the shape of the house.

EXTERNAL ALTERATIONS

Can I build an extension to my house?

If the outside appearance is affected the alteration constitutes a 'development', but may be a 'permitted development', in which case again planning permission is not required. Painting the exterior of a house, so long as you are not painting up advertisements, not surprisingly comes under this category.

You can, however, do far more than this. You are also entitled to extend your property – within strict limits – without first obtaining planning permission. You may add up to 10 per cent or 50 cu. m/1,766 cu. ft, whichever is the greater, to the original dwelling house if it is a terraced house; or 70 cu. m/2,472 cu. ft or 15 per cent if it is not terraced. The original dwelling house is the house as it was on the 1 July 1948 if it was built by then, or its original size if built since. So be careful, as the house may have been extended before you bought it so that earlier work will already count towards the permitted development.

In no case may the addition:

- Exceed 115 cu. m/4,061 cu. ft.
- Exceed the height of the original building.
- Be nearer to the road than the existing building, unless it is still 20m/66ft away.
- Be more than 4m/13ft high, if it is within 2m/6½ ft of the boundary of the house or garden.
- Occupy more than half the garden.
- If it is built near the front of the house, extend beyond the house's nearest point to the road, and may not be nearer to the road than 2m/6½ft.

Can I build a porch?

You are allowed to build a porch without planning permission, but again there are limitations. It must not occupy more than 3 sq. m/32⅓ sq. ft of ground space, or be more than 3m/10ft high. It must not be within 2m/6½ft of the boundary of the garden.

Can I erect a garage?

You can build outbuildings such as a garage, or carport, or construct a swimming pool, without obtaining special permission, but only within certain limitations:

- It must not be for living purposes, and must be incidental to the enjoyment of the existing home. This includes providing a kennel for the dog, or a home for other domestic pets.
- It must not be nearer to the road than the house, or must be at least 20m/66ft away. If it is bigger than 10 cu. m/353 cu. ft, it must not be within 5m/16½ft of the house.
- The height may not exceed 3m/10ft (or 4m/13ft if the roof is ridged).
- The total area covered by outhouses may not be more than half the garden. You can also make a hard surface, e.g. to provide hard standing for a car.

Can I put up a satellite dish?

You may have one satellite dish installed, so long as it obeys certain requirements:

- If it is attached to a chimney, it must not exceed 45cm/17¾in in any direction including mountings.
- If it is attached anywhere else it must not exceed 70cm/27½in or 90cm/35½in, depending on the county in which you live.
- It must not exceed the height of any chimney or roof to which it is attached.

Is there any limit on the height of fences?

Any fences, gates or walls must not exceed 2m/6½ft in height. If the wall or fence is adjacent to a road used by vehicles, it must not exceed 1m/3¼ft.

OBTAINING PLANNING PERMISSION

If your property is a listed building or is in a conservation area, you cannot assume that your ideas will constitute 'permitted development'. Special provisions apply, and any alterations may be very restricted.

How do I apply for planning permission?

You must apply to the planning department of your local authority. Your application will set out details of your proposals and should include, as far as possible, drawings and specifications. These may be compiled by you, or by an architect employed by you. Outline drawings are sufficient, and the authority will tell you if further details are required.

Interested parties are given an opportunity to object to what you have in mind. If, for example, you have proposed an extension that affects your neighbour, you may have to amend your original proposal before you are given permission. Permission may be conditional on carrying out particular work.

If you have omitted to apply for planning permission when you should have done so, you may do so in retrospect, and if granted it will have the same effect as if granted in advance. It is risky to adopt this course deliberately, however, as the local authority has the power to order you to stop. If you fail to comply, you can be fined. Furthermore, the local authority can order you to pull down any construction, which is contravention of the planning laws. So you could be liable for a great deal of expense without any result.

Change of use

You also require planning permission for any change of use of a property. You may not, therefore, without permission use a dwelling house for another purpose, such as a fish-canning factory or a hairdressing shop. You may have a room which you use as a personal office or study within it, however. A dwelling house is one used as a sole or main residence by a single person or family, or by not more than six residents who are not part of a family but are living together as a single household.

Planning permission, or not?

If you are not sure whether planning permission is required, for any job, apply to the local council for a certificate that planning permission is not required; you are then safe from the suggestion that you acted without it, and cannot be required to remove the structure.

It is, in particular, a change of use to convert a single dwelling house into two or more separate houses or flats.

Party walls

If your extension affects your neighbour's property directly, special considerations apply. For example, your loft conversion may involve an RSJ going into a wall that divides your neighbour's house from your own. If this is so, you should obtain his or her consent before the work begins. You may obtain a 'party wall award', which means that a surveyor will inspect the other property before and after the work to ensure that no damage has been caused by it, for which you would be liable. This procedure protects you as well as your neighbour, since if defects already exist, they could not then be attributable to the construction of your extension.

BUILDING WORK

There is no way of being sure that the work you have done in your home is of high quality, but at least you can minimise the risks involved.

HOW TO GET A GOOD JOB

First, you should get more than one quotation for the cost of the work. Once you have obtained, say, three quotations, you can choose the contractor, not necessarily selecting the cheapest, but also taking into account his approach to the work to be done, and any recommendation you have had from others. A good builder will be happy to show you work he has recently completed locally.

Once you have chosen your builder, make sure that he is covered by insurance. Then, if the house collapses because he provided insufficient support while pulling down a wall, you will have some comeback even if the builder goes bankrupt.

He may also belong to one of the recognised trade associations e.g. the Federation of Master Builders (www.fmb.org.uk), or to the Building Guarantee Scheme (www.cefni.co.uk), which offers a guarantee to cover the quality of his work.

Then tie up the legal side. Before the work starts it is important to have the main terms of your agreement with the builder clear. Reputable builders often have their own standard terms. If so, read them carefully before agreeing to anything. Otherwise you could use a standard form of contract such as the RIBA contract for small building works. With any standard form, you will have to fill in the details applicable to your own particular project.

Whether you use a standard form contract or not, it is best to have something in writing. The principal terms of the agreement should be set out. You should have a written agreement setting out the work to be done and the price to be charged. The work required should be set out in a schedule. The term concerning the price should also specify how it is to be paid. It should say whether any money is required in advance and whether payment is to be in stages during the work. If so, it should say who is responsible for deciding the value of work completed at any stage. If an architect is involved, for example, he should decide on the value of the work completed.

Sometimes it is difficult to quote accurately as it is not apparent until work begins exactly what is required. For example, if you are having work done on the roof it may not be clear until the tiles and lead are removed that some of the timbers need replacing. If a price is not quoted in advance for any work, you are liable to pay a reasonable amount for the work actually carried out with your agreement. Ideally, however, extra work should be specified, priced and agreed in writing before it is done. So make sure this is written into the contract to avoid expensive surprises.

The agreement should also contain details of when the work should start and finish, what standard of work is required, and on what basis either party can terminate the contract. If the time of finishing the work is important you should specify that 'time is of the essence'. Otherwise you will have no right to sue if work is not begun or ended on time. If time is important you may also specify what damages are payable on the failure of the builder to complete the work in time. If the sum shown is not related to an estimate of the actual cost to you, but is simply intended as a penalty, the clause will not be valid. It will only take effect if it is a genuine attempt to assess the costs likely to be suffered by you.

If the contract is silent on that point, there is an implied term in the agreement that the job will be carried out with reasonable skill and care, and that the builder will use suitable materials of satisfactory quality. If he fails to fulfil either of these stipulations you can sue him for damages to compensate you for the cost of putting the work right. If the defect is fundamental, it would entitle you to set the agreement aside and employ someone else to redo the work.

PROBLEMS WITH BUILDING WORK

My new kitchen is defective; what can I do?

Under the Supply of Goods and Services Act 1982, the contractor owes you a duty. He is failing in this duty if he has not acted with reasonable skill and care.

He also fails in his duty if he does not use materials of satisfactory quality. This means you could take him to court to claim the cost of finishing the work properly. If the materials used are totally unsuitable, and the job as a whole is unfit for the purpose for which it was required, it is open to you to terminate the agreement, and have the whole kitchen replaced.

Check units and materials before installation. Otherwise, once they're incorporated into the building it's more difficult to spot the cause of any problems.

TIP: You must make sure you see a fitted kitchen before it is installed. Showrooms are there so that you can feel the quality, try the drawers, give it a thump to see how substantial it is. At the least, ask for names and addresses of recent customers.

Can I make the plumber pay for the ruined carpet?

If a plumber has not only mended the pipe badly, but an ensuing flood has caused damage to the carpet in the room below, the plumber has been negligent, and has not complied with his agreement to carry out his work with reasonable skill and care. You can therefore bring an action against him for all foreseeable damage directly flowing from what he did. Damage to the carpet is clearly a foreseeable result of permitting the tap to leak badly, causing flooding. This doesn't mean you can claim the full cost of replacing with new – if it was an old carpet you'll have to contribute to the cost of new.

The electrician has overcharged; will I have to pay?

If you have agreed the price with him in advance, you will have to pay the agreed price, even though the job only took a fraction of the time you thought it might take when you agreed. If there was no express agreement as to the price the electrician is entitled to charge you a reasonable price, by reference to what other skilled tradesmen charge. If you think this is excessive you many need to get another trader to comment on what would have been a reasonable amount and use that to bargain.

If you have an emergency, be sure to enquire first whether there is a call-out charge.

Double glazing: can I get my money back?

If the double glazing installed for you fails to work effectively then the same rules apply. The contractor has failed in his duties under the law, and if the failure is fundamental, as a last resort it would be possible to repudiate the contract and insist on the removal of the installation, as well as to claim damages for the inconvenience caused. So if it costs you more for the similar quality replacements than you had originally budgeted for under the first contract, you can claim the excess – you should not be out of pocket as a result of the original faulty workmanship

What if there was a guarantee with the work?

Much specialist work is the subject matter of guarantees. It includes wood preservation treatment, damp-proof course and roofing work. The guarantees are sometimes for as long as 30 years. If there is a repeat of the infestation during the period the company will return and treat the property again. Since a guarantee is part of what was supplied under the contract, you can sue under the guarantee. The guarantee is a valuable asset when it comes to selling the house, since it may be passed on to the purchaser.

Although a guarantee may say that it guarantees that there will be no recurrence of the infestation, it may not be a promise to pay for any damage caused to your house if there is. So although the company will come and retreat the timbers if there is a recurrence,

e.g. of dry rot, the guarantee does not cover the cost of a wall falling down due to a rotten timber. You would have to sue the company on the contract in the normal way and prove that the workmanship was not up to standard, but to take legal action for faulty workmanship under the contract you have to do so within reasonable time of the problem arising, no matter how long the guarantee lasts for.

Furthermore, the guarantee is only as good as the company giving it. The company may have gone into liquidation long before the 30 years are up, leaving any guarantee worthless. You would also need to check if the guarantee is still valid if the property changes hands or whether a transfer fee is payable.

TIP: Try and choose a company whose guarantee is backed by another substantial firm, such as the manufacturer of the product used for treatment, or even better, an insurance company.

Guarantees and warranties

What is the difference between a guarantee and a warranty?

Although the different words have specific legal meanings, in the context in which they are used here, and in which they are used by companies selling goods, they are indistinguishable. They are simply the terms of the contract, setting out the circumstances in which the seller or manufacturer will repair or replace the goods or refund the money. The legal effect on them depends entirely on the words used.

The only point to note is that they will not usually prevent the buyer from exercising his or her statutory or common law rights, if these happen to be more extensive than those offered under the warranty or guarantee.

Directory

SPECIALIST PRODUCTS

1001 Mousse
www.1001carpetcare.co.uk
tel: 08000 27 33 40

Amodex Ink and Stain Remover
Available from The Pen Company,
www.thepencompany.co.uk
tel: 01707 690 273

Bar Keepers Friend
Available from www.homecareproducts.co.uk
tel: 01270 508 980

Bissell OxyKIC Carpet Spot and Stain Remover
www.bissell.com
tel: 0844 888 66 44

Dasco
Available from www.dunkelman.com
tel: 01536 760 760
Fabric cleaners for leather and suede.

De.Solv.It
www.desolvit.com
Natural citrus-based stain remover.

Dylon Stain Removers
www.dylon.co.uk
tel: 01737 742 020

Hob Brite
Available from www.homecareproducts.co.uk
tel: 01270 508 980
Cleaner for ceramic and halogen hobs.

Liberon Floor Sealer
www.liberon.co.uk
tel: 01797 367 555

Liberon Iron Paste
www.liberon.co.uk
tel: 01797 367 555
Black fireplace and grate polish.

Lithofin Oil-Ex and Stainstop
www.lithofin-uk.co.uk
tel: 01962 732 126

HomeServe Furniture Care Kits
www.homeserve.com/advice/care-maintenance-
furniture-care-kit, Mail order only.
tel: 0800 408 0004

Rustins Rust Remover and Clear Metal Lacquer
www.rustins.eu
tel: 0208 450 4666

Stain Devils Stain Removers and Stain Removing Wipes
www.staindevils.co.uk
tel: 0845 017 8000

Sticky Stuff Remover
Available from Lakeland Limited
www.lakeland.co.uk
tel: 015394 88100
For removing chewing gum, sticky tape and labels.

WD-40
www.WD40.co.uk
tel: 01908 555 400

White Wizard
Available from Lakeland Limited
www.lakeland.co.uk
tel: 015394 88100
Excellent all-purpose stain remover.

Wine Away
Available from Lakeland Limited
www.lakeland.co.uk
tel: 015394 88100
For removing red wine and other stains.

MANUFACTURERS, RETAILERS AND SERVICE PROVIDERS

Alno
www.alnokitchens.co.uk

Bath Renovation Ltd
www.bathrenovationltd.co.uk, tel: 0208 894 6464

Conservation Resources
www.conservation-resources.co.uk
tel: 01865 747 755
Provides conservation storage materials.

Green Cone Limited
www.greencone.com
tel: 0800 731 2572
Food waste digesting and composting systems.

Ikea
www.ikea.co.uk
tel: 08453 583 363

Jeeves of Belgravia
www.jeevesofbelgravia.co.uk
tel: 0208 809 3232
Vacuum packing service for wedding dresses and other special garments.

John Lewis
www.johnlewis.com
tel: 0845 604 9049

Leather Master
www.leathermasteruk.com
tel: 0115 973 7280
Supplier of leather cleaning products and repair service.

London Wall Bed Company
www.wallbed.co.uk
tel: 0208 896 3757

Mattress Doctor
www.matdoc.co.uk
tel: 0845 330 6607
Mattress cleaning service to control dust mites.

MOMART
www.momart.co.uk
tel: 0207 426 3000
Storage and transportation of fine art.

National Carpet Cleaners Association
www.ncca.co.uk
tel: 0116 271 9550

Quooker
www.quooker.co.uk
tel: 0207 923 3355

Rentokil
www.rentokil.co.uk
tel: 0800 218 2210

Renubath Services Ltd
www.renubath.co.uk
tel: 0800 138 2202
Bath re-enamelling service.

Royal School of Needlework
www.royal-needlework.co.uk
tel: 0203 166 6932
Repair and restoration of antique textiles.

SECOL
www.secol.co.uk
tel: 01842 752 341
For photographic storage materials.

Servicemaster
www.servicemaster.co.uk
tel: 0845 201 1184
Network of franchised carpet and upholstery cleaning firms.

Smartsoil Limited
www.smartsoil.co.uk
tel: 01639 701 888
Composting systems.

Strachan
www.strachan.co.uk
tel: 0800 0138 139
Convert-a-room fitted furniture.

The Used Kitchen Company
www.theusedkitchencompany.com
tel: 0208 349 1943

USEFUL ORGANISATIONS

Antiques Trade Gazette
www.antiquestradegazette.com
tel: 0207 420 6600

Art Loss Register
www.artloss.com
tel: 0207 841 5780

Association of Master Upholsterers
www.upholsterers.co.uk
tel: 029 2077 8918
Advice and directory of craftspeople for repairs
and restorations of upholstered furniture.

Association of British Insurers
www.abi.org.uk, tel: 0207 600 3333

British Allergy Foundation
www.allergyuk.org, tel: 01322 619 898

British Antique Furniture Restorers' Association
www.bafra.org.uk
tel: 01305 854 822
Directory of specialist craftspeople for repairs and
restoration of all kinds of antiques.

British Association of Removers
www.bar.co.uk
tel: 01923 699 480

British Blind and Shutter Association
www.bbsa.org.uk
tel: 01449 780 444

British Cutlery and Silverware Association
No website
tel: 0114 266 3084

British Plastics Federation Windows Group
www.bpf.co.uk/Windows/Default.aspx
tel: 0207 457 5000

British Security Industry Association
www.bsia.co.uk
tel: 0845 389 3889

British Standards Institute
www.bsigroup.co.uk, tel: 0208 996 9001

British Waterbed Association
www.waterbed.org
tel: 0870 603 0202

Citizens Advice Bureau
www.citizensadvice.org.uk

Consumer Direct
www.consumerdirect.gov.uk
tel: 0845 404 0506
For advice on what to do when things go wrong
when buying goods and services.

Council for Licensed Conveyancers
www.conveyancer.org.uk
tel: 01245 349 599

Direct Marketing Association
www.mydm.co.uk
tel: 0845 703 4599

Electrical Contractors Association
www.eca.co.uk
tel: 0207 313 4800

Energy Saving Trust
www.energysavingtrust.org.uk,
tel: 0800 512 012

English Heritage
www.english-heritage.org.uk
tel: 0870 333 1181

External Wall Insulation Association
Tel: 01428 654 011

Federation of Master Builders
www.fmb.org.uk
tel: 0207 242 7583

Fire Protection Association
www.thefpa.co.uk
tel: 01608 812 500

Freecycle
www.uk.freecycle.org
Freecycle groups match people who have things they want to get rid of with other people who can still use them, thus helping to keep items out of landfill sites. Go online to find your local group.

Furniture Industry and Research Association (FIRA)
www.fira.co.uk
tel: 01438 777 700

The Furniture Ombudsman (previously known as Qualitas)
www.thefurnitureombudsman.org
tel: 0845 653 2064

Gas Safe Register™
www.gassaferegister.co.uk
tel: 0800 408 5500

Glass and Glazing Federation
www.ggf.org.uk
tel: 0207 939 9101

Heating and Ventilating Contractors' Association
www.hvca.org.uk
tel: 0207 313 4900

Historic Scotland
www.historic-scotland.gov.uk
tel: 0131 668 8600

Home Laundering Consultative Council
www.care-labelling.co.uk
tel 0207 636 7788

Institute of Conservation
www.conservationregister.co.uk
tel: 0207 785 3805
Directory of accredited conservators.

The Institute of Plumbing and Heating Engineering
www.ciphe.org.uk
tel: 01708 472 791

Kitchen Bathroom Bedroom Specialists Association
www.kbsa.org.uk
tel: 01623 818 808

Land Registry
www.landregistry.gov.uk
tel: 0844 892 1111

The Law Society
www.lawsociety.org.uk
tel: 0207 242 1222

Mailing Preference Service
www.mpsonline.org.uk
tel: 0207 291 3327

Master Locksmiths Association
www.locksmiths.co.uk
tel: 01327 262 255

National Energy Foundation
www.nef.org.uk
tel: 01908 665 555

National Federation of Roofing Contractors
www.nfrc.co.uk
tel: 0207 638 7663

National Gas Emergency Service
www.nationalgrid.com/uk/Gas/Safety/Emergency/
tel: 0800 111 999

National Inspection Council for Electrical Installation Contracting
www.niceic.org.uk
tel: 0870 013 0382

National Security Inspectorate
www.nsi.org.uk
tel: 01628 637 512

Office of Fair Trading
www.oft.gov.uk. tel: 08457 22 44 99

Problem Solved
www.problemsolved.co.uk
tel: 0207 290 6060
Trusted tradesmen scheme

Property Protection Association
www.property-care.org
tel: 0844 375 4301

Royal Institute of Chartered Surveyors
www.rics.org
tel: 0870 333 1600

Royal Mail
www.royalmail.com
tel: 0845 774 0740

Secured by Design
www.securedbydesign.com
tel: 0207 084 8962

Sewing Machine Trade Association
www.sewingmachine.org.uk
tel: 0870 330 8610

Sleep Council
www.sleepcouncil.com
tel: 0845 058 4595

Society of Book Binders
www.societyofbookbinders.com

Society for the Protection of Ancient Buildings
www.spab.org.uk
tel: 0207 377 1644

Solid Fuel Association
www.solidfuel.co.uk
tel: 0845 601 4406

Textile Services Association (TSA)
www.tsa-uk.org
tel: 0208 863 7755

TrustMark
www.trustmark.org.uk
tel: 01344 630 804
Trusted tradesmen scheme.

The Twentieth Century Society
www.c20society.org.uk
tel: 0207 250 3857

Vitreous Enamel Association
www.ive.org.uk
tel: 01543 450 596

Welsh Historic Monuments
www.cadw.wales.gov.uk
tel: 01443 33 6000

Wood Protection Association
www.wood-protection.org

Index